JUDGMENT AND DECISION MAKING IN ACCOUNTING

Sarah E. Bonner

University of Southern California

PEARSON

Prentice Hall

Upper Saddle River, New Jersey 07458

Library of Congress Cataloging-in-Publication Data

Bonner, Sarah E.
    Judgment and decision making in accounting / Sarah E. Bonner.—1st ed.
        p. cm.
    Includes bibliographical references and index.
    ISBN-13: 978-0-13-863895-5
    ISBN-10: 0-13-863895-0
    1. Accounting—Decision making. 2. Managerial accounting. I. Title.
    HF5636.B66 2007
    658.15'11—dc22   2007007132

AVP/Executive Editor: Steve Sartori
Development Manager: Ashley Santora
Project Manager: Susan Abraham
Editorial Assistant: Marybeth Ward
Associate Director, Production Editorial: Judy Leale
Senior Managing Editor: Cynthia Zonneveld
Production Editor: Melissa Feimer
Permissions Coordinator: Charles Morris
Associate Director, Manufacturing: Vinnie Scelta
Manufacturing Buyer: Michelle Klein
Design/Composition Manager: Christy Mahon
Cover Design: Bruce Kenselaar
Composition/Full-Service Project Management: Karen Ettinger, Aptara, Inc.
Printer/Binder: R.R. Donnelley & Sons, Inc.
Typeface: 10/12 Times Ten Roman

Credits and acknowledgments borrowed from other sources and reproduced, with permission, in this textbook appear on appropriate page within text.

Pearson Education LTD.
Pearson Education Singapore, Pte. Ltd
Pearson Education, Canada, Ltd
Pearson Education—Japan

Pearson Education Australia PTY, Limited
Pearson Education North Asia Ltd
Pearson Educación de Mexico, S.A. de C.V.
Pearson Education Malaysia, Pte.

10 9 8 7 6 5 4 3 2 1
ISBN-13: 978-0-13-863895-5
ISBN-10: 0-13-863895-0

To Mark, Nathaniel, and Kaylee Young

ABOUT THE AUTHOR

Sarah E. Bonner is the USC Accounting Associates professor of accounting and professor of management and organization at the Marshall School of Business at the University of Southern California. She received a B.S. in accounting and mathematics from Wake Forest University, an M.Acc. from George Washington University, and a Ph.D. in business from The University of Michigan.

Professor Bonner's research on judgment and decision making in accounting has been published in the *Journal of Accounting Research, The Accounting Review, Accounting, Organizations and Society, Contemporary Accounting Research,* the *Journal of Management Accounting Research,* the *Journal of Accounting Literature,* and *Accounting Horizons.* She has received several research grants from the National Science Foundation, the KPMG Peat Marwick Research Opportunities in Auditing program, and the KPMG Peat Marwick Research Opportunities in Tax program, as well as many university grants. She also has sat or currently sits on the editorial boards of *The Accounting Review; Accounting, Organizations and Society; Contemporary Accounting Research; Auditing: A Journal of Practice & Theory; Behavioral Research in Accounting;* and *Journal of Accounting Abstracts.* Her dissertation received the best dissertation award from the Accounting, Behavior, and Organizations Section of the American Accounting Association.

In addition to teaching doctoral seminars on judgment and decision making, Professor Bonner teaches courses in financial accounting, research design, and experimental design. She has won a number of teaching awards including the USC-Mellon Award for Excellence in Mentoring, Mortar Board's Most Outstanding Faculty Member, the USC Parents' Association Teaching and Mentoring Award, and Gamma Sigma Alpha Professor of the Year. Professor Bonner also has served on a number of American Accounting Association (AAA) committees, and is a member of AAA, the American Psychological Association, the American Institute of CPAs, the Judgment and Decision-Making Society, and the Canadian Academic Accounting Association.

BRIEF CONTENTS

CONTENTS

PREFACE

Judgment and decision making are pervasive elements of all accounting settings, and judgment and decision-making (JDM) research is one of the largest and most influential areas of accounting research. The area has grown so much that the number of articles in the area has multiplied at least a hundredfold since Bob Libby's original text on accounting JDM research appeared in 1981. The psychology literature on which accounting JDM research is based similarly has exploded. This book was written to provide a contemporary synthesis of both the psychology and accounting literatures related to judgment and decision making.

Perhaps more important, this book grew from an overriding desire to somehow make sense of this vast literature. As such, the book is organized around a framework that has been developed based on many years of teaching and research on accounting JDM. This framework is meant to succinctly describe the key issues in accounting JDM research and to assist the reader in more quickly assimilating the material related to those issues. Additionally, the framework (and the related syntheses of psychology and accounting research) provides a basis for evaluating one's own current JDM research ideas and generating further research questions.

The book is structured around the framework. Specifically, Chapter 1 provides background information about JDM research and introduces the framework. Chapter 2 discusses the first few questions in the framework, those which relate to JDM "quality"; in so doing, the chapter also covers issues related to how to define quality. Chapters 3 through 7 cover factors that affect JDM quality, Chapter 8 discusses others' understanding of accountants' JDM, and Chapter 9 discusses ways of improving JDM. Chapter 10 concludes with a summary and a discussion of future research.

The book is intended for faculty, PhD students, and master's students who are either interested in or currently conducting JDM research in accounting, as well as for non-JDM researchers who want to learn more about the field. In addition, the book may be helpful to accounting practitioners who are responsible for their firms' programs related to effective JDM.

ACKNOWLEDGMENTS

I am grateful to many people who have provided assistance with this book. First, I thank the reviewers: Karim Jamal, Marlys Lipe, Joan Luft, Laureen Maines, Mark Peecher, and most especially, Lisa Koonce, who reviewed the entire manuscript over a very lengthy period and exhibited great patience and kindness in so doing. I also thank other individuals who provided comments on various parts of the manuscript: Mark Young, Bill Kinney, and Geoff Sprinkle. Thanks also to Bryan Cloyd, Molly Mercer, Kathryn Kadous, Frank Hodge, and Reid Hastie for providing helpful references and examples for various portions of the manuscript. I also received wonderful assistance from Audrena Goodie, Susan Young, Sumit Rana, Artur Hugon, Melissa Martin, Terry Wang, Jim Hesford, and especially, Clara Chen, without whom this project most certainly would not have been completed. I am very grateful to Wendy Craven, Susan Abraham, Melissa Feimer, Andrea Howe, and Karen Ettinger for wonderful editorial assistance. Finally, I am most grateful to the individuals who provided enormous encouragement and moral support: Mark Young, Nathaniel Young, Kaylee Young, Joyce and Sidney Bonner, Doreen and Sydney Young, Geoff Sprinkle, Bill Kinney, Ellen Glazerman, and Audrena Goodie.

1

Introduction to Judgment and Decision-Making Research

Accounting at its core is about the judgment and decision making (JDM) of indi-viduals such as investors, managers, and auditors. For instance, investors decide which stocks to buy, and managers decide on methods of accounting for transactions. In other words, individual JDM pervades almost all issues of concern to accounting practitioners and researchers. Although this fact alone is enough to justify the study of individual JDM in accounting, there also is ample evidence that accounting-related JDM is not always of the highest quality.[1] Further, less than high-quality JDM in accounting can have serious consequences for the individuals making the judgments and decisions; their firms; third parties who use their work; and, more generally, our economy and society.

The aims of this book are to discuss the importance of studying JDM issues in accounting; to cover the key issues related to doing research in this area; to summarize both the psychology and accounting literatures related to significant JDM topics; and finally, to provide directions for future accounting JDM research. This introductory chapter defines JDM research in accounting and describes its goals. Next, it provides material on the relevance of JDM to accounting, the quality of accounting-related JDM, and the consequences of less than high-quality JDM. Then the chapter continues with a section on how to do successful JDM research in accounting. This section begins with a framework that is useful in contemplating JDM research projects and continues with information about choosing a good research question and an appropri-ate method for addressing that question. The framework also provides a glimpse of the remaining chapters, which are summarized briefly in the concluding section. Along with this, the section describes the importance of referring to psychology theories when conducting JDM research in accounting.

---

[1]JDM "quality" can be defined in many ways. For example, it can be evaluated based on the extent to which a judgment or decision compares to some normative criterion (e.g., an auditor's judgment about appropri-ate sample size can be compared to the size specified by a sampling formula). As another example, quality can be evaluated as the extent to which a judgment or decision corresponds with some related outcome (e.g., an analyst's earnings forecast can be compared to actual earnings). Chapter 2 provides a detailed discussion of the issues related to defining and measuring JDM quality.

1-1 DEFINITIONS

What is JDM research in accounting? To answer this question, one must first define judgments and decisions. The term *judgment* refers to forming an idea, opinion, or estimate about an object, an event, a state, or another type of phenomenon. Judgments in accounting tend to take the form of predictions about a future state of affairs or event (e.g., bankruptcy) or an evaluation of a current but not completely knowable state of affairs or event (e.g., the extent of misstatements in financial statements).[2] In other words, judgments in accounting, as is the case in many other domains (Hastie and Dawes 2001), tend to be judgments under uncertainty. Further, these judgments tend to take certain forms—either probabilities (e.g., the chance that bankruptcy will occur) or quantities (e.g., the dollar amount of material misstatements).

The term *decision* refers to making up one's mind about the issue at hand and taking a course of action. Decisions typically follow judgments and involve a choice among various alternatives based on judgments about those alternatives and preferences for factors such as risk and money.[3] In other words, judgments reflect beliefs, whereas decisions reflect both beliefs and preferences. For example, an auditor makes a judgment about the fairness of presentation of financial statements based on her beliefs about misstatements present in those financial statements.[4] Then she makes a decision about the type of audit opinion to issue based on both the fairness of presentation judgment and preferences such as those regarding client retention and litigation.

JDM research, then, can be defined broadly as research that focuses on something about judgments or decisions as either the dependent variable or independent variable.[5]

Two elements of judgments or decisions can be examined. First, research can examine simple variation in judgments or decisions. For example, a study may find that, given the same information for a particular investment project, some management accountants judge the project acceptable to pursue, whereas others do not. Further, research may document that an individual management accountant, given the same information at two different times, makes different judgments about the acceptability of a project. That is, variation can be either across individuals or within individuals over time. A second element of JDM that research can examine is the quality of JDM (and variation in that quality). For example, a study could examine the extent to which management accountants find projects acceptable when they should, such as when the projects' actual rates of return exceed a hurdle rate. Again, studies can document quality variation either across individuals or within individuals over time.

---

[2]Auditors are not able to completely ascertain the extent of material misstatements in financial statements for a number of reasons, most notably because they conduct their tests using samples of items from account balances.

[3]Normative JDM theories prescribe that decisions follow judgments. However, descriptively, people sometimes make decisions first then follow with judgments that support or rationalize those decisions.

[4]Throughout this book, I use feminine pronouns to refer to both men and women.

[5]JDM research is a subset of the area called "behavioral accounting research" (BAR). *BAR,* in general, examines something about the behavior or feelings of individuals of interest to accounting researchers (see the next section of this chapter) as either the independent or dependent variable (Hofstedt and Kinard 1970; Birnberg and Shields 1989). Consequently, BAR encompasses a variety of topics beyond judgment and decision making, including job satisfaction and turnover, management control, ethical behavior, and negotiation behavior. For recent reviews of BAR, see Bamber (1993) and Arnold and Sutton (1997).

This book focuses on JDM quality as the element of judgments or decisions to be examined. The focus on quality reflects the notion that researchers and practitioners often want to know more than just whether JDM varies across individuals or within individuals over time; rather, they are interested in answering questions such as whether any individuals are "good" at the JDM task and, more specifically, which individuals. Such focus on the part of practitioners may be driven, for example, by the desire to improve all employees' JDM to the level of their best employees; this obviously requires the identification of such employees.

However, studying simple variation in JDM across or within individuals also is quite important. As discussed further in Chapter 2, one reason for this is that it can be difficult to define and measure JDM quality. In fact, variation across individuals and variation within individuals sometimes are used as definitions of JDM quality.[6] For judgments, the sheer fact that people disagree with others or themselves can indicate that someone (or a person at one point in time) is "wrong." The difficulty lies in identifying which person (or at which point in time an individual) is "right."[7] For decisions, further difficulty arises because differences in decisions may reflect differences in preferences, meaning that no one may be wrong. Overall, then, research that focuses on variation without an eye toward delineating JDM quality has a more difficult time proposing improvement strategies. Nevertheless, its role in improving our understanding of JDM is significant, particularly for situations in which variation in JDM is of paramount importance in its own right, such as for auditors in litigation settings.

Focusing now on quality as the JDM issue to be examined, research that studies JDM quality as the dependent variable is the most common. This research can simply describe the current state of JDM quality of certain individuals in a given task. A more important goal of such research is to understand the factors that cause variation in JDM quality. A follow-on and very practical goal of this line of work, then, is to propose and examine the effectiveness of methods to improve JDM quality in cases where it is lower than what is considered acceptable.[8]

Research can also examine JDM quality as the independent variable. Dependent variables that can be affected by JDM quality include economic consequences for the individuals making the JDM and for the firms for which they work, and reactions by and economic consequences for third parties who use other individuals' JDM. For instance, research could examine the effect of variation in analysts' forecast quality on analysts' pay and job turnover, as well as its effects on investors' reactions to analysts' forecasts and their consequent investment returns.

Finally, JDM research in accounting examines the JDM of individuals of interest to accounting researchers in accounting-related tasks. The next section discusses these individuals (e.g., tax professionals). As to whether a task is "accounting related," this appears to be more a matter of taste than definition. My taste is that the professional and financial JDM tasks performed by the individuals of interest to accounting researchers are accounting related. An additional distinguishing feature of JDM

---

[6]Note that researchers using variation in JDM across or within individuals as a measure of quality cannot examine variation in quality. That is, variation per se is the measure of quality.

[7]As an alternative, research using variation as a measure of quality often compares the quality of two or more groups of individuals in a JDM task (e.g., analysts versus managers).

[8]Some researchers include a prediction role for JDM research, that is, to be able to predict the JDM quality of various individuals (e.g., Carroll and Johnson 1990).

research in accounting is that it often addresses questions that are at least somewhat unique to the accounting domain. These and other questions that include JDM quality as the independent or dependent variable are delineated in Section 1-4.

1-2 JDM AT THE CORE OF ACCOUNTING

Which individuals' JDM is of interest to accounting researchers, and what are the JDM tasks they perform? In general, there are producers, users, auditors, and regulators of accounting information, as well as evaluators of the work products of accountants; all these individuals make important judgments and decisions.[9] Producers of accounting information include managers, management accountants, and financial analysts. Managers decide on methods of accounting for transactions and make choices about the existence, form, and timing of voluntary disclosures. Management accountants make decisions about whether to investigate variances of costs from standards. Users of accounting information include those listed as producers along with brokers and other investment advisors, money managers, investors, creditors, corporate directors, and tax professionals. As examples of users' JDM, investors make decisions about which stocks to buy and sell and creditors make decisions about interest rates on loans.

Auditors can be external public accountants or internal to firms; public accountants who audit financial statements judge whether there are material misstatements in those statements. Regulators of accounting information include the Financial Accounting Standards Board (FASB), the Securities and Exchange Commission (SEC), the American Institute of Certified Public Accountants (AICPA), and others.[10] These regulators decide on the appropriate presentation of financial information, such as whether to expense stock option compensation. Finally, evaluators of accountants' work include plaintiffs' attorneys, judges, and juries, as well as various professional and regulatory bodies such as the SEC and AICPA. As an example of evaluators' JDM, juries evaluating the work of auditors in the context of civil litigation must decide whether auditors have followed professional standards in rendering an audit opinion and, if not, what penalties to impose on them.

Note that the individuals making important accounting-related judgments and decisions are not just top executives or the wealthy. Auditors work in hierarchical teams composed of persons at the partner level down to persons at the staff level. Each member of the team makes important judgments. Similar to this, decision making is being pushed to lower and lower levels of corporations. More generally, the sheer number of individuals who make important accounting-related decisions today is enormous (for example, there are millions of individual investors). Further, the mountain of

---

[9]Another classification for these individuals is that used by Beaver (1998). He groups people based on their role in the financial reporting process: investors, information intermediaries (financial analysts, brokers, and others who provide information to investors), regulators, management, and auditors. Because he focuses only on financial reporting, however, he omits key accounting professionals such as management accountants and tax professionals.

[10]The FASB is a private body that promulgates financial reporting standards. The SEC was created by the federal government (via the Securities Acts of 1933 and 1934) to regulate financial reporting. Although the SEC effectively has ceded some of its authority to the FASB, it ultimately has power to control financial reporting by corporations. The AICPA is the professional organization of certified public accountants. The AICPA performs many functions including promulgating auditing standards via the Auditing Standards Board.

information available for use in accounting-related decision making has created demand for new services to assist people with their decisions. For example, the Special Committee on Assurance Services has proposed services that will assist people in determining which items of accounting or, more generally, business and economic information, from the voluminous set available, are relevant for decision making (AICPA 1996).[11]

1-3 REASONS FOR STUDYING INDIVIDUAL JDM IN ACCOUNTING

The fact that individuals of interest to accounting researchers make many judgments and decisions, in my opinion, offers sufficient justification for studying accounting-related JDM issues. Yet some readers may require further justification, and as a result, questions related to further justification are included in the framework that is introduced in the next section. For these readers, the next question likely is whether these individuals make JDM errors. If the individuals described above have fairly high-quality judgments and decisions, studying their JDM may appear unimportant. This issue is moot, however, because a large body of research shows that producers, users, auditors, and regulators of accounting information, as well as evaluators of accountants' work, do not always make high-quality judgments and decisions.

More important, many JDM errors are systematic (as opposed to random). Systematic errors are differences between actual JDM and high-quality JDM that occur either because certain types of people consistently make mistakes or because individuals consistently make mistakes under certain circumstances. For example, men investors trade more and earn lower returns than women investors (Barber and Odean 2001). Researchers posit this occurs because men are more overconfident than women, and more overconfidence leads to more trading. As another example, when making intuitive sample size decisions, auditors tend to choose samples that are too small for a given level of risk (Bonner and Pennington 1991). One reason this may occur is that auditors use mental shortcuts, or heuristics, that cause them to underestimate the level of risk. There are numerous other examples of such systematic errors.

Further justification for studying JDM in accounting arises from the fact that these systematic errors, and the low-quality JDM they create, can lead to serious economic consequences for the individuals making the decisions and the firms for which they work. Specifically, the quality of an individual's JDM can affect her performance evaluation, compensation, job retention, and promotion. For example, auditors' performance evaluations are related to the quality of their technical judgments (Tan and Libby 1997) and analysts whose forecasts are relatively less accurate than their peers' are more likely to lose their jobs (Mikhail et al. 1999).[12] Further, poor JDM can lead to negative legal outcomes such as payments in civil litigation for both the individual and her firm (Erickson et al. 2000). For example, audit firms and brokerage firms can suffer

---

[11]The Special Committee on Assurance Services was created by the AICPA to explore new services that could be offered by the public accounting profession. The impetuses for this committee's work include flat revenues from traditional auditing services, an explosion of information available for accounting-related decision making, and demand from clients for value-added forward-looking information advisory services.
[12]Accuracy in this setting is defined as the extent to which earnings forecasts correspond to actual earnings. Accuracy can be measured in a number of ways; further, accuracy is only one dimension of JDM quality (see Chapter 2 for further discussion).

losses due to low-quality JDM on the part of their auditor and analyst employees. In addition, the quality of individual JDM can have severe economic consequences for third parties who rely on these individuals' JDM. For example, investors who rely on the JDM of analysts, money managers, and brokers can make inappropriate investment decisions and experience lowered investment returns if those professionals' JDM is not of the highest quality (Hirst et al. 1995; Brown and Mohammad 2001).

A reasonable inquiry at this point regards the role of markets (and the high monetary stakes they carry) in eliminating individual JDM errors. The markets of most relevance for accounting researchers are capital markets, and historically, research has assumed that capital markets eliminate such errors. In recent years, however, researchers have compiled a rather large body of evidence that suggests individual JDM errors persist in and affect the outcomes associated with capital markets, for example, stock prices and trading volume (see Barberis and Thaler [2003] for a review).

There appear to be at least two reasons for this finding. First, there are "limits to arbitrage" in capital markets (Barberis and Thaler 2003). As Barberis and Thaler explain, arbitrage is "an investment strategy that offers riskless profits at no cost"; arbitrage opportunities appear when some individual traders are making JDM errors. *Limits to arbitrage* means that factors exist to render these strategies either risky or costly or both. For example, implementing investment strategies typically requires various search and transactions costs. The second reason individual errors can persist is that markets, and the monetary incentives they provide, do not always resolve problems with individual JDM, either in the laboratory or the real world (e.g., Camerer 1992; Ganguly et al. 1994; Berg et al. 1995; Camerer 1995; Jenkins et al. 1998; Bonner et al. 2000; Bonner and Sprinkle 2002). One explanation for this finding is that markets and incentives do not address all the causes of low-quality JDM.[13] For example, because of the way memory is structured, people tend to focus on the most salient information even if such information is inaccurate or irrelevant to JDM; markets cannot change such fundamental properties of humans. In addition, markets and incentives can include features that, in fact, have negative effects on individuals' JDM quality. For example, incentives can produce arousal, which has an inverted-U relation with JDM quality (see Chapter 7). If markets (and their related incentives) do not resolve JDM errors and such errors tend to be systematic, individuals' errors can aggregate to create market inefficiencies. As such, individual JDM can have far-reaching consequences (e.g., Thaler 1993; Berg et al. 1995; Bloomfield et al. 2003).

Because accounting is an applied field, the practical reasons for studying JDM are important. However, there are theoretical reasons for studying JDM in accounting as well. Accounting settings have unique features for which theories in other disciplines may not be well developed. For example, the review process in auditing is unique in that it combines elements of accountability by subordinates to superiors who face different incentives, group decision making, the need to follow professional standards, and learning through feedback. More generally, accountants, auditors, and others of interest to accounting researchers are subject to the effects of regulations, professional standards, and other restrictions on practice (also see Ashton and Ashton [1995]). These restrictions may not allow for the implementation of seemingly "natural" improvement methods for low-quality JDM (e.g., incentives for auditors

---

[13]Many of these causes are discussed in Chapters 3 through 7.

based on the number of unqualified opinions they render). Understanding how people make judgments and decisions under these conditions, then, is important for improving JDM in other settings that are at least somewhat similar.

1-4   HOW TO STUDY JDM IN ACCOUNTING

Assume that a researcher is interested in studying JDM issues in accounting. The next logical question to ask, then, is: "How does one go about doing this successfully?" There are two important parts to this question. First, the researcher needs to understand how to study JDM issues in general. Second, she needs to consider the practical concerns that distinguish accounting (and other applied fields) from other domains. To address these questions, this section provides a framework for studying JDM issues. Then it continues with a discussion of how to identify an important JDM research question using institutional knowledge. Next, the section discusses the importance of incorporating psychology theories into JDM research. Finally, the section reviews various methods available for conducting JDM research and their particular benefits and disadvantages.

Framework for Studying JDM Issues in Accounting

Figure 1-1 presents a framework that delineates a logical progression of research questions related to individual JDM. As discussed above, the framework uses "quality" as the element of individual JDM to be studied; however, it also is possible to use the framework to focus on sheer variation in JDM rather than JDM quality. The framework also includes key questions about JDM quality as both a dependent variable and an independent variable. Finally, the framework incorporates questions that are pertinent to the applied field of accounting but not necessarily to JDM work in other fields.

The framework serves at least three purposes. A researcher can use the framework to determine, ex post, if there are any holes in the literature related to a particular JDM issue in accounting; these holes would be questions in the framework about which our knowledge is incomplete. Consequently, these holes can suggest particular research projects or series of projects that might be of interest. In particular, the researcher might be most concerned about unanswered questions in the framework that precede questions researchers are studying currently. For example, if research has proceeded to consider methods for improving JDM quality in a particular task without first considering causes of variation in JDM quality in that task, one should be concerned about the quality of inferences we can draw from the studies on improvement methods. Concern would arise from the fact that it is difficult to find (and study) appropriate ways of improving average JDM quality without first understanding what causes variation therein.

The second purpose of the framework is to evaluate a line of research or particular project ex ante. To use the framework for this purpose, the researcher would engage in three tasks. First, she would locate her planned project(s) in the series of questions in the framework. Next, she would determine if there is sufficient literature to address the questions that precede her question. Then, she would try to anticipate the answers to both her question and the questions that follow hers in the framework. If these answers lead her to a part of the framework that states "reconsider the research," the researcher can start the process over by considering a different research question.

FIGURE 1-1   Framework for JDM Research in Accounting

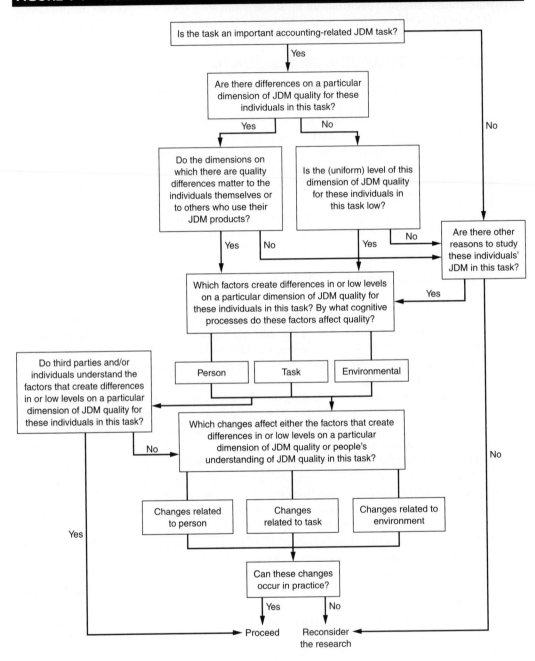

By doing these three tasks (one or more times), the researcher can evaluate a potential project in several ways. One key issue she can address is the positioning of her project within the existing literature. By positioning the project within the literature and anticipating answers to future questions (some of which address the concerns of the applied field of accounting), the researcher can take steps toward ensuring that her project will contribute to the literature from both a theoretical standpoint and an applied standpoint. Another key issue she can address is whether her project may fail to find the hypothesized relations among variables. There are many reasons research studies fail to find hypothesized relations, such as low power of statistical tests, and the framework does not address all of these. However, it can address one major reason for failing to find hypothesized effects, which is whether the research question is premature in the sense that the literature has not addressed preceding questions sufficiently. For example, before examining the determinants of variation in JDM quality in a task, it would be useful to have some evidence that there is, in fact, variation in JDM quality in that task. Otherwise, the project on determinants of variation may not find its predicted effects.

The third purpose of the framework is to serve as an organizing tool for discussing the literature on JDM in accounting. Conceptual frameworks that organize a field can help people learn about the field more rapidly (e.g., Bonner and Walker 1994). Consequently, the remainder of the book is organized around the framework. The next sections develop the framework in detail.

Is the Task an Important Accounting-Related JDM Task?

The first question in the framework is whether the task the researcher intends to study is an important accounting-related JDM task. This question clearly would not appear in frameworks for JDM research in other fields, but the reason for its inclusion here is clear. As accounting researchers, we tend to study accounting-related JDM tasks that are important, typically defined as "practically significant."[14]

There are a variety of ways to determine whether tasks have practical significance. First, the researcher can appeal to empirical research on major (e.g., stock market) reactions to the particular judgment or decision.[15] For example, knowing that the stock market reacts to earnings forecasts (e.g., Gonedes et al. 1976; Givoly and Lakonishok 1979; Brown et al. 1985) gives us evidence of the practical significance of this task.[16] Second, she can appeal to the fact that demand for the task currently exists. Thus, even if there were no observed reaction to earnings forecasts, the researcher could claim that the fact that there are thousands of analysts being paid large salaries to perform this task is evidence of its significance. Third, the researcher can appeal to data that suggest there will be demand for the task in the future (e.g., the assurance services previewed by the Special Committee on Assurance Services [AICPA 1996]).

The framework allows for either a "yes" or "no" answer to this question. A "yes" answer results in proceeding to the question in the next paragraph, whereas a "no"

---

[14]Recall the earlier definition of accounting-related tasks.

[15]Much archival work in accounting already documents such reactions by examining the "information content" or "price informativeness" of a particular judgment or decision (e.g., analysts' stock recommendations).

[16]It could be argued that the stock market is reacting inappropriately to these forecasts if, for example, investors cannot earn substantially higher profits by using the forecasts. However, the fact that the market reacts is evidence of at least the perceived importance of the task.

answer results in proceeding to a question about whether there are other reasons to study JDM in the task. There are several reasons to study tasks that either are not accounting related or are lacking in practical significance; these are addressed below.

Are There Differences on a Particular Dimension of JDM Quality for These Individuals in This Task?

The second question in the framework is whether there are differences on a particular dimension of JDM quality (e.g., accuracy) for certain individuals in the task of interest.[17] The reader should note that this question is narrower than the first; it focuses on a particular dimension of JDM quality and a certain group of individuals.[18] For example, if earnings forecasting is the JDM task of importance, researchers by necessity tend to narrow at this point to focus on, for example, the extent to which forecasts correspond to actual earnings and on analysts as the individuals making these forecasts. Implicit in this narrowing is an assumption that both the dimension of JDM quality and the particular individuals are of significance to accounting researchers, as well as an assumption that the quality dimension is significant for that group of individuals. Important groups of individuals are discussed above. Establishing the significance of a particular JDM quality dimension can be done in a manner similar to establishing the significance of the task. For example, if the market reaction to analysts' earnings forecasts differs based on the extent to which they are predicted to correspond to actual earnings, this quality dimension can be considered significant for analysts. Even if there is no differential market reaction to this quality dimension, if analysts' compensation depends on it, it also can be considered significant.[19]

Most important, this question serves to remind the researcher that, before using JDM quality as a dependent or independent variable, it is important to establish that JDM quality indeed is a variable (not a constant). Differences as to quality can be examined as they relate to, say, average quality and the variation around that average, or with regard to other properties of the distribution, such as the percentage of persons who currently have high-quality levels of JDM. Clearly, it is necessary to learn about the distribution of JDM quality (on some dimension) among a particular group of decision makers (e.g., producers, users, or auditors of accounting information) in the task of interest before moving on to other questions such as those about causes of variation in quality. Surprisingly, despite forty years of research, there are many accounting tasks for which there is no clear answer to this most basic question, at least for certain groups of individuals or on certain dimensions of quality. For example, as recently as just a few years ago, studies continued to address the question of whether there are differences in the accuracy of analysts' earnings forecasts (Sinha et al. 1997). As another example, we know very little about the quality of managerial accountants' JDM in all

---

[17]Again, such differences can be either across individuals at a single point in time or within individuals over time.

[18]There are multiple dimensions of JDM quality that are of interest for accounting-related tasks. Chapter 2 delineates these dimensions and discusses further how a researcher determines the dimensions of significance for a given task.

[19]Before conducting a research project that involves examining a previously studied JDM task with a new group of individuals or using a different JDM quality dimension, it is important to consider whether expected findings may differ from those with an already-studied group of individuals or an already-studied dimension. For example, if internal auditors are expected to have JDM in a particular task that is similar to that of external auditors, it is not clear whether the incremental contribution of a study of internal auditors' JDM in this task is substantial.

the tasks they perform. Again, the framework provides two paths, respectively, for "yes" and "no" answers to this question. The next paragraph addresses the question that follows from a "yes" answer, whereas a later section addresses the question that follows from a "no" answer (i.e., whether JDM quality on a particular dimension for a particular group of individuals is uniformly low).

Do the Dimensions on Which There Are Quality Differences Matter to the Individuals Themselves or to Others Who Use Their JDM Products?

If there is evidence that there is variation in quality in a JDM task either across individuals or within individuals over time, it is appropriate to ask whether the quality dimension(s) on which there are differences (and, obviously, the differences themselves) matter to someone. Important parties who may care about variation in JDM quality include the individuals themselves, the firms for which they work, and other third parties outside firms who rely on the work of these individuals, such as investors and suppliers. This is the second question in the framework that is somewhat unique to the applied field of accounting. One reason is that it is one way of establishing the practical significance of a particular dimension of a JDM task (as discussed above).[20] Second, considering whether quality differences matter to third parties who rely on the products of individual JDM is an important distinguishing feature of the accounting domain because one of the primary purposes of accounting is to provide information for others' JDM.

This question is the first in the framework to examine JDM quality as the independent variable. For JDM quality to matter, there must be economic consequences for the individuals themselves and the firms for which they work, or reactions and associated economic consequences for third parties who use the JDM. Do JDM quality differences have to matter to both the individuals themselves and others to answer "yes" to this question? In my opinion, they do not; if JDM quality differences do not matter to firms or third parties, one can proceed through the framework.[21] Suppose, for example, that studies find that the market reaction to the release of analysts' forecasts does not vary with the accuracy of those forecasts. Why might this occur? It may be the case that individual investors dominate the market and these individual investors are either uninformed about or do not care about the accuracy of analysts' forecasts; perhaps they care more about other factors such as timeliness (Clement and Tse 2003).[22] Nevertheless, it is reasonable to continue to examine issues related to analyst forecast accuracy if differences on the accuracy dimension of JDM quality matter to the analysts themselves. For example, analysts' accuracy relative to their peers is related to job turnover (Mikhail et al. 1999). Further, if variation in JDM quality matters to the individuals themselves, this is a possible clue that variation in quality should matter to third

---

[20]Thus, researchers may answer this question prior to answering the above question as part of establishing the importance of their work.

[21]One cautionary note is that research examining the economic consequences to individuals of their JDM quality is not unique to accounting; such research is common in labor economics, management, and other fields (e.g., Hong et al. 2000). If accounting journals find this work to not be accounting related, the researcher must compete against researchers in other fields for publication in those fields. Nevertheless, accounting researchers likely are those most interested in the factors that affect accounting professionals' work-related outcomes.

[22]Clearly, this result also could occur because of research design, variable measurement, or data analysis problems. These issues are discussed shortly.

parties. For example, research might examine whether attending to variation in analysts' forecast accuracy could result in better decisions and financial outcomes for investors (Brown and Mohammad 2001).

Overall, then, if differences on some dimension of JDM quality matter to someone, if only to the accounting professionals themselves, then one obtains a "yes" answer to this question. A "yes" answer then leads to the next key question in the framework (that relates to the determinants of variation in JDM quality). A "no" answer leads the researcher to consider whether there are other reasons to study JDM in this task.

Is the (Uniform) Level of This Dimension of JDM Quality for These Individuals in This Task Low?

Before coming to the next key question in the framework, however, we must consider the issues that arise if research (or the researcher's best guess if she is using the framework ex ante) indicates there are likely no differences either across or within individuals for a particular group of individuals on some dimension of JDM quality in a given task. To address these issues, the next question in the framework asks whether the (uniform) level of a particular dimension of JDM quality in the task is low. "Low" quality may mean quality, for example, that is low vis-à-vis some absolute standard (see Chapter 2 for further discussion). Another way of phrasing this question is as follows: Is the dimension of JDM quality for this task worth studying from a practical perspective? Recall that one goal of JDM research is to improve decision making. If some dimension of JDM quality in a task is uniformly good, the framework directs the researcher to consider whether there are other reasons to continue research.[23] Stopping and considering this issue is appropriate to remind researchers that accounting is an applied field; hence, certain research topics may be more appealing than others.[24]

Are There Other Reasons to Study These Individuals' JDM in This Task?

A researcher can arrive at this question in the framework in three different ways. First, she can answer "no" to the question of whether the task she proposes to study is an important accounting-related JDM task. Second, she can find that there are differences on a given dimension of JDM quality but these differences do not matter to third parties or to the individuals themselves. Third, she can find that there are no differences on this particular dimension of JDM quality for this task and that the uniform level of quality is high.

If the researcher has arrived at this point because she has answered "no" to the question of whether this is an important accounting-related JDM task, she most likely is using an abstract task to conduct basic research about JDM issues that are of importance to accounting researchers. This is perhaps the most compelling reason to

---

[23]"Good" JDM quality (on a given dimension) means quality that is high but not necessarily perfect. To determine whether improvement efforts would be helpful, one must consider the costs and benefits of improvement (as well as the costs of research to examine appropriate improvements). Further, one must consider that improvements in quality on one dimension may lead to decrements in quality on another dimension. Finally, costs of various remedies such as those that use technology can change dramatically over time. Thus, project ideas that lead to "reconsider the research" at this point may be more feasible at future dates.

[24]It also is important to keep in mind that conducting research on variables that are expected to affect JDM quality or consequences of JDM quality where quality is uniformly high likely will be fruitless, again, because JDM quality is essentially a constant.

continue doing work on the issue. Basic research in accounting is as critical as it is in other fields, and there are many excellent examples of basic research published in accounting journals (e.g., Sprinkle 2000). The principal concern about research using abstract tasks is that accounting researchers may not have a comparative advantage over other researchers who are interested in similar JDM issues. Again, then, if accounting journals will not publish the research (because their taste is that it does not have enough "accounting"), the researcher may be at a disadvantage when seeking publication in journals in another field.

If the researcher has reached this point because the JDM quality dimension(s) on which there are differences do not matter to anyone (including the individuals themselves), it may be difficult to justify continuing the research. One would have to ask why a researcher is examining questions related to these dimensions of JDM quality if they do not appear to matter. Clearly, prior research may have failed to document that these JDM quality differences matter due to measurement problems or other imperfections in the research. If a researcher feels fairly confident that this is the case, then it might be worthwhile to continue looking for evidence that the quality dimensions matter. Otherwise, she should reconsider the research.

The third instance in which a researcher reaches this portion of the framework is when a particular dimension of JDM quality in the task under consideration is uniformly high. There are many valid reasons for continuing to study tasks in which this is the case. For example, if some dimension of JDM appears to be of high quality because of controls already built into the work setting, research could help firms (and researchers) understand why these "natural controls" are effective. This is particularly pertinent if an organization is considering removing or changing some of these controls, say, in an attempt to improve other dimensions of JDM quality. Another important reason for continued study is the prospect of an externally imposed change that has the potential to decrease JDM quality on the dimension under consideration. A typical proposed change of interest to accountants is a financial reporting standard or another type of regulation. A final reason for continued study is that the task may be important for other purposes. For example, one reason there is a great deal of research on the properties of analysts' earnings forecasts is because researchers want to better understand their advantages and limitations when used as earnings expectations in non-JDM studies.

Which Factors Create Differences in or Low Levels on a Particular Dimension of JDM Quality for These Individuals in This Task? By What Cognitive Processes Do These Factors Affect Quality?

Once it has been determined that there are differences in JDM quality that matter or that JDM quality is uniformly low, or the researcher is conducting basic research on JDM issues, the next logical step is to begin to unearth the factors that create variation in or low levels of quality on the JDM dimension of interest for a particular group of individuals doing the task. In other words, this is the first question in which JDM quality serves as the dependent variable. In addition, it is essential to examine the cognitive processes, or mechanisms, by which these factors affect JDM quality. As will be discussed throughout the book, understanding the mechanisms (or mediators) underlying the relationship between a given factor and JDM is critical for identifying changes that can improve JDM.

As shown in the framework, the variables that affect JDM quality can be classified for simplicity into three general categories: person, task, and environmental. *Person variables* relate to characteristics the decision maker brings to the task, such as knowledge and ability. Although these variables (as well as task and environmental variables) affect JDM through various cognitive processes, cognitive processes also are included as a type of person variable because there are systematic errors that occur in these processes per se; as such, processes can have effects on JDM that go beyond their effects as mediators. *Task variables* relate to dimensions of the task, such as its complexity. *Environmental variables* relate to the conditions and circumstances surrounding an individual while she performs a JDM task and are not related to any one person or task. For example, people can be subject to severe time pressure while performing any number of tasks. Person, task, and environmental variables run the gamut from those that are not at all unique to accounting settings, such as personality factors, to those that are at least somewhat unique to professional settings, including accounting. The latter group includes knowledge; repeated (personal) involvement in JDM tasks; accountability to multiple parties, including superiors and clients; large monetary incentives; and the presence of various regulatory and disciplining forces on JDM (also see Ashton and Ashton [1995]). Perhaps it is the confluence of all these factors that makes accounting distinct from other professional fields.

Research that examines variation in one or more of these factors and relates this variation to quality differences is relatively straightforward. Research that attempts to determine reasons for uniformly low levels of JDM quality in a particular task is not. What a researcher might do in this situation is carefully understand the professionals, their task, and their environment, so she can identify, for example, what factors may be completely lacking that plausibly could improve quality. Perhaps people currently lack fundamental knowledge of the task because it is new. An experiment that manipulates training could be conducted to investigate the effects of variation in knowledge on JDM quality in the task. After learning about the factors that are related to variation in quality in a JDM task, there are two logical questions research may address. The following paragraphs discuss these questions.

Do Third Parties and/or Individuals Understand the Factors That Create Differences in or Low Levels on a Particular Dimension of JDM Quality for These Individuals in This Task?

One important question that follows from learning about the person, task, and environmental variables that create differences in or low levels of JDM quality is whether third parties understand these variables' effects. Researchers may proceed to either this question or the next one in the framework because research examining this question can proceed parallel to other work. This question's importance arises because one of the key issues of concern to accountants is how the work of accounting-related professionals is used by and affects others. For example, unsophisticated investors using analysts' earnings forecasts as input to investment decisions appear not to understand completely the factors related to the accuracy of those forecasts (Bonner et al. 2003). One implication of this finding is that unsophisticated investors' returns may suffer as a result of placing too much reliance on inaccurate forecasts.

Whether individuals understand the factors that affect their own JDM quality is important for study from the standpoint that their understanding (or lack thereof) can facilitate (attenuate) the effective implementation of JDM improvement methods. Both "yes" and "no" answers to this question indicate research whose pursuit is worthwhile. However, a "no" answer indicates that it also would be useful to conduct further work on changes to increase the level of understanding of the factors that affect JDM quality.

Which Changes Affect Either the Factors That Create Differences in or Low Levels on a Particular Dimension of JDM Quality or People's Understanding of JDM Quality in This Task?

A second question that arises after investigating variables that affect JDM quality (or understanding of these factors) is which improvement methods can reduce variation in and/or raise levels of quality (or understanding of the factors that affect quality) in a particular JDM task. This question clearly arises if the researcher's ultimate goal is to improve JDM quality and current quality is not high. Again, as shown in the framework, methods for improving low-quality JDM (or low-quality understanding of others' JDM) can be classified as to whether they are changes related to the person, task, or environment. For example, the person can be trained, the task can be restructured, or the environment can be modified to include less time pressure. These categories of improvement methods do not necessarily match up one to one with the categories of variables that contribute to lower-quality decision making. For example, a person variable that can positively affect JDM quality is motivation. A method to improve JDM where motivation is low may be to automate the task; the computer exerts effort unless shut down. Further, there are multiple variants of any given improvement method. Decision aids come in many forms, from simple paper-and-pencil aids to sophisticated and expensive expert systems. Finally, changes to the person, task, or environment can be either not unique (decision aids) or at least somewhat unique to accounting settings (regulation).

Although the development of methods for improving JDM quality may appear to be a practical problem of allocating scarce resources within firms (e.g., between recruiting programs and training programs), research can be helpful on at least two fronts. First, as mentioned earlier, research that examines causes of lower-quality JDM or understanding of others' JDM can examine process explanations. Understanding the process factors that affect JDM quality helps narrow the range of plausible improvement methods. For example, if people tend to engage in poor statistical reasoning while making a judgment, training may not be a plausible fix because statistical reasoning fallacies may be "hardwired." Second, research can examine the as-implemented effectiveness of plausible improvement methods. Even theoretically plausible solutions do not always improve JDM (e.g., Kachelmeier and Messier 1990). Further, methods that actually improve JDM in one task may create problems in other JDM tasks. For example, Bonner et al. (1996) note that a decision aid that improves the quality of particular conditional probability judgments for auditors may create problems in other probability judgments.

Can These Changes Occur in Practice?

The final question in the framework is also the last that is somewhat unique to the applied domain of accounting. This question asks whether the type of change one is proposing to study, and ultimately considering suggesting to practitioners, can occur in practice. Consider a research project that finds time pressure has a negative effect on

JDM quality in a particular auditing task. The logical change to suggest for improving JDM in this situation is to reduce time pressure. Because most auditing firms cannot do this in today's competitive environment, this change likely would not be feasible. At this point, the framework suggests that the researcher reconsider proceeding with a project that results in a "no" answer to this question. The point is for the researcher to think through the entire framework (as it relates to any given research project or line of research) and consider what suggestions about decision improvement she ultimately might make, if indeed this is the ultimate goal of the research. If these suggestions would not be appropriate for practice, a reframing of the project(s) is in order. The previously mentioned study of the effects of time pressure on auditors' JDM could consider examining other variables that could alleviate its ill effects (e.g., knowledge). In this way, the author would be able to discuss not only the time pressure problem, but feasible methods of improving JDM as well.

Identifying an Important JDM Research Issue

Of course, this framework is useful only once the researcher identifies a potentially interesting accounting-related JDM task and an interesting research question related to that task. How does one go about identifying interesting tasks and questions? Identifying interesting tasks involves using general institutional knowledge, and identifying interesting questions involves using detailed, task-specific institutional knowledge, which is gained through a process called "task analysis."

General institutional knowledge typically relates to one of the functional areas of accounting (e.g., financial accounting) or to a particular group of individuals of interest to accountants (e.g., auditors). Having general institutional knowledge about auditors means that one understands the tasks auditors perform as part of their job, the organizational factors that influence their work (e.g., performance measurement and reward systems), the characteristics perceived to be important for their work (e.g., industry-specific knowledge), and the general sources of information they use.

A typical JDM research project, however, focuses by necessity on a single task performed by a particular group of individuals, such as evaluation of internal control systems made by auditors. A successful project, then, also requires task-specific institutional knowledge. Gaining this knowledge through *task analysis* (Newell and Simon 1972; Zemke and Kramlinger 1982; Desberg and Taylor 1986; Schraagen et al. 2000) entails specifying, at a very detailed level, the steps one goes through to perform a task (including the information used) and the characteristics one needs to perform those steps. The techniques used for task analysis include reading various documents and reviewing records that show the actual performance of the task. Documents to read include company manuals and flowcharts, professional standards, textbooks and training materials, practitioner articles, case studies, and work papers and memos completed by practitioners. One also should reference the related archival literature. (For studies that do this, see Hirst et al. [1995] and Libby and Tan [1999].) For example, an archival study that examines the factors investors appear to consider in valuing a particular account (as evidenced by stock prices) might provide some indirect evidence about the actual steps investors go through in making such judgments.

In addition, researchers can ask a small number of individuals to perform the JDM task and think aloud as they do so (or directly after they finish). To provide these *concurrent (retrospective) verbal protocols* (Ericsson and Simon 1996), the researcher asks subjects to describe what they are doing while they are performing (after they perform) the task. For example, a researcher could ask an auditor to think aloud while she performs analytical procedures for a retailing company, specifically to delineate the ratios and other calculations of most relevance. An alternative to gathering protocols that are specific to a given case is to ask questions that are more general in nature; this allows for inquiry about factors that vary across situations. These questions can be asked in the form of structured or unstructured interviews or surveys (e.g., Hirst and Koonce 1996). Finally, it goes without saying that the researcher should perform the JDM task herself.[25]

Task analysis can be painfully detailed (e.g., Bonner and Walker 1994). Keep in mind, however, that each researcher may not have to conduct a thorough task analysis for each JDM study. In many cases, task analyses can be found in previously published studies. However accomplished, task analysis is critical for a successful study. It can help the researcher discover the "big potatoes" for a particular JDM task.[26] "Big potatoes" are the variables that are most likely to explain a large amount of variation in JDM quality. For example, one may note that there is substantial variation in the information individuals purport to examine, leading to an investigation of information search as a key determinant of JDM quality. Without a task analysis, the researcher mistakenly may believe that information search is a trivial component of the task. "Big potatoes" also may refer to the variables that are most unique to the accounting setting of interest; task analysis is helpful for clarifying this issue as well.

Task analysis can also be quite helpful in identifying theories appropriate for hypothesis development. Certain tasks that auditors and other accounting professionals perform have properties similar to those of medical diagnosis tasks, so theories about medical JDM may be appropriate for use in these settings. Choosing appropriate theories, in turn, can lead the researcher to consider variables to either include or control for in a study because the theories indicate that these variables interact with the variable of interest. Next, a thorough task analysis helps a researcher construct successful manipulations or measurements of variables. Finally, as mentioned previously, thorough task analysis forces the researcher to think about constraints on solutions prior to conducting research projects and, in so doing, avoid projects that, in the applied setting of accounting, miss the forest for the trees.

Using Psychology Theories to Study JDM Issues in Accounting

JDM research in accounting and elsewhere typically develops hypotheses on the basis of psychology theories. Clearly, one reason for this is tradition and training; JDM research occupies a prominent place in psychology, and JDM researchers in all fields, including accounting, tend to be trained in psychology. However, because of the significance of economics-based research in accounting, it also is important to consider the value that can be added to JDM studies from reference to and understanding of psychology theories in addition to or instead of economics theories (Koonce and Mercer 2005).

---

[25]Each of these task analysis procedures has its disadvantages. Documents may be out of date or inaccurate. Records that show actual performance of the task may not fully reflect what was done. Verbal protocols are time consuming to gather and difficult to analyze. In answering survey or interview questions, people may have poor memory and/or insight into how they perform the task. For all these reasons, task analysis is an important precursor to, not a substitute for, a rigorous research study.
[26]"Big potatoes" is Bill Kinney's terminology.

In brief, economics theories about individual JDM have weaknesses that can lead to problems in moving JDM research in accounting forward. Psychology theories can at least partially alleviate these weaknesses. The first weakness is that economics theories make various assumptions about individual JDM that are not descriptive or predictive (Koonce and Mercer 2005). Relying on psychology theories in addition to or instead of economics theories would allow the researcher to develop different hypotheses that are more likely to be supported by empirical findings and, thus, that allow us to better understand and improve JDM. For example, economics tends to assume that individuals making decisions behave in a manner consistent with expected utility (EU) theory (von Neumann and Morgenstern 1947; Savage 1954).[27] However, a great deal of research shows that people systematically deviate from this approach to making decisions (Kahneman and Tversky 2000).[28] If researchers rely solely on EU theory to develop hypotheses and those hypotheses are not supported, they may draw incorrect conclusions about individual JDM. For example, researchers may conclude that EU theory is descriptive of JDM, but their studies fail to find it, for example, because of a lack of statistical power.

A second weakness of some economics theories is that they assume away critical parts of the JDM process. Psychology theories address people's behavior in these stages and, thus, at a minimum, draw people's attention to them for consideration while doing research. For example, EU theory assumes that decision alternatives are specified for the individual. This often is not the case; in many real-world situations, individuals have to determine what their alternatives are before making a decision, and indeed, this stage of the process may be the stage that causes the most variation in JDM quality (Einhorn and Hogarth 1981). In other words, perhaps some people have low decision quality because they never identify the best alternative. A study based solely on economics theories would not recognize that this factor may be the "big potato" for a certain task and, thus, focus on a factor of minimal importance.

Third, economics theories tend not to be at the same level of granularity as psychology theories (Koonce and Mercer 2005). Many psychology theories specify in detail, for example, the cognitive processes by which various factors affect JDM quality (e.g., through the search for information).[29] In other words, psychology theories allow the researcher to make more specific predictions than do economics theories. The problem that crops up when economics theories are not detailed about processes is that it is more difficult to prescribe methods for increasing the quality of JDM. For example, if economics-based research does not consider whether abilities have a positive effect on JDM quality because people know what to do at the outset as opposed to, say, learn better from training, it is unclear whether firms should focus employee improvement efforts solely on hiring high-ability people or on providing more training to current high-ability employees.

---

[27]EU theory states that individuals choose the decision alternative that has the highest expected utility. EU for an alternative is the sum of the EU for each possible outcome associated with that alternative. EU for each possible outcome is calculated as the probability the outcome will occur times the utility of the outcome.

[28]A psychology theory that is more descriptive of individual decision making than is EU theory is prospect theory (see Chapter 6).

[29]Barberis and Thaler (2003) note that this is one of the principal reasons that psychology theories have become one of the foundations of behavioral finance.

Methods for Studying JDM Issues in Accounting

Once the researcher identifies an important JDM question, conducts a thorough task analysis, and finds pertinent psychology theories, there remains the issue of which research method to employ for addressing the main research question.[30] The mainstay of most JDM research in accounting is experimentation or passive observation similar to experimentation. (In the latter method, all variables are measured rather than manipulated, but control is similar to that in an experiment; see Bonner and Lewis [1990] for an example.) This is not surprising given that the mainstay method for JDM research in other fields, most notably psychology, is the experiment. Consistent with this, JDM researchers in accounting who study psychology theories tend to learn how to do experiments.

In general, experiments have many advantages over other methods; these advantages pertain to JDM research as well. Experiments allow the researcher to control for alternative explanations for results through random assignment of subjects to treatments; systematic manipulation of variables of interest; control of variables not of interest by, for example, holding them constant; and valid and reliable measurement of variables. These dimensions of experiments allow for better attributions that relations between independent variables and JDM quality or between JDM quality and various consequences are causal in nature, or internally valid.[31] Another advantage of experiments is their ability to examine the processes through which factors affect JDM quality. As described earlier, understanding these processes is critical for proposing and examining changes to the person, task, or environment that are meant to improve JDM.

A more recent impetus for using experiments to address JDM questions in accounting is to conduct ex ante research related to policy issues (e.g., Maines 1994; Schipper 1994; Hussein and Rosman 1997). Because experiments allow the researcher to manipulate just about anything (within the realm of what a human subjects committee considers reasonable), they can provide information about the effects of something that does not exist in the real world; for example, a proposed change in financial reporting standards. This advantage of experimentation is particularly important for examining questions about potentially costly methods for improving JDM prior to their implementation.

However, other methods, in particular archival data analysis, can be very useful for addressing JDM issues in accounting as well. Archival analysis has both general and JDM-specific advantages over experimentation. General advantages are the external validity it provides, the ability to assess the economic significance of variables of interest, and the provision of a representative sample of values for independent variables. Experiments, by necessity, abstract from the real world and sacrifice some external validity.[32] When it comes to the study of JDM in accounting, archival data analysis has further specific advantages. One is that this method may be better at examining the questions in the framework that include JDM quality as an independent variable and economic consequences for individuals, their firms, or third parties as the dependent

---

[30]For a more thorough discussion of the strengths and weaknesses of various research methods, see Kinney (1986).

[31]*Internal validity* is the truth value that we assign to the statement that an independent variable causes a dependent variable (Campbell and Stanley 1963).

[32]*External validity* is the extent to which the causal relationship between an independent variable and a dependent variable, demonstrated in a given study, generalizes to different times, settings, and people (Campbell and Stanley 1963).

variable. For example, it may be difficult to provide severe economic consequences for individuals or third parties in an experimental setting. A second JDM-specific advantage of archival data analysis is that it examines JDM as a product of multiple factors, many of which are correlated in accountants' natural settings. Experiments tend to remove these correlations in order to draw clean inferences. However, many researchers argue that a field gains a better understanding of JDM if studies focus on replicating the settings in which people have learned to do specific JDM tasks because they have adapted their JDM to these environments (Hammond and Stewart 2001). Finally, a practical advantage of archival data analysis is that the researcher forgoes the need to secure the assistance and serious experimental participation of very busy and highly paid professionals. This is a nontrivial issue when considering some of the groups of interest to accounting JDM researchers such as standard-setters and judges.

Unfortunately, of course, archival data analysis has some severe limitations related to the testing of hypotheses about individual JDM. In cases where the researcher is interested in disentangling the effects of correlated variables such as knowledge and information search strategies, it is far more difficult to do so with archival analysis than with experimentation. An experiment can create a situation in which such variables are not confounded by using factorial design. For example, a researcher can direct or teach subjects in different experimental groups (say, formed on the basis of pretest measures of knowledge) to use different search strategies. Conclusions from archival data analysis also may reflect JDM-related selection biases. Consider the inference that sell-side analysts learn from experience based on the finding that experience is related to forecast accuracy. This is problematic in that additional experience may be "granted" to only analysts whom brokerage firms select for retention and promotion based on some other factor such as ability (Mikhail et al. 1997). Because experiments randomly assign individuals to treatments, selection biases such as these can be eliminated.

In addition, variable measurement when conducting archival data analysis is limited by the state of the data (and the researcher's cleverness). This can be a particularly egregious problem for JDM research because few databases contain the typical dependent or independent variable of interest (individual judgments or decisions). Further, when JDM is the dependent variable, important independent variables, such as knowledge, also typically are not available. Thus, archival researchers often must employ weak proxies for both JDM (e.g., stock prices for individual judgments and decisions) and other variables of interest (e.g., general experience for knowledge). Further, they often must omit important correlated variables due to the inability to include measures for these factors. Finally, archival researchers typically cannot examine process factors or conduct ex ante research, both of which are important for suggesting ways to improve JDM.[33]

Researchers may also consider studying JDM using surveys and interviews (Carroll and Johnson 1990). Although these methods are useful for many areas of accounting research and for task analysis leading up to JDM studies, they suffer from some serious disadvantages when it comes to studying JDM.[34] When researchers use

---

[33]Experimentation and archival data analysis are the most typical methods for studying JDM issues in accounting, but mathematical modeling also can be appropriate (e.g., Trueman 1990, 1994; Hayes 1998). Its current lack of popularity likely reflects the background and interests of modelers rather than the usefulness of the method.
[34]This statement does not imply that interviews or surveys should never be used for JDM research. Sometimes other methods are not available. More important, careful use of these techniques can lead to interesting insights (e.g., Nelson et al. 2002).

these methods, people typically do not make judgments or decisions. For researchers to measure JDM quality, then, they must ask people either to recall specific judgments or decisions or to rate their own JDM quality. When people recall judgments and decisions, they may exhibit errors or biases because of flaws in memory. For example, people may simply not remember specific judgments or decisions and, thus, have to guess about or reconstruct their JDM, leading to errors. Also, there are systematic biases such as the *hindsight bias;* this occurs when an outcome related to the decision has occurred since the time of the judgment and people report the outcome as having been their initial judgment when, in fact, it was not (Plous 1993). When people rate their own JDM quality, they may exhibit overconfidence and, thus, overestimate their quality. Although some contend that these biases are not problematic in that they simply increase the average JDM quality, this is not necessarily the case. If some subjects overestimate their capabilities and other subjects underestimate their capabilities, the difference between these two types of subjects is systematic. And if the researcher does not recognize this omitted variable prior to conducting the study, surveys or interviews can lead to incorrect conclusions about the factors that affect JDM. As an example, consider the finding that there are gender-related differences in overconfidence (e.g., Lundeberg et al. 1994).

Finally, there are problems with measurement of independent variables as well when these methods are used. Put simply, people have difficulty explaining and describing their JDM. In other words, people lack insight into their own JDM inputs and processes. Somewhat paradoxically for researchers who would contend that surveys and interviews are acceptable for studying JDM as long as one appeals to highly knowledgeable subjects, lack of self-insight increases with knowledge. As persons increase their knowledge of a particular task, what they do in that task tends to become more automatic and less available for conscious description (Anderson 2005).

Summary of How to Study JDM in Accounting

Conducting a successful JDM research project in accounting requires consideration of a number of key questions. These questions are summarized in a framework that can be used to test the appeal of a proposed JDM project. "Running a project through the framework" requires general and task-specific institutional knowledge, the latter of which can be gained through task analysis. Finally, the researcher must choose an appropriate method for testing a JDM research question.

1-5 SUMMARY OF REMAINING CHAPTERS

The framework serves as an organizing tool for the remaining chapters. As part of addressing several of the earlier questions in the framework, Chapter 2 discusses in detail the issues related to defining and measuring JDM quality. In addition, Chapter 2 describes briefly what we know to date about whether variation in the JDM quality of various parties of interest to accounting researchers (e.g., investors, analysts, and auditors) matters to those individuals or to third parties. Chapters 3 through 7 survey research on variables that affect JDM quality. Chapters 3 through 5 focus on person variables, including the processes individuals employ to make judgments and decisions. Chapters 6 and 7 focus on task and environmental variables, respectively. Following along with the framework, Chapter 8 discusses research on the extent to which individuals and third parties understand the factors that affect JDM quality. Chapter 9 describes the findings of research on various methods of improving JDM quality. Finally, Chapter 10 revisits the framework, briefly summarizes what we have learned about JDM in accounting, and suggests directions for future research.

2

JDM Quality

Among the first several questions in the JDM framework presented in Chapter 1 is whether there are differences on a particular dimension of JDM quality for a given set of individuals in a given task.[1] Further questions ask whether these differences matter to anyone or, if there are no differences, whether JDM quality is uniformly low. Chapter 2 explores these three questions, as highlighted in Figure 2-1. In exploring these questions, the chapter does the following. First, because it is necessary to define and measure JDM quality when addressing these and other questions in the framework, the chapter discusses the many issues related to quality definition and measurement. Most important, the discussion contains a delineation of various dimensions of quality. Along with this, the chapter discusses how a researcher determines JDM quality dimensions worthy of study for a given accounting situation. Next, the chapter briefly surveys the evidence about whether differences in JDM quality for accounting decision makers have economic consequences for the decision makers themselves, their firms, and third parties who use their work products.

2-1 DEFINING JDM QUALITY

The simplicity of the framework may hide the fact that exploring even basic questions about JDM quality in accounting, such as whether there are differences across individuals, can be challenging. This is because researchers must first define JDM quality. Defining JDM quality is an inherently complex undertaking because there are a number of issues that must be resolved in order to fix upon a single definition. In accounting, the matter is further complicated by the fact that individuals of interest to accounting researchers often face multiple constituents for their JDM, and constituents vary as to their characterizations of JDM quality. This means that it is not appropriate for accounting researchers to narrow to a single definition of JDM quality to be used across all studies of accounting-related JDM.

Defining JDM quality presents several challenges per se and, consequently, has been the subject of much discussion in psychology (e.g., Funder 1987; Hastie and Rasinki 1988; Kruglanski 1989; Frisch and Jones 1993; Frisch and Clemen 1994). The first challenge is whether quality should be defined from the perspective of an individual's final answer—the output, or "performance," view—or from the perspective of how she gets to that answer—the input and process, or "process," view. The second issue is that there can be multiple criteria for evaluating either performance or process,

---

[1]Recall from Chapter 1 that narrowing to examine particular individuals and a specific dimension of JDM quality for a given task typically is necessary for constraining the scope of a single research project.

FIGURE 2-1   **Framework for JDM Research in Accounting**

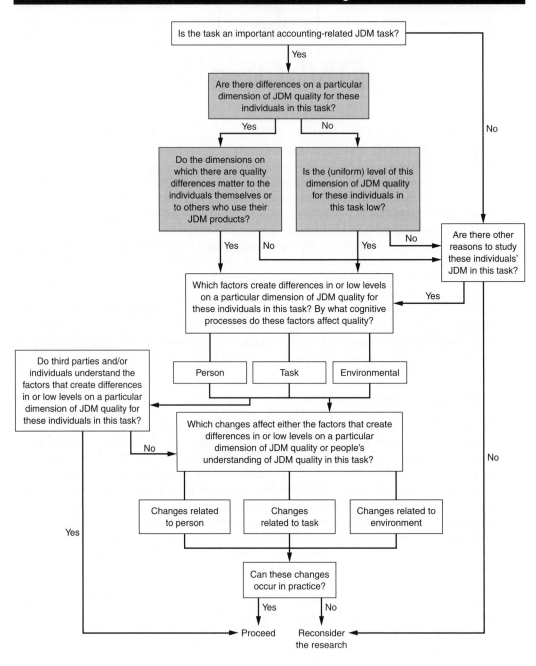

thus creating multiple possible dimensions of JDM quality. For example, a final answer can be evaluated as to whether it agrees with others' answers or as to whether it agrees with a real-world outcome. The researcher must decide which of these dimensions is most important. Along with this, once the researcher chooses a dimension of performance or process for examination, she must determine how to define the dimension conceptually. For example, is agreement with one's peers or with one's superiors the appropriate form of agreement with others to consider? Finally, when discussing differences in JDM quality, oftentimes researchers, and even more frequently practitioners, want to know what "high quality" JDM means. Consequently, the researcher must define high-quality JDM, or who is an "expert," for a given dimension of JDM quality. The resolution of such issues in psychology typically centers around theoretical debate. More important, some psychologists call for this resolution to result in the designation of a single definition of JDM quality on which researchers can agree (e.g., Hastie and Rasinski 1988).

Further difficulty arises when defining JDM quality in accounting. Generally, there are multiple constituents for JDM in professional settings (Hammond 1996), and accounting is no exception. Accounting professionals' constituents include their superiors and peers in their organizations (e.g., partners in public accounting firms), internal "clients" (e.g., marketing managers who use cost information to make pricing decisions), and external clients (e.g., firms who pay for audits, investment banking clients of brokerage houses). They also include third parties who use accounting professionals' work (e.g., creditors who use audit reports, investors who use analyst reports); standard-setters (e.g., the FASB); regulators or, more generally, members of government (e.g., the SEC); and plaintiffs' lawyers, judges, and juries, or, more generally, participants in the legal system who evaluate accounting professionals' work. Further, particular constituents often have multiple goals related to professionals' JDM. For example, audit partners' goals for their personnel include ensuring that audits are done in accordance with professional standards and also that audits are done in minimal time in order to maximize firm and partner profits.[2]

The existence of multiple constituents for accounting professionals' JDM and multiple goals for each of these constituents suggests that there are many relevant JDM quality dimensions for a given accounting-related task, so researchers simply cannot fix on a single dimension based on theoretical arguments. For example, what is high-quality JDM for a tax professional when preparing a tax return? Taxpayer clients likely define this as JDM that saves them the most money. However, tax professionals also must be able to defend their JDM vis-à-vis tax laws to the IRS if clients are audited; not being able to defend their JDM can result in serious consequences such as fines. Given how likely it is that accounting professionals focus on more than one dimension of quality when making judgments and decisions, researchers may need to as well. At a minimum, a researcher who focuses, typically by necessity, on a single dimension should specify for readers the assumed constituent(s) for the individuals of interest in her study and the consequent view of quality she is adopting.

---

[2]Some individuals of interest to accounting researchers, such as individual investors, are not professionals and do not have multiple constituents for their JDM. Individual investors' JDM, for example, affects only the investors (and their families). Nevertheless, these individuals may have multiple goals for their own JDM.

More important, if accounting professionals face multiple constituents, many of whom have multiple goals regarding the professionals' JDM, those professionals likely cannot maximize JDM quality on all relevant dimensions. In other words, accounting professionals must make tradeoffs among various JDM quality dimensions. For example, auditors whose partners expect that they follow professional standards but also minimize time probably cannot do both. So, for example, they may exhibit less than high-quality JDM on the time dimension in order to have high-quality JDM on the following-professional-standards dimension. Again, in order to further our understanding of accounting professionals' JDM, researchers ultimately must incorporate considerations of these tradeoffs when defining JDM quality.

The bottom line is that "JDM quality" in accounting (and other professional settings) cannot be considered a unidimensional construct. For any given JDM task and group of individuals of interest to accounting researchers, there are multiple relevant dimensions of quality (or quality subconstructs) such as agreement with peers or correspondence with a real-world outcome. Thus, accounting research needs first to clearly define JDM quality with an eye toward focusing on multiple dimensions. Once dimensions are defined, accounting (and other) researchers still face the issue of measuring the given dimensions. For example, if JDM quality is to be defined as agreement with peers, how does the researcher determine who are "peers"? Further definitional and measurement issues are discussed in the next two sections.

2-2 PROCESS VERSUS PERFORMANCE VIEWS OF JDM QUALITY

The first issue to address when defining and measuring JDM quality is whether a person's JDM quality should be evaluated based on the extent to which her output, or final judgment or decision, corresponds with some "right final answer" or, instead, based on the extent to which her judgment or decision-making process (e.g., her use of information) corresponds with some "right process."[3] As mentioned above, these views are referred to, respectively, as the performance and process views.

There are compelling arguments for both positions. Starting with the performance view, firms often evaluate their personnel on the basis of final answers (judgment or decision outputs), perhaps primarily because outputs are less costly to observe than are processes and inputs. Observing outputs can be less costly if, for example, outputs are recorded in a firm's information system, whereas inputs and processes are not. Further, outputs likely are easier to measure than processes. Because employees often are evaluated by their firms this way, it makes sense for researchers to evaluate them in the same way.

In addition, third parties who use the JDM of others, particularly that of professionals, frequently care most about whether the professionals are likely to get the right answer. In other words, because third parties use the JDM work products of professionals as an input to their own JDM, they care about having inputs to their own JDM

---

[3]It is important to distinguish between JDM outputs and actual outcomes. An output is a response produced by a person. For the purposes of this book, outputs typically are judgments or decisions. Actual outcomes, on the other hand, are states of nature or events that are related to JDM outputs. For example, auditors make judgments about bankruptcy; the probabilities they estimate are their JDM outputs for this task. Outcomes, on the other hand, are the actual bankruptcies or nonbankruptcies of the firms for which they are making predictions.

that are "right" or, alternatively, relying on professionals who "perform well." In addition, it likely is less costly for third parties to observe outputs than to observe processes. Thus, viewing JDM quality as performance-based is credible from a third-party perspective as well. Finally, characterizing JDM quality in terms of outputs is consistent with research that focuses on the determinants of high-quality JDM by examining the inputs and processes that affect final judgments and decisions.

The process view of evaluating JDM quality also has support. Firms may evaluate their employees based on process rather than or in addition to performance; similarly, researchers may wish to evaluate individuals in this way. One reason firms do this is because focusing on performance or outputs alone as a view of JDM quality can impede learning. Learning requires feedback, and it is natural for firms and individuals to use actual outcomes (e.g., actual earnings) as that output-related feedback.[4] Unfortunately, there are many difficulties associated with learning from outcomes (Hogarth 1987). One problem arises because outcome information may not be available for all JDM outputs. For example, personnel managers have outcomes for only the people they hire, and thus, are unable to learn about the quality of their decisions regarding the people they do not hire. Another difficulty arises because outcomes can be affected by judgments and decisions per se (this is called a *treatment effect*). Personnel managers may pay special attention to the people they hire, thus elevating those individuals' performance vis-à-vis what it would be in the absence of special treatment. This elevation of performance may indicate to personnel managers that their JDM output is better than it really is.

Third parties' use of JDM also supports researchers taking a process view of JDM quality. Although third parties may prefer to use the JDM of professionals who have the "right answer," they also likely care about the process that is used to arrive at that answer. In other words, they want to be assured that professionals have not arrived at correct answers simply by accident. This is because people typically prefer to develop relationships with professionals to obtain ongoing inputs for their own JDM.[5] Consequently, they want to know something about the probability of right answers in the future and likely assess this probability based on the extent to which professionals' JDM processes appear to be systematically sound. For example, many patients would feel uncomfortable with a physician who chooses drugs to prescribe by going to her closet of drug samples and finding the drugs with the prettiest boxes. They would feel more comfortable if the physician chooses drugs based on a thorough understanding of the patients' medical problems and the drugs that address those problems.

In addition, third parties typically want to have recourse against professionals whose JDM leads them astray in their own judgments and decisions. From a legal perspective, it can be quite difficult to obtain recourse based solely on the professional having provided the "wrong answer." In cases against professionals, courts typically employ some sort of negligence standard that requires demonstration that the professional

---

[4]It is natural to use actual outcomes as output-related feedback because actual outcome information may be the least costly to obtain. Further, using outcomes for feedback conforms to commonsense views of what feedback should be. However, outcomes are not the only type of output-related feedback that can be used. For example, a firm could provide feedback to someone on their JDM outputs by comparing them to the JDM outputs of a second person such as a superior.

[5]Note that this is a general formulation of the process by which an individual might rely on a professional in making her judgments and decisions. In specific instances, the process may be far simpler. In the case of reliance on physicians, for example, many individuals do not really engage in any JDM processing of their own. For example, they may simply adopt a physician's recommendation without additional thought.

failed to exercise care in the JDM process. For example, a physician might be considered negligent if she fails to obtain information about drug allergies before prescribing a drug to which a patient happens to be allergic. Finally, it may simply seem unfair to many people to evaluate other individuals on outputs alone, that is, without paying any attention to how they obtain those outputs.[6]

Many accounting academics suggest an additional factor that supports a process view of JDM quality, which is that there sometimes is not a right answer for an accounting JDM task. A better specification of this argument is that there is no actual outcome directly associated with a particular judgment or decision. For example, many studies examine auditors' judgments about the strength of internal controls and suggest that there is no right answer for that task. From the perspective that *answer* means actual outcome, this is reasonable. There typically is no single outcome that can be used to evaluate the quality of auditors' judgments about the strength of controls. Although a financial statement misstatement may be detected later in the audit, it is quite difficult to tie such an outcome to the internal control evaluation because misstatements also can be caused, for example, by judgment errors by management.

However, the lack of a specific outcome related to JDM does not mean that researchers are left to define JDM quality in terms of process. Most of the internal control literature, for example, focuses on the extent to which auditors agree on their evaluations. This agreement on final answers is most decidedly not a process measure. Although it may not be the most desirable output measure, it is an output measure. Further, there are many other criteria (described in Section 2-3) against which researchers can compare JDM outputs to measure quality. Thus, the lack of a right answer as justification for a process view of JDM quality deserves quite a bit of scrutiny. The factors described earlier provide more support for a process view.

Performance and process views of JDM quality persist in accounting. This is not surprising given the earlier discussion about accounting professionals facing multiple constituents, most of whom have multiple goals. For example, investors, as a constituent of auditors, may have a goal of maximizing investment returns. Thus, when using auditors' opinions as part of the investment process, investors likely focus on auditors' performance when thinking about JDM quality. For example, Bouwman and Bradley (1997) note: "Users of financial statements want to be assured that these statements are correct, not whether the auditor has properly documented everything." However, in the event of large losses, investors' goal may change to maximizing losses recouped. In this case, investors may consider litigation and, thus, shift their focus toward a process view of JDM quality because they often have to prove that there are problems with the auditors' JDM process in order to recoup losses. Further, some constituents of auditors (e.g., regulators) may consistently focus more on process than on performance.

Despite the clear importance of the process view, the remainder of this book discusses JDM quality in terms of performance.[7] This is not meant to discourage the use of a process view by researchers, but rather to simplify and streamline the remainder of the

---

[6]Certainly, students have a strong sense that evaluating them based only on their final answers on exams is unfair if their processes are at least partially correct. In other words, people may have some innate sense that it is unfair not to give partial credit.

[7]When using a performance view, a reminder of the earlier cautionary note regarding the distinction between JDM outputs and actual outcomes is in order. Although the use of outcomes as a criterion for evaluating JDM outputs (performance) is quite common, they are different concepts that require separation for a clear understanding of JDM.

book. Further, focusing on the performance view allows for discussion of inputs and processes as determinants of JDM performance, consistent with the framework that is used to organize this book. Finally, the performance view appears to be more consistent with real-world evaluation processes and commonsense views of JDM quality.

2-3 KEY DIMENSIONS OF JDM QUALITY FOR PROCESS AND PERFORMANCE VIEWS

This section introduces the key dimensions of JDM quality viewed from either a process perspective or a performance perspective. This book defines dimensions of JDM quality based on the criteria that can be used for ascertaining "correct" JDM performance or process.[8, 9] In other words, one must have a standard against which to compare a person's JDM process or performance in order to determine whether it is a right process or right final answer, respectively. It is notable that, in many cases, the general type of standard can be used to measure JDM quality from either a process perspective or a performance perspective. This section also notes and explains the customary terms (e.g., *accuracy*) that are used to refer to JDM quality dimensions. Finally, the section covers the issues that arise with regard to specifically defining and measuring the dimensions. Table 2-1 summarizes the JDM quality dimensions and how they can be characterized and measured from both process and performance perspectives.

Normative JDM Theories

This section begins by discussing JDM quality as defined by comparisons of JDM to the requirements of normative JDM theories. These theories have guided much of the history of JDM and continue to pervade the literature today. The theories typically come from economics, statistics, or psychology and pertain to all human judgment and decision making, not just that in accounting. High-quality JDM defined vis-à-vis a normative theory often is termed *rationality*.[10] Rational JDM means that the JDM is exactly, or a close approximation to, what a particular normative theory prescribes.

Expected utility (EU) theory (von Neumann and Morgenstern 1947) and its variants, such as subjective expected utility (SEU) theory (Savage 1954), traditionally have been the most widely accepted normative theories of decision making (there are other theories for judgments). EU theory, in brief, assumes that people face multiple alternatives in decision-making settings and choose the alternative that maximizes their expected utility. The expected utility related to a particular decision alternative is the product of the probability that the outcome(s) associated with that alternative will occur and the utility, or subjective value to the decision maker, of the outcome(s). Decision makers are assumed to calculate the expected utility of the outcome(s)

---

[8]This section does not include self-insight as a criterion because this measure compares a person's statements about her JDM inputs or processes (e.g., her cue weights) to her actual inputs or processes. Thus, it is a measure of how well someone understands her JDM rather than a measure of JDM quality per se. In addition, the framework incorporates an examination of self-insight in the question that asks whether third parties and/or individuals understand the factors that create variation in or low levels on a particular dimension of JDM quality. Self-insight is discussed in Chapter 8.

[9]Given this book's focus on technical judgments and decisions, this section also does not consider the extent to which someone's JDM is ethical as a dimension of JDM quality. Nevertheless, ethical decision making is an important topic in all areas of accounting.

[10]Consequently, departures from high-quality JDM defined in this way are labeled *irrationality*.

TABLE 2-1   Measuring Dimensions of JDM Quality

Dimension of JDM Quality	How to Measure JDM Quality Dimension from the Process Perspective	How to Measure JDM Quality Dimension from the Performance Perspective	Advantages of Focusing on JDM Quality Dimension	Disadvantages of Focusing on JDM Quality Dimension
Normative JDM theories (e.g., EU theories, Bayes' Theorem)	Correlation of decisions to those predicted by EU theory's principles Number of decisions that reflect correct processes based on EU theory Number of judgment processes that are correct according to probability theories Signed or absolute differences between numbers used in judgment processes and those prescribed by probability theories	Correlation of judgments with those prescribed by probability theories Number of judgments that are correct as prescribed by probability theories Absolute or signed differences between judgments and those prescribed by probability theories	Generic theories Widely accepted Mesh well with prescriptively focused research	Normative status questionable Do not compare JDM to reality Omit key JDM processes People have goals other than EU maximization
Actual outcome associated with judgment or decision or predicted outcome from statistical model	NA	Correlation of judgments or decisions with actual or predicted outcomes Comparison of probability judgments to outcomes using probability score, calibration, bias Absolute or signed differences between judgments and actual or predicted outcomes Number of judgments or decisions that match actual outcomes	Reflects commonsense view of "good JDM" Real-world performance evaluations considered Reflects environment in which decision makers learn and work	Factors not under decision makers' control affect outcomes Outcomes can be influenced or manipulated by decision makers Data sometimes difficult to obtain

Professional theories; professional standards and other regulations (e.g., GAAP, GAAS, IRS regulations, SEC regulations, ethics codes)	Correlation of JDM processes to those prescribed by theories or standards Number of JDM processes that are correct according to theories or standards	Correlation of judgments or decisions with those prescribed by theories or standards Number of judgments or decisions that are correct as prescribed by theories or standards Signed or absolute differences between judgments or decisions and those prescribed by theories or standards	Real-world evaluations considered Reflects characteristics of unique accounting environment Useful when no related outcomes exist	Difficult to obtain agreement on meaning Research subjects may "game" answers toward these
Time or costs to do JDM task	Absolute time spent or costs incurred during JDM processing Difference between time or costs and standard or budget	Absolute time spent or costs incurred to reach judgment or decision Difference between time or costs and standard or budget	Real-world evaluations considered Consistent with commonsense views of "good JDM"	Difficult to measure
Other persons' JDM (e.g., peers or "expert panel" or comparison between "experts" and "novices")	Correlation of JDM processes to those used by other persons Number of JDM processes that are the same as those used by other persons	Correlation of judgments or decisions with those given by other persons Number of judgments or decisions that are the same as those given by other persons Signed or absolute differences between judgments or decisions and those given by other persons	Real-world evaluations considered Easier to use than professional standards criterion Useful when no related outcomes exist	Agreeing individuals can all be wrong Defining "peers," "experts," and "novices" is difficult Among disagreeing individuals, do not know who's right and wrong, nor how wrong

TABLE 2-1   Measuring Dimensions of JDM Quality *(Continued)*

Dimension of JDM Quality	*How to Measure JDM Quality Dimension from the Process Perspective*	*How to Measure JDM Quality Dimension from the Performance Perspective*	*Advantages of Focusing on JDM Quality Dimension*	*Disadvantages of Focusing on JDM Quality Dimension*
Person's previous JDM	Correlation of JDM processes to those used previously Number of JDM processes that are the same as those used previously	Correlation of judgments or decisions with those given previously Number of judgments or decisions that are the same as those given previously Signed or absolute differences between judgments or decisions and those given previously	Real-world evaluations considered Easier to use than professional standards criterion Useful when no related outcomes exist Removes need to designate "peers," "experts," and "novices"	Person who agrees with herself can be wrong on all occasions When person disagrees with herself, do not know on which occasions she is correct and on which she is wrong, nor how wrong Disagreement can reflect unmeasured changes in environment May not be important in team environment

associated with each particular decision alternative according to their own utility functions then to choose the alternative with the highest number.

EU theory assumes that decision makers conform to rules of probability theory when calculating the probability portion of expected utility (i.e., they use objective probabilities based on previous frequency of occurrence).[11] With regard to utilities, EU theory makes no particular prescriptions about the contents of the utility function. Research typically focuses on utilities related to money and risk, but EU theory does not limit people to having preferences related to only these factors. However, EU theory does prescribe that preferences conform to certain principles. (See Hastie and Dawes [2001] for a description of all the principles.) For example, a decision maker can violate one of the principles ("transitivity of preferences") by being intransitive in her preferences. *Intransitivity* occurs when someone prefers alternative A to alternative B (because A's expected utility is higher) and alternative B to alternative C (because B's expected utility is higher) but also prefers alternative C to alternative A (despite C's expected utility being lower than that of A).

Notwithstanding the assumptions of EU theory, operationally defining decision quality from a performance perspective using this theory can be difficult. As an example, a decision maker might be asked to choose between two gambles—one offering a 20% chance of receiving $10,000 (or nothing otherwise) and another offering a 15% chance of receiving $15,000 (or nothing otherwise). Expected utility theory suggests that the person will choose the gamble that maximizes her expected utility. However, predicting which gamble this will be and, thus, knowing which gamble is the right answer for a given individual can be problematic. For example, although the expected value of the second gamble is higher than that of the first gamble ($2,250 versus $2,000), the expected utility of that gamble may not be higher if the decision maker has essentially equivalent utility for $10,000 and $15,000 as, say, an extremely wealthy individual might have. Thus, an individual who chooses the first gamble may be maximizing her expected utility and, thus, giving the right answer. Because of these difficulties, then, "incorrect" decision making from an expected-utility standpoint normally is defined from a process perspective.[12] In other words, researchers define correct decision making as that involving a process that does not violate one of the principles of EU theory (e.g., transitivity of preferences). Measurement of JDM quality from this perspective typically involves comparing people's decisions to those that would be predicted based on EU theory's assumptions. Such a comparison can be done, for example, by examining the correlation of a number of decisions to the EU theory answers or by simply counting the number of answers that reflect correct versus incorrect processes.

Probability theory (including Bayes' Theorem) serves as a normative criterion for evaluating probability judgments. (See Hogarth [1987] and Yates [1990] for excellent summaries.) For example, we can compare people's conditional probability judgments (the probability of event A given condition B) to those derived from a correct calculation using a mathematical formula. In addition, Bayes' Theorem specifies a

---

[11]SEU theory allows for subjective rather than objective probabilities.

[12]It is conceivable to ask individuals to directly specify their utilities for the dollar amounts involved in these gambles and, as such, calculate a right answer for each individual. However, it often is difficult for people to directly express such utilities. Further, expressing such utilities prior to answering the gamble question may lead to an answer that is made to be consistent with the just-expressed utilities, and expressing the utilities after answering the gamble question may lead to expression of utilities that rationalize the answer to the question.

mathematical formula for revising prior probability judgments when people obtain new information.[13] Low-quality probability judgments can be defined as either those that do not match the output of probability formulas such as Bayes' Theorem or those that derive from a process that does not match the process implicit in the formulas. Thus, people can be said to violate probability theory because their final probability judgment is incorrect or because, for example, when revising probabilities, they fail to consider prior probabilities of occurrence (as specified by Bayes' Theorem).

To examine judgment quality from the process perspective, then, the researcher can count the number of correct judgment processes people exhibit (e.g., the number of times they include a certain item in their conditional probability calculations). An alternative way of counting correct judgment processes would be to score people as either "correct" or "incorrect" on a single or multiple questions based on whether they engage in the prescribed processes. Also, because probability judgments require calculations, researchers can calculate mean absolute or signed differences between these intermediate calculations and those prescribed by probability theories. To examine judgment quality from the performance perspective using probability theories, researchers can focus on correlating multiple judgments to theory-specified solutions, or they can calculate the number of judgments that are correct based on probability theories. They can also calculate mean signed or absolute differences between judgments and theory-specified solutions.

From a researcher's perspective, there are several advantages of using normative theories as criteria for evaluating JDM in accounting (see Waller and Jiambalvo [1984]). First, these theories make prescriptions for all human JDM; thus, they cannot be criticized as home-grown criteria that accounting researchers have developed to justify accountants' JDM as being of high quality. Second, they are widely accepted, perhaps because, as Waller and Jiambalvo (1984) note, they provide quite reasonable prescriptions. That is, most people do not debate that the expected desirability of outcomes, as well as the probabilities of obtaining those outcomes, should affect decision making (Yates 1990). In fact, Libby (1995) notes that, although it is rarely specified, some expected utility criterion underlies much of accounting JDM research. Third, because one of the goals of JDM research in accounting is to prescribe how to improve accountants' JDM, starting with a normative theory as a criterion allows researchers to learn very clearly how far actual JDM has to go before being of high quality.

There are numerous criticisms of the use of normative JDM theories as the standard for defining JDM quality, however. First, abundant research demonstrates that decision makers are incorrect or irrational when correctness is determined with reference to EU or probability theories (Kahneman et al. 1982; Shafir and LeBoeuf 2002).[14] Given that humans have survived despite such flaws in their JDM, many question whether these are the correct prescriptions for JDM behavior.[15] Second, many believe that the objective of assessing JDM quality is to determine its closeness to reality, and that reality cannot be assessed by reference to normative theories, for example, the

---

[13]Further discussion of Bayes' Theorem appears in Chapter 5.

[14]As a consequence of these findings, researchers have developed many other descriptive theories of JDM, such as prospect theory (Kahneman and Tversky 1979) and adaptive decision-making theory (Payne et al. 1993; Gigerenzer et al. 1999). These theories are discussed in later chapters. In addition, researchers have called for the development of new normative theories of JDM (e.g., Frisch and Clemen 1994).

[15]As Waller (1995) notes, people need only to be "fitter" than others to survive, not necessarily the "fittest" (vis-à-vis EU theory).

internal consistency of an individual's processes for calculating utilities.[16] For example, a person could decide to sit in a desert all night long awaiting the arrival of an alien spacecraft because the expected utility of that outcome is higher to her than the expected utility of staying home and sleeping. Yet others might not view this as a realistic or correct decision (Hogarth 1987). On the other hand, a person may violate a normative theory but make a judgment or decision that still conforms to reality. For example, Asare and Wright (1995) show that auditors violate probability theory when evaluating hypothesized causes of a ratio fluctuation from a real-world case, yet most of them identify the actual cause.

Third, EU theory omits many of the processes involved in JDM and, consequently, provides an incomplete standard by which to determine JDM quality (Frisch and Clemen 1994). In particular, EU theory assumes a world in which decision alternatives already are specified. Often, decision makers have to specify these alternatives. Issues that arise in this process cannot be evaluated vis-à-vis EU theory. Finally, EU theory specifies that a decision maker's goal is expected utility maximization. However, many researchers (e.g., Lopes 1981; Loomes and Sugden 1982) argue that decision makers often have multiple goals, including ensuring their security, minimizing regret, and "playing fair." As such, EU theory's emphasis on EU maximization creates a very narrow view of "good decision making."[17]

Because of the generality of normative theories, they are applicable for evaluating JDM in all areas of accounting. However, their use to date is fairly limited. Expected utility theory has been used mostly to evaluate managerial accounting JDM (see Waller [1995] for a review), whereas probability theory has been used mostly to evaluate auditors' JDM. Further, their use has declined over time. Despite problems with traditional normative theories, researchers should not dismiss this criterion entirely. Instead, it could be fruitful to consider newer normative theories that are being developed as alternatives to EU and other traditional theories (e.g., Frisch and Clemen 1994).

Actual Outcomes and Predicted Outcomes from Statistical Models

Another very common dimension of JDM quality is its correspondence with an associated actual outcome or with a predicted outcome from a statistical model based on previous actual outcomes. This dimension can be used only with an output or performance view of JDM quality because the focus is on the degree to which a person's final judgments or decisions correspond with what ends up happening (or what is predicted to happen) in the real world.

Measuring JDM quality vis-à-vis actual or predicted outcomes takes many forms and, to some extent, depends on whether the researcher is considering judgments or decisions. Furthermore, if she is examining judgments, the type of judgments she is examining will also have an effect. Decisions involve a choice among alternatives; as such, they typically are measured in categorical fashion. For example, the auditor can

---

[16]Note that probability theory does not suffer from this criticism because its calculations are based completely on objective figures (e.g., actual frequencies of occurrence of events), whereas EU theory includes utilities specified by the decision makers themselves.

[17]One way of dealing with this problem, of course, is to allow the utility function to include arguments related to security, regret, and so forth. However, at some point, the inclusion of a large number of arguments reduces the formal appeal of EU theory.

choose an unqualified opinion, a going-concern modified opinion, an adverse opinion, a disclaimer, and so forth. The analyst can choose a recommendation of buy, hold, or sell. The typical comparison of these decisions to related outcomes essentially involves a correlational technique, many times in the form of a contingency table.[18] Standard parlance often refers to JDM quality measured in this way as *empirical accuracy* (e.g., Hammond 1996) or just *accuracy*.[19] For example, the researcher can compare bankruptcy versus nonbankruptcy outcomes with the auditor's choice of a going-concern modified opinion versus other types of opinions (cf. McKeown et al. 1991). In addition, statistical models of such events can be constructed and people's choices can be compared to the categorical outcomes predicted by those models (e.g., Libby 1975). Researchers can also count the number of decisions that correspond to actual or predicted outcomes.

Judgments in accounting settings can be of two basic types. First are judgments of the probability of future events or states (e.g., tax professionals' judgments about the probability of clients being audited). Second are estimates of future quantities (e.g., analysts' earnings forecasts) or current but unknowable quantities (e.g., auditors' estimates of the dollar misstatement in clients' financial statements).

There are several ways of comparing probability judgments to outcomes to measure judgment quality. If these judgments are made in probability terms, the researcher can use a *probability score* (Yates 1990), which is the squared difference between the probability judgment and the actual probability the outcome being predicted occurred (which is always one or zero), typically averaged over several probability judgments.[20] A second measure is *calibration,* which examines the extent to which probability judgments of given levels (e.g., 10%) match the percentage of times the predicted event or state actually occurs. (See Tomassini et al. [1982] for an application in accounting.) Thus, if 10% of the firms that a loan officer believes have a 10% chance of defaulting on a loan indeed do default, that loan officer is said to be perfectly calibrated (for that category of probability judgments). A third measure is *bias,* which is simply the signed difference between the person's average probability judgment and the sample base rate (i.e., the proportion of times a predicted event such as bankruptcy actually occurs).[21]

Estimates of future and current quantities can be compared to outcomes (actual quantities) as follows. First, the estimates and actual quantities can be correlated; again, this type of measure often is referred to as an accuracy measure. Second, the researcher can measure the average absolute difference between individuals' judgments

---

[18]Correlations can be based on all individuals' judgments taken together or on multiple judgments made by a single individual.

[19]Lens model terminology refers to this as *achievement* (Cooksey 1996). The lens model is discussed in Chapter 5.

[20]Probability judgments often are cast in different forms. First, they can be reduced to zero-versus-one predictions. For example, some experimental studies ask auditors or loan officers to predict whether a company will go bankrupt. Second, people can be asked to make what are essentially probability judgments on scales, such as seven-point scales labeled "highly probable" to "not at all probable." When probability judgments are cast in these forms, the measures discussed in this paragraph do not apply. Rather, the researcher typically uses some sort of correlation analysis to compare the judgments to actual outcomes.

[21]Yates (1990) also discusses "discrimination," "slope," and "scatter," which will not be discussed here. Note that all these measures can be extended to determine the quality of probability distributions in addition to that of point estimates.

and the actual quantities; much of the literature on analysts' earnings forecasts measures JDM quality in this way (and calls it "accuracy" as well). Third, the researcher can measure the average signed difference between predicted quantities and actual quantities to examine systematic departures from actual outcomes; again, the literature on analysts' forecasts uses this measure frequently and refers to it as "bias." Fourth, she can simply count the number of judgments that match actual or predicted outcomes.

A specific type of future quantity that people estimate as part of JDM is expected utility for a particular outcome. As discussed above, JDM quality can be assessed vis-à-vis expected utility theory by examining the extent to which those utility assessments conform to the axioms of the theory. Recently, however, researchers have proposed comparing these estimated or expected utilities against the utilities actually experienced for various outcomes (e.g., Frisch and Jones 1993; Kahneman 1994). In other words, research would focus on estimated utilities but compare them to related outcomes (experienced utilities) rather than to the principles of expected utility theory. Estimated utilities and experienced utilities can be compared through correlational techniques, by examining average absolute differences between them, and so forth.

There are several advantages of focusing on JDM quality vis-à-vis actual outcomes (the accuracy dimension). First, this dimension reflects a commonsense view of "good JDM," in particular that of third parties who use professionals' work products. For these evaluators of JDM, the extent to which JDM matches "reality" likely is far more important than the extent to which JDM matches, say, that of another professional. For example, third parties likely are more interested in the degree to which auditors' decisions to issue going-concern modified opinions versus unmodified opinions correspond to the bankruptcy versus nonbankruptcy outcomes of the audited firms than the degree to which auditors agree with other auditors' opinions. Second, as mentioned earlier, firms frequently evaluate JDM quality by reference to actual outcomes. Consequently, the use of actual outcomes makes sense from this perspective as well.

Third, the use of actual outcomes reflects a view that JDM quality should be evaluated based on an understanding of the environment people face. More specifically, evaluation based on outcomes focuses on the extent to which people have adapted to this environment rather than on whether they make judgments and decisions in accordance with normative theories that do not necessarily consider various characteristics of the environment, characteristics that can be either detrimental to JDM or helpful to JDM. For example, oftentimes people make judgments and decisions on the basis of multiple indicators of a future event. Many times these indicators are correlated with each other because of features of the environment. In situations where indicators are correlated, people can make judgments and decisions that correspond fairly well to actual outcomes even if their processes do not conform to those prescribed, for example, by a statistical model. For instance, investors who are attempting to predict the accuracy of analysts' forecasts may choose to rely on only the number of years of experience the analyst has rather than on this measure along with other experience measures such as industry experience. Given that these experience measures are highly correlated, investors who predict analyst accuracy using only years of experience can make judgments very similar to those derived from a statistical model that includes multiple experience measures (Bonner et al. 2003).

Clearly, there are disadvantages to evaluating JDM quality on the basis of actual outcomes. The most obvious is that individuals of interest to researchers are making judgments and decisions under uncertainty, which means that many factors that are not under their control affect outcomes. Many argue that people should not be held accountable for factors that are not under their control, and firms sometimes try to build this notion into performance evaluation systems. For example, an auditor may judge it highly unlikely that a company will go bankrupt, yet the company ends up failing because an earthquake destroys its main manufacturing facility. If JDM quality is evaluated for relatively short time periods, as it often is, such factors can have a large impact on measured quality. The flip side of this is that factors outside people's control can affect outcomes positively as well as negatively, meaning that people can be given undue credit for having high-quality JDM. One situation is when people's judgments and decisions themselves affect outcomes (the treatment effect). For example, an auditor may decide to issue an unqualified opinion for a company not because of good JDM processes, but just the opposite, because she ignores information that indicates impending going-concern problems. However, because she chooses to give an unqualified opinion on the firm's financial statements, the firm is able to obtain a bank loan and the loan provides enough of a cash influx for the business to remain in existence for a year.

A further disadvantage is that some outcomes are partially under the control of the individuals whose JDM might be compared to the outcomes. For example, one way of evaluating managers' earnings forecasts is to compare them to actual earnings. However, managers also have some influence on actual earnings via earnings management (and also, of course, through fraudulent manipulation of earnings). If managers' earnings forecasts correspond to actual earnings because managers have managed or manipulated earnings, it does not seem reasonable to term this "high-quality JDM."

A final disadvantage is that outcome data often are very difficult to obtain for research purposes. For example, unless a researcher has access to information in audit firms' work papers, she likely will not be able to obtain outcomes such as misstatements uncovered during audits. When available, archival outcome data may be incomplete, such that only a partial and potentially biased evaluation of JDM quality can occur. For example, a researcher wishing to evaluate management accountants' choices of investment projects will have outcome information for only the projects the management accountants choose. Further, such archival data collection may not be familiar to many JDM researchers, who typically employ experiments. An alternative is to create experimental materials for which outcomes are known. For example, bankruptcy prediction studies frequently use information about real firms, so the bankruptcy or nonbankruptcy outcomes are known (e.g., Libby 1975). Another way of doing this is to create fictitious materials but to seed outcomes such as financial statement misstatements into the materials (e.g., Bonner and Lewis 1990; Bedard and Biggs 1991b). This approach clearly differs in many ways from using real outcomes, however, because the outcomes are controlled by the researcher and, thus, not subject to environmental uncertainty.

Accuracy vis-à-vis actual outcomes is an applicable JDM quality dimension for many accounting judgments and decisions because they have some sort of outcome associated with them. However, the use of this quality dimension in accounting appears to be dictated more by the availability of data rather than by its importance in various settings. By far, the most frequent accounting task for which actual outcomes are used to evaluate JDM quality is financial analysts' earnings forecasts; this likely occurs because of the archival availability of both forecasts and actual earnings (the outcome). Given the frequent use of outcomes for evaluating JDM quality by key constituents, however, it may be useful for researchers to attempt to obtain outcome data or at least attempt to develop reasonable proxies for outcomes for other accounting tasks. In other words, using this performance criterion can increase the external validity of accounting JDM studies.

Professional Theories; Professional Standards and Other Regulations

In accounting research, another dimension of JDM quality is the extent to which JDM corresponds to a professional "theory" or body of knowledge (e.g., the COSO report for internal controls), or professional standards and other regulations (e.g., auditing standards, SEC rules). Similar to this, researchers can compare JDM to firm policies, which normally are based on professional standards. These criteria are used for a couple of reasons. First, as described earlier, there are some accounting JDM tasks that have no closely associated actual outcome. Second, in accounting environments, these theories and standards are prescriptions for behavior that likely carry more weight than, say, the fact that individuals agree with each other. For example, a chief financial officer's (CFO's) accounting choices can be compared to SEC regulations for "correct" presentation of financial information. In these situations, whether the CFO makes decisions that agree with those of the president of the firm may be of little import if the rules made by the SEC, a regulator with the capability to sanction the CFO with penalties such as fines, indicate that the presentation is not correct.

Because they can specify both correct processes and correct answers, professional theories, standards, and regulations, along with firm policies, can be used to evaluate either JDM processes or performance. For example, auditing standards incorporate the COSO report and, thus, specify for auditors both the process of evaluating internal controls as well as what good controls should look like. A comparison of accountants' JDM processes to those specified by professional standards often is referred to as *justifiability*. For example, auditors' JDM may be considered justifiable if they have gathered sufficient, competent evidence as specified by auditing standards (Emby and Gibbins 1988).[22]

The manner in which a researcher uses professional theories, standards, regulations, or firm policies to measure JDM quality depends on the setting. Some examples are illustrative. Bonner and Lewis (1990) ask auditor subjects to examine an internal control evaluation checklist showing which control procedures a firm has in place then list two errors that could occur because of weaknesses in the controls as well as two substantive tests that might detect those errors. Answers are coded as right or wrong based on auditing theory that specifies relations among control weaknesses, financial statement errors, and substantive tests. Cloyd (1997) examines how many relevant information items tax professional subjects detect in a case. "Relevant" items are the facts highlighted in a solution provided in the Income Tax Regulations for a tax issue

---

[22]Justifiability may be considered a separate dimension of JDM quality (e.g., Emby and Gibbins 1988; Kennedy et al. 1997). It is not presented separately here because the JDM quality dimensions that involve comparison with professional standards and with other persons' JDM incorporate elements of justifiability. Nevertheless, if justifiability incorporates other factors, such as the degree to which one consults with peers (Kennedy et al. 1997), further investigation of its status as a separate JDM quality dimension is warranted.

similar to that in the case. Researchers can measure JDM quality from a process perspective either by obtaining correlations of these sorts of measures to measures of processes prescribed by theories or standards or by simply counting the number of responses that contain correct processes. To measure this JDM quality dimension from a performance perspective, researchers can correlate judgments or decisions to those that would be prescribed by theories or standards, or again, count the number of correct judgments or decisions. An alternative measure is the absolute or signed mean differences between individuals' judgments or decisions and the correct judgments or decisions.

There clearly are advantages to using professional standards, regulations, and firm policies for evaluating JDM quality in accounting research, and researchers strongly advocate their use (e.g., Ashton 1983; Bédard 1991). Perhaps the most important advantage is that the evaluation maps directly into important real-world evaluations of accounting-related JDM. These include firms' performance evaluations and evaluations made in sanction and litigation settings by regulators, judges, and juries. For example, the IRS and tax courts can evaluate tax professionals' JDM as to whether they have followed professional standards and adhered to tax regulations. Again, then, this is an externally valid quality dimension. Also, because the accounting environment is unique in some ways, it is fair to question whether normative JDM theories developed to apply to relatively generic settings are the best for evaluating JDM quality in accounting. Finally, as mentioned earlier, there are situations for which actual outcomes are not available for evaluating JDM.

Naturally, there are disadvantages as well. Evaluating JDM against professional standards requires that all parties involved in the research (the researcher and each individual decision maker) agree on the meaning of the professional standards, so this meaning can be operationalized for study. This sometimes is not the case because of the complex nature of accounting-related standards. Joyce et al. (1982) provide an excellent example of this point; they found that members of the FASB and Accounting Principles Board (APB) exhibited little agreement on the meaning of the qualitative characteristics for accounting information specified in Statement of Financial Accounting Concepts No. 2. In order to facilitate clarification of standards for use as a criterion, it may be useful to employ a panel of "experts," as done by Cloyd and Spilker (1999) to clarify the term "substantial authority," which is a criterion for justifying choices of tax positions in the Internal Revenue Code.

An additional disadvantage is that some professional subjects, if able to determine that their JDM from an experiment will be compared against professional standards, may make judgments or decisions that are different from those they make in their jobs. For example, if CFOs participating in an experiment are able to guess that their disclosure choices will be compared to Generally Accepted Accounting Principles (GAAP) requirements, they might make choices much closer to GAAP than they otherwise would.[23] A clever way to get around such a problem is to employ experimental subjects familiar with the intended subjects' behavior but who have less incentive to misrepresent it. For example, Hackenbrack and Nelson (1996) examine auditors' application of accounting standards when they have clients for whom the risk

---

[23]Of course, another problem is obtaining the participation in experimental studies of professionals whose behavior can be compared to professional standards and regulations.

of litigation is higher versus lower. Auditors are more aggressive in their application of the standards when client litigation risk is lower. From these results, we can infer that managers of firms generally prefer aggressive applications of accounting standards; that is, auditors' choices in the lower risk condition reflect their knowledge of what managers prefer because the auditors do not have incentives to the contrary.

Given the importance of professional standards, theories, regulations, and firm policies in most accounting environments (auditing, tax, and financial accounting, in particular), it appears that correspondence with professional standards could be quite an important JDM quality dimension. It also appears that researchers have not fully explored this quality dimension. The current environment, in which the failure to follow professional standards, at least in part, led to the demise of a large accounting firm and in which there are increased calls for standardization and regulation, suggests that a heightened focus by researchers on this quality dimension would be worthwhile.

Time or Costs to Do a JDM Task

Because firms that employ accounting professionals are in business to make money, another frequently suggested criterion for evaluating JDM quality is the time or costs incurred to do a JDM task. This criterion particularly applies in fixed-fee situations such as auditing where profits grow as costs decrease; in fact, auditing firms use this criterion, labeled *efficiency*, in performance evaluations (Tan and Libby 1997). In other areas such as tax, where professionals charge by the hour, this criterion may be less applicable. This criterion can be used to measure quality from both process and performance perspectives—either as the time to do something or the time to get to an answer. More specifically, time and costs can be measured in absolute fashion or vis-à-vis budgets or standards.

Third parties also focus on time and costs to do JDM as an important dimension of quality; thus, it is consistent with commonsense views as well. For example, a patient with a grave illness would not consider a doctor's JDM to be of high quality if the doctor takes a month to make a decision about treatment. Similarly, an investor wants prompt recommendations from her broker. Because of its importance in some accounting settings—in auditing in particular—it seems quite reasonable for researchers to use time as a criterion for evaluating professionals' JDM. Although time may be difficult to measure archivally if, for example, accounting firms have confidentiality concerns related to providing such data, it is relatively easy to measure in experimental or survey settings. One disadvantage is drawing participants' attention to this dimension of JDM, thus potentially having their JDM not reflect efficiency's relative importance to their real-world JDM. This can be overcome by measuring time surreptitiously rather than overtly.

Other Persons' JDM

Yet another dimension of JDM quality that can be investigated is the extent to which an individual's JDM corresponds to the JDM of other persons. Other persons can be peers (e.g., auditors at the same rank as the individual) or an "expert panel" (e.g., auditors nominated by their firm to be the best and brightest). An individual's final answers (judgments or decisions) can be compared to the answers of other persons, or an individual's JDM process, such as the information she uses, can be compared with other persons' processes. The measure of JDM quality that compares one person's answer to others' typically is referred to as *consensus*. Measures that compare one person's JDM process to other persons' sometimes are referred to as *agreement* on the process element being examined (e.g., "cue weighting agreement") and also are referred to under the rubric of "justifiability." For example, a tax professional's JDM process might be considered justifiable if it matches that prescribed by an expert panel. "High quality" JDM in these situations is determined based on the extent of agreement among people. Finally, another way of using this criterion is to compare the JDM of one group of persons dubbed "experts" to the JDM of another group of persons dubbed "novices." Here, we obviously would look for disagreement rather than agreement, and the assumption would be that the "experts" would be more "correct."[24]

To measure JDM quality from a process perspective, researchers can correlate various measures of processes, for example, cue weights, with those measures of processes for peers, an expert panel, and so forth. Researchers can also count the number of processes that are the same as those used by other persons, for instance, the number of cue weights that match. To measure JDM quality from a performance perspective, researchers again can correlate judgments or decisions with those given by other persons. They can also count the number of judgments or decisions that match those given by other persons (e.g., by an expert panel). Finally, they can measure agreement using the signed or absolute differences between a person's judgments or decisions and those of other individuals. Comparing the JDM of experts to that of novices typically takes the form of examining differences in the groups' average judgments or decisions or processes.

This criterion is similar to the professional theories or standards criterion in the sense that professionals ostensibly make their judgments and decisions on the basis of these bodies of knowledge. Consequently, if professionals disagree with each other, it may be the case that one or more of the individuals is not adhering to professional standards. Also like the professional standards criterion, perhaps the most important advantage of using other professionals' JDM as a criterion is that this evaluation technique maps directly into the evaluation of accounting professionals' work in litigation or sanction settings. A key part of audit litigation, for example, is determining whether auditors exercised due care in their JDM. One way of determining this is by reference to the judgments and decisions other auditors would have made under the same circumstances. This is a frequent way of evaluating due care because of the complexity of extracting "right answers" from professional standards. Further, as noted earlier, operationalizing the meaning of professional standards for use in research studies may involve obtaining the consensus of a group of professionals. Perhaps because of this similarity, and because they avoid the need to specify the standards' meaning, researchers frequently use measures of agreement in JDM work in accounting. In addition, of course, this is a useful measure when there exists no outcome that is directly associated with JDM.

---

[24]There may be other situations where one group's judgments or decisions are compared to those of another group but not because the groups are designated as "experts" and "novices." Rather, there may be some situations where normative theories do not apply, there are no clear professional standards against which to compare JDM, and there are no actual outcomes. A typical example of this is a study that examines the effects of a proposed financial accounting standard (vis-à-vis the current standard) on investors' judgments.

The most obvious disadvantage of measuring JDM in terms of agreement is that people who agree with each other may all be incorrect. In this situation, it would not be appropriate to refer to people who agree with others as having high-quality JDM. Also, there are serious operational disadvantages to using agreement with others as a criterion and to examining differences between experts and novices. These involve how to designate peers, experts, and novices. This issue is discussed further in Section 2-4, but the key point is that this designation often involves a choice of some proxy such as rank or experience, and these proxies often are incomplete or even incorrect. Thus, a researcher can end up with peers who really are subordinates or experts who really are novices. Agreement with a subordinate would not necessarily indicate the same quality JDM as would agreement with a peer. Along the same lines, assuming that experts who really are novices are more correct than others would also lead to inappropriate conclusions about JDM quality.

Perhaps the most important disadvantage of using this JDM quality dimension is that the researcher interested in improving JDM cannot determine which individuals are right and which are wrong. That is, disagreement among individuals indicates that someone is wrong but not which particular individual.[25] Even if a researcher feels comfortable guessing which individual or individuals are wrong, it is not clear how wrong they are because it is not clear whether any individual is completely correct.

Agreement with others and disagreement between so-called experts and novices are applicable criteria for evaluating just about any type of accounting JDM, despite their disadvantages. They are used most often in auditing, likely because of the difficulties of using actual outcomes for much of auditing JDM and the difficulties of interpreting professional standards. Further, agreement is an important real-world criterion for evaluating JDM in auditing. There are other areas in which the agreement criterion can be useful, however. For example, analysts' agreement with other analysts' earnings forecasts or with a consensus earnings forecast can be assessed. (See Hong et al. [2000] for an example.)

Person's Previous JDM

In addition to comparing one professional's JDM to that of other professionals, researchers can compare a professional's JDM at one point in time to her JDM at a later point in time. High-quality JDM is indicated when a person gives exactly or virtually the same judgments or decisions on different occasions when facing the same situation; this measure of JDM quality is known as *test-retest reliability* or *stability*. Stability refers to the degree of agreement at two relatively distant points in time, whereas test-retest reliability refers to agreement within a single experimental session. Researchers can measure this dimension of JDM quality from a process or performance perspective, using measures that are similar to those used for the agreement-with-other-persons'-JDM criterion.

As Ashton (2000) notes, agreement with oneself over time is a very important dimension of JDM quality in professional settings because of the large stakes involved and because disagreement implies that the JDM at one point is incorrect. For example, an investor probably would like to know that an auditor who observes the same level

---

[25]In theory, an individual who disagrees with the JDM of experts can be considered the one who is wrong. However, this is based on the often questionable assumption that the designated experts are right.

of misstatement in a client's financial statements in two different years would render the same type of audit opinion in those two years. If the auditor, in fact, makes different decisions given the same circumstances, this could play negatively in a litigation setting. This criterion has the same advantages that the "other professionals" criterion has; further, it removes the need to designate peers or an expert panel, as is required in measuring agreement among professionals.

A clear disadvantage of this criterion is the same as that above—a person could agree with herself over time but be consistently wrong; consequently, designating someone who agrees with herself over time as a high-quality decision maker could be incorrect. Further, even if a person exhibits disagreement with herself, the researcher cannot specify on which occasion the person is wrong and/or how wrong she is. Also, disagreement over time may simply reflect changes in the environment that a researcher has not captured rather than lower-quality JDM. Clearly, this is not a problem when researchers measure agreement within a single experimental session and carefully control the materials decision makers view. However, in less controlled settings, which are far more representative of what decision makers face, this is a viable disadvantage. Finally, much of the JDM we observe in the accounting environment reflects a team process—either individuals working together or individuals' work being reviewed and possibly changed by superiors. In these cases, whether an individual agrees with herself over time likely is less important than the extent to which she agrees with her peers or superiors.

Perhaps it is for these reasons that accounting studies rarely employ agreement with oneself as their JDM quality dimension. Ashton (2000) includes only 14 studies in his review that spans almost 30 years of work; most of these examine auditors' JDM. However, there may be situations today where this criterion is particularly meaningful. For example, research shows that analysts' earnings forecasts and stock recommendations for a given firm frequently are not consistent with each other. Francis and Philbrick (1993) suggest that this may be due to analysts facing multiple constituencies and incentives. First, analysts have incentives to forecast accurately vis-à-vis actual earnings because, for example, their firms value it enough to include it in their compensation contracts. However, analysts have another important constituent—management of the firms they follow. Management may prefer negatively biased—and, thus, inaccurate—forecasts so actual earnings can meet or beat these forecasts (Brown 2001; Matsumoto 2002). Inconsistency between forecasts and recommendations is not an exact analog to disagreement with oneself because earnings forecasts and recommendations are different outputs; further, they are frequently given at the same time. However, one would expect that these two outputs would be strongly positively related given that they ostensibly both are based on a firm's underlying financial position (i.e., the same information). Casting this in an agreement-with-oneself framework suggests that an analyst may intentionally alter either her forecast or her recommendation and, thus, intentionally create inconsistency, due to the multiple constituencies she faces.

Choosing JDM Quality Dimensions

How does a researcher determine which process or performance dimensions are important for a particular JDM task? She can use task analysis techniques (see Chapter 1) to learn about important quality dimensions, and she can do so from the perspective of multiple constituents. First, the researcher can learn how firms view

JDM quality by learning about the parameters of the compensation and performance evaluation systems or, more generally, the formal and informal incentives faced by the accounting professionals of interest. Some researchers have recent experience working in the field they are studying, so they have firsthand knowledge of the formal and informal parameters of these systems. For example, people who have worked as auditors know that auditors' job promotions focus formally on technical performance, the extent to which they meet time budgets, managerial skills, and client development (Tan and Libby 1997) but also probably informally on pleasing clients.

If the researcher does not have recent firsthand knowledge of the performance evaluation and compensation schemes, she can interview or survey professionals about JDM quality dimensions that are important in these schemes or read already-published interviews or surveys. Although many professionals shy away from revealing details of proprietary systems, the researcher should be able to obtain some general information about how JDM is viewed within a firm. For example, she can ask professionals to identify the decision makers viewed as best by their organizations then to describe the characteristics that likely cause these people to be viewed as best. Further, in many cases, popular press articles reveal information about compensation and performance evaluation schemes, obviating the need for interviews or surveys. For example, the *Wall Street Journal* has published many articles stating that central elements of sell-side analysts' performance evaluation and compensation are the volume of trade and investment banking business they generate (e.g., Gallagher 1996; Gasparino 2002).

In the best of all possible worlds, the researcher discovers that empirical research has documented that certain JDM quality dimensions are important because they are related to important outcomes such as performance evaluations, pay, or job turnover. In other words, research already has proceeded to answer the question of whether differences on a certain JDM dimension matter in some way.[26] For instance, Mikhail et al. (1999) show that the extent to which analysts' earnings forecasts correspond to actual earnings (relative to their peers) is related to their job turnover. This result suggests that relative accuracy is an important JDM quality dimension for analysts from the perspective of their employers.

In addition to understanding how firms view their professionals' JDM quality, the researcher should also learn how other constituents view JDM quality for the professionals. Clearly, the researcher can interview or survey third parties to gain this understanding. For example, researchers can interview marketing managers who use managerial accountants' work as to their views of the important dimensions of the accountants' JDM. In addition, competitive honors and awards for professionals that are reported in the popular press can suggest important dimensions of JDM quality. For sell-side analysts, for example, *Institutional Investor Magazine* awards "All-American" status to analysts based on the profitability of stock picks and forecast

---

[26]In fact, one might consider combining the questions in the framework and simply asking which dimensions of performance matter to someone; demonstrating that a particular performance dimension matters inherently requires demonstrating variation in that dimension. For example, to show that auditors' meeting time budgets matters in performance evaluations, one would have to show that the extent to which time budgets are met varies and that, as a consequence, performance evaluations vary. The reason for showing these questions separately and in the reverse direction in the framework is that it is difficult to demonstrate that a performance dimension for a particular JDM task matters empirically if there are no differences on that dimension; thus, a project that set out to do both could fail. Consequently, research typically proceeds in the direction suggested by the framework.

accuracy, as well as other factors such as client responsiveness (Institutional Investor Web site 2003).[27]

Again, if empirical research has examined relations between certain dimensions of accounting professionals' JDM quality and outcomes for third parties, the researcher has a great fund of information from which to draw. For example, Brown and Mohammad (2001) show that investors can trade profitably based on an understanding of analysts' forecast accuracy. This suggests that, from the investors' perspective, forecast accuracy should be an important dimension of JDM quality for analysts. Finally, the researcher should attempt to determine whether there are important constituents for particular accounting professionals' JDM beyond their firms and various clients or third parties; typically there are. For auditors, for example, the most important JDM quality dimension may be the one focused on by plaintiffs' attorneys, judges, and juries.

Summary

There are a number of dimensions of JDM quality (using either a process or performance view) that can be investigated. Which is (are) most important for a particular accounting JDM task or setting should depend on the characteristics of the task and its constituents. In the past, researchers may have focused more on the availability of data or the ease of measurement than on these factors when choosing criteria for measuring JDM quality. Prior research also has tended to use a single process or performance dimension rather than considering that there are multiple JDM quality dimensions of importance to accounting decision makers. Future research should seek to improve our understanding of JDM quality by clearly specifying task characteristics and constituents in order to choose the appropriate dimension or dimensions of JDM quality for study. Also, research should focus specifically on the extent to which accounting decision makers either attempt to maximize quality on multiple dimensions simultaneously or, instead, are forced to make tradeoffs in quality because they cannot maximize on all dimensions.

2-4   WHAT IS HIGH-QUALITY JDM OR "EXPERTISE"?

In accounting, people often want to know more about JDM quality than just whether there are differences among professionals on some important process or performance dimension(s) of quality. Because one of the goals of accounting JDM research is to improve JDM, researchers (and practitioners) often want to know who has "high" JDM quality, that is, who is an expert decision maker. Of course, this requires defining high-quality JDM on some dimension. Again, this is not a trivial task; consequently, it has engendered a great deal of debate in both psychology and accounting.

The debate involves three main questions.[28] First, should *expertise,* or high-quality JDM, be defined in relative or absolute terms? Second, if expertise is defined in absolute terms, what is the threshold above which someone is an expert? Third, should

---

[27]These awards can also be elements of compensation schemes, as in the case of *II* All-American awards (Stickel 1992).

[28]Some of the debate in accounting relates to whether expertise should be measured as to process or performance. I will not repeat that debate here, as the issue was discussed earlier. The interested reader may find discussions in Davis and Solomon (1989), Bonner and Lewis (1990), Marchant (1990b), and Bouwman and Bradley (1997), among others.

expertise be defined in objective terms or, rather, in subjective terms as specified by the constituents for expertise? The latter is termed a "socially constructed view" of expertise (e.g., Agnew et al. 1997; Stein 1997).[29]

With regard to whether to use a relative or absolute definition of expertise, there are arguments on both sides. Certainly, in many real-world settings such as professional sports, chess, and so forth, people consider expertise in terms of relative rankings. This may be due to the fact that, in these fields, participants think in competitive terms. Further, these fields have published rankings of participants' JDM quality, and there are continual competitions among the members of the field, so the rankings are meaningful and up to date. In addition, people naturally tend to think of expertise in terms of status or position vis-à-vis others (Frank 1985). Perhaps, as mentioned earlier, this is because being "fitter" than others is what counts, not being the theoretically "fittest."

A relative definition has a potential downside, however, in that the people who are the best in a situation and, thus, would be designated experts, could have mediocre-quality JDM. Consider whether you would designate as an expert a mutual fund manager who is ranked number one in his firm but whose best annual return is 10% below the market return. This example illustrates the importance of considering the absolute level of JDM quality when designating someone an expert, in particular, the "theoretically fittest," or absolute level of JDM quality believed possible.[30] If the persons who would be designated experts using a relative definition have JDM quality that falls far short of such an absolute ideal (e.g., the market return), it is worth considering whether an expert designation is appropriate. An expert designation may be appropriate, for example, in a field that is relatively young. Here, people may not have had the experience to develop the highest levels of JDM or science may not have advanced sufficiently to enable people to have high-quality JDM (Shanteau 1992a).

Considering an absolute definition of expertise also means operationally determining the absolute level above which someone is an expert. This is the second key issue related to defining high-quality or expert JDM. How close to some ideal level of JDM quality should this level be? Should it be a certain distance from the ideal or a certain percentage of the ideal? How much farther from the ideal should the level be for a young field (i.e., how much slack should we give people in this situation)? What if we cannot calculate an ideal level of JDM quality for a given task or field; how do we set the level then? Is the criterion valid if most people turn out to be experts? These sorts of questions illustrate many of the difficulties with operationalizing an absolute definition of expertise, even if theory and common sense support its use. They may also explain why prominent expertise researchers rely principally on a relative definition of expertise, with only a nod to an absolute level in noting that experts typically are "outstanding" (e.g., Chi et al. 1988; Ericsson and Smith 1991).

A third major issue related to deciding which persons are experts at JDM is whether to define quality in terms of objective criteria (e.g., actual outcomes, a normative theory, other people's JDM, time and costs, etc.) or whether to designate as experts

---

[29]A more general way of viewing this issue is that JDM quality can be thought of vis-à-vis objective criteria or in subjective terms (i.e., as viewed by people). That is, Section 2-3 could include "society's beliefs" as a further criterion against which to evaluate JDM quality. I have chosen to restrict my discussion of this social construction issue to this section because it is most frequently discussed when debating notions of expertise (high-quality JDM) rather than JDM in general.

[30]This can be done either with or without consideration of environmental constraints such as transactions costs.

the people particular social groups believe are experts. One would hope that social groups would designate as experts people who are, in fact, the most accurate vis-à-vis outcomes, the most rational vis-à-vis normative theories, the most consistent over time, and so forth. In this case, the definitions would coincide. In fields that have continual competitions that are based on quality of some sort and published rankings (e.g., professional sports), the groups of experts designated by objective criteria versus the groups designated by subjective criteria likely overlap substantially.

However, most fields of endeavor, particularly professions, do not have continual tournaments and published rankings. Further, research indicates that people think about professionals' expertise using a variety of factors, such as experience, communication skills, and self-confidence, some of which may not be related to JDM quality (e.g., Shanteau 1987; Hastie and Rasinski 1988). Also, many people think of all professionals as experts because they have extensive education, certification, and other trappings of expertise (Mieg 2001). Anecdotally, however, we can think of professionals who are such "socially constructed experts" but whose JDM quality is questionable. Consistent with this, a great deal of research shows that people designated as experts (the socially constructed group) in a variety of fields do not have high-quality JDM on average. (Shanteau [1992a] provides a list of these fields.)

Does a socially constructed view of expertise have any merit in professions, then? It does because it fits with both the sociology and the economics of professions. As Mieg (2001) notes, much of what so-called professional experts are doing is providing people with explanations of and recommendations about issues that require specialized knowledge. People are willing to pay for these professional services because they believe the cost of acquiring the knowledge themselves exceeds the cost of buying it from professionals. Professions exist, in part, to lay claim to the distribution of this specialized knowledge (Abbott 1988). If we assume that markets for knowledge are efficient, then we can assume that the recommendations (i.e., the JDM) that come from the professionals who currently have claim to a field are the best available. Their JDM may not be of the highest possible quality (i.e., the "fittest"), but it should be "fitter" than the rest. The key issue, of course, is whether the markets in which professionals distribute knowledge are efficient. Anecdotally, at least, it appears they often are not.

These general issues regarding how to define expertise (high-quality JDM) pertain to accounting as well. Most of the individuals accounting researchers are interested in studying are professionals, but they do not participate in continual, full-population tournaments, so there are no rankings of their relative JDM quality. As such, there likely is some social construction of expertise by the users of accounting professionals' work, meaning that there are some professionals designated as experts who do not have high-quality JDM. The exception may be securities analysts; they can receive the *Institutional Investor* or *Wall Street Journal* All-American designation at least partially based on JDM quality. These rankings occur once a year, and most analysts are eligible for them; further, award-winning analysts do have higher-quality JDM on average (Stickel 1992). Also, investors appear to place more reliance on the JDM of analysts who are experts using this objective measure, meaning that socially constructed experts would be true experts in this setting, at least relatively speaking. However, investors also appear to place more reliance on the JDM of analysts who receive quite a bit of media coverage, although media coverage does not appear to be related to JDM quality (Bonner et al. 2006). Consequently, in the one instance in accounting where there are published rankings, there still seems to be social construction of expertise that ends up designating as experts individuals whose JDM quality may not be the highest.

As to whether a relative or absolute definition of expertise (or some combination thereof) makes the most sense in accounting, it depends on the JDM of interest. For evaluating the expertise of investors and money managers, some consideration of absolute quality in addition to relative quality makes sense because there is an absolute ideal that can be calculated (the market return). In addition, these individuals make judgments and decisions in competitive markets, suggesting that the best investors and money managers should not have mediocre JDM. The same is true of securities analysts; we can calculate an ideal for their earnings forecasts, for example (zero error vis-à-vis actual earnings). Research in these areas could focus more on this absolute aspect in the future. For auditors, tax professionals, management accountants, and others, consideration of expertise from an absolute perspective is much more difficult. Thus, we likely will continue to see expertise being considered from a relative perspective for research on these accounting professionals.

2-5   RESEARCH ON JDM QUALITY DIFFERENCES AND THEIR CONSEQUENCES

The final section of this chapter briefly discusses what research shows regarding whether differences on particular dimensions of JDM quality matter to the individuals themselves and others and in what ways they matter. Economic consequences associated with JDM quality for individuals can include promotions, pay raises, and the like. For third parties, economic consequences typically involve financial gains or losses. Note that this section does not discuss what research shows about differences in JDM quality, as it is difficult to concisely summarize the findings. It is a relatively safe assumption at this point that, for a given accounting task, there are differences on at least some dimension of JDM quality. This is a safe assumption because research has proceeded to investigate factors that cause differences in JDM in many accounting-related tasks.[31] This also implies that, for most tasks, there is not uniformly low-quality JDM. However, there are a few tasks where accounting-related professionals do appear to have relatively low JDM quality, supporting the need for this question in the framework. For example, most mutual fund managers' returns do not exceed the market return (Gruber 1996; Carhart 1997).

This section classifies the research findings by the types of individuals accounting researchers study. Producers of accounting information include managers and management accountants and financial analysts. Very few studies examine whether JDM quality differences among managers and management accountants matter to the individuals themselves or to others who use their work.[32] A few studies examine the economic consequences of managers' detection of financial reporting fraud. The presence of fraud indicates that some manager(s) have low-quality decisions (where quality is

---

[31]For a JDM task or quality dimension thereof for which little to no prior research has been conducted (e.g., tax savings for clients related to tax professionals' planning), it is reasonable to expect variation in quality. However, it also is worthwhile to be cautious and make at least a preliminary investigation to ascertain that this is the case before proceeding with work on causes of quality variation.

[32]For management accountants, this may be due somewhat to the lack of criteria for evaluating JDM quality (e.g., professional standards).

defined by comparing the decisions to what professional standards dictate). Karpoff and Lott (1993) find that there are negative abnormal returns for these firms in a short window, whereas Livingston (1997) finds significant turnover among senior management and finance officers in this case. For management accountants, Stone et al. (2000) and Hunton et al. (2000) find that job rank and performance evaluations are related to management accountants' knowledge and abilities. Because prior research indicates that knowledge and abilities are related to managerial JDM quality (Dearman and Shields 2001), we can infer that job rank and performance evaluations are related to JDM quality in this setting.

Work on the effects of JDM quality differences for financial analysts is more plentiful. Differences in earnings forecast accuracy are associated with job terminations and promotions, significant consequences for analysts (Mikhail et al. 1999; Hong et al. 2000; Hong and Kubik 2003), and with profitable trading by investors, a significant consequence for users of analysts' work (Brown and Mohammad 2001). Other work indicates that differences among analysts on the extent to which their forecasts agree with others' forecasts (the consensus forecast) are related to job terminations and promotions (Hong et al. 2000; Hong and Kubik 2003). Research examining analysts' stock recommendations indicates that investors cannot earn abnormal returns based on the quality of recommendations, however (Barber et al. 2001; Mikhail et al. 2004).

Users of accounting information include those listed above as well as brokers and other investment advisors, money managers, investors, creditors, corporate directors, and tax professionals. Research on investment newsletters finds that JDM quality, as measured by the returns of stocks recommended by those newsletters and the extent to which they predict the direction of the market (actual outcome measures), is negatively related to newsletters going out of business (Graham and Harvey 1996; Jaffe and Mahoney 1999). Further, agreement across newsletters as to their recommendations is negatively related to market volatility (Graham and Harvey 1996). Studies of mutual fund managers (Khorana 1996; Chevalier and Ellison 1999b) find that JDM quality, as measured by fund returns (an outcome measure) and agreement with others' portfolio choices, is negatively related to termination or movement to a smaller mutual fund.

With regard to economic consequences of investors' JDM, several papers show that investors' JDM quality is related to the "quality" of market prices—actual prices vis-à-vis equilibrium prices as predicted by theory (Calegari and Fargher 1997; Tuttle et al. 1997; Bloomfield et al. 2003). Further, a large body of archival work on investor psychology implies that there are serious economic consequences associated with variation in investor JDM, although JDM is not measured directly. (See Daniel et al. [2002] for a review.) Finally, there are no studies that examine the effect of creditors', corporate directors', or tax professionals' JDM quality on economic consequences.

Although there is much anecdotal evidence about the consequences of low-quality auditing JDM to auditors, their firms, or third parties, very little research evidence exists.[33] Tan and Libby (1997) show that auditors' performance evaluations are related

[33] There are research studies from which we might draw inferences about the relation of auditors' JDM quality and various economic consequences, but such inferences likely are premature. For example, Bonner et al. (1998) find that the probability of auditor litigation is related to the extent to which (undetected) financial statement fraud involves fictitious transactions. It is conceivable that this implies that auditor litigation is related to the quality of auditors' technical JDM regarding fraud. Audit fee studies find that audit firms earn higher fees when they possess industry "expertise" (e.g., Craswell et al. 1995); again, this may indicate that the amount of fees is related to the quality of auditors' technical industry-specific JDM.

to the quality of their technical judgments (likely vis-à-vis professional standards and firm policy) and efficiency, among other factors, and Erickson et al. (2000) find the presence of low-quality technical judgments in an audit case that resulted in litigation and large payments for an auditing firm.

Regulators of accounting information and accountants include the Financial Accounting Standards Board (FASB), the Securities and Exchange Commission (SEC), the American Institute of Certified Public Accountants (AICPA), and others. Evaluators of accountants' work include plaintiffs' attorneys, judges, and juries, as well as various regulatory bodies such as the SEC. There are no studies that directly examine the relation between regulators' or evaluators' JDM quality and economic consequences. The only indirect evidence on evaluators is provided by Palmrose (1991), who documents that auditors are more likely to be successful in judge trials than in jury trials. If we believe that judges have higher JDM quality, then this result would suggest a link between evaluators' JDM quality and litigation outcomes for auditors.

This section clearly indicates the need for further study of the relation between JDM quality and various economic consequences to the decision makers themselves (such as job turnover and litigation) as well as consequences to others who use their work (such as investment returns). Although this work is difficult to do because of data restrictions and other factors, it is critical in firmly establishing the practical importance of accounting-related JDM quality differences.

2-6   Summary

The main purpose of this chapter is to discuss the issues related to defining and measuring JDM quality. In particular, it discusses whether JDM quality should be considered from a process or performance perspective. In addition, it examines various dimensions of process and performance that can be used to define quality and both the theoretical and operational advantages and disadvantages of each. Along with this, the chapter provides some thoughts about how one defines high-quality or expert JDM. Finally, this chapter briefly examines research findings to date on the relation between JDM quality and various economic consequences for decision makers and others who use their work.

Perhaps the most important conclusion from the chapter is that, unlike psychologists, accounting researchers cannot focus on a single dimension of JDM quality because accounting decision makers typically face multiple constituents who have different views of JDM quality. Even in cases where there are not multiple constituents, single constituents typically have multiple goals for JDM, thus creating multiple relevant dimensions of quality. Researchers should begin to address these issues by gaining a better understanding of the relevant quality dimensions for tasks under study. Also, researchers should examine, likely over the course of a number of studies, questions about JDM quality using different dimensions of quality. Finally, researchers should examine how accounting decision makers react to the facts that there are multiple dimensions of quality for their JDM and, as a consequence, they often cannot maximize quality on all dimensions.

CHAPTER

3

Knowledge and Personal Involvement

Which factors cause variation in or low levels of JDM quality in accounting tasks? This chapter is the first of five that survey research on these factors (this research question is highlighted in Figure 3-1). The chapters identify and define the key factors, explain their importance, and describe both psychology and accounting findings regarding their effects. The description of psychology findings also includes discussion of the cognitive processes through which the factors operate as well as the variables that can moderate the factors' effects on JDM quality. In addition, each section describes how to operationalize the factor for study. In describing accounting findings, the chapters organize material using the producers, users, auditors, regulators, and evaluators scheme developed in Chapter 1.

This chapter begins by reminding the reader of the person/task/environmental variables scheme for classifying the factors that affect JDM quality. It then describes the various processes through which these variables can affect JDM. Next, it introduces person variables and provides information about two key person variables—knowledge and personal involvement in a task—and their effects on JDM in accounting.

Discussion of these variables, as is the case with other variables covered in future chapters, covers a number of issues related to each variable. Each section begins with definitions and classifications of the variable. The sections then describe findings from psychology about the variable's effects on JDM quality and the mediators of these effects (the mechanisms through which the variable operates on JDM). Each section also covers factors that moderate the variable's JDM quality effects. Moderators change the relationship between some independent variable and JDM quality. For example, they can change the sign of the relationship or instead weaken or strengthen the magnitude of the relationship. Additional discussion relates to how to study each variable, specifically whether it can be studied using manipulation and/or measurement because both these techniques are available to experimentalists. Further, to encourage the use of multiple methods to address JDM questions, each section notes how archival and survey researchers can measure the variable (if plausible). The sections then review accounting research related to the variable and conclude with suggestions for future research.

FIGURE 3-1   **Framework for JDM Research in Accounting**

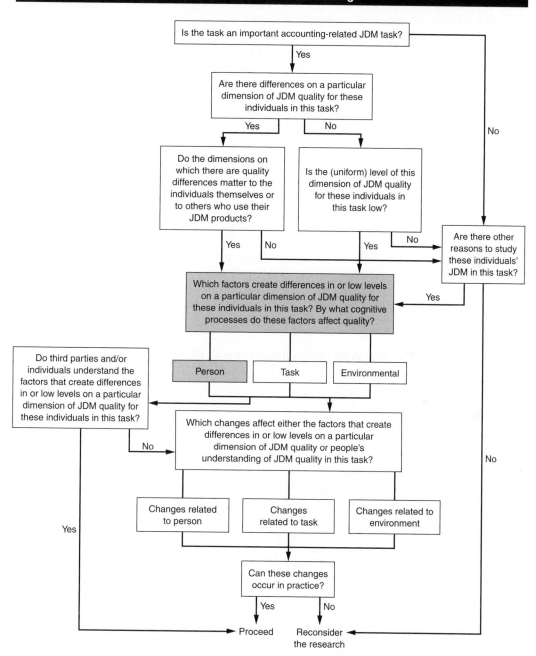

3-1 FACTORS THAT AFFECT JDM QUALITY

The framework used in this book classifies into three general categories the factors that create variation in or low levels of JDM quality. *Person variables* relate to characteristics the decision maker brings to the task or the cognitive processes she uses while making a judgment or decision. *Task variables* relate to dimensions of the task per se. *Environmental variables* relate to the conditions and circumstances surrounding an individual while she performs a JDM task and are not related to any one task.

Person variables include a number of factors that vary across the individuals of interest to accounting researchers. In particular, people vary as to their knowledge content and structure and personal involvement in a task. People also vary in abilities, intrinsic motivation, affect, confidence, risk attitudes, cognitive style, gender, and cultural background (these variables are discussed in Chapter 4). Finally, people vary as to the cognitive processes they use while doing tasks. Research demonstrates that people make systematic errors in cognitive processes per se, meaning that cognitive processes can have effects on JDM quality that are separate from the effects they have as mediators of person, task, and environmental variables. Chapter 5 discusses the separate effects of processes, whereas the next section discusses the processes as mechanisms through which other variables affect JDM quality.

3-2 PROCESSES THROUGH WHICH FACTORS AFFECT JDM QUALITY

This book classifies cognitive processes as follows: memory retrieval, information search, problem representation, hypothesis generation, and hypothesis evaluation.[1] *Memory retrieval* refers to accessing knowledge from memory, whereas *information search* refers to seeking data from sources other than memory (e.g., databases or professional standards). The *problem representation* process entails understanding a situation in order to build a model or framework in memory that specifies the key issues in the judgment or decision problem. Problem representations often include information about how to make a judgment or decision. *Hypothesis generation* involves thinking of a possible explanation or explanations for a given set of facts; this process occurs in diagnostic tasks such as ratio analysis. *Hypothesis evaluation* involves evaluating the validity of the hypotheses already generated or hypotheses provided by another source. The evaluation process also may require planning of hypothesis-testing strategies if the problem representation does not specify means for making the judgment or decision. Finally, some tasks do not require the explicit evaluation of hypotheses, but simply the evaluation of evidence. These issues are discussed under hypothesis evaluation.[2]

---

[1]Many discussions of processes involved in JDM include, as a first stage, recognition that a judgment or decision must be made (e.g., Einhorn and Hogarth 1981). This book does not consider this stage because accounting professionals are working in situations where it typically is clear that they must make a judgment or decision.

[2]Note that although these processes are listed in a particular order, this is not necessarily the order in which they occur. For example, people often form a problem representation before engaging in information search. In addition, people can cycle through the processes multiple times. As an example, people may search for information then revise an earlier problem representation. The sequencing of cognitive processes is discussed further in Chapter 5. Finally, judgments or decisions may sometimes involve only some of the processes. For example, someone may be able to retrieve a judgment directly from memory.

Cognitive processes are considered to be intermediate steps in arriving at a final judgment or decision for which some dimension of quality, such as accuracy vis-à-vis an actual outcome, can be assessed (see Chapter 2). That is, discussions normally portray a particular variable as affecting, say, information search, which, in turn, affects JDM quality. For example, as discussed below, knowledge content operates principally through the retrieval process. However, there are varying levels of granularity psychologists invoke in discussing the processes that intervene between a particular person, task, or environmental variable and an ultimate judgment or decision. For some variables, additional detail about these processes is necessary. Two key factors that may intervene between a specific variable such as incentives and the cognitive processes that ultimately affect JDM quality are motivation and affect. Although Chapter 4 provides more detailed information about the mechanisms by which these factors operate, it is important to provide a brief overview here.

Current research in JDM recognizes the importance of "motivated reasoning" (e.g., Kunda 1990, 1999). *Motivation* generally is defined as "an internal state of an organism that impels or drives it to action" (Reber 1995). In particular, motivation is an intermediate state that may derive from a number of variables in accounting settings, including people's desire to maintain their reputations, monetary incentives, and accountability demands.[3] These factors create two types of (intermediate) motivation that can affect JDM quality. More important, the effects of the motivation occur through cognitive processing, or reasoning. In particular, Kunda proposes that reasoning can reflect motivation to reach an "accurate" judgment or decision, whatever that turns out to be, or motivation to reach a particular desired (and known) judgment or decision.[4] Both types of motivation and the related reasoning can be present in accounting settings. For example, an auditor can be accountable to a superior with unknown views, in which case she is motivated to reach the most "accurate" possible conclusion. On the other hand, an auditor may also feel accountability to a client who has known views, so she is motivated to reach a particular (the client's) conclusion. Note that a decision maker engaging in "motivated reasoning" of the latter type does not simply accept the strategically appropriate judgment or decision without cognitive processing, but engages in directed (biased) cognitive effort to reach and support that judgment or decision.[5]

Accuracy-motivated reasoning affects cognitive processes by increasing the effort people put into those processes. In other words, people expend more effort in retrieving and searching for information, creating a representation of the situation, and generating and evaluating hypotheses and evidence. This effort is directed toward doing the best they can in each process. Reasoning motivated by a particular desired

---

[3]An intermediate state means that the factor is relatively malleable in the short term. For example, motivation can be affected rather quickly by monetary incentives. Factors such as knowledge cannot be classified as intermediate states because they are relatively fixed in the short term.

[4]Kunda (1990, 1999) does not specify what she means by "accuracy." Recall that "accuracy" of JDM typically refers to the correspondence of a judgment or decision with an actual outcome. However, Kunda also may mean to include correspondence of JDM with other criteria, for example, professional standards and normative theories.

[5]It sometimes is difficult to distinguish between strategic adoption of a particular desired conclusion and conclusion-motivated reasoning. In the former case, a person may adopt the JDM then engage in ex post rationalization if there is an incentive to provide such rationalization. In the latter case, the person does not adopt the JDM ex ante, but only after reasoning directed at supporting it. Given that people typically can find evidence that supports a particular judgment or decision, it is highly likely that they will adopt it in these situations. In other words, the outcomes of these very different processes can be similar.

conclusion results instead in biased processing of information. The mechanisms that allow for biased processing include the intentional search for, attention to, overweighting of, or reconstruction of information that supports the desired judgment or decision (Kunda 1990, 1999). In other words, motivated reasoning may seep at least indirectly into all cognitive processes.

Psychology also is increasingly recognizing the importance of affect to JDM. *Affect* refers to positive or negative evaluative reactions to stimuli such as events and results from a number of factors relevant to accounting settings such as people's moods and parameters of monetary incentives. In addition, a recent model proposes affective reactions to accounting numbers (Kida and Smith 1995). Like motivation, affective reactions play a role in the cognitive processes that determine JDM (e.g., Forgas 1995; Mellers and McGraw 2001). In some situations, affect can influence the retrieval or reconstruction of affect-congruent information from memory. Affect can also influence JDM-related cognitive processes in that people use current or predicted future affect as an important information cue. Further, affect can influence initial choice of processing strategies; positive affect typically leads to the use of heuristic, or less effortful, processes, whereas negative affect tends to lead to more systematic, effortful processes.

3-3 KNOWLEDGE AND PERSONAL INVOLVEMENT—PRODUCTS OF EXPERIENCE

The bulk of research on person variables in accounting pertains to knowledge content and structure (the specific items someone knows and the way they are organized in memory). This likely has occurred because of the unique requirements for knowledge placed on professionals including accountants. Not only do professionals need great amounts of knowledge, they also need many different types of knowledge to have high-quality JDM. Further, knowledge must be integrated and organized in multiple ways. These stringent requirements imply that there is variation in knowledge across accounting professionals; people do not come into these positions possessing all the knowledge they need or having the knowledge organized in all the necessary ways. Consistent with this, much of professional practice is aimed at increasing and organizing employees' knowledge. For example, accounting firms screen on knowledge during hiring (using proxies such as grades), have extensive training programs, and provide decision aids that are meant to help people use the knowledge they have (see Chapter 9). Finally, lack of knowledge has been implicated as one source of poor JDM in lawsuits against accounting professionals (e.g., Berton and Adler 1992), meaning that lack of knowledge can have serious economic consequences for accounting decision makers and third parties. Consequently, this chapter discusses research on the effects of knowledge in detail.

The chapter also discusses the effects of personal involvement with a task. Personal involvement means that someone has previously made a judgment or a decision in that setting; it is an important variable in accounting because many accounting settings require repeated involvement in JDM tasks. In fact, accountants may have higher average levels of personal involvement with JDM tasks than other professionals. For example, auditors (analysts) make the same judgments about clients (followed firms) year after year. Management accountants make decisions about whether to continue with investment projects that they have initially chosen. Yet because of employee turnover, as well as rotation of personnel among tasks, personal involvement can vary dramatically across individuals. More important, regulators and other evaluators of accountants' work frequently view high levels of personal involvement as being a serious impediment to JDM (e.g., Levitt 2003). In fact, one requirement of recent audit reform (mandatory rotation of audit partners) clearly seeks to reduce the perceived negative effects of personal involvement on auditors' JDM because of the economic consequences of lower-quality JDM for third parties such as investors (e.g., Levitt).

Both knowledge and personal involvement derive from "experience" in a task, yet they may have opposite effects on JDM quality. Thus, it is important to discuss their effects in tandem. *Experience,* in its strictest sense, refers to the actual performance of a task, a concept that also is referred to as *practice.*[6] However, *experience* often is used to refer to other concepts, including university and firm instruction, and feedback received after doing a task. Thus, subsequent discussion includes all these concepts. Instruction, practice, and feedback typically are thought of as mechanisms for imparting knowledge. Because of this, many studies in both psychology and accounting use direct or indirect measures of instruction, practice, and/or feedback as proxies for knowledge. For the most part, studies use a single proxy—years of time spent in a job— which incorporates instruction, practice, and feedback. Using these factors as proxies for knowledge is problematic because they can also create or affect other person variables, and these other person variables may or may not have the same effects on JDM quality as knowledge does. For example, feedback can negatively affect a person's motivation. Consequently, when these proxies are measured rather than manipulated, they may reflect variables other than knowledge. For example, the finding from archival research that financial analysts with more experience make more accurate earnings forecasts may simply reflect the fact that analysts with more innate ability both make more accurate forecasts and continue in their jobs longer than analysts with lesser ability (e.g., Mikhail et al. 1997). Most important for our purposes is that experience, in addition to mostly having positive effects on knowledge (which typically has positive effects on JDM quality), creates personal involvement in a task, which can have negative effects on JDM quality. Consequently, it is important not only to consider knowledge and personal involvement as separate constructs, but also to consider them separately from the concepts embedded under the term "experience."

3-4 EFFECTS OF KNOWLEDGE CONTENT AND STRUCTURE ON JDM QUALITY

This part of the chapter discusses the effects of knowledge content and structure on JDM quality.[7] The first section defines these concepts and gives some background on classifications and measurement of knowledge content and structure. The next section discusses what psychology tells us about the effects of knowledge content on JDM quality, including mediators and moderators of these effects, and the third section discusses accounting studies that examine knowledge content. The following sections discuss psychological and accounting findings regarding knowledge structure effects.

---

[6]The effects of experience are discussed in Chapter 9.
[7]Recall that, throughout the remainder of the book, JDM quality will be defined from a performance/output perspective. If variables have different effects on JDM quality depending on which dimension of JDM quality is considered, the discussion will note such differences.

Definitions and Background

Knowledge is information stored in long-term memory; *long-term memory* is memory that is relatively permanent.[8] *Knowledge content* refers to the quantity and specific pieces of information stored in long-term memory, whereas *knowledge structure* refers to the extent to which and the ways in which that information is organized in memory.[9] Knowledge content and knowledge structure clearly are interrelated, but they can have separate effects on JDM quality.

There are many ways of classifying the knowledge content that can be relevant to accounting-related JDM. A basic classification in psychology is episodic versus semantic knowledge (Klatzky 1980). *Episodic knowledge* is for personal experiences; this type of knowledge includes temporal, spatial, and other sensory features of those experiences, including affective reactions in many cases. For example, a person might remember that she wore a black dress to her college graduation on May 19, 1980, or that XYZ Company ensures that sales are not recorded twice by punching a hole in sales invoices once they are recorded. *Semantic memory* extracts the underlying meaning of experiences and preserves the meaning in the form of concepts, principles, and the like. In addition, semantic memory may include affective factors such as whether the concept is generally a "good" or "bad" thing. Examples of semantic knowledge include an understanding of the concept of graduation and knowledge of appropriate general internal controls for sales recording. Semantic knowledge clearly is relevant to JDM in all areas of accounting. However, episodic knowledge is important for many accounting tasks as well. For example, Moeckel and Plumlee (1989) examine auditors' episodic knowledge of work papers for a particular client, and McDaniel et al. (2002) examine audit committee members' episodic knowledge related to financial reporting quality.

Semantic (conceptual) knowledge can be of two types: declarative and procedural.[10] *Declarative knowledge* is composed of facts (e.g., that a red light means stop or that debits go on the left). *Procedural knowledge* consists of if-then rules for performing a skilled task (e.g., if a stoplight is red, then press the brake pedal to bring the car to a stop or if a transaction increases an asset account, then debit the account). Declarative knowledge typically is thought of as being consciously available, whereas procedural knowledge is not always available for description (Reber 1995). In addition, instruction can be sufficient for creating declarative knowledge, whereas some combination of instruction, practice, and feedback normally is necessary for creating procedural knowledge. Again, both declarative and procedural knowledge are important for accounting-related JDM tasks.

Another way of classifying knowledge content is by the topic area covered. Some examples of the classifications used in accounting JDM studies are illustrative, although other classifications clearly are acceptable. Bonner and Lewis (1990) distinguish among general accounting and auditing knowledge, specialized industry knowledge, and

---

[8]Decay of this information does occur but at a very slow pace. In contrast, *short-term memory* holds information that someone is currently attending to; decay of information in short-term memory is very rapid unless people continuously rehearse the information (Anderson 2005).

[9]Knowledge structure refers to the way(s) in which a particular set of information is "naturally" organized in memory. This is in contrast to problem representation, which is the way in which a particular set of information is organized for a particular decision-making purpose. Problem representations are influenced heavily by knowledge structures, but they also can be influenced by other factors such as task format. The creation of a problem representation is considered a cognitive process and, as such, is discussed in Chapter 5.

[10]Some authors classify procedural knowledge as a third type of knowledge separate from episodic and semantic knowledge (Tulving 1985).

general business knowledge when discussing the knowledge relevant for various auditing tasks. Bonner et al. (1992) characterize tax planners' knowledge in terms of technical knowledge (knowledge of tax rules) and functional knowledge (knowledge of corporate transactions). More generally, *technical knowledge* refers to an understanding of the facts, rules, and relationships within a domain, whereas *functional knowledge* refers to knowledge of the operations of the entities that are pertinent to a particular task. Finally, Tan and Libby (1997) examine the effects of *tacit managerial knowledge* (knowledge of how to manage oneself, manage others, and manage one's career) versus technical accounting and auditing knowledge on auditors' JDM. (See Sternberg and Horvath [1999] for a discussion about the role of tacit knowledge in many professions.)

There also are many classifications of knowledge structures that can apply to both episodic and semantic knowledge (Markman 1999). However, psychologists envision different types of knowledge structures depending on whether semantic knowledge is declarative or procedural in nature. Many believe that procedural knowledge (if-then rules) is stored in a simple list format (Anderson 2005). In contrast, there are many theories about how declarative knowledge is structured in memory.[11]

One common type of declarative knowledge that is important for judgment and decision making is knowledge about categories—what the important categories are, which items belong to which categories, and what the important features of categories are. One popular belief about category knowledge is that it is structured in the form of a *hierarchical network* (Markman 1999; Anderson 2005), also referred to as a *taxonomic structure*.[12] The category at the highest level of abstraction (e.g., toys) is at the top of the network; beneath it are categories at the next most detailed level of abstraction (e.g., dolls and games). Membership in categories is based on similarity along some dimension(s). Beneath these categories are further categories, if applicable, or individual members of categories; differences at this point can occur due to the level of expertise of the individual. For example, under games, a game aficionado may have further categories such as "board games," "card games," and "physical games," whereas someone less interested in games may simply list "Monopoly," "Crazy Eights," and other members of the game category. Hierarchical networks typically have "basic level" categories; this is the level of categories people refer to most frequently because it is the most useful.[13] For example, people more frequently refer to "birds" and "fish" than to "animals," or to "sales controls" and "purchases controls" than to "internal controls." Also, a network structure has the potential to incorporate a great deal of information about categories such as features of the categories at each level of abstraction in the network. For example, a feature of birds is "has wings," and a feature of "robin" is "has a red breast." Much accounting research assumes a network (taxonomic) structure for knowledge of categories such as those for internal controls and financial statement errors (e.g., Libby 1985; Tubbs 1992; Nelson et al. 1995).

Another popular belief about how people represent category knowledge is via schemas. Anderson (2005) defines a *schema* as a representation of categorical knowledge that contains particular types of objects, the parts of those objects, and their

---

[11]For recent reviews of the literature on knowledge structures, see Conway (1997), Lamberts and Shanks (1997), and Markman (1999).

[12]Many theories propose that affective reactions are stored in a networklike structure as well (Bower and Forgas 2001).

[13]The category level that is considered basic also can differ based on the amount of knowledge people have.

typical attributes.[14] A schema is similar in level of abstraction to a basic-level category in a network representation, and it includes reference to higher-level categories. However, it does not refer to specific lower-level instances that are members of the category. Instead, schemas record regularities about a category by incorporating slots that contain typical values for that category. Thus, for example, a schema for bird would specify that a bird is a member of the animal category and also would specify features such as "can fly." Having these slots filled in with typical values allows people to make inferences about an item by just knowing the category to which it belongs. However, schemas are flexible in that they allow typical values to be overwritten. For example, a person can overwrite "can fly" in the bird schema if she encounters a penguin. Also, schemas can incorporate reference to other schemas for items that serve as slots in the original schemas. For example, a schema for a house could be connected to a schema for a kitchen because kitchen would be a part in the house schema.

Similar to schemas are *scripts*—knowledge structures that represent regularities about event categories. For example, people may have scripts in memory for events such as going to a doctor's appointment. Like schemas, scripts contain slots filled with typical values for an event that can be overwritten. In addition, scripts can be linked to other scripts. For example, the "going to the doctor" script could be linked to another script about "getting your temperature taken." The key differences between scripts and schemas are that scripts contain information about actions that are part of an event category, whereas schemas contain information about features of an object or concept category; further, scripts link those actions in a temporal sequence, whereas temporal issues are not important in schemas. In accounting, Frederick (1991) compares taxonomic and script structures when examining auditors' knowledge of internal control categories.[15]

As mentioned earlier, there are a number of theories about how knowledge is structured in memory, and the above are but a few. Accounting researchers have depended on a small number of widely known theories in their work to date. Although predictions based on the selected theories largely have been supported, it is conceivable that findings support more than one theory. In addition, psychologists continue to debate the validity of even the most popular theories (Markman 1999). If the ultimate goal of work on knowledge structures is to better understand them in order to suggest methods of improving JDM quality deficiencies associated with knowledge structures, it is important to continue testing new theories from psychology. Even though predictions about JDM behavior may be similar across two or more theories, improvement methods related to different types of knowledge structures may not be. For example, improvement methods related to a taxonomic structure may include reminding people of category members (e.g., Bonner et al. 1996), whereas those related to a script may include reminding people of events that occur directly prior to the events to be remembered.

A final note relates to how to study knowledge content and knowledge structure. As mentioned earlier, the preponderance of both experimental and other (archival or survey) research in accounting uses some sort of instruction, practice, or feedback proxy to measure knowledge because these factors affect knowledge.[16] Most typically,

---

[14]Although this definition is stated in terms of objects, it applies equally to concepts such as those of interest in accounting.

[15]Also see Choo (1989) for a discussion of the relevance of scripts in accounting.

[16]As mentioned in Chapter 1, survey researchers also may ask participants to rate their own knowledge. However, there are many problems with this, so it is not recommended.

the proxy is years of experience in a job or doing a particular task, which incorporates instruction, practice, and feedback.[17] There are more direct ways of measuring or manipulating knowledge content and structure in experimental settings that deserve mention.[18]

Researchers can measure knowledge content with recognition tests. *Recognition tests* measure knowledge content in memory by providing people with a series of stimuli that allow them to retrieve that knowledge. These tests include the normal types of questions given on exams (e.g., true-false, matching, and multiple-choice questions). Researchers can derive measures of knowledge content by counting the number of right answers. Typically, recognition tests work best for measuring the declarative form of semantic knowledge, but it is conceivable they can measure procedural knowledge as well. (See Bonner and Walker [1994] for an example.) *Recall tests* require people to "reproduce material previously learned" (Reber 1995); the only stimuli that aid retrieval are the words in the recall question. A recall test might ask someone to "list as many corporate transactions as you can think of" (Bonner et al. 1992). Recall tests can also present people with information to read (e.g., a list of corporate transactions) then ask them to reproduce that material after doing a "distractor task." *Distractor tasks* such as multiplication problems clear short-term memory; people cannot simultaneously rehearse the material and complete the distractor task. Thus, they allow recall tests to measure knowledge truly stored in long-term memory. Recall tests can measure both episodic and semantic knowledge. Knowledge content can be measured from recall tests by counting the number of correct items recalled.[19]

Researchers can also use recall tests to measure knowledge structure—the extent to which and the ways in which knowledge is organized in memory. For example, there are standardized measures that examine the amount of clustering of items predefined to be similar. In addition, researchers can examine the contents of the clusters to determine the underlying organizing principles. In accounting, Weber (1980) was the first to use these techniques to measure auditors' knowledge structures for internal controls. Another method of measuring knowledge structure is *card sorting.* In this method, people are asked to form clusters by sorting cards into piles of "related items," where the people doing the sorting define relatedness. Each card contains a single item such as the name of an animal or an internal control procedure. Measures here include a quantitative comparison of the contents of piles to a theoretically correct structure, if one exists (see Nelson et al. [1995] for an example), or more qualitative measures that involve the researcher's examination of the contents of the sorted piles.[20] Many other methods for measuring knowledge content and structure are available as well. (See Bonner et al. [1991] for more information.)

---

[17]Chapter 9 discusses in detail the relations between instruction, practice, and feedback and knowledge content and structure.

[18]It is plausible, albeit highly unlikely, for researchers to obtain these measures of knowledge in archival form. For example, audit firms measure auditors' knowledge after training courses. However, firms are unlikely to provide such information to researchers because of privacy and other concerns.

[19]Recognition and recall tests can produce different results with regard to knowledge content because of their effects on memory retrieval processes. This issue is discussed further in Chapter 5.

[20]A related method is paired comparisons. Paired comparisons is a more detailed, time-consuming version of card sorting in which people are asked to rate the similarity of all possible pairs of items represented on the cards. In card sorting, an assumption is made that all items in one pile are equally similar to all other items in the pile.

Finally, researchers can manipulate knowledge content or structure by varying one or more of the factors that influence these variables. For example, an experiment could manipulate the content and amount of instruction people receive in order to manipulate knowledge content (e.g., Bonner and Walker 1994) or knowledge structure (e.g., Bonner et al. 1997). Manipulation is costly in terms of subject time, however, so it is rarely used.

Knowledge Content Effects

What are the effects of knowledge content on JDM quality? Knowledge content typically is thought to have a positive effect on JDM quality, but there are many moderators of these positive effects (discussed below). Positive effects of knowledge content on JDM quality appear for all JDM quality dimensions—accuracy, agreement with others and oneself, correspondence with normative theories or professional standards, and time and costs to do a task.

Before describing the effects of knowledge content on JDM quality, it is important to provide a brief overview of the cognitive processes through which knowledge content can operate. Knowledge content is brought to bear on JDM tasks first through retrieval from memory; retrieved knowledge can affect information search, problem representation, hypothesis generation, and hypothesis evaluation processes as well.[21] The speed and probability of retrieval of knowledge from memory are a function of the level of activation of that knowledge (Anderson 2005). *Activation* is a function of two factors: the strength of the knowledge in memory and information provided by the task at hand. *Strength* refers to the long-term durability of knowledge in memory; it is determined by the frequency and recency of previous activations of that knowledge. In other words, every time someone uses a piece of knowledge, it gets stronger in memory. However, strength decreases as a function of the time since a piece of knowledge was activated. Information provided by a task also affects activation. For example, if a task mentions a particular auditing standard and an auditor has knowledge of that standard stored in memory, the knowledge likely will be activated. In addition, other pieces of knowledge that are related to the activated piece of knowledge in memory also will be activated; this is known as *spreading activation.* "Related" knowledge typically refers to knowledge that is related conceptually. However, activation can also spread to knowledge that is tagged with a similar affective reaction (Bower 1981; Bower and Forgas 2001).

Research examining the positive effects of knowledge content for JDM comes largely from the expertise literature (Chi et al. 1988; Ericsson and Smith 1991; Hoffman 1992; Ericsson 1996).[22] This literature typically indicates that positive effects occur through the above process mechanisms. That is, people with greater and stronger knowledge content are more likely to retrieve the knowledge and be able to use it to arrive at a high-quality judgment or decision than are people with lesser and weaker knowledge content.

---

[21]Although this chapter does not discuss the processes by which knowledge becomes stored in memory, clearly people must have knowledge in long-term memory in order to retrieve it and apply it to a JDM task. For further discussion of memory encoding and storage issues, see Klatzky (1980), Baddeley (1990), Schacter (2001), and Chapter 9.

[22]The expertise literature does not always define expertise or high-quality JDM in terms of performance. I make note of this where it is likely to be pertinent to the issue of under what conditions knowledge content has positive effects on JDM quality.

However, this research also indicates several reasons knowledge content may not have a consistent positive effect on JDM quality, that is, moderators of its effects. First, knowledge content can have a positive effect on JDM quality only if the knowledge is relevant to the specific task under consideration. For example, an auditor who generally is highly knowledgeable about internal control evaluation may not do well at evaluating the internal controls of a financial institution because its controls are somewhat different from those of other businesses. One of the central findings of the expertise literature is that task-specific knowledge is an important determinant of high-quality JDM (e.g., Chi et al. 1988; Ericsson and Lehman 1996). Knowledge related to other tasks in the domain or even the specific area generally is not helpful.[23] This is a particularly important point for accounting research as accounting tasks, even within a broad functional area such as auditing or even within a very narrow area such as internal control evaluation, can vary greatly as to the types of knowledge they require.

Second, many tasks require multiple types of knowledge, and different types of knowledge may interact to affect JDM quality in some tasks.[24] In particular, one type of knowledge may not have a positive effect on JDM quality unless another type of knowledge is present in memory as well. In other words, the absence of other required knowledge can moderate the positive effects of a given type of knowledge. For example, studies of computer programmers find that the interaction of technical knowledge of programming concepts and functional knowledge of the entities for which programs are being designed affects JDM quality (Adelson and Soloway 1985; Pennington 1987a, 1987b). The fact that knowledge content may have only positive effects on JDM quality in interaction with other knowledge content also is important in accounting. There are a number of contexts in which accountants need multiple types of knowledge and must integrate such knowledge to exhibit high-quality JDM. An example is assurance services. It is possible that auditors who know how to conduct assurance engagements will have low JDM quality unless they also possess a great deal of knowledge about the information for which assurance is being provided, such as customer satisfaction information. (See Vera-Muñoz et al. [2001] for a related example.)

The first two reasons knowledge content may not have a positive effect on JDM quality are that people do not have in memory either a specific type of knowledge or all the types of knowledge relevant to a given task. A third reason knowledge content may not have a positive effect on JDM quality is that it exists in memory but is not retrieved. The most striking example of this is people's failure to use statistical knowledge, particularly that for prior probabilities (base rates) of occurrence.[25] People tend to interpret situations as unique, so they perceive that base rates are not relevant (Meehl and Rosen 1955; Kahneman and Tversky 1973). Here, then, cognitive process errors serve to moderate positive effects of this type of knowledge. If people can see the relevance to a task of base-rate knowledge, they are more likely to retrieve and use

---

[23] There are situations in which people can transfer knowledge across tasks and make high-quality judgments and decisions, but transfer occurs only under fairly restrictive conditions (Singley and Anderson 1989).

[24] Shanteau (1992b) and Camerer and Johnson (1991) also argue that knowledge content may not have a positive effect on JDM quality unless other person variables are present, for example, various cognitive process characteristics or abilities.

[25] People also sometimes fail to use base-rate knowledge when it is present in the problem because they do not see its relevance (Kahneman and Tversky 1973). In these cases, failure to use knowledge obviously is not the result of memory retrieval issues.

it. One way of fostering this is by detailing the causal relation of base rates to outcomes because people naturally tend to think in terms of cause–effect relations (e.g., Ajzen 1977; Bar-Hillel 1980). Another situation in which knowledge may exist in memory but not be applied to the task at hand is when a person is engaging in conclusion-motivated reasoning, as discussed earlier.

Next, knowledge may not be retrieved because of the interference of other knowledge, specifically knowledge activated by task information. Here, factors inherent in the memory retrieval process may moderate the positive effects of knowledge. There are at least two theories about interference examined in the accounting literature. One theory relies on the spreading activation mechanism. Task information activates a particular piece of knowledge in memory, and activation spreads to closely related pieces of knowledge. Because retrieval is a function of relative activation, knowledge related to the information in the task then has a higher probability of being retrieved, and less related knowledge has a lower probability of being retrieved (Collins and Loftus 1975; Meyer and Schvaneveldt 1976). If the less related knowledge is necessary for the task, then JDM quality may suffer. For example, an auditor retrieving financial statement errors from memory may inherit an initial hypothesis from a superior or previous work papers. That initial hypothesis may interfere with the retrieval of the correct hypothesis if the correct hypothesis is not closely related to the inherited hypothesis in memory. For example, the correct hypothesis may be an error in inventory purchases recording, whereas the inherited hypothesis may be an error in sales recording, which spreads activation to other sales errors and makes their retrieval more likely.

An alternative view of interference paints the retrieval process as being akin to sampling with replacement. Under this scenario, the initially activated piece of knowledge increases in strength simply because of its activation. Even though spreading activation is occurring, the initial activation of the particular piece of knowledge increases its strength relative to those other pieces and, consequently, increases the probability it will be retrieved again and again. Essentially, the person gets "stuck" on the activated knowledge and never gets to the pertinent piece of knowledge, even if it is closely related (e.g., Rundus 1973; Raiijmakers and Shiffrin 1981). Using the error generation auditing example, this form of interference suggests that an auditor's inheritance of a sales hypothesis would make it less likely that she would retrieve further sales errors. Finally, if a person has activated an affective reaction to knowledge, she is more likely to retrieve affect-congruent knowledge than affect-incongruent knowledge (Bower and Forgas 2001).

Fourth, particular types of knowledge can have negative effects on JDM quality per se. This phenomenon is known as the "curse of knowledge." As Kennedy (1995) notes: "the *curse of knowledge* occurs when, in predicting others' knowledge or forecasts, individuals are unable to ignore knowledge they have that others do not have (Camerer et al. 1989) or when they are unable to disregard information already processed (Fischhoff 1977)." The former situation typically involves people knowing actual outcomes but having to evaluate the JDM of others who did not know actual outcomes at the time of their JDM. In this situation, people should ignore outcomes when making their evaluations; not doing so is labeled an *outcome effect*. For example, jurors must evaluate whether auditors' JDM is in agreement with professional standards, not whether auditors' JDM is accurate with regard to outcomes. The latter situation also involves cases in which actual outcomes are normatively irrelevant to the

JDM task at hand, but no evaluation of others' JDM is involved. For example, when using analytical procedures, auditors must form expectations of what account balances should be then judge whether unaudited account balances are substantially different from expectations. Unaudited account balances are normatively irrelevant for forming expectations.

Closely related to the "curse of knowledge" is *hindsight bias,* which occurs when people say that they would have judged a higher probability of occurrence for an event ex ante when they know that event has occurred (Plous 1993). The curse of knowledge and hindsight bias occur partially because people associate outcome information with previously stored knowledge; consequently, outcome information is activated and retrieved when other knowledge about the situation is used. Outcome knowledge can also affect information search and hypothesis evaluation (Hawkins and Hastie 1990). Regardless of the process mechanism, outcome effects cause people to make judgments and decisions that they otherwise would not make, thereby decreasing JDM quality.

Fifth, particular types of knowledge do not have uniformly positive effects across all dimensions of JDM quality. One key finding in this regard is that declarative and procedural knowledge have different effects on time and costs to do tasks. People develop procedural knowledge by using declarative knowledge repeatedly and compiling it into automated rules. These rules effectively combine various elements of declarative knowledge; further, they can be accessed from memory and applied very rapidly. Because of rapid access, procedural knowledge typically has significant positive effects on the efficiency dimension, whereas declarative knowledge does not (Anderson 2005). In addition, as Libby (1995) notes, procedural knowledge may also have a greater effect than declarative knowledge on quality dimensions such as accuracy and agreement with professional standards when people are under time pressure. This would occur because procedural knowledge's incorporation of multiple elements of declarative knowledge in single rules allows people to get more "right answers" in a fixed amount of time. Time pressure is a key element in many accounting settings, most notably auditing.

Finally, the expertise literature indicates that there are several domains in which persons designated to be experts do not have higher-quality JDM than those designated to be novices (e.g., clinical psychology), despite obvious differences in knowledge content (e.g., Shanteau 1992b). Clearly, these findings could indicate problems with the choice of experts and novices; however, they could also indicate that people possess and retrieve knowledge relevant to a particular task but characteristics of the task or environment prevent that knowledge from having a positive effect on JDM quality. For example, Shanteau proposes that task complexity may moderate the effects of knowledge content on JDM quality. However, he also notes that the fields in which this occurs may be in their infancy (e.g., they have not accumulated enough information to make tasks less complex through the provision of decision aids). This also implies, however, that "high knowledge content" is a relative term applied to those with higher knowledge content than others. Nevertheless, for some reason, knowledge content differences are not associated with JDM quality differences in these domains.[26]

---

[26]Another reason knowledge content may not have a positive effect on JDM quality is that it has not been measured properly. See Bonner et al. (1992) for an example of how knowledge content measured in different ways has varying effects on JDM quality.

Accounting Studies on Knowledge Content

A large number of studies in accounting examine the effects of knowledge content on JDM quality. However, many of these studies use some measure of "experience" as a proxy for knowledge content, most typically years of time spent in a job or task. Also, many studies use students as surrogates for accounting professionals, implying that students possess the knowledge necessary for the tasks the studies examine. Studies using an experience proxy are included in this section only if they can provide strong support that the proxy captures knowledge content rather than a correlated variable such as ability. For example, Bonner (1990) uses a design that involves two auditing tasks. In one of these tasks, there should be experience-related knowledge differences, but in the other there should not. However, experience-related ability differences would occur in both tasks. As such, the design allows her to assert with more credibility that experience proxies for knowledge (if the predicted results occur). Studies using students are included only if there is strong evidence that at least some of the students possess the appropriate knowledge.

Studies of knowledge content effects for producers of accounting information include the following. Vera-Muñoz (1998) finds that students with greater financial accounting knowledge (as proxied by coursework) identify fewer theoretically correct opportunity costs. Hunton et al. (2000) find that general management accounting knowledge is related to job performance for junior and senior management accountants but not managers. They also find that specialized industry knowledge and tacit managerial knowledge are important for seniors' and managers' performance but not juniors'. Dearman and Shields (2001) report that managers' knowledge of activity-based costing (ABC) is positively related to the agreement of their judgments with ABC theory, whereas knowledge of traditional volume-based costing is negatively related to this performance measure. Vera-Muñoz et al. (2001) find that management accountants' procedural knowledge (as proxied by management accounting experience), in interaction with their knowledge structures for cash flow information, is related to the theoretical correctness of their judgments regarding opportunity costs.

Several studies examine outcome effects in performance evaluation contexts. Brown and Solomon (1987) show that students do not ignore outcome information when evaluating a capital budgeting committee's JDM performance if they have no prior involvement in the JDM; with prior involvement, they ignore outcome information. Brown and Solomon (1993) use a similar task and find that subjects ignore outcome information in evaluating the capital budgeting committee when they agree with the committee's JDM but not when they disagree; observed effects appear due to memory retrieval. Lipe's (1993) student and management accountant subjects attend to outcomes when evaluating another person's variance investigation decision; outcome effects occur because they are incorporated into problem representations.

Tan and Lipe (1997) report that outcomes affect both students' and managers' evaluations of others' project investment decisions. Outcome effects are attenuated but not removed for students when they have information about outcome controllability. Frederickson et al. (1999) find that students making evaluations of others' managerial decisions are most prone to ignore outcome information when they have learned to make evaluations under a system that evaluates processes. Ghosh and Lusch (2000) report that regional managers' evaluations of store managers are influenced by outcomes over which store managers have no control. Finally, for analysts, Fisher and

Selling (1993) find that analysts ignore outcome information in evaluating others' bankruptcy predictions only when they make correct predictions themselves. Note that there are no other studies that examine the effects of knowledge content on JDM quality for analysts.[27]

For users of accounting information, there are also relatively few studies about knowledge content. Herz and Schultz (1999) report that students (proxying for investors) who have higher procedural knowledge related to converting cash-based income into accrual-based income perform better at this task (where performance is defined vis-à-vis accounting theory). DeZoort and Salterio (2001) find that audit committee members' auditing knowledge is associated with the extent to which they agree with the auditor's position (versus management's position). However, their financial reporting knowledge has no effect on this dimension of JDM quality. McDaniel et al. (2002) examine the effect of audit committee members' (as proxied by auditors and managers) semantic and episodic financial reporting knowledge on their identification of financial reporting choices that do not conform to professional standards. Higher semantic financial reporting knowledge leads to higher JDM quality, but higher episodic financial reporting knowledge does not. Finally, Buchman (1985) finds that student users of financial information do not ignore bankruptcy outcome information when asked to predict the probability of bankruptcy.

Most studies of users' knowledge relate to tax professionals. Bonner et al. (1992) examine JDM quality in tax planning using two measures: number of theoretically correct tax issues identified and difficulty of issues identified (a proxy for expected utility maximization). Declarative but not procedural tax knowledge is related to number of issues identified. However, neither declarative nor procedural corporate transaction knowledge is related to this element of JDM quality. Only the three-way interaction of procedural tax knowledge, procedural transaction knowledge, and problem-solving ability is related to the difficulty measure. Spilker (1995) finds that both declarative and procedural tax knowledge affect performance in a tax research task, where performance is defined as the ability to find theoretically relevant tax authorities. Cloyd (1995, 1997) similarly reports that declarative tax knowledge is related to this measure of research performance and demonstrates that the effect occurs at least partially through information search activities and reduced processing time. Roberts and Ashton (2003) find that declarative knowledge of the tax code increases efficiency and accuracy in a tax research task. Finally, Helleloid (1988) finds that tax professionals' use of outcome information is in accordance with tax law; they ignore it when evaluating clients' prior beliefs but use it when recommending tax treatments.

Studies of auditors' knowledge content are more plentiful. Most studies focus on the effects of semantic auditing and accounting knowledge, for example, knowledge about internal controls, financial statement errors, accounting principles, and substantive tests. It is unclear whether most studies measure declarative knowledge or procedural knowledge. Nevertheless, research shows consistent positive effects of semantic knowledge when it is relevant to the specific task at hand. Frederick and Libby (1986) find that knowledge of internal control weaknesses and their relations to accounting errors, along with knowledge of the relations among accounts, leads to judgments that agree more with accounting and auditing theory and are less likely to violate probability

---

[27]Several studies examine analysts' cognitive processes. These are discussed in Chapter 5.

theory. Bonner (1990) reports that auditors' knowledge of internal controls and analytical procedures result in judgments of control risk and analytical procedures risk that agree more with the judgments of other auditors; process results indicate this occurs mostly through differential weighting of cues.

Bonner and Lewis (1990) find that different types of knowledge relate to the agreement of judgments with auditing theory, depending on the auditing task involved. They examine knowledge of internal controls, analytical procedures, and business in general. Coincidentally, they find little correlation among the different types of knowledge for experienced auditors. Again, this suggests the subtlety involved in detailing the types of knowledge needed for a specific task and the importance of measuring the knowledge directly rather than assuming, for example, that all experienced auditors possess it. In a study that attempts to differentiate between declarative and procedural knowledge, Bonner and Walker (1994) show that procedural knowledge (but not declarative knowledge) about ratio analysis is related to students' choice of errors that can explain financial ratio fluctuations. Choo (1996) finds that both declarative and procedural knowledge positively affect the accuracy of auditors' going-concern judgments; his subjects exhibit greater variation in declarative knowledge than do Bonner and Walker's subjects.

Other studies investigate more specialized types of semantic knowledge. Tan and Libby (1997) examine technical and tacit managerial knowledge and find that staff and senior auditors whose work performance is rated higher have higher technical auditing knowledge but not higher tacit managerial knowledge than others, whereas managers with higher performance evaluations have higher tacit knowledge but not higher technical knowledge. Several studies examine the effects of specialized industry knowledge on JDM quality and find mostly positive effects as measured by agreement with auditing and accounting theories and professional standards. They also find positive effects on accuracy as compared to actual outcomes (Bonner and Lewis 1990; Bedard and Biggs 1991a; Bédard 1991; Johnson et al. 1991a, 1993; O'Keefe et al. 1994a; Jamal et al. 1995; Wright and Wright 1997; Owhoso et al. 2002; Thibodeau 2003; Low 2004). Although most of these studies use industry-specific experience as a proxy for knowledge, we can infer from the findings of Solomon et al. (1999) that this proxy captures specialized knowledge. Finally, Thibodeau reports that auditors with more specialized knowledge related to loan collectibility are better able to assess the going-concern status of firms. This is the only study in accounting that demonstrates that knowledge relevant for one task can have positive effects on JDM quality in another task. Thibodeau acknowledges the restrictive conditions typically necessary for transfer of knowledge and finds that they are met in his setting.

Several studies investigate the lack of positive effects of auditors' semantic knowledge on JDM quality due to the inability to retrieve that knowledge from memory. Four (Libby 1985; Libby and Frederick 1990; Church and Schneider 1993, 1995) examine the "output interference" phenomenon in an analytical procedures task that provides auditors with an error that can explain ratio fluctuations and asks them to generate further errors. As described above, *output interference* means that one piece of knowledge interferes with the retrieval of other pieces of knowledge. These studies examine only the hypothesis generation phase of the task but find evidence that output interference occurs. Libby and Frederick's auditors generate more errors from the transaction cycle to which the provided error belongs, meaning that they then generate fewer errors from other transaction cycles. Libby does not find such results but attributes this to the choice of prompt. Church and Schneider find that auditors generate fewer errors from the provided error's transaction cycle.[28] Anderson et al.'s (1992) auditors generate fewer error explanations in this type of task if they generate them after having provided nonerror explanations rather than before, but Bedard and Biggs (1991a) report that auditors given an incomplete explanation from management are no less able to generate the correct hypothesis than those given no explanation. Frederick (1991) also finds that auditors experience output interference for internal controls knowledge when prompted with controls from the same transaction cycle. In all these cases, if output interference prevents a relevant piece of semantic knowledge from being retrieved, there is the potential for a lack of a positive relation between knowledge content and JDM quality.[29]

A few studies focus on the effects of auditors' episodic knowledge on JDM quality. One particularly important type of episodic knowledge is that of base rates of occurrence of financial statement errors. Although many studies examine the effects of such knowledge on hypothesis generation and hypothesis evaluation in analytical procedures tasks (e.g., Libby 1985; Libby and Frederick 1990; Tuttle 1996), only Nelson (1993a) and Asare and Wright (1995) examine the effect of base-rate knowledge on judgments. Nelson finds positive effects of this knowledge on auditors' judgment quality vis-à-vis accounting theory, and Asare and Wright find positive effects on the accuracy of error detection. However, it may not be prudent to generalize from these two studies' findings given that people do not always use base-rate knowledge (as discussed above). In addition, although base-rate knowledge may lead auditors to generate frequently occurring errors as hypotheses for ratio fluctuations, various problems in the hypothesis evaluation phase may not lead them to ultimately choose the "right answer" (Bonner and Pennington 1991). Further, Asare and Wright find that base-rate knowledge does not have a positive effect on the extent to which auditors' judgments conform to (normative) probability theory.

Kennedy (1995) documents negative effects of episodic knowledge. She finds that auditors estimating the going-concern or dollars-of-sales judgments of other auditors, such as they might do in a litigation setting, are unable to ignore knowledge of bankruptcy outcomes or actual dollars of sales. Similarly, several previous studies find that auditors are unable to ignore their knowledge of unaudited account balances when conducting tests (e.g., Kinney and Uecker 1982; Biggs and Wild 1985; Heintz and White 1989). However, Wright (1988a) shows that auditors with knowledge of the prior year's auditing procedures are more effective at identifying appropriate current procedures than those without such knowledge.

There are no studies of knowledge content effects for regulators. For evaluators of accountants' work, the focus is exclusively on the negative effects on JDM of outcome knowledge. As might be expected, jurors' and judges' and other users' evaluative judgments of auditors' work are negatively affected by knowledge of negative outcomes

---

[28] There are several differences between these studies that may account for the results. For example, Church and Schneider (1993, 1995) restrict the number of transaction cycle categories from which subjects can generate errors, whereas Libby and Frederick (1990) do not. Nevertheless, the findings suggest that there may be different forms of output interference, consistent with the psychology literature.

[29] Moser (1989) also examines output interference in an investment setting but does not specifically examine it as a result of the activation of related pieces of knowledge.

(Anderson et al. 1993; Lowe and Reckers 1994; Kinney and Nelson 1996; Anderson et al. 1997b; Kadous 2000, 2001).

Overall, accounting studies' findings on knowledge content mostly parallel findings from psychology. First, accounting researchers are now well attuned to the idea that knowledge can have a positive effect on JDM quality only if it is relevant to the specific task. Consistent with this, most studies of knowledge content investigate the main effects of knowledge relevant to specific tasks. It should be noted, however, that for some accounting professionals, such as analysts, research has not yet documented the knowledge relevant to their JDM. Second, a handful of studies investigates interactive effects of different types of knowledge or knowledge and other person variables and finds results consistent with those for similar settings in psychology. These studies may become more important in the future if the accounting profession moves toward the provision of services that require accountants to have and integrate several types of knowledge.

Third, a few studies indicate that accountants are subject to knowledge retrieval problems and curse of knowledge and hindsight bias problems, similar to others. However, these issues continue to deserve study because of their clear importance in litigation settings, as well as because of some contrary findings. Fourth, there are situations in which accounting professionals' JDM seems to be of relatively low quality, yet these professionals also likely have a great deal of knowledge. However, research has not investigated why this may be the case. For example, most mutual fund managers routinely fail to beat the market but clearly are highly knowledgeable individuals (Gruber 1996; Carhart 1997).

Next, it is extremely important to understand how factors that are peculiar to accountants' experience affect the acquisition of knowledge. For example, do various characteristics of accounting systems facilitate or hinder knowledge acquisition (e.g., Luft and Shields 2001)? Along with this, it is important to empirically examine the effectiveness of improvement methods that are in place in practice specifically to enhance knowledge acquisition and use. Research discussed in Chapter 9 indicates that it cannot be assumed that these methods are universally effective. In other words, although improvement methods such as training and decision aids often have positive effects on knowledge, various factors can moderate these effects.

Knowledge Structure Effects

Similar to knowledge content, knowledge structure typically is thought to have a positive effect on all dimensions of JDM quality. Indeed, the expertise literature indicates that experts have better organized knowledge—structures that are more extensive and that organize knowledge using more substantive principles (Chi et al. 1988). Knowledge structures operate on JDM principally through the retrieval process, which then can influence other cognitive processes as well. Because of the way knowledge structures affect retrieval and other processes, however, it is more realistic to say that knowledge structures sometimes have positive effects on JDM quality and sometimes have negative effects. In other words, the retrieval process itself often moderates the positive effects of knowledge structures.

As mentioned earlier, when knowledge is activated in memory, activation spreads to related items in a knowledge structure. Thus, the presence of a knowledge structure tends to affect activation and retrieval of several items of knowledge, most particularly for the items closely related to the originally activated item. Further, the more organized and more frequently accessed is the knowledge structure, the greater is the retrieval effect brought by spreading activation.

Knowledge structures' potential positive effects on JDM quality include the following. First, people with high-quality knowledge structures typically can retrieve more information from memory or, at a minimum, can retrieve a given amount of information more quickly. Part of this, of course, is due to the fact that they simply know more. However, having knowledge structured means that people can retrieve sets of information (called "chunks") rather than individual pieces of information. Spreading activation obviously facilitates the quick sequential retrieval of items in a set of information; however, people with high-quality knowledge structures sometimes store pieces of information in groups. For example, chess experts tend to retrieve from memory entire board arrangements rather than the positions of individual chess pieces (DeGroot 1966; Chase and Simon 1973).

Second, in attempting to retrieve detailed episodic knowledge, people often retrieve a generic knowledge structure that is related to the episode and infer details from that knowledge structure. Thus, instead of directly retrieving details about a particular visit to a restaurant, for example, a person may infer details from her script for typical visits to restaurants. Such inference helps JDM if what the person infers happens to be consistent with the original details and relevant to the JDM task. Of course, if the person infers information that is not consistent with the original details, her use of the inferred information can lead to lower-quality JDM. Similarly, Kida and Smith (1995) argue that people may first retrieve the affective reaction to an episode and infer details about the episode by invoking an affect-consistent schema.

Third, knowledge structures often contain not only linked items of knowledge, but also JDM strategies and plans or even outputs related to particular situations (Chi et al. 1988). Hence, activation of a knowledge structure can lead to the immediate construction of a problem representation or even an immediate judgment or decision, thus affecting the efficiency of JDM (at a minimum). For example, chess experts have knowledge structures that link certain combinations of pieces with moves. Thus, when these knowledge structures are activated, these experts can immediately choose their next move (Chase and Simon 1973). Similarly, physics experts have knowledge structures that contain solutions to particular types of physics problems (Chi et al. 1981). The fact that knowledge structures contain decision strategies and solutions again tends to help JDM if the activated knowledge structure is well suited for a task, that is, the decision strategies and solutions it contains are appropriate.

Unfortunately, people do not always activate knowledge structures that are well suited for tasks. Knowledge structures develop with experience; thus, in their early stages, they may not contain appropriate decision strategies and/or solutions. Retrieval of inappropriate decision strategies or solutions clearly can harm JDM. In addition, even experienced people develop knowledge structures that are not consistent with the structure of all tasks they face. This can occur, for example, because people naturally structure knowledge around causes, and some tasks relate to effects rather than causes (e.g., Nelson et al. 1995). When knowledge structures do not match the structure of a task, people often restructure the task to create a problem representation that matches their knowledge structures; this, in turn, harms their JDM.

Finally, there are several potential downsides of the spreading activation that occurs in well-developed knowledge structures. One is the output interference phenomenon discussed earlier. A second is the curse of knowledge and hindsight bias effects; these are thought to occur because people incorporate the "bad knowledge" into existing knowledge structures. A third potential downside of spreading activation occurs for people with high-quality knowledge structures, such as experts, because those structures also tend to be quite complex. Complex knowledge structures have multiple paths from one item to other items. Because a given amount of activation spreads through the knowledge structure, the larger the number of paths over which it spreads, the smaller the activation for any given path. Thus, people with more paths in their knowledge structure may be less likely to retrieve a particular knowledge item than people with fewer paths; this phenomenon is called the *fan effect* (Anderson 2005).

Accounting Studies on Knowledge Structure

There are very few accounting studies that directly examine the effects of knowledge structure on JDM quality.[30] Two studies examine producers' knowledge structures. Dearman and Shields (2001) show that the extent to which managers have activity-based knowledge structures as opposed to physical-resource-based knowledge structures positively affects the agreement of their judgments with activity-based costing theory. Vera-Muñoz et al. (2001) find that accountants who have a cash-flow-based knowledge structure (as proxied by management accounting experience) have more appropriate problem representations for a relevance assurance task; however, both a cash-flow-based knowledge structure and procedural management accounting knowledge must be present for judgments regarding opportunity costs to be of the highest quality.

Two studies examine users' knowledge structures. Pratt (1982) shows that students whose knowledge about annual reports is better structured have more accurate predictions of net income in a complex task but not in simpler tasks. Kida et al. (1998) find that managers using financial data to make investment choices incorporate affective reactions to specific numbers into their knowledge structures and have better retrieval of those affective reactions than they do for comparisons of numbers and the numbers themselves. Further, when they are unable to retrieve specific numbers or comparisons, they infer these from their retrieved affective reactions, consistent with the inference of details from a schema, for example. Also, because the affective reactions are stronger than numbers in the knowledge structures, they have more influence on subsequent judgments. Kida et al. then show that this feature of knowledge structures leads to investment decisions that do not conform to investing theory.

Studies of auditors typically examine knowledge structures for internal controls or financial statement errors. Plumlee (1985) assumes a schema structure for internal auditors' knowledge of controls and finds that auditors with such a structure are better able to identify theoretically correct control weaknesses than those without such a structure. Frederick (1991) finds that auditors organize their knowledge of internal controls both taxonomically and in script form. However, a script organization better facilitates retrieval and is less likely to lead to output interference, although it does not entirely prevent output interference. Frederick does not examine the ultimate impact

---

[30]Several studies examine the effect of experience on knowledge structures. These are discussed in Chapter 9.

of knowledge structure on judgments. Choo (1996) assumes a script structure for going-concern knowledge and finds that various qualitative aspects of the script structure are positively related to the extent to which going-concern probability judgments correspond with bankruptcy outcomes. Thibodeau (2003) finds that knowledge structures related to loan collectibility evaluation have positive transferable effects on the accuracy of auditors' going-concern judgments vis-à-vis actual outcomes.

Consistent with the discussion above, several studies find negative effects of knowledge structures. Choo and Trotman (1991) assume a schema structure for knowledge of going-concern factors and find that the extent of organization of knowledge is related to inferences made at retrieval, some of which are inconsistent with the original material. In turn, inferences affect going-concern probability judgments. In this study, there is no stated criterion for determining JDM quality; however, we can infer that judgments that are affected by incorrect inferences may be of lower quality. Nelson et al. (1995) and Bonner et al. (1996) illustrate another negative effect of knowledge structures. They show that auditors tend to structure their knowledge of financial statement errors by audit objective as opposed to transaction cycle (although they are able to structure by transaction cycle when asked). Thus, when auditors make conditional probability judgments and budgeting decisions that require a transaction cycle structure, as is the case in audit planning, their JDM quality suffers. JDM quality in these studies is measured as the extent to which probability judgments and budgeted hours decisions correspond to probability theory.[31] Finally, Moeckel and Plumlee (1989) and Moeckel (1990) examine negative effects of knowledge structures on auditors' accuracy of and confidence in their memory for information in audit work papers. Knowledge structures cause auditors to make inferences in retrieval; consistent with this, Moeckel and Plumlee find that auditors are inaccurate when presented with inferences that are contradicted by the original work papers, and Moeckel finds that more experienced auditors are more inaccurate. Although these studies do not examine the ultimate effects on judgments, this finding clearly has negative implications for JDM quality.

In sum, accounting studies of knowledge structure effects report results that are consistent with those from psychology. Specifically, accountants' knowledge structures sometimes have positive effects on JDM quality and sometimes have negative effects. Knowledge structures play a prominent role in high-quality JDM and, as such, deserve further scrutiny in accounting. A topic of particular interest would be the impact on JDM of different types of knowledge structures that are encouraged by different professional theories, such as traditional costing theories versus activity-based costing theory (Dearman and Shields 2001). For example, auditors who structure their knowledge around business processes, an idea currently in vogue (Eilifsen et al. 2001), may have different JDM than auditors who structure their knowledge more traditionally (e.g., by transaction cycle). Another question that is somewhat unique to accounting settings is whether accountants can use multiple knowledge structures when they perform tasks that require different structures and, if not, how to help them do so (e.g., Bonner et al. 1996).

---

[31]Similarly, Bonner et al. (1997) train auditing students to have an audit objective or transaction cycle-based knowledge structure for financial statement errors and find that budgeted hours correspond less to probability theory when the structure needed for decisions does not correspond to the trained knowledge structure.

3-5 EFFECTS OF PERSONAL INVOLVEMENT ON JDM QUALITY

Personal Involvement Effects

Personal involvement means that a person who is currently making a judgment or decision for a particular task has made a judgment or decision previously for that task. She could have done this either by completing the task herself or by participating in a group who completed the task; in other words, the person has experience with the task. However, the key focus here is on the fact that the person has made a previous judgment or decision. This is as opposed to the focus being on the knowledge that can be gained from the experience of having done the task and received feedback on the JDM.

Personal involvement can lead people to make the same judgment or decision as in previous periods. If the previous JDM was of low quality, then it is likely that the current period's JDM will be as well.[32] Thus, personal involvement normally is thought to have negative effects on JDM quality. Although most studies in this area examine JDM quality as accuracy vis-à-vis outcomes or correspondence with normative theories, it clearly is possible to examine personal involvement's effects on other quality dimensions, particularly given their unique importance in some areas of accounting.

Personal involvement can lead people to make the same judgment or decision as in the previous period through a variety of processing mechanisms. Some of these mechanisms are unintentional, that is, they result from the way memory works. Others reflect motivated reasoning—biased processing of information that results from the intent to reach and support a particular preferred conclusion, here the previous judgment or decision.[33]

Memory-related mechanisms include people directly generating last period's JDM as the leading hypothesis for this period's JDM because of its strength in memory. Alternatively, people may initially generate multiple hypotheses but then search for or retrieve from memory only information that is consistent with last period's JDM. This occurs because they are most likely to incorporate information that is consistent with last period's JDM into a knowledge structure related to that JDM. Consequently, this supporting information is activated in memory when last period's JDM is activated, and it is natural that last period's JDM for a particular task is activated when people start to do the task again in the following period. In turn, because of the apparent support it has, last period's JDM becomes the most prominent hypothesis for this period's JDM. Similarly, people may retrieve from memory a schema related to last period's JDM and reconstruct supporting information rather than directly retrieving it.

Motivated reasoning also plays a strong role in prior involvement's negative effects on JDM as well. Research finds that people who have previously made judgments or decisions become committed to those judgments or decisions. Commitment initially derives from people's motivation to justify their previous JDM to themselves or to others (e.g., Staw 1976; Staw and Ross 1986; Brockner 1992). However, commitment (and subsequent motivated reasoning) can increase with several other factors, including the length of prior involvement, the extent to which the JDM is public and explicit, and

---

[32]It is not certain that current JDM will be of low quality because the meaning of high-quality JDM can change from period to period. For example, a judgment in the previous period that did not agree with professional standards may agree with those standards in the current period if standards have changed.

[33]Again, this is as opposed to strategically adopting last year's judgment or decision without an attempt to support it through reasoning.

the importance of the JDM to the individual (Salancik 1977). These factors typically are present in professional settings, suggesting that motivated reasoning is important in explaining the effect of personal involvement on accountants' JDM. Further, commitment seems to increase when people whose prior JDM is of low quality receive negative feedback regarding that JDM; this is the phenomenon known as *escalation of commitment* (Staw and Ross). Escalation of commitment occurs because people now are more motivated to rationalize their behavior. Escalation of commitment is particularly dangerous in accounting settings given the large economic consequences that can result from low-quality JDM. Motivated reasoning mechanisms that occur in personal involvement settings include the directed search for, attention to, overweighting of, or reconstruction of information that supports the previous JDM (Kunda 1990, 1999; Ditto and Lopez 1992; Ditto et al. 1998). In addition, people may exert effort to develop counterarguments against information inconsistent with prior JDM (Tan 1995).

Although the effects of prior involvement on JDM quality generally are negative, there are some factors that can moderate these effects. Specifically, evaluating people's performance on the basis of their JDM processes as opposed to on the basis of JDM-related outcomes can reduce escalation of commitment (e.g., Simonson and Staw 1992). Further, asking people to specify goals that, if not reached, will automatically force changes in JDM can reduce escalation (e.g., Simonson and Staw; Cheng et al. 2003b). Formatting tasks to clearly focus on future economic benefits and providing precise feedback about negative outcomes to date also may reduce escalation (Ghosh 1997). In addition, if further investments would exceed a project budget, escalation may be reduced (Tan and Yates 2002). Finally, factors unique to accounting settings such as experienced auditors' skepticism may reduce the negative effects of personal involvement (Jeffrey 1992).

Prior involvement typically is a manipulated variable. Measuring prior involvement requires using experience with a judgment or decision as a proxy. As discussed earlier, this measure could capture the effects of many other variables such as knowledge content. Experimental studies that manipulate involvement can attempt to control for these correlated factors, for example, by not providing feedback on earlier JDM to minimize learning from experience. The most direct manipulation of involvement requires some subjects to make a judgment or decision once, whereas other subjects make the judgment or decision at least twice. Other studies ask some subjects to assume they have made a previous judgment or decision and tell other subjects to assume someone else made it (e.g., Harrison and Harrell 1993). Another manipulation is to have everyone make judgments or decisions but tell some subjects that they have no responsibility for their previous JDM and tell other subjects they do (e.g., Schulz and Cheng 2002). Because the latter two types of manipulations do not necessarily elicit the motivational or cognitive effects described above, the next section discusses only those using the most direct manipulation.

Accounting Studies on Personal Involvement

Despite the clear importance of personal involvement effects in accounting, there are few studies that examine the issue using the clearest manipulation of involvement. In a management accounting setting, Brown and Solomon (1987) find that students are less prone to hindsight bias in evaluating the JDM of a capital budgeting committee when they have prior involvement with that JDM. Although this result appears to suggest that prior involvement improves JDM quality, it may simply reflect motivation to justify one's previous work.

Other studies examine the effects of external or internal auditors' personal involvement with tasks. In a study of internal auditors, Plumlee (1985) shows that those who originally design a particular internal control system are less able to identify (theory-based) weaknesses when reviewing the system than those with no prior knowledge about the system. Note that, technically, his subjects are not making the same judgment twice, but the judgments are related. Jeffrey (1992) examines auditors' classification of loans as troubled or not troubled when they have either made previous judgments that the loan was not troubled or been told that another auditor made such a judgment. She finds that inexperienced (senior) auditors are more likely to continue to classify the loan as not troubled when they have made that judgment previously, although experienced (senior manager) auditors are not. Note that, in this study, the previous judgment (not troubled) is considered high-quality JDM; it becomes low-quality JDM if subjects continue to make it when circumstances have changed.

Tan (1995) examines the effect of prior involvement on experienced auditors' going-concern judgments. He finds that auditors with prior involvement recall relatively more information that is consistent with a previous judgment when they make that judgment than when they read someone else's previous judgment. In addition, the auditors with prior involvement are more likely to make a second judgment that is consistent with the first, although their second judgments are not on average different from those without prior involvement. Thus, whether prior involvement results in lower-quality JDM is not clear from this study. Brody and Kaplan (1996) investigate whether internal auditors with prior involvement in a judgment about whether an acquisition target requires extensive review of internal controls are less likely to make a theoretically correct second judgment than those without prior involvement. They manipulate prior involvement by having one group of subjects make two judgments—one after receiving mostly favorable information and one after receiving further negative information. The other group of subjects makes only one judgment. Those who make a first judgment then receive negative information are less likely to propose the extensive review (the theoretically correct judgment) as their second judgment.

The studies above examine the effects of personal involvement in a variety of settings. Those that come closest to the original psychology literature (Jeffrey 1992; Tan 1995) find little evidence that personal involvement has negative effects on JDM quality. Jeffrey finds that experienced auditors are not subject to these negative effects, and Tan finds that auditors with personal involvement versus those without make the same ultimate judgments. These findings suggest that experienced auditors are less prone to the negative effects of personal involvement, in contrast to the anecdotal evidence offered by regulators and in contrast to psychology research. However, these studies do not examine the original escalation-of-commitment scenario in which previous JDM quality is low and auditors make the same judgment in a subsequent period despite negative feedback; this is considered to be the most serious effect of personal involvement. Further, personal involvement effects likely occur in many other accounting settings (e.g., for management accountants). Consequently, it seems very important to continue studying these effects in accounting settings and, in particular, the unique features of accounting settings that may mitigate them, such as auditing standards that emphasize professional skepticism.

3-6   SUMMARY

This chapter begins the discussion of key person, task, and environmental variables that affect JDM quality. In particular, it discusses the effects of knowledge content and structure and personal involvement. To date, results regarding knowledge content and knowledge structure generally parallel findings from psychology. However, a few studies examining personal involvement show that auditors are less prone to its negative effects. This is a tentative conclusion given the small amount of work to date.

Future research on all these variables should first fill out our understanding of unexplored tasks, such as financial analysts' forecasts, then exploit what is unique about these factors in accounting. Many professional tasks require high knowledge content and well-structured knowledge and also are repeated multiple times. However, accounting tasks may require the largest, most diverse, and most integrated set of knowledge and knowledge structures. This calls for research that proceeds beyond main effects to understand more complicated interrelationships. Personal involvement in accounting settings is somewhat unique in that there likely are institutional arrangements such as the review process that work against its ill effects. Thus, the most relevant questions likely will focus on how personal involvement works in combination with these arrangements.

4

Abilities, Intrinsic Motivation, and Other Person Variables

This chapter continues the survey of person variables begun in Chapter 3. The chapter examines the effects of characteristics other than knowledge and personal involvement that people bring to accounting-related JDM tasks. In particular, it discusses the effects of abilities, intrinsic motivation, affect, confidence, risk attitudes, cognitive style, gender, and cultural background.[1,2] Each section in this chapter covers a specific person variable.[3]

To date, knowledge has been queen among person variables examined by accounting research; this emphasis certainly is and will continue to be appropriate because intellectual capital may be the biggest asset professional firms and individuals possess (e.g., Stewart 1994). Further, the myriad knowledge requirements distinguish accounting settings from many others. However, other person variables clearly can be important in explaining JDM quality in accounting as well. For example, behavioral finance researchers have explored the importance of affect and confidence to investor behavior (e.g., Saunders 1993; Barber and Odean 2001). In addition, as discussed in Chapter 3, in complex tasks such as those accountants face, superior knowledge may not result in superior JDM quality unless other personal characteristics such as abilities are present.

Because person variables other than knowledge and personal involvement clearly are not unique to accounting settings, it makes sense to begin by considering justifications for investigating their effects. Three situations lend the most credence to

---

[1]This classification of person variables is similar to that used in psychology texts. It should be noted, however, that many of these variables overlap in substantial ways. For example, most discussions of motivation invoke concepts related to affect (e.g., Kanfer 1990; Beck 2000). Also, many variables discussed in this chapter, such as motivation and cognitive style, frequently are considered part of the larger construct of "personality." Space constraints prohibit anything but a rudimentary introduction to and classification of the variables.

[2]This chapter does not discuss the effects of moral development. Research documents differences among auditors on this factor (e.g., Ponemon and Gabhart 1990), and moral development clearly is important to the ethicality of decision making among auditors, analysts, and others. However, because it is difficult to determine the quality of JDM that involves reliance on ethics and morals, it also is difficult to determine the extent to which moral development has a positive or negative effect on JDM quality.

[3]Note that each section covers the issues covered in Chapter 3—the variable's definition and classifications, its effects on JDM quality, mediators and moderators, how to study the variable, and accounting research on the variable.

doing so. The first is that there is some practical importance associated with the variable. For example, researchers may want to investigate whether one of the factors, for example, abilities, can partially substitute for knowledge because these kinds of substitutabilities have implications for firms' resource allocations. If this issue is of interest, it also is imperative that the individuals of interest either possess uniformly high amounts of the variable or, at least, exhibit some variation. Although factors such as abilities vary in the general population, it is not clear this will be the case for a particular group of individuals of interest to accounting researchers because of self-selection biases. For example, because of their focus on numbers, it may be the case that auditors are low in other types of abilities such as spatial abilities (the abilities to detect patterns visually). The most likely place to find variation is in groups that are the most representative of the general population (e.g., investors and jurors).

The second situation that calls for considering these variables is when one of them can be an alternative explanation for knowledge effects. This is frequently the case with abilities and motivation, for example. In this case, examining the effects of the variable is important if only for control purposes. The third situation in which these factors are most interesting to investigate is when they have interactive effects with knowledge, in particular interactions that prevent knowledge from having a positive effect unless a high level of the other factor is present.

4-1   EFFECTS OF ABILITIES ON JDM QUALITY

The term *abilities* refers to talents that are relatively fixed once people reach adulthood (Carroll 1993). Unlike knowledge, then, abilities tend not to change within individuals due to learning opportunities; however, abilities do vary across individuals, including those of interest to accounting researchers.[4] This section's focus is on the cognitive abilities that are relevant to JDM.

Classifications of cognitive abilities abound, and considerable debate regarding these classifications continues (e.g., Sternberg and Kaufman 1998). Intelligence tests typically classify cognitive abilities as verbal abilities, reasoning abilities, and spatial abilities (Anderson 2005). *Verbal abilities* include talents related to reading comprehension, spelling, and the like. *Reasoning abilities* include deductive and inductive thinking abilities, as well as talents related to reasoning with quantitative and mathematical concepts. *Spatial abilities* refer to the capacity to identify and comprehend patterns in visual stimuli, as well as the ability to manipulate visual patterns. Perhaps more important, this classification views these abilities as all subsumed under one factor of "general intelligence."

Most research on abilities includes categories beyond these. For example, Carroll (1993), in pulling together almost all studies conducted on intelligence, proposes that there also are differences across individuals as to the speed with which they can retrieve and process information. Carroll includes these abilities under general intelligence as well. Sternberg (1996) goes away from these traditional notions of intelligence, as they tend to focus on the prediction of academic success, and instead proposes

---

[4]It may not seem intuitive that professionals such as auditors vary greatly as to any type of abilities, but empirical evidence indicates they do (e.g., Bonner and Lewis 1990).

types of intelligence that are predictors of job success.[5] He proposes one overarching concept—"successful intelligence"—that includes three components: analytical abilities, creative abilities, and practical abilities. Analytical abilities are similar to reasoning abilities, whereas creative abilities relate to idea generation. Practical abilities relate to implementing ideas; Sternberg includes tacit managerial knowledge in this category. Because Sternberg notes that people can acquire practical abilities through experience, it seems appropriate to consider them a type of knowledge rather than a talent (and, as such, tacit knowledge is discussed in Chapter 3). Many standardized tests for measuring traditional abilities exist (see Carroll [1993] and Benson [2003] for details), whereas Sternberg has developed measures for the additional abilities he proposes.[6]

Although not unique to accounting settings, most of the abilities described above are relevant to accounting JDM tasks. Accountants have to read and decipher complex documents such as SEC filings, so verbal abilities seem relevant. Reasoning abilities clearly are relevant to many accounting tasks because of their quantitative nature. Spatial abilities could come into play when people make accounting judgments or decisions at least partially on the basis of visual stimuli such as graphs or charts. For example, analysts who practice technical analysis use charts as key pieces of information in their JDM (Malkiel 1999). Clearly, accountants' abilities to retrieve and process information are important to most tasks. Creative abilities could be particularly important in areas such as tax planning, where accountants' principal function is to come up with novel strategies on behalf of their clients. Finally, as noted in Chapter 3, practical abilities are important in accounting settings.[7]

What are the effects of cognitive abilities on JDM quality? There are widely differing points of view as to whether cognitive abilities are important to high-quality JDM. Much of the expertise literature (e.g., Glaser and Chi 1988; Posner 1988; Ericsson 1996) suggests that cognitive abilities are not important in distinguishing experts from novices; rather, knowledge content and structure differences that have developed through experience in a domain are critical. On the other side of the coin is evidence from a large body of work in industrial psychology (summarized in Hunter [1986]). These studies show that cognitive abilities have a significant impact on job performance across a wide variety of jobs, many of which include JDM tasks. Cognitive abilities in these studies are the standard abilities included on intelligence tests. Job performance is measured using supervisor ratings and by comparing individuals' actual work

---

[5]Gardner (1999), on the other hand, proposes that there is not one intelligence that subsumes all others, but rather that there are multiple independent intelligences. Gardner proposes the following types of intelligences: verbal, reasoning, spatial, musical, bodily-kinesthetic (physical), interpersonal (related to understanding others), intrapersonal (related to understanding oneself), and naturalist (related to understanding nature). Note that the cognitive abilities included here are similar to those measured on intelligence tests; Gardner's contribution is to add noncognitive abilities to the list of intelligences and to consider various types of intelligence to be independent.

[6]Manipulation of abilities is not a viable alternative because abilities tend to be fixed in adults. Obtaining archival measures of abilities typically is not feasible either because firms do not measure them or because they would not want to disclose such data. Occasionally, archival researchers use proxies for abilities such as college attended (e.g., Chevalier and Ellison 1999a), but these clearly are poor proxies in that they reflect a number of factors, including knowledge. Thus, abilities tend to be measured in experimental or survey settings.

[7]I am not aware of any research or anecdotes suggesting economic consequences that occur due to a lack of abilities, but such consequences clearly are plausible.

to preestablished standards. In addition, intelligence research such as that by Sternberg (1996) provides evidence that abilities are related to job performance. However, as noted above, this research defines abilities differently.

This book adopts the perspective that abilities have a positive effect on JDM quality. Although research on abilities tends to examine accuracy and agreement with professional standards, it seems reasonable to expect abilities to have a positive effect on other JDM quality dimensions as well. Hunter (1986) hypothesizes that the positive impact of cognitive abilities on job performance occurs for two reasons. The first is that cognitive abilities aid in the acquisition of knowledge, which subsequently can have a positive impact on performance (Ackerman 1989). However, abilities' effect on knowledge is moderated by other factors. First, abilities affect the acquisition of declarative knowledge but only to the extent they match the to-be-learned material. For example, spatial abilities do not aid the acquisition of verbal material. Abilities also affect declarative knowledge acquisition less as the to-be-learned material is simpler, the quality of instruction increases, and the particular individuals involved have consistently high abilities. In later stages of learning, when people are turning their declarative knowledge into procedural knowledge, Ackerman proposes that cognitive speed abilities enhance learning. Although not part of Ackerman's theory, it also seems plausible that people who possess certain types of abilities are better able to see patterns in things and, thus, can more quickly and/or accurately create knowledge structures. Hunter's meta-analysis of hundreds of studies shows that abilities are related to training success for many types of jobs. His evidence cannot speak to the varying impact of abilities under different instruction and knowledge complexity conditions, however.

The second effect of abilities on performance that Hunter (1986) proposes occurs because job-related tasks vary quite a bit; in particular, they can differ greatly from the standardized tasks people practice during instructional periods. Consequently, people must invoke various abilities in order to apply their knowledge to disparate instantiations of a standard task. Although Hunter does not explicate which abilities are important for doing this, it appears that he implicates reasoning abilities, which include the capabilities to identify problems, recognize relationships, interpret information, and reason analytically. Along with this, Hunter's evidence supports the idea that the positive effect of reasoning abilities on job performance is moderated by task complexity. This makes sense because complex tasks have attributes such as the need to process large quantities of information that call on reasoning abilities, whereas simpler tasks do not (Bonner 1994). Consequently, people can perform well on simple tasks even if they lack abilities. Further, although not part of Hunter's theory, it seems clear that abilities cannot have a positive effect on JDM quality if people lack knowledge. For example, a highly able auditor cannot make high-quality medical judgments unless she happens to possess medical knowledge.

Accounting research on cognitive abilities tends to take one of two paths. Many studies follow the lead of Bonner and Lewis (1990) and use measures of reasoning abilities from standard tests. Other studies focus on a particular form of spatial ability called *perceptual differentiation (PD) ability*. As Awasthi and Pratt (1990) note, this "represents an individual's ability to perceptually abstract from a complex setting specific familiar concepts or relationships." PD ability is measured using the embedded-figures test, which requires people to find simple figures that are hidden within more complex figures (e.g., Witkin et al. 1971). Although this may appear to be a narrow measure, it correlates with general abilities measured by intelligence tests (Ho and Rodgers 1993).[8]

Research on the effect of accounting information producers' abilities is sparse. Chesley (1977) finds that PD ability affects MBA students' accuracy in producing subjective probability distributions for information related to supplier performance as to materials usage. Vera-Muñoz (1998) finds that reasoning ability has a positive effect on student subjects' detection of theoretically relevant opportunity costs. Her measure of ability is similar to that used by Bonner and Lewis (1990), that is, a series of questions from the Graduate Record Examination that measure analogical reasoning ability (the ability to recognize relationships and when these relationships are parallel), data interpretation ability (the ability to synthesize information and to select the appropriate information to answer the question), and analytical reasoning ability (the ability to analyze a given structure of relationships and to deduce new information from that structure). Ghosh and Whitecotton (1997) find a positive effect of analysts' PD ability on forecast accuracy. Jacob et al. (1999), in an archival study of analysts' forecast accuracy, examine the effect of analysts' ability by including dummy variables for individual analysts. They find that ability is related to analysts' survival in the sample (through job retention) but only when analysts follow companies for which their abilities are suited.

A number of studies examine the effect of PD ability on users' JDM quality. Benbasat and Dexter (1979) find a positive effect of PD ability on accounting students' and professors' profit maximization and efficiency in a task that requires decisions about raw materials ordering and inventory production. In addition, they find that PD ability has a greater effect as task complexity increases. Benbasat and Dexter (1982) find a similar positive effect of PD ability in the same task but do not find an interaction with task complexity, as defined by the provision of a decision aid. Otley and Dias (1982) find no effect of PD ability on JDM quality in a similar production-planning task.

Bonner et al. (1992) use the Bonner and Lewis (1990) measure of reasoning abilities and find that tax professionals' reasoning abilities have no relation to the number of theoretically correct planning issues identified but do have a positive effect on the difficulty of issues identified, a proxy for expected utility maximization. However, this effect occurs only when tax professionals' knowledge content is low. DeZoort and Salterio (2001) find no effect of reasoning abilities on the extent to which audit committee members' judgments agree with the auditor's judgments.

Studies of auditors' abilities include several that examine PD ability. Pincus (1990) finds that PD ability is positively associated with the propensity to detect a misstatement in an audit case and that this is due to initial recognition of a problem and subsequent search for information that indicates the problem. However, Bernardi (1994) finds no association of PD ability with misstatement detection, and Mills (1996) finds no differences in auditors' reliance on internal auditors as a result of PD ability.

Bonner and Lewis (1990) examine the effect of auditors' reasoning abilities on the production of theoretically correct answers for four different audit tasks. They predict that reasoning abilities will be important only in the two most complex tasks: one that

---

[8]PD ability is also referred to as "field dependence." Many authors describe field dependence as a cognitive style characteristic, but as Ho and Rodgers (1993) note, it is more aptly described as a type of ability. Consistent with this, PD ability is measured on standard intelligence tests.

requires the generation of an explanation for a pattern of ratio fluctuations and one that requires the generation of an explanation for an observed accounting irregularity. They find support for their prediction for only the first task. Libby and Tan (1994) reanalyze the Bonner and Lewis data to examine effects of reasoning abilities on both knowledge and JDM quality. Their findings are consistent with Bonner and Lewis's predictions. Also, Libby and Tan predict that abilities have a positive relation to the knowledge needed for the ratio analysis task, the irregularity task, and another task requiring understanding of interest rate swaps but not the knowledge needed for an internal control evaluation task. Their prediction is based on Ackerman's (1989) ideas about the complexity of the knowledge and the quality of instruction available for such knowledge and Bonner and Pennington's (1991) analysis of the quality of instruction available for audit tasks. They find support for all predictions except for the knowledge needed for ratio analysis. Bonner and Walker (1994) find that reasoning abilities are related to the acquisition of the procedural knowledge needed for ratio analysis. However, they are not related to the number of theoretically correct answers given in ratio analysis; this may be due to the fact that their ratio analysis task is simple.

Tan and Libby (1997) extend these studies by examining the relation of auditors' abilities to JDM quality as defined by performance evaluations. They predict that staff and senior auditors with superior performance evaluations have higher reasoning abilities, but there are no differences in abilities among managers evaluated differentially because accounting firms promote auditors to manager level partially on the basis of abilities. They find support for their predictions regarding seniors and managers but not for staff. They conjecture that abilities may not matter to staff performance evaluations if these evaluations mostly reflect work on simple tasks. Bierstaker and Wright (2001) examine a measure of abilities called "practical problem-solving ability," which measures people's ability to handle everyday problems. They find that this ability is positively related to auditors' and students' detection of an explanation for ratio fluctuations and their detection of internal control weaknesses. The latter is not inconsistent with the findings of Bonner and Lewis (1990) because of differences in the complexity of the internal control tasks. Finally, Chang and Monroe (2001) use gender as a proxy for general information processing abilities and find that women auditors are better able to detect an account misstatement than are men under high-complexity conditions but not under low-complexity conditions.

Overall, the effects of abilities in accounting tasks appear somewhat consistent with theories that posit positive effects of abilities on knowledge acquisition and JDM quality, and greater positive effects when the quality of instruction is low and/or task complexity is high. Further, studies show experience-related differences in abilities, suggesting that firms select people for promotion partially on the basis of abilities (Lusk 1973; Bonner and Lewis 1990; Tan and Libby 1997). This finding also implies that studies using experience as a proxy for knowledge may capture ability effects as well, again emphasizing the need to consider abilities as an alternative explanation when examining knowledge issues.

Research on abilities in accounting seems somewhat stagnant, however. Studies tend to use fairly narrow measures of abilities. It is important to consider other types of abilities and extend and improve these measures. Future research may find that Bonner and Lewis's (1990) measure of reasoning abilities or the embedded-figures measure of spatial ability are as predictive of knowledge acquisition or JDM quality as are other measures, but this is an empirical question. Further, accounting research tends to assume that these narrow abilities are relevant for most accounting tasks, and findings do not always support this. A better approach would involve a task analysis that seeks to determine which abilities are likely to play a role in a particular task. Along with this, researchers should consider whether the relevant abilities likely vary in a particular subject group. Most important, researchers must consider what the most vital issues regarding abilities in accounting settings are; one example may be understanding the circumstances under which abilities can at least partially substitute for knowledge.

4-2 EFFECTS OF INTRINSIC MOTIVATION ON JDM QUALITY

Generally, *motivation* is defined as "an internal state of an organism that impels or drives it to action" (Reber 1995). In particular, motivation is an intermediate state that is initiated or invoked by other factors. A number of factors can create motivation, including people's internal needs, drives, and motives, often collectively referred to as "intrinsic motivation." In addition, motivational states can be elicited by external factors such as monetary incentives, accountability demands, and goals.[9]

Intrinsic motivation—motives that people bring with them to tasks—can vary across individuals of interest to accounting researchers. Although there are many types of intrinsic needs, such as hunger, this section discusses only those that are relevant to JDM in a professional setting. Kanfer (1990) characterizes intrinsic motives as being of three types: motives related to having a certain level of stimulation or arousal, motives related to achievement and competence (and the avoidance of failure), and motives related to power and control over one's environment.[10] Also, other researchers include motives related to the attainment of fairness in outcomes and procedures, particularly those related to employer–employee relationships (e.g., Adams 1963, 1965; Thibaut and Walker 1975; Greenberg and Folger 1983), and to the maintenance of one's reputation with others, particularly superiors and colleagues (e.g., Asch 1956; Moscovici 1985).[11]

Most of these forms of intrinsic motivation appear relevant, albeit not unique, to accounting-related JDM. First, although it seems plausible that people who self-select into professional accounting positions have uniformly high needs for stimulation and, consequently, that this type of motive is not relevant, research documents that the stimulation provided by these environments may be too high for some individuals. For example, Ashton (1990) documents that the stimulation provided by the combination of factors present in auditing positions (e.g., incentives and decision aids) degrades JDM quality for some auditors. In turn, this suggests that some auditors have lower needs for stimulation than other auditors. Further, other groups such as investors probably vary quite a bit as to their stimulation motive, suggesting this factor could play a major role in affecting JDM in those areas. Second, persons of interest to accounting researchers, including professionals, may vary in their achievement and competence motives. For example, staff accountants in public accounting firms probably are not uniformly high in these motives; this could affect the quality of the decisions they make

---

[9]Research on these variables is discussed in Chapter 7.
[10]Power and control motives will not be discussed further because they typically affect job-related behaviors such as treatment of others and choice of positions rather than JDM quality (Beck 2000).
[11]The need to maintain one's reputation, instead of being a characteristic a person brings with her to a JDM task, may derive from external factors such as monetary incentives.

and their consequent performance evaluations and promotions. Third, motivation related to attaining fairness and to maintaining one's reputation is relevant to accounting situations because accountants work in organizations in which professional relationships are important (Luft 1997). For example, research documents that analysts are concerned about maintaining their reputations and that one way in which they seek to do so is by making their earnings forecasts conform to consensus forecasts (Cote and Sanders 1997).

What are the effects of differences in these types of intrinsic motives on JDM quality? If people self-select into positions to obtain a particular level of stimulation, then they typically have high JDM quality if indeed those positions provide this level of stimulation. However, as mentioned above, particular features of work environments, such as accountability demands, may provide stimulation in addition to that provided by the tasks one performs. Theory posits that performance starts to decrease if people end up in situations with more stimulation than is optimal (Yerkes and Dodson 1908; Easterbrook 1959; Broadbent 1971; Eysenck 1982, 1986; Humphreys and Revelle 1984). Research also documents that achievement motivation is positively related to current task performance and job success (Alper 1946; McClelland 1961) as well as to acquisition of knowledge that will enhance performance later (White 1959; Lawler 1994).

Research related to fairness motives typically examines the effects of unfairness perceptions elicited by inequities in incentive or performance evaluation systems. This work sometimes finds that the larger the perceived unfairness, the larger the negative effect on task performance; however, overall results are mixed (Kanfer 1990). Although this work does not speak directly to the effects of variation in people's need for fairness on performance, it may suggest that persons with higher needs for fairness exhibit larger negative (positive) effects in their task performance under conditions perceived to be unfair (fair). Finally, people with strong motivation to maintain their reputations may move their JDM toward whatever JDM is considered "acceptable" (e.g., the consensus or majority JDM of a group of colleagues or superiors) (Asch 1956; Moscovici 1985). Thus, the quality of an individual's JDM here depends on the quality of the acceptable JDM. However, reputation-related motivation may, in the long run, be directed at creating accurate JDM (vis-à-vis outcomes) given that pay and promotions often are affected by such accuracy criteria. Note that research on intrinsic motives tends not to specify the JDM quality dimensions affected by these motives, but it seems safe to assume all dimensions can be affected.

What are the process mechanisms by which differences in intrinsic motives affect task performance? Unfortunately, we know very little about the specific processing effects of these intrinsic motives (Kanfer 1990). However, we can discuss the effects of motivation in general on processing. Kunda (1990, 1999) proposes that motivation has different effects depending on whether the motivation is to be accurate or the motivation is to reach a particular conclusion that is known prior to JDM, irrespective of its accuracy.[12] Recall that Kunda's definition of motivation to be accurate refers to the desire to obtain the "correct answer," and "correct" is defined in varying ways. The most important

---

[12]It appears that achievement motivation would be akin to an accuracy motive. Fairness and reputation motives may lead to motivation to obtain an accurate result or to reach a specific conclusion, depending on the situation (Cialdini and Trost 1998). In the absence of further information, stimulation motives will be assumed to be accuracy-type motivation.

element of this type of motivation is that the correct answer is not known a priori. In general, accuracy-related motives are thought to operate on JDM quality by increasing cognitive effort, which in turn leads to increased quality in current JDM. Kunda posits that greater effort is directed toward current performance of the task. However, others note that effort also can be directed toward acquisition of knowledge, which would lead to increased JDM quality in future periods (Kanfer; Locke and Latham 1990). Like abilities, then, accuracy-related motivation can affect JDM quality in two ways: by promoting the acquisition of knowledge or through more direct mechanisms.

Increases in cognitive effort related to current performance of a task can occur in direction, duration, or intensity. An increase in *effort direction* means that a person is more likely to engage in a particular activity than she would without the antecedent motivation. An increase in *effort duration* means that the person devotes more time to being actively engaged in the task, and an increase in *effort intensity* means that the person devotes more attention to an activity during a fixed period of time than she would otherwise (Kanfer 1990). Theory tends not to specify which cognitive processes are the beneficiaries of increased effort, so this chapter assumes that people may put more effort into all the processes.

There are two popular theories that explain the processes by which motivation operates on effort direction, duration, and intensity. Goal-setting theory proposes that motivation translates into effort through personal goals (Locke et al. 1981; Locke and Latham 1990). Specifically, highly motivated individuals may be more likely to set specific and/or challenging goals than less motivated individuals. Further, highly motivated individuals may be more committed to their personal goals. Specific and challenging goals lead to greater effort than do vague, easy, or no goals, and goal commitment is positively related to effort. Social-cognitive theory (Bandura 1997) posits that motivation affects effort through *self-efficacy,* or an individual's belief about whether she can execute the actions needed to attain a specific level of performance. Self-efficacy, in turn, operates on effort through several mechanisms including goals.[13]

Overall, then, theory proposes and much empirical research supports that accuracy-related motivation has a positive effect on current task performance via increases in cognitive effort and that increases in cognitive effort occur through a variety of mechanisms including personal goals and self-efficacy. However, empirical results also indicate systematic reasons motivation may not have a positive effect on current task performance (or JDM quality). First, if people direct effort toward learning, they take resources away from and decrease current task performance. Second, several factors can moderate a positive relation between effort and performance.[14] For example, persons lacking knowledge or abilities may not perform well at a task even if they exert great effort (Lawler 1994; Camerer 1995; Bonner et al. 2000; Bonner and Sprinkle 2002). They may direct effort toward the wrong activity or work long or intensely doing

---

[13]The difficulty with self-efficacy as an explanation for effects of motivation on current effort is that self-efficacy for a particular task is unlikely to be high unless a person has experienced the task sufficiently to expect a high level of performance currently. Consequently, it is unlikely that high motivation leads to high self-efficacy in a single-trial situation, but rather only over a period of time.

[14]Further, alternative theoretical accounts posit an inverted-U relation between motivation and effort. Such theories (e.g., Yerkes and Dodson 1908; Easterbrook 1959; Broadbent 1971; Eysenck 1982, 1986; Humphreys and Revelle 1984) propose that motivation initially increases effort but, beyond some moderate point, decreases effort. This also implies an inverted-U relation between motivation and JDM quality. These issues are discussed further in Chapter 7.

the wrong things. Third, many factors also can moderate a positive relation between motivation and effort. For example, people who have high motivation but who lack knowledge or abilities may not have higher effort than people with low motivation because they realize that increases in effort will not lead to performance increases (Lawler). There are a number of variables that can moderate the motivation–effort and effort–performance relations, thereby causing motivation to not have a positive effect on performance (see Bonner and Sprinkle).

Motivation directed toward reaching a particular conclusion has different effects on JDM quality than accuracy-related motivation. The effect of such motivation on JDM quality depends on the quality of the desired conclusion. If the desired conclusion happens to be right (wrong), then this motivation will have a positive (negative) effect on JDM quality. Recall that motivation to reach a desired conclusion can derive from intrinsic motives to maintain one's reputation with others who hold a particular point of view or for a particular outcome that is perceived as fair, as well as from external factors such as accountability to a client with a particular view.

Kunda (1990, 1999) posits that people engage in biased cognitive processes in an attempt to create a rationale for the desired conclusion, but the extent to which they can construct such a rationale moderates this behavior. The particular cognitive processes she posits as most affected by conclusion-related motivation are memory search and problem representation. That is, people search memory to find information that supports the desired conclusion and bring that information into their problem representation. She notes that people also may "creatively combine accessed knowledge" or creatively use rules for operating on information to construct beliefs that form the basis for a problem representation (1990). For example, in one instance, people may access a rule that tells them to use base rates when using those base rates would support the desired conclusion but, in another instance, access a rule that tells them to focus on situation-specific information when using base rates would work against the desired conclusion.

Kunda (1990, 1999) also discusses research that shows that motivation to reach a particular desired conclusion may first affect the hypothesis generation process in that the desired conclusion also becomes the most plausible conclusion. In turn, a person's search for information from memory and other sources is biased toward finding support for that hypothesis, but this occurs because of the cognitive mechanism of activating information related to the hypothesis. Finally, she acknowledges that motivation may affect the hypothesis evaluation process if people encounter information that is contradictory to the desired conclusion; here, people look for reasons not to use the information.

What happens to effort when motivation relates to a desired conclusion? Effort can be reduced or increased depending on the circumstances (Kunda 1999). Effort may be smaller if someone is able to quickly access enough information from memory to construct a sufficient rationale (vis-à-vis effort that would occur without such motivation). However, if evidence that does not support the desired conclusion crops up, effort may be far greater than without such motivation because people will work hard to justify ignoring or underutilizing the evidence. Therefore, the relation between effort and JDM quality also is not clear under these circumstances. Low effort may lead to high JDM quality if the desired conclusion is correct, and high effort may lead to low JDM quality if the desired conclusion is wrong.

The measurement of intrinsic motives and related process mechanisms in experimental and survey settings is fairly well established.[15] Researchers can use the Sensation Seeking Scale to measure need for stimulation (Zuckerman 1994). Researchers tend to measure need for achievement with the Thematic Apperception Test (McClelland et al. 1953). As discussed above, because research on needs for justice and fairness tends to relate to perceptions of fairness generated by situational factors, this motive typically is manipulated. Motives related to maintaining one's reputation can be measured with the Social Desirability Scale (Crowne and Marlowe 1960). With regard to the process mechanisms through which motivation operates, researchers tend to measure effort duration and intensity with self-reports or using time as a proxy (e.g., Sprinkle 2000).[16] Effort direction is easily measured by observing choice of activities. Research has extensively studied how to measure goal and self-efficacy theory constructs (see Locke and Latham [1990] and Bandura [1997]).

Accounting research on the effects of motivation on JDM quality tends not to examine the effects of intrinsic motives such as the need for achievement. Instead, it tends to focus on motivation elicited by environmental factors such as accountability demands (e.g., Tan 1995) and monetary incentives (e.g., Sprinkle 2000). One likely reason for this is that the accounting environment contains a number of such entrenched institutional factors that create variation in motivation, and researchers may believe that the variation in motivation created by these factors is greater than the variation created by intrinsic motives. For example, some researchers note that intrinsic motivation can be assumed to be constant at a relatively high level among accounting professionals (e.g., Libby 1995). Another possibility is that researchers believe there is variation in intrinsic motives but consider the ultimate methods that might be suggested to directly reduce this variation (e.g., extensive screening on motivation at hiring) less practical for firms than improvement methods that address other issues. Consequently, there are few studies to discuss in this section. Included are those that examine the intrinsic motives discussed above or general process models of motivation. Studies that examine perceptions of fairness also are discussed. Although these studies elicit fairness motives through external means rather than studying subjects' intrinsic needs for fairness, the studies are so few in number that they are more easily discussed here.

Studies of users, producers, and auditors of accounting information include Cote and Sanders (1997), who examine the effects of analysts' need to maintain their reputations on their earnings forecasts. They use investors to proxy for analysts and measure this motivation with the Social Desirability Scale (SDS). They find that this motive affects self-reported herding behavior but not actual movement in earnings forecasts toward a consensus. Hammersley et al. (1997) also use the SDS scale in a study where students assume the role of an accountant explaining an inventory fluctuation either privately or publicly. Students with high SDS scores exhibit the "explanation effect" in the public condition but not the private condition, whereas students with low SDS scores are unaffected by whether the explanation is private or public.[17] Kadous and Sedor (2004)

---

[15]Research on intrinsic motives and process factors tends to be limited to experimental and survey studies because archival data on these variables are hard to obtain. Archival studies tend to focus on other antecedents to general motivation such as accountability and monetary incentives; Chapter 7 discusses how to study these variables.
[16]For an alternative technique, see O'Donnell (1996).
[17]The *explanation effect* (see Chapter 5) occurs when individuals assign a higher probability to an event when they have explained it as compared to when they have not explained it.

measure students' self-monitoring tendencies in an experiment where students make project continuation recommendations. Self-monitoring refers to the extent to which individuals engage in behaviors in order to present themselves as socially acceptable. Persons high in self-monitoring are less likely to recommend discontinuing an obviously unprofitable project. In auditing, Jiambalvo (1979) finds that the intrinsic value of audit activities, a proxy for general motivation, predicts auditors' effort and performance evaluations, and Becker (1997) finds that auditors' general intrinsic motivation has a positive effect on the quality of their bankruptcy predictions vis-à-vis actual outcomes.

Studies that elicit perceptions of fairness and examine their effects on JDM quality include the following.[18] Kachelmeier et al. (1991) manipulate perceptions of fairness through the type of tax system imposed on buyers and sellers of hypothetical goods in an experimental market. They find some support for the notion that subjects who believe the equilibrium price is fair are more likely to offer it. Evans et al. (1994) find that subjects are willing to sacrifice money for fairness when choosing systems that control managers' behavior. Moser et al. (1995) examine the effects of fairness perceptions on tax reporting decisions. Taxpayer subjects' reporting of income is negatively related to tax rate changes when they perceive unfairness in the tax system but not when they perceive fairness. Luft and Libby (1997) find that managers engaging in negotiation to decide transfer prices are affected by perceptions of fairness regarding division profits that result from chosen prices. This contrasts with the predictions of normative theories. In addition, they find substantial variation among managers' judgments about prices, suggesting variation in intrinsic motives for fairness. Finally, Greenberg and Greenberg (1997) find that students doing a transfer pricing task are concerned about fairness in the division of profits and perceive different types of outcomes to be fair depending on the context.

Overall, accounting studies on the effects of intrinsic motives or general motivation on JDM quality are fairly consistent with extant theory. However, they are few in number and focus mostly on motives related to fairness. Although a general focus on external factors rather than intrinsic motives may be justified in most accounting settings, the work on fairness motives indicates these are important in many situations involving accountants. It also seems clear that motives related to maintaining reputation are critical for many individuals of interest, particularly auditors, managers, and analysts, yet only a few studies examine this issue to date. Future research should further investigate the effect of these intrinsic motives on JDM quality. Of additional interest is the impact of these motives on JDM quality when they conflict with one another. For example, accountants need to maintain their reputation with different constituents such as clients and regulators, and these constituents may view reputation differently.

4-3 EFFECTS OF AFFECT ON JDM QUALITY

Like motivation, affect is an intermediate state that can be induced by a number of factors. In general, *affect* refers to an evaluative reaction to a stimulus (a person, event, etc.) that has either positive or negative valence (Fiske and Taylor 1991). Affective reactions can be induced by moods and emotions that people bring to tasks as well as

---

[18]A number of studies examine the effects of perceptions of fairness on the performance of a physical task, such as constructing models (e.g., Lindquist 1995). These studies are not discussed.

by external factors such as monetary incentives. People's affective reactions to stimuli appear to be a hardwired, sometimes unconscious function (Zajonc 1998).

People vary in the moods and emotions they bring to JDM tasks, and these variations create differences in affect and JDM quality. Moods are thought to be simply valenced, low-intensity feelings that have no specific target associated with them; people are thought to be in a good or bad mood, or sometimes a neutral mood (Fiske and Taylor 1991; Reber 1995). Emotions, on the other hand, are thought to be richer in their valences and complexity, as well as more intense and short lived than moods. For example, people can be angry, frustrated, disgusted, or disappointed. Further, emotions may have targets (e.g., someone can be angry with a work-averse colleague). Clearly, moods and emotions and affect more generally are relevant to accounting-related JDM because accounting professionals experience many factors that influence affect. Kida and Smith (1995) posit that people have affective reactions to numerical data itself, so it may be the case that there are unique affect issues in accounting settings. Most important, as discussed further below, research in finance suggests that affective reactions may have negative economic consequences such as lowered investment returns.

There is a great deal of research on the effects of moods on JDM quality. Some research indicates that people in good moods tend to make more positive judgments than people in neutral or bad moods and vice versa (Fiske and Taylor 1991; Schwarz 2002). For example, people in good moods tend to make higher (lower) estimates of the probabilities of positive (negative) events than do people in neutral moods (e.g., Johnson and Tversky 1983; Wright and Bower 1992). Whether these effects end up denoting good or bad JDM depends on the criterion by which JDM quality is determined. In this instance, the higher or lower estimates of probabilities may be low-quality JDM when compared to statistical theory. However, if higher (lower) estimates lead to a decision to choose (not choose) an alternative for which an attractive (aversive) outcome happens to occur in a particular instance, JDM could be considered high quality vis-à-vis the outcome. Other research indicates, however, that mood has little or no effect on JDM quality. (See Forgas [1995] for a review.)

We can understand the situations in which moods or emotions will or will not influence JDM quality by reviewing the process mechanisms through which affect induced by moods, emotions, or other factors generally influences JDM. Current thinking about affect revolves around the "affect infusion model" (Forgas 1995). Forgas predicts that the influence of affect on JDM depends on the situation and the consequent cognitive processing strategies people employ. In familiar situations with low stakes, people tend to make judgments through direct retrieval of nonaffective information from memory. In these cases, affect is inconsequential to JDM, so JDM quality depends on the quality of knowledge in memory. Forgas predicts that affect will also have little impact on JDM motivated to reach a certain conclusion, for example, the client's desired decision. Here, motivation overrides affect and leads to biased processing that has the goal of reaching the desired conclusion, and JDM quality depends on the quality of the desired conclusion.

In other situations, affect is proposed to have a substantial effect on JDM. However, the effect occurs through different mechanisms depending on the processing strategies people employ. In situations in which people rely on shortcuts or heuristics to reach a judgment or decision, such as when they are under time pressure or have little other information, affect can influence JDM through the "affect heuristic" (e.g.,

Schwarz 2002; Slovic et al. 2002). People are using the *affect heuristic* when they ask themselves how they feel about a particular alternative and use the answer as information to make their judgment or decision as opposed to doing an extensive search for information about the alternative. Unfortunately, this heuristic can lead to low-quality JDM because the answer to the question may be influenced by feelings generated by something other than the decision alternative, and people may not realize that their feelings derive from the unrelated source, a phenomenon referred to as *mood misattribution.* Schwarz and Clore (1983) provide the classic example of this. They show that people report higher life satisfaction if asked on a sunny day rather than on a rainy day. However, if people realize that their affect relates to the weather because the researcher prompts them by asking them about the weather, there are no differences in satisfaction reported on sunny versus rainy days. An example that is more relevant to accounting is that people using the affect heuristic expect an inverse relationship between risk and return (e.g., Finucane et al. 2000). Because this misunderstanding could lead people such as investors to make choices they otherwise would not make, it indicates the possibility for low-quality JDM.

When people engage in more systematic processing because, for example, the task is complex or they are motivated by monetary incentives, affect tends to influence JDM through the retrieval of affect-congruent information from memory. Memory theories related to affect propose that people store information in memory with related affective reactions and that spreading activation occurs not only to conceptually related information, but also to information that has the same affective reactions as the activated item (Bower 1981; Bower and Forgas 2001). In other words, a positive (negative) affective state leads to the retrieval of information items that have positive (negative) affect associated with them, although the findings regarding the effects of negative affective states on retrieval tend to be mixed (Fiske and Taylor 1991). If JDM-relevant information has an affective tag attached to it that differs from the current affective state, people may not retrieve it and have lower-quality JDM. Although not part of Forgas's (1995) model, other research demonstrates that people reconstruct information to be consistent with an affect-laden schema if they are unable to retrieve the information directly (Fiske and Taylor 1991). Of course, reconstructed information can be inaccurate and, consequently, can lead to low-quality JDM.

Further research shows that affect can directly shape the choice of cognitive processing approaches in addition to seeping in once people choose approaches (Kunda 1999; Schwarz 2002). People in positive affective states tend to employ heuristics and, thus, engage in less effort, which may lead to lower-quality JDM. Kunda speculates that this occurs because people do not want to disrupt positive affective states by engaging in effortful processing. However, people in positive affective states tend to be more creative and more willing to take risks, so JDM quality could be enhanced in some situations. People in negative affective states, on the other hand, tend to employ more systematic and effortful processing, which typically would have a positive effect on JDM quality. Kunda proposes that this may occur because people engage in effortful processing to deal with negative affect and this effortful processing then carries over to a given JDM task.

To this point, the influence of affect on JDM occurs because of affective reactions that occur while judgments or decisions are being made. A different view of the influence of affect on JDM is that people predict the affective states they would experience for various consequences of decision alternatives and incorporate predicted affect into decision making just as they incorporate predicted utility.[19] Unfortunately, in some situations people make systematic errors when predicting affect, and these errors lead to systematic errors in JDM (Loewenstein and Schkade 1999; Mellers and McGraw 2001). Loewenstein and Schkade provide several reasons people make inaccurate predictions of affect. For instance, people have inappropriate theories about the factors that influence affect (e.g., "money brings happiness") that persist despite disconfirming feedback.

Some experimental studies manipulate affect, often through a mood-inducing technique such as having subjects read a sad or happy newspaper article. Other experimental studies, along with archival and survey studies, tend to use proxies to measure affect. In particular, behavioral finance studies (see below) rely on psychological evidence supporting the relation to affect of proxies such as weather. Manipulations and measurements are simplistic; they tend to assume two (three) affective states: good or bad (or neutral).

Research on the effects of affect on JDM in accounting is new and, thus, sparse. Although affect is induced by a number of factors in these studies, it is most expedient to discuss them in this section. Kida and his colleagues have three studies that examine affect. Kida et al. (1998) find that managers presented with financial ratio information can more accurately recall affective reactions to those ratios than the actual values of the ratios themselves or the sign of how a ratio compares to last year's ratio or the industry average. In a second study, they find that managers identify items not previously seen as having been seen, that is, they reconstruct memory to be consistent with their affective reaction. In a third study, they find that managers rely on affective reactions when making investment decisions and consequently make decisions that are inconsistent with what investing theory would predict based on the numerical data.

Kida et al. (2001) examine managers' affective reactions in a capital-budgeting context. They manipulate affect by providing negative or neutral descriptions of characteristics of people with whom the managers would work on a particular project; these characteristics influence only the working relationship and not the economic value of the projects. Managers overwhelmingly choose the neutral affect alternative despite its having lower economic value. Moreno et al. (2002) manipulate affect to be negative, positive, or neutral in a similar capital-budgeting task. They also manipulate whether projects are expected to produce a gain or loss in order to examine the predictions of prospect theory. Prospect theory indicates that people are risk averse in gain situations and risk seeking in loss situations (see Section 4-5). With neutral affect, most managers choose as predicted by prospect theory; however, with positive or negative affect, most managers choose opposite to the predictions of prospect theory. Because prospect theory is not a normative theory of JDM, it is not possible to say whether affect is having a negative or positive influence on JDM quality in this situation.[20]

Several finance studies examine the effects of affect on investor JDM as measured by stock returns. The studies predict mood misattribution, that is, that when investors are in a good (bad) mood for some reason unrelated to their investments, stock returns will be higher (lower). Saunders (1993), Kramer and Runde (1997),

---

[19]Mellers and McGraw (2001) note that expected affect is not part of expected utility but rather a separate factor that affects JDM.
[20]Although not manipulated in her study, Luft's (1994) subjects appear to be anticipating affective reactions when choosing between incentive contracts framed in terms of bonuses/gains and penalties/losses.

Trombley (1997), and Hirshleifer and Shumway (2003) find some evidence that stock returns are higher on sunny days. Other studies examine the effects of sunlight (Kamstra et al. 2003), changes in daylight savings time (Kamstra et al. 2000), daily bio-rhythms (Kramer 2000), and lunar phases (Dichev and Janes 2003; Yuan et al. 2006) and find some support for the predicted effects of moods on stock returns.

Most of the research on the influence of affect on accounting-related JDM finds that affect plays a role in JDM. However, the research is in its infancy. All but one of the studies (Kida et al. 1998) examines the role of affect through mood misattribution. Perhaps this has been of importance in archival studies because data on factors that affect moods such as weather are readily available; also, because these factors should have no theoretical bearing on decisions, results clearly indicate low-quality JDM. However, as noted above, affect can derive from a number of factors and can have many different effects on JDM other than those attributable to mood misattribution, as well as no effects in some cases. Kida and Smith's (1995) propositions regarding affective reactions to numerical data deserve particular attention because accounting JDM involves such data. Further, there are a number of negative implications of their suggestions that pertain to decision makers other than investors. For example, if auditors rely on initial affective reactions to client-provided information to guide testing, they may seek evidence that supports those affective reactions in cases where client-provided information is misleading. As a consequence, they may ultimately give an inappropriate audit opinion.

4-4   EFFECTS OF CONFIDENCE ON JDM QUALITY

Confidence is another factor of considerable importance to JDM. *Confidence* typically refers to "assuredness," either in one's JDM or in one's knowledge (Reber 1995). Confidence can be a dependent variable of interest in JDM studies or a factor that a person brings to a task or experiences as an intermediate state while performing a task. Although this section briefly touches on research related to the former characterization, the latter is of most relevance.

Why discuss confidence issues in accounting settings? Plous (1993) claims that "no problem in judgment and decision making is more prevalent and more potentially catastrophic than overconfidence." Overconfidence may be the most frequently discussed problem in anecdotal accounts of investor JDM (e.g., Belsky 1995; Clements 1996; O'Reilly 1998) and also appears to have the most credence as an individual-level factor that can create inefficient markets (e.g., Rubinstein 2001). As discussed further below, although many people are overconfident, there are systematic differences in confidence across individuals such as investors. Further, the high monetary and reputation stakes associated with accounting-related JDM makes it critical to consider whether overconfidence affects JDM in accounting settings.

The traditional literature on confidence examines confidence as a dependent variable, in particular whether people are overconfident in either their predictive judgments or their answers to knowledge questions. Overconfidence is demonstrated when people have higher confidence ratings, on average, than accuracy. Most of this literature indicates that people, including experts, are overconfident about their judgments and knowledge and that overconfidence is greatest when tasks are the most difficult (Lichtenstein et al. 1982). However, there are domains such as meteorology in which overconfidence does not appear. High-quality, prompt feedback in these domains may prevent overconfidence (Plous 1993).

This literature is unsatisfactory for understanding the effects of confidence on JDM quality for several reasons. First, studies that examine confidence in predictive judgments elicit confidence ratings after JDM. Consequently, they may tell us that JDM affects confidence or that various cognitive processes affect both JDM and confidence rather than that confidence affects JDM. Second, studies that examine confidence in knowledge tend not to examine any effects of this confidence on subsequent JDM. Further, these studies tend to use restricted types of questions and confidence ratings and assume that these choices have no effect on results. Recent research shows that this is a highly vulnerable assumption. Gigerenzer et al. (1991) find that knowledge overconfidence occurs in laboratory studies because of unrepresentative sampling of questions from domains. Further, overconfidence may be greater when confidence is rated for a single decision rather than for a group of decisions. (For example, see Griffin and Tversky [1992], but see also Brenner et al. [1996]).

More important, Klayman et al. (1999) find substantial individual differences in overconfidence and that the most confident individuals are also the most overconfident. Given these differences, the next question is why there are differences. Are some people just born overconfident? Little is known about which individuals are more versus less overconfident. For example, levels of knowledge and abilities have very low associations with overconfidence (Lichtenstein and Fischhoff 1977; Mabe and West 1982; Oskamp 1982). There is some evidence that men are more overconfident than women (e.g., Lundeberg et al. 1994), although this typically occurs only in domains perceived to be "masculine" (Deaux and Emswiller 1974; Deaux and Farris 1977; Lenney 1977; Beyer and Bowden 1997).[21] At any rate, these findings suggest that people may bring varying levels of overconfidence in their knowledge to JDM tasks.

Other theories posit differences in knowledge overconfidence that occur as an intermediate state. One theory proposes that overconfidence results from knowledge structures (e.g., Koehler 1991). People first search memory for a tentative hypothesis then retrieve information about that hypothesis. Retrieved information tends to be consistent with the hypothesis because of spreading activation.[22] Confidence in the hypothesis increases when people find confirming evidence because they do not realize that memory is set up to produce this result; however, quality of knowledge is not necessarily related to the extent to which one finds confirming information in memory. The finding that overconfidence increases with experience in a domain (e.g., Paese and Sniezek 1991) is consistent with this theory because experienced people tend to have more extensive knowledge structures. A second theory proposes that overconfidence results from a mismatch between the structure of the task and people's knowledge structures (Gigerenzer et al. 1991). A third proposes that overconfidence results from people placing too much weight on strength of information and too little weight on credibility of information (Griffin and Tversky 1992). However, this theory also predicts that underconfidence can occur in some situations. Finally, a fourth theory posits that knowledge overconfidence occurs because of self-attribution biases in which

---

[21] Also, some studies find no differences between men and women (e.g., Jonsson and Allwood 2003).
[22] See Chapter 3 for a discussion of this phenomenon.

people attribute high-quality JDM to their own knowledge and low-quality JDM to external factors (e.g., Langer and Roth 1975).

What effects do these differences in knowledge overconfidence have on JDM quality, and what are the further process mechanisms through which overconfidence affects quality? In general, studies that examine confidence as an independent or intermediate variable find that higher overconfidence is associated with lower JDM quality, typically defined as accuracy or agreement with normative theories (Arkes 2001).[23] There are several proposed mechanisms through which overconfidence is seen to affect JDM, but a common element of most theories is that overconfidence causes people to rely too much on their own knowledge. In turn, this causes them either to fail to search for further information or to place too much weight on their knowledge vis-à-vis other, readily available information during hypothesis evaluation (e.g., Odean 1998). This can be seen, for example, in findings that overconfidence has a negative relation with reliance on decision aids (e.g., Arkes et al. 1986) and failure to use base rates (e.g., Vallone et al. 1990).

Typically, overconfidence is thought to be a robust phenomenon and to have substantial negative effects on JDM quality. Are there ways of moderating these effects? As mentioned earlier, the way in which confidence is elicited may affect overconfidence—asking people to rate confidence for a group of decisions versus a single decision can lower overconfidence (Griffin and Tversky 1992). In addition, providing people with information about their actual level of knowledge may reduce overconfidence (e.g., Tramifow and Sniezek 1994). Asking people to list reasons their knowledge or judgments may be wrong also may reduce overconfidence (Arkes 2001). Finally, if possible, providing people with complete, timely, and accurate information about outcomes may reduce overconfidence (Plous 1993).

For experimental researchers, the study of confidence is a thorny issue. Many researchers are concerned that measuring confidence prior to experimental tasks will lead to hypothesis guessing.[24] Consequently, even when confidence is treated as an independent variable or intermediate state, experimental researchers tends to measure it postexperimentally. There are several traditional methods for measuring confidence and overconfidence. Researchers can ask, for example, for direct ratings on 100-point scales or for ranges within which they are X% certain the correct answer will fall. As mentioned earlier, however, the manner in which confidence is measured can affect findings, so care must be taken in choosing a method. As an alternative, it is plausible to manipulate confidence by varying situational factors that elicit varying degrees of confidence. Another alternative is to measure differences in behavior determined by confidence and control for other possible determinants. For example, Nelson et al. (2003) use trade size measures of behavior. In archival studies, measurement of confidence typically is accomplished by using some factor that is correlated with confidence (e.g., gender) as a proxy. The problem with this approach is that these proxies may reflect multiple differences among individuals. For example, in addition to being

---

[23]Studies that examine confidence as a dependent variable typically find little relation between overconfidence and JDM quality (Plous 1993), although there is great debate about these findings (e.g., Sporer et al. 1995).

[24]*Hypothesis guessing* means that subjects figure out the hypotheses being tested in the experiment. The danger is that they then intentionally behave consistently with the hypotheses when they otherwise would not or behave inconsistently with the hypotheses when they otherwise would not(Cook and Campbell 1979).

less overconfident than men, women may be more risk averse (Barber and Odean 2001).

Like work in psychology, accounting research on confidence examines confidence both as a dependent variable and with regard to its effects on JDM. Studies on producers of accounting information include Tyszka and Zielonka (2002), who find that analysts are quite overconfident. Whitecotton (1996) finds that the confidence of analysts and accounting students making earnings forecasts is negatively related to reliance on a decision aid, and decision aid reliance positively affects the accuracy of those forecasts. Cote and Sanders (1997) find that the confidence of analysts (as proxied by investors) is negatively related to their agreement with a consensus earnings forecast.

A number of studies examine the effects of investor confidence on JDM. Several behavioral finance studies model market inefficiencies as being principally the result of investor overconfidence (e.g., Kyle and Wang 1997; Odean 1998; Daniel et al. 1998; Gervais and Odean 2001). Most of these models assume individual differences in overconfidence but do not explain why some individuals are more overconfident than others. These models predict many market-level effects of overconfidence, including excessive trading volume and price volatility; they also predict reduced returns for overconfident investors. Several archival papers test predictions of these models, relying on their assumptions about which investors are overconfident, and find support for the proposed effects of overconfidence (e.g., Odean 1999). The most direct test of the effects of overconfidence on individual investor JDM quality comes from Barber and Odean (2001), who examine differences between men's and women's trading and profits relying on the finding that men are more overconfident than women in traditionally masculine domains such as investing. Indeed, men trade more and have lower returns.

Other studies related to investor overconfidence are experimental in nature. Estes and Hosseini (1988) examine factors related to investor confidence viewed as a dependent variable. Gender provides the most explanation of variance in confidence, with women being less confident than men. Similarly, Selling (1993) examines the effect of several factors on MBA students' confidence in their bankruptcy predictions. He finds that subjects with high predictability tasks are more confident with experience, with less frequent feedback, and with less information. Also, subjects with low predictability tasks are more overconfident than subjects with high predictability tasks. Lichtenstein and Fischhoff (1977) and Yates et al. (1991) find that student investors are overconfident about stock price predictions, and Moore et al. (1999) find that MBA students allocating money among mutual funds are overconfident in their forecasted returns and in judgments about past returns.

Bloomfield et al. (1999) examine the effects of investor overconfidence on trading in an experimental market. Investors (MBA students) with less information, who are posited to be too confident vis-à-vis more-informed investors, create biases in prices in line with whether their information is favorable or unfavorable and transfer wealth to more-informed investors. In other words, confidence has a negative effect on their JDM quality. However, warning less-informed investors about their informational disadvantage reduces their confidence and increases JDM quality. Bloomfield et al. (2000) examine individual and market effects of over- and underconfidence predicted by Griffin and Tversky's (1992) theory. They find that inappropriate confidence leads to inappropriate individual reservation prices and inappropriate market prices. Nelson et al. (2001) find similar results.

Nelson et al. (2003) examine the effect of MBA student investors' overconfidence on their reliance on a decision aid (a disciplined trading strategy) in an experimental market. They manipulate overconfidence by asking subjects to make investment decisions either on a security-by-security basis or on a portfolio basis. Consistent with findings in psychology, they expect investors to be less overconfident when they make decisions on a portfolio, or aggregated, basis and, consequently, to rely more on a decision aid and make higher profits when they make portfolio-based decisions. Findings are consistent with expectations. A second experiment finds that investors receiving negative feedback about their investment decisions are less confident and rely more on the decision aid than investors receiving positive feedback.

Early studies of auditor confidence examine whether auditors are overconfident in their subjective probability distributions for account balances and whether the manner in which their confidence ratings are made affects the level of confidence (e.g., Corless 1972; Felix 1976; Crosby 1981; Solomon et al. 1982; Tomassini et al. 1982; Solomon et al. 1985). The typical finding is that auditors tend to be underconfident in their accounting probability distributions. Further, the manner in which confidence ratings are elicited affects the level of underconfidence observed. Mladenovic and Simnett (1994) suggest that the difference in findings between auditing and psychology studies is due to the lower difficulty of the tasks used in the auditing studies.

Other auditing studies examine a variety of issues regarding confidence. Moeckel and Plumlee (1989) find that auditors are as confident in inaccurate memories related to the contents of work papers as they are in accurate memories. Pincus (1991) finds substantial overconfidence among auditors making a decision about the existence of a material misstatement in inventory. Kennedy and Peecher (1997) find that auditors are overconfident in their own technical knowledge and in subordinates' knowledge. The latter result occurs because auditors use their knowledge to evaluate subordinates' knowledge. Boatsman et al. (1997) find that auditors' confidence is positively associated with the tendency to ignore a decision aid when making fraud judgments. None of these studies examines the effects of confidence on JDM quality.

Where does the accounting literature stand on confidence effects? With the exception of early work on auditors' probability distributions for account balances, individuals of interest to accounting researchers are overconfident on average, similar to the general population. However, there is variation in overconfidence that results both from individual differences and other factors. Further, to the extent that the effects of confidence or overconfidence on JDM quality have been studied, the effects tend to be negative and due to overreliance on one's knowledge vis-à-vis other information such as that provided by decision aids. The most promising avenues for future research seem to be work on the factors that cause differences in overconfidence and studies that examine methods for reducing overconfidence. Of most interest would be research on factors and methods that are particularly relevant to accounting such as whether investment decisions are made on a case-by-case or portfolio basis, as examined by Nelson et al. (2003).

4-5 EFFECTS OF RISK ATTITUDES ON JDM QUALITY

In addition to varying as to abilities, motivation, and other factors, people may vary in attitudes about risk, and these attitudes may affect JDM quality. A person's *risk attitude* is simply her feeling about risk, where risk is anything that "threatens something of value" (Reber 1995). In particular, we are concerned with the feelings people have about the risks or uncertainties associated with receiving or losing money, feelings that they incorporate into their utility functions. Some theories, most notably expected utility (EU) theory (von Neumann and Morgenstern 1947), suggest there are individual differences in risk attitudes. Other theories, such as prospect theory (Kahneman and Tversky 1979), assume that people inherently do not vary in their attitudes toward risk, but rather change their risk attitudes because of external factors. In other words, these theories view risk attitudes as an intermediate state.

In either case, people can be classified as risk averse, risk neutral, or risk seeking (Hogarth 1987). *Risk-averse* individuals do not like risk. Thus, in choosing between two alternatives with the same expected value, they prefer a sure thing to a choice that occurs only with some probability. Often, risk-averse individuals prefer a sure thing even when it has a lower expected value. *Risk-seeking* individuals prefer the risky choice to a sure thing, sometimes when the risky choice has lower expected value, whereas *risk-neutral* people are indifferent between the two choices. Risk attitudes clearly are relevant (albeit not unique) to accounting research because most accounting tasks involve decisions under uncertainty. Further, in many accounting settings, it would be preferable to have invariance across people in risk attitudes to ensure consistency of choices. For example, auditing firms likely prefer their personnel to have similar attitudes toward risk and, consequently, make similar opinion choices so they can demonstrate consistency of thinking in a litigation setting (or, otherwise, possibly face severe negative consequences). In addition, the popular press frequently discusses the impact of risk attitudes on investors' decision making (e.g., Clements 1996; O'Reilly 1998).

Many theories of decision making, most notably EU theory, assume that there are differences across people in risk attitudes but do not specify why such differences exist. Other theories draw on a combination of motivational and affective factors to explain these differences. (See Larrick [1993] for a review.) For example, regret theories (e.g., Bell 1982, 1983; Loomes and Sugden 1982; Josephs et al. 1992) assume that people are motivated to avoid regret in their JDM because regret worsens their self-image. People feel regret when they compare the outcome from the decision alternative they choose with outcomes that might have been associated with other alternatives and it appears that their alternative has produced a worse outcome. Further, these theories predict that people anticipate the negative affect brought by regret and that some people react worse to anticipated regret because, for example, they lack self-esteem. Differences in vulnerability to anticipated regret lead to differences in risk attitudes, with those most vulnerable individuals being the most likely to be risk averse. More recent work (e.g., Damasio 1994; Lo and Repin 2002; Loewenstein et al. 2001; Smith et al. 2002) suggests that people experience immediate affective reactions to risky situations and that these affective reactions then influence people's risk attitudes. Further, characteristics other than the parameters of the risky alternatives such as the vividness with which those alternatives is described influence affective reactions, meaning that risk attitudes are influenced by irrelevant factors. Empirical evidence related to the causes of differences in risk attitudes is mixed (Larrick 1993), but it seems clear that many prominent researchers support the idea that there are such differences. (See Bromiley and Curley [1992] for a review; also see Lopes [1987].)

What are the effects of risk attitudes on JDM quality under theories that specify individual differences? EU and other theories do not specify any particular effects of varying risk attitudes on JDM quality. That is, they do not indicate that risk-averse individuals make lower-quality decisions than do risk-neutral individuals, for example. The role of risk attitudes is simply to explain why people make different choices.

Other theories assume that people tend to be risk averse unless situational factors impel them to change these risk attitudes (e.g., Arrow 1971; Kahneman and Tversky 1979). The most prominent of these is prospect theory, which has substantial empirical support (Kahneman and Tversky 1979, 2000). Prospect theory proposes that irrelevant task format characteristics can induce different attitudes about risk both across and within individuals. This is because people tend to think about situations in terms of changes from a reference point rather than thinking in terms of final states of wealth. As a result, people tend to view choices as creating gains or losses. Further, when tasks are formatted to involve a choice between a sure gain and a gain that occurs with some probability, people tend to be risk averse. That is, they prefer the sure gain to the risky gain. However, when tasks are formatted to involve a choice between a sure loss and a loss that occurs with some probability, people tend to be risk seeking; they prefer the risky loss to the sure loss. People who change their risk attitudes in response to task characteristics violate EU theory principles and, thus, from a process perspective, have low-quality JDM. More important, if a person makes different decisions when she receives the same information but in different formats, this indicates low-quality JDM from the perspective of stability over time. That is, she must be "incorrect" on one occasion. By extension, then, people who normally have the same risk attitudes and make the same choices given certain information will disagree if they are given information in different formats. This means at least one of them has lower-quality JDM.

What are the process mechanisms through which risk attitudes operate? It depends on the theory. EU theory proposes that risk attitudes affect the subjective evaluation of choices. Prospect theory proposes that risk attitudes operate first through the problem representation process, that is, through the representation of a situation as involving a gain or loss. Recent theories that incorporate affective reactions to risky alternatives (Loewenstein et al. 2001) do not specify the particular cognitive processes through which risk attitudes operate.

As mentioned earlier, many experimental and archival studies assume that people are uniformly risk averse. In addition, some studies ignore risk attitudes or, in the case of experiments, assume they are equivalent across treatments because of random assignment of subjects. Yet other experimental studies ensure that risk attitudes are constant by inducing them to be so. A popular induction technique in accounting is that introduced by Berg et al. (1986); Selto and Cooper (1990) review the accounting studies that use this technique. As Selto and Cooper note, studies may use the assumption or inducement approaches because measurement of risk attitudes can be difficult. They review a number of measurement methods, including certainty equivalent techniques, that require subjects to state how much they would be willing to pay for a particular risky alternative. Finally, of course, many experimental studies, such as those examining the predictions of prospect theory, manipulate risk attitudes. In addition to manipulating risk attitudes by wording of the task, some studies attempt to induce different risk attitudes with mood manipulations (e.g., Isen and Patrick 1983; Isen and Geva 1987).

Accounting studies examining the effects of differences in risk attitudes are not plentiful, with the exception of studies that manipulate risk attitudes using task wording; these are reviewed in Chapter 6.[25] Newton (1977) and Lewis (1980) find differences in risk attitudes across auditors. Greer (1974) examines corporate managers' risk attitudes and their choices of investment projects and finds that managers are more risk averse in their actual choices than they indicate ex ante they will be. Hilton et al. (1988) find that risk-neutral student subjects choose product prices closer to the theoretically optimal price than do risk-averse subjects. Maital et al. (1986) find that the risk aversion of student investors is negatively related to the riskiness of the portfolios they choose. Finally, Shapira (1995) finds differences in risk attitudes among managers.

Surprisingly little work in accounting examines the effects of risk attitudes, despite the fact that they may vary across individuals and have substantial practical importance in some areas such as auditing and investing. Risk-seeking behavior when faced with losses could be particularly devastating in these areas. Consider the auditor faced with a sure loss of the revenues from a client if the auditor disagrees with the client's accounting treatment versus a probable loss from third-party lawsuits that could result later if the auditor agrees with the accounting treatment and it is subsequently discovered to not be in compliance with accounting standards. Recent theories regarding individual differences in risk attitudes, along with the ways they arise and the effects they have on JDM, deserve further attention in these very important accounting settings.

4-6 EFFECTS OF COGNITIVE STYLE AND OTHER PERSONALITY CHARACTERISTICS ON JDM QUALITY

Previous sections describe the effects of a number of factors that can be considered part of personality, such as confidence and intrinsic motives. This section considers the effects of factors that routinely appear in discussions of personality and JDM. Personality psychology generally is concerned with understanding the determinants and effects of differences in the ways people, think, feel, and act (Funder 2001). One of the tenets of personality psychology is that people exhibit relatively permanent consistencies in their behavior that can be labeled "traits." In particular, the traits of interest here are cognitive style, tolerance for ambiguity, and locus of control. *Cognitive style* is the "characteristic . . . manner in which cognitive tasks are approached or handled," whereas *tolerance for ambiguity* is the "degree to which one is able to tolerate lack of clarity in a situation" (Reber 1995). Finally, *locus of control* pertains to the "perceived source of control over one's behavior" (Reber). Internal-locus-of-control individuals believe that they have some control over outcomes through their actions, whereas external-locus-of-control individuals believe that outcomes occur mostly because of external, chance forces.

---

[25]Also, several studies that examine risk attitudes employ non-JDM tasks (e.g., Young 1985), so they are not reviewed here.

Clearly, these personality traits are not unique to accounting. Whether these traits are relevant to a particular accounting task depends on whether they vary among the people performing the task and whether any variation in the traits has an impact on JDM quality (e.g., Chatman et al. 1999). These are questionable assumptions. First, there may not be much variation in some of these characteristics in accounting settings. For example, studies of the cognitive style of public accountants find that these professionals are predominantly of two types out of a possible sixteen (e.g., Schloemer and Schloemer 1997). Second, even if there is variation, it does not appear to account for much variation in JDM quality in professional tasks (e.g., Huber 1983). In other words, personality characteristics may be small potatoes to accounting JDM. Nevertheless, because several studies examine these variables, this section reviews the extant work, starting with cognitive style.

Perhaps the most frequently applied definition of cognitive style originates from Jung (1923). Jung's theory, as modified by Myers (Myers and McCaulley 1985), includes four traits that are part of cognitive style. However, only two are relevant to JDM. The first—sensing versus intuition—relates to how people prefer to perceive their environment. Sensors prefer to process details and to do so in a sequential fashion, whereas intuitives prefer to "think globally." The second—thinking versus feeling— relates to how people prefer to make decisions. Thinking types prefer to decide based on logical, objective analysis, whereas feeling types prefer to decide more subjectively and consider the effects of decisions on other people. Most discussions and findings related to cognitive style and JDM are akin to those related to risk attitudes; that is, differences in cognitive style result in differences in JDM, but no particular cognitive style is said to result in higher-quality JDM (Ruble and Cosier 1990). This means, however, that people with different cognitive styles will make different judgments and decisions given the same information, suggesting at least some of them must have lower-quality JDM. The most specific prediction relating cognitive style to JDM quality is that intuitives will have higher JDM quality than sensors in tasks that require understanding the "big picture" to perform well (e.g., Casey 1980a). Many accounting tasks such as ratio analysis have such a requirement. Although research does not indicate the processes through which cognitive style operates, its definition suggests it affects problem representation and information search.

Another personality trait that is thought to influence JDM is tolerance for ambiguity. There are two possibilities for the influence of tolerance for ambiguity on JDM quality. As Pincus (1990) describes, people with low tolerance may exert more effort to resolve the ambiguity because it is unpleasant to them (also see Ashford and Cummings [1985]). Although she does not specify which cognitive processes are the beneficiaries of greater effort, overall the prediction is that greater effort leads to higher JDM quality. Ghosh and Whitecotton (1997) draw on work by Guilford (1959) and posit, instead, that people with high tolerance for ambiguity have higher JDM quality because they generate more hypotheses during cognitive processing. However, they also note that tolerance for ambiguity may be positively correlated with measures of cognitive abilities. Consequently, the effects of this trait on JDM quality (and on which dimensions of quality) are not clear.

Locus of control is the final trait of interest here. Typically, studies examine the relation of locus of control to job performance rather than JDM quality. It is generally presumed that "internals" are more motivated than "externals." Consequently, they are assumed to exert more effort and have higher job performance (e.g., DuCette and Wolk 1973; Freeman and Miller 1989). However, some research indicates that the key to predicting the effect of locus of control on performance is the fit between a person's locus and the job environment, with internals doing better in jobs that allow them to control their work and externals doing better in jobs that impose control on them (e.g., Brownell 1981, 1982; Sandler et al. 1983).

Psychologists typically measure cognitive style with the Myers-Briggs Type Indicator (MBTI) (Myers and McCaulley 1985), which requires subjects to answer a number of questions about their preferences in various situations. However, a number of accounting studies use a measure developed by Driver (1971), who proposes that cognitive style consists of the extent to which people focus on multiple alternatives when making decisions and the amount of information they use. Yet others use a measure called "category width," which measures the extent to which people are able to distinguish finely among items in a group of stimuli (e.g., Pettigrew 1958; Bruner and Tajfel 1961). Tolerance for ambiguity can be measured with scales developed by MacDonald (1970) or Budner (1962). Finally, measurement of locus of control typically is accomplished with Rotter's (1966) scale.[26]

Cognitive style studies in accounting include the following studies that use the Driver (1971) measure of style. Mock et al. (1972) find that students and businesspeople who focus on multiple alternatives and use extensive information generate greater profits and lower costs than others in a task requiring production and marketing decisions. However, Driver and Mock (1975) and Vasarhelyi (1977) find no effect of cognitive style on information usage and performance in a similar task, and Savich (1977) finds no effect on amount of information used in an investment decision setting. Further, McGhee et al. (1978) find no effect of cognitive style on analysts' (as proxied by MBA students') judgments about whether particular stocks should be included in an investment portfolio.

Other studies include Casey (1980a), who classifies loan officers using the intuition scale of the MBTI and finds that intuitors are more accurate at predicting bankruptcy than are sensors. Chenhall and Morris (1991) also find that intuitor managers recognize more theoretically relevant opportunity costs in a resource allocation situation than do sensors. Eggleton (1976) finds that the category width measure of style has no relation to students' and business people's estimates of production costs. Pincus (1990) uses the same measure and finds no relation to auditors' detection of a material error.

Studies related to tolerance for ambiguity include Ghosh and Whitecotton (1997), who find that analysts with higher tolerance for ambiguity make more accurate earnings forecasts. However, Pincus (1990) finds that auditors with lower tolerance for ambiguity are more likely to detect a material error, and Reckers and Schultz (1993) find no effects of ambiguity tolerance on auditors' fraud judgments.

Hirsch (1978) reports that managers making choices between two gambles are less likely to choose the gamble with the highest expected value if they have an internal locus of control. Maital et al. (1986) find that student investors with an internal locus of control choose riskier portfolios of stocks. Bernardi (1994) predicts but does

---

[26]Measures tend to come from surveys or experiments because archival measures typically are not available. Manipulation of these factors is not plausible given that they are considered fixed personality traits.

not find that internal-locus-of-control auditors are more likely to detect fraud. Hyatt and Prawitt (2001) show that internal- (external-) locus-of-control auditors have higher performance evaluations when they work in firms with unstructured (structured) audit technologies.

Studies of personality factors in accounting have not been particularly successful from the standpoint that many of them find no effects on JDM quality. Why might this have occurred? First, there may be little variation in these factors among the individuals of interest. Second, although these characteristics may be important for other behavioral issues, they may be relatively unimportant for JDM. Studies that do find effects may be detecting effects of correlated omitted variables given that these personality factors can be correlated with abilities and other person variables (e.g., Pincus 1990).

4-7 EFFECTS OF GENDER AND CULTURAL BACKGROUND ON JDM QUALITY

Research often examines whether there are JDM differences between men and women or among people of varying cultural backgrounds. In addition, the popular press frequently discusses these issues, particularly as they pertain to investors (e.g., Thomas 2001; *Wall Street Journal* 2002). In fact, many brokerage firms are developing programs geared toward women because they believe there are clear gender-related differences in investor JDM (e.g., Gutner 2001). Given the mix of genders and cultural backgrounds among groups of interest to accounting researchers, this topic clearly is relevant to accounting JDM. Further, preliminary evidence indicates that these factors may be related to economic consequences such as lowered investment returns (Barber and Odean 2001).

Gender refers to the psychological and sociological differences related to maleness or femaleness (Halpern 2000).[27] *Cultural background* can refer to a person's nation of residence, her ethnic background, her race, and so forth (Shiraev and Levy 2001). Much JDM research examines very crude differences between people from Western cultures and people from Eastern cultures (Nisbett 2003). The most common way of viewing culture in accounting is using Hofstede's (1980) five-dimension scheme and related scales for classifying the cultural factors relevant to work environments.[28] These include Confucian dynamism, masculinity versus femininity, individualism versus collectivism, power distance, and uncertainty avoidance. *Confucian dynamism* refers to whether a culture has a long- or short-term focus. *Masculinity* versus *femininity* reflects the extent to which individuals behave in what is seen as a stereotypically male fashion by being, for example, responsible, decisive, and goal oriented. *Individualism* versus *collectivism* pertains to the degree to which individuals within the culture focus on their self-interests versus those of the larger group. *Power distance* is the degree to which members of a cultural group accept inequality among individuals within organizations. *Uncertainty avoidance* refers to the extent to which individuals dislike uncertainty. Studies of culture's effects tend to compare Westerners to

---

[27]Note that *sex*, which refers to the biological differences between women and men, typically is used as a measure of gender. That is, it is assumed that all women are of female gender and all men are of male gender.
[28]Note that there is substantial debate about the validity of this measure (e.g., Baskerville 2003).

Easterners and focus on only some of the dimensions from Hofstede's scheme. These studies tend to posit that Eastern cultures are higher as to collectivism, power distance, femininity, uncertainty avoidance, and Confucian dynamism.

Instead of discussing findings regarding the effects of gender and cultural background on JDM quality, this section discusses what research tells us about gender- and cultural background–related differences in cognitive and other factors that can affect JDM quality.[29] Because there are a number of such differences, studies that examine gender or cultural background as the construct of interest run the risk of effectively examining the impact of multiple, completely confounded constructs. More prevalent in JDM research is the use of gender or cultural background as a proxy for a single construct such as overconfidence (e.g., Barber and Odean 2001). These studies run the risk of having correlated omitted variables. For example, Barber and Odean acknowledge that, instead of proxying for overconfidence in their study, gender may proxy for other variables, most important risk attitudes. Because of this, they attempt to rule out risk attitudes as an alternative explanation for their findings.

What are the differences between men and women that can affect JDM quality? There is evidence that men and women differ in cognitive abilities. Although there are no differences in overall intelligence, men tend to score higher on tests of spatial and reasoning abilities, whereas women tend to score higher on tests of verbal abilities (Halpern 2000). In particular, men tend to score higher on the embedded-figures test of spatial ability used in many accounting studies. Further, Geis (1993) cites evidence that men tend to have more power and control in job situations and that these factors lead to greater motivation for men. Consistent with this, Bandura (1997) notes that women have lower self-efficacy than men for traditionally masculine jobs. However, when the jobs are decomposed into their component tasks, there are no gender-related differences in self-efficacy. Thus, it is unclear whether there are gender-related differences in motivation.

There appear to be gender differences in affect, with women experiencing a greater number of both positive and negative affective states than men (Nolen-Hoeksema and Rusting 1999). Further, as mentioned earlier, men tend to be more confident and, thus, more overconfident, than women, particularly in masculine domains. Although less overconfidence would tend to give a JDM quality edge to women according to the research reviewed earlier, Geis (1993) suggests that lower confidence in women, in combination with gender stereotyping, can lead to lower task performance. Men and women clearly differ in risk attitudes as well, with women being more risk averse on average (Byrnes et al. 1999; Slovic 2000; Olsen and Cox 2001). Gender differences on the thinking-feeling trait of the Myers-Briggs measure of cognitive style also exist, with men tending more toward thinking (Myers and McCaulley 1985). However, there appear to be few gender-related differences in locus of control (Feingold 1994). Finally, Halpern (2000) reports evidence that women have better short-term memory and episodic memory than men, and Meyers-Levy (1986) suggests that women have greater information processing abilities than men.

Do people from different cultural backgrounds differ in factors that can affect JDM quality? Research documents differences in overall intelligence and in verbal,

---

[29]This chapter does not discuss the bases for these differences, that is, whether they are physiological or sociological.

reasoning, and spatial abilities among people with different ethnic backgrounds (Shiraev and Levy 2001), although there is enormous controversy about the source of these differences. For example, Sternberg (1996) suggests that one reason there may be differences is that certain cultures care very little about developing some of the abilities tested on standard intelligence tests. His examination of culture-related effects in creative and practical abilities shows fewer differences. A specific finding is that people from Eastern cultures are less able to disembed figures from background, as is required by the embedded-figures test (Nisbett 2003). Research to date on culture-related ability differences does not relate them to Hofstede's (1980) dimensions, however.

People from different cultures may also differ as to intrinsic motives as well as their reactions to external motivators. People in low power distance cultures may have greater intrinsic motives related to fairness (Bond and Smith 1996). Further, there appear to be differences across cultural groups in motives related to achievement and concern with reputation; however, these differences are not necessarily related to individualism (Bond and Smith; Shiraev and Levy 2001). With regard to external motivators, many accounting studies use Hofstede's (1980) dimensions and find that people from different cultures differ in the motivation they feel from management control devices such as participative budgeting and goals (e.g., Chow et al. 2001).[30] Finally, the motivation of people from both individualistic and collectivistic cultures operates through self-efficacy; however, self-efficacy concepts differ in line with cultural differences (Bandura 1997).

Current research indicates that there are cultural differences as to positive and negative affect and that greater positive affect and lower negative affect are found in cultures with greater individualism (Diener and Suh 1999). Several studies also demonstrate differences in overconfidence in knowledge among cultural groups. Easterners, with the exception of Japanese, tend to be more overconfident than Westerners (Yates et al. 2002). It is unclear which cultural dimensions may be related to overconfidence, however. There also are differences in risk attitudes across cultural groups; one specific finding is that people who are high in power distance appear to be less risk averse (Slovic 2000). It is not known whether there are systematic differences in cognitive style and locus of control across cultures. Tolerance for ambiguity seems strongly related to the uncertainty avoidance dimension of culture.

Finally, and perhaps most important, people from different cultures differ in their knowledge, knowledge structures, and cognitive processes. People from different cultural groups categorize things differently and also differ in their need to categorize information (Shiraev and Levy 2001; Nisbett 2003). In particular, people from Eastern, collectivistic cultures tend to group objects in terms of relationships among them, whereas Western, individualistic cultures tend to group objects on the basis of rules that are related to shared attributes. For example, Easterners would group cow and grass together because a cow eats grass, whereas Westerners would group cow and pig together because they are both farm animals. In addition, people from collectivistic

---

[30]This section does not review specific accounting studies of culture differences because the vast majority of them examine management control system research questions and variables rather than JDM quality issues. Further, this section does not discuss other taxonomies of cultural differences because accounting studies routinely employ Hofstede's (1980) work. (See Harrison and McKinnon [1999] for a review of this literature.)

cultures are less prone to overlook situational factors when attempting to understand the causes of outcomes. Finally, Westerners are more likely to use logic in everyday reasoning, although it is not clear which cultural dimension accounts for this.

In sum, people of different genders and from different cultural backgrounds differ on a large number of factors that can influence JDM quality. These include many of the factors reviewed in this chapter and others related to memory and information processing capabilities, knowledge structures, and reasoning processes. Some of these differences indicate higher-quality JDM is likely for one subgroup, whereas other differences indicate lower-quality JDM is likely for that same subgroup. Further, some of the differences, such as those in abilities, are important to JDM quality in some situations but not in others. Consequently, it seems critical to focus on the particular construct of interest (e.g., motivation) for which gender and cultural background may proxy rather than focusing on gender and cultural background as constructs themselves. Further, because gender and cultural background are effectively amalgams of multiple constructs, studies that use them as proxies for a single construct must attempt to rule out alternative explanations.

4-8 SUMMARY

This chapter continues the discussion of key person variables that affect JDM quality. In particular, it discusses the effects of abilities, intrinsic motivation, affect, confidence, risk attitudes, cognitive style and other personality factors, gender, and cultural background. Findings for these variables in accounting tend to parallel psychology findings, with the exception of studies indicating no effect of PD ability and early studies indicating auditor underconfidence in assessing probability distributions for account balances.

For many of these variables, there are only a few accounting studies. With the exception, perhaps, of personality variables, the lack of research does not seem to be due to the variables' lack of practical significance. Further, when studies examine these variables, they tend to find variation, so the lack of research also does not appear due to self-selection biases among groups of interest to accounting researchers. Finally, many of the variables, most notably abilities and motivation, can interact with knowledge and other important variables such as task complexity to affect JDM quality.

Perhaps the lack of research indicates that these factors' effects are not perceived to be unique to accounting contexts. However, this is an empirical question. Further, there may be factors that are unique to accounting contexts that work by inducing one of the variables discussed here, such as overconfidence, as an intermediate state. For example, Nelson et al. (2003) focus on an issue unique to the world of investing when they examine investors' thinking about securities on an aggregated versus individual basis. Also, there may be interactions of these variables with other variables that are unique to accounting tasks. For example, it might be interesting to examine the effects on auditors' JDM quality of the interaction of motivation to be accurate due to, say, litigation concerns, and motivation to reach a desired conclusion due to, say, accountability to a client. Overall, then, research that focuses on the ways in which these factors alone or in combination with other factors most uniquely affect accounting JDM seems to be of the most interest for the future.

CHAPTER
5
Cognitive Processes

This chapter completes the survey of person variables by discussing the effects of cognitive processes on JDM quality. Specifically, the chapter examines the effects of the five cognitive processes introduced earlier: memory retrieval, information search, problem representation, hypothesis generation, and hypothesis evaluation. Although person, task, and environmental variables partially dictate the character of cognitive processes, there also are certain regularities in these processes that affect JDM quality per se. Cognitive processing factors are not unique to accounting settings, but understanding their effects is critical because one of the ultimate goals of accounting JDM research is to improve judgments and decisions. Methods for improving low-quality JDM are most effective if they directly target the responsible cognitive processes. Further, accountants may not exhibit the same process regularities as do other individuals.

The chapter begins with an overview of cognitive processes and a discussion of how to study them using measurement and/or manipulation. Each of the following sections examines a particular cognitive process. These sections begin by describing various dimensions of the process that are pertinent to JDM quality. For example, during information search, people vary as to the amount of information they search for as well as their order of search. The sections then describe the effects of the process on JDM quality and the mediators through which these effects occur, as well as any factors that moderate their effects. Finally, the sections describe accounting research on the particular cognitive process and conclude with suggestions for future research.

5-1 OVERVIEW OF COGNITIVE PROCESSES

For simplicity, this book classifies cognitive processes into five types. *Memory retrieval* refers to searching memory for information pertinent to a particular JDM task, whereas *information search* refers to looking for information in external-to-memory sources, such as companies' annual reports. During *problem representation* people construct a mental interpretation of a situation that reflects their understanding of the key issues. *Hypothesis generation* involves thinking of possible explanations or predictions given a set of information cues; this process is most pertinent to diagnostic tasks such as determining possible causes of ratio fluctuations.[1] *Hypothesis evaluation* involves appraising the likelihood of the hypotheses already generated or provided by another source and, typically, choosing the most plausible as the favored explanation, that is, as

---

[1]Diagnostic tasks are those that require reasoning from "symptoms" (information cues) to ascertain an underlying cause for those symptoms, like medical diagnosis tasks.

the final judgment.[2] The hypothesis evaluation process may also require the design of tests to gather further information. Evaluation of evidence that is unrelated to specific hypotheses also is discussed in this section. The chapter discusses the cognitive processes in the following order: memory retrieval, information search, problem representation, hypothesis generation, and hypothesis/evidence evaluation.[3] Although people sometimes do not work through all the processes or work through them in this sequence, this is one typical sequence assumed by psychology and accounting researchers (e.g., Bonner and Pennington 1991). Perhaps more important, people often iterate through these processes multiple times. For example, they may search for information, then generate some hypotheses, then search for further information.[4]

All these processes are affected by the fact that people are boundedly rational (Newell and Simon 1972). This means that, even if people do their best to make judgments and decisions that are of the highest quality, there are limits to how well they can do. One constraint people face is limited *short-term memory,* the memory store that holds information currently being processed.[5] Typically, people can hold between five and nine items in short-term memory (Miller 1956). This means that most people do not process large amounts of information simultaneously because they simply cannot do so. In situations where they should process more extensively, JDM quality may suffer. Another constraint people face is their computational capabilities; people process much more slowly and laboriously than computers (Simon 1990). Given that people typically cannot use unlimited amounts of time and energy for JDM, this means they will not process as intensively or extensively as they should for a given task; again, JDM quality may suffer.

In other words, because of these constraints, people's cognitive processes are simplified vis-à-vis those of "rational man." Processes are not simplified in random ways, however. Instead, processing is adaptive, meaning that people have developed particular mechanisms to deal with the constraints they face (e.g., Newell and Simon 1972; Payne et al. 1993; Gigerenzer et al. 1999). The first several of these mechanisms are relatively unconscious, that is, people's minds simply operate in these ways. To deal with the short-term memory constraint, people store and organize knowledge in long-term memory and rely on retrieval of this knowledge as a first line of defense. This is adaptive because people can retrieve knowledge up to the limit of short-term memory then continue to retrieve sequentially as previous information is used or discarded. Further, knowledge organization allows for the effective use of more information cues than the number held by short-term memory because people can retrieve cues in groups, or "chunks."[6] If possible, people directly retrieve a task-specific strategy or solution; highly knowledgeable people are most likely to be able to do so (Simon 1990). This

[2]If choice follows judgment, the process normally entails combining the judgment with information about utilities for various possible outcomes.

[3]Assuming that cognitive processes occur sequentially is consistent with the information-processing paradigm that underlies most psychology and accounting research (Newell and Simon 1972).

[4]The search process likely is subject to the most debate about its sequence in the process. Consequently, this chapter discusses what we know about information search behavior that either precedes or follows hypothesis generation.

[5]In contrast, long-term memory typically is thought to be relatively unlimited in its capacity (Anderson 2005).

[6]Further, because highly knowledgeable individuals tend to have larger chunks than less knowledgeable individuals, they may be less subject to the short-term memory constraint.

type of knowledge also helps deal with the processing speed constraint. If people directly retrieve solutions, other processing is reduced.

If people lack task-specific strategies and solutions but have other relevant knowledge, they may employ task-independent strategies called *heuristics* that tap into that knowledge and provide structure for JDM (Gilovich and Griffin 2002). Heuristics rely on relatively small numbers of information cues and only a few processing steps (Hastie and Dawes 2001); in this way, they are adapted to both the short-term memory constraint and the processing speed constraint. Further, information cues called for by heuristics sometimes are aggregates of many pieces of related knowledge (e.g., counts of instances of occurrence of some event), so again, heuristics (when piggybacked on organized knowledge) allow for the use of more information than can theoretically be held by short-term memory. Those who lack relevant knowledge obviously cannot rely on these adaptive mechanisms. The final line of defense for these individuals is *weak methods*—generic, somewhat innate processing strategies that rely on task information and short-term memory (Newell and Simon 1972). For example, people sometimes work backward from a problem's goal to find a solution. These generic methods are termed weak because they cannot avoid the short-term memory or processing speed constraints.

As compared to the unconscious adaptive mechanisms described above, people sometimes consciously deal with the computational speed constraint. Specifically, based on task demands, they choose processing strategies from among an arsenal that they either have stored in memory or construct on the spot. If the task has few demands, people can use all the task information and process it in a slow and effortful way but still complete the task with overall cognitive costs (effort spent) that do not exceed benefits (the level of JDM quality and its related consequences).[7] However, if the task imposes greater cognitive costs itself, for example, by containing many alternatives among which to choose, people often adopt strategies that do not use all task information in order to keep cognitive costs lower than benefits. People may simplify, for example, by not considering all alternatives (Payne et al. 1993). Essentially, people consciously anticipate costs and benefits and adapt by choosing strategies for which anticipated costs do not exceed anticipated benefits. People using this adaptive mechanism typically can use more complicated strategies and will use them if the cost–benefit comparison changes, such as when monetary incentives are tied to JDM quality (Arkes 1991). Further, these strategies are not always task independent; highly knowledgeable individuals develop task-specific simplified processing strategies. (See Bonner et al. [2003] for an example.)

Although all people are boundedly rational, there is variation in processing and JDM quality across individuals because people vary in the extent to which they possess the adaptive mechanisms that target the short-term memory and processing speed constraints. Specifically, people vary as to knowledge content and organization and, thus, the ability to use task-specific solutions and strategies as well as heuristics. Further,

---

[7]Payne (1982) considers both effectiveness and efficiency elements of JDM quality. Throughout the rest of this chapter, JDM effectiveness refers to high-quality JDM defined vis-à-vis normative theories, outcomes, others' JDM, professional standards and theories, and one's earlier JDM, whereas JDM efficiency refers to high-quality JDM defined vis-à-vis time. The literature on processes, with the exception of that on hypothesis evaluation, provides little information about the differential effect of process regularities on various JDM quality dimensions, so the discussion here is necessarily more general.

adaptive mechanisms, although largely helpful to JDM, have unavoidable costs in that they create predictable errors in JDM (Hogarth 1981; Arkes 1991). Specifically, knowledge organization, task-specific strategies, and heuristics all can create systematic errors. Somewhat paradoxically, then, people with more adaptive mechanisms are better able to circumvent processing constraints but also are more prone to certain types of errors. In addition to variation in adaptive mechanisms, people vary as to the level of constraints they face. That is, people vary in their abilities related to short-term memory and processing speed (Carroll 1993). The effects on JDM of processing constraints, regularities in people's responses to them, and differences across individuals in their possession of adaptive mechanisms will be discussed in each process section.[8] Before examining individual processes, however, it is important to understand how to study cognitive processes. The next section provides this information.

5-2   METHODS FOR STUDYING COGNITIVE PROCESSES

Chapters 3 and 4 discuss various methods for studying person variables other than cognitive processes. These methods can be categorized as involving either manipulation or measurement, with the latter being done directly or indirectly. In this text, "indirect measurement" refers to the use of a proxy for a variable, with proxies typically being factors that are determinants of that variable. For example, researchers can measure knowledge content directly with a variety of methods, such as recall tests, or indirectly by asking people to report prior instruction in the topic area. The study of cognitive processes, however, is notoriously more difficult than the study of other person variables. This is because researchers are attempting to get at dynamic thinking processes rather than static factors such as abilities that people bring to JDM tasks. Consequently, researchers have devised alternatives to the traditional approaches in order to study cognitive processes.

Direct Measurement

This section begins by discussing direct measurement methods and their advantages and disadvantages for studying cognitive processes. These methods typically are available only in experimental settings.[9] The broadest technique for measuring processes directly is verbal protocols (Ericsson and Simon 1996). *Verbal protocols* are spoken accounts that people produce when researchers ask them to think aloud about what they are doing while performing a task. Protocols can be taken concurrently, while the task is being performed, or retrospectively, shortly after people finish the task. Because this technique does not constrain what people discuss, it has the advantage that it can provide measures of all cognitive processes. There has been great debate, however, about whether protocols provide valid measures of processes. A key criticism is that

---

[8]For succinct listings of process regularities as they pertain to investors, see Olsen (1998) and Rubinstein (2001).

[9]These methods tend to be available only in experimental settings because archival records of cognitive processes normally maintain only a portion of information about processes. For example, auditors' work papers document the information they end up using to form a judgment about whether a particular account contains a material misstatement. They may have searched for or retrieved other information before making their judgment but concluded ultimately that much of the information was not relevant. In addition, they may have generated multiple hypotheses about the size of material misstatements but document only the one that survives the evaluation phase of processing. Further, firms tend to keep these records private for legal and other reasons. It also is difficult to obtain such information via surveys.

the requirement to verbalize substantively changes the cognitive processes in which people engage. However, evidence compiled from hundreds of studies indicates that this occurs only when researchers ask people to do something other than verbalize their thoughts (e.g., explain their thoughts) or when they deviate from standard procedures in other ways (Ericcson and Simon 1996). A viable disadvantage of protocols is that they may provide an incomplete picture of experts' processes, which often are not consciously available (Anderson 2005). Also, protocols require a great deal of subject time, so studies using protocols tend to have small numbers of subjects. Finally, protocols provide qualitative data, which can be difficult to convert to quantitative form. This is particularly problematic for accounting researchers because quantitative data historically has been the norm in accounting.

Researchers can also ask postexperimental questions of subjects. If the questions ask subjects to report their thoughts during the experiment, they are akin to retrospective protocols. However, other approaches can be used. One approach is to posit a particular process explanation and ask questions that would be indicative that such a process is operating. For example, Hopkins (1996) posits that the financial statement classification of hybrid financial instruments influences JDM first through subjects' categorization of those instruments as debt or equity. To examine this explanation postexperimentally, he asks subjects to calculate a debt-equity ratio using a list of the account balances viewed earlier in the study; subjects' ratio values reflect how they categorize the instruments. Postexperimental questions are advantageous in that they can work for any of the processes. However, these questions can be tricky to employ because subjects may experience memory problems by this point in the study (Ericsson and Oliver 1988). Also, the questions must be sufficiently specific that they capture processes used during the experiment but not so leading as to create biases in subjects' answers.

Direct measurement methods other than verbal protocols and postexperimental questions tend to be narrower in that they pertain only to particular cognitive processes. Methods for measuring memory retrieval are those discussed in Chapter 3 for the measurement of knowledge—recognition and recall tests. Recognition tests provide people with information previously seen to examine to what extent the information is in memory and can be retrieved. They also provide *distractors,* or items not previously seen, so people cannot appear to have perfect retrieval by simply responding in the affirmative to all items. A standard measure of memory retrieval for recognition tests is the number of correct answers minus the number of wrong answers (Klatzky 1980; Baddeley 1990), although better measures can be developed using signal detection theory (Green and Swets 1966; see Sprinkle and Tubbs [1998] for an example in accounting). *Recall tests* ask subjects to retrieve information about a particular topic or from a particular document and typically measure retrieval as the number of correct items recalled.[10] *Free recall tests* provide no information other than these instructions, whereas *cued recall tests* provide prompts. For example, a researcher asking auditors to recall internal controls might provide a sample control as a starting point. These methods are less time consuming than protocols and easily provide quantitative data.

---

[10]There are a variety of methods for determining "correctness" of recall. Some researchers require verbatim recall, whereas others use a "lenient gist" criterion, which scores material based on whether people produce answers that are substantively similar to the original material (Fiske et al. 1983). Note, however, that the use of a lenient gist criterion may capture affective reactions to material and reconstructions from an affective schema.

However, there are at least four disadvantages of recognition and recall measures. First, they provide a joint measure of knowledge and the retrieval process. To focus solely on retrieval issues, psychologists create nonsense materials; this is not a viable alternative for accounting researchers. Second, recall and recognition tests invoke different retrieval processes, so they produce different results regarding the quality of retrieval (Klatzky 1980; Baddeley 1990). The subject's basic task in a recognition test is to figure out which items are "previously seen" or "known" versus which are "new" or "unknown." In recall tests, by contrast, the subject's basic task is "reproducing all the members of a designated set" (Klatzky 1980). The most common differential result is that people tend to show greater retrieval on recognition tests than on recall tests because the retrieval process is easier. However, recognition tests do not always indicate higher-quality retrieval; for example, people tend to retrieve low-frequency items better than high-frequency items when given a recognition test, inconsistent with their being of higher strength in memory and with recall test results. Third, a particular problem related to cued recall that can exacerbate these differences is that the prompts are a form of task information that can create output interference. Fourth, although subjects may be able to recall experimental information when asked, they may focus on information they generate themselves when making a judgment or decision. As a consequence, recall may show no relation to JDM simply because the experimenter does not realize subjects are doing this (Moser 1992). The bottom line is that a researcher choosing a method for measuring retrieval needs to be familiar with the factors that differentially affect recognition and recall (as well as with the effects of cues and experimenter instructions on recall) and whether these factors interact with her independent variables.

Direct measurement of information search can be accomplished with protocols or computerized search monitoring methods.[11] Software records many facets of information search such as the specific information items accessed and the order in which people search for items (Payne et al. 1993). These systems can present information items in a variety of ways; one is as icons on a screen. Subjects typically click the mouse on an icon to acquire an item. Recent technological developments also allow subjects to seek information displayed on computer monitors using only their eyes; staring at an information item for a certain amount of time is tantamount to a mouse click (e.g., Lohse and Johnson 1996; Hunton and McEwen 1997). Software then records the same types of data about information search based on eye movements.

Interestingly, research indicates that choice of method matters when studying information search processes. Earlier studies indicate that verbal protocols provide different inferences about search behavior than do manual search monitoring methods (e.g., Payne et al. 1978), whereas more recent studies indicate that there are differences even between eye-movement- and mouse-click-driven computerized methods (Lohse and Johnson 1996). Because of the difficulties associated with protocols and the

---

[11]Earlier studies used manual versions of these monitoring methods. For example, many studies used information boards to track subjects' information search (e.g., Payne 1976). *Information boards* are pieces of cardboard or similar material with pieces of information attached, for example, in envelopes. They typically arrange information by decision alternative and attribute of decision alternative, and subjects choose the pieces they want. Researchers can observe various aspects of subjects' choices that computers now can record automatically. Information boards are obviously far more costly in terms of subject and researcher time than are computerized methods.

prohibitive cost of eye-movement systems, researchers typically use mouse-click systems to measure information search processes. Consequently, they need to be aware of these issues, in particular the extent to which the method-related differences in search behavior interact with independent variables of interest.

When measuring problem representations, researchers can employ verbal protocols or ask subjects to provide written analyses (Gentner and Stevens 1983; Rouse and Morris 1986). These written analyses can take the form of numerical calculations, narrative descriptions, or pictures, depending on the task. As an example, Vera-Muñoz et al. (2001) ask subjects to write a memo that provides advice to a hypothetical client about a disinvestment decision. They use subjects' memos and supporting calculations to classify subjects' problem representations as being focused on cash flows or earnings. Researchers can also ask subjects to interpret provided analyses (Anzai 1991). Written analyses take less time than protocols; are easier to code; and, most important, are consistent with people's normal JDM procedures. However, consistency with day-to-day work can create a disadvantage in that people may be used to documenting only a partial record of their processes (see note 9). Note that a few studies (e.g., Hammersley et al. 1997; Kadous and Sedor 2004) use recall or recognition tests to measure problem representations. These techniques can work as long as researchers have specific predictions about recall or recognition that distinguish the findings from those that would be predicted based solely on memory retrieval outcomes.

Researchers can take measures of the hypothesis generation process with protocols or simply by asking subjects to generate, with or without prompts, a set of explanations or predictions for a given set of cues. Prompts can be sample hypotheses or hypotheses ostensibly proposed by another source such as a superior. Asking people to directly generate hypotheses requires little time for subjects; outputs also are relatively easy to code. However, researchers need to consider whether the output interference potentially created by prompts interacts with other variables.

There are at least two techniques beyond protocols for measuring hypothesis or evidence evaluation processes; as above, these techniques are easier to code and less time consuming for subjects.[12] First, researchers can examine various dimensions of information search such as depth (see Section 5-4) to identify whether individuals are using certain types of evaluation strategies (Payne et al. 1993). Second, researchers can ask subjects to evaluate hypotheses or evidence directly. This strategy requires a number of design choices to ensure experimental control, however, and these design choices may affect the findings regarding the quality of evaluation and its link to JDM quality. For example, if the researcher wishes to ensure that subjects are serious when evaluating hypotheses, she may give them a set of hypotheses purportedly generated by a particular superior. If subjects perceive this superior to be highly credible, they may engage in different evaluation processes than they would in the absence of such information. For example, they may exert little effort and simply rate all the hypotheses as highly plausible (Petty and Wegener 1998). The key point again is that the researcher needs to be aware of how such factors affect the hypothesis or evidence evaluation process and, specifically, whether they interact with her variables of interest.

---

[12]In some domains such as auditing and medicine, hypothesis evaluation may involve the design of tests to collect further information. Measuring this part of the process involves asking people to list the tests they would use (e.g., Bonner and Lewis 1990) or to evaluate tests on a list (e.g., Brown and Solomon 1991).

Indirect Measurement and Manipulation

Each of the direct measurement methods has serious disadvantages, so researchers often have to look for alternatives. Is "indirect measurement," or the measurement of factors that determine processes, a possibility? Theoretically it is, but there are considerable problems with this approach, especially deciding which level of determinant the researcher should use. For example, if information search is largely determined by knowledge structure, which is largely determined by instruction and experience, does the researcher indirectly measure information search with knowledge structure or with instruction and experience? If she uses knowledge structure as her proxy, she faces the difficult task of attributing any JDM quality effects to information search processes rather than to other processes that also are affected by knowledge structure, such as memory retrieval. If she uses instruction and experience, JDM quality effects may be due to differences in search, other processes, and to other factors that are correlated with instruction and experience. For example, experienced people may have higher abilities because of firm selection procedures. Consequently, measuring cognitive processes using proxies is difficult.

What about studying cognitive processes via manipulation? This is possible, although researchers have to be quite clever to ensure that various difficulties are avoided. One difficulty is the possible blatancy and consequent triviality of the manipulation and findings. For example, a researcher could manipulate information search by telling one group of subjects to read information in the order in which it is presented and telling another group of subjects to read information in a different order. Another difficulty is that subjects may ignore such manipulations if their knowledge or other personal characteristics suggest otherwise. For example, auditors with well-structured knowledge might search for information in an order suggested by their knowledge structures irrespective of an experimenter's instructions to do otherwise. Yet another potential difficulty is that manipulations directed at a cognitive process may simultaneously affect other variables, making it difficult to separate out the effects of the process. For example, one way of manipulating problem representations is to format a JDM task in different ways, for example, as involving a loss or gain. However, this manipulation also can induce differential risk attitudes in subjects.

Some examples of manipulations of processes illustrate what researchers need to do in order to address the above difficulties. Sedor (2002) manipulates the format in which management's future plans are presented to analysts in order to induce analysts to process in different ways, specifically to evaluate evidence differentially. She ensures that the presentation format manipulation has an effect on evidence evaluation by asking subjects several manipulation check questions about the manner in which they thought about the material. She also uses subjects' responses to these questions as a mediator in her analyses and finds that the predicted ways of thinking are related to subjects' judgments. Kadous and Sedor (2004) manipulate assigned JDM purpose and posit effects on problem representations and JDM quality. They measure problem representations and ensure that the manipulation has its predicted effect and also relate problem representations to subsequent judgments. Although they measure problem representations using a recognition test, it is unlikely in their setting that this measure instead reflects memory retrieval. Further, other processes such as information search are held constant.

Because direct measurement, indirect measurement, and manipulation of processes can be difficult, researchers have developed alternative methods for studying processes. These are discussed in the next two sections.

Inferring Processes by Manipulating JDM Improvement Methods

One approach involves inferring processes underlying JDM by studying the effects on JDM of improvement methods targeted at hypothesized processing difficulties.[13] If JDM quality with these methods is higher than JDM quality without the presence of the methods, the researcher can infer that the hypothesized processes are operating. This approach is distinct from direct measurement in that it makes hypotheses about processes and infers support or lack of support for the hypotheses rather than examining actual processes. Advantages of this approach are that researchers can use it to study all types of processes and can do so with relatively small amounts of subject time. In addition, coding of responses typically is not difficult. However, critical to the validity of inferences is that the researcher rule out alternative explanations for the observed effects of the JDM improvement methods.

As an example, Bonner et al. (1996) provide auditors with decision aids for probability judgments they make during audit planning.[14] Based on the findings of Nelson et al. (1995), they hypothesize that auditors have low-quality JDM in these judgments because of difficulties in memory retrieval and hypothesis evaluation. They provide auditors with either no aid or one of two aids. One aid targets only memory retrieval, whereas the other aid targets both memory retrieval and hypothesis evaluation. The authors also rule out a number of alternative explanations for differential JDM across aid conditions. The retrieval-aid group has higher-quality JDM than the no-aid group and the retrieval/evaluation-aid group has higher-quality JDM than the retrieval-aid group, suggesting that both retrieval and hypothesis evaluation problems contribute to lower-quality JDM for this task.

Modeling Processes

Another popular alternative for studying cognitive processes is to model them quantitatively using subject-provided data.[15] This approach is distinct from direct measurement in that modeling studies view processing as something of a black box. They assume that certain elements of processing are both fixed across individuals and simplistic then provide "as if" measures about the elements allowed to vary. It is distinct from the improvement method approach in that assumptions oftentimes are not based on prior research or task analyses; rather, their purpose is to make modeling more tractable. Experimental studies that examine processes with modeling normally require quantitative responses such as scale ratings to facilitate their work; as a

---

[13]Typically, researchers must conduct an experiment to use this approach, as it is difficult to find archival data. First, such data would have to be available within one firm to avoid confounding characteristics of the JDM improvement methods with characteristics of firms. Normally, firms implement a single method such as an incentive plan or decision aid on a firm-wide basis. Second, even if a researcher discovers a single firm that has implemented multiple improvement methods, there is still possible confounding of these methods with other factors. For example, a firm might give inexperienced people a particular decision aid and give experienced people a different decision aid. Finally, it is unlikely that firms have in mind the goal of disentangling cognitive processes when choosing methods for improving JDM.

[14]See Baron (2000) for a discussion of using training methods to understand cognitive processes.

[15]This section discusses modeling that is used as the primary technique for studying cognitive processes. Some researchers develop "cognitive computational" or "process tracing" models based on other measures of processes such as protocols, but they often create these models with purposes other than the further study of processes. For example, some researchers create them as the basis for expert systems (e.g., Biggs et al. 1993).

consequence, data coding issues that occur with protocols tend not to arise. In addition, these studies use structured tasks because tasks are set up to be consistent with assumptions of simplistic processing. Structuring of tasks can allow subjects to display their highest-quality JDM. The modeling approach is also advantageous because it can be used with archival data. (See Bonner et al. [2003] for an example.) The most important disadvantages of the approach derive from the models' restrictive assumptions. Because many factors are assumed to be constant, model-based studies provide somewhat limited insights into processes. Further, the assumptions about processes allowed to vary may not be consistent with actual behavior (Hoffman 1960); if so, model-based studies have limited potential to suggest methods for improving JDM that target actual processing difficulties. These criticisms are explored further below.

The most frequently used technique to model cognitive processes is linear regression. Within the family of models that employ regression analysis, the most popular is the lens model (Brunswik 1952; Hursch et al. 1964; Tucker 1964). The lens model is unique in that it models the task environment in addition to decision makers' processes. Brunswik's purpose in including the task environment in the lens model is to make the important point that cognitive processes do not develop in a vacuum; rather, they are products of the environments people face.[16]

Figure 5-1 depicts the key elements of the lens model. First is a set of information cues (X_1, X_2, etc.) designated by the researcher as relevant to a specific judgment or decision. These cues can be correlated with each other (depicted as r_{ij}). For example, cues could be financial ratios. Second is the person's judgment or decision (Y_s). For example, this could be an auditor's decision about whether to issue a going-concern audit opinion.[17] Third is the actual outcome (Y_e), or *criterion event,* such as whether a company goes bankrupt.[18] A lens model study regresses a person's judgments on the information cues to construct a model of her processes (formula (2) in Figure 5-1), and the actual outcomes on the cues to construct a model of the task (formula (1) in Figure 5-1).[19] Even if the researcher includes a large number of cues, these cues are not expected to account for all the variation in outcomes or JDM. That is, the lens model recognizes the uncertainty inherent in tasks and the inconsistency in people's JDM processes, as well as the fallibility of cues themselves.

Researchers then calculate several statistics to study processes as well as other JDM issues. The *achievement index* (r_a), or the correlation of JDM and outcomes,

---

[16]People developing processing strategies that reflect task characteristics is another form of adaptation that is referred to as "vicarious functioning" (Hammond and Stewart 2001).

[17]Clearly, different forms of regression must be used depending on the criterion of interest. In examples such as this with a dichotomous dependent variable, the researcher must employ logit regression.

[18]There is an alternate version of the lens model, called the "social judgment theory" version, that can be used when there is no actual outcome associated with a judgment or decision (Hammond et al. 1975). This version of the model includes one person's judgment or decision on one side of the model and a second person's judgment or decision on the other side of the model and, thus, examines the processes related to agreement between people. It also is conceivable to model people's judgments vis-à-vis a correct answer derived from professional standards or theories.

[19]Models such as the lens model that use regression analysis are the most general version of process models because they allow for varying correlations among cues. There are equivalent ANOVA versions that can be used when information cues are systematically crossed in a factorial design, that is, when they are uncorrelated (e.g., Ashton 1974a, 1974b).

FIGURE 5-1   Lens Model

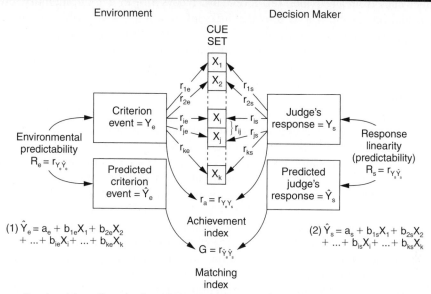

Source: Reprinted from Organizational Behavior and Human Performance, Vol. 1, Issue 1, Linda Dudycha and James Naylor, *Characteristics of the Human Inference Process in Complex Choice Behavior Situations,* Page No. 110–128, Copyright 1966, with permission from Elsevier.

serves as a measure of JDM quality. *Environmental predictability* (R_e) is the correlation between actual outcomes and the predictions made by a statistical model of the task. This serves as an indicant of the extent to which the cues can predict outcomes. Next are various statistics that examine process issues. The coefficients from the regression model of the person (b_{1s}, b_{2s}, etc.) tell us which cues the person uses in JDM (those with nonzero weights). The second measure of processing is the *matching index* (G). This is the correlation between predictions from the environmental model and the person's model. G reflects the extent to which a person's cue weights, taken as a set, match those in the environmental model, or to what extent people have adapted their cue weights to those dictated by the environment.[20] The final measure is *response linearity* (R_s), the correlation between actual JDM and the predictions made by the model of the person. This shows the extent to which the person is consistent in applying her cue weights.[21] Note that a person's JDM quality can be expressed as a multiplicative function of environmental predictability, her consistency, and her cue-weight matching ($r_a = GR_eR_s$).

---

[20]An excellent feature of the lens model is that it correlates the predictions from the environmental model and the predictions from the person's model rather than focusing on specific cue weights. This allows for the notion that people can exploit correlation, or redundancy, among cues when making judgments and decisions. For example, the current ratio and the quick ratio are two highly correlated cues used to predict bankruptcy. Suppose that an environmental model of bankruptcy outcomes puts more weight on the current ratio. However, a lender making a judgment about bankruptcy could put more weight on the quick ratio and make predictions that are very similar to the environmental model. In this case, G would indicate high-quality processing, whereas an alternative technique such as protocols that focus on individual cue weights might indicate otherwise.

[21]Other statistics include the univariate correlations between cues and outcome (r_{1e}, r_{2e}, etc.), known as *ecological validities,* and those between cues and JDM (r_{1s}, r_{2s}, etc.), known as *cue utilization coefficients.*

Overall, then, what does the lens model tell us about processing? It specifies which cues, from a provided set, people use. It says little else about memory retrieval or information search. It also provides little information about problem representation and hypothesis generation other than the fact that these cues enter representations and may affect the set of plausible explanations. It says the most about hypothesis or evidence evaluation, delimiting the extent to which people's cue weights match the weights in an environmental model, and the extent to which people are consistent in using their weights.

Several assumptions underlie what the lens model can tell us about processing. First, the lens model assumes that the small set of information cues the researcher chooses are all those relevant to a given judgment or decision, and also that people would not use irrelevant cues if unconstrained. Second, and more important, the lens model assumes that these cues and their situation-specific values are available to all decision makers. In an experimental setting, this clearly is the case.[22] However, researchers using the lens model with archival data must recognize that there are further assumptions implied by this assumption. One further assumption is that information cues are publicly disseminated to all decision makers at the same time. Another is that all decision makers can obtain the proper situation-specific values of cues (i.e., measure them) through memory retrieval or information search.

Third, in largely ignoring retrieval and search processes, the lens model assumes that various facets of these processes, such as the order of search, are either unrelated to JDM quality or constant. Fourth, the model assumes that information cues have a linear relation both to outcomes and people's JDM rather than being of some other functional form. Fifth, the lens model typically assumes that cues do not interact to affect outcomes and also that people do not consider interactions among cues. A further implication of this is that the lens model assumes a compensatory process of combining weighted cues. That is, people add up cues, so a high value on one cue can compensate for a low value on another cue. Essentially, the lens model assumes that people select some information cues, obtain their values (which normally are given), multiply cues' values by weights reflecting their perceived importance, and add up the resulting numbers.[23]

How valid are the assumptions of the lens model and, thus, the resulting inferences about processes? It turns out that many of them provide a reasonable reflection of actual processing behavior (and task environments). First, although it sometimes appears that there is an unending amount of information available to use in JDM, many contexts contain information cues that are redundant with other cues. For example, investors often hear multiple media reports regarding companies that may appear to be separate cues but that are simply repetitions of companies' press releases (Shiller 2001). Further, in many contexts, a small number of cues can account for much of the variation in outcomes. For instance, Altman's (1968) model of bankruptcy prediction

---

[22]Experiments typically provide the situation-specific values of cues (e.g., they tell subjects that the current ratio is 2.0 for a company). In some instances, the "values" of cues are provided in words such as "yes" or "no" or "high" or "low" (Cooksey 1996). The latter occurs in situations where the cues' values typically are not stated in numbers (e.g., internal controls are either absent or present). However, it is possible to conduct lens model studies where subjects first have to determine the values of the cues from experimenter-provided descriptions. (See Bonner [1991] for an example.)

[23]Because the lens and other models portray cognitive processes this way, researchers often use a simpler taxonomy of processes that includes cue selection, measurement, and weighting (e.g., Bonner 1990).

contains only five cues. Along with this, people tend to use only a small number of cues in their JDM (Brehmer and Brehmer 1988). The part of this assumption that most likely does not match reality is that people often perceive nondiagnostic cues to be relevant to JDM (e.g., Nisbett et al. 1981; Dawes et al. 1989), so if unconstrained by the researcher's choice of cues, they would use (or are using in an archival setting) cues not included in the model. Note, however, that there is nothing in the setup of the lens model that precludes the inclusion of normatively irrelevant cues.[24]

The second assumption is perhaps the most problematic, particularly if the lens model is to be used with archival data. Although it is often the case that experiments provide measured values of cues, this clearly does not match the reality that decision makers face. Cue measurement is thought to be one of the most difficult components of JDM, one where knowledge plays a big role (Einhorn 1972, 1974). In an archival setting, matters are more complicated because information cues may not be available to all decision makers at a given time. For example, prior to Regulation FD, it was commonly thought that financial analysts had access to company information prior to investors (Shiller 2000).[25] Even if available, not all decision makers have the resources they need to obtain cue values such as access to databases. To deal with these problems, researchers can vary the requirement to measure cues within a lens model–based experiment (Bonner 1991) or they can conduct additional analyses that attempt to deal with differential access in an archival study (Bonner et al. 2003). The third assumption also is problematic. As discussed below, people vary as to the "quality" of their retrieval and information search, and this variation can affect JDM quality. The lens model cannot deal with this issue.

The fourth and fifth assumptions regarding linear relations and interactions have some support. First, in many contexts, cues have linear relations with outcomes. Along with this, many cues have conditionally monotone relations with outcomes, which means that, as they increase, outcomes increase irrespective of the values of other cues (Dawes and Corrigan 1974). In other words, cues do not interact to affect outcomes in these situations. Further, if there are interactions, most can be approximated by linear models (Hastie and Dawes 2001). Second, people generally prefer to think in terms of linear relations and main effects and sometimes have difficulty detecting nonlinear relations of cues to outcomes and interactions among cues (Brehmer and Brehmer 1988; Hammond 1996). However, in situations that call for it, people sometimes can use nonlinear relations and consider interactions; the latter is called *configural processing* (Brehmer and Brehmer 1988). Most important, the lens model can be adapted to deal with nonlinear relations and interactions.

However, the compensatory processing assumption of the lens model can be problematic because people often use noncompensatory JDM processes (Einhorn 1970; Payne et al. 1993). In these situations, a high value on one cue does not necessarily make up for a low value on another cue. For example, people sometimes use an *elimination-by-aspects* (EBA) rule, in which they eliminate alternatives based on whether cues meet a minimum threshold (e.g., graduate schools eliminate all candidates

[24]Thus, admonitions to find out which cues are available to people for JDM when determining what to include in a lens model study (e.g., Carroll and Johnson 1990) may be more appropriate than those that suggest determining the most relevant cues (e.g., Cooksey 1996).
[25]Regulation FD requires that companies disclose material information to all interested parties simultaneously (Opdyke et al. 2000).

with GMAT scores below a certain number irrespective of their other attributes).[26] Fortunately, two frequently used noncompensatory rules (conjunctive and disjunctive) can be incorporated into a lens model analysis (Cooksey 1996). In situations where it is expected that people may use other noncompensatory rules such as EBA, the lens model's assumptions are not appropriate.

It appears, then, that the assumptions of the lens (and other regression-based) models are somewhat realistic and, where they are not, researchers often can make adjustments to reflect alternative assumptions. However, some of its assumptions such as no variation in information search are rather significant and limit what can be learned about cognitive processes. Thus, the researcher must consider the goals of her research on processes to determine if the modeling approach makes sense. If the research is relatively preliminary or does not seek to understand processes in order to suggest methods for improving JDM, this approach may be appropriate. Further, if the researcher is interested mostly in hypothesis or evidence evaluation, a modeling study may make sense.

There are a number of alternatives for studying cognitive processes; the most promising are direct measurement, modeling, and using improvement methods as a way of "backing into" inferences. With direct measurement methods, researchers must bear in mind that seemingly innocuous choices such as cued versus free recall may significantly affect their findings. Quantitative modeling, specifically the lens model, has serious limitations as well, but researchers should consider this approach in appropriate circumstances. Perhaps the most important feature of the lens model is that it allows for people to adapt to environments that have correlated cues. Many accounting settings contain such cues, but this issue and the related use of the lens model have not been fully appreciated to date. The "backing into" method also has great potential as long as researchers exercise careful control; it is particularly handy when subjects' time is constrained. The next sections discuss research on the effects of various processes on JDM.

5-3 EFFECTS OF MEMORY RETRIEVAL ON JDM QUALITY

This section discusses *memory retrieval,* or the process of recovering items stored in long-term memory through either recall or recognition. In particular, it discusses the extent to which memory retrieval has a causal effect on JDM, as opposed to simply being correlated with JDM. In order for memory to have a causal influence on JDM, judgments or decisions must require the retrieval of previously viewed information rather than be "on-line" (Hastie and Park 1986). On-line JDM occurs when people form judgments or decisions as they view information; in these situations, memory and JDM may be correlated because the information being used affects JDM and also affects memory, or because JDM affects memory. Thus, in discussing memory retrieval issues, the first question to explore is to what extent accounting-related JDM is memory-based versus on-line.[27]

Clearly, much experimental work in accounting induces memory-based JDM. As Hastie and Park (1986) note, JDM definitely requires memory when it comes as a surprise. Indeed, many accounting experiments do not explain to subjects why they are

---

[26]Other noncompensatory strategies are discussed later in this chapter.
[27]This section restricts its discussion to the effects of memory on JDM, but this does not imply that the effects of JDM on memory are unimportant. To some extent, studies that examine the latter issue are reviewed elsewhere (e.g., Libby and Trotman 1993).

viewing the information that precedes a request for a judgment or decision. If subjects cannot anticipate the requested judgment or decision, they are forced to rely on memory. On the other hand, subjects can operate in an on-line mode if the experimenter tells them JDM is coming or if the context makes it apparent. For example, subjects reading items that indicate a going-concern problem may be able to anticipate that they will be asked to make a going-concern judgment (Choo and Trotman 1991).

A key question is to what extent memory-based versus on-line JDM occurs in real-world accounting contexts. There likely are instances of all points along the continuum. Take the example of the staff auditor making a judgment about the quality of a client's internal control system. To do so, she gathers information, makes a judgment, and documents the information she deems most relevant in her work papers. This sounds like on-line JDM. However, suppose her senior, in reviewing her work, raises a number of questions that are not addressed in the work papers. The staff auditor may attempt to answer the questions by gathering more information from the client. However, she also may rely on memory if, for example, she feels particularly confident (Moeckel and Plumlee 1989; Koriat 1993) or if she feels the items in question are not very important (Sprinkle and Tubbs 1998). Thus, any revised judgment she makes while addressing the reviewer's questions may be at least somewhat memory based. As mentioned earlier, people prefer to rely on long-term memory to circumvent processing constraints, and highly knowledgeable people do so more frequently (Simon 1990). Further, in accounting settings such as auditing, it frequently is not feasible for decision makers to review all previously seen information because of efficiency concerns (Libby and Trotman 1993). Overall, then, memory-based JDM is an important issue in accounting. There is variation in the extent to which it occurs and, furthermore, if used in settings such as auditing, obviously can have severe consequences if memory is incorrect.

What is the causal effect of memory retrieval on JDM quality when JDM is memory based? To answer this question, it is necessary to delineate dimensions of memory retrieval; that is, it is not appropriate to say that "more memory retrieval" leads to higher JDM quality. The key dimensions of memory retrieval discussed in the psychology literature are quantity and accuracy of items retrieved (Koriat et al. 2000). For episodic memory, accuracy means that the retrieved memories are the same as actual experiences; for semantic memory, accuracy means that people have correct factual information. In JDM settings, there likely are other important dimensions of retrieval, specifically, the relevance to the task of the items retrieved; the speed of retrieval; and, possibly, the order in which items are retrieved.[28]

When JDM is memory based, what are the relations of various dimensions of retrieval to JDM quality? The relation of quantity of items retrieved to JDM is unclear. On the one hand, experts in many domains retrieve a larger quantity of items than novices (Chi et al. 1988). However, this likely reflects greater and more structured knowledge. When experts are given nonsense materials to retrieve, they do no better than novices (Chase and Simon 1973). Further, quantity and quality of items retrieved are not necessarily associated. For example, people who watch television directly after

---

[28]Note that these dimensions of memory retrieval refer to products of the retrieval process rather than the process per se, which is consistent with the psychology literature (Koriat et al. 2000). The effects of the retrieval process are discussed in Chapter 3. In particular, Chapter 3 discusses many of the factors that lead to breakdowns of the retrieval process, such as lack of strength, output interference, misunderstanding of the items' relevance to JDM, and so forth.

an airplane crash may be able to retrieve a larger number of instances of such crashes than people who do not watch television. However, the quality of their retrieval may be diminished because their focus on instances of crashes may mean that they are unable to recall instances of safe landings. If higher quantity retrieval does not imply higher quality retrieval, retrieval quantity may not be positively related to JDM quality. In fact, efficiency may be negatively affected if quantity of items retrieved is more than is necessary to make a judgment or decision.

If we define accuracy of items retrieved as an average across all items, accuracy should be positively associated with JDM effectiveness (Hastie and Park 1986). Relevance of items retrieved can be defined, for example, as the proportion of items retrieved that are relevant to the task, as well as the completeness of the retrieved set vis-à-vis a set of all possible relevant items. Here, as relevance increases, JDM effectiveness should increase. Note that positive effects of retrieved item accuracy and relevance encompass the negative effects of knowledge discussed in Chapter 3. For example, if people infer items from schemas that are inconsistent with what actually occurred, accuracy of retrieval is diminished and, thus, JDM quality can be diminished. As another example, if people retrieve knowledge of outcomes, relevance of items retrieved can be lessened because outcomes typically are irrelevant to JDM. Speed of retrieval obviously has a positive effect on efficiency measures of JDM quality but also could have a positive effect on other measures if people are under time pressure. Finally, the order in which items are retrieved also may have an effect on JDM quality if people are under time pressure. People who retrieve the most relevant items early are likely to have higher-quality JDM than people who retrieve those items later and, thus, may not retrieve them at all under time pressure.

The products of memory retrieval can affect JDM quality directly or through other cognitive processes. The relation of memory retrieval to JDM may have no mediators if retrieval leads directly to the "right answer." This is likely to occur for highly knowledgeable individuals (Simon 1990). In other cases, memory retrieval has an effect on JDM quality by working through other processes. One theory is that retrieved items are incorporated into problem representations, which can influence hypothesis generation, information search, and hypothesis evaluation (e.g., Pennington and Hastie 1988). Another theory relates to the use of retrieved items in judgments about probability or frequency. Here, people often use the *availability heuristic,* which means they judge probability or frequency based on ease of recall of relevant instances (Tversky and Kahneman 1973). In this scenario, people count the number of retrieved items favoring particular hypotheses rather than organizing them into a problem representation (Wolfe and Pennington 2000). The use of the availability heuristic is what can lead quantity of items retrieved to have a negative effect on JDM quality because quantity, for example, can be influenced by factors such as recency of experience that lead to biased, or low-quality, retrieval (as discussed in the airplane example above).

What factors moderate the positive effects of various dimensions of retrieval on performance? That is, once the products of retrieval are established, what might cause them to have a lesser positive effect? Quickly retrieved items and early-to-be-retrieved items likely have little effect on JDM effectiveness when people are not under time pressure. This is because people often retrieve more items when given more time to try (Klatzky 1980). Moderators of positive effects of accuracy and relevance of items retrieved include task complexity and conclusion-related motivation induced by factors such as accountability. Complex tasks require a larger number of and/or more complicated processing steps (Bonner 1994). In these situations, people are less likely to be able to apply what they have retrieved from memory (Shanteau 1992b). Also, if people are motivated to reach a particular conclusion, they may ignore or rationalize away accurate and relevant retrieved items that do not support the conclusion (Kunda 1990, 1999).[29]

There are relatively few accounting studies that examine the relation of memory retrieval to JDM quality, despite essays about its importance (e.g., Birnberg and Shields 1984; Libby 1989). Many examine problems in the retrieval process such as output interference; these studies are discussed in Chapter 3. Studies examining producers and users of accounting information include Luft (1994), who finds that the accuracy of students' memory for their past performance is not related to their JDM quality. Moser (1989) asks investor subjects to generate reasons that support and do not support a specific amount of increase in a company's earnings then to judge the probability of this increase. Subjects who generate relatively more supporting reasons make higher probability judgments, consistent with memory retrieval affecting JDM through availability. Moser (1992) provides similar findings. Finally, Kida et al. (1998) find that the quality of managers' investment decisions is strongly influenced by affective reactions to numerical information about the investment alternative, which are remembered more accurately than the numerical information itself. Unfortunately, the affective reactions are biased because of the manner in which the managers view investment alternatives in the experiment; these biases lead to lowered JDM quality.

The following auditing studies examine retrieval issues. Anderson et al. (1992) examine whether the extent of retrieval of nonerror versus error explanations for a ratio fluctuation affects judgments about the probability of error; inconsistent with Moser (1989) and an availability process, there is no relation. Libby and Lipe (1992) examine whether recall accuracy improves more than recognition accuracy with monetary incentives. Their premise is that recall requires more effort; thus, incentive-related effort increases have more potential to affect recall accuracy. Results are consistent with this premise. Moeckel and Williams (1990) show that auditors make no better inferences from work papers when they are able to access those documents versus when they rely on memory. Johnson (1994) finds that auditors retrieving information from work papers have better memory after one hour than after one day.

Bonner et al. (1996) find that auditors have difficulty with memory retrieval when faced with a conditional probability judgment structured around transaction cycles because their knowledge tends to be structured around audit objectives. When given a retrieval aid, auditors' difficulties are lessened. Further, the extent of retrieval difficulties is related to the extent to which judgments correspond to probability theory.

Rau and Moser (1999) examine whether performing a seemingly unrelated audit task affects auditors' memory for information related to going-concern judgments as well as the judgments per se. Some subjects do not perform the unrelated task; subjects who perform the unrelated task receive information that either positively or negatively reflects on the company's ability to remain a going concern. Consistent with auditors' general tendencies to focus on negative information (Smith and Kida 1991), there are

---

[29]It may be more likely, however, that the items are not retrieved in the first place because people are more likely to retrieve items consistent with the conclusion of interest.

no differences in memory for such information across conditions. However, subjects who perform the positive unrelated task remember significantly more positive information than others. Further, these subjects make significantly more positive going-concern judgments than others, and this effect is due to their memory errors.

Finally, analogous to Rau and Moser's (1999) examination of the effects of working on multiple tasks within one audit, Lindberg and Maletta (2003) study the effects on memory of working on multiple audit clients. Subjects read information about the inventory audit at two different companies, make judgments about the likelihood of misstatement, and take recognition tests. The authors vary the extent to which previously unseen statements about one client on the recognition tests are consistent with information provided about the other client. Auditors make a number of memory errors in which they attribute evidence to one client when it relates to the other client. These errors increase as the evidence from one client becomes more consistent with the other client's situation; further, memory is associated with judgments about misstatements, suggesting memory errors may affect the quality of JDM in this task.

The accounting literature on memory retrieval generally is consistent with the psychology literature. First, as discussed in Chapter 3, accounting professionals have difficulties during the retrieval process such as output interference. Second, there are differences in memory retrieval results depending on how retrieval is measured. Third, most accounting studies find that the accuracy and relevance of memory retrieval, but not necessarily its quantity, are related to JDM quality. The importance of these studies depends, however, on their common assumption that the individuals of interest rely on memory to complete the JDM tasks under consideration when outside the laboratory. Further investigation of this assumption is warranted, given Sprinkle and Tubbs's (1998) finding that auditors are less likely to rely on memory for the information they deem more important. More generally, it is critical for researchers to conduct thorough task analyses to fully understand the environments in which the decision makers of interest work and the conditions under which they rely on memory then examine memory retrieval effects under these conditions. Rau and Moser's (1999) examination of the effects of performing unrelated audit tasks on memory and going-concern judgments is an excellent example of a study that does this. The authors recognize that auditing standards' requirements regarding the going-concern task create a situation in which auditors must rely on memory.

5-4 EFFECTS OF INFORMATION SEARCH ON JDM QUALITY

Information search is another critical aspect of cognitive processing, particularly in accounting contexts. Many JDM tasks in accounting cannot be completed solely on the basis of information retrieved from long-term memory; in other words, they invoke on-line processing of some information. This information frequently comes to the decision maker through active search, and in many instances, search for particular information is prescribed. For example, to follow auditing standards, auditors must search for up-to-date information related to client risks. Nevertheless, the extent to which individuals search for information likely varies for a variety of reasons including knowledge differences (see below). More important, if decision makers do poorly at information search and, thus, miss important pieces of information, they clearly can make low-quality JDM that can have consequences for themselves and others. For example, if auditors miss information about serious violations of debt covenants, they may incorrectly conclude that a company's going-concern status is not in question; give the wrong audit opinion; and, ultimately, face litigation.

As with memory retrieval, it is important to specify the dimensions of information search that are of interest. The dimensions psychologists study are amount of information searched for (called depth of search), order of search, speed of search, and types of information for which people search (Ford et al. 1989). *Depth of search* can refer to the total amount of information searched or the proportion searched. *Order of search* can be defined in many ways. Some researchers characterize search as "sequential" versus "directed"; *sequential search* means that people work through information in the order presented, whereas *directed search* means they do not (e.g., Hunton and McEwen 1997). Studies of decision behavior also examine the extent to which people search within a decision alternative as opposed to across alternatives (Payne et al. 1993). Under types of information searched, it seems prudent to consider relevance of items, although some researchers are interested only in describing which items people examine. Finally, *speed of search* refers to the time spent per item or the total time taken to search for all items.

Much of the literature relating information search to JDM quality contains conflicting findings. Starting with depth of search, people generally prefer to limit search and rely instead on memory (Simon 1990). Further, knowledgeable individuals tend to search for less information than do less knowledgeable people (e.g., Johnson 1988), although there are notable exceptions (Elstein et al. 1978; Phelps and Shanteau 1978). The explanation for this finding is that the former use their knowledge to zero in on the most relevant information; further, they already have a greater store of knowledge in memory on which they can rely. Thus, depth-of-search differences partially reflect knowledge differences, and knowledge has a positive effect on JDM quality. However, depth of search also reflects adaptation to processing speed constraints. For example, as tasks increase in complexity, depth of search tends to decrease (Payne et al. 1993). In these cases, decreased depth of search likely leads to less effective JDM, although decreased depth typically would increase efficiency.[30] Thus, the overall relation between depth of search and JDM quality dimensions other than efficiency is unclear.

With regard to order of search and specific information searched for, knowledgeable individuals tend to use directed search because they are seeking specific pieces of information that do not appear sequentially. Less knowledgeable people tend to use sequential search. Knowledgeable individuals also better distinguish between relevant and irrelevant information (Chi et al. 1988), although this does not mean they never search for irrelevant information (Shanteau 1984). However, in decision situations, knowledgeable people sometimes search in different sequences and for different pieces of information for each alternative, whereas less knowledgeable people tend to search in the same way for each alternative (e.g., Camerer and Johnson 1991). This reflects the former's attempts to develop sophisticated hypothesis evaluation strategies, which can underperform simple strategies because they introduce inconsistencies into JDM. Further, directedness of search and specific items searched for also are affected by the ways people adapt their hypothesis evaluation strategies to processing constraints (Payne et al. 1993). For example, time pressure can cause people to evaluate

---

[30]These findings are discussed in detail in Chapter 6.

only a subset of information. As a consequence, they appear to be using directed search. However, because this directed search may be forced by task demands rather than informed by knowledge, it may not lead to high-quality JDM.

In addition, these search dimensions can be affected by whether search precedes or follows hypothesis generation in tasks that contain this process. If people search after generating hypotheses, that is, during the evaluation phase, they tend to exhibit *confirmation bias* (e.g., Snyder and Swann 1978; Snyder and Cantor 1979; Nickerson 1998). This is the tendency to search for information that is likely to support the favored hypothesis and may be one of the costs of relying on organized knowledge as an adaptive mechanism (Arkes 1991). Direction of search toward confirming information means that people may miss relevant items. Along with this, people tend to search for information related to a favored hypothesis rather than for information related to all hypotheses generated (Fischhoff and Beyth-Marom 1983; Robinson and Hastie 1985). Both of these forms of directedness typically do not lead to higher-quality JDM, whereas directed search preceding hypothesis generation can. As expected, then, people who use directed search and people who include more relevant items in the set they search for only sometimes have higher JDM effectiveness (Camerer and Johnson 1991). However, directed searchers typically are more efficient.

Speed of search has a positive effect on the efficiency dimension of JDM quality and potentially on other dimensions under time pressure because fast searchers can obtain more pieces of relevant information in a fixed time period. However, because speed of search is affected by depth and directedness of search, it is difficult to make predictions about its independent relation with JDM quality except as to efficiency. Overall, all four dimensions of search vary because of people's differential capacities to overcome processing constraints. In addition, people may exhibit individual differences in search strategies (e.g., Payne 1976). Unfortunately, it is frequently unclear how these differences in search dimensions affect JDM quality.

The mediators of information search effects, where positive, likely are similar to those for memory retrieval. Information search may lead directly to a "right answer," in which case there are no mediators between search and JDM. If search occurs prior to hypothesis generation, persons who search for relevant information and do so in a directed way will more quickly create problem representations and the representations will be of higher quality. These representations then lead to higher-quality hypothesis generation and evaluation processes. These mediators also explain depth of search findings assuming that depth of search reflects knowledge rather than adaptation to processing constraints. The mediators of negative search effects include the following. If dimensions of search reflect adaptive mechanisms, their ill effects occur because they provide incomplete inputs to the other phases of processing. If information search follows hypothesis generation and is prone to confirmation bias, search provides biased inputs to the hypothesis evaluation phase.

What moderates the effects of information search on JDM quality, both positive and negative? In other words, once the products of search are created, what might cause them to have decreased effects on JDM quality? Some of the moderators are similar to those for memory retrieval. High levels of task complexity may make it difficult for people to apply the information they have gained through search to the remaining phases of JDM. Time pressure may do the same. Finally, if people face motives to reach a particular judgment or decision, they may not utilize some of the information obtained through search (Kunda 1990). Note that these moderators may have a positive effect on JDM quality if they reduce a negative effect of some dimension of search.

There are quite a few papers that examine information search in accounting settings. In managerial accounting, San Miguel (1976) finds that students adapt their depth of search to environmental uncertainty. Shields (1980) finds some evidence that managers doing performance evaluations adapt their search order and depth to task complexity. Shields (1983, 1984) reports little agreement among managers and students as to the items of information they search for and as to final judgments. Swain and Haka (2000) find that managers and students adapt their search to task conditions in a capital budgeting context. Managers' search behavior is also more homogeneous than that of students. Finally, Harrison et al. (1988) find that managers exhibit confirmation bias in search related to a variance investigation.

Many studies examine the search behavior of analysts. Biggs (1984) finds that analysts use directed search when choosing a company with the greatest earnings power; however, there are differences in the specific items they examine. In addition, their depth of search is fairly limited. Jacoby et al. (1985, 1986) report that analysts whose price predictions are closest to actual outcomes have greater depth of search, search for different types of information, and search in a more directed fashion than analysts with lower-quality JDM. Bouwman (1984) shows that accountants proxying for analysts search for more information than students, engage in directed search (whereas students use sequential search), and vary more as to specific items searched than students. Bouwman et al. (1987) find that analysts use directed search but vary as to the contents, depth, and speed of search. Anderson (1988) compares the search behavior of analysts and investors making a stock recommendation. These groups have similar depth and speed of search, but analysts exhibit more directed search than investors. In addition, analysts search for both confirming and disconfirming information, whereas investors exhibit confirmation bias. Johnson (1988) compares analysts' and students' search behavior and predictions of stock prices; analysts search for less information and are faster, but the accuracy of their price predictions is no different. Hunton and McEwen (1997) find that directedness and speed of search are related to analysts' forecast accuracy. Finally, in a study of municipal analysts predicting bond ratings, Lewis et al. (1988) find that analysts who search for information are less accurate than those given information.

Several studies pertain to investors' and creditors' search processes. Abdel-Khalik and El-Sheshai (1980) and Chalos and Pickard (1985) find results similar to Lewis et al. (1988) with loan officers making default judgments. Biggs et al. (1985) report that loan officers adapt their search depth to task complexity. Bricker and DeBruine (1993) find that students proxying for investors seek information in order to reduce risk but decrease information search as the costs of information increase. Ackert et al. (1996) find that students proxying for investors adapt the type of information they search for to environmental uncertainty.

Tax professionals' search behavior is the subject of a number of studies. Spilker (1995) reports that knowledgeable tax students doing a tax research task adapt search to time pressure by increasing speed and depth, whereas less knowledgeable students do not. Spilker and Prawitt (1997) find similar results with tax professionals and students, and they provide evidence that knowledgeable subjects adapt to time pressure by focusing more on search than on building a problem representation. Cloyd (1995) measures tax professionals' JDM quality as the number of relevant items less the number of irrelevant items (where relevance is defined by professional tax standards) that subjects use to evaluate a case; depth of search is negatively related to this measure of JDM quality. Cloyd and Spilker (1999) find that tax professionals doing research exhibit confirmation bias when they know clients' preferences regarding tax positions, although Cuccia and McGill (2000) find no such relation between general advocacy positions and search. Finally, Cloyd and Spilker (2000) report that both law and accounting students exhibit confirmation bias in tax research, but law students are less prone to do so, ostensibly because of their training.

In auditing, Biggs and Mock (1983) and Biggs et al. (1988) examine search in internal control evaluation and audit program design settings, respectively. Biggs and Mock find that seniors vary as to the directedness, depth, and contents of search, as well as in their final judgments. Biggs et al. find that managers are faster in search than seniors. In Knechel and Messier's (1990) study, audit seniors with lower depth of search make more extreme judgments about the probability of collecting an account; it is not known whether these extreme judgments are of higher or lower quality. Bédard and Mock (1992) compare computer audit specialists to nonspecialists doing a control evaluation task; specialists search faster, for less information, and in a more directed manner. Rosman et al. (1999) find that auditors who are more accurate at predicting bankruptcy outcomes have less depth of search and are more likely to use the most relevant cues. Further, search patterns are adapted to environmental uncertainty. Other studies include Simnett and Trotman (1989), who report results similar to Lewis et al. (1988) with auditors predicting bankruptcy. Bedard and Biggs (1991b) and Bedard et al. (1998) find that one cause of auditors' inability to determine the true error cause of ratio fluctuations is because they fail to search for some of the relevant cues. Davis (1996) finds that experienced auditors select more relevant cues than inexperienced auditors; however, they do not have control risk assessments closer to the firm's solution. Asare and Wright (2003) show that auditors who receive evidence regarding a correct hypothesis ultimately are more likely to choose that hypothesis than auditors who conduct their own search.

Finally, several studies examine confirmation bias among auditors. Kida (1984b) finds that audit partners and managers do not exhibit this bias when searching for information relevant to going-concern judgments. Trotman and Sng (1989) report that auditors consistently choose more failure cues than those indicating viability in this setting; however, there is some evidence of confirmation bias toward viability when auditors start with a viability hypothesis. Kaplan and Reckers (1989) report that experienced auditors are not prone to confirmation bias when seeking information to explain ratio fluctuations, whereas inexperienced auditors are. In McMillan and White's (1993) ratio fluctuation setting, auditors exhibit (do not exhibit) confirmation bias when they propose an error (a nonerror). Bamber et al.'s (1997) experienced and inexperienced auditors show confirmation bias in two auditing tasks. Brown et al. (1999) find that auditors exhibit confirmation bias in interpreting audit evidence unless they are told to emphasize audit effectiveness. Finally, Peterson and Wong-on-Wing (2000) find strong evidence of confirmation bias in auditors' selection of test results after hypothesizing possible errors; their study differs from previous studies in that they ask auditors to provide intermediate hypotheses and classify information search as it relates to the most recent hypothesis rather than to the first hypothesis. They also find that the confirmatory strategy is beneficial to JDM efficiency.

Overall, the accounting findings regarding the relation of information search to JDM quality are fairly similar to those in psychology. Depth of search has varying relations to JDM quality, consistent with its reflecting both knowledge structure differences and adaptation to processing constraints. Accountants who use directed search typically have higher JDM quality than those who do not. Further, there is great variation in the items people access.[31] Accountants exhibit confirmation bias in managerial and financial accounting settings but may be less likely to do so in auditing settings, consistent with auditors' requirement to exercise professional skepticism. However, further research that elicits auditors' intermediate hypotheses is needed to determine whether earlier findings are due to this methodological issue. Along with this, research needs to examine under what conditions confirmation bias in search has negative effects on JDM quality; it may be an adaptive mechanism that works well in many cases. Finally, research on information search should focus more on issues that are unique to accounting. For example, auditors must search for "sufficient competent evidence" to comply with professional standards; this implies that they will execute deep search. Yet they also experience conditions such as time pressure that lead to decreased search. Research could examine how auditors' search reflects these countervailing forces.

5-5   EFFECTS OF PROBLEM REPRESENTATION ON JDM QUALITY

Problem representations come into play when people are unable to retrieve a solution for a JDM task directly from memory or find one through information search. Because many accounting tasks are novel and unstructured, accountants frequently cannot retrieve ready-made solutions. In these situations, the quality of problem representations plays a major role in the quality of accountants' JDM. Also, researchers suggest that third parties try to manipulate decision makers' problem representations in an attempt to exploit them (Kahneman and Tversky 1984). For example, management may attempt to manipulate auditors' problem representations to prevent them from detecting fraud (Johnson et al. 1991a). Clearly, if auditors succumb to this manipulation, they can face severe consequences.

A *problem representation* is a mental framework that organizes a decision maker's understanding of a JDM task and, as such, provides a road map for completing the task (Anderson 2005). The creation of a representation involves several processing steps, so there are several dimensions of representations that are related to JDM quality. Typically, it is not simply the presence of a representation that predicts JDM quality because people spontaneously form representations to simplify and structure their work (Bédard and Chi 1993; Nicholson 1998).

When forming representations, people start by incorporating the information cues they gather from memory and search.[32] As part of this step, they may have to

---

[31]Some studies identify specific items associated with JDM quality. For example, see McEwen and Hunton (1999) for information about analysts' use of specific items.

[32]Some theories of evidence evaluation suggest that problem representation is a stage within the evidence evaluation process (e.g., Pennington and Hastie 1986, 1988, 1992, 1993). These theories are discussed in the evidence evaluation section.

measure some cues, that is, convert qualitative information into quantitative form. For example, an auditor who obtains a description of a client's internal control system must translate that description into a level of risk. The as-measured accuracy and relevance of the cues included in the representation, then, are the first elements of problem representations related to JDM quality. Typically, these elements are positively related to JDM effectiveness, largely because they are products of knowledge, memory retrieval, and information search. In particular, the expertise literature finds that experts' cue measurement quality is one of the keys to their superior JDM (Einhorn 1972, 1974; Elstein et al. 1978; Johnson et al. 1981; Lesgold et al. 1988).[33] Experts have more cue measurement knowledge because they have had greater experience with the range of qualitative characteristics cues can take on and greater feedback regarding their conversions of these characteristics into quantitative form.

Second, people organize information in the representation in a meaningful way. This step does not entail simply activating a stored knowledge structure. People also must integrate current information into the retrieved knowledge structure and infer further relationships among cues (Pitz and Sachs 1984).[34] These relationships then may activate solution strategies if they exist in memory. People may also place constraints into the representation; constraints are additional pieces of information that simplify the task (Voss and Post 1988). For example, in a tax planning setting, the goal for the tax professional normally would be to minimize taxes. Suppose that a client is not interested in using charitable contributions as a way of reducing taxes; this then becomes a constraint on the tax professional's representation.

Based on these steps, the second and third dimensions of problem representations that affect JDM quality are the type of organizing principle that forms the basis for the representation and the extensiveness of its contents, in particular whether it contains solution strategies and constraints in addition to the basic information cues. Organizing principles can be "deep" (substantive) or superficial. For example, physics students represent problems in terms of the items described in the problem such as inclined planes, whereas knowledgeable physicists represent problems in terms of the principles involved (Chi et al. 1981). In addition, substantive organizing principles can be appropriate or inappropriate for a task, depending on whether they match or fail to match the objective of the task. For example, people should use cash flows rather than accounting earnings representations for investment decisions, but both may appear relevant.

The expertise literature also indicates that problem representations based on the appropriate substantive principles typically lead to more effective but not more efficient JDM (Newell and Simon 1972; Chi et al. 1988). The use of representations based on substantive principles reflects superior knowledge structures as well as an ability to activate the most relevant knowledge structure when more than one appears appropriate. The latter reflects better knowledge of task objectives. Also, knowledgeable individuals tend

---

[33]This does not mean that people who would normally be classified as "experts" never experience difficulties in cue measurement. For example, even experienced individuals have difficulty measuring cues that are characteristics of other people because they attend to irrelevant factors when doing so (Petty and Wegener 1998). Many accounting tasks require measurement of such cues; as such, this topic is discussed more completely in Chapter 8.

[34]One way of representing information in a meaningful way is to construct a "story" (e.g., Pennington and Hastie 1986, 1988, 1992, 1993) or a "scenario" (e.g., Schoemaker 1991, 1993; Hastie and Dawes 2001). Because the construction of stories and scenarios typically is thought to occur during evidence evaluation, these issues are discussed in that section.

to stick with their representations, whereas less knowledgeable people continually change theirs (Anzai 1991). Further, knowledgeable individuals expend greater effort to integrate cues and determine meaningful relations (Glaser and Chi 1988).

However, even knowledgeable people can have difficulties choosing the appropriate representation. One manifestation of this is called *functional fixation,* which means people are unable to represent an object in terms of a novel function rather than in terms of its typical function (Anderson 2005). A well-known example comes from a study by Duncker (1945) in which subjects are asked to use a candle, box of tacks, and matches to fix a candle to a door. People have difficulty determining that the box can be used as a platform because they fixate on its use as a container. Also, one representation may become so dominant in memory with experience that it is difficult to invoke a more appropriate representation (Adelson 1984; Nelson et al. 1995).[35] For example, people prefer to structure knowledge around causes rather than effects, but some tasks may require a structure based on effects. Finally, people can fall prey to *mental accounting,* which means they naturally create certain types of representations about financial issues; these representations, although potentially adaptive, can reduce JDM quality in many situations (Thaler 1999). For example, people represent expenditures as costs if they can include benefits related to the expenditures in their mental accounts, but as losses otherwise (Kahneman and Tversky 1984; Lipe 1993).

The extensiveness of problem representations, or the extent to which they include solution strategies and constraints, typically has a positive effect on JDM quality (Chi et al. 1988). This normally occurs because knowledgeable people are the individuals who include these extra components in their representations, so their inclusion partially reflects the activation of better knowledge structures. It also reflects the additional effort these individuals expend building up the representation initially. Again, however, even knowledgeable individuals may have difficulties because their automatic linking of a certain solution strategy to a task interferes with their ability to see a novel strategy that is more efficient and effective (Anderson 2005); this is called a *set effect.*

How do these dimensions of problem representations lead to higher-quality JDM? In diagnostic tasks, having the right cues in the representation leads people to have a better chance of generating the correct hypothesis. Having the right organizing principles and relationships among cues allows people to detect patterns of cues more easily; in turn, this leads to a higher likelihood of generating the correct hypothesis. Incorporating solution strategies and constraints means that people are more likely to gather additional relevant information, if needed, and to combine information to choose the best hypothesis from the set generated. In nondiagnostic tasks, having the right cues, cues organized properly, and solution strategies lead to high-quality JDM through evidence evaluation.

Factors that moderate the effects of problem representations on JDM quality depend on the dimension of representations of interest. Relevant and accurate cues are less likely to have a positive effect if they are contained in a representation that is organized around inappropriate principles. The same is true of solution strategies and constraints. Even when people have the correct organizing principles, they may not be able to achieve the highest-quality JDM if they lack certain elements of knowledge.

---

[35]This phenomenon may be a cost of the use of knowledge structuring as an adaptive mechanism.

Specifically, people who exhibit the best JDM typically have both well-developed knowledge structures that lead to appropriately organized representations and situation-specific procedural knowledge that leads to better solution strategies than broad rules invoked by representations (Anzai 1991; Bédard and Chi 1993; Vera-Muñoz et al. 2001).

Relatively few accounting studies examine problem representations directly.[36] Lipe (1993) examines the effects of mental accounting in students' and management accountants' evaluations of a variance investigation decision; she finds that representations based on losses lead to different evaluations than representations based on costs. Vera-Muñoz et al. (2001) study the effect of representations on the extent to which management and public accountants can identify theoretically correct opportunity costs in a disinvestment timing task. Accountants with more public or management accounting experience tend to choose a cash flow–based representation. Further, those with the cash flow representation identify more theoretically correct opportunity costs but only when they have extensive experience in management accounting. This is consistent with people needing both correct representations and task-specific procedural knowledge for high-quality JDM. Kadous and Sedor (2004) report that students given the express purpose of making a project recommendation have problem representations that better incorporate threats to project viability than do students given other purposes. Further, these representations are related to higher-quality JDM. Asking subjects to justify their recommendations does not increase JDM quality when subjects are given other purposes. Thus, the authors conclude that giving subjects a particular purpose is critical and that it is critical because of its role in creating the appropriate problem representation.

Pratt (1982) reports that the quality of students' problem representations related to financial statements, in particular whether they focus on the most relevant cues, is positively related to the accuracy of predictions of income but only in a complex version of his task. Bouwman (1984) finds that analysts (proxied by accountants) spend a great deal of time creating a mental picture of "what is going on" in the firm being analyzed, whereas students focus only on linking related financial facts. Analysts also focus on building contradictions into their representations, whereas students do not. Hopkins (1996) finds that analysts represent hybrid financial instruments as debt or equity or as some combination of these instruments, depending on their financial statement classification. When these instruments are classified clearly, analysts appear to invoke a representation based on an existing knowledge structure; when the classification is less clear, analysts must construct a representation by integrating cues. These representations then affect stock price judgments. Hammersley et al. (1997) report that students acting as accountants construct different problem representations when they explain (versus do not explain) the cause of an inventory fluctuation and, consequently, estimate a higher probability for the explained cause.

In auditing, Biggs and Mock (1983) find that senior auditors differ in the ways they represent internal control evaluation judgments. For example, some auditors focus more on risk as an organizing principle than do others. Biggs et al. (1988) report that managers focus on building a thorough representation of the client's situation

---

[36]There are several studies related to the functional fixation issue; however, their results cannot be attributed clearly to problem representations. These studies are discussed in Chapter 6.

during information search, whereas seniors focus simply on completing the task at hand. Bedard and Biggs (1991b) and Bedard et al. (1998) find that auditors who create inappropriate problem representations cannot detect the error that is the cause of ratio fluctuations; inappropriate representations occur because of the failure to use all relevant cues or the failure to integrate them properly. Bierstaker et al. (1999) use the same task and find that auditors who can shift problem representations with the aid of prompts are better able to detect the error. Christ (1993) examines how auditors' problem representations change with experience; experienced auditors' representations are more extensive, include more relationships among items, and reflect more abstract knowledge. Similarly, Moeckel (1991) finds that experienced auditors are better able to identify relationships among items in work papers than inexperienced auditors; however, they also struggle to integrate when items are not close in proximity within the work papers. Johnstone et al. (2002) find that auditors facing higher litigation risks have better developed problem representations; no information is given about the relation of representations to JDM quality.

Two studies examine problem representations in auditors' fraud judgments. Johnson et al. (1991a) present audit partners with one fraud case and one error case, both of which contain information that management provides to create a misleading representation. The partners who detect (fail to detect) the fraud or error outcome change (do not change) from this initial representation to one that leads them to the correct solution. Jamal et al. (1995) examine partners' detection of fraud; partners who detect fraud outcomes change management-provided information into a different representation.

A few studies demonstrate that problem representations do not affect JDM quality. This may be because subjects' representations do not vary. Shields et al. (1987) find that the accuracy of auditors' judgments about misstatement in accounts is not influenced by whether the task is formatted in terms of book values or misstatements. Postexperimental questions reveal that auditors' representations likely are organized around misstatements irrespective of task information. Similar findings occur in several going-concern studies; here, auditors appear to create "failure" representations irrespective of whether tasks are formatted in terms of survival or failure (e.g., Kida 1984b). Professional standards and litigation exposure likely lead auditors to focus on the conservative representation in these cases. Finally, Bonner (1991) examines the cue measurement component of representations and finds that inexperienced and experienced auditors do not differ as to the quality of their measurement of control risk and analytical risk cues; this is predicted based on the timing of auditors' training regarding these cues.

Consistent with psychological findings, accounting studies demonstrate the importance to JDM quality of problem representations based on appropriate substantive principles as well as representations that are complete. Accountants are more likely to invoke such representations as they gain and structure knowledge; however, knowledgeable individuals do not always invoke the appropriate representation. Further, it appears that, at least in the case of auditors and fraud detection, people can manipulate accountants' representations through the information they provide or the format of the task. On the other hand, in situations where auditors have extensive experience with JDM tasks (going-concern evaluations and account misstatements), they are less susceptible than the general population to having their representations influenced by external factors because they consistently adopt the conservative, skeptical representation. Finally, appropriate problem representations may not be sufficient for high-quality JDM in accounting tasks that require many different types of knowledge (e.g., assurance services). The most promising areas for future research are those that seek to understand the factors that affect whether accountants choose the appropriate representation, particularly in the face of potential manipulation, and those that examine the characteristics people must possess in addition to high-quality problem representations in order to use those representations properly.

5-6 EFFECTS OF HYPOTHESIS GENERATION ON JDM QUALITY

Many accounting tasks, most notably auditing tasks, require hypothesis generation because of their diagnostic nature. Consistent with this, all the accounting studies in this area relate to auditing issues. However, there are other settings in which hypothesis generation is important. For example, investors likely generate hypotheses about price appreciation of stocks. Further, there is variation in the ways in which decision makers generate hypotheses, the number they generate, and so forth. Because the quality of hypotheses in accounting settings can have serious economic consequences such as lowered investment returns and losses in litigation, understanding this process and, in particular, problems in the process, is important.

The *hypothesis generation* process involves thinking of a set of explanations or predictions given a set of cues; people then narrow the set during the evaluation phase.[37] When relating hypothesis generation to JDM quality, research examines the number of hypotheses generated as well as the extent to which the hypotheses fit the evidence. Although people normally do not generate a large number of hypotheses because of processing constraints (e.g., Mehle et al. 1981), quantity generated is positively related to JDM effectiveness and efficiency up to a certain point (e.g., Elstein et al. 1978; Lesgold et al. 1988). This occurs because the probability of including the correct hypothesis in a set increases as the set size increases. However, as the set of hypotheses increases beyond some point, the processing required to evaluate the set pushes the limits of people's capacities and they reduce their hypothesis evaluation efforts. In turn, this reduces the probability of accepting the correct hypothesis and rejecting incorrect ones; it also can lead to inefficiency. Having the correct hypothesis in the original set also leads to higher JDM quality as to both effectiveness and efficiency. Order of generation of hypotheses also may be relevant; if people become committed to the first hypothesis they generate and it is wrong, effectiveness and efficiency can suffer (Heiman-Hoffman et al. 1995).

Theories of hypothesis generation specify that people first generate hypotheses based on information in memory then subject them to a plausibility assessment in which they reason backward to check the consistency of the hypotheses with the cues to determine whether they are viable enough to evaluate (Gettys and Fisher 1979).[38] There are

---

[37]People may "inherit" hypotheses from others such as superiors. In these cases, the ensuing memory retrieval phase of hypothesis generation may be subject to output interference from these inherited hypotheses. Further, people may not generate any further hypotheses if they inherit hypotheses (Mehle et al. 1981; Gettys et al. 1986).

[38]If people are unable to generate hypotheses using memory, they may rely on weak methods such as analogical reasoning (Simon 1990). When people use memory for hypothesis generation, this implies that they may experience memory retrieval problems during hypothesis generation as well.

several techniques people use when consulting memory to generate hypotheses, however (Kassirer 1989), so it is important to understand how these techniques may or may not lead people to generate a large number of and the correct hypotheses.

First, people may search memory for instances of occurrence of individual hypotheses related to cues and generate the hypotheses they perceive to be most frequent. For example, auditors can generate a list of possible misstatements for a particular account by retrieving instances of occurrence of specific misstatement causes. This reflects implicit use of the *availability heuristic,* or the strategy of thinking about ease of recall, to judge probability (Tversky and Kahneman 1973). The availability heuristic does not necessarily lead to problems in hypothesis generation because the ease with which people can retrieve instances of hypotheses is affected by actual base rates (frequencies of occurrence). Because people gain such knowledge relatively easily through experience, experienced individuals have relatively complete and accurate knowledge of frequencies and, thus, accurate ease-of-recall perceptions (Nelson 1993b).[39] However, ease of recall also can be affected by recency and salience of experiences. Consequently, even experienced, knowledgeable individuals may generate as hypotheses items that do not frequently occur.[40] Overall, this technique leads to the generation of a larger number of hypotheses when people have extensive frequency knowledge, which is more likely as experience increases. This technique also tends to lead to the generation of the correct hypothesis when two conditions exist: people have accurate frequency knowledge—also more likely with experience—and the right answer is a high-frequency event.

Second, people may match sets of cues to patterns stored in memory and retrieve associated hypotheses. For example, auditors who observe an increase in both sales and bad debts may match this pattern to a hypothesis that the client has loosened its credit policy. When using this technique, people are implicitly using the *representativeness heuristic,* in which they judge probability based on the extent to which cues resemble or are representative of a particular hypothesis (Kahneman and Tversky 1972).[41] For example, when asked to generate hypotheses about another person's job, people think about the extent to which the person's characteristics (e.g., detail oriented and compulsively neat) resemble stereotypes for various jobs (e.g., accountant). They then generate the hypotheses for which the cues appear most representative. Again, this heuristic can work well because cues often "resemble" hypotheses; for example, increased bad debts "looks like" a credit policy issue. However, the use of this heuristic leads to predictable errors. The most notable is that people do not attend to base rates; thus, they may generate all hypotheses for which the pattern of cues appears representative irrespective of their base rates. They then may use similarity as a basis for ordering

---

[39]However, see Ashton (1991) for a different perspective and findings.

[40]These individuals may not explicitly consider ease of recall when making their probability judgments; instead, they may directly retrieve the items with greatest strength in memory. In other words, their judgments may not be mediated by the use of the availability heuristic. That is, they may not explicitly substitute judgments about ease of recall for judgments about frequency (Kahneman and Frederick 2002). Nevertheless, recency and salience have the same effects because they affect strength, which in turn affects ease of recall.

[41]Again, this does not imply that knowledgeable individuals are explicitly using this heuristic in the sense that they may not think about the extent to which cues resemble hypotheses but rather directly match to patterns stored in memory. That is, they do not necessarily substitute judgments of similarity for judgments about probability (Kahneman and Frederick 2002).

hypotheses as to plausibility; although this does not affect hypothesis generation quality, it may affect the effectiveness and efficiency of the hypothesis evaluation process.

Knowledgeable individuals frequently use pattern recognition because they store thousands of patterns in memory and prefer to tap the patterns if possible (Simon 1990). Consequently, they normally can generate a relatively large quantity of and correct hypotheses. However, a cost of such structured knowledge is that these individuals may overly or too quickly rely on routinized associations of hypotheses with patterns that work most, but not all, of the time (e.g., Elstein et al. 1978; Lesgold et al. 1988). Less knowledgeable individuals do not have as many stored patterns, so they typically generate fewer hypotheses. Further, their patterns are not refined through a large sample of experiences. Instead, theirs tend to be inaccurate patterns created by a small sample of experiences or intuitive theories and stereotypes (Nisbett and Ross 1980; Kunda 1999). For example, a staff auditor may generate a hypothesis that a youthful-looking employee is stealing from a company after seeing her with an expensive car and applying a stereotype that someone so young could not afford such a car. In these cases, hypotheses clearly can be incorrect because the "patterns" are inferior.

Third, people sometimes use memory to retrieve a global hypothesis associated with a situation then reason causally to generate more detailed hypotheses related to specific cues.[42] For example, an analyst may retrieve a hypothesis that a stock is a growth stock then interpret accounting numbers in light of this model. This technique typically does not lead to the generation of a large number of hypotheses even for knowledgeable individuals. It also is less likely to lead to the correct hypothesis than the other techniques. Both these findings occur because the use of a single global model limits the number of detailed hypotheses that can fit both the cues and the model (Clancey 1988; Kassirer and Kopelman 1989).

What can moderate the positive effect of number and correctness of hypotheses generated on JDM quality? Once a large number of hypotheses is established, which implies that a correct hypothesis likely is included in the set, JDM effectiveness can suffer only if something goes awry in the hypothesis evaluation process. This process can go awry because of the factors mentioned earlier; either task complexity or time pressure can keep someone from finding all the evidence she needs to distinguish among hypotheses. Further, incentives that lead to reasoning motivated toward supporting an incorrect hypothesis can cause people to search only for confirming evidence or inappropriately evaluate evidence (Kunda 1990, 1999). Also, as discussed in the next section, there are a number of regularities in the evaluation process that can lead to errors, for example, further use of heuristics. JDM efficiency can be reduced if people evaluate hypotheses in order based on similarity, and this order is different than one based on base rates.

As mentioned earlier, all the accounting literature about hypothesis generation relates to auditing. The first study is by Libby (1985), who finds that auditors generate hypotheses regarding error sources of ratio fluctuations in accordance with their perceived frequencies. Further, perceived frequencies of occurrence correspond well to actual frequencies. However, recency of experiencing errors also positively affects the probability of their being generated as hypotheses. Also, as discussed in Chapter 3,

---

[42]This behavior also may be considered an instance of "story" or "scenario" construction (see note 34). The evidence evaluation section discusses this type of reasoning.

Libby examines output interference caused by an inherited hypothesis and finds no interference; however, he attributes this to his choice of prompt. Libby and Frederick (1990) use a similar task and find that managers generate more theoretically correct and fewer incorrect hypotheses than do staff auditors and students. Further, a higher proportion of their hypotheses are high-frequency errors. This study uses a different prompt from Libby and finds output interference with auditors but not students.[43]

Most other studies examine hypothesis generation using ratio analysis tasks as well. Biggs et al. (1988) report that managers generate more hypotheses than seniors and are more likely to generate the correct narrow hypothesis (the outcome), although seniors identify the general problem area. Bedard and Biggs (1991b) report that managers are better able than seniors to identify the correct hypothesis. Inability to generate the correct hypothesis is partially a function of errors in information search or problem representation. However, many auditors recognize the key pattern of cues yet still make errors. Results indicate this is due to the inability to propose hypotheses that explain all parts of the pattern simultaneously; many auditors focus on one cue at a time. Bonner and Lewis (1990) use the Bedard and Biggs task and find that senior managers are better able to generate the hypothesis than seniors. In a somewhat different study, Marchant (1989) examines whether audit seniors use analogical reasoning (a weak method) to generate hypotheses based on ratios. He finds that auditors first rely on knowledge of frequencies then turn to analogical reasoning.

Bedard and Biggs (1991a) show that auditors provided with a correct explanation from management are more likely to generate the correct hypothesis (the outcome). Nelson (1993a) finds that auditors use both pattern recognition and frequency knowledge to generate hypotheses. Heiman-Hoffman et al. (1995) report that auditors generate highly frequent errors more often than less frequent errors. Further, auditors who initially generate a highly frequent and theoretically correct error are more likely to make the correct judgment later than those who generate a less frequent but correct error. On the other hand, auditors who generate a highly frequent but incorrect error are the least likely to make the correct judgment later. Wright and Wright (1997) find that industry specialist auditors generate more theoretically correct hypotheses than nonspecialists; however, these hypothesis generation differences have little effect on decisions about audit testing. Bedard et al. (1998) find that auditors who generate more hypotheses have a higher probability of generating the correct one (the outcome). Bierstaker et al. (1999) find that some auditors are unable to generate correct hypotheses even with prompts to change problem representations, possibly because of interference from inherited hypotheses. Bhattacharjee et al. (1999) report that auditors asked to generate three hypotheses are more efficient and more likely to have the correct hypothesis than those asked to generate either one or six hypotheses. Finally, Asare and Wright (2003) find that auditors who inherit the correct hypothesis are more likely ultimately to choose it than those who inherit an incorrect hypothesis or generate their own.

The remaining studies use other types of tasks. Johnson et al. (1991a) find that auditors who are able to generate a correct hypothesis in a fraud detection task can do so because of the quality of their problem representations; further, once they generate a correct hypothesis, they are able to make the correct judgment. Wright and Bedard

---

[43]Please refer to Chapter 3 for other studies' findings regarding output interference.

(2000) examine hypothesis generation in a risk assessment and audit-planning task. Auditors who generate more hypotheses and who include the true hypothesis in their set have higher JDM quality, measured as whether they choose audit tests that can detect an error. Johnstone et al. (2002) examine auditors' generation of financial reporting alternatives. High-knowledge auditors generate more alternatives under high litigation risk than under low litigation risk, whereas low-knowledge auditors' generation is not affected by risk. Also, when low-knowledge auditors receive an inherited alternative, they generate fewer alternatives than with no inherited alternative; high-knowledge auditors are not affected by the inherited hypothesis.

Most accounting studies examine regularities in the hypothesis generation process rather than the effects of hypothesis generation on JDM quality. These studies' results are consistent with prior work: hypothesis generation sometimes is based on perceived frequencies and sometimes based on patterns. Although no work in accounting examines hypothesis generation based on global models, Bouwman's (1984) findings are suggestive of analysts using this technique. Further, perceived frequencies are affected by actual frequencies, which become more accurate with experience but also are affected by other factors. The few studies that examine effects on JDM quality indicate that the frequency-based generation technique works well when the correct answer is a high-frequency event but less well otherwise and that, when accountants use pattern recognition, the presence of a correct hypothesis in the initial set is associated with higher JDM quality. Further studies should examine the effects of hypothesis generation on various measures of JDM quality because people in general are better at coming up with lists of possibilities than they are at finding the right one (Bonner and Pennington 1991). Also, these findings come only from auditing tasks; research should examine hypothesis generation in other settings.

5-7 EFFECTS OF HYPOTHESIS AND EVIDENCE EVALUATION ON JDM QUALITY

The final cognitive process of interest is hypothesis evaluation. In this phase, people typically gather further information that serves as evidence in support of or against initially generated hypotheses. Based on this evidence, they choose one or more hypotheses to serve as their final judgment(s). The hypothesis evaluation process clearly is important in tasks that require earlier hypothesis generation, such as ratio analysis in auditing. However, many accounting tasks that do not require explicit generation of hypotheses require processing that is akin to hypothesis evaluation. For example, auditors assessing control risk may not generate hypotheses about the risk level before collecting evidence. Nevertheless, their evaluation of evidence is similar to the process of evaluating an explicit hypothesis; further, the choices available for assessments of control risk such as "low," "medium," and "high" may be considered implicit hypotheses. Most important, people make a number of errors during hypothesis and evidence evaluation that can lead to low-quality JDM and serious consequences. For example, mutual funds have used the strategy of betting against people's hypothesis evaluation biases on the assumption that these biases affect market prices and, thus, create opportunities for abnormal returns (Sorenson 1988; Wysocki 1996). Further, the extent to which people make errors in hypothesis and evidence evaluation varies across individuals and circumstances. This section discusses what we know about hypothesis and evidence evaluation, in particular the regularities in the process that affect JDM quality.[44]

As with other processes, hypothesis and evidence evaluation involves multiple steps, so JDM quality can be affected by what happens in each step. First, people may need to design tests to gather evidence, so the quality of test design is relevant to JDM quality. Second, people typically conduct further information search and, possibly, further information measurement using these customized tests or other methods such as standardized checklists. Consequently, the quality of search and measurement during hypothesis evaluation is relevant to JDM quality. Third, people must assess the evidence in light of explicit or implicit hypotheses; this involves determining how much weight to place on measured cues and how to combine the weighted values of cues. Weighting and combination techniques, thus, are relevant to JDM quality.

Effects of Test Design

Hypothesis evaluation may require the design of tests. For example, auditors must choose the specific tests to use for each account, the sample size for each test, and the timing of each test. The quality of design normally is positively related to JDM effectiveness but not necessarily efficiency (Morris and Rouse 1985). Specifically, knowledgeable test designers choose a larger number of relevant, diagnostic tests and a smaller number of irrelevant tests than others. These tests lead to search that has a higher likelihood of producing a complete set of relevant information cues that can then be weighted and combined; thus, problems in weighting and combination may reduce the impact of test design on JDM quality.

Further, knowledgeable individuals do not always exhibit high-quality design. For example, they may fall prey to confirmation bias in their choice of tests (Skov and Sherman 1986). The main manifestation of this is focusing on tests that are likely to provide evidence that supports the favored hypothesis (Klayman 1995). In turn, this can lead to an incorrect hypothesis being accepted and, thus, lessen JDM effectiveness or, at a minimum, lessen efficiency if the incorrect hypothesis is maintained for some time. The use of standardized checklists that force individuals to consider the implications of each piece of evidence for each hypothesis under consideration could alleviate this problem.

Effects of Search and Measurement

Information search and measurement are vital elements of hypothesis evaluation as well, and the dimensions of these activities mentioned earlier continue to be relevant to JDM quality at this stage. Additional variation in search and measurement may occur because of facets of the evaluation process. One facet of this process is that people may evaluate explicit hypotheses they generate themselves; explicit hypotheses provided to them by someone else, such as a superior; or hypotheses that are implicit in a judgment, such as those that are part of control risk assessment. People who generate their own hypotheses are more likely to search for confirming evidence and to

---

[44]This section differs from other sections in that it discusses the relation of various facets of the hypothesis evaluation process to JDM quality rather than the relation of the products of this process to JDM quality. This is because the product of hypothesis evaluation is the final judgment.

measure cues in a way that supports their hypotheses (Klayman 1995).[45] People who receive hypotheses from a particular source may also behave differently in search and measurement, depending on the credibility of and accountability to the source (Petty and Wegener 1998; Lerner and Tetlock 1999). For example, people who know that the inherited hypothesis is the source's favored hypothesis may bias their search and measurement toward accepting that hypothesis, particularly if the source is perceived as credible.[46] Further discussion of cue measurement problems appears below. Clearly, such biased search and measurement can reduce JDM effectiveness and efficiency. A second facet, as mentioned earlier, is that people may search for cues related only to the most favored hypothesis rather than looking for cues that can distinguish among hypotheses. This can lead to acceptance of an incorrect hypothesis when they fail to realize that the evidence also supports other hypotheses (Fischhoff and Beyth-Marom 1983). In this situation, if search continues till the correct hypothesis is found, efficiency is diminished. Such behavior may be reduced when people have extensive experience evaluating hypotheses or training that urges skepticism (Asare and Wright 1995).

Effects of Weighting and Combining Cues during Hypothesis Evaluation

The final steps in hypothesis evaluation are the weighting and combination of measured cues. One convenient way of discussing regularities in these steps when part of hypothesis evaluation is to classify them as to how they relate to Bayes' Theorem, the statistical norm (Fischhoff and Beyth-Marom 1983). Because people typically have difficulty with statistical hypothesis evaluation (e.g., Peterson and Beach 1967; Fong et al. 1986; Plous 1993), the use of this framework indicates that a long list of errors is forthcoming. Indeed, there is such a list, and these errors translate into problems with JDM quality defined vis-à-vis normative theory. However, they do not necessarily lessen JDM quality defined in other ways, for example, vis-à-vis outcomes. This is extremely important to consider because, as discussed in Chapter 2, conformity with normative theories may be a relatively unimportant JDM quality dimension for some individuals and tasks of interest to accounting researchers. This section discusses findings regarding other JDM quality dimensions to the extent they are known.

Bayes' Theorem specifies that the revised probability that a hypothesis is correct should be a multiplicative function of its prior probability and the extent to which an information cue indicates that the hypothesis is correct. It is stated as:[47]

$$\frac{P\,(H/D)}{P\,(\hat{H}/D)} = \frac{P\,(D/H)}{P\,(D/\hat{H})} \times \frac{P\,(H)}{P\,(\hat{H})}$$

The rightmost term provides the probability that H is the correct hypothesis (versus $\hat{H}$, or the complement to H) prior to the receipt of a particular information

---

[45]Factors that can mitigate such negative effects of personal involvement are discussed in Chapter 3.
[46]The effects of accountability are discussed in Chapter 7, and the effects of source credibility are discussed in Chapter 8.
[47]An alternative form of Bayes' Theorem is:

$$P\,(H/D) = \frac{P\,(D/H) \times P\,(H)}{P\,(D)}$$

cue.[48] The middle term, called the likelihood ratio, gives the relative odds that H (versus $\hat{H}$) is correct when a particular cue is observed. A likelihood ratio of one indicates that a cue is perceived not to distinguish between H and its complement; that is, it is perceived to be nondiagnostic.

As Fischhoff and Beyth-Marom (1983) note, people make errors in each step implicit in Bayes' Theorem. Although some of these errors relate to cue measurement, many lead to incorrect cue weighting and combination. The first step is estimating the prior probability of a given hypothesis as well as of its complementary hypothesis (or set of complementary hypotheses). As described above, people may use heuristics to estimate these probabilities, leading to cue measurement problems. If they use the availability heuristic, even knowledgeable individuals' estimates may be incorrect because recency and salience affect ease of recall in addition to actual frequencies. The use of the representativeness heuristic can lead to errors as well because people judge prior probabilities based on the similarity of cues to a pattern in memory. In some cases, similarity may be associated with frequencies, but in many cases, it is not. More important, the standard use of the representativeness heuristic in hypothesis evaluation is as a global mechanism for updating beliefs. When people use it this way, they base their judgment on the extent to which the situation-specific information (D) is similar to the hypothesis under evaluation; as a consequence, they typically underweight or ignore base rates, even when they are already calculated and provided by the experimenter (Kahneman and Tversky 1972). Theories indicate that judgments of similarity are based on a linear combination of the common and distinctive features of items (here, D and H). However, these judgments also are affected by normatively irrelevant factors such as whether people are thinking in terms of similarity or difference or whether they compare H to D rather than D to H (Tversky 1977; Tversky and Gati 1978).

Another measurement problem is that people tend to be overconfident when making probability assessments, meaning that all probabilities may be overestimated and, thus, the ratio may be incorrect (Lichtenstein et al. 1982). A third (weighting) problem is that because of processing constraints and overconfidence, people may not specify a complete set of hypotheses, so the ratio of prior probabilities is based on incomplete information (Fischhoff et al. 1978; Mehle et al. 1981). A fourth (weighting) problem is that people tend to exhibit supra-additivity with hypotheses, that is, P (H) and P ($\hat{H}$) sum to more than one, meaning that the prior probabilities and, thus, the ratio may be distorted. Perhaps most egregious is that people do not adjust the probabilities of remaining hypotheses when one is eliminated. Supra-additivity is more likely when people evaluate hypotheses one at a time rather than simultaneously (e.g., Robinson and Hastie 1985).

Problems in this phase can be mitigated by various factors. As mentioned earlier, task-specific knowledge tends to reduce the ill effects of heuristics because people may substitute task-specific strategies or because heuristics are piggybacking on good knowledge (Gilovich and Griffin 2002). With regard to base rates, showing their causal relation to the hypothesis can increase their use. Although overconfidence is difficult to reduce (see Chapter 4), requiring people to specify alternative hypotheses can increase the completeness of their hypothesis sets (e.g., Hoch 1985). Supra-additivity

---

[48]P (H) and P ($\hat{H}$) should sum to one.

can be reduced by various types of decision aids (Hastie and Dawes 2001). The more important issue is whether these regularities in generation of prior probabilities affect JDM quality defined vis-à-vis a criterion other than normative theory. One study finds that they do not affect quality defined vis-à-vis outcomes when auditors have task-specific knowledge (Asare and Wright 1995), but there is little evidence otherwise.

The next step is estimating the likelihood ratio or, more generally, assessing the relation between situation-specific information and a given hypothesis. A number of problems can occur in this step. First, people have difficulty estimating conditional probabilities; they sometimes confuse a conditional probability with the reverse conditional or with a joint probability (Fischhoff and Beyth-Marom 1983; Hogarth 1987). Compounding this problem is the manner in which people estimate causal relations between hypotheses and cues. Theories of causal reasoning indicate that people judge whether H causes D based on the strength of the evidence supporting H less the strength of the evidence supporting alternative hypotheses. Strength of evidence is judged by the presence of various "cues to causality," including temporal order (whether H occurs before D), closeness in time of H and D, and the similarity of H and D (Einhorn and Hogarth 1986). Whether these cues are normatively appropriate depends on the situation. People also consider the extent to which H and D have covaried over time if they have such information (Kelley 1973; Kelley and Michela 1980). These *covariation judgments* should be made on the basis of the data from a contingency table formed by crossing D and *not D*, and H and $\hat{H}$. However, people often do not use all these data; in many cases, they focus on only the cell that includes instances of D and H because these are associated in memory (e.g., Shaklee and Tucker 1980; Crocker 1981). Further, people have difficulty detecting low levels of covariation (Jennings et al. 1982). Also, people often must classify instances as D or *not D* and as H or $\hat{H}$; when data are ambiguous, they tend to exhibit confirmation bias in their classifications (Crocker). Finally, judgments of causality can also be affected by seemingly minor factors such as the context or wording of the task.

Second, people can evaluate evidence related to a hypothesis either sequentially, in which case they update their evaluation of a hypothesis after each cue, or as a set, in which case they update after viewing all cues. Research discussed more fully in Chapter 6 indicates that people measure and weight evidence differently depending on whether they view it sequentially or simultaneously. Further, when evidence is viewed sequentially, sequence differences can create different evaluations because people place more weight on early and late cues (Hogarth and Einhorn 1992). Third, when nondiagnostic information is included in a set of cues, people sometimes assume it is relevant and place nonzero weight on it (e.g., Nisbett et al. 1981).[49] Fourth, people differ as to how they weight both negative and positive evidence (Hogarth and Einhorn).

Fifth, further problems arise because of the use of the representativeness heuristic (Kahneman and Tversky 1973). When evidence consists of a summary statistic from a sample, people may not differentially value the evidence derived from samples of different sizes because they focus only on the similarity of the statistic to the hypothesis. Similarly, when people encounter a cue with an extreme value, they tend to associate that cue with an extreme hypothesis or prediction because they fail to understand regression to the mean. Along with this, the evaluation of evidence also can be contingent on the

---

[49]This research also is discussed in Chapter 6.

credibility of the source of evidence, which people often ignore when thinking only about similarity. Appropriate evaluation of evidence conditional on a source is discussed in Chapter 8.

The above problems can relate to both the numerator and denominator of the likelihood ratio. There are additional problems related to the numerator. First, although the likelihood ratio is normatively independent of priors, people who possess strong priors about a hypothesis may overestimate the numerator.[50] For example, Elstein et al. (1978) find that the interpretation of evidence as supportive of a hypothesis when in fact it is not is the most common hypothesis evaluation error among experienced physicians. Second, errors in the measurement of the numerator can be magnified because people tend to place weight on only the numerator; they do not view the denominator as relevant to their evaluation, partially because people tend to evaluate evidence as it relates to each hypothesis independently (Doherty et al. 1979; Beyth-Marom and Fischhoff 1983).

What factors can mitigate problems in this phase? The problem of calculating conditional probabilities is lessened when people's knowledge is structured in a way that facilitates the calculations or the appropriate sample space is otherwise made clear (Eddy 1982; Nisbett et al. 1983; Nelson et al. 1995). Difficulties with covariation judgments are reduced, for example, when people have task-specific knowledge, when data are presented in table form, or when D and H are easy to measure (Crocker 1981). Task-specific knowledge appears to alleviate misunderstandings of the role of sample size, as does highlighting the role of chance in sample results (Nisbett et al.; Smith and Kida 1991). The problem of focusing on only the numerator can be alleviated when there are only two hypotheses to consider; this may be a function of the task or the experimental instructions (Beyth-Marom and Fischhoff 1983). Other moderators are discussed in future chapters. With regard to whether these regularities affect JDM quality defined in relation to a criterion other than a normative standard, problems in covariation judgments can affect quality vis-à-vis actual outcomes (Kunda 1999). Also, individual differences may lead to disagreement. Beyond this, we know little about the effects of problems in this stage on JDM quality vis-à-vis a criterion other than Bayes' Theorem.

The final stage of Bayesian hypothesis evaluation is multiplying the prior odds ratio and the likelihood ratio. This stage can induce problems in JDM, even when people attend to both ratios. First, if people are strongly committed to a particular hypothesis (i.e., the prior odds ratio is high), they may allow this ratio to dominate the final combination process. One reason is simply because the hypothesis is a high-frequency event (Heiman-Hoffman et al. 1995). Second, people sometimes average the ratios rather than multiplying them (Birnbaum and Mellers 1983). Third, people may be asked to express their evaluation that results from this combination in a number of different ways. Again, research on this factor—response mode—is discussed more fully in Chapter 6, but it is important to note the issues related to hypothesis evaluation. For example, people's responses can be different if they are asked to evaluate in terms of numbers (there is a 10% chance) or verbal probability expressions (the chance is remote) (e.g., Budescu et al. 1988; Wallsten et al. 1993). In addition, people interpret

---

[50]People may have strong priors about a hypothesis because, for example, they are being held accountable to someone who is known to favor this hypothesis.

probability expressions such as "remote" quite differently, sometimes producing wide ranges of responses (e.g., Lichtenstein and Newman 1967; Beyth-Maron 1982). Finally, there are various ways of eliciting numerical probabilities (e.g., as direct probabilities or odds), which also create differential responses (Hogarth 1987). Factors that moderate response mode effects are discussed in Chapter 6. Again, we know little about how errors in this stage affect non-normative measures of JDM quality. One example is that overweighting priors can lead to inaccuracy and inefficiency (Heiman-Hoffman et al. 1995). Clearly, individual differences may lead to disagreement as well.[51]

Although Bayes' Theorem serves as a convenient organizing tool for discussing hypothesis evaluation, much research indicates that people do not evaluate hypotheses (or, more generally, evidence) using statistical reasoning. Instead, people make judgments and decisions on the basis of causal or explanation-based reasoning (Shafir et al. 1993; Hastie and Dawes 2001). In this form of reasoning, people think in terms of verbal narratives rather than numbers and calculations. Hastie and Dawes define narratives as "representations of temporally ordered sequences of events glued together by causal relationships." Narratives often are referred to as "stories" (e.g., Pennington and Hastie 1986, 1988, 1992, 1993) or "scenarios" (e.g., Jungermann 1985; Schoemaker 1991, 1993). Sedor (2002) defines scenarios as being "narratives that concretely describe the sequence of events in which proposed actions lead to future outcomes." By contrast, stories typically relate to historical events. Nevertheless, narratives of various forms share certain characteristics: temporal ordering of events, causal relations among events, and the inclusion of concrete, detailed explanations.

As is the case with other cognitive processes, causal reasoning during hypothesis or evidence evaluation can be invoked by various factors such as the presentation format of the task. However, Hastie and Dawes (2001) also posit that one reason this form of reasoning occurs frequently is that the ability to construct such narratives is a relatively hardwired phenomenon. In other words, people also may naturally prefer to reason in this manner, irrespective of various task or environmental factors. In addition, people tend to communicate with others using the narrative form because it is a convenient way of organizing information (e.g., Baumeister and Newman 1994). This suggests the possibility for manipulation of accounting professionals' JDM through this form of communication. For example, managers who communicate to investors in story form may experience different (and more favorable) reactions than those who do not.

No matter how causal reasoning is invoked, the ultimate question of interest is how it affects JDM quality. In general, when individuals provide causal explanations of hypotheses, they assign higher probabilities to those hypotheses than they do otherwise and also are more confident that those events will occur (Kahneman and Tversky 1982). This effect on probability judgments accounts for several violations of normative theories of judgment and decision making (Shafir et al. 1993; Hastie and Dawes 2001). In other words, the use of causal reasoning can lessen JDM quality defined

---

[51]If a decision must be made based on hypothesis evaluation, the normative process is prescribed by expected utility theory (von Neumann and Morgenstern 1947; Savage 1954). As described in Chapter 2, people should combine their subjective probabilities (formed on the basis of Bayesian reasoning) with their utilities and choose the alternative that has the highest expected utility. Of course, people often do not follow this prescribed behavior. For example, people sometimes *satisfice,* which means they choose the first decision alternative that meets a minimum threshold for utility (Simon 1955). Also, people often choose different alternatives depending on how decision alternatives are presented (Hogarth 1987).

vis-à-vis this criterion. Other studies focus on how differences in causal reasoning lead to differences in JDM. In particular, the juror decision-making literature shows that jurors who construct different stories from the evidence they receive choose different verdicts (e.g., Pennington and Hastie 1986, 1988, 1992, 1993). Here, then, JDM quality defined as agreement with others is affected by causal reasoning. Advocates of scenario-based reasoning suggest that the use of multiple scenarios can reduce some of these negative effects of causal reasoning (e.g., Schoemaker 1993); however, empirical evidence does not bear this out (Kuhn and Sniezek 1996). There is little evidence about the effects of causal reasoning on other aspects of JDM quality.

How does causal reasoning affect JDM quality? When causal reasoning is used during hypothesis evaluation, it is used to focus investigation on a particular hypothesis. Focus on that hypothesis leads people to retrieve from memory evidence associated with the hypothesis, search for further confirming evidence, and interpret existing evidence in a way that supports the hypothesis (Koehler 1991). During evidence evaluation, people construct stories or scenarios that best fit the evidence. Although people can construct more than one story, they typically have one they view as most acceptable; it best accounts for all the evidence, is plausible, is complete, and contains no contradictions (Pennington and Hastie 1992). The construction of the story per se then leads directly to a judgment or decision (i.e., causal reasoning effects are not due to differential memory or search for information, but rather due to the organization of the evidence into story form).

Causal reasoning's effects on JDM can be moderated by a few factors. First, narratives are less influential when they are less complete, less detailed, and less plausible, or when it is more difficult to envision a narrative that accounts for the evidence in the first place (Hendrickxx et al. 1989; Koehler 1991; Hastie and Dawes 2001). In addition, asking people to generate counterexplanations can moderate the effects of causal reasoning (Koehler 1991). Counterexplanations do not completely eliminate the effects of causal reasoning in most cases, however. Research indicates that when people first reason about a hypothesis then engage in counterexplanation, there is a primacy effect; counterexplanation is less effective than is the initial causal reasoning.

Effects of Weighting and Combining Cues during Evidence Evaluation

There are a number of additional regularities related to cue weighting and combination during evidence evaluation. First, there are two general ways people can combine evidence (cues) to make judgments or decisions—using compensatory or noncompensatory processes. As discussed earlier, when people use *compensatory processes,* cues can "compensate" for each other. The most frequently assumed compensatory process is that used by the lens model—a *weighted additive rule*—in which people weight each cue by its perceived importance, multiply the cue's value by the weight, then add the weighted values. Compensatory processes are "conflict confronting" (Einhorn and Hogarth 1981); this means that people explicitly determine how to trade off conflicting attributes such as price and quality.

Noncompensatory processes, on the other hand, do not allow cues to compensate for each other; thus, one motive for use of these processes is to avoid conflict. Three general types of noncompensatory processes described by Einhorn (1970) are conjunctive, disjunctive, and lexicographic. *Conjunctive processes* require that all cues exceed a minimum threshold. For example, an investor screening mutual funds may specify that she will not consider any funds with annualized returns below 5% and a manager with less than three years' experience. Thus, funds that have high returns but new managers will not be considered because the high value of the returns cue does not make up for the low value on the manager tenure cue.[52] A *disjunctive process* requires at least one cue to exceed a high threshold and does not attend to other cues. A school that specializes in the arts may employ such a rule for admissions: a student has to be a good singer or dancer or artist, but her other characteristics are irrelevant. A *lexicographic process* determines the most important cue first and chooses the decision alternative with the highest value on that cue; if there is a tie, the process moves on to the second cue and so forth. An additional process delineated by Tversky (1972) is the elimination-by-aspects rule described earlier. Finally, Gigerenzer et al. (1999) posit a very simple process in which people choose the first alternative they recognize; for example, an investor may choose to invest in Microsoft simply because she has heard of it.

There are a variety of factors that propel people toward the conscious use of noncompensatory processes; one is conflict avoidance. People also tend to adopt them when task demands are high and they lack task-specific cue weighting and combination strategies (Payne et al. 1993). High task demands can include complexity and time pressure. As mentioned earlier, people consider the cognitive costs and benefits of processing using either compensatory or noncompensatory schemes, with the latter being less costly. When task demands increase so cognitive costs are likely to go beyond some threshold, people use noncompensatory processes to lower costs substantially. They likely also lower JDM quality, for example, because of the failure to consider relevant cues. Factors that moderate the use of noncompensatory processes are those that increase the benefits of good JDM such as monetary incentives (Arkes 1991) or that lower the costs of processing, such as task-specific knowledge.

People can also use incorrect cue weights and combination rules when they employ compensatory processing. Knowledgeable individuals are more likely to have the correct signs and magnitudes of cue weights because they have received more feedback regarding these weights (Einhorn 1974; Johnson et al. 1981; Johnson 1988; Bonner 1990). However, their cue weights are not always correct when compared to those from a statistical model, for example; nor are they always in agreement with the weights used by other experienced individuals. Another problem that even knowledgeable individuals face is that they sometimes confuse their beliefs with their preferences. That is, because they want a particular judgment outcome to eventuate, they misweight information in a way that makes that outcome appear most likely. This phenomenon, termed "wishful thinking" (Hogarth 1987; Babad and Katz 1991; Babad et al. 1992; Babad and Yacobos 1993; Babad 1995, 1997), is a special case of motivated reasoning (Kunda 1990, 1999) and occurs even when there are monetary incentives to the contrary or people have high amounts of knowledge. Similarly, people generally use linear additive rules to compensatorily combine cues; they tend not to consider interactions or nonlinear relations of cues to outcomes or judgments (Brehmer and Brehmer 1988; Hammond 1996). Knowledgeable individuals may use more sophisticated techniques in situations that call for it; however, they still can exhibit substantial disagreement (Brehmer and Brehmer).

---

[52]The satisficing heuristic is an example of a conjunctive process.

The key issue is to what extent inappropriate cue weighting and combination leads to low-quality JDM. Getting the wrong sign of cues typically reduces JDM quality because people perceive good things to be bad and vice versa. Beyond this, the effect on JDM quality depends on the structure of the task. Getting the magnitude of cue weights wrong often is not a problem for JDM quality because many tasks contain naturally correlated cues. (See Bonner et al. [2003] for an example.) When cues are correlated, different people can use different weights but still agree as to their JDM and also be accurate vis-à-vis outcomes. Further, in these settings, the application of equal or even random weights across cues can lead to JDM that is similar to that based on unequal weights (Dawes 1979). Using linear relations of cues to outcomes or assuming no interactions among cues also is not necessarily bad because linear models often can perform as well as nonlinear models. Overall, then, incorrect cue weighting and combination rules frequently do not reduce JDM quality.

An evidence evaluation process of particular import to accounting is the use of a time series of numbers to predict a future number, such as earnings. Although predictions from time series can be made using statistical models, there are a number of reasons people make these judgments intuitively. For example, they may not have the capability to develop statistical models. Eggleton (1976) characterizes the intuitive time series evaluation process as having three steps. First, people attempt to categorize the process generating the series (e.g., as random). Then they use the category to develop a schema that includes estimates of the mean and variance of the time series. Finally, based on these estimates, people estimate future elements of the series.

There is evidence of judgment errors in all three stages, and these errors lead to incorrect time series judgments. First, people prefer to see patterns in data because structuring tasks makes it easier to reason (Simon 1990). This means that people may categorize time series as being nonrandom when, in fact, they are random. On the other hand, people have difficulty detecting low levels of autocorrelation, meaning that they may fail to categorize time series as nonrandom when, in fact, they are. Further, people are better able to detect positive autocorrelation than negative autocorrelation, suggesting they are less likely to make a correct categorization with the latter (Wagenaar 1972). There also may be differences in the ability to detect different types of generating processes, for example, autoregressive versus moving average. When estimating means, people are relatively accurate with short, low-variance time series. As length and variability increase, accuracy decreases (Peterson and Beach 1967). When estimating variances, people underestimate variances associated with high means because they think of variances as being related to means. They also incorrectly weight deviations from the mean when calculating variance (Peterson and Beach). When extrapolating from these parameters to make a prediction, people rely on their estimates of means and adjust upward or downward; typically, they adjust insufficiently. This is similar to the anchoring and adjustment heuristic (Tversky and Kahneman 1974). Other factors such as noise also can adversely affect time series judgments; the key factor that mitigates process errors in time series predictions is task-specific knowledge (Webby and O'Connor 1996).

A final issue related to hypothesis and evidence evaluation (and other processes) is the extent to which people engage in thinking at all. In some cases, people make judgments and decisions by observing others' judgments and decisions and mimicking them. In particular, they mimic the behavior of a crowd of people. This *herding behavior* is relevant in many accounting settings. For example, analysts can obtain a consensus earnings forecast and investors can observe the consensus of other investors' decisions (the market price). There are many reasons people herd. For example, as discussed in Chapter 4, a lack of confidence in one's JDM or knowledge can lead to herding. It also is suggested that herding is the result of unconscious affective reactions, in particular to stressful situations (Prechter 2001). Whether adoption of others' JDM as one's own leads to high-quality JDM depends on the situation. For example, the consensus analyst forecast may be accurate for a company with high earnings predictability.

Accounting Studies on Test Design

Accounting studies related to hypothesis and evidence evaluation are plentiful; thus, this section groups studies based on phase of the process. The first studies are those related to test design in auditing. Joyce (1976), Abdel-Khalik et al. (1983), and Trotman (1985) find low agreement among auditors as to hours planned for testing. Aly and Duboff (1971), Biggs and Mock (1983), and Kachelmeier and Messier (1990) find low agreement among auditors as to their judgments of appropriate sample size. The last study also finds that auditors sometimes work backward from desired sample sizes to estimate parameters that would produce those sample sizes. Cohen and Kida (1989) find experience-related differences in auditors' choices of sample size, but it is unknown which group has better quality design. Biggs et al. (1988) also find experience-related differences. Managers increase sample sizes for tests related to specific hypothesized error causes, whereas seniors increase sample sizes for all tests related to an account that may be in error; managers' JDM clearly is more efficient, then.

Several studies examine choice of specific tests. Biggs et al. (1987) examine the quality of computer audit specialists' choices as compared to a solution created by firm-designated experts and find a fairly high level of quality among these specialists. Wright (1988a) uses a similar procedure but finds that auditors miss several critical tests related to the inventory account and also include some inappropriate tests. Bonner and Lewis (1990) find that managers choose more theoretically correct tests related to control weaknesses than do seniors. Brown and Solomon (1991) find that auditors understand test substitutabilities, which is important for efficiency purposes.

Brown et al. (1999) examine two key facets of auditors' choice of tests: their expected diagnostic value and the extent to which they are likely to be confirmatory of a given hypothesis. They also examine the extent to which auditors can adapt their choice of tests to differences in relations between a beginning hypothesis and the correct hypothesis. For example, the beginning hypothesis may be "embedded" within the correct hypothesis; in other words, it is too narrow. In their first study, students and auditors doing an abstract hypothesis-testing task under incentives that reward "truth discovery" are more likely to detect the theoretically correct hypothesis if they use tests that can rule out the beginning hypothesis. Further, they show adaptivity in choice of tests and tend to choose diagnostic tests. A second study uses an auditing scenario and finds less evidence of quality in choice of tests. Auditors often choose tests that are likely to confirm client-suggested hypotheses and overestimate the diagnostic value of these tests. Finally, Asare et al. (2000) examine auditors' choice of tests to investigate causes of a ratio fluctuation and find that the number of hypotheses tested, but not the number of tests per hypothesis or overall, affects whether auditors determine the correct cause.

Consistent with psychology, studies of test design in auditing find differences in quality of design among auditors that appear to be knowledge related. Further, even knowledgeable auditors do not always choose the most diagnostic tests and sometimes exhibit confirmation bias in their choice of tests. Unfortunately, we know very little about the effects of the choice of tests on ultimate JDM quality. This is important to investigate because it is not clear how errors in such choices may affect auditors' JDM. That is, do they simply result in efficiency problems because auditors eventually discover the right tests to use, or do they result in effectiveness problems? Do the effects of test design on JDM quality depend on other factors? There is great potential for continuing research in this area.

Accounting Studies on Weighting and Combining Cues during Hypothesis Evaluation

A number of studies examine various facets of cue weighting and combination during hypothesis evaluation.[53] Studies related to estimation and use of priors and likelihood ratios include the following in management accounting. Magee and Dickhaut (1978) and Lewis et al. (1983) examine students' use of heuristics in a cost variance investigation setting. They find that students predominantly use a "control chart" strategy, which is akin to the representativeness heuristic. Further, Lewis et al. measure evaluation with protocols and find very little reference to priors. Brown (1985) examines students' evaluations of possible causes of a cost variance given information about base rates of these causes, and confirming or disconfirming evidence regarding covariation of these causes with the particular variance, or temporal order—whether the cause is present during the time period of the variance. He finds that subjects increase (decrease) their judged probabilities of the initial most likely cause given confirming (disconfirming) temporal order evidence. Confirming (disconfirming) covariation evidence causes no change (a decrease) in these probabilities. Further, students overwhelmingly request the H and D cell of the provided covariation table. Brown (1987), in a similar study, also provides information about the magnitude of deviations from normal of each cause to investigate whether subjects evaluate hypotheses using the similarity (representativeness) of the magnitude of the cause deviation and the magnitude of the variance. Evaluations are affected by both similarity and covariation.

In tax, Johnson (1993) finds that tax professionals place more weight on court cases that are supportive of their client's desired tax treatment than on those that are not; in turn, these confirmatory evaluations lead to higher assessed probabilities of success and stronger recommendations regarding tax treatment. Further, higher priors regarding success also lead to greater confirmation in evaluation of evidence. Marchant et al. (1991) find that tax professionals sometimes are better able than students to use information from a substantively similar precedent to identify facts and issues in a new tax case, and sometimes they are not. Marchant et al. (1993) find that both tax professionals and students can identify a substantively similar case; however, when the predicted outcome of the case goes against the client, both groups rely more on only superficially similar cases to identify facts and issues, consistent with a confirmation bias in evaluation. The ability to use a substantively similar case can indicate

---

[53]Recall that accounting studies related to information search during hypothesis evaluation are summarized earlier.

high-quality JDM from the perspective of compliance with professional standards. However, in a further exploration, Davis and Mason (2003) find that tax professionals focus principally on features common to the taxpayer's situation and the precedent when judging similarity rather than also focusing on features that differ, as called for by professional standards. Barrick et al. (2004) report that tax professionals reviewing a hypothetical staff accountant's memo find a memo biased (incorrectly) toward the client's preferred position is more persuasive than one biased toward the correct tax treatment. However, they also find that a memo that is not biased toward the correct tax treatment is viewed as more persuasive than one that is biased toward this treatment. Finally, Kahle and White (2004) show that tax professionals revise their initial beliefs regarding proper tax treatment more when evidence supports their client's preferred position than when it does not but do not exhibit confirmation bias vis-à-vis their own initial beliefs.

In financial accounting, Johnson (1983) examines whether students predicting bankruptcy use the representativeness heuristic. He finds that they ignore base rates when they believe the ratios are representative of bankruptcy or nonbankruptcy, and underweight base rates when the ratios are viewed as not representative. A number of studies examine the use of base rates by loan officers predicting bankruptcy (Casey 1983; Houghton 1984; Casey and Selling 1986; van Breda and Ferris 1992). These studies follow earlier conflicting studies regarding base rates' effects on accuracy by Libby (1975), Zimmer (1980), and Casey (1980a) and suggest that the reason for the conflict is that Casey does not disclose the population base rates, whereas Libby and Zimmer do. Thus, subjects in Casey's study likely use their own perceived base rates. This is important because these studies use samples in which half the firms are bankrupt firms, far higher than the true population rate. Not surprisingly, these follow-on studies find conflicting findings regarding the use of base rates depending on disclosure thereof. Overall, prediction accuracy is fairly high in these studies, but accuracy does seem to be higher when sample base rates are closer to true population base rates and, thus, to subjects' priors.[54] Finally, Hammersley et al. (1997) find that students who explain a hypothesized cause of an account fluctuation estimate a higher probability for that cause than do students who do not explain it.

Consistent with auditing being a diagnostic process, hypothesis evaluation studies involving auditing tasks are plentiful. Studies on the estimation and use of priors include Swieringa et al. (1976), who find that students do not appear to always use the representativeness heuristic in abstract or auditing cases; thus, they do not always neglect base rates. Joyce and Biddle (1981b) and Holt (1987) show that auditors use base rates in several contexts but underweight them somewhat. Kida (1984a) finds that auditors predicting bankruptcy generally underweight base rates but do so less when they are causally related to the bankruptcy outcome. Kaplan et al. (1992) report that experienced auditors are more likely to rank hypotheses related to ratio fluctuation in terms of base rates than are inexperienced auditors. Asare and Wright (1995, 1997a, 1997b) find that auditors evaluating self-generated or provided sets of hypotheses for ratio fluctuations exhibit supra-additivity, although their priors reflect relative base

---

[54] A few studies (e.g., Ganguly et al. 1994) examine the use of the representativeness heuristic in experimental markets involving abstract tasks. These studies generally find underweighting of base rates even with large monetary incentives.

rates. Tuttle (1996) shows that auditors rate hypothesized causes of ratio fluctuations in the order suggested by their base rates. Mock et al. (1997) find that about half the auditors in their study attend to prior probabilities and the other half rely exclusively on situation-specific evidence. Finally, Heiman (1990) shows that auditors who generate a larger number of alternative hypotheses for ratio fluctuations are more likely to discount the probability of an initial hypothesis, suggesting many auditors generate incomplete sets of hypotheses.

The next several studies examine auditors' estimation and use of the likelihood ratio. First, Nelson et al. (1995) and Bonner et al. (1996) find that auditors who must judge conditional probabilities that are relatively inconsistent with their knowledge structures tend to reverse those conditionals so they are more consistent. Second, Waller and Felix (1987) report that auditors' covariation judgments are correlated more with correct rules for judging covariation than with incorrect rules (such as the use of only one cell), although absolute levels often are over- or underestimated. Several studies find that auditors revise their probability judgments more when they receive negative versus positive evidence, but there is substantial variation in reactions to both positive and negative evidence (Kida 1984b; Ashton and Ashton 1988, 1990; Butt and Campbell 1989; Trotman and Sng 1989; Knechel and Messier 1990; Anderson and Maletta 1994).[55]

Next, several studies examine auditors' use of the representativeness heuristic in this stage of the process. Swieringa et al. (1976) find that students do not always fail to appreciate the importance of sample size. Uecker and Kinney (1977) report that auditors do not consistently use this heuristic when evaluating the results of tests of controls done with sampling. Nevertheless, a substantial portion of the auditors still make theoretical errors because, although they attend to sample size, they underweight it. Nelson (1995) finds that auditors consider sample size in evaluating sample results but underweight it. Finally, two studies examine another effect of the use of the representativeness heuristic—the *conjunction fallacy*. Here, people judge the probability of a conjunction of events to be higher than that of one or both of the separate events, inconsistent with probability theory. Frederick and Libby (1986) and Ho and May (1993) find that auditors and students exhibit this fallacy in auditing judgments.

Several studies examine confirmation bias during hypothesis evaluation. Butt and Campbell (1989) find that auditors given instructions to confirm prior beliefs about an internal control system make higher probability judgments (given the same set of evidence) than those instructed to disconfirm prior beliefs or those given no instructions. Church (1991) finds that auditors who view confirming and disconfirming evidence interpret evidence as consistent with their initially hypothesized control weakness, irrespective of the error they choose. However, McMillan and White (1993) find that auditors attend more to disconfirming than to confirming evidence when evaluating causes of ratio fluctuations. Next, a number of studies find that auditors evaluating causes of ratio fluctuations evaluate hypotheses independently; in other words, they focus only on the numerator of the likelihood ratio (Asare and Wright 1995, 1997a, 1997b). Finally, Heiman-Hoffman et al. (1995) find that auditors who

---

[55]However, see Pei et al. (1992b), who find the opposite result. They conjecture that this occurs because their task is a performance audit rather than a financial audit; in the former setting, positive evidence is atypical, whereas it is not in the latter.

generate a highly frequent error as a hypothesized cause of ratio fluctuations have difficulty moving away from this hypothesis during evaluation when faced with disconfirming evidence.

The remaining studies examine a variety of issues. Anderson and Wright (1988) examine auditors' and students' evaluations of hypothesized errors caused by control weaknesses. Students (auditors) asked to provide explanations for a particular hypothesized error provide (do not provide) higher probability judgments. Koonce (1992) finds that auditors asked to provide explanations (counterexplanations) related to a hypothesized cause of a ratio fluctuation estimate higher (lower) probabilities than do control subjects. Koonce and Phillips (1996) find that client-suggested nonerror causes for ratio fluctuations are judged more probable when they are easy to comprehend.

Studies related to the cue weighting and combination stages of hypothesis evaluation indicate that accounting and business students tend to exhibit many of the regularities found in psychology studies (e.g., the use of representativeness and the consequent neglect or underweighting of base rates and sample size information and the failure to use all information when judging covariation). However, accounting professionals are less likely to exhibit many of these regularities, consistent with knowledge being critical in allowing adaptive mechanisms to work more effectively. For example, auditors are more sensitive to base rates and sample size information than the general population. Further, they are less likely to exhibit confirmation bias during the evaluation phase. Nevertheless, auditors, who are the most likely to acquire knowledge pertinent to Bayesian hypothesis evaluation because of their statistical training and rich experiences, still make systematic errors. For example, they tend to underweight base rates and sample size information, specify incomplete sets of hypotheses, exhibit supraadditivity, estimate the wrong conditional probabilities, and evaluate hypotheses independently. Many of these studies also find that auditors are conservative in their probability judgments; that is, they tend to err on the side of judgments that are too high for negative events such as bankruptcy.

The key question that arises from these findings is that posed by Asare and Wright (1995). If auditors (or other accounting professionals) do not evaluate hypotheses in a Bayesian fashion and, thus, exhibit JDM quality problems when quality is defined vis-à-vis normative theory, what is the impact of such behavior on other dimensions of JDM quality (e.g., accuracy vis-à-vis outcomes)? If there are few ill effects, these errors may not be troublesome. In other words, auditors (and others) may have adapted to deal with their bounded rationality so it aids them on the JDM quality dimensions that matter most to them. On the other hand, errors may have serious consequences that are necessary costs of adaptation (Arkes 1991). Further research should investigate this issue.

Accounting Studies on Weighting and Combining Cues during Evidence Evaluation

Turning now to evidence evaluation studies, several studies examine stock price predictions or investment choices. Slovic (1969) and Slovic et al. (1972) find substantial disagreement among stockbrokers and students as to price judgments, cue weights, and the extent of configural processing, with some brokers exhibiting substantial amounts of the latter. Wright (1977a, 1979) finds relatively low accuracy and moderate disagreement among students, along with moderate matching indexes and response linearity and some nonlinear processing. Anderson (1988) finds that analysts employ different cue weights than investors and make different investment decisions. Olsen (1997) finds that money managers exhibit wishful thinking in rating the probability of several economic events.

Next, Lipe (1998) finds that student investors have difficulty using covariance information when judging the risk of and ranking investments; in particular, their misunderstanding leads to internally inconsistent choices. Amir and Ganzach (1998) examine how analysts may use both the representativeness and anchoring and adjustment heuristics when making earnings forecasts. They find that analysts appear to use anchoring when they have a salient anchor available; previous forecasts are more salient than previous earnings and are particularly salient when the analyst is considering a downward revision in her forecast. Anchoring leads to inaccurate revised forecasts due to insufficient adjustment. In other situations where representativeness is more prevalent, inaccuracies are due to extremeness in predictions. Sedor (2002) examines the effects of causal (or scenario-based) reasoning on analysts' earnings forecasts; analysts make more optimistic forecasts if they engage in causal reasoning than if they do not; this effect is greater for firms in a loss situation than for profitable firms.

A number of studies also examine time series predictions.[56] Eggleton (1976) examines students' predictions of production costs under varying time series conditions. Subjects make similar estimates for random and negatively autocorrelated sequences, suggesting they do not detect the pattern in the latter; however, they make higher estimates for positively autocorrelated series. In addition, subjects' predictions for the series perceived to be random or negatively autocorrelated are close to their estimated means; in turn, these estimates are relatively accurate and too high, respectively, vis-à-vis predictions from a statistical model. Predictions for the positively autocorrelated series reflect their estimated means plus an insufficient adjustment, indicating they are lower than those from a statistical model. Along with this, predictions for high-variance series are higher than those for low-variance series, despite no differences in means. Eggleton (1982) reports similar results.

Andreassen (1987) reports that students predicting stock prices are more prone to be nonregressive in their predictions, consistent with the representativeness heuristic, when they read media stories providing causal explanations for the series. In other words, they move too far from the mean of the series. As a consequence, their trading profits are lower. Andreassen and Kraus (1990) find that predictions are less regressive when students see multiple instances of the same trend; in this case, however, the less regressive predictors are more accurate. Maines and Hand (1996) report that students' predictions of quarterly earnings reflect but underweight the moving average and autoregressive components of time series. They suggest that these errors are due to both misunderstanding of the process and insufficient adjustment from estimated means.

Calegari and Fargher (1997) also find that students underweight time series components in an experimental market setting, consistent with anchoring and insufficient adjustment. Bloomfield et al. (2003) use an experimental market but rely on a different theoretical framework that suggests people place too much weight on relatively

---

[56]A few of these studies examine predictions of production costs rather than financial accounting numbers, but it is most expedient to discuss these studies together.

unreliable information. In an earnings time series context, this would be old information. They predict and find that such overweighting can lead to either an under- or overweighting of time series components, depending on whether current earnings are similar in level to old earnings. Finally, a number of archival studies report that analysts' earnings forecasts are more accurate than statistical time series models' forecasts (Schipper 1991). However, these studies also find that analysts and investors make errors in their time series predictions that are consistent with misweighting of time series components (e.g., Bernard and Thomas 1990; Mendenhall 1991; Abarbanell and Bernard 1992; Ball and Bartov 1996; Brown and Han 2000).

Next, several studies examine bankruptcy predictions or other credit-related judgments. Abdel-Khalik and El-Sheshai (1980) find that cue weighting accounts for a small amount of inaccuracy among loan officers making default judgments. Similarly, Chalos and Pickard (1985) and Lewis et al. (1988) find little effect of cue weighting and response linearity on accuracy vis-à-vis outcomes of default judgments and bond ratings, respectively. Schepanski (1983) finds little evidence of configural processing among students making creditworthiness judgments. Schneider and Selling (1996) find that nonlinear models fit students' bankruptcy predictions better than linear models only when task complexity is low. Biggs et al. (1985) find the use of noncompensatory processes in response to task complexity by loan officers making choices regarding to which company a loan should be granted. Finally, Paquette and Kida (1988) examine accountants' choices of companies with the highest bond ratings from among a set; subjects are trained to use compensatory or noncompensatory strategies. Subjects using noncompensatory strategies are more efficient but no less accurate vis-à-vis actual ratings.

Studies of auditors' evaluation of evidence include many related to control risk assessments. Ashton (1974a, 1974b) finds moderately high agreement among auditors as to their assessments and cue weights; also, there is little evidence of configural processing. Ashton and Kramer (1980) and Ashton and Brown (1980) find similar results with, respectively, students and auditors. Hamilton and Wright (1982) find similar results and that experienced auditors do not exhibit more agreement than inexperienced auditors. Bonner (1990), however, finds that managers exhibit higher agreement than seniors and that this is due principally to higher agreement on cue weights. Brown and Solomon (1990) design cases where configural processing should be present because control procedures have interactive effects on control risk, and they find more such processing than do earlier studies.

Similarly, several studies examine evidence evaluation during other risk and reliance judgments. Brown (1983) and Schneider (1984) find results similar to those of Ashton (1974a, 1974b) with auditors evaluating reliance on internal auditors. However, Maletta (1993) and Maletta and Kida (1993) find configural processing for this judgment under certain conditions. Colbert (1988) finds results similar to Ashton's in an inherent risk setting. Bonner (1990) finds that managers exhibit higher agreement about analytical procedures risk than do seniors and that this is due to higher agreement about cue weights. Brown and Solomon (1991) find results similar to their earlier study with judgments of detection risk.

Along with these studies, Moriarity and Barron (1976) find that auditors' judgments of materiality are mostly linear additive. Raghunandan et al. (1991) find auditors' processing of information related to disclosure and audit reporting on loss contingencies to be compensatory in nature; this is consistent with the auditing standards but not the financial accounting standards. Simnett and Trotman (1989) find that inappropriate cue weights cause errors in auditors' predictions of bankruptcy but only when they use cues provided by the experimenter (rather than choosing their own cues). Rosman et al. (1999) find substantial configural processing in going-concern judgments.

Two studies examine auditors' use of precedent evidence in determining accounting treatments. Salterio (1996) reports that similarity of precedents affects auditors' judgments about accounting treatments but client preferences do not. However, his archival study shows that audit firm research units tend to select only precedents that are consistent with client preferences. In a follow-up study, Salterio and Koonce (1997) report that similarity affects reliance on precedent evidence. Further, when precedents are consistent, auditors' judgments reflect the treatment suggested by the precedents; but when precedents are mixed, auditors interpret them to support the client's position.

Finally, although the finance literature is replete with discussions and analytical models related to herding (e.g., Scharfstein and Stein 1990; Froot et al. 1992; Trueman 1994; Prechter 2001), there is little empirical evidence about the effects of this behavior on JDM quality. Extant evidence mostly relates to the presence of herding or its economic consequences such as stock returns. Shiller and Pound (1989), based on a survey, report that institutional investors exhibit herding behavior for volatile stocks. Grinblatt et al. (1995) find herding among mutual fund managers, but this herding has no effect on returns. Similarly, Wermers (1999) reports herding in small stocks among mutual fund managers; however, herding has positive effects on returns of these stocks. Nofsinger and Sias (1999) document behavior consistent with herding among institutional investors, and herding is positively associated with returns. Graham (1999) finds herding among investment newsletters. In contrast, Lakonishok et al. (1992) finds little evidence of herding by investors. In the lone experimental study, Cote and Sanders (1997) find herding among investors. Finally, Hong et al. (2000) report that inexperienced analysts are more likely than experienced analysts to exhibit herding, and Clement and Tse (2005) find that herding among analysts is positively related to prior accuracy, brokerage size, and experience and is negatively related to number of industries followed. Further, "herding forecasts" are less accurate than are "bold forecasts."

Accounting studies about cue weighting and combination during evidence evaluation report findings similar to psychology studies. In difficult tasks such as stock price prediction, there can be substantial disagreement about cue weights; in simpler tasks such as some of the experimental tasks involving internal control evaluation, there is more agreement. Further, cue weight accuracy (vis-à-vis a model) or agreement is associated with high-quality JDM; however, cue weight inaccuracy or disagreement is not necessarily associated with low-quality JDM. The latter result likely occurs because of the redundancies among cues. Accountants tend to use linear additive processing unless experimental tasks are constructed to allow them to exhibit nonlinear or configural processing. However, studies that demonstrate something other than linear additive processing tend not to examine the effect of this on JDM quality; thus, the importance of such processes remains unclear. Studies of time series predictions find that students make errors similar to those documented in psychology. Professionals tend to make errors as well, although they can outperform statistical models. Finally, some studies document herding among investors and accounting professionals such as money managers, but it is unclear how such behavior affects individuals' JDM quality and the related consequences.

5-8 SUMMARY

This chapter completes the discussion of person variables by examining cognitive processing regularities that affect JDM quality. Many of these process regularities and related errors occur because of the combination of processing constraints people face and the adaptive mechanisms they have developed to circumvent these constraints. That is, the adaptive mechanisms are largely helpful but not perfect; they cannot completely circumvent the constraints, and their use also carries unavoidable costs (Arkes 1991).

Specifically, the chapter discusses the effects of various aspects of memory retrieval, information search, problem representation, hypothesis generation, and hypothesis and evidence evaluation. Many of the findings of accounting studies parallel those from psychological studies of the general population. The largest differences are found in studies of auditors' processes. Auditors may be less susceptible to confirmation bias during information search and hypothesis evaluation. Further, their requirements to exercise professional skepticism (along with the related potential for litigation payments) may make them choose more conservative representations, to focus more on negative information, and to make conservatively negative probability judgments. Auditors also appear to be less susceptible to ill effects of the representativeness heuristic such as base-rate neglect and insensitivity to sample size information either because they are less likely to use the heuristic or because the knowledge on which the heuristic piggybacks is superior. Finally, auditors may process more configurally than other decision makers under the right circumstances.

Future research on cognitive processes in accounting should continue to document process regularities, particularly for individuals whose processes are underexplored, such as management accountants and investors. More important, along the lines of Asare and Wright (1995), research should be extended to examine the effects of processes on various aspects of JDM quality. This is critical to understanding the extent to which accountants' processes are properly adapted to their environments, as well as whether such adaptation comes at significant costs for accountants, as it does for the general population. Finally, work must continue to explore process issues that are of particular significance and perhaps unique to accounting contexts. For example, the use of global models to generate hypotheses typically does not lead to high-quality JDM, yet this may be the favored technique in areas such as financial analysis. Research could explore what factors have influenced the adoption of this technique and whether it has other positive effects that offset its possible negative effects during hypothesis generation.

CHAPTER

6

Task Variables

This chapter examines the effects of task variables on JDM quality (see Figure 6-1). *Task variables* are characteristics or dimensions of tasks that vary across tasks but, more important, can vary within tasks. The latter variation may be more worrisome for JDM because people can exhibit vastly different JDM quality for a single task that varies on a seemingly minor characteristic such as the order in which it presents information cues. The specific variables discussed in this chapter are task complexity, relevance of information, framing of tasks and information, order of information, presentation format, and response mode.[1]

These task variables are not unique to accounting settings, yet their importance cannot be understated. Many psychologists view task characteristics as being one of the principal forces explaining JDM behavior in all fields (e.g., Simon 1990; Shanteau 1992a; Hogarth 1993; Stewart et al. 1997). There are two key reasons task characteristics are important in shaping JDM. First, task characteristics have a static effect on JDM; at a given point in time, task characteristics can hinder or assist JDM. This idea is captured nicely by the "environmental predictability" component of the lens model (see Chapter 5). JDM quality in the lens model is affected not only by people's processing, but also by the ability of the set of information cues to predict a particular outcome. For some tasks, there are sets of cues that predict outcomes very well (not so well); these tasks have high (low) environmental predictability. The higher a task's environmental predictability, the more likely it is people have high-quality JDM because the task essentially is easier. Second, people acquire knowledge and processing strategies over time that are adapted to the tasks they face. For example, when people face tasks for which information cues are highly correlated, they may learn a strategy of focusing on only one or a few cues rather than all cues. Thus, overall, task characteristics can have strong effects on JDM quality. They can limit or assist JDM directly in the short term. They can also affect the knowledge and processing strategies people acquire in the long term and, thus, indirectly affect JDM quality through these person variables. Given the importance of knowledge and cognitive processes to JDM, task variables can have substantial effects on JDM quality.

More important, task variables, as a group, may be those that are most unique to accounting. As Kinney (2001) notes, one of the key value-added activities offered by

---

[1]Consistent with other chapters, each section discusses a single variable, beginning with its definition and classifications. Following this is information about the variable's effects on JDM quality and mediators and moderators of those effects. Then each section discusses how to study the variable through manipulation or measurement and concludes by summarizing accounting studies and offering directions for future research. One exception to this structure is that presentation format and response mode issues are discussed together because of their similarities.

FIGURE 6-1 **Framework for JDM Research in Accounting**

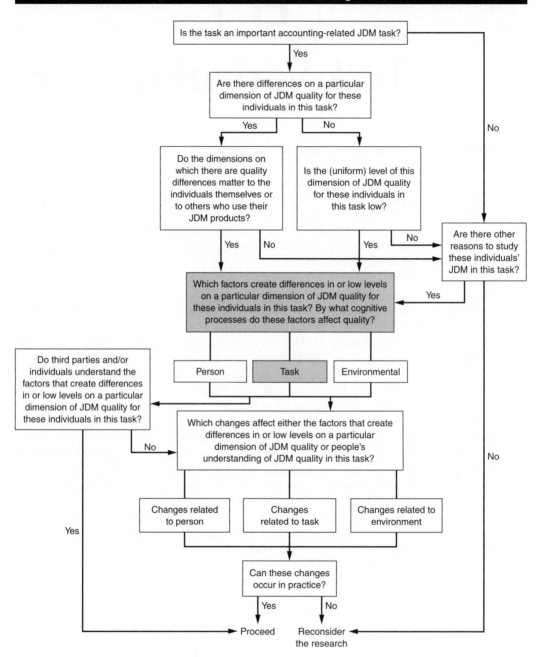

accountants is the standardization of tasks for users of accounting information. There are a number of elements of accounting's standardization of tasks. First, accounting attaches numbers to many items (e.g., Kadous et al. 2005). For example, many items in firms' annual reports appear in numerical format, whereas others are described qualitatively. Second, accounting shapes to what degree numerical items are aggregated and summarized for report purposes. For example, financial statements show the total amount of cash a firm has rather than listing separately, for example, cash in individual bank accounts. Third, accounting dictates how numerical items are presented (e.g., in what categories they are placed and where they appear in reports). For example, accounting dictates whether items are classified as liabilities or equity in the balance sheet.[2]

Consistent with the importance of these task characteristics in accounting, standard-setters and regulators spend a great deal of time debating issues related to the effects of specific standardization mechanisms on users' JDM. Based on their debates, policy makers prescribe particular standardization mechanisms. Empirical research that illuminates the effects of these task variables can be of enormous practical importance for these debates. Specifically, research can examine not only the effects of various characteristics of accounting tasks as currently prescribed, but also how various changes to tasks might improve or worsen the quality of users' JDM. Further, research that investigates factors that affect standard-setters' choices of task characteristics (e.g., their understanding of empirical research) could be useful in improving the standard-setting process. Of additional importance is the fact that individuals other than policy makers can influence task characteristics and perhaps do so strategically to influence accounting professionals' JDM. For example, clients can frame information for auditors in an attempt to persuade auditors to reach a desired conclusion. These issues are discussed in each of the sections that follow.

6-1   EFFECTS OF TASK COMPLEXITY ON JDM QUALITY

Definitions and Background

Task complexity typically is thought to be synonymous with either *task difficulty,* which refers to the amount of attentional capacity or cognitive processing the task requires (Kahneman 1973), or *task structure,* which refers to the level of specification of what is to be done in the task (Simon 1973).[3] Clearly, task complexity can differ across tasks; for example, detecting management fraud likely is more difficult than evaluating internal controls related to the payroll function. Further, complexity can vary within tasks. For example, one bank may require its loan officers to make creditworthiness judgments on the basis of a few financial ratios and a credit rating, whereas another bank requires its officers to use 10 ratios and a number of other information cues. Thus, task complexity can result from natural characteristics of tasks or from requirements imposed by humans.

---

[2]These standardization choices can have effects on numerous task characteristics, including complexity, framing, and presentation format.
[3]Research debates whether task complexity is a function of the task per se, or rather a joint function of the task and the person doing the task (Hackman 1969; Fleishman 1975; Wood 1986; Campbell 1988). This section discusses the variable as a function of the task and describes how various person variables interact with complexity.

The difficulty element of task complexity relates to the amount of cognitive processing a task requires (Bonner 1994). Amount of processing can vary as a result of several factors. First, the number of processing steps people must go through can vary (Wood 1986); for example, multiplication problems differ as to the number of steps required based on the number of digits being multiplied. Second, amount of processing can vary due to the number of distinct information cues available; the number of hypotheses or judgment solutions to consider; or for decisions, the number of alternatives to consider (Schroder et al. 1967; Kahneman 1973; Steinmann 1976; Beach and Mitchell 1978; Wood 1986; Campbell 1988; Payne et al. 1993). The number of information cues available often is referred to as *information load* (Schroder et al. 1967). Although increases in the number of distinct information cues can increase load and complexity, correlation among cues decreases load and complexity because people may be able to ignore many cues.[4] This is important to keep in mind in accounting environments where information cues often are correlated. Finally, amount of processing varies with the number of goals present in a task (Campbell 1988). For example, an auditor may have goals related to both effectiveness and efficiency.[5] Amount of processing can increase if each goal carries unique information cues (to the extent these cues are correlated, of course, number of goals does not increase complexity).

The structure element of task complexity relates to the clarity of cognitive processing created by elements of the task (Bonner 1994). Clarity is affected first by the extent to which information cues are specified. For example, radiologists examining X-rays do not view a neat list of information cues, but instead have to find those cues. (Is the black spot on the film a cue to disease or just bad photography?) Whether cues are measured already also affects clarity. Further, if cues are presented in a form similar to that stored in memory, clarity is greater.[6]

The relations between information cues and outcomes (or, more generally, task outputs) also affect clarity of processing. Research indicates that four aspects of these relations are particularly important: magnitude, sign, consistency, and functional form (Steinmann 1976; Wood 1986; Campbell 1988).[7] Cue-criterion relations that are of higher magnitude (individually or collectively for the set of cues) are easier for people to detect, understand, and incorporate into JDM (e.g., Naylor and Clark 1968; Brehmer 1973). For example, predicting bankruptcy one year ahead is easier than predicting bankruptcy two years ahead because the overall relation between cues and bankruptcy is of greater magnitude in the former case (Simnett and Trotman 1989). Cue-criterion relations that have positive signs are clearer for people to process because people naturally think in terms of positive relations (e.g., Naylor and Clark; Brehmer 1972, 1973). Cues that, as a set, have consistent relations with a criterion are clearer to process than are cues that have inconsistent relations with a criterion (Brehmer 1972). Because people naturally think in terms of linear functions, this functional form is easier to process than other forms (e.g., Brehmer 1973; Schmitt and Dudycha 1975). Finally, if processing

---

[4]This assumes that people can recognize redundancy among cues. Clearly, this is an empirical question; such recognition likely is affected by many factors such as knowledge of the domain.

[5]More generally, it may be the case that task complexity increases whenever two or more JDM quality dimensions are important to a decision maker. However, multiple quality dimensions may affect factors other than task complexity. For example, they may create conflicting incentives.

[6]Certain presentation formats, such as graphs versus tables, may affect clarity of processing as well (Hwang and Wu 1990; Vessey 1991). See Chapter 9 for further discussion.

[7]Further, if these characteristics change over time, complexity increases (Wood 1986).

steps are prespecified or independent of each other, processing is clearer than if steps are not specified or are interdependent (Simon 1973; Greeno 1976; Campbell and Gingrich 1986; Wood 1986; Campbell 1988; Smith 1988).

Given that research on task complexity spans a wide range of domains, this variable clearly is not unique to accounting. There is no doubt, however, that it is relevant to accounting JDM. As described earlier, complexity can vary both across and within accounting JDM tasks. Further, standard-setters, politicians, and others in positions to dictate accounting tasks' requirements (e.g., the bank loan officer's superiors described above) have the conscious capability to make tasks less complex but inadvertently may make them more complex when attempting to achieve other goals. For example, in using rules-based standards as a way of constraining strategic financial reporting behavior, the FASB may make standards more complex (Nelson 2003). As another example, Congress may increase the complexity of the tax system when attempting to reduce inequities (Plumlee 2003). These changes to more complex standards may lead to lowered JDM quality for users of the systems (e.g., investors and taxpayers) and related economic consequences such as lowered investment returns or overpayment of taxes. The next section discusses the effects of task complexity on JDM quality.

Task Complexity Effects

On average, task complexity has a negative effect on JDM quality beyond some level; this level may differ depending on the element of complexity involved. Typically, studies show that task complexity has a negative effect on JDM quality defined as accuracy vis-à-vis outcomes or correspondence with either normative theories or professional standards. However, it also is possible to examine the effects of task complexity on agreement with others and with oneself over time; again, the prediction would be that complexity has a negative effect on these elements of quality.

Whether task complexity has no effect or a positive effect on JDM quality prior to the level at which its negative effects begin is debatable. For example, Wood (1986) proposes that increases in task complexity initially have a positive effect on JDM quality because such increases provide motivation in the form of arousal (see Chapter 4), which has an inverted-U relation with quality (Yerkes and Dodson 1908; Eysenck 1982). As another example, empirical findings related to the information load element of task complexity often indicate higher initial JDM quality with increases in load. However, these effects likely are confounded by the fact that, as the number of cues increases, people have not only greater processing to do, but also better information to process. This occurs because additional cues are relevant (associated with the judgment or decision in question) and they are not completely correlated with already existing cues. Thus, positive effects of task complexity in these studies (up to some point) likely are positive effects of information content instead. Because of these issues, further discussion portrays task complexity as having no effect on JDM quality till some point; after this point, it has a negative effect.

How do these effects of task complexity occur? Some of the effects occur because task complexity plays into the processing limitations described in Chapter 5. That is, complexity can have negative effects on JDM when it is high enough to tax the short-term memory constraint and/or the computational speed constraint, and no effects prior to these points. The short-term memory constraint may be exceeded due to difficulty elements of complexity such as information load. Task structure/clarity elements of complexity also can tax the short-term memory constraint because people may need to hold both "unclarified" and "clarified" information in short-term memory. Further, as complexity increases, computational speed constraints increase the probability of not completing a task in a given time period. When these constraints are taxed due to complexity, people may end up not using all relevant information because they simply cannot, and failure to use relevant information can reduce JDM quality. For example, if an auditor has five hypotheses under consideration, she may focus on only one information cue per hypothesis in order not to exceed the short-term memory constraint. However, if she has two hypotheses under consideration, she may be able to examine up to four cues per hypothesis simultaneously.

Complex tasks can also lessen JDM quality because they do not match people's knowledge structures or the ways in which they think. As mentioned previously, some tasks contain cues that have nonlinear relations to outcomes, but people appear to be hardwired to think in terms of linear relations (e.g., Summers and Hammond 1966; Brehmer et al. 1974). When such a mismatch occurs, people attempt to clarify tasks, that is, make them less complex. Clarification consists either of adjusting knowledge structures or thinking to meet task characteristics or adjusting task characteristics to comply with natural structures or modes of thinking. People tend to prefer the latter technique because it is easier than attempting to adjust memory. Unfortunately, this mode of clarification can change tasks in substantive ways, and these changes can lessen JDM quality. Further, such effects occur irrespective of processing constraints because amount of processing is not an issue. For example, Nelson et al. (1995) find that auditors appear to restructure conditional probability judgments that are not consistent with preferred knowledge structures to be consistent with those structures and, as a consequence, make incorrect judgments.

A third way in which complexity can lessen JDM quality is through conscious choice of processing strategies. As complexity increases, people are more likely to choose noncompensatory processing strategies (Payne et al. 1993).[8] When people use noncompensatory strategies, they search for and use a smaller percentage of the information available; they also search for different pieces of information across judgment or decision alternatives (Payne 1976; Ford et al. 1989). The reasoning behind this is that people attempt to keep total cognitive costs below benefits. Complexity increases cognitive costs (and not necessarily benefits) unless people change strategies to be less costly, that is, noncompensatory.[9] When people use noncompensatory strategies, they do not search for all relevant information and, as a consequence, can have lowered JDM quality.[10] Another reason people may switch to such strategies for complex tasks is that they know they lack the knowledge needed for these tasks and, thus, cannot make high-quality judgments or decisions. In other words, they anticipate benefits to be very low, so they keep costs low as well. In either case, people likely switch to noncompensatory strategies when they expect processing constraints to be exceeded; as such, this choice-of-processing strategies mediator of task complexity effects explains negative effects beyond some level of complexity.

---

[8]Clearly, an assumption underlying this explanation is that people recognize complex tasks as such.
[9]This assumption may not hold in some settings because the rewards for performing well at complex tasks may exceed those for performing well at simple tasks. For example, the relative magnitude of CEO compensation to employee compensation (Crystal 1991) may partially reflect the relative complexity of the tasks these individuals perform.
[10]Typically, these effects occur through information search rather than other processes because the studies present all relevant information to subjects. Thus, memory retrieval, for example, is not an issue.

Finally, task complexity can have a negative effect on JDM quality in the short run because people respond to highly complex tasks by trying to learn the complicated strategies that ultimately will lead to higher-quality JDM (e.g., Campbell and Ilgen 1976; Creyer et al. 1990). They are particularly likely to do so when they have incentives related to long-run JDM quality. In this case, short-term JDM quality can suffer because people frequently change strategies while learning (e.g., Naylor and Clark 1968; Naylor and Schenck 1968). These negative effects of task complexity likely occur beyond the point at which people perceive tasks to require strategy development.

What factors can moderate the negative effects of task complexity? First, when these negative effects occur because of the taxing of processing constraints, knowledge content and structure can lessen them. Also, task complexity effects become negative at different points for different people because they vary in abilities related to short-term memory and processing speed (Carroll 1993). Thus, negative effects of complexity are attenuated as average abilities increase.[11] When complexity effects occur because of a mismatch between knowledge structure or mode of thinking and task characteristics, increases in knowledge content and structure likely exacerbate the problem. Attenuation can occur only with decision aids that maintain the substantive characteristics of the task but allow people to use their knowledge in appropriate ways. For example, Bonner et al. (1996) find that auditors are able to make high-quality conditional probability judgments under mismatch conditions when given such a decision aid.

When task complexity effects occur because people consciously switch to noncompensatory strategies, moderators depend on the reason for switching strategies. If people believe they can make high-quality judgments or decisions, they tend to switch just to keep costs below benefits. In these cases, one way of reducing the effects of task complexity is to increase benefits, for example, by providing monetary or other types of incentives (Payne et al. 1993). If people switch strategies in complex tasks because they believe they cannot make high-quality JDM, increasing possible benefits will not moderate these effects. Instead, moderation can occur only by providing people with the attributes they believe they lack (e.g., knowledge); this can be done through the provision of decision aids or instruction, for example. Finally, if task complexity provides incentives that lead to lowered short-term JDM quality in favor of long-term JDM quality, such effects could be reduced by providing incentives related to short-term quality. However, this may lead to perverse behavior that is not acceptable from a practical perspective. For example, people may engage in fraud in order to make short-term quality appear to be high when in fact it is not, rather than attempt to do their best.

Task complexity can be studied either through manipulation or measurement, and thus experimental, archival, and survey studies of complexity effects appear in the literature. However, measurement of task complexity makes it more difficult to focus on individual elements of complexity, if desired. Either method comes with the following precautionary note: when considering complexity from the perspective of multiple tasks, there are possible confounding factors. That is, tasks can vary on complexity but also on a number of other factors such as the extent to which JDM quality is sensitive to effort, their presentation format, and so forth. Of particular note here is

---

[11]Schroder et al. (1967) also posit that a personality factor ("conceptual structure") moderates the negative effects of task complexity. It is not clear, however, whether this is part of personality or some sort of ability.

the effort-sensitivity confound, as illustrated by a study by Libby and Lipe (1992). This study examines the effects of monetary incentives on auditors' recall and recognition of internal controls and finds that incentives have a greater effect on recall. Although task complexity is not the main thrust of the study, they posit that the recall task is both more sensitive to cognitive effort and more complex, implying that incentives have greater effects on tasks that have either greater effort sensitivity or greater complexity or both. As described above, incentives typically do not have greater effects on JDM in tasks that are more complex (Bonner et al. 2000), with the exception of the situation where people possess the characteristics they need for high-quality JDM and believe they possess these characteristics but do not want to use costly compensatory strategies to process information. This is not the situation in Libby and Lipe's study because processing consists of only memory retrieval.

To ensure that such confounds do not appear, then, it is better to conduct initial examinations of task complexity by focusing on a single task, and indeed, many accounting studies do so. Unfortunately, many of these studies examine the information load element of complexity and, consequently, may introduce a confound (information content) even in this more restrictive setting. Fortunately, recent studies (e.g., Simnett 1996) demonstrate how to disentangle the effects of load and content. For other elements of task complexity such as number of processing steps, it is less likely that there are confounds, so careful manipulation should produce interpretable results.

Accounting Studies on Task Complexity

This section discusses accounting studies on complexity. Because studies of information load frequently confound complexity and information content, the following discussion separates studies that examine information load as an element of (or proxy for) task complexity from those that examine other elements of complexity. Studies on information load effects among producers of accounting information include Shields (1980), who examines the effects of the number of responsibility units and the number of performance parameters per unit on managers' search for information while analyzing performance reports. He finds that complexity induced by an increase in the number of responsibility units (performance parameters) is (is not) related to more variability in search across units, one element of noncompensatory processing. Shields (1983) shows that both types of complexity lead to decreases in the percentage of information used; further, complexity increases initially lead to increases in judgment accuracy because more information is available for JDM, but they lead to decreases beyond some point.

Otley and Dias (1982) give student subjects a production planning task that requires them to maximize plants' contributions to profits. Subjects with greater numbers of information cues are less accurate vis-à-vis simulated results. Iselin (1988) reports that manager and student subjects are less likely to make the theoretically correct capital investment decision and take more time as the number of dimensions of information and the number of values per dimension increase; however, these effects of task complexity are reduced after subjects gain knowledge through participating in multiple trials. Iselin (1989) finds that subjects managing a simulated business take significantly more time when the number of dimensions is higher but do not earn lower profits. Finally, Swain and Haka (2000) report that managers search a smaller proportion of the information (and more variably) as the number of alternatives and the number of dimensions per alternative increase in a capital budgeting task.

Other studies of task complexity in management accounting settings include Hilton et al. (1988), who find no effect of linearity in cost functions on the extent to which students' prices correspond to profit-maximizing prices. Chenhall and Morris's (1993) survey of managers finds higher JDM quality in tasks with less uncertainty. Gupta and King (1997) vary the complexity of tasks subjects face when making product cost forecasts and find that profits based on these forecasts are lower in more complex settings. Hirst and Yetton (1999) show that greater task interdependence leads to lower outputs in a simulated production management task.

Several studies examine the impact of task complexity on analysts' JDM. First, a number of studies find negative effects of the number of firms and industries followed, proxies for information load, on forecast accuracy (Clement 1999; Jacob et al. 1999; Bonner et al. 2003; Clement and Tse 2003, 2005). Next, several studies indicate a negative relation between the length of the horizon between analysts' forecasts and the earnings announcement (called "forecast age") and the accuracy of those forecasts, ostensibly because the function relating the available information and earnings is of lower magnitude when horizons are longer (e.g., O'Brien 1988; Mikhail et al. 1997; Sinha et al. 1997; Clement; Jacob et al.; Bonner et al.; Clement and Tse 2003). Other studies examine earnings predictability as a component of task complexity by measuring either the variability in earnings or the magnitude of errors from time series model predictions; these studies find that analysts' accuracy increases as predictability increases (Lys and Soo 1995; Dowen 1996; Ackert and Athanassakos 1997).[12] Finally, Plumlee (2003) reports that analysts use less complex tax law information to a greater extent than more complex information when making effective tax rate forecasts.

Studies related to investors and other users of accounting information include several about information load. Dickhaut (1973) reports that students' (businesspeople's) estimates of stock prices vis-à-vis Bayesian estimates are negatively (not) affected by load. Students' and accountants' levels of agreement in cash flow predictions also are not affected by information load in Snowball's (1980) study. Casey (1980b) finds an initial increase in loan officers' bankruptcy prediction accuracy with a load increase, then no effect. Time taken increases steadily with load.[13] Biggs et al. (1985) find that loan officers choosing companies as loan candidates are more prone to use noncompensatory strategies and, thus, search more variably and for smaller percentages of information under conditions of higher information load. Paquette and Kida (1988) report that accountants attempting to choose the company with the best bond rating are less accurate and take more time as the number of alternatives increases. Umanath and Vessey (1994) report no differences in students' accuracy at bankruptcy prediction due to load. Finally, Stocks and Harrell (1995) show that loan officers agree more with each other and themselves over time with lower information load. However, there are no differences in the accuracy of their bankruptcy predictions.

Further studies examine various elements of task complexity. Houghton's (1984) and Casey and Selling's (1986) student and loan officer subjects are more accurate at

---

[12]In the latter two studies, the authors report that forecasts exhibit more positive bias (optimism) when earnings are highly unpredictable. However, because they document optimism across forecasts, forecasts with higher optimistic bias are, by necessity, less accurate.

[13]This study provides an example of load being confounded with information content. The low load condition includes just ratios; the medium load condition includes ratios plus financial statements; and the high load condition has ratios, financial statements, and footnotes.

predicting bankruptcy with ratios from three years prior to bankruptcy rather than five years prior; in the former case, the magnitude of the relation between the ratio cues and the bankruptcy outcome is higher. Chang et al. (1997) examine the extent to which students' judgments in two accounting tasks conform to theoretically correct responses. Subjects' responses are more likely to be correct in the less complex task. Also, experience (a proxy for knowledge) affects JDM quality in the more complex task but not in the less complex task. In the tax domain, Milliron (1985) indicates that taxpayers make different decisions depending on the complexity of the tax situation; it is unclear how JDM quality is affected, however. Krawczyk (1994) reports that tax professionals agree more with each other in a more complex setting (one with imprecise rules) than in a less complex setting, contrary to her prediction.

Auditing studies on information load include Blocher et al. (1986), who find that internal auditors' judgments conform more to auditing theory under low-load conditions. However, load also interacts with tabular versus graphic presentation; under high complexity, tabular presentation leads to more theoretically correct responses, whereas the opposite obtains for low complexity. Chewning and Harrell's (1990) subjects vary in their responses to increases in information load in a bankruptcy prediction task; some subjects exhibit negative effects of load on consensus and consistency, and others show no effects. Trotman and Wood (1991) provide a meta-analysis of internal control judgment studies and indicate that number of cues provided in these studies has no impact on JDM quality; however, this may occur because subjects typically possess the necessary knowledge. Simnett (1996) finds that information load has a negative effect on auditors' bankruptcy prediction accuracy. Finally, Chung and Monroe (2001) report that auditors more accurately detect an inventory misstatement under low load.

Boritz (1985) and Abdolmohammadi and Wright (1987) find that auditors' judgments differ depending on whether tasks are structured or unstructured. Simnett and Trotman (1989) vary magnitude of the cue–output relation in a bankruptcy prediction task; auditors facing a higher magnitude relation are more accurate. McDaniel (1990) varies the structuredness of audit programs and finds that auditors are more effective and take less time under structured conditions; effectiveness is defined as the extent to which auditors detect seeded errors and choose sample sizes that conform to requirements of professional standards. Asare and McDaniel (1996) vary the structuredness of review procedures and find either no effect or a positive effect of complexity on detection of errors in preparers' work papers. However, the latter finding may be due to auditors' reviewing the work of familiar preparers. Nelson et al. (1995) and Bonner et al. (1996) find that auditors faced with a mismatching task structure make conditional probabilities that are less correct vis-à-vis probability theory than do auditors faced with a task structure that matches their knowledge structure.

Wright (1995) examines two elements of complexity: the amount of information needed to make a loan collectibility judgment and the clarity of that information, as operationalized by tables versus graphs. Auditors' judgments agree more with those of an expert panel when the amount of information needed is lower and when graphs are presented. Further, the clarification of information through graphs has a larger impact when tasks are more complex due to information load. Goodwin (1999) reports that auditors who view consistent evidence make different accounting treatment choices than do those who view inconsistent evidence, although it is not clear which choices are of higher quality. Tan et al. (2002b) find that auditors' JDM quality (defined in accordance with auditing theory) declines as task complexity increases. Knowledge moderates the negative effect of complexity, but accountability does not. Along with this, Prawitt (1995) and Abdolmohammadi (1999) report that audit firms assign more experienced (a proxy for more knowledgeable) auditors to more complex tasks, consistent with knowledge moderating the effects of task complexity.

For the most part, accounting research on task complexity parallels that in psychology. Task complexity generally has a negative effect on JDM quality beyond some point, with one notable exception. Studies that examine the information load component of complexity often show positive or no effects of complexity; however, this likely is due to the information content confound that occurs in many of these studies. To the extent mediators of complexity have been studied, the mediating forces in accounting settings appear similar to those proposed in psychology. Also consistent with psychology, knowledge is an important moderator of task complexity effects in accounting tasks.

Research on task complexity in accounting is somewhat disjointed, so it is important to step back and define the key complexity issues in accounting. The world faced by accounting decision makers today can be characterized as one involving huge amounts of information, tasks with multiple goals, and a focus on regulation. All of these elements of today's environment can increase accounting tasks' complexity and potentially lead to lower-quality JDM. However, the accounting world also can be characterized as one where information cues often are correlated; this factor reduces task complexity. Thus, research on task complexity seems more relevant than ever in accounting, particularly in the contexts where many of the forces above converge (e.g., financial accounting and analysis). Research could examine the effects of these elements of complexity more thoroughly, in particular how the effects of the various elements combine to affect JDM. Research should also continue to consider whether there are responses to task complexity by accounting decision makers that can harm the JDM of users of those decision makers' JDM. For example, if managers respond to rules-based standards by reinterpreting evidence so it is consistent with those standards, investors may be harmed if they assume that the rules prevent managers from behaving in this manner. Finally, given that the forces creating increases in complexity, for example, technology that provides greater amounts of information, are not likely to abate, research on factors that can attenuate task complexity's negative effects is particularly important, especially if there are "natural" improvement methods already in place in accountants' environments. For example, the greater knowledge of reviewers may serve to moderate complexity effects in auditing. Also, it is important to understand the factors that lead to task complexity being increased by standard-setters and others.

6-2   EFFECTS OF INFORMATION RELEVANCE ON JDM QUALITY

Another important task variable is the *relevance* of the information available, or the extent to which the information is directly concerned with or informative about a particular judgment or decision. In particular, there are two important questions that arise with regard to information relevance: Do people use all relevant information when making judgments and decisions, and do people ignore all irrelevant information during JDM? Naturally, the answer to both questions is "no." However, this section focuses on only the second question—the effects of irrelevant information on JDM quality. Many studies that examine the first question are asking whether accountants' JDM is of high quality vis-à-vis professional standards. Other studies are demonstrating bounded rationality effects (e.g., the use of heuristics).

This section highlights three lines of research on irrelevant information. The first relates to the effects of anchors on numerical judgments; *anchors* are salient but irrelevant numbers that are present at the beginning of the judgment process and typically are the sole information cue (Chapman and Johnson 2002). The second line of research relates to the effects of theoretically irrelevant information that can be quantitative or qualitative in form but that is included in a larger set of information that also includes relevant information. Such information often creates a *dilution effect,* meaning that it lessens the effects of the relevant information on JDM (Nisbett et al. 1981). The third line of research relates to qualitative or quantitative information that has theoretical relevance to a judgment or decision when taken on its own but empirically does not because it is redundant with other information in a larger set. Specifically, this chapter focuses on a particular form of *redundancy* i.e., the situation in which information already provided to the decision maker is repeated.[14]

Anchors

The effect of anchors on JDM is a widely established finding (Chapman and Johnson 2002). A classic example of this comes from the work of Tversky and Kahneman (1974). They spin a number wheel then ask subjects to estimate whether the percentage of African countries that belong to the United Nations is higher or lower than the number on the wheel. Although the number on the wheel has no logical bearing on the requested judgment, subjects who receive a high anchor make higher judgments on average than subjects who receive a low anchor.

It is important to distinguish anchors on several dimensions. First, anchors can be relevant or irrelevant to the task; consistent with this section's focus, the discussion centers on irrelevant anchors.[15] Psychology research examines only one type of irrelevant anchor—those that are uninformative for a task (Tversky and Kahneman 1974). In accounting, however, there is a second type of irrelevant anchor. These anchors are informative, but their use has been proscribed by professional standards. For example, in developing expectations of account balances, auditors should not use client-provided, unaudited figures as anchors (AICPA 2004). Second, anchors can be externally provided or generated by the decision maker. This section focuses on the former type of anchor because the literature on self-generated anchors to date focuses on relevant anchors (Epley and Gilovich 2002). Finally, anchors can be plausible, meaning they are within the realm of possibility (e.g., 65 degrees as an average temperature), or implausible, meaning they are so extreme as to be outrageous (e.g., 300 degrees as an average temperature). The mediators of such anchors' effects differ, so they are discussed separately.

The effects of anchors occur in a plethora of contexts, so this issue clearly is not unique to accounting. However, its relevance cannot be questioned. Much of accounting JDM is numerical in nature (e.g., auditors' predictions about account balances and

---

[14]Another form of redundancy discussed in the literature is correlation among information cues. This chapter considers the correlation form of redundancy to be an element of task complexity.
[15]There clearly are real-world tasks, including many in accounting, for which there are relevant (informative) anchors. For example, an earnings forecast made by management likely is a relevant anchor for analysts making earnings forecasts.

auditors' decisions about achieved risk during sampling), and either proscribed or uninformative anchors for these judgments exist (e.g., client-provided account balances and allowable sampling risk). In proscribing certain anchors, standard-setters likely understand their possible ill effects. For example, a client could attempt to manipulate an auditor's JDM by providing an unaudited account balance anchor that is far from the correct balance and, as a result, cause auditors who move toward that anchor to conclude that a less extreme, but still materially incorrect, balance is acceptable. As another example, a plaintiff's attorney could influence the amount of damages auditors or other professionals have to pay as a result of litigation by suggesting a clearly outrageous figure that then serves as an anchor (Hastie and Dawes 2001). The severity of possible economic consequences in the latter example is clear.

The typical effect of anchors shown in JDM studies is that subjects who receive different (uninformative) anchors make substantially different judgments or decisions, and more important, these judgments or decisions are biased in the direction of the anchors. People with high anchors produce higher numerical responses than people with low anchors. Thus, anchors are thought to have a negative effect on JDM quality when quality is viewed from the perspective of agreement with others. Further, anchors can decrease quality as defined by correspondence with normative theories because these theories indicate that irrelevant information should receive no weight in JDM. In accounting, it also is possible that anchors have negative effects on JDM from the perspective of agreement with professional standards (i.e., they affect JDM when professional standards say they should not). Finally, when used strategically as in the case of clients interacting with auditors, anchors could lead to JDM that is inaccurate. Consistent with research to date in psychology, this section focuses on the negative effects of anchors on agreement with others and describes research that employs uninformative anchors. However, issues related to other quality dimensions and informative but proscribed anchors are discussed where pertinent.

The early literature on uninformative, externally provided anchors' effects proposed that these effects occur because people start with the anchor then adjust insufficiently from that anchor when giving a numerical judgment (Tversky and Kahneman 1974). However, reasons for the insufficient adjustment either have not been offered or have since been refuted (Chapman and Johnson 2002).[16] More recent accounts propose alternative mediators. The typical study employing externally provided anchors asks subjects a "comparative question" (e.g., Is the average temperature in Los Angeles greater than or less than 65 degrees?) After answering the comparative question, subjects then are asked an "absolute question" (e.g., What is the average temperature in Los Angeles?) The current literature indicates that the effects of these anchors occur through hypothesis evaluation and related memory retrieval. The specific hypothesis evaluation and retrieval mechanisms depend on whether the anchor is plausible or implausible.

Plausible anchors affect JDM as follows. When answering the comparative question, subjects appear to first evaluate the hypothesis that the anchor is the correct number (Strack and Mussweiler 1997; Chapman and Johnson 1999; Mussweiler and Strack 1999, 2000a, 2001). When people evaluate hypotheses using memory, they tend to seek

---

[16]Recent research revives the insufficient adjustment explanation for the effects of self-generated anchors in contexts where anchors are informative (Epley and Gilovich 2002).

information that is consistent with the hypothesis (e.g., Snyder and Swann 1978; Snyder and Cantor 1979). In the typical experimental scenario, they must seek information in memory because no other information is available. In other scenarios, this confirmation bias might play out through information search. The retrieved (or searched for) information related to the comparative question—information consistent with the anchor being the correct answer—is then more available in memory when subjects answer the absolute question. As a consequence, people who receive different anchors retrieve different information at the stage of the comparative question and, thus, have different information available when answering the absolute question.

Implausible experimenter-provided anchors also have a negative effect on JDM quality, but it often is lesser in magnitude than the extremity of the anchors would suggest (Chapman and Johnson 1994; Wegener et al. 2001). The mediators of these effects also differ. Rather than retrieving or searching for specific information consistent with the hypothesis that the anchor is correct, people need only access categorical knowledge related to the question (Mussweiler and Strack 2000b).[17] For example, when asked if the average temperature in Los Angeles is greater or less than 300 degrees, people can answer by noticing that 300 degrees is beyond the upper boundary of an average temperature distribution associated with the category Earth. In other words, they do not need to retrieve or search for any information that is consistent with the hypothesis that the average temperature in Los Angeles is 300 degrees because they know that Los Angeles is a member of the category "cities on Earth." However, these implausible anchors still create differences in judgment among individuals because they affect memory retrieval (or information search) at the stage of the absolute question. Specifically, at this point, people appear to test the hypothesis that the boundary of the category that is closest to the anchor is the correct hypothesis (Mussweiler and Strack). Thus, in the temperature example, if a person's category knowledge indicates that 100 degrees is the highest average temperature of any place on Earth, she would start with this hypothesis then retrieve hypothesis-consistent information, which in turn influences her judgment.

Finally, as mentioned earlier, the psychology literature does not examine the effects of anchors that are proscribed but potentially informative. Thus, what causes people to use such anchors is unknown. Perhaps auditors, for example, are not aware that they are affected by these anchors or, if they are aware that they are affected, believe that their professional skepticism will eliminate the anchors' effects. However, it seems plausible that these anchors affect JDM through cognitive processes that are similar to those invoked in the face of uninformative anchors.

There are few factors that moderate the effects of anchors; studies describe anchors' effects as among the most robust in psychology (Chapman and Johnson 2002). With experimenter-provided anchors, the evaluation of the anchor as a hypothesis and the resulting confirmation-prone memory retrieval are thought to be automatic processes; consequently, little can disrupt them. The only approach that appears to at least decrease the effects of anchors, that is, decrease the differences in judgments between people with different anchors, is asking people to think of reasons the anchor may not

---

[17]Mussweiler and Strack (2000b) also discuss situations where people are unable to access category knowledge because they do not know to which category a presented anchor belongs (e.g., whether it is a person or a city). These situations are unlikely in accounting because decision makers of interest normally have this minimal level of knowledge.

be the correct hypothesis (Chapman and Johnson 1999; Mussweiler et al. 2000). This causes people to retrieve from memory information that is inconsistent with the anchor being correct as well as information that is consistent with the anchor being correct.

Experimental studies of anchoring manipulate anchors and carefully control other information so the effects of the anchor are not confounded. It might be difficult to study the effects of anchors through measurement because there normally would be only one anchor related to a particular task at one point in time. For example, auditors state only one allowable risk figure in work papers for a given time period and sampling application (this risk figure might serve as an anchor for auditors' achieved risk judgments). In such settings, therefore, anchors are confounded with many other factors, such as client type and time period. If adequate controls are not available to deal with these confounds, then archival and survey methods are not viable for studying anchoring.

Accounting studies on anchoring are fairly limited. In a cost variance investigation context, Brown (1981) finds that uninformative cost anchors affect investigation decisions. Remaining studies relate to auditing JDM. Joyce and Biddle (1981a) conduct several experiments on the effects of anchors. Although some of the studies find results consistent with typical anchor effects, some do not. However, these experiments employ relatively unrealistic tasks; further, some of them may confound anchors with other task variables such as order of information. Butler (1986) varies the amount of allowable risk in a sampling context and finds that auditors' judgments of achieved risk are affected by the allowable risk anchor (which is uninformative as to achieved risk); however, auditors are affected less by anchors than are students.

A few studies examine the effects of proscribed anchors on the prediction of account or ratio balances.[18] Kinney and Uecker (1982) employ an analytical procedures task. Auditors given different unaudited values but the same prior audited values for the gross margin ratio give different investigation boundaries for that ratio; means of the boundaries are biased in the direction of the anchors. However, auditors appear to be less affected by anchors that suggest a trend reversal than by those that do not. Biggs and Wild (1985) provide similar findings. Heintz and White (1989) also report similar findings, except anchors suggesting a trend reversal have greater effects on their subjects' judgments than those that do not. Shields et al. (1988) similarly find that unaudited values affect auditors' estimates of account balances. Further, they measure accuracy of responses using calibrationlike measures (see Chapter 2) and find that auditors who receive unaudited values with material errors are less accurate than auditors who do not receive these anchors; when the unaudited values do not contain material errors, there is no effect of anchors on accuracy.

Research in accounting on anchor effects is consistent with that in psychology. That is, studies typically find differences in JDM that are in the direction of differences in either uninformative or proscribed anchors. In other words, anchors can have a negative effect on accounting JDM quality defined as agreement with others and defined as correspondence with normative theories. This line of research appears to have

---

[18]Client-provided unaudited values should not be used for forming expectations about current account or ratio balances during analytical procedures. Instead, auditors should develop independent expectations about these numbers then compare them to unaudited balances.

ceased, however, and it is not clear why. We know little about how accounting decision makers use anchors in real-world settings. What sorts of uninformative and proscribed anchors are present? How do these anchors enter accountants' environment? Such questions examining anchors as a dependent variable are especially important to consider if anchors can be used as a way of manipulating accounting professionals. Further, the possibility for strategic use makes it important to examine the effects of anchors on JDM quality criteria such as accuracy more closely. Along with this, given that recent research better explicates the mechanisms through which anchors produce their effects, accounting researchers might be able to study such issues then quickly proceed to examining factors that may attenuate anchors' effects (e.g., conditions that allow accounting professionals to ignore them or see through their strategic use). Finally, there may be additional moderating variables that are related to particular features of accounting contexts that have not been investigated by psychologists. For example, differential reactions to anchors that indicate a reversal in trend versus no reversal may be tied to litigation concerns or other forms of incentives that are unique to accounting.

The "Dilution Effect"

Many studies examine the effects of irrelevant information other than anchors. This information can be quantitative or qualitative; studies normally focus on a particular effect of such information called the "dilution effect" (discussed below). Irrelevance (uninformativeness) to JDM typically is established by appeal to researchers' knowledge of contexts and by ratings of the relevance of information cues from a separate subject group. The difference between these studies and those of anchor effects is that the irrelevant information is contained in a set that also contains relevant information. For example, a study may compare the judgments of car buyers who have information about only relevant aspects of this purchase such as price and gas mileage to the judgments of those who also have information about clearly irrelevant factors such as the color of the car salesperson's hair. In contrast, studies of anchors present the anchor — one irrelevant information cue — as a starting point and, in many cases, as the only cue. Although anchors and other irrelevant information can be construed to have similar effects on JDM quality, irrelevant information used as a starting point may induce different mental processes than does irrelevant information embedded in a set. Thus, it is important to discuss these two streams of research separately.

Irrelevant information and its dilution effect have been studied in a number of settings, including accounting. This factor is important to study in accounting because many accounting JDM tasks can present irrelevant information to decision makers. This can occur in a number of ways. First, accounting decision makers may ask subordinates to gather information relevant to a particular judgment or decision; if subordinates lack knowledge of the situation, they may inadvertently include irrelevant information. Second, accounting decision makers may have irrelevant information thrust on them by various third parties such as the media and clients. Third, many settings require the use of a subset of information for each of several judgments or decisions. For example, auditors must choose subsets of information from work papers for different judgments and decisions. Having that information all in one place (such as work papers) and using various parts of it for multiple tasks may make it difficult to ignore information that is relevant for one judgment or decision when making another judgment or decision for which the information is not relevant (Rau and Moser 1999). Clearly, the use of irrelevant information can have substantial economic consequences. For example, investors who attend to irrelevant information provided by the media may have lowered investment returns (e.g., Bonner et al. 2006).

Studies of irrelevant information indicate that this variable tends to create a dilution effect, which is considered a negative effect on JDM quality. There are two ways in which such an effect can occur. First, a dilution effect can decrease JDM quality defined as agreement with others. Here, people who receive irrelevant and relevant information make different judgments and decisions than people who receive only relevant information. In particular, people who receive irrelevant information make less extreme judgments than those who do not. The dilution effect is said to occur because the irrelevant information receives nonzero weight in this group's JDM, thus diluting the effect of the relevant information as well as the extremity of the judgment. Second, a dilution effect can decrease JDM quality defined as agreement with normative JDM theories such as Bayes' Theorem or defined as agreement with oneself over time. In these studies, the finding is that people change their initial judgments or decisions after they view irrelevant information; again, the change is to a less extreme judgment. Finally, although research has not examined other elements of JDM quality, it is conceivable that irrelevant information could have negative effects on these other elements. For example, if clients use irrelevant information to persuade auditors about the accuracy of a materially incorrect account balance, the result could be an inaccurate audit opinion.

Most studies of the dilution effect characterize it as resulting from the hypothesis evaluation process. In particular, many theoretical accounts posit that people use the representativeness heuristic to evaluate a hypothesis (Kahneman and Tversky 1972). In so doing, people are thought to make an assessment of the similarity of the set of information cues to the hypothesis that is implicit in the judgment being requested (Troutman and Shanteau 1977; Nisbett et al. 1981; Zukier 1982; Zukier and Jennings 1983–1984). Similarity judgments are based on the extent to which the set contains cues that are considered similar to the hypothesis versus cues that are considered dissimilar to the hypothesis. The higher the ratio of similar cues to dissimilar cues, the higher the similarity judgment and the resulting judgment of the probability that the hypothesis is correct (Tversky 1977; Tversky and Gati 1978). Thus, when a set contains irrelevant cues that are not similar to the hypothesis, similarity and probability judgments are lower than they are if the set contains only relevant (and similar) cues, creating "dilution." For example, a loan officer predicting the probability that a company will go bankrupt would be expected to make a lower probability judgment if confronted with both relevant cues such as financial ratios and irrelevant cues such as the gender of the CEO than if confronted only with relevant cues.

Recent studies propose alternative accounts of the dilution effect that also relate to the hypothesis evaluation process. One set of studies proposes that the effect occurs simply because experimental subjects believe that researchers would not give them irrelevant information as part of a research study; thus, they give this information nonzero weight during hypothesis evaluation because they assume it is relevant (e.g., Schwarz et al. 1991; Tetlock et al. 1996). A more recent study (Meyvis and Janiszewski 2002) characterizes the dilution effect as resulting from a confirmation-biased evaluation process. Decision makers test the hypothesis embedded in the judgment task and classify irrelevant information as not supportive of the hypothesis (rather than as unrelated), thus lowering their judgments about the probability the hypothesis is correct.

Are there any factors that can lessen the dilution effect? If the dilution effect is caused by the use of the representativeness heuristic, task-specific knowledge may serve as a moderator. This is because the heuristic can piggyback on good knowledge (Gilovich and Griffin 2002). If the effect is, instead, caused by confirmation-prone processing, asking decision makers to consider an alternative hypothesis (and, thus, evaluate information as to whether it pertains to both the original and alternative hypotheses) can reduce the effect because people realize that the information neither supports nor fails to support the original hypothesis (Meyvis and Janiszewski 2002). Similarly, subjecting people to time pressure may reduce the effect because people are forced to be more prudent about the information they use when time is limited; as a consequence, they may ignore the irrelevant information (Glover 1997).

Studying the dilution effect requires that irrelevant information be present in a setting. Thus, it is conceivable to study this information archivally or with surveys; clearly, there is irrelevant information present in many real-world contexts. For example, investors appear to react to media coverage of financial analysts even though this factor is not relevant to analysts' forecast accuracy (Bonner et al. 2006).[19] The difficulty, of course, is finding situations in which irrelevant information is present sometimes and not present otherwise (it may always be present) and also controlling for any other differences between those situations. Experimental studies can manipulate the presence of irrelevant information and control for other important factors.

Accounting studies related to the dilution effect all are set in auditing contexts. Hackenbrack (1992) finds that auditors' judgments about the probability of fraud differ (are less extreme) when they view relevant information coupled with irrelevant information versus when they view only relevant information. Hoffman and Patton (1997) replicate these findings and also report that accountability does not moderate the dilution effect. Glover (1997) finds that time pressure reduces the dilution effect in judgments about the chance of material misstatement. These three studies use senior-level auditors. Shelton (1999), on the other hand, compares the going-concern judgments of partners and managers to those of seniors. She finds that seniors exhibit the dilution effect, whereas partners and managers do not. Waller and Zimbelman (2003) examine data collected from actual audits. Because they cannot control the sets of information auditors view, they define dilution as occurring when auditors' risk assessments underweight a critical information cue, specifically, the existence of a prior year misstatement. Underweighting is analyzed based on a comparison of the auditors' judgment models to a regression model. Auditors' judgment models indicate that they underweight this critical cue, consistent with dilution. Finally, Asare and Wright (1995), although not focusing specifically on the dilution effect, examine the effects of irrelevant information on auditors' revisions of their probability judgments for each of a set of hypotheses about the cause of a ratio fluctuation. They find that audit seniors tend not to revise their probability judgments in the face of irrelevant evidence, whereas students do.

---

[19]Recall the suggestion from Chapter 5 that studies examining decision makers' use of information with archival data should consider incorporating irrelevant information because decision makers may, in fact, use such information.

To a large extent, research in accounting parallels psychology with regard to the dilution effect. That is, accounting decision makers sometimes allow irrelevant information to affect their JDM. Consistent with the hypothesized process mechanisms above, knowledge and time pressure may moderate these effects. However, research to date relates solely to auditing issues; irrelevant information may have different effects in other contexts, for example, investing. Further, theories explaining the dilution effect appear to be still under construction; accountants could help advance theory development. Perhaps most important is to identify the contexts in which accounting decision makers are most likely to encounter irrelevant information and to understand the factors that lead to irrelevant information being present and salient in these contexts (e.g., media coverage of irrelevant information or incentives related to pleasing the provider of irrelevant information). Again, such investigations are particularly important for situations in which irrelevant information can be used strategically. Beyond this, research needs to further explicate the mechanisms behind the effects of irrelevant information, as well as moderators that can lessen its effects.

Redundant Information

A recent type of irrelevant information examined by accounting and psychology research is information that repeats, or is redundant with, other information in a set provided to a decision maker. A common setting in which such information appears is media coverage of events. For example, a newswire service may release an article about a company that is then reprinted, verbatim, by a number of newspapers. By contrast, a story about another company may be printed only by the newswire service (i.e., never reprinted). For this example, repeated information clearly is a form of irrelevant information because the contents of repeated articles clearly are not informative to any judgment or decision that could be based on the first article.[20]

In other situations where information is subject to measurement and, thus, to measurement error, repeated information is not completely irrelevant because it may serve to reduce measurement error. For example, it may be helpful to measure a person's weight twice with the same scale when there is error in the scale's readings (Soll 1999). Nevertheless, even in these situations, nonredundant information is preferable to redundant information because nonredundant information can reduce both measurement error and bias. Continuing the example, it would be preferable to measure a person's weight using two different methods than to use the same scale twice (Soll). Scales, for example, may always overestimate people's weights (and do so with error). Assuming that another technique to measure weight (e.g., water displacement) does not suffer from the same type of bias (but does measure with error), measuring weight with these two methods should reduce both bias and error.

Repetition of information, although not unique to accounting, clearly is important. Repeated information appears in a number of accounting contexts, most notably the media context mentioned above. The business media, like financial analysts and others, appears now to be an important information intermediary linking accounting information and stock prices (e.g., Busse and Green 2002; Gadarowski 2004; Bonner et al. 2006). As another example, auditors write memos that repeat information contained

---

[20]This statement assumes that media outlets' choices to feature these articles do not represent signals that those media outlets have private information about the events in question.

in work papers, and reviewers of work papers may examine both the original information and the memos. Further, anticipating the potential effects of repeated information, third parties may try to manipulate accounting decision makers through simple repetition of statements. Repetition is a common technique used by advertisers in persuading consumers of the validity of product claims, for example (e.g., Roggeveen and Johar 2002).

Studies of repeated information tend to indicate that this variable decreases JDM quality defined either as agreement with others or as agreement with normative JDM theories such as Bayes' Theorem. In studies examining agreement with others, people who receive repeated information make different judgments and decisions than people who do not receive repeated information. In studies examining agreement with normative theories, the normal finding is that people change their initial judgments or decisions after they view repeated information. Again, although research in psychology has not examined other elements of JDM quality, it is plausible that repeated information could have negative effects on these other elements. For example, if clients use repeated information in an attempt to convince auditors of the fair statement of a materially incorrect account balance, the result could be an inaccurate audit opinion.

One common account of the mechanism behind the effect of repeated information on JDM quality comes from studies of the *truth effect,* or the *validity effect.* These studies require that subjects read and rate the truthfulness of plausible but uncertain statements during multiple sessions; some statements are repeated in second and later sessions. The studies demonstrate that repetition of information increases perceived truthfulness or validity (e.g., Hasher et al. 1977; Bacon 1979; Begg et al. 1985; Arkes et al. 1991; Begg and Armour 1991; Begg et al. 1992; Hawkins and Hoch 1992; Boehm 1994; Hawkins et al. 2001; Roggeveen and Johar 2002). Researchers posit this occurs because people trying to answer a question about truthfulness ask themselves whether the statement "rings a bell"; in other words, they attempt to retrieve the statement from memory. If the statement seems familiar based on memory retrieval, they evaluate it as more likely to be true than if it does not seem familiar. Although these studies stop short of demonstrating the impact of perceived validity of information on JDM quality, the implication is that repeated information would have a larger effect on JDM than would nonrepeated information or than it should given the prescriptions of some normative theory; as a result, JDM quality suffers.

Joe (2003) posits an alternative view of the effects of repeated information. She suggests that repetition effects can occur through hypothesis evaluation in a manner similar to the way that dilution effects occur. Specifically, she posits that people use the representativeness heuristic and, thus, make an assessment of the similarity of the presented information to a particular hypothesis. People evaluate information cues as to their similarity to the hypothesis and calculate a ratio of similar cues to dissimilar cues. Assuming that repeated information is viewed as similar to the hypothesis, people who view repeated information are viewing a seemingly increased number (and ratio) of similar cues; therefore, they attach a higher probability to the hypothesis than do others who do not see the repeated information.

The studies above examine the effects of information when it is provided to subjects. An alternative account provides an information-search view of the effects of redundancy (Soll 1999); note that this account does not focus on information that is repeated verbatim, but rather on specific measurements or tests (inputs) that are repeated in a certain situation to produce a particular piece of information. Thus, for example, Soll examines whether people prefer to obtain the weight of an object by weighing it twice on the same scale or once on each of two different scales. This account proposes that people have intuitive theories about the relevance of redundant information that guide the extent to which they search for information that is redundant (that is, comes from repeated measurements or inputs). Specifically, people are assumed to be relatively sophisticated and understand the value of reducing both measurement error and bias in information. However, people also tend to believe that obtaining measurements from different input devices reduces only bias rather than both bias and error. Thus, they perceive a tradeoff between reducing measurement error and bias where none exists; as a consequence, people appear first to evaluate whether error or bias is the larger problem in a particular situation. If they deem error the larger problem, they will seek redundant information; that is, they prefer to use the same input repeatedly. Again, this line of work stops short of tying the intermediate processes related to repeated information to JDM quality. The implication here would be that, in situations where measurement error is perceived to be the bigger issue, JDM quality would be diminished because people would seek and give inappropriate weight to repeated information.

What can attenuate the ill effects of repeated information? Truth effect studies indicate that people must have something besides a feeling of familiarity to go on when judging the validity of information. Specifically, they must have other information available either in memory or at the time of the JDM. One way in which subjects could have more information available is if they engage in a higher level of initial processing of the information (Hawkins and Hoch 1992); for example, subjects could be encouraged to list reasons the statements may not be true. Similarly, domain knowledge may reduce the truth effect (Srull 1983; however, see Arkes et al. [1989] and Boehm [1994] for contradictory results).[21] Finally, Soll (1999) suggests that statistical training can reduce the ill effects of repeated information that occur due to incorrect intuitive theories.

Studying the effects of repeated information normally requires the use of an experiment to ensure that repetition is the only variable captured. Archival or survey studies that examine repetition's effects (e.g., Ho and Michaely 1988) can confound repetition of information with many other factors. For example, an archival researcher examining the effects of newspaper articles that contain repeated information cannot hold constant the format of the articles, other information present in the articles, the credibility of the newspapers, and so forth. However, to date, experimental studies also have confounded repetition with other factors. (See Hugon [2006] for further discussion.) One type of study compares the JDM of subjects who receive baseline information to the JDM of subjects who receive the baseline information plus repeated information. Because these two groups differ in the amount of data they receive, any effects attributed to repetition could be due instead to data quantity. Another type of study compares the JDM of subjects who receive baseline information plus further, nonredundant information to that of subjects who receive baseline information plus repeated information. These two groups have the same quantity of data, but one group has a greater amount of information on which to base their judgments or decisions.

---

[21]The same moderator would be suggested if this effect is caused by use of the representativeness heuristic.

Again, then, the effects of repetition could be confounded, this time with information content. A better design employs both types of comparisons along with other conditions to rule out confounds (Hugon).

Accounting studies related to the effects of information repetition or redundancy are few in number and examine widely varying issues. Davis et al. (1994) find that students' accuracy at predicting earnings per share is negatively affected by repeated information. However, because accuracy also is negatively affected by nonredundant information, there is the possibility that any repetition effect is due to information overload (in other words, there is an information quantity confound). Two studies examine the effects of repeated information on auditors' decisions to issue going-concern opinions. Mutchler et al. (1997) archivally examine the effect of news items reported in the *Wall Street Journal* on this decision and find that the reporting of extreme negative news items, which likely repeats information available to auditors in their work papers, increases the probability that audit firms give a going-concern opinion.[22] More specifically, the reporting of a default, which clearly is known to firms, increases the likelihood of modifying the opinion. These findings could reflect heightened litigation concerns rather than an increase in the perceived truthfulness of the information. To address this issue, Joe (2003) experimentally examines the impact of the presence of a news article that repeats information about a loan covenant violation included in the work papers. Auditors are more likely to issue a going-concern opinion with repeated information; further, Joe finds that this is due to their estimating the probability of bankruptcy to be higher and not due to higher perceived litigation risk.

Results in accounting are similar to those in psychology; repeated information has an effect on JDM when it should not, thereby decreasing JDM quality. However, at this point, it is difficult to determine whether these findings reflect the effects of repeated information or, instead, a confound such as the amount of data or the amount of information. Nevertheless, this task characteristic seems important in accounting, particularly for investors' decision making. Structural features of the media environment such as the need to fill space create incentives to repeat information, yet investors may not understand that these incentives exist (Bonner et al. 2006). Thus, continued research about both the antecedents and effects of repeated information seems useful both theoretically and practically.

6-3 EFFECTS OF FRAMING ON JDM QUALITY

Definitions and Background

Another characteristic of tasks that can have a profound influence on JDM quality is the "framing" of the information in the task. Although the term *framing* sometimes is used loosely, this section restricts discussion to what Levin et al. (1998) term "valence framing," in which the wording of the task can portray the judgment or decision either in positive or negative terms. For example, an auditing firm can frame the going-concern judgment such that it asks auditors to consider whether a company will continue in existence or, instead, to consider whether a company will go out of existence. The framing

---

[22]This book typically does not discuss firm-level studies; an exception is made here to better understand the Joe (2003) paper.

of tasks clearly is not a natural phenomenon; humans construct JDM tasks and, thus, have control over whether they are worded in a positive or negative light.[23]

In particular, in accounting, there are many different types of individuals involved in constructing and wording tasks that could influence the framing thereof. For example, standard-setters can create frames through the wording of standards; for the going-concern judgment, the frame is to "evaluate whether there is substantial doubt about the entity's ability to continue as a going concern" (AICPA 2004). Policy makers within firms also can create frames. For example, one bank may direct its loan officers to evaluate loan applicants for weaknesses, whereas another bank directs its loan officers to search for strengths. As described further below, a consequence of this is that the two banks could evaluate loan applicants quite differently and potentially draw different conclusions about granting a loan. Such framing effects would be unintentional but still could have economic consequences for both the banks and loan candidates. Framing effects can be intentional as well. For example, audit clients could use framing to try to affect auditors' JDM (Jamal et al. 1995). Such intentional use of framing is common in many areas such as marketing and politics (Kahneman and Tversky 1984; Turk 1995; Hastie and Dawes 2001). As such, although not unique to accounting, framing clearly is an important issue to accounting JDM.

To further clarify the effects of framing, this section adopts Levin et al.'s (1998) taxonomy of framing that distinguishes three types of framing based on the object thereof: risky choice framing, attribute framing, and goal framing. *Risky choice* framing is the original type introduced by Tversky and Kahneman (1981) with their "Asian disease" problem. This type of framing study asks subjects to make a choice between a riskless alternative (one in which a single outcome is guaranteed) and a risky alternative (one with multiple possible outcomes, each of which occurs with some probability); these alternatives have equal expected values. Both the riskless and risky alternatives can be described in positive or negative terms (in the "Asian disease" problem, descriptions are in terms of lives saved or lives lost). *Attribute framing* refers to positive or negative wording of a key element of a single object or event about which subjects are asked to make a judgment. For example, Levin and Gaeth (1988) ask people to rate the quality of ground beef given frames that are in terms of percentage lean or percentage fat. Finally, *goal framing* is defined as variation in the wording of the goal related to the decision to engage in a particular behavior. An example of this type of framing might occur in a study that describes the goals of quitting smoking and examines the extent to which subjects do so. Specifically, the goal wording can be positive and focus on the gains to be obtained by engaging in the behavior (e.g., lowered risk of heart disease), or it can be negative and focus on the losses to be incurred by not engaging in the behavior (e.g., increased risk of heart disease).

Framing Effects

The typical effect of framing of any sort is that people who receive positive frames make different judgments and decisions than people who receive negative frames; thus, frames can have a negative effect on JDM quality defined as agreement with

---

[23]Sometimes, framing is imposed on a task by a decision maker as a consequence of her knowledge structure, goals, and so forth. This section discusses the effects of task framing and the extent to which frames brought by individuals can moderate task framing effects.

others. Some studies show within-subjects effects of frames, suggesting that JDM quality defined as agreement with oneself over time can be impaired as well. Further, if frames have an effect on decisions, then JDM quality is considered to be degraded according to normative theories such as expected utility theory. Finally, although psychology research tends not to examine the effects of framing on accuracy dimensions of JDM quality, it is entirely possible that it could have a negative impact on accuracy. For example, if auditors make a going-concern judgment by focusing on reasons a client may continue in existence, they may judge the probability of going-concern problems to be below a threshold that would trigger a going-concern modification to an opinion in a case where the client subsequently goes bankrupt.

The means by which framing effects occur and their manifestation in judgments and decisions depend on the type of framing. The mediators and JDM effects of risky choice framing effects are spelled out by prospect theory (Kahneman and Tversky 1979).[24] Prospect theory proposes that framing affects decisions because framing affects the problem representations that people adopt. Specifically, prospect theory says that people adopt problem representations that are either positive or negative depending on the frame of the task. The theory proposes that this occurs because people naturally prefer to think about outcome alternatives in terms of changes (gains or losses) from some reference point, which typically is the status quo, rather than in terms of final states. In turn, positive or gain-oriented problem representations create different risk preferences than negative or loss-oriented problem representations; these risk preferences then factor directly into decisions. When people think in terms of gains, they tend to be risk averse; that is, they prefer the riskless option to the risky alternative. With losses, people tend to be risk seeking and prefer the risky alternative.[25]

The impact of attribute framing on JDM is thought to occur principally through memory retrieval and information search (Kühberger 1995; Levin et al. 1998). When a person reads a positively (negatively) framed description of an item, she keys on that positive (negative) description in memory as well. If the person has knowledge in memory about the item, focus on the positive (negative) description causes activation to be spread to other positive (negative) items. If the person is searching for information instead, confirmation bias in search leads to the search for positive (negative) items when there is a positive (negative) frame. As a consequence, people with positive frames make more positive judgments than do people with negative frames.[26] However, it is not clear whether attribute framing's effects flow from judgments to decisions (Kühberger 1998).

Goal framing effects, although less well understood, may occur through the hypothesis evaluation process (Levin et al. 1998). When people are informed of the negative consequences of not engaging in a behavior, for example, not quitting smoking, that negative information appears to receive more weight in their evaluation of the desirability of the behavior than does comparable positive information that is given in

---

[24]For alternative theoretical perspectives, see Reyna and Brainerd (1991) and Kühberger (1995).

[25]Note that prospect theory addresses the effects of framing only on decisions (final choices) rather than on both judgments (evaluations) and decisions. In addition, there are other aspects of prospect theory that are important to decisions. One of these is that people tend to think in terms of percentage differences rather than in terms of absolute differences. Thus, for example, people value a savings of $10 on a $40 purchase more than they do a savings of $10 on a $200 purchase.

[26]It also is conceivable that an attribute frame can be used to create a problem representation, which then dictates memory retrieval and information search.

a positive version of the message. Thus, people who receive the negative goal frame are more likely to choose to engage in the behavior than are people who receive the positive goal frame.[27] Note that the applicability of the goal-framing literature to accounting is tentative given that studies to date mostly examine behaviors rather than technical JDM.

Moderators of framing effects are not well understood in psychology (Levin et al. 1998). Several studies indicate factors that appear to attenuate or reverse risky choice framing effects, but it is not clear for what these factors proxy and, thus, why they moderate framing effects. For example, when choices between a riskless outcome and a risky outcome involve probabilities other than the specific ones used by Tversky and Kahneman (1981), people are less likely to exhibit framing effects (Fagley and Miller 1990; Miller and Fagley 1991; Schneider 1992; Wang 1996; Kühberger et al. 1999). Similarly, choices between risky options (rather than between a riskless and a risky option) show fewer framing effects (Schneider and Lopes 1986; Kühberger 1998).

Logic suggests that risky choice framing effects can be reduced by factors that cause people to adopt the same problem representation irrespective of the frame presented by the task. Similarly, the effects of attribute framing might be reduced by factors that cause people to adopt the same starting point for memory retrieval or information search irrespective of the task's frame.[28] Such factors might include incentives related to the positive versus the negative outcome. For example, auditors appear to think about the going-concern judgment using a negative frame no matter how the task is set up. This may reflect their perception that there are smaller costs associated with initially deeming a client a going-concern risk and engaging in extra audit tests as a result than with deeming a client not to be a going-concern risk and issuing an unqualified opinion that later turns out to be inaccurate. Another factor may be professional skepticism; auditors are trained to be skeptical of information presented by the client. In addition, training and experience may create a strong knowledge structure that relates to one frame, and this knowledge structure overrides frames provided by tasks.

Studies of framing tend to be experimental so frames can be manipulated. As is the case with anchors, examining framing effects through measurement is difficult because there normally is only one frame associated with a particular task at a particular point in time. For example, companies release one annual report with a letter from the president that can be framed either positively or negatively (but not both). Again, then, the researcher would need to control for firm, time period, and other such confounds, in order to study framing through measurement.

Accounting Studies on Framing

Accounting studies on framing include the following related to producers of accounting information.[29] Lipe (1993) finds that students and management accountants who adopt a positive frame vis-à-vis variance investigation (that such investigation is a cost)

---

[27]Yaniv and Schul (1997, 2000) propose a specific process by which goals related to including or eliminating alternatives can create framing effects.
[28]Factors that may moderate the effects of goal framing are not discussed because the processes underlying these effects are not well understood.
[29]Note that many accounting studies of framing rely on prospect theory yet examine judgments or decisions under uncertainty rather than a choice between a riskless alternative and a risky alternative.

make more positive performance evaluations than do subjects who adopt a negative frame (that variance investigation is a loss). Although Lipe does not directly manipulate framing, differential frames result from the manipulation of other task information. Luft (1994) finds that, when presented with incentive contracts with equal expected value, students prefer positively framed contracts to negatively framed contracts. Further, students with negatively framed incentives recall that they have lower past performance than do other students; in actuality, their past performance is equivalent. Shelley (1994) and Shelley and Omer (1996) find that students choose larger discount rates for investment projects when incentive contracts are framed negatively than when they are framed positively. Chang et al. (2002) utilize a risky-choice scenario related to an investment and find the standard risk-averse (risk-seeking) choices in the positive (negative) condition.

Studies of users of accounting information include two related to analysts. Hunton et al. (2001) find that analysts placed in a gain frame make less risk-seeking future earnings forecasts than do analysts placed in a loss frame. They manipulate the frame by telling subjects that their previous earnings forecast is either close to or far above actual earnings. Tan et al. (2002a) examine the effects of firms' earnings announcements on analysts' earnings forecasts. Firms that present positive news regarding earnings (actual earnings are greater than analysts' forecasts) lead analysts to make higher earnings forecasts if they present that news in two pieces that appear to be gains than if they present the information in two pieces that are framed either as a gain and no change or as a gain then a loss.[30] For firms that present negative news regarding earnings, analysts make higher earnings forecasts if firms present that news in two pieces that appear to be a loss then a gain, as opposed to two pieces that appear to be a loss and no change or two losses. Although not direct examinations of framing, studies that indicate that firms either manage or round up reported earnings to meet or exceed benchmarks such as prior period earnings and analysts' forecasted earnings are assuming that investors use these benchmarks as reference points and encode current earnings as gains or losses vis-à-vis those reference points (e.g., Burgstahler and Dichev 1997; Degeorge et al. 1999; Das and Zhang 2003).

A number of studies examine the effects of framing on taxpayers' JDM. Schadewald (1989) explains how the decision to claim a deduction (or to not report a receipt) where taxability is uncertain is akin to a risky-choice problem. Not taking a deduction is akin to a riskless option; taking the deduction is akin to the risky option because there are two possible outcomes, each of which occurs with nonzero probability: the deduction is either allowed or disallowed. Schadewald finds that students' decisions about taking a deduction are not affected by the framing of taxes due or taxes to be refunded as a gain or loss unless the terms *gain* and *loss* are used; however, he finds standard framing effects with nontax problems. White et al. (1993) and Dusenbury (1994), however, find that subjects become more risk seeking in their decisions about how much income to include when they are in a payment due (loss) situation than when they are in a refund due (gain) situation. Christensen and Hite (1997) find that taxpayer subjects' deduction/income inclusion decisions are not affected by attribute framing of the probability of taxability (as either winning or losing vis-à-vis the IRS).

---

[30]Presenting two gains is accomplished by firms announcing that earnings will be somewhat higher than the forecasts then announcing actual earnings that are higher than previously announced earnings.

Other studies examine framing effects in tax evasion situations. Chang et al. (1987), Robben et al. (1990), Schepanski and Kelsey (1990), and Schepanski and Shearer (1995) find that taxpayers are more likely to take a nonallowed deduction (the risk-seeking choice) when they are in a loss position.

Two studies examine tax professionals' JDM. Newberry et al. (1993) find that tax professionals are more willing to support an ambiguous deduction for a client (which would be somewhat akin to risk-seeking behavior) in a negatively framed situation than in a positively framed situation. Negative (positive) framing is accomplished by portraying the client as an existing (potential) client with the implication that the client might be lost (not be gained). Schisler (1994), however, finds no effect of the client's tax-due (loss) versus refund-due (gain) status on judgments of the probability of recommending an ambiguous deduction unless clients are described to be aggressive.

In auditing, Kida (1984b) examines attribute framing effects on going-concern judgments. Although auditors given a positive frame list more positive cues as relevant to their judgments than do auditors given a negative frame, there are no differences in negative cues listed or in final probability judgments. Trotman and Sng (1989) report that auditors' choices of relevant cues are (are not) affected by framing when they have strong (weak) prior beliefs about the client's going-concern status; however, framing does not affect final probability judgments in either case. Asare (1992) also finds no effects of framing on auditors' going-concern judgments. These studies suggest that auditors use a standard problem representation for going-concern judgments (the failure frame) which overrides any task-related framing effects. Emby (1994) studies the effects of framing internal control judgments as related to the strength or risk of the system; auditors with the risk frame require more substantive testing. Emby and Finley (1997) replicate this finding but also show that asking auditors to rate the relevance and sign of each piece of evidence eliminates the framing effect. They suggest that this occurs because the technique creates a similar problem representation for all auditors.

McMillan and White (1993) indicate that auditors' information search and judgments of the probability of financial statement error based on analysis of ratios are affected by attribute framing, specifically whether they are asked to think about whether ratio fluctuations indicate an error cause or an environmental cause. Mueller and Anderson (2002) examine goal framing in a ratio analysis task. Auditors asked to evaluate a list of fluctuation causes under an inclusion-of-likely-causes goal retain fewer causes than do auditors with an elimination-of-unlikely-causes goal. Finally, Shields et al. (1987) indicate no effect on auditors of framing financial statement account value judgments as audited values versus book value misstatements.[31]

Although some accounting studies find framing effects similar to those documented elsewhere, a significant number do not. In cases where there are no framing effects, researchers speculate about their causes (e.g., incentives that lead to constant problem representations). However, there is little direct evidence about this issue. It seems important for researchers to understand clearly the factors that differ between situations where accounting decision makers are affected by framing and those where they are not and how these differences affect the JDM process. Such an understanding

---

[31]Studies by Johnson et al. (1991a) and Jamal et al. (1995) that contain the term "framing" in their titles are not included here because framing does not vary in these studies.

can lead to research that examines whether instituting the factors that appear to be responsible for no framing effects in some situations will improve JDM quality in other situations. This research is particularly important given that framing of tasks often is under the control of standard-setters and other policy makers. Finally, the fact that clients and other individuals who deal with accounting professionals can strategically frame tasks and information to their advantage strongly supports research both on antecedents of framing and methods for attenuating framing effects.

6-4 EFFECTS OF INFORMATION ORDER ON JDM QUALITY

Information Order Effects

This section examines the JDM quality effects of the sequential *order* in which individual information cues are received and processed. Specifically, the section discusses the effects of varying the order of information cues (or choice alternatives) such that one group of subjects sees particular cues in order *A-B,* whereas another group sees the same cues but in order *B-A*. For example, one investor could read a *Wall Street Journal* article about a company then an analyst's report, whereas another investor might read the analyst's report followed by the article.[32] Much of the literature on order effects instead discusses the extent to which cues received early (late) in a sequence of cues receive greater weight in JDM vis-à-vis other cues in that same sequence when cues appear in one order. Although this section discusses only the former issue, it should be noted that both literatures refer to order effects as "primacy effects" and "recency effects." *Primacy effects (recency effects)* means that information received early (late) in the sequence receives greater weight than information received later (earlier) in the sequence information. In addition, this section discusses the effects of the order in which choice alternatives are viewed on choices. For example, does driving a Mercedes before driving a Honda cause people to make different car-buying choices than they would if they were to drive a Honda first?

How is it that order of information or choice alternatives can vary in accounting settings? As in the investor example above, order of information can vary because individual decision makers often construct the sequence in which they view information. For example, investors may view information in different orders because they accumulate reports, articles, and various other sources of information until the point at which they are ready to make a decision, and they read through the information in the order in which it occurs in their pile. Differential placement in a pile might occur unintentionally, for example because of the way mail is delivered; instead, people may consciously construct the order of information. For example, people who believe that the *Wall Street Journal* is the most credible source of information about companies may always read its articles first, whereas other people may start with analysts' reports. Further, third parties could be strategic in creating the order of information they provide to decision makers. For example, a manager trying to convince a superior to continue investing in her pet project may strategically place positive information about the

---

[32]This example uses the term "information cue" loosely; it is likely that the newspaper article and analyst's report each contain multiple cues. Nevertheless, it is feasible that one investor could read one *set* of cues followed by the other set of cues and another investor could read the sets in reverse order.

project at the end of the sequence (based on the belief that recency effects will occur). If the superior does not consider the order issue, she may make an inaccurate decision about the project and end up experiencing losses. The order of choice alternatives, for example, two mutual funds being presented by a broker to an investor, can vary for similar reasons. Thus, although not unique to accounting, order of cues or alternatives clearly can have an important effect on JDM quality in accounting tasks and related economic consequences.

Order of information or of choice alternatives often has a negative effect on JDM quality, where quality is defined as agreement with others. That is, people who view information (choice alternatives) in one order make different judgments or decisions than other people who view the same information (choice alternatives) in a different order. It also is possible that a single decision maker may not agree with herself over time if she views information (choice alternatives) in different orders on different occasions. Further, to the extent order has an effect on decisions, order effects would be said to lower JDM quality defined vis-à-vis normative theories such as expected utility theory. Finally, third parties using order strategically may lower decision makers' JDM quality as to accuracy.

The predominant model regarding the effects of the order of information cues is the "belief-adjustment model" (Hogarth and Einhorn 1992). This model predicts that order effects occur because people process sequential information using an anchoring-and-adjustment strategy. The anchor in this case is not an irrelevant information cue (as is the case in the literature on anchor effects); rather, it is the current state of belief. A given state of belief is adjusted for an information cue then becomes the anchor, or starting point, for the next belief adjustment. Further, such a process does not always produce order effects; these effects depend on a number of factors. First, like prospect theory, this model proposes that people encode each information cue vis-à-vis some reference point. However, reference points can be either a particular hypothesis under consideration, in which case information is encoded as confirming or disconfirming of the hypothesis (irrespective of one's current belief about the hypothesis's truth), or the current state of belief, in which case evidence is encoded vis-à-vis that anchor. Hogarth and Einhorn refer to the first type of task as an "evaluation task" and the second type as an "estimation task." Whether a task is of the evaluation or estimation type depends on, among other things, the type of judgment required (e.g., a dichotomous judgment such as guilty or not guilty typically appears in an evaluation task) and the manner in which cues are presented.

Second, when presented with information in a given order, people can make judgments sequentially (after each piece of information) or simultaneously (after seeing all the information). The former mode is referred to as *step-by-step processing,* whereas the latter is called *simultaneous processing.* Hogarth and Einhorn (1992) posit that people will use the step-by-step mode when asked to do so but also may use it to simplify processing of complex tasks when asked to use the simultaneous mode. They define complex tasks as those that have either a large number of cues or those that have "cues" that must be constructed from a number of pieces of evidence (other cues).

Third, information cues can vary as to sign. Some cues are encoded as positive (or confirming) vis-à-vis a reference point, whereas other cues are considered negative (or disconfirming). Further, cues vary as to the strength with which they confirm or disconfirm a belief. From the perspective of the belief-adjustment model, both these factors combine to affect the way a belief is adjusted. When a cue is negative, the weight it receives reflects its own strength but also is proportional to the anchor. Thus, bigger anchors get reduced more by negative evidence than do smaller anchors. When a cue is encoded as positive, the weight it receives also reflects its strength but is inversely proportional to the anchor. Thus, bigger anchors get increased less by positive evidence than do smaller anchors. These weighting outcomes are referred to as the *contrast effect*. Hogarth and Einhorn (1992) make predictions about order effects based on whether a set of cues is consistently positive or negative or mixed as to positive and negative signs. Further, they allow for individual differences in sensitivity to negative and positive cues.

Thus, the effects of the order of information cues occur through problem representation (the choice of a reference point) and hypothesis evaluation (processing of the cues). Hogarth and Einhorn's (1992) model predicts the following specific order effects. For evaluation tasks (where the reference point is a hypothesis), it predicts some type of order effect unless cues are consistently positive or negative and the tasks are simple. If evaluation tasks are complex and contain consistent cues, the model predicts primacy effects. If evaluation tasks contain mixed cues, the model predicts recency effects when step-by-step processing is used for simple tasks and mostly primacy effects otherwise. For estimation tasks, step-by-step processing is predicted to yield recency effects for mixed and consistent cues unless the task is complex, in which case primacy effects are predicted. Simultaneous processing mostly yields primacy effects. All these predictions assume that people have nonzero sensitivity to both positive and negative cues.[33]

Order of choice alternatives affects decisions through other mechanisms. Bruine de Bruin and Keren (2003) posit that the first choice alternative (e.g., a Mercedes) is compared either to some category (e.g., "cars") or to some other alternative generated by each decision maker, whereas the second alternative (e.g., a Honda) is compared to the first. They propose that people make similarity judgments during such comparisons (Tversky 1977), so they focus on the similar and unique aspects of each alternative. Alternatives that have unique positive features are more likely, therefore, to be chosen when they appear second, whereas alternatives with unique negative features are less likely to be chosen when they appear second.

Little seems to be known in psychology about what moderates order effects. Accounting studies (described further below) find some evidence that knowledge and having to justify one's JDM may attenuate negative effects of order. For choice situations, asking people to simultaneously process the choices can eliminate order effects because each choice can be compared to the other, or at least to the same category of items (Bruine de Bruin and Keren 2003).

As is the case with other task variables, studies of order effects tend to be experimental because there normally would be only one order of information associated with a given task at a given point in time. For example, the earnings forecast of one analyst comes either before or after the earnings forecast of another analyst. Thus, researchers wishing to study order effects through measurement would have a number of confounds for which to control.

---

[33]Please see Hogarth and Einhorn (1992) for the mathematical derivation of these predictions.

Accounting Studies on Information Order

Order effects studies in accounting tend to assume that accounting tasks are evaluation tasks; thus, they assume or set up the tasks such that information cues are encoded relative to a hypothesis.[34] Studies of information producers include Dillard et al. (1991), who present students with several hypotheses to evaluate using step-by-step processing and related decisions to make. Their findings mostly support Hogarth and Einhorn's (1992) predictions. However, they find that order effects, where present in judgments, have little impact on decisions. Rutledge (1995) reports that students exhibit recency effects with mixed cues when evaluating a hypothesis that a budget will be met. However, if information is framed inconsistently with its sign (e.g., it is framed as negative when it is a positive cue), recency effects are moderated.

Studies of information users include Libby and Tan (1999), who report that analysts who receive a warning about lower earnings sequentially prior to learning actual earnings make lower earnings forecasts than do analysts who receive the warning and the earnings report simultaneously. They contend that this is due to the analysts' interpreting the warning as a negative cue in the first case but as a positive cue in the second case. In tax, Pei et al. (1990) report that tax professionals exhibit recency effects when they view mixed cues related to an ambiguous tax treatment; these effects occur with judgments about the probability of audit and with recommendations to a client. Pei et al. (1992a) find similar results with experienced tax managers but not with inexperienced tax managers. Schadewald and Limberg's (1992) student subjects also exhibit such recency effects; however, asking subjects to justify their judgments eliminates the order effects. Cuccia and McGill (2000) find that tax professionals exhibit recency effects with mixed cues when order of cues is imposed on them. However, when they have the ability to choose the order in which they view cues, recency effects disappear.

A number of studies examine order effects in auditing tasks. Ashton and Ashton (1988) ask auditors to make judgments regarding the hypothesis that internal control systems will prevent or detect material errors. They find no order effects for consistently positive or negative cues and recency effects for mixed cues, and they also find the predicted contrast effect. Butt and Campbell (1989) manipulate order of mixed cues and level of prior beliefs. Order effects occur when auditors have low priors; when they have high priors, there are no order effects. Trotman and Wright (1996) find that students and senior auditors exhibit recency effects in an internal control task with mixed cues that is done using step-by-step processing, and students exhibit primacy effects in this task when done with simultaneous processing. Managers exhibit no order effects.

Trotman and Wright (1996) find similar order effects with mixed cues in a going-concern scenario. Kennedy's (1995) manager subjects show no recency effects in a similar going-concern task (although students do). On the other hand, Asare's (1992), Cushing and Ahlawat's (1996), and Ahlawat's (1999) manager, partner, and senior subjects show recency effects in going-concern judgments; Asare's subjects also exhibit these effects in opinion choices. Asking subjects to explain their judgments eliminates recency effects in Cushing and Ahlawat's study.

---

[34]Kerr and Ward's (1994) study is an exception to this, although they investigate other aspects of the model's predictions regarding evaluation versus estimation tasks.

Several studies examine order effects in judgments about errors in account balances. Tubbs et al.'s (1990) senior auditors exhibit no order effects with consistent positive and negative cues and recency with mixed cues processed in a step-by-step mode. When mixed cues are processed simultaneously, recency occurs with a series of four cues but not a series of two cues. Messier and Tubbs (1994) find that seniors exhibit recency in a similar task but managers do not. Krull et al. (1993) and Reckers and Schultz (1993) report that auditors exhibit recency effects with mixed cues when judging the probability of an account write-down; more experienced auditors demonstrate greater recency effects. Anderson and Maletta's (1999) auditors exhibit primacy in their judgments about the probability of error and audit hours when they see mixed cues and inherent risk is low; when inherent risk is high, there are no order effects.

Other studies examine a variety of tasks. Pei et al. (1992b) find recency (no) effects in auditors' judgments of the effectiveness (efficiency) of a social program. Koonce (1992) documents recency effects when auditors doing analytical procedures see varied orders of explanation and counterexplanation for a hypothesized cause of a ratio fluctuation. Hirsch (1978) demonstrates that order of new product line choices affects students' decisions, although to a lesser extent than occurs in a generic choice task.[35]

Studies of order effects in accounting produce results that mostly are consistent with Hogarth and Einhorn's (1992) model and other theories in psychology. Also consistent with psychology, we know little about factors that attenuate order effects. What seems essential at this juncture is a thorough understanding of why order varies in accounting contexts. Some order variation is due to inconsequential factors such as mail delivery (as described earlier); however, it is likely that some order variation occurs for strategic reasons. That is, individuals may present information to others in the order they believe is most likely to elicit a desired response, and this order can change with the task and circumstances. A better understanding of the contexts in which accounting decision makers can control versus not control the order of information can point researchers to the most fruitful areas for conducting research on order effects. Along with this, we need to consider whether there are "natural" improvement methods related to order effects already in the environment. For example, can the review process moderate order effects in audit tasks? If such methods do not exist, then further research on the factors that can moderate order effects seems in order.

6-5 EFFECTS OF PRESENTATION FORMAT AND RESPONSE MODE ON JDM QUALITY

Two final task characteristics of import to accounting JDM are presentation format and response mode. *Presentation format* refers to the manner in which information is provided to the accounting decision maker. For example, information about a particular accounting issue may be found either in the financial statements or in a footnote.[36] *Response mode* refers to the manner in which the accounting decision maker is asked to make a judgment or decision. For example, an auditor can be asked to rate inherent

---

[35]Four studies examine the effects of order of choice alternatives using nonaccounting tasks (Ronen 1971, 1973; Lewis and Bell 1985; Moser et al. 1994).

[36]Some presentation format issues, such as graphical versus tabular presentation, are subsumed under task complexity because specific predictions about the relation between format and complexity can be made.

risk numerically (e.g., 20%, 50%, or 80%) or using words (e.g., low, medium, or high). In accounting, presentation format and response mode are created by persons who construct tasks (e.g., standard-setters and firm policy makers). To the extent that these characteristics are controllable by such individuals, then, it may be more feasible to deal with their adverse effects on JDM quality.

The typical effect of variation in presentation format or response mode is that people who view different formats or response modes make different judgments; therefore, JDM quality measured as agreement with others is decreased. Similarly, it is conceivable that individuals could disagree with themselves over time if presented with different formats or response modes, and to the extent that normative theories imply that such characteristics are irrelevant to JDM, JDM quality is lessened vis-à-vis these theories. Although not studied as much, it also is conceivable that presentation format or response mode could be used strategically when dealing with accounting decision makers, in which case their effects could be more problematic. For example, managers may present information numerically in an attempt to persuade superiors of the viability of their proposals (Kadous et al. 2005). If superiors do not understand such strategic uses of format, they may make incorrect decisions regarding projects in which to invest.

Unfortunately, studies of presentation format and response mode are not united by theory. As a consequence, this section simply discusses the studies grouped by the issues they address. Recent studies (e.g., Hopkins 1996) make strong advances on the theoretical front, but it is not clear that theories used in these studies pertain to all presentation format and response mode issues. To better understand particular issues, researchers must engage in careful task analysis (as described in Chapter 1). Further, researchers may have to develop separate theories for various facets of presentation format such as categorization and aggregation issues. Typically, researchers also must use an experimental approach because it is relatively rare when multiple formats or response modes are used in the real world. For example, standard-setters normally dictate that certain accounting information must appear in the financial statements or the footnotes, rather than giving companies a choice. Similarly, auditing firms make a policy decision about whether their auditors make risk judgments using numbers or words. Although researchers might be able to compare the JDM of auditors from one firm to that of auditors from another firm who respond differently when making risk judgments, it would be difficult to control for all other differences between the firms that might cause them to choose numerical or verbal response modes.

Accounting Studies on Presentation Format

This section groups presentation format studies by issues examined. The first group of studies examines aggregation of information, a key function of accounting systems. Aggregation is a presentation format issue from the standpoint that aggregated numbers may provide no more or less information than do disaggregated numbers. However, some studies suggest that aggregation reduces information content and also may reduce information load (an element of task complexity). Thus, aggregation may be related to task variables other than presentation format. Hence, its effects on JDM quality can be difficult to interpret.

Stallman (1969) reports that analysts who receive disaggregated segment information make similar stock price judgments as those who do not; however, Ortman's (1975) analyst subjects make different price judgments. Harvey et al. (1979) find that analysts prefer disaggregated financial data when making investment recommendations and tend to recommend allocating more funds to the investment for which disaggregated information is provided. Barefield (1972) finds that student subjects do not differ in the accuracy of their judgments about whether labor is used efficiently when given disaggregated variance information versus aggregated information. Abdel-Khalik (1973) finds that loan officers are more consistent in their decisions about whether to grant loans and are also more accurate vis-à-vis outcomes when they use disaggregated versus aggregated financial statement information. There are no differences in consensus due to aggregation, however.

Benbasat and Dexter (1979) examine students with high and low perceptual differentiation (PD) ability, respectively (see Chapter 4). Students with high PD ability take more time to make decisions with disaggregated inventory production and profit information than with aggregated information, but their achieved profits are no different. Low-PD-ability students make less profit with aggregated information. Patton's (1978) municipal finance officer subjects make similar estimates of interest rates for a governmental entity regardless of whether they receive disaggregated fund information or consolidated information. However, Ramanathan and Weis (1981) find that students and loan officers make different judgments about universities' performance (albeit not financial condition) when they view financial information in a disaggregated fund-by-fund format versus a format that also includes consolidated numbers. Consistent with the notion that aggregation may reflect both presentation format and other task-related issues, these studies find very mixed results about its effects.

The second group of studies covers various accounting information presentation issues, including accounting method chosen. The general idea here is that, if accounting methods reflect the same underlying economic circumstances, method chosen should not affect JDM. However, this is not always the case, and unfortunately, many studies examine JDM under situations where accounting method and underlying economics are related. Dyckman (1964b) reports that students make different stock price judgments when they view financial statements that differ as to the use of LIFO versus FIFO to value inventory. Jensen's (1966) analyst subjects make different portfolio allocation decisions and stock price judgments when faced with FIFO versus LIFO and also when faced with accelerated versus straight-line depreciation. However, Dyckman's (1964a) and Bruns's (1965) subjects are not affected by inventory valuation method when making various business decisions such as inventory production and pricing. These studies appear to assume no economic effects due to accounting methods (and their related income effects), such that different JDM when faced with different methods is "inappropriate." Dopuch and Ronen (1973), on the other hand, use students who have training related to the cash flow effects of LIFO and predict that students will allocate more dollars in a portfolio to LIFO firms. However, many students do not do so.

Barrett (1971) reports that analysts' stock price judgments are not affected by the cost versus equity method choice for investments. McIntyre (1973) shows that students' investment choices are not affected by whether they see historical cost or current cost financial information. A recent study by Hopkins et al. (2000) finds that analysts' stock price judgments are different when firms use pooling versus purchase accounting. However, presenting goodwill amortization as a separate line item in the income statement mitigates these effects. Luft and Shields (2001) report that students predicting profits are less accurate vis-à-vis simulation results and agree less with others and themselves over time when intangibles are expensed rather than capitalized.

Other studies examine the effects of placement of financial information and invoke the ideas that placement matters because certain placements of information are more salient to decision makers (e.g., within the financial statements) and that decision makers emphasize salient information. Belkaoui (1980) reports that loan officers and accountants, but not students, are affected by the placement of pollution abatement cost information in the balance sheet versus in the balance sheet and footnotes. Wilkins and Zimmer (1983) examine loan officers' judgments about clients' ability to repay loans and decisions about amounts to loan when they view lease information in the balance sheet or in the balance sheet and footnotes, and they find that placement has no effect on JDM. Harper et al. (1987) show that students and loan officers are more likely to include a pension liability in their calculation of the debt-equity ratio when it appears on the balance sheet and in the footnotes rather than just in the footnotes. Similarly, Sami and Schwartz (1992) report that loan officers have different judgments and decisions about loans depending on the placement of pension liability information.

Hopkins (1996) finds that analysts' stock price judgments are affected by the classification of mandatorily redeemable preferred stock on the balance sheet as debt, equity, or in the mezzanine. He carefully analyzes the effects of classification and applies psychology theory related to categorization and related retrieval processes to predict these findings. Hirst and Hopkins (1998) report that analysts' stock price judgments for a firm that manages earnings through the sale of marketable securities and a firm that does not manage earnings differ when no comprehensive income information is provided and when such information is provided in the statement of changes in equity. However, when comprehensive income information is presented in a separate statement accompanying the income statement, stock price judgments do not differ. Maines and McDaniel (2000) develop a psychology-based framework for understanding the Hirst and Hopkins results that focuses on initial encoding of information and evidence evaluation. Their student subjects encode comprehensive income information similarly when such information is presented in the statement of changes in equity versus in a separate statement. However, they make different stock risk and management effectiveness judgments (albeit not stock price judgments) because they weight information differently in these two formats. Finally, Hirst et al. (2004) find that analysts are able to recognize different interest rate risk among banks (as reflected in their risk and value judgments) based on financial statements that recognize all fair value changes in income. However, when some fair value changes are disclosed in footnotes instead, analysts are unable to detect differential risk.

Other studies examine a variety of financial accounting presentation format issues. Oliver (1972) and Keys (1978) present loan officers with either standard financial statements or confidence-interval financial statements; lending decisions are not affected by format. Bell (1984) finds no effect on financial analysts' judgments about firm performance due to numeric versus nonnumeric presentation of president's letter comments. Klammer and Reed (1990) report that loan officers and bank analysts are more variable in judgments about amounts to be loaned when they use cash flow statements prepared in the indirect format than when they use direct format statements; in the former situation, subjects also make more errors calculating operating cash flow.

Kachelmeier (1996) demonstrates that students who view profit calculated vis-à-vis unavoidable costs rather than redemption values of assets make different bids and asks in a laboratory market; however, final market prices are not affected.

Maines et al. (1997) report that analysts view segment reporting as more reliable when it is congruent with internal segment classifications and also when firms group similar products (rather than dissimilar products). Analysts' confidence in their stock price judgments and recommendations is affected similarly. Maines et al. do not report the effects of these presentation format issues on JDM. Hirst et al. (1999) find that student subjects' earnings predictions do not differ depending on whether they receive management earnings forecasts presented in the form of point estimates or ranges; however, their confidence in management forecasts is affected. Koonce et al. (2005a) show that student subjects who see a financial instrument labeled as a "hedge" view that instrument as less risky than when it is labeled as a "swap." Providing information that the instruments have the same fair value and cash flows does not attenuate this effect.

Finally, two studies examine more general format issues. Hodge (2001) demonstrates that hyperlinking unaudited information to audited information, as opposed to presenting the materials in hard copy form, increases students' perceptions about the credibility of the unaudited information and judgments about earnings potential. Format effects are attenuated by labeling the information as either audited or unaudited. Sedor (2002) shows that analysts who receive information in a scenario format are more optimistic in earnings forecasts than analysts who receive information in a list; further, this difference is larger for loss firms than for profitable firms. Sedor attributes this effect to analysts' being able to reason causally when a scenario format is used.[37]

The next group of studies relies on a literature in psychology related to "functional fixation." The original meaning of *functional fixation* is that people have difficulty finding alternative uses, or functions, for objects once they use them in a particular way. A well-known example of this comes from Adamson (1952): subjects who receive boxes containing matches and thumbtacks are less able than subjects who receive empty boxes to determine that the boxes can be used as platforms to mount candles on a wall, ostensibly because they view the boxes as functioning as containers. As discussed by Ashton (1976), however, accounting researchers have used the term to refer to people being unable to adjust their JDM to a change in accounting method that affects the financial data they see (e.g., a change from FIFO to LIFO).[38] Oddly enough, however, only one study examines fixation in a financial accounting setting. Vergoossen (1997) examines analysts' and media reports for companies who disclose material accounting changes in their annual reports. He defines fixation as occurring if analysts or reporters either do not mention the accounting change or mention it but do not quantify its effects; such fixation occurs in nearly one-half of the reports. Fixation is more likely to occur with less disclosure about the changes, but analysts and reporters are no different in their levels of fixation.

---

[37]See Chapter 5 for further information on causal reasoning.
[38]Note that a number of archival studies use the term *fixation* to refer generally to investors' lack of understanding of accounting information (e.g., Hand 1990). This section includes only studies that examine decision makers' reactions to changes in accounting methods.

The remaining studies examine fixation issues in management accounting contexts. Ashton (1976) reports that many students who establish selling prices for products first using full cost data then using variable cost data (or vice versa) do not adjust their decision processes after being informed of the accounting change. (Also see Dyckman et al. [1982], Barnes and Webb [1986], and Marchant [1990a].) Chang and Birnberg (1977) demonstrate that student subjects who view a change from an inaccurate to an accurate variance investigation standard adjust their JDM about manager performance somewhat but still exhibit some fixation. There have been a number of criticisms of these studies, however, so it is not clear whether fixation exists nor to what extent it indicates poor JDM quality (e.g., Wilner and Birnberg 1986).

A final group of studies covers various presentation format issues in management accounting and auditing. Vera-Muñoz et al. (2001) report that management and public accountants are less likely to choose a cash-flow analysis (the appropriate) method when they are presented with information about a disinvestment decision in a historical earnings format rather than a future cash flow format. However, more public accounting or management accounting experience attenuates this effect. Lipe and Salterio (2002) report that student subjects who view performance evaluation information in a balanced scorecard (categorized) format give less extreme evaluations than subjects who view the information in a list format when multiple positive (or negative) results are concentrated in one category. There are no differences in evaluations when multiple positive (negative) results are distributed across categories. Buchheit (2004) varies the format in which fixed cost information is reported and finds that subjects' selling price choices differ depending on format. Kadous et al. (2005) demonstrate that quantification of information in a proposal regarding changes to a firm's operating procedures makes the proposal more (less) persuasive when the underlying information is objective (subjective) and the person who prepares the proposal has incentives to report fairly (mislead). Finally, Ricchiute (1984, 1985) examines the effects of visual and auditory formats on auditors' JDM. External and governmental auditors' judgments about the probability of adjusting an account or the proper recording of a transaction are affected by format.

It is impossible to summarize the findings of presentation format studies in any meaningful way. The first problem is that "presentation format" encompasses a variety of issues such as placement of information and accounting method. Thus, this section may be mixing not only apples and oranges, but also apples and airplanes. Second is the lack of theory for each separate presentation format issue or for format more generally. Specifically, we do not know whether presentation format is simply an amalgam of several task variables including, most prominently, task complexity, or a construct (or several constructs such as aggregation and categorization) unto itself. Along with this, we know little about how cognitive processing is affected by some elements of format, for example, aggregation. Recent theory development such as that by Hopkins (1996), Maines and McDaniel (2000), Lipe and Salterio (2002), Sedor (2002), Kadous et al. (2005), and Koonce et al. (2005a) should continue because it will provide researchers with answers to these types of questions. Third, findings in this area are truly mixed—nearly half of the studies find no effects of presentation format—and we know little about why this is the case. Perhaps there are factors at work in accounting settings such as large monetary incentives that motivate people to "work around" format issues. Nevertheless, it cannot be overemphasized how important continued work on presentation format issues is in accounting because they are at the core of what is unique to accounting scholarship and the practice of standard-setting (Kinney 2001). Further, if presentation format is used strategically to manipulate accounting decision makers by individuals such as clients, studying its effects takes on added importance.

Accounting Studies on Response Mode

A number of studies in accounting examine response mode effects. There are three general types of studies included here. First are those related to the effects on JDM of interpreting verbal probability expressions such as "probable" versus "likely" when responding. Many settings require accountants to make judgments and decisions using verbal expressions such as "probable" or "reasonably possible." These expressions sometimes are included in professional standards such as the Statements of Financial Accounting Standards or the Internal Revenue Code. Even if only one term is speci-fied, difficulty with JDM arises because interpretation of that term can vary across decision makers (e.g., Lichtenstein and Newman 1967). For example, some managers may interpret the term "remote" to mean that there is a 10% or less chance of some event occurring, whereas others managers interpret this term to mean a 1% or less chance. As a result, these managers may make different judgments and decisions; for example, a manager who deems the probability of a contingent claim as "remote" and follows SFAS No. 5 would provide no disclosure related to that claim, and another manager who deems the probability "reasonably possible" would provide footnote dis-closure related to that claim. Thus, JDM quality defined as agreement with others can be decreased. Further, interpretation of terms can vary across contexts; a given man-ager may interpret the term "remote" to mean different things depending on the con-text. Thus, JDM quality defined as agreement with oneself over time also can be decreased. Because both of these factors frequently are invoked when evaluators are determining the quality of auditors' work, such JDM effects could lead to litigation payments.

A number of studies examine variation in interpretation of verbal expressions. Schultz and Reckers (1981), Jiambalvo and Wilner (1985), and Harrison and Tomassini (1989) report that auditors exhibit substantial variation in their interpretation of the terms used in SFAS No. 5; the first two studies also show variation in recommendations for disclosure. Raghunandan et al. (1991) show variation across individual auditors, audit firms, accounting contexts, and materiality levels (the last finding is reported by Schultz and Reckers also). Amer et al. (1995) extend results on accounting contexts to show that variation in interpretation of SFAS No. 5 terms is related to the base rates of the events under consideration. Chesley (1986) reports that students exhibit large vari-ation in interpretation of many probability terms. Amer et al. (1994) find similar results with auditors; further, auditors do not have a good understanding of how other auditors interpret these terms. Finally, Cuccia et al. (1995) report that tax managers interpret verbal expressions quite differently; further, they interpret them in line with incentives related to client preferences for aggressive reporting.

A second set of studies examines the effects of requiring numerical versus verbal responses. Professional standards often allow either numerical or verbal responses for important judgments; for example, the Statements on Auditing Standards allow audi-tors to make judgments about the components of audit risk in either way. As a result, there is variation in practice as to response mode and, thus, possible variation in JDM.

These studies sometimes draw on the notion that the requirement for numerical responses ought to result in more agreement among individuals and with oneself over time, that is, higher JDM quality. This might occur because numerical responses are less subject to interpretation (e.g., Budescu et al. 1988). However, empirically, this often is not the case (e.g., Wallsten et al. 1993).

Three studies examine this issue in audit risk judgment contexts. Reimers et al. (1993) find that auditors make higher control risk judgments using a verbal rather than a numerical response mode. Although auditors do not make decisions in this study, their judgments likely would translate into less audit testing with the verbal response mode. However, auditors agree more with each other when they use the verbal response mode. Stone and Dilla (1994) find that auditors exhibit more agreement with others and with themselves over time when using numerical responses for inherent risk judgments. Students' judgments are not affected by response mode. Dilla and Stone (1997) report similar findings and examine the effects of presenting cues in either numerical or verbal form. Auditors agree more with each other when cues are in verbal form and are no different in agreement with themselves or time taken.

Another set of studies examines various methods of eliciting numerical responses, particularly probability distributions, and their effects on JDM. Although the manner in which probability distributions are estimated should not affect those estimates, substantial research indicates that this is the case (e.g., Winkler 1967; Chesley 1975). Abdolmohammadi (1985) describes the most common elicitation methods. These include the *cumulative distribution function* technique (CDF), in which subjects are asked to estimate a value such that the probability that an amount less than that value occurring is a given percentage, and the *probability density function* method (PDF), in which subjects are asked to specify the probability of an amount falling into a certain range of values. Another technique is the *equivalent prior sample* information technique (EPS), in which subjects are asked to specify a sample size and the number of "successes" (e.g., sales invoices without an error) in that sample that would be the same as a hypothetical sample of given size and number of successes. With the *hypothetical future samples* method (HFS), a fourth technique, subjects estimate a most likely value for an amount then revise those estimates based on findings from hypothetical samples. Occasionally, studies also use techniques related to betting and odds estimation.

Several studies examine the effects of these techniques among producers and users of accounting information. Chesley (1976, 1977, 1978) reports that students' distributions related to manufacturing performance do not differ depending on CDF or alternative elicitation techniques, some of which involve odds estimation. Eger and Dickhaut (1982) examine students' judgments about whether a department is in or out of control using betting and odds techniques. The betting technique produces judgments closer to those prescribed by Bayes' Theorem but also produces less agreement among subjects. Wright (1988b) compares PDF and CDF methods for students creating distributions for financial ratio values. The PDF method produces distributions that are more accurate vis-à-vis actual values of the ratios.

Studies examining the effects of these techniques on auditors' probability distributions include Corless (1972), who reports that auditors' distributions for control system error rates differ under CDF and PDF methods. Felix (1976) and Crosby (1980) report similar findings for CDF versus EPS. Crosby further reports that intuitive sample size decisions do not correspond to those that would be derived from the auditors' probability distributions under either method. However, Crosby (1981) reports no differences due to CDF versus EPS. Abdolmohammadi and Berger (1986) show that auditors assessing account balance distributions have higher agreement when using PDF than when using HFS, CDF, and EPS. They also are more accurate vis-à-vis simulation results with PDF. However, Shields et al. (1987) find no differences due to PDF versus CDF elicitation in account balance distributions. Abdolmohammadi and Wright (1992) report that auditors agree most with themselves and other auditors when using HFS (versus PDF and CDF) but that PDF takes less time than CDF and HFS.

Summarizing the findings of response mode studies is somewhat easier than is the case for presentation format. There are only a handful of practically significant response mode issues that crop up in accounting settings. The most prominent of these are the effects of different verbal expressions (or of a single verbal expression on different decision makers) and the effects of verbal versus numerical response modes on individuals making probability judgments. These response mode issues are at the core of much of standard-setting and regulation in accounting because accounting decision makers working under uncertainty frequently must estimate probabilities. Further, response mode studies appear to be fairly consistent in showing that response mode has a negative effect on JDM quality, indicating that continued work on response mode issues is important. In particular, research needs to develop better theories about why JDM quality is affected by response mode. Understanding the mediators of response mode effects then allows for a better understanding of potential methods for improving JDM if it is negatively affected by response mode. For example, suppose that standard-setters currently believe that variation in interpretation of verbal phrases occurs because of their imprecision; if so, they may recommend switching to numerical, "bright-line" standards (Nelson 2003). However, suppose that research indicates that variation in interpretation of verbal phrases is largely due to cultural differences and that research also indicates that cultural differences similarly affect the way people estimate numerical probabilities. In this case, it seems unlikely that changing verbal phrases to a numerical response mode would enhance JDM.

6-6 SUMMARY

This chapter examines the effects of task variables on accounting JDM quality. Specifically, it covers the effects of task complexity, irrelevant information, framing, order of information, and presentation format and response mode. Findings for many variables are similar to those in psychology. However, accounting decision makers sometimes are not affected by framing or presentation format. We know little about why these findings occur. Thus, it is important to better develop theories relating to the mediators of these variables in order to make better predictions about their effects. More generally, accountants can make a contribution to psychology by further developing theories about task variables, specifically focusing on moderators of the variables' effects that may be unique to accounting. In the case of presentation format, accountants can also make a contribution by clearly specifying the elements of format that have effects on JDM quality (such as quantification and aggregation) and investigating whether these elements are individual constructs for which separate theories should be developed (e.g., Kadous et al. 2005).

More generally, task characteristics are important to JDM quality because of their direct effects on JDM and also because they shape the knowledge and cognitive processes people bring to tasks. If only because of the critical role of knowledge and processes in JDM, task variables deserve more prominence in accounting research. Further, some task variables that have a negative effect on JDM quality seem to be increasing in the world faced by accounting decision makers, for example, complexity created by massive amounts of information and multiple task goals and repetition of information by the media. However, these characteristics' effects may be offset partially by the positive effects of other task variables that also appear to be prevalent or increasing in today's environment, such as correlation among information cues.

Task variables have further significance in accounting because one of the roles of accounting is to standardize task information for users. Thus, many task characteristics (e.g., complexity, framing, and presentation format) that affect JDM quality either directly or through learning are created by policy makers who establish and regulate accounting systems. Perhaps these characteristics can be changed more easily than other factors that affect JDM (e.g., abilities and risk attitudes). In addition, given the enormous resources devoted to task standardization, it behooves researchers to produce relevant findings in this area. Along with this, it is important to explore whether there are factors currently in the environment, such as time pressure or the review process, that already serve to mitigate the negative JDM effects of many task variables, particularly those created by accounting systems per se. Further, it seems important to investigate the JDM processes of standard-setters in order to understand how they make task standardization decisions.

The possibility for the strategic use of task characteristics for manipulating users' JDM in accounting settings is worrisome and, thus, also deserving of further study. People can manipulate many task factors, including the presence of irrelevant information and framing. For example, clients can manipulate these factors when providing information to auditors. Many research questions stem from this issue. For example, do people such as firm managers understand that they may be able to manipulate others such as auditors through task characteristics? If so, under what conditions will they make such manipulation attempts? Do auditors understand that clients may try to manipulate their JDM through task characteristics and how clients may do this? If so, how do they attempt to undo any negative effects on their JDM quality that may result? Are these attempts successful? Examining both the antecedents and effects of the strategic use of task variables seems particularly important in an era of corporate fraud, enormous litigation against auditors and analysts, and regulatory attempts to stem these problems. Perhaps improvement methods other than or in addition to regulation are necessary to undo strategically induced negative effects of task variables.

CHAPTER

7

Environmental Variables

This chapter examines the effects of environmental variables on JDM quality. Environmental variables are factors that surround individuals while they perform JDM tasks. They do not pertain to specific people or specific tasks, but are general to all people and all tasks in a particular environment. For example, some audit firms place their auditors under more time pressure than others. The environmental variables discussed in this chapter are monetary incentives, accountability and justification, assigned goals, feedback, groups and teams, time pressure, and standards and regulations.[1] Studies related to the review process are contained under the section on groups and teams.[2] As shown in Figure 7-1, this chapter completes the series of chapters that examine factors creating differences in or low levels of JDM quality.

Many of these environmental variables (e.g., monetary incentives, feedback, and regulations) appear to be methods for improving JDM that is not of the highest quality, but they also are critical and ubiquitous parts of the environment faced by accounting decision makers. Further, although individually these variables may not be unique to accounting settings, their confluence may be (Ashton and Ashton 1995). More important, the confluence of these factors may create JDM conflicts for accounting decision makers that are not faced by other decision makers. Recent scrutiny of environmental variables by regulators and policy makers suggests that such conflicts also may have serious economic consequences both for the decision makers themselves and for third parties who use their JDM, for example, investors. In addition, scrutiny may reflect the fact that many environmental variables are under the control of regulators, policy makers, and firms. As such, to the extent these factors are not effective methods for improving JDM, they can be altered in order to be more effective. Interestingly, however, alterations often create further negative (and unintended) effects on JDM, making research on environmental variables all the more important.

Each of the following sections discusses a single environmental variable, beginning with its definition. The sections then describe the variable's effects on JDM quality and how these effects occur. Moderating factors and methods for studying the variable also are discussed. The sections conclude with accounting research related to the variable of interest and suggestions for further research.

---

[1]These are not the only important environmental variables for accounting JDM, simply those with sufficient accounting research to discuss. For example, variables such as organizational culture likely are important to the JDM of managers, auditors, analysts, and others.

[2]Some studies that refer to the review process are discussed under the section on accountability because they examine the effects of the awareness that someone will be reviewed, that is, held accountable.

FIGURE 7-1   Framework for JDM Research in Accounting

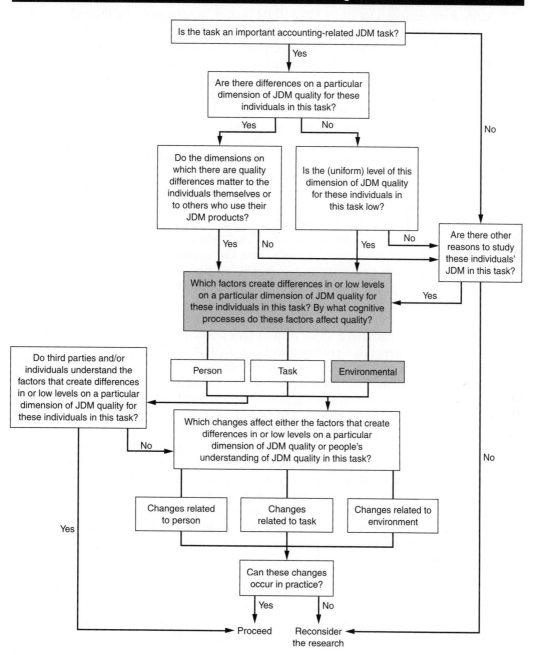

7-1 EFFECTS OF MOTIVATION ON JDM QUALITY

Many environmental variables affect JDM quality, at least partially, through increases in motivation (and consequent cognitive effort). Therefore, this chapter begins with a review of the material from Chapter 4 on motivation and its effects on JDM quality. The sections for each environmental variable then note whether motivation is thought to be the main mediator of the variable's effects; in cases where factors other than motivation also are mediators, those mediators are discussed. Finally, each section describes variable-specific moderators.

To review, *motivation* generally is defined as an intermediate "state of an organism that impels or drives it to action" (Reber 1995).[3] Current thinking suggests there are two types of motivational effects that can occur in JDM (Kunda 1990, 1999). First, motivation can be directed toward reaching the "correct" judgment or decision, where this "correct answer" is not known prior to the JDM process.[4] Second, motivation can be directed toward reaching a particular (known) desired judgment or decision. As described in Chapter 4, both types of motivation can occur in accounting settings. Further, some of the environmental variables described here can manifest themselves to operate through both types of motivation. For example, accountability can be to a superior whose views are unknown, in which case the subordinate is motivated to be correct, or to a superior whose views are known, in which case the subordinate may be motivated to reach the superior's desired conclusion.

Motivation directed toward reaching a correct answer generally is thought to positively affect cognitive effort, which in turn positively affects JDM quality. Kunda (1990, 1999) proposes that greater effort can occur in all the cognitive processes that affect the quality of a particular judgment or decision in the current period, including memory retrieval, information search, problem representation, hypothesis generation, and hypothesis and evidence evaluation. However, other studies indicate that people instead may increase effort related to learning so they can improve JDM quality in future periods (Kanfer 1990; Locke and Latham 1990).

Research suggests that there are three possible positive effects of motivation to be correct on cognitive effort related to current performance of a JDM task. First, people may increase *effort direction;* this means that a person is more likely to engage in a particular cognitive process than she would without the antecedent motivation. Second, people may increase *effort duration* by spending more time working actively on the task. Third, people may increase *effort intensity;* this means that they devote more attention to a task during a given time period than they would otherwise (Kanfer 1990).

In addition to positing specific effort effects of motivation to be correct, the psychology literature goes further to propose mediators of the motivation–effort relation. There are two theories about these mediators that appear frequently in the literature.[5] Goal-setting theory posits that personal goals are the main mediator of the motivation–effort relation (Locke et al. 1981; Locke and Latham 1990). Specifically, motivation is

---

[3]Intermediate states are those that can be altered in the short run.
[4]Again, Kunda (1990, 1999) does not specify what she means by a "correct answer." Thus, any number of criteria could be used to define "correctness," such as accuracy vis-à-vis outcomes, correspondence with professional standards, etc.
[5]For broad overviews of motivation theories, see Miner (1980), Kanfer (1990), Locke (1991), and Eccles and Wigfield (2002).

positively related to the setting of specific and/or difficult goals, and specific, difficult goals result in more effort than do vague, easy, or no goals.[6] In addition, motivation may have a positive effect on the extent to which a person is trying to achieve a goal (called *goal commitment*), and goal commitment also positively affects effort.

Social-cognitive, or self-efficacy, theory proposes that self-efficacy is an additional mediator of the motivation–effort relation (Bandura 1997). *Self-efficacy* refers to a person's belief about whether she can do what is necessary to achieve a specific level of performance in a given task. The effect of motivation on self-efficacy is complex and can occur only over multiple trials or periods. Motivation presumably leads to greater effort and improved JDM quality in the first period (assuming that no moderators attenuate these relations). In turn, improved JDM quality implies that knowledge has increased, and knowledge has a positive relation to self-efficacy. Thus, self-efficacy in later periods is enhanced. The effects of self-efficacy on effort also are complex. Self-efficacy can affect effort through personal goal level and goal commitment but also through other mechanisms. For example, self-efficacy increases the use of high-quality cognitive processes and can alleviate negative affective states (Bandura).

Alternative theoretical accounts posit an inverted-U relation between motivation and effort and, thus, an inverted-U relation between motivation and JDM quality, with the highest JDM quality occurring at moderate levels of motivation. Such theories (e.g., Yerkes and Dodson 1908; Easterbrook 1959; Broadbent 1971; Eysenck 1982, 1986) propose that motivation initially increases effort because motivation either creates or is akin to arousal, and arousal increases effort direction and intensity (Eysenck 1982). Specifically, arousal leads to more attention to the task and acceleration of cognitive processing (Miller 1960). JDM quality can increase as a result of acceleration because people simply do more work in a given time period than they would otherwise.

At some moderate point of motivation, however, arousal is coupled with anxiety.[7] Anxiety tends to decrease effort direction because people remove part of their attention from the task and instead focus on worrying. Clearly, taking attention away from the task can decrease JDM quality. Anxiety also can decrease effort intensity. In particular, people begin to narrow their use of available information; this is called *filtration* (Miller 1960). Filtration appears to occur mostly in memory retrieval, information search, and evidence evaluation. Initially, this anxiety-induced decrease in effort intensity has positive effects on JDM quality if people otherwise might use irrelevant information. However, filtration then leads to the failure to use relevant information, which can be harmful to JDM quality. Where pertinent, both perspectives on the motivation–effort relation are considered throughout this chapter.

Motivation directed toward a desired conclusion can lead simply to strategic adoption of the conclusion (and, thus, the exertion of minimal effort). However, consistent with the focus of this book on cognitive explanations for behavior, this chapter posits that desired-conclusion motivation often leads to effort aimed at finding support for or otherwise rationalizing that conclusion (Kunda 1990, 1999) and reviews studies

[6]Clearly, the level of goals that is "difficult" is hard to define ex ante because the level may vary across individuals and over time within individuals. Difficulty normally is established based on pilot tests that document the distribution of performance in a given task.
[7]The arousal and anxiety concepts often are referred to instead as "pressure" (e.g., Ashton 1990; DeZoort and Lord 1997). Further, some researchers consider arousal to be akin instead to effort intensity rather than an antecedent thereto (e.g., Humphreys and Revelle 1984; Locke and Latham 1990).

related to this premise.[8] The theory is that effort is put into biased processing such as the intentional search for confirming information, the "creative" use of knowledge retrieved from memory, or the ignoring or biased interpretation of disconfirming information that crops up. It is unclear whether effort aimed at supporting the desired conclusion is greater or smaller than it would be in the absence of the motivation to reach the desired conclusion. In some situations, a person may encounter enough evidence to support a conclusion very quickly. In other situations, however, she may have to search through far more evidence than she normally would to find support for the desired conclusion. Further, it is unclear whether effort has a positive relation to JDM quality when desired-conclusion motivation is present. JDM quality in these circumstances depends on the quality of the desired conclusion. If it is correct, then this type of motivation has a positive effect on JDM quality, but motivation's positive effect may occur in conjunction with any level of effort.[9] Similarly, if the desired conclusion happens to be wrong, desired-conclusion motivation has a negative effect on JDM quality, but this may not be due to decreased effort. Instead, a person may exert a great deal of effort to construct a rationale for the desired conclusion.

Overall, then, motivation is an intermediate state that can be created by many factors, including many of the environmental variables described below. People can be motivated to reach a correct (unknown) judgment or decision or to reach a particular desired judgment or decision. In the former case, motivation generally is thought to have a positive effect on effort, which in turn has a positive effect on JDM quality. The effect of motivation on effort may occur through goals, self-efficacy, and other mechanisms. The latter type of motivation may or may not increase effort and JDM quality. Instead, motivation leads to effort that is biased toward supporting the desired conclusion.

7-2   EFFECTS OF MONETARY INCENTIVES ON JDM QUALITY

Definitions and Background

This section discusses the effects of monetary incentives on JDM quality. *Monetary incentives* are financial rewards that typically are contingent on current period performance.[10] In the case of JDM, performance may be defined as accuracy vis-à-vis outcomes, correspondence with normative theories, correspondence with professional standards, and so forth. For example, auditors' compensation may be tied to the extent to which their JDM conforms with professional standards (Tan and Libby 1997).

Monetary incentives are not unique to accounting but are an important environmental variable affecting JDM in accounting settings. Although the presence and

---

[8]A situation in which this may not be the case is when a person is unable to construct a rationale for the desired conclusion. In this case, a variety of JDM outcomes can occur. First, the person may strategically adopt the desired conclusion. Instead, however, she may increase effort toward making the correct judgment or decision because the lack of a rationale for the desired conclusion may be considered prima facie evidence that the conclusion is incorrect.

[9]We can speculate about the circumstances under which this may be the case. For example, if the desired conclusion comes from a person with high ability, it is more likely to be correct than if it comes from someone with low ability. In brief, the quality of the desired conclusion potentially is affected by all the factors discussed in Chapters 3 through 7.

[10]This section focuses on incentives as rewards. Some incentives schemes, by contrast, embody penalties that are imposed for inferior performance, however defined. Although it is possible that rewards and penalties have different effects on JDM (e.g., Luft 1994), little is known about differences in the mediators and moderators for reward-based versus penalty-based incentives.

structure of incentives can vary dramatically across firms, overall, firms have increased their use of monetary incentives in recent years (*Wall Street Journal* 1999). Some of these incentives, particularly for managers and analysts, can be rather large (Hausmann 1999; Munk 2003). Further, regulators have begun to increase their focus on such incentives (Cohen and Kelly 2003; Munk). Specifically, regulators are considering the deleterious effects that monetary incentives can have on the quality of managers', auditors', and analysts' JDM, and the consequent effect the use of these individuals' JDM by investors can have on their investment returns (Cohen and Kelly).

This section includes studies that examine the effects of "direct incentives" and "indirect incentives." Studies examining direct incentives are traditional studies that investigate the effects of tying pay to JDM performance in the current period. Indirect incentives studies differ from the traditional studies in two important ways. If experimental, they do not pay subjects based on their JDM; thus, the incentives must be imagined by subjects. A key question that arises because of this attribute of the studies is whether subjects internalize the imaginary incentives; in most accounting studies, this appears plausible. A second way in which these studies differ from traditional studies is that the pay effects of the incentives may not be felt (if they were to be actually felt) until future periods. Thus, for example, an auditor who faces an experimental scenario in which the client is described as having financial difficulties may think that there is a nonzero probability that the client will go bankrupt in a future period, in which case there also is a nonzero probability that she will be sued and/or lose her job some time after the bankruptcy would occur. Thus, these incentives are probabilistic, and studies typically manipulate them by varying the probabilities that pay would be affected in some future period. In addition, many indirect incentives are at least implicitly associated with a desired conclusion. For example, some auditing studies manipulate incentives related to client retention. Implicit in these studies is that client retention is more likely if the auditors' JDM agrees with the client's desired JDM, typically the accounting treatment that increases net income. Because these types of incentives are extremely important to accounting decision makers of various sorts, the literature is replete with examples of such indirect incentives studies. The next section discusses how incentives of either sort affect JDM.

Monetary Incentive Effects

Consistent with the motivated reasoning framework, monetary incentives can reward people for correct JDM or for a particular desired judgment or decision. For instance, analysts may be rewarded based on the accuracy of their earnings forecasts vis-à-vis actual earnings, but they also may be rewarded for generating trading volume, which typically is best facilitated by issuing buy recommendations (Friedman 2002). Monetary incentives related to being correct typically are thought to have positive effects on JDM quality, which is most often defined in psychology as accuracy vis-à-vis outcomes or as correspondence with normative theories. For example, many studies examine whether subjects with incentives adhere more to Bayes' Theorem than do subjects without incentives. However, it clearly is possible to consider the effects of incentives on other measures; indeed, accounting studies tend to focus on these. In particular, many accounting studies of incentives define JDM quality as agreement with others, although oftentimes there is an implication that a specific group is more correct than another group. For example, in studies that examine financial reporting decisions, incentives can affect the aggressiveness of chosen alternatives. Although the aggressive choices typically still conform to professional standards, the implication is that these choices are worse. Monetary incentives related to obtaining a desired conclusion have a positive effect on JDM quality only if the desired conclusion is correct.

Most theories posit that incentives related to getting the correct answer affect JDM quality principally through increased motivation and effort. Alternatively, if incentives are viewed more generally as affecting arousal, then incentives of this sort may have an inverted-U relation with effort. Incentives related to a desired conclusion increase motivation to get to that conclusion, which then may lead to effort that is aimed at supporting the conclusion. This effort can be greater or smaller than it would be otherwise and, further, may have no relation to JDM quality.

Why do incentives increase motivation? Expectancy theory (e.g., Vroom 1964) proposes that people make judgments and decisions that they expect will lead to outcomes that are maximally satisfying. Under expectancy theory, motivation is affected by the expectancy about the effort–outcome relationship and the attractiveness (or utility) of the outcome. The attractiveness of a monetary outcome is clear, particularly vis-à-vis no pay. JDM quality–contingent monetary incentives also may be more attractive than flat pay, depending on the expected value of each. Further, the effort–outcome expectancy should be higher with incentives than with no pay or with noncontingent pay. This is because greater effort is thought to lead to greater JDM quality and, thus, greater pay.[11]

Because the JDM effects of incentives to reach desired conclusions are unclear, moderators also are unclear. However, there are many factors that can moderate positive JDM quality effects of incentives related to correct answers. These factors disrupt either the positive link between incentives and motivation and consequent effort or the positive link between effort and JDM quality. First, people with high intrinsic motives, such as need for achievement, may have high motivation irrespective of the presence of other motivators in the environment (e.g., Atkinson and Reitman 1956; Mawhinney 1979). Thus, intrinsic motivation can attenuate the incentives-motivation/effort link. The other main person variable moderators are knowledge and ability, collectively referred to in this chapter as "skill." If JDM tasks require that people have skill and also exert effort, then lack of skill can moderate the effects of monetary incentives. If people lack skill, they may exert more effort when faced with incentives but work long and hard at the wrong activities (Kanfer 1987; Arkes 1991; Smith and Walker 1993; Camerer 1995; Bonner et al. 2000). Here, skill serves as a moderator of the effort–JDM quality link. Further, if people lack skill and are aware that their lack of skill will render them unable to attain high-quality JDM, they may not respond to incentives with higher motivation and effort. In other words, they may give up because they know that they need both effort and skill to attain high-quality JDM (Lawler 1994). In this case, lack of skill disrupts the incentives-motivation/effort link.

Skill may not be a moderator of incentive effects, however, if people are allowed to select their own incentive contracts (e.g., Demski and Feltham 1978). In this case, people lacking skill tend not to choose contracts that tie pay to current JDM quality. This occurs because skill affects self-efficacy (Bandura 1997), which in turn affects

---

[11]It may be the case, however, that noncontingent pay is as motivating as pay tied to performance. This is particularly true when people form reputations that affect their market wage (Fama 1980).

people's choices to take on particular jobs, where *jobs* is defined to include both the tasks people perform and the incentive schemes tied to those tasks. Thus, people who choose incentives that tie pay to JDM quality likely are those with adequate skill, in which case lack of skill does not lead to misuses of effort.

Two task variables also can moderate the positive effects of incentives on JDM quality.[12] First, although it normally is assumed that skill and effort both affect JDM quality in accounting, some JDM tasks are not particularly sensitive to effort variation. For example, recognizing the errors that are responsible for patterns of ratio fluctuations may depend mostly on ability (Bonner and Lewis 1990). If JDM quality is relatively uninfluenced by effort, then incentives may have no effect. A second task variable that can moderate incentive effects is task complexity. Complexity can moderate these effects because it is positively related to tasks' skill requirements (Wood 1986; Campbell 1988; Bonner 1994). Thus, in the short run, people are less likely to possess the skill needed for complex tasks than for simple tasks, so either the incentives-motivation/effort link is attenuated or the effort–JDM quality link is attenuated, as described above.[13] Further, in the face of complex tasks, people may attempt to develop strategies to improve JDM quality in the long run (Locke and Latham 1990). When people engage in strategy development, short-term JDM quality can suffer because they frequently change strategies, and some of these changes are to inappropriate strategies (e.g., Naylor and Clark 1968; Naylor and Schenck 1968; Naylor and Dickinson 1969). Here, then, the effort–JDM quality link is disrupted. Finally, both incentives and task complexity can create arousal, which has an inverted-U relation to JDM quality (Eysenck 1986). Thus, the combination of incentives and a complex task may create a higher level of arousal and a lower level of effort than the combination of incentives and a simple task.

Finally, the term "monetary incentives" does not refer to a single way of tying pay to JDM quality. There are a number of schemes for doing so, and these schemes differ on both financial and nonfinancial attributes that can affect JDM quality. This section discusses these attributes using the categories of schemes from Bonner et al. (2000): flat rate, piece rate, variable ratio, quota, and tournament. The key financial attributes on which incentive schemes vary are whether they tie pay to current JDM quality at a global level and whether they tie pay to JDM quality at the more disaggregated level of individual units of output. *Flat-rate schemes* provide a fixed salary for a given period; thus, they do not tie current pay to current JDM quality at any level.[14] *Piece-rate schemes* pay a specified amount for each unit of output; thus, they tie pay to quality at both global and output-unit levels. For example, a factory worker might be paid two dollars for each toy part produced. *Variable-ratio* (VR) *schemes* also pay based on units of output but only part of the time. For example, a VR-5 scheme would reward the worker two dollars for one out of each five toy parts produced, on average. Thus, VR schemes tie pay to quality globally but not at the individual unit level. *Quota schemes* pay a flat rate until some desired level of quality is reached (the quota); at that point, people receive a bonus. Some quota schemes pay a piece rate for output beyond the quota, whereas others pay

---

[12]It also is possible that framing and task "attractiveness" moderate the effects of incentives. See Bonner and Sprinkle (2002) for further discussion.

[13]Clearly, if people possess skill, task complexity may not moderate the positive incentives–JDM quality relation.

[14]In the field, future periods' flat pay often is tied to current JDM quality, so flat-rate schemes can provide indirect incentives.

additional bonuses for hitting higher quotas. At any rate, quota schemes link pay to performance at a global level but not at the unit-of-output level. *Tournament schemes* link rewards to JDM quality based on competitive rankings, with the highest performer receiving the highest pay and so on. Because rankings rather than units of output are used to determine pay, pay is linked to performance only at a global level.

Schemes that tie pay to current JDM quality at a global level should lead to higher motivation and JDM quality, ceteris paribus. Thus, flat-rate schemes should be less likely than other schemes to produce positive JDM effects, assuming that they do not allow for the possibility of raises. Schemes that tie pay to JDM quality at a unit level (i.e., piece-rate schemes) also should lead to higher motivation and JDM quality than other schemes (again, ceteris paribus). Higher motivation likely occurs because people have higher effort–outcome expectancies.

Unfortunately, the above predictions are based on an assumption of ceteris paribus, which typically does not hold with these incentive schemes. That is, they differ on nonfinancial attributes as well as on financial attributes. For example, quota schemes include a specific, assigned goal (the quota); other schemes typically do not. Assigned goals provide motivation and, thus, can have positive effects on JDM quality per se (see Section 7-4). This means that quota schemes may be more likely than other schemes to result in positive incentive effects because they include two motivators: goals and monetary incentives (Bonner et al. 2000). This assumes, however, that the goals embedded in quota schemes are challenging but not too difficult. When goals become too difficult, people may give up because they believe they cannot reach the goal (Locke and Latham 1990). In this case, the presence of assigned goals in incentive schemes could decrease the probability of positive incentive effects because they could disrupt the incentives-motivation/effort relation.

The above incentive schemes also differ in that tournament schemes explicitly embody competition, whereas other schemes do not. Although competition can enhance motivation (e.g., Lazear and Rosen 1981), there are at least two reasons competition can erase the positive motivational effects of incentives. First, people who lack skill may not be motivated by a tournament scheme because they believe they will not rank high enough to receive pay whose benefits exceed the cost of the effort they would exert (Dye 1984; Bull et al. 1987). Second, competition may have negative effects on motivation for people of all skill levels because competition is viewed as controlling, and people can be demotivated by feeling controlled (Deci et al. 1981). Further, even if tournaments do not diminish the incentives-motivation/effort relation, they may diminish the effort–JDM quality relation because they can cause people to make excessively risky decisions.

There are other characteristics of incentive schemes that can vary within a single type of scheme, such as a piece-rate scheme, and that can moderate positive effects of incentives. For example, most accounting JDM tasks have several important dimensions of quality. Incentive schemes can attempt to reward all or only some of these dimensions. If incentives are tied to only some dimensions of quality, it is unlikely that incentives will have a positive effect on the unrewarded dimensions (Jenkins et al. 1998; Bonner and Sprinkle 2002). Perhaps a more important issue is the effect on JDM of incentives rewarding multiple dimensions of quality but that provide conflicting recipes for JDM. For example, auditors may be rewarded both for efficiency (e.g., time spent) and for effectiveness (e.g., correspondence with professional standards). Other than the expected utility of achieving high quality on each dimension, it is unclear what factors affect JDM under such circumstances. Finally, if people are informed about incentives after they process information but before making a judgment or decision, incentives cannot have a positive effect on JDM quality because people can no longer increase processing effort (Bonner and Sprinkle).

Researchers can study direct incentive effects through both manipulation and measurement.[15] The typical experimental study compares one or more incentive schemes to either a flat-rate control group that has no prospect of receiving a raise or to a no-pay group. A flat-rate group normally is a better control because the expected value of the pay can be equalized across treatments; this means that the variable being isolated is whether pay is tied to JDM quality. Further, the experimentalist can hold constant various person and task variables that may interact with incentives and also use the design or postexperimental questions to address incentive scheme attributes that may serve as moderators. For example, to try to disentangle the effects of an assigned goal and the tie of pay to JDM quality in quota schemes, it may be useful to include a treatment that includes both pay for performance and an assigned goal that is not part of the incentive scheme. Much archival and survey research examines the effects of incentives, at least implicitly, on JDM. These studies suffer from their usual problems, which are exacerbated by the fact that incentive schemes themselves differ so widely. Archivalists and survey researchers must take care, then, to measure as many attributes of the schemes as possible.

Studying indirect incentives also can be done through manipulation or measurement. The typical manipulation of such incentives, as mentioned earlier, is one that affects the probability that subjects' pay would be affected in future periods. Manipulation of the probability depends on the context. For example, analysts can be given information about the chance of investment banking business for their firm or auditors can be given information about the chance of providing additional services for an existing client. This information normally is not stated numerically or even verbally, but rather to be inferred from experimental materials. That is, subjects typically are not told that the probability is ".90" (or "high") versus ".20" (or "low"), but rather must first determine such from cues related to those probabilities. These incentives are studied somewhat similarly when measured; for example, studies examine the effects of the presence or absence of current investment banking relationships on analysts' JDM under the assumption that current banking relationships imply higher probabilities of future banking relationships. The next section discusses accounting studies on incentives.

Accounting Studies on Monetary Incentives

Accounting studies on incentives, construed broadly, are extremely numerous. This section restricts its coverage to studies that examine the effects of either direct or indirect monetary incentives on individuals' accounting JDM, consistent with the objectives of this book.[16] Studies on producers of accounting information include Mock (1973), who

---

[15]See Chapter 4 for a discussion of measuring the mediators of incentive effects.
[16]Omitted from coverage, then, are studies that examine incentive effects in non-JDM tasks, such as physical or clerical tasks (e.g., Chow 1983), studies that examine incentive effects in nonaccounting tasks (e.g., Bloomfield 1997), and studies that examine incentive effects at the firm level (e.g., studies of earnings management). (See Healy and Wahlen [1999] for a review.)

finds that students doing a business simulation game make production decisions that lead to more profits and take more time when they have direct incentives. Magee and Dickhaut (1978) report that students facing different direct incentives use different heuristics to make variance investigation decisions. Waller and Mitchell's (1984) student subjects select more reliable variance investigation systems when they face direct incentives than when they face flat pay. Luft (1994) finds no effect of bonus versus penalty-framed direct incentives on students' responses to general business questions; she notes that this is expected because the task of memory retrieval is relatively insensitive to effort. Sprinkle (2000) shows that students with a direct piece-rate scheme exert more effort than do students with a flat-rate scheme when doing a production decision task and, after several periods of learning, make normatively more correct decisions. Finally, Sayre et al. (1998) vary the number of subjects involved in a tournament scheme related to future promotion (an indirect incentive) as either two or six; promotion is based on the outcome of a project decision. More subjects in the larger tournament choose the most risky project; this project is assumed to be a worse choice.

Two studies examine incentive effects on producers in situations that include implicit desired conclusions. Harrell and Harrison (1994) find that students given indirect incentives related to future pay are more likely to decide to continue an unprofitable project when the project information is known only to them. The desired conclusion here is the subject's previous decision to accept the project. Cloyd et al. (1996) report that managers are more likely to choose financial accounting treatments that conform to aggressive tax treatments (the desired conclusion) when incentives related to defending these aggressive treatments are higher.

Studies of the effects of direct incentives on users of accounting information include Wright and Anderson (1989), who report that students facing a tournament incentive scheme are no more accurate in their probability distributions related to management fraud than those facing no monetary incentives; however, they are affected less by irrelevant anchors. Tuttle and Burton's (1999) student subjects spend more time making stock price predictions under a piece-rate incentive; further, they use more information when faced with incentives (JDM quality is not assessed in this study).

There are a number of studies related to the effects of incentives on analysts. Analysts face a number of direct and indirect incentives, some of which relate to desired conclusions. Their current pay can be a function of, for example, the accuracy of their forecasts; in this case, incentives are of the "be correct" type because analysts are trying to get as close as possible to an unknown earnings figure.[17] Their current pay also can be a function of the volume of trade they generate; as mentioned earlier, trade volume is best facilitated by issuing buy recommendations, a desired conclusion. Analysts are compensated also for the volume of investment banking (IB) business they are associated with; future IB business may be facilitated by optimistic earnings forecasts and recommendations in the current period (Munk 2003), that is, desired conclusions.[18]

---

[17]It can be argued that these incentives are not completely of the "be correct" variety given that firms provide analysts with a great deal of guidance on what earnings will be (e.g., Richardson et al. 2004) and also because firms often manage earnings to meet their managers' (and subsequent analysts') forecasts (e.g., Degeorge et al. 1999).

[18]Under recent legislation (e.g., Munk 2003), investment banking and research functions of securities firms must be separated. Thus, these incentive issues may now be of less relevance.

A number of archival studies examine the effects of indirect incentives on analysts' JDM in situations with implicit desired conclusions. Dugar and Nathan (1995) document that the earnings forecasts and investment recommendations of analysts whose firms have IB relationships with companies are more optimistic than those of analysts working for non-IB firms; however, there is no difference in forecast accuracy or recommendation profitability. Lin and McNichols (1998) find that underwriter-related analysts make more optimistic growth forecasts and recommendations than do unaffiliated analysts, but their earnings forecasts are no different. Hayward and Boeker (1998) document similar findings for analysts affiliated with debt, equity, and acquisitions deals. Dechow et al. (2000) report that analysts working for the lead underwriter make growth forecasts that are more optimistic than do other analysts. Further, there is a positive relation between the amount paid to the lead underwriter firm and the level of their analysts' growth forecasts. Finally, Hunton and McEwen (1997) experimentally examine the effects of indirect incentives related to having an underwriting relationship with or following a particular firm on analysts' JDM quality. Analysts given underwriting incentives are more optimistic than those given firm-following incentives, who are more optimistic than subjects with no incentive information. Further, because mean forecasts are optimistic in all conditions, greater optimism means lower accuracy.

Other archival studies of the effects of indirect incentives on analysts' JDM include Francis and Philbrick (1993), who conjecture that Value Line analysts have incentives to please firm management so they can obtain information and, thus, improve forecast accuracy. Findings indicate that analysts are more optimistic in their earnings forecasts when other analysts in their firm issue sell (hold) recommendations than when those analysts issue hold (buy) recommendations. However, Eames et al. (2002) report that these results reverse when analyses control for actual earnings, a correlated omitted variable. Their finding—that analysts issue more optimistic earnings forecasts when there are buy recommendations—is consistent with incentives related to increasing trade volume and the related desired conclusion. Eames et al. also find that this behavior may be due to biased processing related to the trade volume incentive rather than to intentional (strategic) boosting of forecasts.

Das et al. (1998) report findings consistent with the notion that analysts' forecasts are more optimistic when earnings are less predictable; this is purportedly due to their having greater incentives to gain information from management in order to improve future accuracy in this case, and because pleasing management currently means providing optimistic forecasts. However, Eames and Glover (2003) document that these findings disappear when earnings level is included in analyses.[19] Willis (2001) finds that mutual fund managers issue optimistic forecasts for stocks they hold, consistent with incentives for having their funds appear to be good performers. Further, his findings also suggest that optimism is due to motivated reasoning rather than to strategic increases in forecasts.

One study (Cuccia 1994) manipulates direct incentives to tax professionals; some subjects have penalties subtracted from pay for reporting a liability less than that suggested by the IRS, whereas others do not. He finds that CPAs (non-CPAs) facing the

---

[19]Further, studies document that managers may prefer pessimistic analysts' forecasts so actual earnings will meet or beat those forecasts (e.g., Brown 2001; Matsumoto 2002).

penalty exert more (less) effort than those who do not, but there are no effects of incentives on aggressiveness of recommendations. A number of studies examine indirect incentives and tax professionals' JDM.[20] Typically, there is a desired client conclusion implicit in these studies, which is the more aggressive tax treatment. However, some studies also manipulate incentives related to IRS audits. It is unclear whether these incentives imply the opposite conclusion—the conservative tax treatment—or whether they are of the "be correct" variety. Kaplan et al. (1988) report that a higher audit probability results in less aggressive positions being taken by tax professionals. Pei et al. (1990) find no effect of client preferences on recommendations. However, Pei et al. (1992a) report that this result is driven by experienced professionals; inexperienced professionals are affected by client preferences. Reckers et al. (1991) find that the effects of incentives related to client revenues (IRS penalties) positively (negatively) affects the extent to which tax professionals agree with the client's desired position. Newberry et al. (1993) document similar findings. However, Schisler (1994) finds that professionals respond to client preference incentives but not to IRS penalties.

Cuccia et al. (1995) document that tax professionals interpret vague standards in line with client-related incentives and consequently make recommendations that also are in line with those incentives. When standards are unambiguous, tax professionals instead interpret evidence in a manner consistent with client preferences and, again, make recommendations consistent with those preferences. These are two different forms of motivated reasoning resulting from incentives with desired conclusions. Cloyd and Spilker (1999) extend Cuccia et al. to show that client preference incentives can also affect the search for support for a client's desired tax treatment and, in turn, ultimate recommendations. Kadous and Magro (2001) report that tax professionals facing high risk of litigation related to a client attend relatively more to disconfirming evidence than do those facing a low-risk client, and this differential attention affects the aggressiveness of recommendations. Barrick et al. (2004) examine whether tax professionals reviewing hypothetical memos regarding proper tax treatment are more influenced by the incentive to be accurate or by the client's preferred treatment (and related incentive). When comparing memos that do not suggest the client's desired conclusion, the incentive to be accurate affects reviewers' conclusions regarding the memos' persuasiveness. However, when comparing memos, one of which contains the client's preferred (and incorrect) tax treatment and one of which does not, reviewers find the former more persuasive. Similarly, Kahle and White (2004) find that tax professionals find evidence more persuasive if it supports the client's preferred position.

Three studies provide direct incentives to auditors in experimental settings. These studies have no implicit desired conclusions. Ashton's (1990) study has auditors making bond ratings under a tournament scheme or under no monetary incentives and manipulates the presence of a decision aid. Auditors receiving the incentive and no decision aid are more accurate than those with neither the incentive nor the aid. When auditors receive the decision aid, however, incentives have no incremental effect on the accuracy of ratings. Libby and Lipe (1992) provide subjects with either a flat-rate scheme or a piece-rate scheme related to the recall and recognition of previously

---

[20]Studies of the effects of incentives on taxpayer behavior (see Fischer et al. [1992] and Jackson and Milliron [1986] for reviews) are not included because they typically examine intentional (strategic) noncompliance with the tax law given a desired conclusion, rather than incentive effects that may occur through motivated reasoning.

viewed internal controls.[21] Some subjects are informed of the piece-rate scheme prior to encoding, whereas others are informed after encoding but prior to retrieval. Subjects with monetary incentives prior to encoding spend more time than other groups studying the internal controls, whereas both incentive groups spend more time than the flat-rate group attempting to retrieve controls from memory. Further, subjects with incentives recall more items than flat-rate scheme subjects and those with incentives prior to encoding recognize more than flat-rate subjects. The differential incentive effects for recall and recognition are consistent with the prediction that recall is a more effort-sensitive task and, thus, incentives have a greater effect in recall than in recognition. Boatsman et al. (1997) examine the effects of various incentive schemes on auditors' reliance on an aid when making decisions about whether to extend an audit because of the probability of fraud. Incentives affect reliance on the aid, but the effects on JDM quality are not reported.

There are numerous studies of indirect incentives and auditors' JDM quality. Many of these studies incorporate desired conclusions. Jiambalvo and Wilner (1985) examine incentive effects on the evaluation of contingent losses. Incentives in this case relate to clients' preferences that loss contingencies not be recorded or disclosed; decisions consistent with clients' preferences are more likely to lead to client retention. However, there also are penalties related to not referencing loss contingences; in the event of a problem, litigation and other sanctions may be more successful, resulting in losses for the auditor. Jiambalvo and Wilner find no effects of client preferences. Nelson and Kinney (1997) compare the judgments of auditors and students (proxying for investors) about the need to reference a contingent loss in the audit report, under conditions of varying ambiguity about the probability of that loss. They posit that auditors face greater incentives than do users for not referring to the loss, so ambiguity causes auditors to react less conservatively than do users. Consistent with this, results indicate that users are more likely to suggest report reference given ambiguous information about moderate probabilities, whereas auditors are unaffected by ambiguity at this level of probability.

Other studies examine the effect of indirect incentives on auditors' judgments about a variety of financial reporting issues. All these studies examine accounting choices that apparently are in accordance with GAAP, but some choices are more "aggressive" than others, and these aggressive accounting choices are implicit desired conclusions. Farmer et al. (1987) find that auditors agree more with the client when litigation risk is low and threat of client loss is high. Windsor and Ashkanasy (1995) report similar findings. Trompeter (1994) examines the effects of the extent to which auditors' compensation is tied to local office profits and perceived litigation risk. In three cases that vary as to the restrictiveness of applicable GAAP, auditors with higher compensation incentives (higher litigation risk perceptions) are more (less) likely to allow the client to use more aggressive accounting. The compensation incentive effects appear only in the less restrictive cases, however. Hackenbrack and Nelson (1996) manipulate incentives through engagement risk and find that auditors make reporting decisions related to uncollectible accounts receivable consistent with these incentives. Further, similar to the idea of motivated reasoning, auditors justify their reporting choices through their interpretation of the applicable accounting standards.

---

[21]The piece-rate scheme also incorporates elements of a tournament scheme.

Salterio (1996) manipulates client preferences related to accounting for a contract as being either one of two accounting treatments or the client wanting the "accurate" treatment along with various aspects of precedents related to this issue and finds no effect of client preference. However, in an analysis of archival data, he finds that an accounting firm's research staff tends to provide auditors with precedents that support the client's preferred position. In practice, if only supporting precedents are passed along to field auditors, then client-preference incentives could affect their judgments. Salterio and Koonce (1997) conduct similar experiments and find that client-preference incentives have no effect on choice of accounting treatment when precedents all suggest the same outcome. However, when precedents are mixed, auditors' choices are in line with client preferences. Cohen and Trompeter (1998) find a negative effect of engagement risk on willingness to bid on a client, which then positively affects willingness to accept the client's preferred treatment. Gramling (1999) reports that auditors rely more on internal auditors described to be of moderate quality when clients provide incentives related to reducing fees versus obtaining a high-quality audit.

Libby and Kinney (2000) examine the effects of incentives related to managers' wanting to meet or exceed (versus falling below) analysts' consensus earnings forecasts on auditors' decisions regarding corrections of immaterial earnings overstatements. These incentives exist because the stock market typically "rewards" firms that consistently meet or beat forecasts with higher stock prices (Bartov et al. 2002). Auditors recommend larger corrections when earnings would continue to beat the consensus versus fall below the consensus (managers' desired conclusion). Braun (2001) studies the effects of several incentives on the extent to which auditors' decisions to waive adjustments for errors are in compliance with GAAS. The incentive related to the importance of the client's fees to the local office has no effect on auditors' decisions, whereas the incentive related to the client's financial health leads to more GAAS decisions in some cases but not in others.

Johnstone et al. (2002) find that auditors with high knowledge generate more alternatives to a client-preferred aggressive accounting position when engagement risk is high than when it is low; auditors with low knowledge are not affected by this incentive. Further, high-knowledge auditors process information more deeply for riskier clients, as evidenced by problem representations containing more inferences. Moreno and Bhattacharjee (2003) report that staff and senior auditors rate the risk of inventory obsolescence as lower when presented with an incentive for additional client revenues than when no such incentive is present; managers and partners do not react differentially to the incentives despite the fact that the client position is known. Staff and seniors' reasons for providing their risk assessments are consistent with motivated reasoning. Kadous et al. (2003) manipulate client-related incentives by telling one group that the client already has announced earnings using an aggressive method but telling the other group they are in the middle of the audit. They also manipulate whether subjects must separately identify the most appropriate accounting treatment for the circumstances. Auditors with incentives are more likely to accept the client's aggressive method but only when they perform the separate assessment of appropriateness. Further, these incentive effects operate at least partially through goal commitment.

Several studies examine the effects of indirect incentives (with no desired conclusions) on time budget and other audit planning decisions. Pratt and Stice (1994) manipulate several factors related to litigation risk of clients and find that only some of these factors affect auditors' decisions about the necessary amount of audit evidence. Walo (1995) finds similarly mixed evidence for various litigation-related incentives on several planning judgments. Houston et al. (1999) document an effect of litigation risk on planned hours in a situation where irregularities exist but not in a situation where errors exist. Houston (1999) manipulates incentives related to reducing fees and related to litigation and finds that auditors increase budgeted hours when faced with higher litigation risk but only when there are no cost-cutting incentives in place. Further, part of this effect occurs through assessments of inherent risk. Bedard and Johnstone (2004) report that litigation risks related to earnings manipulation and client financial condition are positively related to planned audit hours. Finally, Anderson et al. (2004) find that auditors are less likely to rely on client explanations when planning audit tests for clients who have high incentives for earnings management.

Other studies examine a variety of issues. Holt and Morrow (1992) document that indirect incentives related to taking on a potentially unsuccessful client have no effect on the extent to which auditors' probability assessments correspond to Bayesian estimates, whereas they do have an effect for lenders' assessments. They posit this is due to the incentive structure faced by lenders in which penalties for taking on unsuccessful clients are higher. Lindberg and Maletta (2003) find that memory errors related to working on multiple audit clients increase in the presence of high litigation risk, but they do not examine JDM quality effects.

Findings of incentives studies in accounting largely are consistent with those elsewhere. Studies examining the effects of incentives where there is no particular desired conclusion mostly find positive effects, although factors such as skill and the competition embedded in tournament schemes can moderate these effects. Further, some studies not finding positive effects relate to auditors not adjusting evidence collection to be consistent with the risks indicated by incentives. This finding is at odds with audit standards requiring the use of the audit risk model in planning audits and those that require the collection of sufficient, competent evidence (AICPA 2004).

Accounting studies on incentives associated with desired conclusions (many of which also examine indirect incentives) overwhelmingly find that people who face these incentives make judgments and decisions that are closer to the desired conclusions than do people who do not face the incentives. These findings are important due to the prominence of such incentives in accounting professionals' environments. They also are important given that they are at odds with many standards and regulations that prohibit or at least discourage such behavior. In particular, studies of auditors' JDM report that auditors are affected by desired-conclusion incentives. In their role as independent assurance providers, auditors are supposed to evaluate evidence and draw conclusions in a manner that is free from bias that draws them toward any particular conclusion (AICPA 2004). Analysts' reports also are meant to be objective evaluations of company's prospects (Financial Analysts Federation and Institute of Chartered Financial Analysts 1988). Regulators appear to have recognized these issues. Recent regulations have prohibited accounting firms from accepting many types of consulting work that are thought to create incentives to reach desired conclusions during the audit. Other regulations have split the investment banking and brokerage functions of investment firms. It is too early to determine whether these regulatory interventions will reduce the negative effects of desired-conclusion incentives on auditors' and analysts' JDM.

Future research on incentives in accounting could take several directions. It seems likely that studies will continue to focus on indirect incentives, if only because it is difficult to provide professional subjects with a meaningful amount of pay. Indirect incentives studies tend to manipulate only one desired conclusion, typically that of the client. However, in some cases, accounting professionals face multiple indirect incentives, some of which carry desired conclusions and some of which encourage being correct. We know little (other than anecdotally) about how accounting professionals respond to multiple incentives, particularly when they conflict. (See Fields et al. [2001] and Nelson [2005] for reviews.) Of particular interest are the factors (other than expected utility) that distinguish between the situations in which professionals tilt more toward the desired-conclusion incentives and the situations in which they respond more toward the be-correct incentives. For example, perhaps individuals whose reputations are more established (e.g., All-Star analysts) respond more to be-correct incentives because they are under less pressure to please clients.

Future research on direct incentives should continue to examine the various attributes of incentives that affect JDM quality, including nonfinancial attributes such as goals and competition. Specifically, research should try to disentangle the effects of these attributes from the effects of the link of pay to JDM quality. For example, it may be both more effective and less costly for firms to employ goals alone rather than incentives that embody goals.[22]

7-3 EFFECTS OF ACCOUNTABILITY AND JUSTIFICATION ON JDM QUALITY

Definitions and Background

This section describes the effects of accountability and justification on JDM quality. *Accountability* is the "implicit or explicit expectation that one may be called on to justify one's beliefs, feelings, and actions to others" (Lerner and Tetlock 1999). Under conditions of accountability, a person prepares to justify her judgments and decisions, but she may not actually have to do so. For example, staff auditors are accountable for all their work on an audit, but they may receive review notes relating to only some of the work. *Justification* is the process of providing an explanation to support one's beliefs. Continuing the example, staff auditors may have to respond to review notes by writing a clarifying memo.

Accountability exists in many professions; thus, it is not unique to accounting settings. However, it is an extremely important element of the environment for accounting professionals because they are accountable to many different parties. For example, managers are accountable to shareholders, creditors, boards of directors, auditors, and regulators. Further, accountability is an important feature of auditors' environment because GAAS requires the review of subordinate auditors' work (AICPA 2004). Recent scrutiny of and related litigation against managers, analysts, and auditors indicates that accountability may be at an all-time high for these professionals (e.g., France 2004). Yet the level of accountability and the manner in which it is implemented varies

---

[22]Meta-analyses of various motivational techniques implemented in the field find that goals have a larger average effect size than do incentives, whose average effect size sometimes is not significantly different from zero (e.g., Guzzo et al. 1985; Pritchard et al. 1988).

across time periods and firms. Corporate governance is stronger for some firms than for others, for example (e.g., Langley 2003; Spors 2004).

An important question about accountability is how it differs from monetary incentives. That is, what are the consequences of satisfying or not satisfying accountability requirements? Lerner and Tetlock (1999) note that satisfying (not satisfying) accountability requirements often leads to monetary rewards (penalties), but they also suggest that people can receive other nonmonetary rewards (penalties) such as pleasant (unpleasant) interactions with other people or the reduction (increase) of jail time. Accounting professionals may be more concerned about the monetary incentives associated with accountability, such as keeping or losing the revenues related to a client, than about the nonmonetary issues, such as saving or losing face with a client. Yet having the approval of and appearing competent before important others are strong nonmonetary motives (Tetlock 1985; Curley et al. 1986; Baumeister and Leary 1995; Tyler 1997).[23] More generally, as Sprinkle (2003) notes, motives concerning interpersonal relationships can have strong effects on JDM. Overall, then, it is important to consider to what extent accountability effects reflect the influence of these nonmonetary motives rather than reflecting monetary incentive effects in future research. This section reviews accountability studies assuming they reflect nonmonetary motives.

Accountability Effects

Again, consistent with the motivated reasoning framework (Kunda 1990, 1999), accountability theorists (e.g., Lerner and Tetlock 1999) distinguish between accountability to a party who has a known view (desired conclusion) and accountability to a party whose view is unknown. Accountability to a party with an unknown view typically is thought to have positive effects on JDM quality. JDM quality can be measured as accuracy vis-à-vis outcomes, correspondence with normative theories, and so forth. Accounting studies examine the effects of accountability on a variety of JDM quality dimensions. Accountability to a party with a known view obviously will have a positive effect on JDM quality if the known view is correct.

How does accountability affect JDM quality? As mentioned previously, the main mediators are thought to be motivation and consequent effort. Accountability to parties with unknown views increases motivation to be correct, which then leads to increased effort in cognitive processes relevant to a particular task. Specifically, theory suggests that accountability-induced motivation increases "self-critical" effort (Lerner and Tetlock 1999). Not only do people work harder, but they direct some of their effort toward anticipating and preparing for possible criticisms of their conclusions. Theory predicts that this leads to more complex cognitive processing because people must consider different perspectives. Why does accountability to parties with unknown views increase motivation to be correct? Work in psychology does not directly address this question, but expectancy theory or expected utility theory clearly can provide an explanation if the outcomes associated with satisfying accountability requirements are monetary, and additional effort is thought to increase the chance of receiving the monetary incentive. Further, if we allow for people's utility functions to include arguments related to pleasing and appearing competent before others (or, more generally, social

---

[23]Indeed, Evans et al. (1994) find that there is demand for control systems that include accountability features, even when those features do not increase people's wealth.

motives) and assume that people believe additional effort will increase the chances of these outcomes occurring, both theories can explain a positive accountability-motivation/effort relation for outcomes that are nonmonetary (Sprinkle 2003).[24]

For accountability to a party with a known view, the key mediator is motivation to reach a desired conclusion. The accountability literature indicates that such motivation often leads to strategic adoption of the known view (Tetlock 1983; Tetlock et al. 1989). In other words, people exert minimal cognitive effort; they simply conform. However, in many cases, people engage in motivated reasoning. That is, they bias their effort toward finding support for the known view. Again, this may manifest itself in searching for supporting evidence, ignoring contradictory evidence, and so forth.[25] Lerner and Tetlock (1999) note that little is known about the circumstances under which people accountable to a party with a known view strategically adopt the view rather than engage in motivated reasoning.

As is the case with incentives, because it is not possible to predict directional JDM quality effects of accountability to a party with known views, discussion of moderators for this type of accountability is speculative. Therefore, this section discusses only moderators of the positive effects of accountability to parties with unknown views. These moderators disrupt either the link between accountability and motivation/effort or the link between effort and JDM quality.

The moderators of accountability effects are somewhat similar to those for incentives. One of the key moderators again is skill (knowledge and/or ability), specifically lack of skill. Lack of skill can moderate the effects of accountability in two ways. First, lack of skill can attenuate the link between effort and JDM quality because people exert additional effort in the wrong activities. Second, if people realize they lack the skill required for successful completion of a task, they may not be motivated by accountability. Another moderator relates to the task. In some situations, people view normatively irrelevant cues. For example, auditors often are aware of proscribed anchors (e.g., the unaudited balance for an account). In these situations, accountability may decrease JDM quality because people may increase their effort related to processing all information cues, including the irrelevant ones. In other words, irrelevant cues may have a greater influence under accountability than they would otherwise.[26]

Accountability normally includes certain elements: another party is involved, a person's JDM is traceable to her, there is some sort of evaluation involved, and there is possibility for justification (Lerner and Tetlock 1999). Like incentives, however, such accountability requirements can be implemented in a number of ways, and these varying attributes can serve as moderators of positive accountability effects. First, similar to incentives, people can be informed of accountability requirements prior to JDM or after JDM. If people are made accountable post-JDM, accountability is less likely to have positive effects. This is because accountability cannot lead to self-critical effort. In this situation, people instead engage in "defensive bolstering"; they may increase

---

[24]Pleasing others is but one outcome from which people may derive utility and, as such, but one explanation for why accountability may increase motivation. Lerner and Tetlock (1999) discuss several other possibilities, such as avoiding regret and meeting conversational norms.
[25]Gibbins and Newton (1994) present a more detailed view of various responses that may occur among auditors in this situation.
[26]As is the case with incentives, other person and task variables may moderate the effects of accountability. For example, intrinsic motivation, task complexity, and effort-sensitivity are viable moderators. They are not discussed in this section because there is little relevant research in psychology.

effort, but the effort is directed at rationalizing their JDM. Post-JDM accountability, therefore, is akin to accountability to a party with known views, but the party is oneself and the known view is one's JDM.

Accountability, albeit to a party with unknown views, can specify a dimension of JDM quality that is important (e.g., correspondence with professional standards). Clearly, if a particular dimension of quality is emphasized, accountability may not lead to improvements in other dimensions of quality.[27] Finally, the party to whom someone is held accountable must be perceived as having legitimate authority. Otherwise, accountability may have no effect on motivation and self-critical effort.

Accountability is difficult to study using archival or survey methods because accountability and monetary incentives (and other environmental variables such as goals) frequently are confounded in real-world settings. For example, managers are accountable to investors but also face monetary incentives related to investors such as the threat of litigation. To study accountability using these methods, then, researchers would have to measure other factors that may be confounded with accountability and hope that the correlations of these factors with accountability are not high. Most studies of accountability, then, employ experimental manipulation. Manipulating accountability requires informing subjects that they will be held accountable to someone. Normally, a particular person is not named, but rather someone from a group of individuals. For example, auditing studies may tell subjects that "a partner from your office may review your work." When only accountability is manipulated, subjects do not have to verbalize or put in writing any justification. They merely face the possibility of doing this later. Some studies also manipulate justification by requiring some subjects to provide explanations for their judgments or decisions, normally in writing. One of the important characteristics of successful manipulations of accountability is that the experimenter follows up and actually holds some subjects accountable. That is, if she tells subjects that a partner will review their work, a partner should review at least some of the subjects' work. Given that researchers frequently use subjects from the same subject pool (e.g., one auditing firm), the threat of contaminating future manipulations of accountability is large if a particular researcher does not follow up (Dopuch 1992; Gibbins 1992).

Even when accountability is manipulated, however, there remains the possibility that subjects react to accountability manipulations with differential perceptions of both accountability and monetary incentives. For example, staff auditors who are told they are accountable to a partner may think about both losing money (e.g., by losing their jobs) and losing face. Thus, it also is important for experimental researchers to ensure that accountability and monetary incentives are not confounded through such perceptions. The first step along these lines is to do an extensive manipulation check to ensure that perceptions of accountability differ as intended by the manipulation. (See Brazel et al. [2004] for an example.) A second important step is to obtain measures of self-critical effort, as accountability is thought to operate through this mediator, but monetary incentives are not. Another possible technique would be to include postexperimental questions about perceptions of incentives that may be elicited by the accountability manipulation. The next section reviews accounting studies related to accountability and justification.

---

[27]There is some evidence that making people accountable for their JDM process rather than the judgment or decision per se leads to higher-quality JDM (e.g., Siegel-Jacobs and Yates 1996). However, there also is evidence showing the opposite result (Lerner and Tetlock 1999).

Accounting Studies on Accountability

Only a handful of studies examine the effects of accountability on the JDM of producers and users of accounting information. Schadewald and Limberg (1992) report that student subjects judging the strength of tax cases make different judgments when order of cues is varied; however, the requirement to justify their judgments eliminates these differences. Cloyd (1997) finds that tax professionals exert more effort doing a tax research task when told their work will be reviewed. In turn, increased effort leads to better JDM quality, defined as the number of relevant items identified less the number of irrelevant items identified, for subjects who possess knowledge. Chang et al. (1997) find no effect of requiring students to justify their answers to several JDM questions.

A number of studies examine the effects of accountability on auditors' JDM. Johnson and Kaplan (1991) report that auditors held accountable for their inventory obsolescence judgments agree more with each other than do nonaccountable subjects but do not agree more with themselves over time. Lord (1992) finds that accountable auditors are less likely to give an unqualified opinion to a client with a questionable accounting choice than are nonaccountable auditors. In other words, they act more conservatively. Kennedy (1993) examines the effectiveness of accountability at reducing order effects in a going-concern task. She finds no effect of accountability for auditors because they exhibit no order effects. Students are affected by order; for them, pre-JDM accountability eliminates order effects, whereas post-JDM accountability does not. Kennedy (1995) finds that auditors and students predicting others' going-concern or sales judgments and given outcome information are not affected by accountability; they use outcome information similarly in all conditions, even though it is normatively irrelevant.

Hoffman and Patton (1997) find that accountability has no effect on the extent to which auditors use irrelevant cues when making fraud risk judgments. However, accountable subjects make more conservative judgments than do nonaccountable subjects. Glover (1997) finds similar results. Tan and Kao (1999) employ three auditing tasks that vary in complexity. Accountability has no effect on correspondence with professional theories for the low-complexity task. For the medium-complexity (high-complexity) task, accountability has a positive effect on correspondence with professional theories only when subjects have high knowledge (high knowledge and ability). Brazel et al. (2004) manipulate whether auditors expect a face-to-face review, electronic review, or no review of their going-concern judgments with the first type of review expected to create the highest accountability. They find that face-to-face subjects take more time and give more accurate judgments (vis-à-vis those of an expert panel) than do other subjects. Electronic and no review subjects do not differ.

Four studies examine the effects of accountability with known views. DeZoort and Lord (1994) report that auditors accountable to either a manager or partner who wishes to allow latitude to a client are more likely to indicate that they would allow clients to circumvent audit procedures than are subjects under no accountability.[28] Cohen and Trompeter (1998) hold audit managers accountable to an aggressive or conservative partner and find that the former group is more likely to accept a client's proposed aggressive accounting treatment. Brown et al. (1999) ask auditors to evaluate

---

[28]The authors characterize the study as being related to obedience pressure rather than accountability. It is included here because there are no other studies of obedience pressure.

client explanations for unexpected fluctuations and rate the diagnosticity of tests; all subjects are held accountable. Some are held accountable under conditions supporting the client's view, whereas others are asked to be skeptical and discount the client's view. A third group is given instructions to be "accurate." Auditors given the client's view tend to find more tests that support the client's explanation and judge this explanation more likely than other groups. Skeptical-condition auditors are prone to request more tests of all types in an attempt to gather information. Wilks (2002) reports that audit managers given a partner's view on a going-concern judgment pre-JDM shift more toward that judgment than do managers given the view after evidence evaluation, although the latter group's judgments reflect the partner's view. The effect of accountability in the pre-JDM group is driven partially by biased evaluation of evidence, consistent with motivated reasoning.

The remaining studies manipulate justification, often along with accountability. Ashton (1990, 1992) requires auditors to make bond ratings, some under conditions of justification (but no accountability). Ashton (1990) finds no effect of justification on the accuracy of these ratings, but Ashton (1992) finds that auditors required to justify are more accurate and consistent over time. Church (1991) manipulates accountability and justification in a test planning task. Accountable subjects allocate relatively more hours to the transaction cycle they select for testing than do nonaccountable subjects; further, they assign more weight to cues that support their hypothesis. Tan (1995) compares the judgments and recall of subjects justifying versus not justifying going-concern judgments; however, justification is confounded with prior involvement. Although justifying subjects recall relatively more information consistent with their judgments, there are no differences in final judgments between the groups. A second experiment manipulates justification and accountability (again, however, confounding this with prior involvement). With the threat of review, auditors recall relatively more inconsistent information and make different judgments than control subjects.

Koonce et al. (1995) require all auditors to justify their decisions regarding tests for an unexpected fluctuation while holding some accountable as well. Accountability has no effect on budgeted hours but increases the number and breadth of justifications written. Asare et al. (2000) ask auditors to determine the cause of a ratio fluctuation. Auditors held accountable and asked to justify exert more effort as evidenced by conducting more tests. Accountable subjects also examine more hypotheses, consistent with greater self-critical effort, and are more conservative in their testing, focusing relatively more on error causes than nonerror causes. Finally, accountable subjects are more accurate, and this appears to be due mostly to increased self-critical effort. Agoglia et al. (2003) manipulate the form of justification while holding all subjects accountable. Auditors asked to provide supporting evidence of their fraud judgments provide less information than those asked to provide balanced evidence.

Three studies examine justification and accountability effects on auditors when views are known. Peecher (1996) uses a task and accountability manipulation similar to that in Brown et al. (1999) and also asks subjects to justify their judgments. Auditors given the client's view make higher judgments about the likelihood that the client's explanation is correct than do the other two groups. Tan et al. (1997) also hold all auditors accountable for their inventory obsolescence judgments but provide some with a partner's judgments as well. All subjects must justify their judgments. Subjects with known views make judgments closer to those views and exhibit less effort in the form of fewer justifications provided. Finally, Turner (2001) uses an accountability manipulation similar to Peecher and Brown et al. and asks all auditors to provide justification. Auditors with client views search relatively more for client-prompted evidence than do those in other groups and, overall, search for less evidence.

In summary, results regarding accountability and justification are similar to those in psychology. When held accountable to persons with known views, accounting professionals make judgments and decisions that are closer to those views than individuals not held accountable. Oftentimes, these judgments and decisions are more aggressive and, again, contrary to standards that call for objectivity in judgments (as discussed above). Accountability with unknown views often produces positive effects on JDM quality, but it can have no effect if subjects lack skill or if irrelevant information is contained in a task. The last finding is somewhat unlike that in psychology, where accountability frequently has a negative effect on JDM quality under irrelevant information conditions. Perhaps there are countervailing forces in accounting settings that mitigate this tendency.

Future research should consider several issues related to accountability and justification. First, it is important to be more specific about possible consequences associated with accountability. These consequences likely differ depending on the party to whom an accounting professional is held accountable. Further, because many of the consequences are monetary in nature, it is crucial to attempt to separate the effects of social and other consequences from the effects of monetary consequences when studying accountability. Separation of accountability and incentives effects can be accomplished perhaps through design or the use of postexperimental questions. Further, there are a number of recent practice developments related to accountability that deserve attention. One of these is that audit firms are making changes in the review process in order to increase its efficiency (Rich et al. 1997b). Some of these changes may create accountability conditions that have lesser positive effects than do those embedded in the traditional review process. For example, firms are making the review process more interactive and "real time." These changes make it more likely that the superior's views will become known, in which case accountability will have positive effects on JDM quality only if these views are correct.

7-4 EFFECTS OF ASSIGNED GOALS ON JDM QUALITY

This section discusses the effects of assigned goals on JDM quality. *Goals* are "the aim or end of an action" (Locke and Latham 1990), and theory distinguishes between personal goals and assigned goals. *Assigned goals* are those that an organization or an individual attempts to impose on a person, whereas *personal goals* are those actually adopted by the person. Although there are many types of goals, for example, career goals and life goals (Austin and Vancouver 1996), this section focuses on task-specific assigned goals, consistent with the focus of this book on JDM in accounting-related tasks. For example, a staff auditor might be given a goal to complete a particular area of the audit in 20 hours or, alternatively, in less time than spent last year in that area. Thus, goals can be quite specific or relatively vague.

Assigned goals are an environmental variable that is not unique to accounting. Yet the relevance of assigned goals to accounting JDM is enormous. For example, one purpose of management accounting systems is to provide information that can be used to motivate individuals, and one key piece of such information is goals embedded in budgets and standards, such as goals for total product costs (Sprinkle 2003; Atkinson et al. 2003). Further, as mentioned earlier, assigned goals are an explicit part of quota-based incentive schemes, and quota schemes are used in both research and practice (Bonner et al. 2000; Sprinkle). Although the use of goals is widespread, organizations likely vary in the extent to which they attach goals to all JDM tasks performed by their employees and also in various attributes of goals, such as how specific they are. Further, attaining goals can have economic rewards (e.g., if they are part of quota incentive schemes). For example, managers may receive bonuses for meeting revenue goals. Even if pay is not directly tied to meeting goals, reputation, interpersonal relationships, and other factors may be affected by whether people achieve or miss goals.

Assigned goals typically are thought to have positive effects on performance. Much of the literature in psychology examines the effects of assigned goals in physical production tasks, measuring performance as the quantity of acceptable output and the extent to which that quantity meets or exceeds the assigned goal. Less work examines the effects of goals on JDM quality. Further, JDM-related goals often reflect an outcome that is the product of the quality of one or more judgments and decisions (along, possibly, with other factors such as environmental uncertainty) rather than being related to JDM quality per se. For example, a division manager given a goal of increasing revenues over the prior year makes several judgments and decisions that then may or may not lead to the goal being met. She may decide to introduce new products, discontinue some products, or increase marketing expenditures. Such decisions are based on judgments such as the potential customer base for products and the effectiveness of advertising for a particular product. Thus, measuring whether JDM meets assigned goals often means measuring whether one or more outcomes associated with JDM meet assigned goals.[29] Based on this, it is not appropriate to characterize the effects of goals in terms of the motivated reasoning framework. That is, although goals may appear to be "desired conclusions," the measure of JDM quality typically is some outcome associated with JDM rather than the JDM itself. In other words, goals impose "desired outcomes," not "desired conclusions."

Goal-setting theory does not explicitly posit that assigned goals affect JDM quality and related outcomes through motivation. However, the theoretical account is similar to one that would include motivation as a mediator.[30] In particular, Locke and Latham (1990) propose that assigned goals positively affect both personal goals and self-efficacy. Assigned goals affect personal goals simply because goals tend to be accepted when assigned by an authority figure. Assigned goals positively affect self-efficacy because goals provide information about the performance level someone is expected to achieve and, thus, the performance level they think they can achieve (Meyer and Gellatly 1988). In turn, self-efficacy and personal goals both positively affect performance via effort direction; effort duration; effort intensity; and, in some cases, strategy development. Self-efficacy also has an indirect effect on effort and

---

[29]This also raises the issue of how one determines JDM quality of individuals who may have the power to manipulate outcomes so they meet assigned goals. For example, managers seeking to meet assigned earnings goals may do so by managing earnings rather than by making high-quality judgments and decisions that lead to earnings that actually meet the goal.

[30]Further, motivational concepts and the term "motivation" often are used in discussions by the key goal-setting theorists (Locke and Latham 1990).

performance by positively affecting personal goals; people with higher self-efficacy believe they can achieve higher goals (Locke and Latham 1990; Earley and Lituchy 1991).

Considering motivation as a mediator of a positive goal–JDM quality relation raises the question of why goals increase motivation. Again, this question can be answered using expected utility or expectancy theory concepts. Under these theories, attaining a goal must be considered to have more than zero attractiveness or utility. This certainly is the case if pay is tied to reaching a goal. However, it appears that people derive utility simply from meeting goals (even if there are no associated financial consequences). People feel a sense of achievement or pride in attaining goals, particularly if they attribute goal attainment to themselves rather than to external factors (Weiner 1986; Locke and Latham 1990). People also may derive utility from trying hard and accepting challenges, even if they do not meet goals (Matsui et al. 1981). In addition, the effort–outcome expectancy is affected by the presence of goals. People should have a clearer and stronger idea that effort will allow them to achieve a desirable outcome (meeting a goal) when a goal is present than when it is not.

As is the case with other environmental variables, there are a number of moderators of the positive effects of assigned goals on JDM quality (or performance, more generally). Skill is a moderator of goal effects; if people lack skill for a given task, assigned goals may increase motivation and effort, but the effort–quality relation will be attenuated because effort is misplaced. Also, as above, the goal–motivation/effort relation may be attenuated if people give up, knowing they lack skill. Task complexity moderates goal effects for similar reasons (Wood et al. 1987). In particular, the goal-setting literature focuses on the idea that task complexity leads to effort directed at strategy development, which harms quality in the short run (Locke and Latham 1990). In addition, feedback can moderate the effects of goals in multiple-trial situations (Tubbs 1986). Specifically, if people are not provided with feedback in order to monitor how well they are progressing toward goals, assigned goals may have no positive effects because people give up, attenuating the goal–motivation/effort relation (Locke and Latham). If they do not give up, they may misdirect effort, attenuating the effort–JDM quality relation.[31]

Like incentives and accountability, goals can be implemented in a number of ways. In other words, goals vary on a number of dimensions, and these dimensions can attenuate their positive effects, as evidenced by a large volume of studies and a number of meta-analyses (Locke and Latham 1990; Austin and Vancouver 1996).[32] First, the difficulty level of the assigned goal has a positive effect on JDM quality up to the point at which goals become overly difficult. Beyond this point, quality may either level off or decrease. Thus, easy assigned goals, on average, have a smaller effect on JDM quality than do difficult assigned goals and may have no different effect than no goals. This occurs because easy assigned goals lead to lower motivation and easy personal goals, which in turn create lower effort, than would more difficult goals. Second, specific difficult goals have a greater effect on quality than do vague difficult goals, such as "do your best," or than no goals, which sometimes are assumed implicitly to provide instructions to "do your best." This occurs because variation in motivation, personal

---

[31]Clearly, another possible moderator of the effect of a single goal is the presence of other, conflicting goals. However, little is known about how people make tradeoffs among conflicting goals, particularly in JDM tasks and professional settings (Locke and Latham 1990).

[32]This section discusses the dimensions about which much is known. There are other dimensions of goals that may serve as moderators, such as goal complexity (Austin and Vancouver 1996).

goals, effort, and, thus, JDM quality is greater under "do your best" or no goal conditions. Because these factors are uniformly high under specific difficult goal conditions, they are higher than for other types of goals or no goals.

Another factor that attenuates the effects of assigned goals is the level of goal commitment. When commitment to assigned goals decreases, motivation, effort, and quality decrease as well. In many early experimental studies, goal commitment was not an issue because subjects apparently felt that they had to be committed to goals assigned by the researcher, who served as an authority figure (Locke and Latham 1990). However, more recent research indicates that there are a number of attributes of goals that affect the level of goal commitment and, thus, moderate the relationship between assigned goals and motivation/effort. First, as goals become more difficult, a person's expectation of reaching the goal and, thus, her level of commitment to doing so may decrease.[33] Goal commitment can be influenced by the credibility of the person assigning the goal. Locke and Latham note that commitment is highest when the person is perceived as a legitimate authority figure, is physically present, is considered trustworthy and competent, and provides reasonable justification for the goal. Clearly, these conditions are met in most laboratory settings but may not be met in the field. A number of other dimensions of goals can affect commitment. For example, if a goal is made public, people are more likely to be committed to these goals.

One final issue vis-à-vis goal commitment that is important in accounting is whether goals are "purely" assigned, that is, handed down from a supervisor, or the subordinate who is trying to reach the goal participates somewhat in the setting of the goal ultimately assigned. Again, this is a particularly salient topic in management accounting because goals in the form of budgets are one major use of management accounting information. Research to date indicates that participation in the setting of budgets or goals typically does not increase motivation, effort, or JDM quality when compared to no participation (Tubbs 1986; Locke and Latham 1990). However, participation may have cognitive effects because a subordinate may acquire information about how best to perform a task while discussing a budget or goal with a superior.[34]

As is true with incentives and accountability, studying the effects of goals using measurement is quite difficult. Goals typically are confounded with other environmental variables such as incentives. For example, a manufacturing firm may implement differential goals across divisions but also implement differential rewards for achieving those goals. As a consequence, much assigned goal research is done experimentally; further, several things are known about studying goals experimentally because of the depth of the literature. Locke and Latham (1990) make a number of suggestions, among them the following: researchers examining assigned goals should measure subjects' personal goals and level of commitment to those goals; otherwise, a manipulation of assigned goals may not be known to have worked. Scales for measuring these variables are well established. Further, because there is little theory that can aid researchers when studying the effects of goal difficulty, it is important to conduct pilot tests to ensure that the expected levels of difficulty are consistent with reality. In

---

[33]Note that this effect of goal difficulty may offset positive effects of difficulty. Alternatively, goal difficulty may simply create arousal, which has a U-shaped relation to effort and JDM quality.

[34]Participation in goal-setting also may have negative effects on JDM quality if people build "slack" into goals so they can have a high probability of attaining the goals. In this case, people may make the goals so easy that they exert little effort, thus lowering JDM quality.

multiple-trial situations, it is also important to provide feedback due to its strong moderating role. Finally, researchers should carefully consider other known moderators of goal effects such as skill.

Unfortunately, most accounting studies that examine the effects of assigned goals do not examine these effects in JDM tasks.[35] Thus, there are few studies to review in this section. Kenis (1979) surveys managers about various characteristics of goals, including difficulty and specificity, and examines their relation to self-reported performance measures. Performance is defined as the degree to which managers meet the goals. Specificity, but not difficulty, is related to performance. Hirst and Lowy (1990) also survey managers regarding the effects of goal difficulty and feedback on performance, measured as self-ratings of either overall job performance or meeting goals. Goal difficulty and feedback interactively affect performance measured as meeting goals but not overall job performance.

Several survey studies examine the effect of participation in the setting of goals on motivation and managers' self-reported performance. Kenis (1979) finds a positive relation between participation and performance at meeting goals. Merchant (1981) and Brownell (1983) report mixed evidence linked to the relation between participation and either motivation or performance. Brownell and McInnes (1986) find that participation is positively related to performance, but this finding is not due to participation's effects on motivation. Further, Brownell and Hirst (1986) and Dunk (1989) find no relation of participation to performance. Mia (1988) finds a positive relation of participation to performance only for individuals with high self-reported intrinsic motivation; for individuals with low motivation, participation has a negative effect. Mia (1989) reports an interaction between participation and job complexity, indicating that participation has a greater effect on performance as jobs become more complex. Brownell and Dunk (1991) and Lau et al. (1995) report similar findings. Finally, Nouri and Parker (1998) find a positive relation between participation and both budget adequacy and organizational commitment, which are positively related to performance. Budget adequacy measures managers' feelings about the extent to which they have resources to meet goals.

Although some of these studies find a relation between participation and managers' self-reported or supervisory-rated performance, the results do not appear to be attributable to motivation increases. Instead, they could be attributable to the cognitive effects of participation in goal setting (acquisition of information), consistent with the conclusions of Locke and Latham (1990). Kren (1992) demonstrates just this. In a survey, he finds that participation has a positive relation to the amount of information managers report having, which then has a positive relation to performance. The relation between participation and information is larger when managers have complex jobs. Chong and Chong (2002) also report survey findings indicating positive relations between, respectively, participation and goal commitment, goal commitment and information, and information and performance.[36]

[35]Typical dependent variables are performance in a production or clerical task (e.g., Chow 1983) or budgetary slack created (e.g., Young 1985). This section includes articles examining managers' performance as a dependent variable based on the assumption that an important part of this performance is JDM quality. For larger perspectives on the effects of budgets, see Covaleski et al. (2003), Luft and Shields (2003), and Sprinkle (2003).
[36]Many of these studies also examine the interaction of participation and firms' emphasis on goals and sometimes find that these interactions are significantly related to managers' performance.

The lone experimental studies include Harrell (1977), who demonstrates that subjects given "policy statements" (goals) related to the importance of various criteria to judgments make judgments more in line with those goals than do other subjects.[37] Hirst and Yetton (1999) compare the effect of specific, difficult goals and "do your best" goals; students with the former have higher-quality JDM in a resource allocation task. JDM quality here is defined as the percent of the maximum possible output achieved in a simulated production decision task. Variance in quality also is reduced by specific, difficult goals.

The few studies in accounting related to goals and JDM produce results that mostly are consistent with those in other fields. That is, specific, difficult goals tend to lead to better JDM quality (or general job performance) than do vague, easy, or no goals. In addition, feedback and task complexity may be moderators of these effects. Further, where participation in the setting of assigned goals has a positive relation to JDM quality or performance, this relation likely is due to information acquisition rather than increased motivation.

Because the use of goals as a motivational mechanism is so widespread (particularly when their use in incentive contracts is considered), it seems extremely important to further understand their effects on professionals' JDM (Sprinkle 2003). In particular, it may be interesting to examine the effects of goals that are stated specifically in terms of JDM quality dimensions. That is, it does not seem necessary for all goals to be stated in terms of outcomes that are reflective of multiple judgments and decisions. It is especially intriguing to understand how professionals make tradeoffs when they face goals that create conflicts in the appropriate JDM. Of course, when examining goals, it is important to disentangle them from accountability and incentives, factors with which they often are confounded in practice. This is important for both research purposes and organizational efficiency purposes. Perhaps goals (combined with feedback) are sufficient for producing desired levels of motivation. As mentioned earlier, organizations may not need to append monetary incentives to goals. In fact, appending monetary incentives to goals may reduce individuals' JDM quality and firm performance vis-à-vis what they would be with goals alone (Jensen 2001).

7-5 EFFECTS OF FEEDBACK ON JDM QUALITY

Definitions and Background

This section explores the effects of feedback on JDM quality. *Feedback* is information about some element of JDM that comes to the decision maker after the JDM task has been performed (Reber 1995). Feedback can come from people; a staff auditor might receive feedback from a senior auditor about the extent to which her work complies with GAAS, for example. Feedback can also come from systems; lights on the instrument panel of a machine may illuminate if the machine is overheating.[38]

There are several different types of feedback, so it is important to begin with definitions. *Outcome feedback* provides information about some dimension of JDM quality. In other words, outcome feedback gives the correct judgment or decision, using a given criterion for "correctness" such as accuracy vis-à-vis outcomes or correspondence with

---

[37]This study does not use an accounting task but is included because it is widely cited.
[38]Feedback may be sought actively by individuals as well (e.g., Ashford and Cummings 1983).

professional standards (Kluger and DeNisi 1996). Thus, outcome feedback in a bank-ruptcy prediction task might be the actual outcome for the firm being examined—bankruptcy or no bankruptcy. In a sample size decision task, outcome feedback might consist of the normatively correct sample size. With outcome feedback, an individual is provided with only this correct answer; there is no further elaboration.

Outcome feedback can be contrasted with *cognitive feedback,* which provides information about JDM processes or tasks rather than about the quality of JDM out-puts (Balzer et al. 1989). In other words, cognitive feedback can inform people about JDM without informing them about correct answers.[39] There are three elements of JDM processes or tasks that feedback can describe. First is *task properties* (or task information); this type of feedback provides information about factors such as the appropriate weights for cues or the functional form of the relation between cues and outputs. For example, an individual doing bankruptcy prediction can be given informa-tion about the appropriate weights to place on various financial ratios. Second is *cognitive information;* this type of feedback provides information about the individ-ual's cognitive processes such as the cue weights she is using. Third is *functional valid-ity information;* here, feedback pertains to the relationships between task properties and cognitive processes, such as the extent to which an individual's cue weights match the appropriate cue weights.

The provision of feedback is one of the key elements of accounting systems. Thus, although feedback is not unique to accounting settings, the effects of feedback are of supreme importance in understanding accounting JDM quality. Management account-ing information, in particular, often is described as having either motivational (deci-sion-influencing) or knowledge-acquisition (decision-facilitating) properties (Sprinkle 2003). Management accounting information in the form of feedback is somewhat unique in that it can play both roles. Further, accounting professionals receive feed-back on their work that can vary across tasks or superiors within a firm or across firms (Belkaoui and Picur 1987; Bonner and Pennington 1991). Because feedback can play multiple roles, it clearly can have substantial effects on JDM quality and related conse-quences. For example, firms who do not provide proper feedback to employees may not be maximizing their profits. The next section discusses psychology research on feedback.

Feedback Effects

Feedback typically is thought to have positive effects on JDM quality. Although JDM quality frequently is operationalized as accuracy vis-à-vis outcomes in psychology studies, it is conceivable to study the effects of feedback on all dimensions of JDM quality. For example, in accounting, it may be particularly appropriate to examine whether feedback affects the extent to which JDM corresponds with professional stan-dards. Consistent with the importance of multiple JDM quality dimensions, accounting studies examine the effects of feedback on a number of such dimensions.

Feedback is thought to positively affect JDM quality through at least two mecha-nisms, one of which is increased motivation and effort (Kluger and DeNisi 1996). Here, the motivation is of the "be correct" variety because feedback is being given over mul-tiple trials with varying task characteristics and, thus, varying judgments or decisions. In

---

[39]Cognitive and outcome feedback can, of course, be combined.

other words, there is not the possibility for motivation to be oriented toward a desired conclusion because there are multiple conclusions that relate to multiple instantiations of the task. Given this, the motivational effects of feedback can affect JDM quality through increases to effort direction, duration, or intensity, or effort put into strategy development.

Feedback (either outcome or cognitive) can increase motivation and effort for at least two reasons. First, feedback may indicate that the person has either low JDM quality or problems in her JDM processes, which imply the possibility for low JDM quality. In this case, if a person wants to achieve some attractive consequences associated with high JDM quality such as money or pleasant interactions with a superior, she is motivated to increase her effort because the current level of effort is not leading to the desired level of JDM quality. Second, if feedback indicates that the person currently has either high JDM quality or appropriate JDM processes, self-efficacy can increase. In turn, this can lead to the setting of higher personal goals, which then lead to greater effort.[40]

As mentioned above, feedback can also have decision-facilitating properties. In other words, it can provide information to people that can help them acquire knowledge. Acquired knowledge then can have a positive effect on JDM quality (Kluger and DeNisi 1996). The learning effects of either outcome or cognitive feedback can be direct or indirect. Indirect effects are those that occur through motivation and related strategy-development effort. That is, people sometimes acquire knowledge from feedback because they are motivated to learn so they can increase JDM quality in the future and experience more attractive consequences; thus, they work harder at learning. For example, motivation may lead people to generate hypotheses for appropriate cognitive processes then test those hypotheses in future encounters with the task. Direct learning effects of feedback occur in different ways depending on the type of feedback. With outcome feedback, learning can take place by people reasoning backward from the outcomes and determining the necessary corrections to their cognitive processes. Because outcomes are influenced by many process factors (and many task and environmental factors as well), however, learning from outcome feedback can be quite difficult (this is discussed further below). With cognitive feedback, acquisition of knowledge is expedited because the feedback gets directly at the cognitive processes that need improvement. For example, if a person is given feedback about appropriate cue weights (task properties feedback), all she need do is compare those weights to her own cue weights.[41] To the extent there are discrepancies, she can adjust her cue weights.

Feedback often does not produce positive JDM quality effects, however, despite its potential for positive effects on both motivation and knowledge acquisition. In fact, feedback often can have negative effects on JDM (Kluger and DeNisi 1996). Moderators of feedback effects can disrupt the link between feedback and motivation/effort or the link between effort and JDM quality. Instead (or in addition), they can disrupt the link between feedback and knowledge or between knowledge and JDM quality.

---

[40]Alternatively, feedback may create motivation leading to arousal (DeZoort and Lord 1997), so it may have a U-shaped relation with effort and JDM quality.
[41]This assumes that the individual has insight into her cue weights. This sometimes is not the case.

Skill can be a prominent moderator of feedback effects, as it is for other environmental variables. This is particularly true for outcome feedback. Outcome feedback often has negative effects on JDM quality because it seldom allows for knowledge acquisition. In order for a person to be able to acquire knowledge in an outcome feedback situation, she must be able to infer appropriate cognitive processes from outcomes. If she lacks skill, she is unlikely to be able to do so unless the task is extremely simple. Envision a situation in which a task is simple because it has high environmental predictability and two cues. In this case, learning from outcome feedback is possible because outcomes are affected almost entirely by two cues (i.e., virtually not at all by random error). Thus, people can relatively easily determine appropriate cue weights and also are more likely to be consistent in the application of those weights. However, even slightly more complicated tasks may make learning from outcome feedback for people lacking skill nearly impossible. In other words, lack of skill can disrupt the feedback–knowledge link unless tasks are simple.

Further, if a person knows she is unable to learn from feedback, the feedback–knowledge and feedback–motivation/effort links may be disrupted because she may give up. Skill can be a moderator of both cognitive and outcome feedback effects for an additional reason: if people already possess knowledge, then feedback cannot have further positive effects on knowledge. In addition, high levels of skill likely translate into high current levels of JDM quality and highly attractive consequences associated therewith, so the motivational effects of feedback likely are moot as well. For similar reasons, task complexity can moderate feedback effects, particularly the effects of outcome feedback. Specifically, certain elements of task complexity can diminish learning from feedback, for example, the presence of nonlinear rather than linear relations and negative rather than positive relations (Hogarth 1987).

Self-efficacy also can moderate the effects of feedback. People who are low in self-efficacy are more likely to have a disruption of the feedback–motivation/effort link, particularly in the face of negative feedback (Kluger and DeNisi 1996). This occurs because people high in self-efficacy are more likely to believe they can be successful at the task and persist, whereas people low in self-efficacy instead may turn their attention away from the task and toward something for which they have high self-efficacy (e.g., another task). Similar arguments can be made for self-esteem (Luckett and Eggleton 1991). Of course, a number of factors affect self-efficacy or self-esteem, including feedback itself (see below). In addition, feedback normally is associated with the use of goals or standards for determining what is "high quality" JDM. Thus, feedback without goals is less likely to have positive effects because people have more difficulty determining whether their JDM is of high or low quality based on the feedback (Pritchard et al. 1988; Locke and Latham 1990; Kluger and DeNisi). As a consequence, for example, people may give up, attenuating the feedback–motivation/effort link.

As is the case with other environmental variables, feedback can be implemented in a wide variety of fashions, and various dimensions of feedback can attenuate its positive effects. First, the time lag between JDM and the receipt of feedback can attenuate feedback effects (Anderson 2005). Such lags occur frequently in accounting. For example, auditors must wait about a year before obtaining feedback on bankruptcy outcomes associated with going-concern judgments. The longer the lag, the less likely feedback is to have positive effects. This occurs because feedback must be compared to a judgment or decision in order to both learn and be motivated by it, and longer time lags make it less likely that people will recall their judgment or decision. Even if the JDM is recorded somewhere, the longer lag may make it more costly to find.

Second, the less complete feedback is or the less completely people process it, the less likely it is to have positive effects on JDM quality (Hogarth 1987). Feedback, particularly outcome feedback, often is not complete. Consider a situation in which there are two possible judgments and two possible outcomes (e.g., the going-concern situation). Auditors can judge that there is a going-concern issue or that there is no issue; along with this, going-concern problems (e.g., bankruptcy) can either occur or not occur. Complete outcome feedback includes information about the four possible combinations of judgments and outcomes. However, people often do not get all four types of feedback. For example, when accounting firm recruiters hire staff auditors, they likely do not receive feedback on their JDM about the individuals they do not hire. Instead, they receive only two of the types of feedback—whether the persons they judged as likely to succeed (and consequently hired) either succeed or fail.

Along with this, even in situations where all four types of outcome feedback are provided, people often do not use it completely (Einhorn and Hogarth 1978; Brehmer 1980; Einhorn 1980). People have a tendency to focus on only the feedback related to the combination of a positive judgment and a positive outcome (called a "positive hit") when processing feedback. This occurs because these two items are associated in memory and also because of people's general tendencies to seek confirming information (e.g., Shaklee and Tucker 1980; Crocker 1981). Focusing on positive hits alone is problematic because people are not using all the feedback and, more important, they fail to realize the problems inherent in the feedback they do use. For example, an audit firm that is extremely litigation conscious in its choice of clients may accept very few clients who ultimately experience bankruptcy. Individual auditors at that firm who make judgments that there are no going-concern issues then experience no-bankruptcy outcomes may fail to realize that their judgments are almost always going to be accurate because of their firm's client acceptance policies. Instead, they attribute the accuracy of their judgments to themselves (Einhorn and Hogarth 1978). Based on these attributions, people can become increasingly overconfident, which lessens their motivation to learn from future feedback (Einhorn 1980).[42] A final problem that arises from focusing on only the positive judgment–positive outcome type of feedback is that the positive judgment can create the positive outcome (called a treatment effect). For example, a judgment that there is no going-concern issue likely leads the auditor to give the client an unqualified opinion. In turn, the unqualified opinion, even if inaccurate, may allow the client to borrow enough cash to continue as a going concern. Overall, then, failure to obtain complete feedback or completely use existing feedback can lead to a disruption of either the feedback–knowledge link or the feedback–motivation link.

Third, the quality of feedback can serve as a moderator. Both outcome and cognitive feedback can be incorrect. For example, the outcome of actual earnings that an analyst might compare to her earnings forecast may be misstated. Feedback given by a senior auditor to a staff auditor about the importance of various factors in judging going-concern issues may be inaccurate because the senior auditor is not knowledgeable about this task. Further, feedback can be perceived to be inaccurate. Continuing

---

[42]See Gervais and Odean (2001) for a model that develops how investors become overconfident in a similar fashion.

the example, if the staff auditor believes for some reason that the senior is not knowledgeable, she may perceive the senior's feedback to be inaccurate. In the case where feedback is truly inaccurate, the feedback–knowledge relation can be attenuated. In the case where feedback is perceived to be inaccurate, both the feedback–knowledge and feedback–motivation/effort relations can be disrupted because the person receiving the feedback perceives low benefits to using the feedback. However, the power of the source may undo the effects of the feedback accuracy moderator. That is, people may draw conclusions from feedback known or perceived to be inaccurate and, thus, negatively affect their knowledge if the source is very powerful (Luckett and Eggleton 1991).

Fourth, the frequency with which feedback is given can moderate feedback's effects (Luckett and Eggleton 1991). More frequent feedback may lead to better JDM quality than does less frequent feedback. Less frequent feedback can attenuate the feedback–knowledge relation because of memory problems due to time lags, for example. Further, if time period is held constant, less frequent feedback means a lower amount of feedback and, thus, fewer opportunities for learning. Less frequent feedback, particularly if the feedback is positive, means fewer chances for a person to be informed about the quality of her JDM and, thus, fewer chances for self-efficacy and consequent motivation to increase. Thus, frequency can disrupt the feedback–motivation/effort link as well. These statements must be tempered, however, in the case of outcome feedback. If a person is receiving outcome feedback related to a complex task, frequent feedback may impede the acquisition of knowledge because, under outcome feedback, people tend to change strategies in an attempt to find high-quality cognitive processes and, in so doing, fail to learn well. Further, frequent feedback, particularly if negative, can impede motivation; people give up because they believe that learning in such a situation is quite difficult.

A number of other dimensions of feedback are pertinent to its positive relation to JDM quality (e.g., Luckett and Eggleton 1991; Kluger and DeNisi 1996). For example, elements of feedback that negatively affect either self-efficacy or self-esteem can moderate feedback effects. In particular, feedback that is overly discouraging, feedback that is made public, or feedback given in person can lower self-efficacy or self-esteem. Along with this, research indicates that task properties feedback likely is better than cognitive information feedback (Balzer et al. 1989, 1992). This may occur, for example, because task properties feedback draws attention and effort toward high-quality processes, whereas cognitive information feedback draws attention and effort away from low-quality processes but does not provide any direction on how to improve. Thus, the feedback–knowledge link can be attenuated when feedback provides cognitive information.

Feedback effects can be studied through manipulation or measurement. However, the issues related to measuring other environmental variables apply here as well. In the field, feedback frequently is confounded with goals, and goals instead may be responsible for observed effects of feedback (e.g., Locke 1967). Feedback can be confounded also with accountability and monetary incentives. Further, obtaining measures of feedback archivally seems tricky, so that measurement might require surveys. In this case, the specific problems that arise when using surveys to study JDM are particularly salient (see Chapter 1). For example, people may have to recall particular elements of feedback long after the feedback occurred, and memory problems may make this difficult. Consequently, feedback is more often studied through manipulation.

Experimental study of feedback cannot only remove confounds such as accountability, but also control for or manipulate many elements of feedback that serve as moderators, such as its timeliness and completeness.

Accounting Studies on Feedback

Accounting studies on the effects of feedback mostly relate to producers and users of accounting information. Cook (1967, 1968) reports that students' and managers' rate of return in a simulated business game increases with frequency of feedback. Mock (1973) provides feedback just on profits (outcome feedback) to some students doing a business simulation, whereas other students receive feedback on profits plus the extent to which they meet self-set goals. Because only the students receiving the latter type of feedback set goals, feedback and goals are confounded. Those with the more extensive feedback have higher profits, lower costs, and spend more time making production decisions. However, there are no differences in learning due to feedback, suggesting goals may be responsible for the findings. Hoskin (1983) also examines feedback effects in a business simulation; feedback that includes information on opportunity costs leads to more theoretically correct decisions than does feedback without this information.

Harrell (1977) provides some subjects with no feedback. Other subjects receive feedback indicating that superiors agree with the recommendations of a policy statement, feedback indicating that managers ignore the policy statement, or feedback that is random in nature. All groups receive the policy statement as well. Subjects' cue weights and judgments are closer to (farther from) those prescribed by the policy statement in the superior-agreement (superior-ignoring) feedback condition than in other conditions. Random feedback's effects are similar to those of no feedback. Ashton (1981) compares the effects of task properties feedback about cue weights to the effects of what he terms "general feedback," which consists of a lengthy memo from management about the task, and finds no effect of either type of feedback on learning or product pricing decision quality (measured as theoretical correctness). Arunachalam and Beck (2002) find similar results.

Gupta and King (1997) examine the effects of cost report accuracy and feedback on the profits subjects make based on product cost forecasts. All subjects receive feedback about profits (outcome feedback), whereas some subjects also receive information about products' use of resources (akin to task properties feedback). Subjects with both types of feedback obtain higher profits than those with just outcome feedback. However, outcome feedback appears to be used somewhat effectively by subjects for learning; their profits with outcome feedback are higher than they would be with the cost information alone. Following up on this study, Briers et al. (1999) provide all subjects with relatively inaccurate cost information but vary the type of feedback they receive. Results are consistent with those of Gupta and King. Ghosh (1997) reports that subjects are less likely to decide to continue with an unprofitable project when the negative feedback they receive is precise rather than ambiguous. Finally, Sprinkle (2000) does not vary the availability of outcome feedback but documents that subjects with monetary incentives use feedback more than do flat-wage subjects and are able to make more normatively correct production decisions.

Survey studies of managers include Kenis (1979), who finds no relation between managers' self-reported amount of feedback and performance. Brownell (1983) presents evidence that the extent to which negative feedback is emphasized (management by exception) has no relation to motivation. Hirst and Lowy's (1990) survey finds that feedback affects self-rated performance interactively with goals but has no main effect.

Other studies of users and producers of accounting information include Kessler and Ashton (1981), who examine students making bond ratings under four cognitive feedback conditions. One group receives information about how many ratings are correct and the number of ratings that miss the correct ratings by only one category. A second group receives this information plus cognitive information. A third group receives the summary information plus task-properties feedback, and a fourth group receives all three types of feedback. Subjects with task-properties feedback are more accurate at predicting bond ratings than are those with cognitive information feedback, but they are not more accurate than those with only the summary information. Jacoby et al. (1984) make outcome feedback available to analysts performing a stock selection task. There is a negative relation between profits made and the extent to which outcome feedback is accessed; analysts with the highest-quality JDM access outcome feedback least frequently. Tuttle and Stocks (1998) manipulate both outcome and task-properties feedback in an experiment that requires students with prior knowledge to make predictions of financial distress. JDM quality is measured as either the correlation to or the difference from a panel of loan officers' judgments. Outcome feedback consists of the loan officers' judgment, and task-properties feedback is the ranking of cues by weight. Students' JDM quality is higher with outcome feedback than without. Further, after several trials, task-properties feedback also improves JDM quality.

A few studies examine feedback effects for auditors. Waller and Felix (1984) provide auditors with either complete or incomplete outcome feedback related to internal control evaluations; in the latter group, subjects receive feedback only when they decide to rely on the control system. They also manipulate the extent to which positive outcomes (strong control systems) occur in the environment and measure subjects' self-perceived judgment quality. They find that incomplete-feedback subjects' self-perceived JDM quality is positively related to the occurrence of positive hits (reliance judgments and good outcomes), whereas complete-feedback subjects' self-perceived JDM quality is not related to positive hits. Further, the strength of the environment per se has a positive relation to self-judged quality for incomplete-feedback subjects but not for complete-feedback subjects. Bonner and Pennington (1991) document that the amount of task-specific feedback auditors receive through the performance evaluation process is positively associated with their experimentally documented performance in those tasks.

Ashton (1990) examines the effects of outcome feedback (the actual bond rating) and the presence of decision aids on the accuracy of auditors' bond ratings. Subjects with outcome feedback and no aid are more accurate than those with neither feedback nor the aid. Outcome feedback has no effect on the accuracy of subjects with the decision aid, however, Bonner and Walker (1994) compare the theoretical correctness of students' answers to ratio analysis problems under conditions of no feedback, outcome feedback (the correct answer), and "explanatory feedback." The latter consists of the correct answer plus an explanation of why that answer is correct. Outcome feedback does not allow subjects to acquire knowledge unless it is combined with extensive pretask instruction. On the other hand, explanatory feedback allows subjects to acquire knowledge irrespective of the type of pretask instruction they receive. Earley (2001) extends Bonner and Walker with auditor subjects and a task that requires evaluation of the reasonableness of the assumed discount rate for commercial real estate. She manipulates both explanatory feedback and the requirement that subjects generate explanations that clarify the actual outcomes. Both treatments result in higher accuracy than no feedback, and the combined feedback–explanation treatment results in higher accuracy than either treatment alone. Finally, Earley (2003) uses a similar task and manipulates the timing of outcome feedback. Auditors who receive the theoretically correct answer, generate explanations, then receive explanatory feedback (including the correct answer) exert more effort in the explanation phase and have higher JDM quality than do auditors who do not receive outcome feedback prior to the explanation phase. Further, effort mediates the feedback timing effect.

Findings for feedback effects in accounting are somewhat similar to those in psychology, although accounting studies appear more likely to find positive effects for outcome feedback. This may occur because accounting studies use very simple tasks or, more plausibly, because they employ subjects who have prior knowledge and, thus, are able to use outcome feedback. Nevertheless, cognitive feedback often results in higher JDM quality than does outcome feedback, consistent with psychology. Moderators of feedback effects appear similar to those in psychology as well (e.g., goals and knowledge).

Feedback is a critical element of accounting environments, yet our knowledge of feedback effects is somewhat disjointed and limited. Studies to date focus mostly on the knowledge acquisition effects of feedback rather than its motivational (or demotivational) properties.[43] Both effects are important and, further, may offset each other in the field. In addition, although there is some evidence of the type of feedback faced by accounting decision makers (e.g., Bonner and Pennington 1991), this evidence is out of date. Studies that document attributes of feedback in today's environment would therefore be useful. For example, it is likely that changes in the review process in auditing also have created changes in the feedback auditors receive. Finally, incomplete feedback abounds in accounting settings, yet we know very little about its potential negative effects on accounting decision makers' JDM.

7-6 EFFECTS OF GROUPS AND TEAMS ON JDM QUALITY

Definitions and Background

This section examines the effects of groups and teams on JDM quality. Much of the research relates to the JDM quality of groups and teams versus the JDM quality of individuals.[44] The section also covers the accounting literature documenting factors that affect group JDM quality.[45] Further, the section discusses accounting research on the audit review process, some of which involves group decision making and some of which involves individual JDM that occurs while people serve in the role of reviewer,

---

[43]For an example of a non-JDM study that examines the motivational effects of feedback, see Young et al. (1993).

[44]Clearly, this section is out of sync with other sections that examine the effects of a particular environmental variable on individual JDM, but I would be greatly remiss if I were to omit the literature on group JDM because of its importance in accounting. However, the literature on negotiation among individuals, although also important in accounting, is beyond the scope of this section. See Bazerman et al. (2000) for a review and Gibbins et al. (2001) for an example of negotiation research in accounting.

[45]Because the primary emphasis in this text is on individual JDM, this section does not discuss psychology theories about factors affecting group JDM.

an integral member of the audit team.[46] Finally, although there is literature on the effects of participating in a group on individual JDM quality and this is an important issue in some accounting settings, the literature is too scant to be reviewed.[47]

This section adopts the definitions of groups and teams used by Solomon (1987) and Rich et al. (1997b). The term *group* typically is used to refer to a collection of two or more individuals who work interactively and concurrently to perform some JDM task. Although not necessary, individuals in a group often are at the same rank in an organization and are somewhat homogeneous as to their skill and other personal characteristics (Cannon-Bowers et al. 1993). Further, groups typically are formed for short periods of time to accomplish specific objectives. For example, a group of audit partners may be convened to resolve a contentious accounting issue. Another type of group—the *composite group*—is not really an interacting group, but rather a statistical combination of individual judgments and decisions. Nevertheless, because individual JDM frequently is compared to that of composite groups and interacting groups, both types are discussed in this section.

A *team* refers to a collection of people who work interactively and sequentially to perform some JDM task. In a team, people may have hierarchical relationships to each other. For example, an audit team may include a staff auditor, a senior, a manager, and a partner. Work begins with the staff, is passed to the senior, and so on. Teams in accounting settings often work iteratively as well (e.g., work passes from the senior back to the staff after it is reviewed). If teams are hierarchical in nature, members are not at the same rank in the organization and likely are more heterogeneous as to their personal characteristics. Further, teams often work together for extended periods of time; for example, auditors can work together for many years on a particular engagement. Note, however, that because of recent changes in the review process (see the accountability section above) as well as changes in organizational structures and technology, the distinction between groups and teams is becoming blurred (e.g., Guzzo and Dickson 1997; Sutton and Hayne 1997; Kerr and Tindale 2004).

The use of interacting groups and teams in organizations is widespread (e.g., Guzzo and Dickson 1997); thus, this variable is not unique to accounting.[48] However, group JDM is of particular importance in many areas of accounting because group JDM produces important outputs such as audit opinions.[49] In addition to auditors, mutual fund managers, tax professionals, loan officers, management accountants, and investors sometimes make judgments and decisions in groups; however, the extent to which groups are utilized for JDM varies across firms, making this an important organizational design choice. Further, using group JDM rather than individual JDM can

---

[46]Recall that studies examining the effects of the threat of review from an unspecified reviewer on the JDM of the person being reviewed are discussed in the section on accountability.

[47]For example, members of investment clubs make individual investments in addition to those made by the clubs (Hodge 2003). These investors likely are influenced by having participated in the clubs. For examples of psychology research that examines the effects of being in a group on individual JDM, see Castellan (1993), Levine et al. (1993), and Heath and Gonazalez (1995). Examples of such studies in accounting include Schultz and Reckers (1981), Reckers and Schultz (1982), and Abdel-Khalik et al. (1983).

[48]This section assumes that groups have been formed either voluntarily, as in the case of investment clubs, or by superiors in firms, as in the case of audit teams. The factors that affect the formation of groups are beyond the scope of this section but clearly are of interest given that group composition has an effect on JDM quality. For more information, see Levine and Moreland (1990) and Thibaut and Kelley (1991).

[49]The term "groups" will be used to refer to interacting groups, teams, and composite groups where distinguishing among these types is not necessary.

have important economic consequences. For example, Fidelity mutual fund managers are required to share information with each other based on the belief that this improves all funds' performance (Smith 1994). On the negative side, the use of groups frequently is blamed for the failure of business projects and associated losses (e.g., Sandberg 2004). In addition to placing people in groups, firms also often reward people using group-based incentive schemes (Sprinkle 2003). If pay is tied to group JDM, the economic consequences become more important for all individuals. Finally, composite groups also are used in accounting settings. In particular, consensus analysts' forecasts are used both by investors for JDM and by researchers to proxy for earnings expectations. Further, analysts themselves can be affected by consensus forecasts. For example, Hong et al. (2000) document that inexperienced analysts who stray farther from consensus forecasts are more likely to lose their jobs than those who forecast closer to the consensus. The next sections discuss various streams of research on groups.

Group Effects

Naturally, group JDM is thought to be superior to individual JDM, although this frequently is not the case (e.g., Steiner 1972; Hill 1982; Kerr and Tindale 2004). Group JDM can be compared to individual JDM (or to the JDM of groups with different attributes) on many dimensions of quality, although accuracy vis-à-vis outcomes and correspondence with normative theories appear to be the dimensions most frequently examined. Studies in accounting examine these dimensions of JDM, along with agreement. It also is important to examine the time and costs associated with group versus individual JDM (or that of groups with varying attributes) given the importance of these dimensions in accounting settings, and given that group JDM can be far more time consuming than individual JDM.

When comparing either interacting or composite group JDM to individual JDM, it is important to specify how quality is to be measured because this specification affects the conclusion about whether group JDM is superior to that of individuals (Einhorn et al. 1977; Solomon 1987; Gigone and Hastie 1997). There are a variety of ways in which groups can be compared to individuals. Assume that accuracy is the dimension of JDM quality being examined. First, group JDM accuracy can be computed, for example, as the absolute difference between the group's response and an actual outcome. This measure of accuracy then can be compared to the average accuracy of individual group members. Second, the accuracy of the group response can be compared to the accuracy of one or more individuals randomly chosen from the group. Third, the group's accuracy can be compared to that of the "best individual," that is, the person whose accuracy ex post is the highest. Finally, Gigone and Hastie suggest that the most appropriate comparison of interacting group JDM to individual JDM may be that of the interacting group to a composite group. Their suggestion is based on the notion that the time and costs associated with convening a group ought to yield gains beyond those that can be obtained from simply averaging or otherwise combining individuals' JDM.

Composite group JDM quality frequently exceeds or equals individual JDM quality irrespective of whether the comparison is made to the average of individuals, the best member, or a random individual (McNees 1992). These outcomes occur because composites of individual judgments and decisions cancel random errors and also can cancel bias if individuals have JDM biases that go in opposite directions. When composite group quality exceeds that of individuals, it is effectively because of higher knowledge (or, more generally, skill) or higher-quality cognitive processes. The skill and processes of a composite group can be significantly better than those of individuals if group members have diverse backgrounds and, thus, possess unique skills and processes (Armstrong 2001a). Composites do not affect JDM quality through other mechanisms, in particular motivation, because people do not interact. Research also shows that composites formed by equally weighting individual judgments or decisions often perform as well as or better than composites formed using either intuitive weights or unequal weights determined mechanically, for example, by regression analysis (Einhorn and Hogarth 1975; Ashton and Ashton 1985; Lawrence et al. 1986; Clemen 1989; Webby and O'Connor 1996).

There are moderators of the superiority of composites' JDM quality, however. The most prevalent is the diversity of individuals included in the composite. As diversity decreases, so do the advantages of composites. Further, individuals often use similar cognitive processes (e.g., heuristics) despite diversity in other personal characteristics. This means that biases go in the same direction, in which case composite group JDM can be of lesser quality than that of many individuals because the biases are amplified (Armstrong 2001a). For example, if all analysts are optimistic in their earnings forecast, a composite forecast will be more optimistic than that of many individuals.

By contrast, interacting group JDM quality sometimes exceeds the average of individuals and randomly chosen individuals but seldom exceeds that of the best individual (McNees 1992; Gigone and Hastie 1997; Kerr and Tindale 2004). Further, to the extent that interacting group JDM is superior to individual JDM, this is thought to occur because of both enhanced skill and cognitive processes and enhanced motivation (Kerr and Tindale).[50] Again, skill and cognitive processes can be enhanced in interacting groups due to the diversity of individuals, and diversity may be more likely to occur in interacting groups, particularly teams, than in composites. In addition, interacting groups may also have higher-quality cognitive processes than composite groups that occur due to interaction (Hinsz et al. 1997). For example, memory retrieval often is facilitated in interacting groups because discussion prompts the retrieval of items that might not be retrieved otherwise.[51] As another example, groups can generate a greater number of hypotheses than can individuals and are more likely to generate the correct hypothesis. This occurs partially because group members can correct the erroneous hypotheses of other members.

Motivation in an interacting group can be of the "be correct" variety or the "desired conclusions" variety. For example, auditors trying to resolve a contentious accounting issue may be working toward finding the treatment that is most in line with professional standards. On the other hand, auditors working in a team may realize that the partner on the engagement tends to support client-proposed accounting treatments and, thus, be working with a desired conclusion in mind. The "be correct" type of motivation can be greater in an interacting group than for the average individual for several reasons. First is *social compensation,* a phenomenon said to occur when some individuals exert substantially more effort in the group setting because they fear others

[50]This section does not discuss separately theories related to team JDM or, more specifically, to the audit review process because of the infancy of this literature. For examples of such theory development, see Guzzo et al. (1995), Rich et al. (1997a), and Gibbins and Trotman (2002).
[51]Groups also can have better memory than individuals after they perform a JDM task (Hinsz et al. 1997).

in the group may harm the group's performance (Kerr and Tindale 2004). In addition, if the utility of the outcome or the expectancy about the effort–outcome relationship is higher for groups than individuals, motivation and effort may be higher in a group. The utility for a group outcome may be greater than that for an individual outcome because, for example, incentives are larger. However, even if incentives are held constant, people may derive utility from being part of a group accomplishment (Levine and Moreland 1990; Karau and Williams 1993). Further, concern about being evaluated by fellow group members may increase arousal, motivation, and effort (Davis 1969; Steiner 1972). Presumably, increased effort in a group translates into greater JDM quality vis-à-vis individuals. When motivation is of the desired-conclusions variety, group JDM likely will be no different than individual JDM because everyone faces the same desired conclusion.

Unfortunately, interacting group JDM quality often can be inferior to individual JDM quality. Specifically, as mentioned earlier, interacting groups frequently are not as good as the best individual in the group. Further, interacting group JDM quality can be below that of the average individual because of motivation issues; the positive relation between group processing and motivation/effort is attenuated, or the positive relation between effort and JDM quality is disrupted. In addition, of course, a positive relation between groups and knowledge (or skill) or between groups and quality of cognitive processes can be attenuated. Finally, a positive link between knowledge (or skill) and group JDM quality can be disrupted, as can positive links between various processes and group JDM quality.

Characteristics of the members of the group, the task, and attributes of groups can serve as moderators of these relations for interacting groups.[52] Starting with attributes of individual members, the less diverse are group members' skills and cognitive processes, the less likely group JDM quality is to exceed individual JDM quality (Sniezek and Henry 1989; Guzzo and Dickson 1997; Sutton and Hayne 1997).[53] Further, interacting groups often can exacerbate the use of certain processes, such as heuristics (e.g., Stasser and Titus 1985; Argote et al. 1986, 1990; Tindale 1993; Kerr et al. 1996). As is the case with composites, lack of diversity can disrupt a positive relation between groups and knowledge (or skill) or groups and high-quality processes for interacting groups. Also, if members of interacting groups realize they do not possess these characteristics, lack of diversity can disrupt a positive group-motivation relation because members give up.

---

[52]Discussion of moderators here does not focus on *process losses* and *process gains* (Steiner 1972). The former term is used to refer to factors that explain group JDM that is inferior to idealized group JDM, and the latter term was developed to discuss factors that can undo or counteract some of the "losses." Instead, the discussion here focuses on factors that make group JDM quality and, thus, the probability that group JDM quality will exceed individual JDM quality vary. This focus reflects the fact that there are two main types of issues related to groups in accounting settings. First, groups are fixed in some accounting settings (e.g., the review process in auditing). In these settings, research questions tend to focus on factors that affect group JDM quality. Second, in some settings, groups are considered as a method for improving inferior individual JDM. Here, research questions focus on whether group JDM quality is superior to that of individuals and, if not, why. In other words, research questions related to optimal group quality are of lesser practical importance in accounting.

[53]Sutton and Hayne (1997) mention that diversity also may reduce the probability of *groupthink,* or the phenomenon in which group members focus strongly on achieving unanimity and, consequently, think very similarly and narrowly. This would occur because one of the preconditions for groupthink is homogeneity of group members (Janis 1982). However, it is not clear how prevalent a problem groupthink is (Aldag and Fuller 1993).

In addition, even in diverse interacting groups, the best knowledge often is not shared with or used by the group, in which case group JDM can suffer (Stasser et al. 1989; Hinsz et al. 1997; Kerr and Tindale 2004).[54] One reason for this is that the best knowledge also may be unique knowledge (possessed by only one group member), and unique knowledge is less likely to be shared with or used by the group than is knowledge that is common to two or more group members (Stasser and Titus 1985; Gigone and Hastie 1993; Larson et al. 1994). There are several possible reasons for this; one is that people with unique knowledge may realize that unique knowledge can be treated by a group as opinion and dismissed accordingly (Stewart and Stasser 1995). People appear to prefer knowledge that is held by two or more individuals, perhaps because they consider it more valid and credible (Wittenbaum et al. 1999; Kerr and Tindale).[55] High-quality and/or unique knowledge also may not be used in interacting groups (if shared) because these groups often cannot identify their most knowledgeable member (e.g., Einhorn et al. 1977; Kerr and Tindale). This occurs because people use inappropriate cues to judge the knowledge of others, for example, confidence, talkativeness, etc. (e.g., Steiner 1972; Einhorn et al.; Littlepage et al. 1995; Littlepage and Mueller 1997).[56] These problems, then, can disrupt either the group–knowledge relation or the knowledge–JDM quality relation for interacting groups.

Similar results can be found with interacting groups and motivation. That is, group members can have lower motivation and exert less effort than they would working individually. This phenomenon, dubbed *social loafing* (Latané et al. 1979), has a number of possible causes (Karau and Williams 1993). For example, groups of men are more likely to exhibit lower motivation in groups (versus individually) than are women because women place more value on collective efforts (Karau and Williams). This is an example of group members having lower utility for the group outcome than they would for individual outcomes. Group members also may have lower effort–outcome expectancies than they would as individuals (Shepperd 1993).[57] Lower effort–outcome expectancies can result, for example, from homogeneity of group members' knowledge, resulting in a feeling of being redundant with other members.

The groups literature also focuses on the type of task as a moderator. Specifically, for tasks with "demonstrable solutions," interacting groups often have higher JDM quality than do individuals, whereas, for tasks not having such solutions, groups often have lower JDM quality than individuals (Laughlin and Ellis 1986; Tindale 1993; Guzzo and Dickson 1997). Tasks with demonstrable solutions typically are problem-solving tasks that do not involve uncertainty but that require reasoning to complete. In this case, as long as someone in an interacting group can solve the problem, the group normally is willing to adopt what appears to be a "correct" answer. For other tasks,

[54]Possible methods for dealing with this moderating factor include group training (Larson et al. 1994). Note that methods for improving group JDM issues are discussed in this chapter because Chapter 9 focuses only on methods for improving individual JDM.
[55]This finding may be related to findings on the effects of repeated information (see Chapter 6).
[56]It may be possible to improve groups' ability to identify their most knowledgeable member by providing instructions to do so (Yetton and Bottger 1982; Henry 1995; Henry et al. 2002) or by providing feedback regarding group members' JDM quality (Henry et al. 1996).
[57]Utility for group outcomes can be increased through incentives or accountability related to group JDM. However, such techniques also must be tied to the capability to evaluate individual JDM (Shepperd 1993), which often is difficult to accomplish in practice. Group effort–outcome expectancies can be increased, for example, by instructing people that their contributions are important to the group outcome (Shepperd). Again, however, if such instruction is deceptive, it will not be effective in practice for more than one period.

because the solution is not necessarily clear, groups tend to determine correctness through a majority voting process. In these cases, if the majority is "wrong," for example, because they lack knowledge, then group JDM will be lower than individual JDM. Unfortunately, accountants typically encounter JDM tasks with uncertainty; in other words, they encounter tasks that do not have demonstrable solutions. Thus, the nature of accounting tasks per se can impair group JDM. This task characteristic can attenuate the group–knowledge relation, the group–processes relation, or the processes–JDM quality relation.

Interacting groups can vary on a number of dimensions; these dimensions also can moderate the JDM quality of one type of group versus another, or groups versus individuals. First, groups can vary as to cohesiveness, or the extent to which members stick together (Steiner 1972); less cohesive groups have lower-quality JDM (Evans and Dion 1991; Mullen and Copper 1994; Gully et al. 1995) because of a lowered groups–motivation relation.[58] Second, groups can vary as to size; beyond some point, increases in size can lead to decreased JDM for groups (Steiner), meaning they are less likely to outperform individuals. Optimal group size is somewhere around three to five members (e.g., Libby and Blashfield 1978; Ashton 1986; Solomon 1987).[59] One reason for this result is that the size of the group attenuates the effects of group cohesiveness (Mullen and Copper).[60] In addition, people in interacting groups are more likely to think their knowledge and/or effort is redundant with that of another group member, leading to a lower effort–outcome expectancy and, thus, reduced motivation and effort. In other words, the groups–motivation relation is attenuated for groups of large size.

Third, interacting groups can make judgments and decisions in a number of ways. They can meet face-to-face or in some other manner such as by phone or by computer. Groups that meet face-to-face can have lower task-related motivation than groups that meet in other ways because the presence of other people can motivate individuals to focus on self-presentation, interpersonal relations, and the like (Shepperd 1993; Hinsz et al. 1997). Further, face-to-face group members may be less likely to identify the most knowledgeable group member because they experience more cues that can erroneously be used to judge knowledge (e.g., facial expressions). Thus, face-to-face interaction can moderate the groups–knowledge relation. Some of the problems with face-to-face interaction may be mitigated by using computer-mediated interaction; however, results regarding this factor are mixed. For example, computer-mediated groups may be better at hypothesis generation, whereas face-to-face groups may be better at hypothesis evaluation (e.g., Hollingshead et al. 1993; Strauss and McGrath 1994; Kerr and Tindale 2004; however, see McLeod [1992]).

Another way of dealing with the decreased motivation that may occur in face-to-face groups is to not allow them unrestricted interaction. Freely interacting groups are more prone to socialize and focus on other off-task activities. However, there are many ways of restricting the interaction of groups; these techniques can lead to better group JDM quality (Sniezek 1989). The most restrictive is the *Delphi technique,* in which

---

[58]Mullen and Copper (1994) find, however, that the link from JDM quality (performance) to cohesiveness is stronger than the link from cohesiveness to JDM quality (performance). Further, Steiner (1972) asserts that cohesiveness is a consequence of motivation rather than a separate attribute of groups.
[59]These findings apply to composite groups as well.
[60]Initially, increases in group size can be beneficial to JDM quality because, for example, size increases lead to a higher chance of having a knowledgeable group member (Davis 1969; Steiner 1972; Hill 1982), and larger groups are better able to identify the most knowledgeable member (Littlepage and Silbiger 1992).

groups have minimal interaction (Rohrbaugh 1979). Group members receive feedback about other members' JDM and continue to revise their individual JDM until consensus is reached. More interaction is allowed by the *nominal group technique,* in which individuals make judgments then provide them to the group for an initial round of voting. Voting is followed by discussion then further voting (Sutton and Hayne 1997).

Studying group JDM can be difficult for a variety of reasons. First, experimental studies typically form ad hoc groups. In these groups, individuals are brought together for purposes of the research study and may have no experience working together. In the field, however, natural groups prevail. That is, most groups consist of individuals who have some experience working with other members of the group. Because natural groups are prevalent, researchers would like for results from experimental studies to generalize to such groups. Unfortunately, however, research comparing natural and ad hoc groups often finds different results regarding factors affecting their JDM (Solomon 1987; Sutton and Hayne 1997). Experimental studies of groups also must consider which moderating factors to hold constant and which to manipulate. The rather large number of moderators of group JDM quality (e.g., group size, group cohesiveness, diversity of members' knowledge, interaction processes) suggests that this could be challenging. Further, experimentalists are faced with obtaining much larger numbers of subjects for groups studies, exacerbating the difficulties of obtaining the serious participation of professional subjects. Researchers employing measurement techniques (surveys or archival data analysis) can study natural groups and do not have to be concerned about obtaining experimental subjects. However, they must take care to measure the many moderating factors. More important, many of these moderators and/or the presence of groups per se may be confounded with other important variables such as incentives and accountability.

Accounting Studies on Groups

A number of studies examine group JDM quality (versus individual JDM quality) or various elements of group JDM per se in accounting settings. Beginning with studies that examine group JDM among producers and users of accounting information, Uecker's (1982) student subjects make sample size choices that correspond to information system choices first individually, then in groups. Groups' sample size choices, although not theoretically correct, are better than average individual choices. Hunton's (2001) student and manager subjects participate in groups making a recommendation about replacing a system. Within groups, the extent to which information is known by all group members varies. That is, some information is shared by all group members, whereas some is known by fewer members, and finally, some information is known by only one member. In addition, one set of groups receives training that directs them to attend to less-shared information, and the other set receives no training. Without training, groups tend to discuss highly shared information more than less shared information. With training, this finding is diminished, and subjects also increase the amount of information they discuss. No JDM quality effects are discussed.

Further studies include that by Daroca (1984), who has individuals make choices about budgets to allocate to research and development versus marketing then make those choices again in groups. Groups vary as to their composition, that is, the number of science and engineering students (who presumably would tend to allocate more to research and development) and the number of marketing majors. Further, some groups have a designated leader, whereas others do not. Groups with leaders make less extreme allocations than do leaderless groups, and groups with more science and engineering students allocate more to research and development. Bloom et al. (1984) compare functional fixation in product pricing decisions of individuals and groups. Groups exhibit more functional fixation. Rutledge and Harrell (1994) examine individual versus group judgments related to continuing an unprofitable project. Groups are more risk averse (less likely to continue) than individuals when they view a positively framed case but more risk seeking than individuals when they view a negatively framed case. Further, groups told of their prior involvement are more likely to continue a project than individuals, whereas groups told of no prior involvement are less likely to continue.

Chalos and Poon (2000) document that degree of participation in setting goals is positively related to the self-rated performance of groups of project managers; part of this effect is due to increased sharing of information. Scott and Tiessen (1999) find similar results using superior-rated performance. In addition, when group performance is given higher weight in incentive schemes, performance is enhanced. Cheng et al. (2003a) have pairs of students do a production scheduling task and measure JDM quality as the output of the simulated production system. They vary whether the pairs are similar in cognitive style. Groups containing students with different cognitive styles outperform one type of homogeneous group but not the other. Finally, Ashton (1982) and Ashton and Ashton (1985) report that a composite of managers' predictions of advertising pages outperforms all individuals as to accuracy. In addition, equally weighted composites are very similar in accuracy to unequally weighted composites, and most gains vis-à-vis individuals come from combining a small number of judgments.

Several studies examine the group JDM of loan officers. Chalos (1985) compares the JDM of individuals, individuals formed into groups, and a statistical composite. Subjects make various judgments and decisions about loans. Both the statistical composite and interacting group are more accurate in default predictions and loan decisions than the average individual, and the interacting group is more accurate than the most accurate individual. Chalos and Pickard (1985) report similar findings with students; these findings appear to be due to groups being better able to use financial statement information and being more consistent in the application of cue weights. However, the appropriateness of groups' cue weights does not differ from individuals'.

Libby et al. (1987) ask loan officers to predict bankruptcy. Individuals make judgments then join ad hoc or natural groups. Ad hoc and natural groups do not differ as to accuracy, but both these types of interacting groups, as well as statistical composites, are more accurate than the average individual. Interacting groups and composites do not differ from each other or from the most accurate individual. They also examine variation in group accuracy and find that group accuracy increases with the extent to which the most influential individual (the person with whom the group most often agrees) is also the most accurate individual. Stocks and Harrell (1995) have individuals and groups judge the probability of financial distress under a medium or high information load condition. Under medium load, individuals and groups do not differ as to accuracy; under high load, groups are more accurate. In addition, groups use more cues, are more consistent in their cue weighting, and agree more with each other than do individuals at both levels of load. Finally, studies of composite groups include Libby (1975) and Libby and Blashfield (1978), who document that composites of loan officers are more accurate than the average individual, as well as most individuals alone, at predicting corporate failure. The largest gain in accuracy comes when moving to three-member composites. Zimmer (1980) reports similar findings. However, Casey (1980a) finds no difference in the accuracy of predicting bankruptcy by individual loan officers and composite groups.

Turning to other studies of users, Bloomfield et al. (1996) report that investors' ability to communicate confidence in their individual judgments affects the accuracy of the group at estimating security values based on answering general business questions. Investors who participate in markets (groups) where number of shares traded is revealed are more accurate than those who participate in markets (groups) where only the number of traders is revealed. A second experiment demonstrates that number of shares traded is used by subjects to judge others' confidence. In addition, group judgments are more accurate than the average individual and the statistical composite, although they are no more accurate than the best individual. Carnes et al. (1996) find that tax professionals' group judgments regarding the probability of taking a pro-client position are more extreme than the average of the individuals' judgments prior to joining the groups. Finally, studies of composite groups include O'Brien (1988), who documents that composite (consensus) analysts' forecasts are less accurate than the single most recent forecast. However, composites are more accurate than individual forecasts if only recent forecasts are included. Brown (1991b) also finds that composites of more recent forecasts are more accurate than composites including all forecasts (the consensus). Staël von Holstein (1972), Ebert and Kruse (1978), and Wright (1979) report that composite predictions of stock prices are more accurate than mean student, faculty, or analyst subjects' forecasts. Ebert and Kruse also report that composite predictions are more accurate than those of an environmental model and that a composite with weightings based on past performance is more accurate than an equally weighted composite.

Studies of auditors include those examining group JDM and review-process issues. Starting with group studies, Trotman et al. (1983) report that the statistical composites of students making internal control evaluations exhibit more consensus and consistency over time and use more cues than do average individual judgments and interacting group judgments. In addition, three-person composites exhibit greater consensus with other composites than do two-person composites. Trotman and Yetton (1985) find no differences in consensus of internal control evaluations for senior auditors in interacting groups versus composite groups. Trotman (1985) employs a task that requires estimation of dollar error in inventory based on audit test results. Interacting groups of seniors give answers that are closer to the error amount derived from a simulation than does the average individual and the composite. These results are attributed to interacting groups reducing both systematic bias and error by greater amounts than does the composite.

Solomon (1982) compares the calibration and consensus of probability distributions for account balances provided by individuals or groups processing in one of two modes. Groups are composed of auditors of different ranks (staff, seniors, and managers). Group probability distributions are more extreme and exhibit greater consensus than do individuals' distributions, but they are also more miscalibrated. However, interacting groups' distributions are better calibrated than composite groups'. Reckers and Schultz (1993) find that individual auditors adhere more to professional standards when making fraud judgments than do interacting groups. Bamber et al. (1996) find that auditors in groups require a lower probability threshold for disclosing contingent losses than do individuals, consistent with conservatism, and exhibit greater consensus. They also manipulate whether groups interact face-to-face or using a computerized group support system that preserves anonymity. There are no differences between these group modes, except that those using the computerized system tend to generate more ideas. Bedard et al. (1998) report that groups of auditors doing a ratio analysis task are no more likely than individuals to detect the theoretically correct error. Groups are superior to individuals at acquiring information cues and recognizing a pattern of cues as well as generating greater numbers of hypotheses and being more likely to generate the correct hypothesis. However, during hypothesis evaluation, groups are no more likely than individuals to correct errors, leading their ultimate JDM quality to be no different. Johnson's (1994) groups of auditors have more accurate recall and recognition for information from previously read work papers. Ahlawat (1999) reports that individual auditors exhibit order effects when making going-concern judgments, whereas groups do not and are less accurate at recognizing previously presented items. However, groups choose fewer qualified opinions than do individuals, exhibiting less conservatism.

Remaining studies examine the effects of various aspects of groups on group JDM quality among auditors. Arnold et al. (2000) compare the materiality judgments of students in groups who interact face-to-face versus using a computerized support system. Those using the computerized system provide judgments that are less correct theoretically; they also take more time to make judgments. Murthy and Kerr (2004) ask groups of students to answer two questions related to a client's accounting issue under one of three groups modes: face-to-face, using "chat" software that immediately posts all comments, or using "bulletin board" software that sequentially posts comments and organizes them. Further, subjects receive information that either is shared with other group members or is not shared. Groups using the bulletin board system have a higher number of correct answers than the other groups. These findings reflect the bulletin board system groups being better at conveying and processing unshared information. However, bulletin board groups take the most time to complete the task. Finally, King (2002) manipulates whether groups of student subjects serving as auditors are more or less cohesive. Groups that are more cohesive are less trusting of management representations and choose more stringent audits than do less cohesive groups. Group cohesiveness, in fact, counteracts the self-serving bias (the propensity of auditors to trust clients due to their relationship).

Turning now to studies of the audit review process, this section separates studies into those that examine judgments given by individuals acting in the role of reviewer versus individuals acting as preparer, those that examine differential characteristics of reviewers at various hierarchical levels, and those that examine factors that affect reviewers' JDM.[61] The first group of studies includes Trotman and Yetton (1985), who document that individual managers doing internal control evaluation exhibit more consensus as reviewers than individual seniors do as preparers. However, reviewer judgment consensus is no different than the consensus of seniors in either interacting

---

[61]Note that many of the latter type of studies are included in other chapters or other sections of this chapter as well because they examine the effects of a particular person, task, or environmental variable on individual JDM. They are repeated here because individuals are serving in the role of reviewer.

or composite groups. Trotman (1985) finds similar results. Libby and Trotman (1993) compare the recall of information by auditors (of the same ranks) acting as either preparers or reviewers in a going-concern task. Reviewers are told of a preparer's judgment. Recall is scored as to whether it is consistent or inconsistent with the going-concern judgment. Preparers recall relatively more consistent information, whereas reviewers recall relatively more inconsistent information. A second experiment demonstrates that decreases in the amount of inconsistent information documented by a preparer increases its relative recall by reviewers. Ricchiute (1999), in a follow-up study, finds that partners' going-concern judgments are influenced by seniors' judgments when seniors document only a subset of evidence that is supportive of their judgments.

Messier and Tubbs (1994) document that seniors and managers acting in a reviewer role are similarly subject to order effects as are seniors acting in a preparer role. Ismail and Trotman (1995) compare the number of theoretically correct hypotheses generated in an analytical procedures task of seniors acting as preparers versus either seniors or managers acting as reviewers. In addition, some reviewers are allowed discussion with preparers, whereas others are not. Review with discussion leads to a greater number of correct hypotheses being generated, whereas senior versus manager review has little effect on JDM (seniors spend more time). However, reviewers generate more correct hypotheses than preparers under all conditions. Reimers and Fennema (1999) report that auditors serving as reviewers (preparers) are (are not) sensitive to the objectivity of the source of evidence.

Studies examining how reviewers at different hierarchical levels vary include Ramsay (1994), who reports that managers are better able to detect conceptual errors while performing overall reviews of work papers, whereas seniors are better able to detect mechanical errors (errors are defined vis-à-vis professional theory). Bamber and Ramsay (1997) compare seniors and managers making overall reviews to seniors making specialized reviews for mechanical errors and managers making specialized reviews for conceptual errors in a similar task. There is no effect of specialization instructions on either seniors' or managers' detection of mechanical errors. However, both groups are better able to detect conceptual errors during an all-encompassing review. Harding and Trotman (1999) compare the JDM quality of staff versus seniors serving as reviewers using a similar task. Seniors detect more conceptual errors than staff, whereas staff detect more mechanical errors than seniors. Owhoso et al. (2002) replicate these findings with seniors and managers working on a case consistent with their industry specialization but not when working outside their area. Finally, Bamber and Ramsay (2000) document that seniors and managers performing overall reviews take less time than those performing specialized reviews.

Another group of studies examines the effects of various factors, including elements of the review process, on reviewer JDM. Research on person variables includes Ballou (2001), who documents that self-reported effort is positively related to the number of review notes auditors generate. Jamal and Tan (2001) show that managers, high-performing seniors, and "mediocre" seniors do not differ in the accuracy of their predictions of other individual auditors' choices in two tasks, contrary with the prediction that tacit job knowledge affects these judgments. However, managers are more accurate than top seniors, who are more accurate than mediocre seniors, at predicting the number of correct choices made by other groups of auditors. Further, these accuracy differences occur only for the high-complexity task.

Studies of task variables include Ricchiute (1997), who documents that audit partners serving as reviewers of evidence related to going-concern judgments make judgments that are more in line with those of preparers when they receive an incomplete set of evidence that is consistent with preparers' judgments than when they receive a complete set of evidence. Boritz (1985) documents that auditors serving as reviewers make different review judgments under tasks of varying complexity. Asare and McDaniel (1996) manipulate task complexity and preparer familiarity and examine reviewers' ability to detect errors in work papers. Overall, reviewers detect many of the preparers' "conclusion errors" (inappropriate evaluations of evidence). In complex tasks, reviewers familiar with preparers are better able to detect these errors than those unfamiliar with preparers, whereas there is no difference on the simple task. Further, reviewers familiar with the preparer detect more errors in the complex task. Gupta et al. (1999) report survey findings indicating that audits are more effective when the review process is consistent with the level of complexity of the audit.

Bamber and Bylinski (1987) manipulate time pressure by telling one group that there is sufficient time to complete the audit, whereas others are told that the audit must be completed "shortly." They find no effect of time pressure on time budgeted for review procedures. Gibbins and Trotman (2002) document a number of factors that affect JDM in the review process. For example, auditors write more review notes for riskier clients (those for whom disincentives are potentially large), but do not spend more time reviewing.

Finally, several studies examine the effects of characteristics of the preparer or her work on reviewers' JDM. Bamber (1983) examines the effects of the described reliability of a preparer on reviewers' judgments about reliance on an internal control system. Reviewers rely less on systems investigated by less reliable preparers. Kennedy and Peecher (1997) document that managers (seniors) who are evaluating the knowledge of seniors (staff) are affected by their confidence in their own knowledge. Overall, reviewers are overconfident about subordinates' knowledge, and more so when the gap in their knowledge is larger (this occurs for seniors evaluating staff). Agoglia et al. (2003) report that the form of documentation used by preparers (see the accountability section above) also affects reviewers' judgments.

Yip-Ow and Tan (2000) find that reviewers generate fewer error hypotheses and assign a higher probability to a nonerror cause of ratio fluctuations when they receive justification from the preparer for the nonerror cause. This effect is moderated by having reviewers generate and/or explain alternative hypotheses or make judgments before reading the preparer's justification. Tan and Yip-Ow (2001) manipulate whether reviewers receive a neutral or stylized memo from a preparer related to a judgment regarding the collectibility of an account receivable. The neutral memo presents a balanced view of the evidence underlying the judgment, whereas the stylized memo focuses on evidence supporting the conclusion. The preparer's conclusion (collectible or uncollectible) influences the reviewer's judgment in the neutral memo condition but not in the stylized memo condition, consistent with reviewers placing less weight on preparers' judgments when accompanied by a stylized memo.

Tan and Trotman (2003) manipulate the known focus of the preparer, which is to stylize work papers toward either documentation or conclusions, based on the preferences of a reviewer. They examine the review judgments of managers versus seniors and also measure these auditors' "stylization sensitivity," or the extent to which reviewers focus on errors that may occur because of the preparer's focus. They find that managers' ability to find documentation errors in the condition in which preparers focus on conclusions (documentation) first increases then decreases with stylization sensitivity (is unaffected). There is no effect (a positive effect) on their ability to detect conclusion errors in the conclusion (documentation) condition. Seniors detect more (no more) documentation errors in the conclusion-focus (documentation-focus) condition as their sensitivity increases, but sensitivity has no effect (an initial positive then a negative effect) on their detection of conclusion errors in this condition. These results reflect rank-related differences in mental representations related to the review process.

Wilks (2002) asks auditors to estimate the going-concern judgment of a manager faced with a partner reviewer who is known to be concerned about either undue pessimism or undue optimism. Subjects are told also that the manager learns of the partner's view either prior to or after evaluating evidence. Subjects expect managers to make going-concern judgments consistent with the partner's views. However, they do not anticipate that this effect is larger when managers receive the views prior to evidence evaluation. However, when asked to explicitly consider the timing issue, auditors anticipate this larger effect. Rich (2004) manipulates whether the preparer is not under time pressure or known to be under time pressure and, thus, likely to have lower-quality work. As described above, he also manipulates accountability to users of financial statements. Reviewing auditors decrease their level of agreement with the preparer's work from prereview to postreview more when the preparer is more likely to make errors, and this decrease is larger when accountability to users is high. Further, reviewers generate greater numbers of and more critical ideas when the preparer is thought to be under pressure.

The study of group JDM in accounting encompasses three different lines of research. First, research on group JDM versus individual JDM largely is consistent with work in psychology; groups sometimes outperform individuals and sometimes do not (and, to some extent, mixed results depend on how individual JDM quality is defined). Second, research on the review process also indicates that the review process sometimes improves JDM quality and sometimes does not. Many of the findings reflecting improved JDM quality (vis-à-vis individual preparer JDM quality) appear to reflect the hierarchical nature of the review process and, specifically, the fact that reviewers, who are higher in the hierarchy, possess greater knowledge and also may differ as to other characteristics, for example, abilities. However, there do appear to be additional effects of being placed in the role of reviewer, such as greater search for or weighting of evidence that is inconsistent with hypotheses or conclusions. Third, a number of studies examine various person, task, and environmental factors that affect group JDM. These studies are too disparate to summarize easily.

Given the increasing use of groups in organizations and the importance of the review process to auditing, continued research on group and team JDM is vital to a clear understanding of accountants' JDM. In particular, we first need a better understanding of the characteristics of groups in various accounting settings. For example, recent changes in the review process and the use of technology for group JDM in auditing have been documented, but we know little about other group settings. Because many important accounting decisions are made in groups, it behooves researchers to gain a better understanding of the composition and processes of these groups. Then, given such an understanding, research needs to focus on the attributes that are unique to groups (versus individuals). For example, the interactive nature of the review process and the opportunities it provides for impression and reputation formation need to receive more attention. (For recent examples of such research, see Tan and Trotman [2003] and Rich [2004], among others.) Research on the review process also needs to consider how the various elements of the review process (e.g., accountability to the reviewer, differential knowledge of reviewer and preparer, etc.) interactively affect JDM. As would be expected, extant research tends to focus on the main effects of each factor, but work on interactive effects may reveal interesting and unique aspects of the review process that can lead to further theory development. Researchers developing theories related to the review process also may want to consider research in psychology related to "judge–advisor" JDM, in which group members are not peers but rather have differentiated or hierarchical roles (Sniezek and Buckley 1995).

Next, although it is important to understand the effects of various person, task, and environmental variables on group JDM quality, researchers should consider whether these variables and/or their effects are unique to the group setting. In other words, researchers should think about whether such variables' effects are likely to be different in group settings than in individual settings. If it is likely that there are few differences, the importance of such research is not clear. Research on groups also needs to continue the trend of using natural groups in experimental settings rather than ad hoc groups, given the prevalence of natural groups in accounting settings. Another important issue to examine is how the setup of groups varies with other organizational choices such as structuring of tasks, assignment of employees to various tasks, and the like. Research to date tends to examine group effects in isolation. (For an exception, see Watson [1975].) Finally, given that groups normally are prescribed as a method for improving low-quality individual JDM, it makes sense for researchers to step back and consider whether groups are a good choice, given all the factors that moderate their JDM quality. There may be other ways of improving JDM that are both more effective and less costly (Gigone and Hastie 1997). In situations where groups are required (e.g., the review process), it makes sense to focus on factors that can be changed in the environment so groups will have higher-quality JDM (e.g., King 2002).

7-7   EFFECTS OF TIME PRESSURE ON JDM QUALITY

This section examines the effects of time pressure on JDM quality. There does not appear to be any universally accepted definition of time pressure, yet there is consistency in the literature that there are two key types of time pressure (e.g., Solomon and Brown 1992; DeZoort and Lord 1997). The first type is caused by deadlines; people are given a specific point in time by which something must be done. For example, auditors often must complete audits by a certain date in order to allow clients to release actual earnings figures. The second type of pressure comes from time budgets. Here, pressure is caused by being given a certain amount of time in which to complete a task, and the amount of time is considered too meager. Again, auditors face time budgets not only for completing audits, but for each subsection of the audit as well. Solomon and Brown also distinguish between time pressure that is anticipated versus pressure that is unanticipated. As they note, much time pressure faced by accounting professionals is anticipated. For example, auditors typically know going into audits that their time will be constrained. However, research to date focuses on unanticipated pressure. Consequently, this section discusses only the effects of unanticipated time pressure. Issues related to anticipated pressure are discussed in the summary section.

Deadlines and time budgets occur in many professional settings, including those in which accounting professionals work. In fact, time pressure often is cited as one of the most challenging environmental features auditors in particular face (e.g., Cook and Kelley 1988; Waggoner and Cashell 1991). Auditors face time budgets because of fee pressure that causes them to focus heavily on keeping costs down. However, at the same time, auditors must comply with professional standards and be aware of other important factors in their environment, such as the threat of litigation. Cost-cutting due to time pressure in such an environment can be very difficult and, if implemented, can be disastrous. For example, in the Comptronix case, time pressure contributed to the failure to gather sufficient audit evidence and the resulting failure to detect a massive fraud (Boockholdt 2000). Fortunately, high levels of time pressure are not a foregone conclusion in auditing; time pressure can vary across accounting firms, clients, supervisors, and the like.

Time pressure normally is thought to have an inverted-U relation with JDM quality, except when JDM quality is defined as time or costs to do a JDM task.[62] That is, time pressure at first increases JDM quality, where quality normally is defined as accuracy vis-à-vis outcomes or correspondence with normative theories. Beyond a moderate level of time pressure, JDM quality begins to decrease. When JDM quality is defined as efficiency (time or costs to do a task), time pressure typically has a positive effect. The more pressure people are under to hold down time and/or costs, the more likely they are to do so. In accounting, studies tend to focus on the effects of time pressure on accuracy, correspondence with normative theories or professional standards, and time spent or budgeted. However, it clearly is plausible to examine the effects of time pressure on agreement with others and with oneself over time, measures of JDM quality that are important in settings such as auditing.

Time pressure is thought to affect JDM quality through several mechanisms. Most theoretical accounts posit that time pressure operates at least partially through arousal/motivation (Miller 1960). Research on time pressure specifically indicates that there is a sequence of responses to time pressure that is consistent with arousal theory. Typically, the first response is to accelerate processing, or increase effort intensity (e.g., Ben Zur and Breznitz 1981; Payne et al. 1993). Again, this initially helps JDM quality because people do more work than they otherwise would in a given amount of time. However, at some point, acceleration may result in careless errors and inconsistencies in processing, thereby decreasing JDM quality (e.g., Rothstein 1986). After acceleration, people tend to move to filtration, or selective use of information (e.g., Wright 1974; Ben Zur and Breznitz; Wallsten and Barton 1982; Edland and Svenson 1993; Payne et al. 1993). Initially, again, this effect of time pressure can lead to increased JDM quality because filtration tends to target irrelevant cues. If people do not attend to irrelevant cues (when they otherwise would), their JDM quality normally is improved. However, with increasing filtration, people begin to ignore relevant cues, thus decreasing JDM quality.

---

[62]Some researchers note that the construct should be "perceived time pressure" rather than "actual time pressure" because it is the feeling of being under pressure that leads to the behaviors thought to mediate time pressure's effects on JDM (e.g., Maule and Hockey 1993).

Time pressure also appears to affect JDM quality through a change in JDM strategies from compensatory to noncompensatory (Edland and Svenson 1993; Payne et al. 1993).[63] This response is thought to occur after acceleration and filtration. However, this response is related to the filtration response. Noncompensatory JDM strategies, by definition, do not use all cues and, thus, do not allow for people to make tradeoffs between positive and negative features of a situation. Thus, it may be the use of noncompensatory strategies at moderate to severe levels of time pressure that leads people to ignore relevant cues. At any rate, noncompensatory strategies typically are less effortful, so people may believe they can process more information in a constrained time period using these strategies. That is, they are trading off trying to get to many aspects of the JDM task versus processing completely on each aspect.

Discussion of moderators of the effects of time pressure must focus on factors that can attenuate its positive effects, as well as those that can relieve the negative effects that occur beyond some moderate level. Moderators of initial positive effects of time pressure likely are factors that do not allow people to have higher JDM quality through their cognitive responses. Little research exists on this issue in psychology, so this discussion is speculative. For example, if people lack knowledge about the task, they will put more intense effort into inappropriate processes. Along with this, if people lack knowledge of which cues are irrelevant, they are less likely to use filtration effectively to weed out inappropriate cues. Clearly, lack of knowledge is more likely to occur when tasks are complex, so task complexity may serve as a moderator as well. Further, if tasks are simple, responses to time pressure such as acceleration may not improve JDM quality because it already is uniformly high (e.g., Rothstein 1986; Zakay 1993). When time pressure starts to have negative effects on JDM quality, knowledge again may be a moderator. That is, people with greater knowledge may have well-developed responses to JDM tasks such that they do not have to resort to noncompensatory strategies. Clearly, there are other possible moderators, but theory is scant. (See Weick [1983] and Edland and Svenson [1993] for further discussion.)

It is conceivable to study time pressure both through manipulation and measurement. Manipulation of time pressure requires extensive pilot testing to determine what amounts of time constitute various levels of time pressure. There is little in the way of theory that can inform a researcher about the manipulation of time pressure. It is mostly a process of trial and error and, consequently, is somewhat circular (MacGregor 1993). Measurement of time pressure effects on JDM quality, although difficult, should be something researchers consider. It may be possible to use a survey-like instrument to gather time pressure data related to specific tasks. For example, researchers have used this technique to examine time pressure and underreporting behavior (e.g., Kelley and Margheim 1990). Measurement of time pressure may also be the most feasible way of examining the effects of anticipated time pressure; as mentioned by Solomon and Brown (1992), such effects may be more important than the effects of unanticipated pressure.

A few studies examine the effects of unanticipated time pressure among producers and users of accounting information. Eggleton's (1982) study of time-series judgments manipulates time pressure; subjects have either 15 seconds or two minutes to view each series. Estimates of positively autocorrelated and random series are closer to

---

[63]See Chapter 5 for further discussion of compensatory and noncompensatory strategies.

those from a statistical model under low time pressure than under high time pressure; there is no difference in estimates of negatively autocorrelated series. Spilker (1995) reports the effects of time pressure on tax professionals' selection of theoretically correct key words during search for relevant cases. Some subjects receive 11 minutes for a case, whereas others receive 25 minutes, although the authors analyze only what happens in the first 11 minutes of the latter group's work. Subjects with procedural knowledge select more relevant words under time pressure, whereas subjects with declarative but not procedural knowledge are unaffected by pressure. Subjects lacking both procedural and declarative knowledge select fewer relevant key words under time pressure. Spilker and Prawitt (1997) use a similar procedure with a different tax case and use experience as a proxy for knowledge. Although experienced tax professionals spend more time overall building a problem representation, they reduce this time more than do inexperienced professionals under time pressure. Further, under time pressure, experienced professionals increase the importance of the items they search per unit of time, whereas inexperienced professionals are not affected. In other words, knowledgeable professionals focus their search more intensively on relevant information under pressure.

Several studies examine auditors' JDM under time pressure. Bamber and Bylinski (1987) manipulate time pressure by telling one group that there is sufficient time to complete the audit, whereas others are told that the audit must be completed "shortly." Surprisingly, they find no effect of time pressure on time budgeted for review procedures. McDaniel (1990) varies time pressure at four levels, allowing from 45 minutes (high pressure) to 75 minutes (low pressure) to complete tests related to inventory. Subjects also receive either a structured audit program, which has detailed audit tests and sample selection procedures, or an unstructured program, which provides no details about testing. JDM quality is measured with an "effectiveness" score, which combines the extent to which auditors detect seeded errors in inventory and the adequacy of their sample size selections vis-à-vis professional standards and sampling formulas. JDM quality is measured also with an "efficiency" score, computed as the effectiveness score divided by time spent. Time pressure has a negative effect on effectiveness; further, the effect of pressure is worse for the structured audit program group. Time pressure effects are due to auditors missing more errors and choosing smaller sample sizes. Compared to a normatively optimal sample size, all groups choose samples that are too small; time pressure exacerbates this problem. Efficiency is greater for the high-pressure group than for the low-pressure group. Braun (2000) uses a similar task and time pressure levels but adds information that points to possible fraud and asks auditors to attend to cues that may indicate fraud and follow up on them. His subjects, however, do not have to do sampling procedures. Thus, time pressure is expected to be lower in this setting. Braun finds no effect of time pressure on the extent to which auditors miss errors. However, time pressure has a negative effect on the extent to which auditors detect and follow up on indicators of fraud.

Choo (1995) also manipulates time pressure at four levels from high (eight minutes) to low (32 minutes) for auditors answering various questions about audit tests. The extent to which auditors provide theoretically correct answers initially increases with time pressure (between the low and moderately low conditions) then decreases. Specifically, tests of various models indicate that the best fit is provided by an inverted-U, consistent with time pressure initially creating arousal. Glover (1997) reports that time pressure reduces the extent to which auditors allow irrelevant information to influence their misstatement risk judgments. Asare et al. (2000) provide some auditors with a time budget when planning audit tests related to the cause of an unexpected ratio fluctuation and provide others with no budget. Auditors with time pressure plan for fewer tests to be conducted (less effort). However, time pressure has no effect on the number of hypotheses tested or on the extent to which error versus nonerror causes are tested. Given that number of hypotheses tested is the main determinant of auditors' finding the actual error, time pressure has no effect on accuracy.

Time pressure studies in accounting contain mixed results, finding positive, negative, and no effects of time pressure on JDM quality. However, these findings are consistent with time pressure having an inverted-U relation with JDM quality and with earlier speculation that knowledge may moderate the effects of such pressure. To date, studies have examined unanticipated pressure. However, as Solomon (1987) notes, time pressure often is anticipated in practice. If anticipated and unanticipated time pressure have different effects on JDM, it seems crucial to begin to study the effects of anticipated pressure. It seems likely that firms have different strategies for dealing with anticipated time pressure, such as the assignment of more knowledgeable employees to tasks and changes to JDM processes. A study such as that conducted by Prawitt (1995)—about how staffing assignments are related to task structure—could shed light on firms' responses to anticipated time pressure. It also seems important to understand the effects of unanticipated time pressure that comes from parties other than one's superiors. For example, clients may strategically place deadlines on auditors in order to force them to narrow their cognitive processing when making decisions by the deadlines. Clients may hope that such narrowing causes auditors to miss key information and, thus, make decisions which are advantageous for them, but which may be incorrect for auditors. It would be important to understand whether auditors understand such tactics and, if not, how their JDM is affected by them.

7-8   EFFECTS OF STANDARDS AND REGULATIONS ON JDM QUALITY

This section discusses the effects of standards and regulations on JDM quality. *Standards* and *regulations* are rules put in place by regulatory or other rule-making bodies that define appropriate behavior in many contexts. For example, the government issues water quality standards with which water providers must comply. The accounting environment is characterized by a large number of standards and regulations and an increasing focus on them (Cohen and Kelly 2003; Nelson 2003; Schipper 2003; France 2004). For example, financial accounting is governed by standards issued by the FASB, regulations promulgated by the SEC, and other such rules. Tax accounting is governed by IRS regulations. Auditing is governed by auditing standards promulgated by the AICPA. There are numerous other standards and regulations that apply to many accounting contexts. Further, the incidence, complexity, and other dimensions of standards and regulations vary across tasks. For example, auditors must comply with a specific standard related to going-concern judgments but do not have such specific standards for many other audit tasks. Along with this, standards and regulations change over time due to political and economic forces.

Clearly, although standards and regulations are not unique to the accounting environment, they are one of its defining characteristics. More important, violation of standards and regulations can have serious economic consequences. For example, one of the largest public accounting firms is now defunct due to, among other factors, the consequences of an audit that failed to comply with auditing standards (Venuti et al. 2002). At the individual level, auditors who violate standards or regulations can lose their jobs, their savings, and their right to audit public clients. In addition, individual auditors can pay fines and spend time in jail.

In fact, because the monetary consequences associated with the failure to comply with standards and regulations are so severe, it is tempting to consider studies of regulations and standards as relating simply to monetary incentives. However, standards and regulations incorporate the effects of many other variables. For example, as Nelson (2003) suggests, standards can vary as to complexity. Some standards include a large amount of information and a number of rules, whereas others do not. Further, standards can vary as to the response mode they require (e.g., whether they include numerical or verbal information in rules). Nelson contrasts SFAS No. 13, which includes a rule that leases must be capitalized if the lease term is 75% or more of the property's estimated life, and SFAS No. 5, which requires that losses should be accrued when they can be reasonably estimated and it is probable that they will occur. Standards also vary as to presentation formats required. In fact, one of the major reasons for changes in standards by the FASB is to change presentation formats for particular accounting items. Finally, standards can vary as to the types of JDM processes they prescribe (e.g., Zimbelman 1997).

Given the number of variables incorporated by standards and regulations, it is difficult to discuss their effects on JDM quality and the mediators through which these effects occur. Instead, then, this section simply reviews the literature to date that examines the effects on JDM quality of the presence versus absence of standards or variation in some dimension of the standards and refers the reader to earlier sections of the text related to task complexity, presentation format and response mode, monetary incentives, and various cognitive processes.

Studies of the effects of standards and regulations on JDM can use measurement or manipulation. In fact, many "event studies" measure the effects of changes in standards; however, most of these studies examine aggregate effects rather than individual JDM effects because of a lack of data at the individual level. Consequently, studies of the effects of standards and regulations on individual JDM to date use experimental manipulation. Experiments are particularly useful because of all the potential confounds present in event studies related to standards. For example, when accounting standards change, firms may alter compensation plans or restructure transactions. Experiments can hold such factors constant.

Some of the presentation format studies related to users of accounting information described in Chapter 6 are relevant here. To briefly summarize those studies, variation in placement or classification of information in the financial statements (as mandated by various standards) tends to lead to variation in analysts', investors', and loan officers' JDM (Belkaoui 1980; Harper et al. 1987; Sami and Schwartz 1992; Hopkins 1996; Hirst and Hopkins 1998; Maines and McDaniel 2000; Dietrich et al. 2001). Accounting standard variation also affects JDM. For example, Hopkins et al. (2000) find that analysts make different stock price judgments when viewing pooling versus purchase accounting.

Other studies of standards and regulations include Anderson et al. (1990a), who report that managers (proxied by students) who face the threat of IRS access to audit work papers are less likely to disclose information about the tax liability than those who do not; however, there is no effect on the accuracy of tax liability estimates. In tax, Cuccia et al. (1995) report that standards that contain either numerical or verbal information result in tax professionals' recommendations being in line with client preference incentives. Tax professionals use different forms of motivated reasoning depending on the type of standard. Spilker et al. (1999) find that tax professionals in a compliance context are more likely to recommend an aggressive, pro-client position when a rule is vague rather than precisely stated. However, these results reverse in a planning context.

Studies of auditors include Trompeter (1994), who finds that the restrictiveness of GAAP reduces the extent to which partners' accounting treatment choices correspond to client incentives. However, Libby and Kinney (2000) find that a standard requiring management to either correct misstatements or represent that they are material has little effect on auditors' judgments of recommended corrections to earnings, unless corrections would allow earnings to continue to be above analysts' consensus forecast. Dopuch et al. (2001) document that students proxying for auditors are less likely to issue audit reports that are consistent with management's desired conclusion (a high financial outcome) when management is required to rotate auditors periodically. Ng and Tan (2003) report that auditors who have access to standards related to revenue recognition are more likely to recommend audit adjustments that will make earnings fall below analysts' consensus forecast. However, in the presence of an effective audit committee, guidance availability has no effect. Kadous et al. (2003) find that a suggested regulation requiring auditors to make a separate assessment of the appropriateness of accounting treatments renders it more likely that auditors will respond to client-related incentives.

Zimbelman (1997) examines the effects of SAS No. 82 on auditors' fraud risk assessments. This standard requires auditors to make a separate assessment of fraud risk rather than include the fraud risk assessment in overall risk assessments. Auditors directed to process in a manner in accordance with SAS No. 82 (versus follow the old standard) spend more time reading fraud-related cues; however, they are not differentially sensitive to actual fraud risk when making risk judgments or selecting audit tests. Hronsky and Houghton (2001) examine the effect of different wordings of a standard related to extraordinary item accounting. Auditors attach different meanings to the standard depending on wording and also make different decisions regarding classifying items as extraordinary.

Standards and regulations are an extremely important part of accounting decision makers' environment and typically are thought to constrain "bad behavior" (here, low-quality JDM caused by factors such as monetary incentives with associated desired conclusions). However, results of studies to date indicate mixed results of standards on JDM quality. One possible reason for these findings is that standards incorporate so many variables, including task complexity, presentation format, and incentives. In some studies, variables having negative effects on JDM may dominate, whereas in other studies, variables having positive effects may dominate. Without disentangling the various attributes of standards and appealing to theories related to those attributes, it is difficult to move forward in this area. JDM researchers stand to have a significant impact on both practice and theory development by making attempts along these lines.

Another possible reason for the mixed findings is that changes in standards and regulations intended to constrain "bad behavior" can have unanticipated consequences. For example, one impetus for recent debates regarding a requirement by the Sarbanes-Oxley Act to study "principles-based" versus "rules-based" financial accounting standards is that rules-based standards can encourage firms to structure transactions so they get around the rules (Nelson 2003; Schipper 2003). On the other hand, principles-based standards may allow clients to report aggressively for different reasons, such as motivated reasoning on the part of auditors (Nelson). Again, research that examines the various attributes of standards in detail and seeks to develop theory regarding the possible effects of such attributes is critically important in accounting.

7-9   SUMMARY

This chapter reviews the literature on environmental variables and accounting JDM quality. In particular, the chapter discusses the effects of monetary incentives, accountability and justification, assigned goals, feedback, groups and teams, time pressure, and standards and regulations. In addition, because many of these variables affect JDM quality via motivation, the chapter also includes a brief review of the motivation material from Chapter 4.

Findings for environmental variables' effects in accounting are relatively consistent with those in psychology. First, studies examining the effects of variables that work through motivation of the "be correct" variety show that these variables can result in higher-quality JDM, although their effects often are moderated by many factors, most notably skill. Given the prevalence in the accounting environment of monetary incentives, accountability, and regulations that should motivate people to make the "correct" judgment or decision, findings of significant moderator effects are practically important. Further, we know little about whether these factors have additive or interactive effects on JDM quality. Accounting professionals face multiple motivators of this sort, and their additive or interactive effects on JDM quality may be less positive (or more negative) than are their individual effects, for example, if they cause pressure (Ashton 1990). In addition, research should examine accounting-specific moderators of these factors' effects. For example, monetary incentives may appear to be leading to higher JDM quality for managers whose pay is tied to earnings when earnings meet prespecified targets. That is, one way in which this can occur is through high-quality JDM about products, customer relationships, and the like. Of course, this can occur also because of the flexibility allowed by GAAP and the resulting opportunity for earnings management. That is, the accounting system per se may be allowing for what appear to be positive effects of monetary incentives but that clearly may not be positive for at least some constituents such as investors.

Even more worrisome than the findings about environmental variables operating through the "be correct" type of motivation are findings related to their effects when operating through the "desired conclusions" type of motivation. These findings are highly consistent with those in psychology; that is, such variables tend to result in reasoning that is motivated toward supporting a given conclusion and the resulting adoption of that conclusion. More important, the desired conclusion is sometimes incorrect from the standpoint of correspondence with actual outcomes or correspondence with professional standards, among other criteria. These findings are worrisome because many accounting decision makers are subject to standards and regulations that require that they make unbiased judgments and decisions. Further, as mentioned above, these professionals also face motivation to be correct, which does not appear to offset the effects of the desired-conclusion motivation. Again, then, research on how accounting professionals make judgments and decisions under conflicting motivations is extremely important.

These findings are of further interest because they are, at least implicitly, the subject of recent regulatory and public scrutiny. This scrutiny has resulted in substantial changes in the environment accounting decision makers face, changes apparently aimed at mitigating negative effects of environmental variables such as incentives that can result in motivation toward reaching desired conclusions. For example, audit partner rotation is now required, and research analysts must be separated from the investment-banking arms of their brokerages. Other environmental changes are being considered (e.g., a focus on standards that are more principles based). Yet recent studies (e.g., Libby and Kinney 2000; Kadous et al. 2003) find that some of these proposed or already instituted environmental changes have either no effect or negative (unintended) effects on JDM quality. Consequently, continued research on environmental variables, especially those under scrutiny by regulators and other policy makers, is critical both theoretically and practically. In particular, researchers need to think carefully about both intended and potential unintended JDM consequences of alterations to environmental variables.

Further, researchers need to focus not only on changes to a relatively small subset of changes (e.g., regulation) as a way of mitigating currently observed negative effects created by desired-conclusion motivation. For example, King's (2002) finding that group cohesiveness can mitigate auditors' potentially inappropriate trust of clients is intriguing and suggests that other environmental changes are viable JDM improvement methods. Also, to date, researchers have tended to adopt the position that many environmental variables have positive effects, possibly because they underemphasize the notion that these variables can result in desired-conclusion motivation. Given that policy makers appear to be thinking of environmental variables, at least as currently implemented, as being causes of low-quality JDM, researchers probably should shift their focus as well.

Next, work on environmental variables that operate through mediators other than or in addition to motivation clearly continues to be relevant. Recent emphasis on desired-conclusion motivation issues should not overshadow the importance of this work. For example, recent theory development related to the review process shows great promise. Accounting researchers should continue this work because of the relatively unique nature of factors such as the review process. Finally, work that addresses the confounding of these environmental variables is critical. One type of work along these lines would be to simply document the extent to which they are confounded in real-world settings. Then, experimental work can attempt to parse out their separate effects.

8

Understanding the Factors that Affect JDM Quality

This chapter examines whether third parties who use accounting professionals' judgments and decisions, as well as the accounting professionals themselves, understand the factors that cause variation in (or low levels) of JDM quality for a particular task. As shown in Figure 8-1, this question follows the examination of factors that create differences in JDM quality (as discussed in Chapters 3 through 7). This ordering of questions reflects the notion that, as researchers, we first must identify the factors that affect JDM quality in order to examine whether third-party users and accounting professionals understand their effects. However, it is only one of two questions that can follow the "which factors create differences?" question. The other issue that naturally follows the study of JDM determinants is reflected by the question regarding the sorts of changes that can improve JDM quality; this issue is addressed in Chapter 9. Whether researchers proceed to examine third-party understanding of accountants' JDM or to examine methods for improving accountants' JDM after examining the factors that affect JDM is a matter of taste. This book begins by discussing third-party (and personal) understanding of JDM quality then covers improvement methods because methods for improving individuals' JDM also may be appropriate for improving third parties' understanding of others' JDM.

There are a variety of contexts in which third-party understanding of others' judgments and decisions arise; this chapter covers two contexts that are of particular importance in accounting. The first context is that in which users of accounting professionals' JDM are predicting the quality of the professionals' JDM in order to determine to what extent they should rely on the JDM as an input to their own decision making. For example, investors may view several analysts' earnings forecasts and attempt to predict which of those forecasts will be the most accurate vis-à-vis actual earnings when making a decision about buying or selling a stock. As another example, loan officers review audited financial statements when making decisions about loans. As part of their loan review, the loan officers likely attempt to predict whether an auditor's opinion about financial statements will be accurate vis-à-vis the key outcome of bankruptcy occurrence.

FIGURE 8-1   **Framework for JDM Research in Accounting**

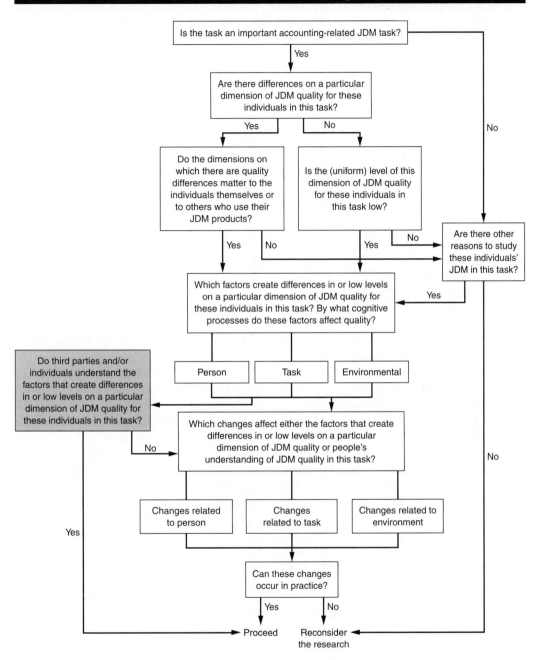

The second important context in which third-party understanding of JDM occurs is the ex post assessment of accounting professionals' JDM quality. Sometimes this assessment is done as part of a standard review of work. For example, auditors' work is reviewed as part of quality control procedures performed by the Public Company Accounting Oversight Board. In other cases, ex post assessment occurs because users of professionals' JDM have suffered losses. The latter type of assessment often results in the attribution or nonattribution of responsibility to the accounting professionals for low-quality JDM that is associated with the losses. Along with this, accounting professionals may experience serious monetary and other penalties. For example, judges and juries evaluate auditors' and analysts' JDM quality as part of litigation brought against auditors and analysts by clients, investors, and others, and auditors and analysts may have to make large payments, lose their jobs, or even serve jail time.

Common to these contexts is that third parties are attempting to understand professionals' JDM from "afar." That is, third parties likely do not have strong personal relationships with accounting professionals in these settings. Individual investors using the work of sell-side analysts, for example, typically do not ever meet those analysts. Loan officers using the work of auditors may know a few auditors in the accounting firm's local office but typically do not have relationships with all the auditors in a global or national firm who may have contributed to the JDM leading to an audit opinion. Jurors, judges, and regulators also typically do not (and should not) have long-standing personal relationships with the professionals being evaluated.

This characteristic of third-party evaluation of the JDM of accounting professionals distinguishes it from other types of JDM evaluation in which the evaluator and the evaluated party have an interpersonal relationship. For example, performance evaluation of subordinates by their superiors within organizations often involves an assessment of JDM quality, and superiors likely know subordinates fairly well. In other words, this type of third-party evaluation is done "nearby." Because interpersonal relationships can alter the evaluation process, such "nearby" evaluations are not discussed in this chapter. Instead, the main type of these evaluations—performance evaluation—is considered part of the "personnel screening" improvement method, which is discussed in Chapter 9. Along with "afar" evaluations of JDM quality by third parties, this chapter covers people's understanding of their own JDM, because self-insight often is affected by the same factors and cognitive processes as is third-party understanding.

This chapter is organized as follows. The next section discusses general issues related to third-party evaluation, including methods for studying related research questions and to what extent spontaneous third-party evaluation of accounting professionals' JDM quality occurs. The following section covers how third parties evaluate professionals' JDM. Specifically, it discusses the factors they consider when evaluating JDM quality, as well as the cognitive processes they use. This section also contains a brief discussion of what is known to date about methods for improving the quality of third-party understanding. Section 8-3 considers whether there are differences among third parties as to their understanding of professionals' JDM and what may cause these differences. For example, more knowledgeable investors may evaluate analysts' JDM differently than do less knowledgeable investors. The chapter continues with a discussion about individuals' understanding of their own JDM quality (self-insight). Following this, the chapter reviews research that examines third parties' understanding of accounting professionals' JDM. This section is organized by the type of professionals whose JDM is being evaluated, specifically managers and internal auditors, analysts, and external auditors. The next section covers accounting research on self-insight, and a final section summarizes.

8-1 OVERVIEW OF THIRD PARTIES' UNDERSTANDING OF ACCOUNTING PROFESSIONALS' JDM

As mentioned above, third parties have important reasons to understand accounting professionals' JDM. In accounting, *third parties* are defined as persons who are connected to accounting professionals' JDM from "afar" and *third-party understanding* is defined as these persons' evaluations of which factors affect accounting professionals' JDM quality. Third parties may engage in this activity in order to predict the quality of a professional's current judgment or decision that they are using as an input to their own decision making, or they may want to determine these factors as part of an effort to evaluate the quality of a professional's past JDM.[1]

The use of professionals' JDM in personal decision making or the ex post evaluation of professionals' JDM, particularly in situations where people have experienced losses, is not unique to accounting; people use the JDM of doctors, lawyers, and other professionals in their decision making and also question these professionals' JDM ex post. However, the extent to which third parties understand the factors that affect professionals' JDM quality is of particular relevance to accounting for several reasons. First and foremost is that the function of accounting is to provide information that is useful for decision making. Given that accounting information comes from accounting professionals or from systems created by accounting professionals and, therefore, is affected by the professionals' JDM, it makes sense that persons using accounting information would want to understand the JDM quality of the professionals who have provided it.

In addition, third-party understanding of accounting professionals' JDM is particularly relevant to accounting researchers because third parties such as investors can suffer financial losses if their understanding is poor. Along with this, if accounting professionals realize that third parties do not properly understand the factors that affect JDM quality, the professionals may be strategic in presenting themselves to those third parties. For example, if a professional knows that third parties focus heavily on a particular factor that is irrelevant to JDM quality (e.g., confidence) as being a key cause thereof, the professional may attempt to increase the quantity of that factor she possesses. Further, if accounting professionals are evaluated by third parties who do not fully understand the professionals' JDM, the professionals themselves also can suffer financial losses. For example, a jury may believe that an auditor's consulting relationship with an audit client negatively affected the quality of her audit judgments and consequently find the auditor liable for investor losses when the consulting factor actually had no effect on the auditor's JDM. Further, because it is done from afar, third parties' understanding of accounting professionals' JDM also is of theoretical relevance.[2]

---

[1]Note that third parties may not be actively attempting to understand causes of others' JDM quality; instead, they may simply be (somewhat passively) influenced by various factors when reacting to others' JDM. The discussion throughout this chapter encompasses both of these types of "understanding."

[2]Having compared these two types of third-party evaluation, I must note for the reader that some of the theories and findings discussed later in the chapter (and used in accounting research) relate to nearby evaluations rather than afar evaluations.

That is, it likely differs from third parties' understanding of many other professionals' JDM that is done nearby. It is not clear how third-party understanding is affected by this element of the accounting context. Nevertheless, the accounting context provides a unique opportunity for building theory that may contrast with theory about nearby understanding.

At this point, it is worthwhile to consider whether third parties who use or evaluate accounting professionals' JDM vary in any way in their understanding of the JDM. There are many levels at which third-party understanding could vary or fail to vary, with the most fundamental of these being whether third parties make any attempt to understand the causes of professionals' JDM quality (or react differentially to varying determinants of quality). It is quite plausible that third parties who use accounting professionals' work consider professional JDM to be of uniformly high quality. That is, third parties may consider all accounting professionals to be experts because professionals generally must endure rigorous training and credentialing processes, and third parties may assume that these processes lead to expert levels of knowledge (Stein 1997; Mieg 2001; Shanteau et al. 2002). In other words, third parties may exhibit "blind trust in professionals" (similar to "blind trust in numbers"; see Kadous et al. [2005]). Consistent with this, the key role of professionals in our society often is thought to be the distribution of expert-level knowledge (Abbott 1988). Professionals also possess many trappings of expertise, such as membership in societies and exclusive titles, as well as a compelling air of authority (Sherden 1998). If third parties consider all professionals to be experts (i.e., to have high-quality JDM), they likely will not exert any effort to understand factors that may affect the professionals' JDM quality (or be influenced by any factors in their reactions to the professionals' JDM) because they believe JDM quality to be a constant.

Anecdotally, many of us can think of times when we assumed that a given professional had high-quality JDM simply because she was a professional. Further, there is frequent public discussion about this issue, particularly with regard to which professionals can be considered expert witnesses in litigation settings or whose opinions on significant events should be considered expert (e.g., McCartney and Evans 1995; Simon 1996; Schmitt 1997; MacDonald 1999). The question for accounting researchers is whether this is a pervasive phenomenon among third parties who use accounting professionals' JDM. For example, do most investors consider sell-side analysts to have high-quality JDM simply because they are professionals? Fortunately, existing research suggests otherwise; investors react differentially to the judgments and decisions of analysts who differ in either prior or predicted JDM quality (e.g., Bonner et al. 2003; Clement and Tse 2003; Gleason and Lee 2003). More generally, as discussed in Chapter 2, research indicates that JDM differences among accounting professionals do matter to third parties.[3] In other words, these third parties do not appear to believe that all accounting professionals are experts.

Assuming that at least some third parties attempt to understand (or are affected by) the factors that determine accounting professionals' JDM, then, why might the quality of this understanding vary in any way that makes it of interest to researchers?

---

[3]Given that studies addressing this question are not plentiful, it is important for researchers to consider whether there is sufficient evidence that JDM quality differences matter to third parties before considering questions about third-party understanding of these differences.

First, some people have systematic beliefs about factors that affect JDM that are not consistent with reality, meaning that the quality of their understanding of professionals' JDM can be lowered. For example, some people focus on factors such as confidence and communication skills when attributing high-quality JDM to others, and these factors often are not related to JDM (e.g., Shanteau 1987; Hastie and Rasinski 1988; Agnew et al. 1997; Stein 1997; Sniezek and Van Swol 2001). Second, third parties who use accounting professionals' JDM can vary as to a number of other personal characteristics that can influence the quality of their understanding of others' JDM. For example, sophisticated investors may be more able than unsophisticated investors to understand the factors that affect analysts' forecast accuracy because they have superior knowledge about analyst forecasts (Bonner et al. 2003). Third, situational characteristics may cause variation in the quality of third-party understanding of accounting professionals' JDM. For example, JDM that is unusual in some way (e.g., substantially different from that of other professionals) may attract more third-party understanding attempts than other JDM (Weiner 1986; Försterling 2001) and, thus, potentially more variation in the ultimate quality of understanding.

How can researchers go about conducting research to examine the quality of third parties' understanding of the factors that affect accounting professionals' JDM? First, it is necessary to define "quality of third parties' understanding." In many ways, the issues related to this definition are similar to those related to defining the quality of individuals' JDM (see Chapter 2). One issue is whether quality should be defined as to process or performance. For example, third-party understanding could be assessed as to whether third parties conduct extensive information search when evaluating others' JDM (a process method of assessing quality). Instead, third-party understanding could be assessed as to whether third parties ultimately focus only on "correct" determinants of JDM, for example, those empirically shown to be related to professionals' JDM in a particular setting, and ignore irrelevant factors (a performance method of assessing quality). This chapter assumes that a performance perspective is used to assess the quality of third-party understanding, consistent with other chapters that assume a performance perspective is used to assess the quality of individuals' JDM.

A second issue is which criterion should be used to assess the "correctness" of third parties' performance. For example, to examine whether third parties focus on the correct determinants of JDM, should correctness be defined vis-à-vis actual outcomes, professional standards, normative theories, other third parties' beliefs, or their own beliefs at a prior point in time? As is the case when measuring individual JDM performance, there are advantages and disadvantages that accompany the choice of any of these criteria for measuring third-party understanding of JDM. Unfortunately, the psychology and accounting literatures diverge somewhat on this point. Much of the psychology literature implicitly defines quality of third-party understanding by examining the extent to which third parties agree with others or with normative theories, whereas most of the accounting literature defines quality based on whether third parties' understanding matches actual outcomes or professional standards. Although these differences create opportunities for theory development (in both psychology and accounting), they also make comparison of psychology and accounting findings somewhat difficult. For example, a third party could diverge from a normative theory's prescription regarding how to evaluate others' JDM yet come to an overall prediction of a particular professional's JDM that is close to the professional's true JDM. In this case, it seems inappropriate to say that the third party has low-quality understanding. These issues will be discussed further in later sections.

The preceding example points to another issue that arises with regard to how researchers should evaluate the quality of third-party understanding. This issue arises even if the researcher adopts a performance perspective and, for example, a criterion of actual outcomes for defining correctness of performance. This issue is whether quality of understanding should be assessed as to its components or at a global level. An illustration clarifies this issue: Suppose that an investor is attempting to understand the factors that affect analysts' earnings forecast accuracy. Further suppose that she concludes that knowledge and ability are the primary determinants of forecast accuracy and that they are equally important determinants. She then uses experience and brokerage firm as her measures of these factors and weights them equally when predicting the accuracy of each analyst. Based on this process, the investor predicts the following: Analyst A's earnings forecast will be highly accurate because she works for a prestigious brokerage firm and has many years of experience, Analyst B's forecast will be somewhat less accurate because she works for a less prestigious firm but also has many years of experience, and Analyst C's forecast will be relatively inaccurate because she works for a low-prestige firm and has only one year of experience.

In this example, there are at least six ways of assessing the quality of the investor's understanding of the factors affecting analysts' JDM (even using a narrow definition of quality of understanding based on performance vis-à-vis actual outcomes). First, the researcher can ask the investor to predict the accuracy of the analysts in terms of, say, the number of pennies per share difference there will be between the analyst's forecast and actual earnings. In other words, the researcher asks the investor to quantify what she means by "highly accurate," "slightly less accurate," and "relatively inaccurate." The researcher then can compare the investor's estimates to the actual number of pennies per share difference between the analysts' forecasts and reported earnings per share. Second, the researcher could use the investor's qualitative predictions to rank the analysts' predicted accuracy and compare these rankings to the analysts' rankings on accuracy vis-à-vis actual earnings. Both of these methods assess understanding at a "global," or overall, level based on the investor's predictions of analysts' accuracy.[4] If the investor makes highly accurate predictions about analysts' forecast accuracy, the researcher can infer that she has a good understanding of the factors affecting analysts' JDM. Further, because the investor's main purpose in this setting is to predict accuracy, it may make sense to assess the quality of her understanding based on these predictions.

Remaining methods of assessing the quality of understanding involve examining components of that understanding.[5] First, the researcher can compare the list of factors used by the investor to an empirically determined list that is derived by relating cues to actual outcomes and finding those with statistically significant coefficients. This method gauges the extent to which the investor is focusing on all factors affecting analysts' JDM and ignoring factors that are irrelevant to JDM; in other words, the

---

[4]The second method can be used only when a third party predicts JDM for multiple accounting professionals, but the first can be used for a prediction of a single professional's JDM.

[5]Note that examining components differs from assessing quality of understanding using a process view. These components are intermediate answers that result from cognitive processes as opposed to the processes themselves. A global assessment of quality, by contrast, relies on some "final answer."

researcher is assessing the quality of the third party's cue selection (see Chapter 5). Second, the researcher can examine whether the investor uses the correct signs for cues, that is, knows the directional relationship between factors affecting others' JDM and that JDM. Many researchers posit that the keys to good JDM (and, thus, perhaps to the understanding of others' JDM) are knowing the right cues and cue signs (e.g., Dawes and Corrigan 1974). Third, the researcher can compare the measurement of JDM-related factors to an empirically determined measurement method. For example, if information is available about the relative abilities of analysts at various brokerage firms, the researcher can determine whether the manner in which the investor uses brokerage firm as a measure of ability is appropriate. Here, the researcher is assessing quality based on cue measurement, and some authors suggest that cue measurement is the most critical component of JDM (e.g., Einhorn 1972, 1974). Finally, the researcher can directly compare the weights used by the investor for various factors to empirically determined weights; this is a cue weighting assessment of quality.[6] The quality of cue weighting also has been shown to be critical to overall JDM quality (see Chapter 5).[7]

If data on factors that affect JDM quality, as well as measures of third parties' understanding of professionals' JDM quality, are publicly available, archival data analysis is a viable method for examining this question. For example, many studies measure investors' understanding (using stock price reactions) of the accuracy of the forecasts of analysts who vary as to experience and several other factors related to forecast accuracy. In addition to being able to examine third parties' understanding under the conditions they typically face, archival work can examine whether third parties understand and use factors that are relevant to JDM quality as well as whether they ignore irrelevant factors (e.g., the hair color of the analyst, assuming this has no relation to analysts' forecast accuracy). One downside of using the archival approach is that measures such as stock price are very noisy proxies for "third-party understanding." More specifically, the researcher is not assessing the quality of third-party understanding directly because stock price reflects buy or sell decisions by investors, which are based both on predictions of professionals' JDM (predictions that reflect the level of understanding of the professionals' JDM) and on other factors such as cash needs. Similarly, measures of factors that affect JDM quality also can be noisy (e.g., years of experience as a measure of knowledge). A second and significant downside of using such measures from archival sources is that researchers often cannot make inferences about individual third parties' understanding of these factors. At best, they may be able to make inferences about only the average understanding of groups of third parties, such as sophisticated and unsophisticated investors (Bonner et al. 2003).[8] Third, it often is difficult to obtain measures of the processes involved in third-party understanding from archival data unless those data consist of newspaper stories or the like (Weiner 1985). If little information about cognitive processes is available, it is difficult to consider appropriate methods for improving third-party evaluations.

---

[6]Another way of operationalizing a cue weighting assessment of quality is to compare predictions based on the third parties' cue weights to predictions based on empirically determined weights. This method likely is superior when factors affecting JDM are correlated (see Chapter 5).
[7]All these methods can be used to assess a third party's understanding of a single professional's JDM or of multiple professionals' JDM.
[8]Again, this book typically would not include such studies. However, because a large proportion of studies on third-party understanding employ this method, they are included in this chapter for completeness.

Researchers can overcome many of these problems by using a survey or an experiment. The survey researcher could ask individuals to respond to questions regarding the JDM of accounting professionals they use. For example, creditors could be asked questions about factors they believe affect auditors' JDM quality. These responses likely would provide measures that are less noisy than those used in archival research and also would provide measures at the level of the individual third party. Responses to such questions could be open ended, in which case respondents spontaneously may list both relevant and irrelevant factors, or structured to include some irrelevant factors that respondents may choose.[9] As mentioned earlier, the determination of factors that are relevant and irrelevant to accounting professionals' JDM quality can be made on the basis of prior empirical research, professional standards, normative theories, and the like.

Researchers could use an experiment in two ways to evaluate third parties' understanding. First, they could manipulate various factors to determine if third parties' evaluations of professionals' JDM vary with these manipulations. These manipulations could include both relevant and irrelevant factors. Manipulations of factors relevant to JDM quality can draw on work cited in the previous chapters of this book, as well as work specifically focused on third-party evaluations of these factors (e.g., Ohanian 1990).[10] Manipulations of particular irrelevant factors may be found in the third-party evaluation literature or may require further development on the part of the researcher. A second way of using an experiment to study third-party understanding would be to manipulate both the factors that affect (or do not affect) JDM quality and JDM quality itself and examine whether third parties can learn the relation of the factors to JDM quality. However, a potential problem with the inclusion of irrelevant factors in an experiment is that they are too obvious to subjects, thereby creating potential demand effects. Finally, researchers using experiments frequently are able to obtain measures of third parties' cognitive processes, thus allowing for work on methods of improving third parties' understanding of others' JDM to move forward.

8-2   PROCCESSES USED BY THIRD PARTIES WHEN UNDERSTANDING PROFESSIONALS' JDM

This section discusses how third parties go about understanding professionals' JDM. In particular, it delineates how third parties explicitly explain the determinants of JDM quality among professionals or how they process reactions to the JDM of professionals. This section discusses the causes that third parties consider (or are affected by) using the framework introduced earlier in this book, specifically person-related causes, task-related causes, and environmental causes.[11] To the extent possible, third parties' cognitive processes are also discussed using the earlier process framework (i.e., in terms of memory retrieval, information search, problem representation, hypothesis generation, and hypothesis and evidence evaluation).

---

[9]See Hewstone (1989) for discussion of how structured questions should be formulated.
[10]See Petty and Cacioppo (1986) and Fiske and Taylor (1991) for extensive discussion of how to manipulate relevant factors that have not been discussed previously in this text, for example, the quality of arguments accompanying a professional's judgment or decision.
[11]Much of the literature on third-party understanding uses a somewhat similar scheme.

Because of the diversity of literatures and theories that relate to third-party understanding of others' JDM, this chapter departs somewhat from earlier chapters in that it discusses findings separately by theory before attempting to integrate these findings. These literatures differ on a number of important attributes. For example, some theories posit that third parties actively attempt to understand others' JDM, whereas other theories suggest that their reaction is more passive. The literatures also differ as to the types of factors they suggest third parties focus on when understanding others' JDM; some suggest that third parties focus heavily on person-related causes of JDM, whereas others suggest that third parties consider person, task, and environmental causes. Relatedly, some literatures examine the extent to which third parties focus on relevant JDM causes, whereas other literatures examine third parties' understanding of irrelevant factors. These attributes of the literatures and theories, along with other attributes, such as how they measure the quality of third-party understanding and the cognitive processes posited to be affected by third-party understanding, are discussed fully in the sections that follow. A summary section then recaps the differences and commonalities among the theories and literatures.

Attribution Theory

One of the key theories related to third-party understanding of others' JDM is attribution theory. (See Försterling [2001] for an overview.) This theory proposes that third parties explicitly attempt to understand JDM quality (or, more generally, people's behavior) in order to determine the causes thereof. More important, these evaluations affect third parties' subsequent judgments and decisions, as well as their beliefs about the professionals whose JDM quality they are considering (Kelley and Michela 1980).[12]

Specifically, attribution theory proposes that third parties evaluate JDM (and behavior) in terms of person causes versus task-related and environmental causes (Heider 1958; Jones and Davis 1965; Kelley 1967, 1971a; Jones and Nisbett 1971; Darley and Goethals 1980; Weiner 1985, 1986).[13] Person causes include "power," which third parties believe to be a function principally of abilities but also believe to be influenced by confidence, fatigue, and mood (Heider). Attribution theory proposes that the other key perceived person-related cause of variation in JDM quality is motivation. Task-related and environmental causes include task difficulty, chance, and incentives (Heider; Jones and Davis; Kelley 1967, 1971a; Jones and Nisbett).

The attribution theory literature documents a number of regularities in the cognitive processes used by third parties when evaluating others' JDM. Early proposals (e.g., Kelley 1967, 1971a) suggested that third parties act like "intuitive scientists" and assess causes of JDM on the basis of covariation, or the extent to which a cause is present when the effect is present and absent when the effect is absent. Specifically, third parties consider the covariation of the effect (here, JDM quality) with, respectively, the person, task, and environment; these three types of covariation are labeled consensus, distinctiveness, and consistency. Further, people use this information about covariation to conduct a mental analysis of variance (ANOVA) in order to ascertain the relative

---

[12]Note that much of the attribution theory literature is based on interpersonal situations, or nearby evaluations. However, to the limited extent comparisons are made in this literature, findings for interpersonal situations seem to parallel those from noninterpersonal situations.

[13]Kelley (1967, 1971a) refers to task-related causes as "entity" causes and environmental causes as "circumstance" causes.

contributions of person, task, and environmental causes.[14] More specifically, then, early proposals suggested that people retrieve from memory or search for information about covariations of a particular effect and various causes then evaluate this evidence using something akin to a mental statistical process. In other words, people do not form an initial problem representation or generate hypotheses that later are evaluated. Rather, they simply retrieve or search for the necessary information then proceed to calculations.

A large body of literature now has refined these early proposals, documenting that people sometimes act in the above fashion and sometimes do not (Nisbett and Ross 1980; Försterling 2001). Specifically, current attribution theory suggests that people are unable to act like "intuitive scientists" unless relevant, unbiased, and already-calculated covariation information is presented to them in an experimental situation along with little to no other information (Nisbett and Ross; Hewstone 1989). People often will not conduct a mental ANOVA due to time pressure, lack of (intrinsic) motivation or (extrinsic) incentives, or if they are unable to obtain complete covariation information because, for example, it is not publicly available (Kelley 1971a, 1971b). Similar to this, if people are not dependent on the outcomes of their evaluations of others, they are less likely to engage in covariation-based thinking (Weiner 1985).

When not using a covariation-based mental analysis, people tend to retrieve information about possible causes by accessing either knowledge structures that contain information about causes linked to effects that are similar to the single effect they observe or intuitive (naive) causal theories that specify cause–effect relationships in propositional form (Fiske and Taylor 1991). In particular, people first may search memory for a knowledge structure or theory that suggests a single cause for a particular effect—here, a particular judgment or decision (Heider 1958; Kelley 1973; Nisbett and Ross 1980; Shaver 1985; Hewstone 1989). People appear to prefer to be able to explain effects in terms of a single cause because of a belief that single effects have single causes. In addition, people may focus on one cause because they use the representativeness heuristic when searching memory; specifically, they search for a cause whose features resemble the features of the effect (see Chapter 5). People typically make this assessment based on whether the JDM effect matches a knowledge structure or an intuitive theory. For example, when investors observe a highly accurate forecast being issued by an analyst with many years of experience, they may believe that the experience is an obvious single cause for the accurate forecast. As another example, when investors observe a buy recommendation from an analyst whose firm has investment-banking ties to the covered firm, they likely believe that the investment-banking incentive is an obvious single cause. More generally, people tend to attribute JDM effects that are consistent with existing incentives to those incentives. If people are able to readily match a JDM event to a knowledge structure or intuitive theory that suggests a single cause, they likely will not engage in further cognitive processing (e.g., further memory retrieval, search for further information, and evidence evaluation) (Kelley and Michela 1980).

---

[14]Kelley (1967, 1971a) also proposes that specific patterns of covariation lead to particular attributions. For example, when consensus and distinctiveness are low but consistency is high, Kelley proposes that third parties will attribute an effect to the person. This would occur because low consensus means that only one person exhibits the effect (e.g., high JDM quality), low distinctiveness means that this person exhibits the effect for all tasks, and high consistency means that the person exhibits the effect at all time periods and under all circumstances. This chapter does not further elaborate on Kelley's original predictions, as later studies have criticized the initial theory for its incompleteness and empirical evidence often does not support Kelley's predictions (Hewstone 1989; Försterling 2001).

If third parties believe there are multiple possible causes of a JDM effect (and they are not using covariation-based processing), they will attempt to retrieve a knowledge structure or intuitive theory that contains multiple causes. The circumstance that most frequently triggers this belief is the existence of an extreme effect; people tend to think that a single cause is not enough to explain an extreme effect (Kelley 1971b).[15] For example, an analyst's earnings forecast may be substantially different from that of other analysts, and an investor may retrieve a knowledge structure that indicates that award-winning analysts with many years of experience tend to deviate greatly from their peers. Such a knowledge structure indicates two causes for the JDM outcome: a good reputation (proxied by the award) and a high level of knowledge (proxied by years of experience). Situations other than extreme events also may trigger a belief that there are multiple possible causes. For example, third parties tend to evaluate good performance on a difficult task, or good performance where there are no (extrinsic) incentives, as being due to both abilities and motivation (Heider 1958; Darley and Goethals 1980; Weiner 1986). Similarly, third parties attribute a person's bad performance at an easy task to multiple causes, such as lack of ability and incentives for bad performance (Hewstone 1989).

Sometimes, third parties are unable to match a particular effect to an existing knowledge structure or naive theory because the effect is unexpected for a given situation; for example, investors may observe an analyst with investment-banking ties making a sell recommendation. In this case, third parties may engage in further memory retrieval and information search, as well as problem representation and hypothesis generation and evaluation, in order to explain the outcome's causes (Kelley and Michela 1980; Weiner 1985; Försterling 2001). In other words, they may engage in more extensive processing than when they simply match effects to knowledge structures or intuitive theories contained in memory. For example, people may search for information in order to revise existing knowledge structures or naive theories. However, if, in addition to the JDM effect being unexpected, the professional's JDM is voluntary (e.g., it is not a required audit opinion) and the JDM is not reflective of the professional's incentives, a third party instead may invoke a knowledge structure that suggests that the cause is person related and, as a consequence, not engage in more extensive processing (Jones and Davis 1965).

Irrespective of whether third parties use covariation-based mental analysis, access knowledge structures or intuitive causal theories, or engage in other types of processing, attribution theory findings show that they tend to make particular errors and exhibit specific biases when evaluating causes of others' JDM. Starting with covariation-based analysis, there are a variety of problems that can occur (Nisbett and Ross 1980; Crocker 1981; Alloy and Tabachnik 1984). First, the covariation information people access from memory or obtain through information search may be biased. As described in Chapter 5, people often do not record in memory or search for all the pieces of information needed to assess covariation, nor is this information always

---

[15]Note that Kelley (1971b) proposes that there are two general types of knowledge structures/theories: those containing "multiple sufficient causes" (MSC) and those containing "multiple necessary causes" (MNC). MSC structures and theories suggest that any one cause or combination of causes is enough to cause an outcome, whereas MNC structures and theories suggest that at least two causes are needed for a particular outcome. This chapter does not discuss these theoretical structures further because Kelley's proposal suggests that they are free of content, that is, not imbued with knowledge about a particular domain. This has been the subject of much criticism (e.g., Hewstone 1989; Fiske and Taylor 1991). This chapter assumes that knowledge structures are domain specific.

archived, say, by the media. For example, the media may report about situations in which auditors issue unqualified opinions for sizable companies that go bankrupt but not report about small companies with similar characteristics. Thus, investors or others attempting to evaluate the quality of auditors' JDM may not have complete information about auditors' JDM in situations in which small companies go bankrupt or in situations in which companies of all sizes do not go bankrupt.

Second, third parties often must classify information as to whether it indicates high or low JDM quality and the presence or absence of a particular cause. In ambiguous situations, people may make errors in these classifications (Crocker 1981), oftentimes because they are influenced by preexisting beliefs (consider the case of ethnic stereotypes). Third, even when people have accurate and complete covariation information, they tend not to use it all when assessing covariation, focusing instead on a biased subset (e.g., Shaklee and Tucker 1980; Crocker). Fourth, people's knowledge structures and intuitive causal theories often intrude on covariation analysis. That is, instead of proceeding from memory retrieval or information search to calculations, people may generate a hypothesized cause based on their prior knowledge then exhibit confirmation bias for this cause during further processing (Kelley 1971a; Hansen 1980; Nisbett and Ross 1980; Alloy and Tabachnik 1984; Hewstone 1989). Overall, then, covariation-based evaluations of the causes of others' JDM often can be incorrect.

Third parties can also make errors or exhibit biases in their evaluations when matching JDM to a knowledge structure or an intuitive theory containing either a single cause or multiple causes. This is due to the simple fact that knowledge structures and intuitive theories can be incorrect because, for example, people have acquired them through incorrect instruction. This seems particularly likely in the case of single-cause evaluations (i.e., it seems unlikely that a single factor frequently accounts fully for JDM). For example, the quality of auditors' judgments likely is affected by both their knowledge and their motivation to produce high-quality judgments. Yet, single-cause knowledge structures and theories likely exist among third parties for many reasons. For example, it is cognitively easier to think in terms of a single cause. Also, repeated accessing of single-cause structures and intuitive theories increases their strength and their future probability of retrieval. Further, people may not learn through experience that their knowledge structures or theories are incorrect (Nisbett and Ross 1980). For example, people may search for evidence that supports their proposed cause(s) of behavior or interpret existing evidence as supportive of these causes. Given the ease with which these confirmatory activities typically can be carried out, people may not change their existing knowledge structures or intuitive theories.

Whether third parties engage in covariation-based analysis, matching to information contained in memory, or another form of cognitive processing, there are further persistent regularities in their evaluation processes documented by the attribution theory literature; these regularities also may lessen the quality of third-party evaluations. The most pervasive of these is the *fundamental attribution error* (also called the *correspondence bias*), in which third parties tend to deem person-related causes, particularly those perceived to be stable characteristics such as personality traits and abilities, as more important in causing effects than task-related or environmental causes (Ross 1977; Darley and Goethals 1980).[16] One of the main reasons this bias can occur is that

---

[16]However, see Quattrone (1982) for situations in which the opposite finding appears.

third parties tend to hold beliefs that "people are how they act" (Jones and Davis 1965). With these beliefs, third parties may spontaneously deem person-related causes as determinants of JDM effects then not adjust or elaborate further. Further adjustment may be suspended because it is too effortful or because people have strong beliefs that certain person causes are necessary for certain outcomes; for example, they may believe that abilities are necessary for a high level of performance (Gilbert et al. 1988; McClure 1998). As mentioned earlier, third parties are especially likely to behave this way if a person's JDM is unexpected or if the person does not appear to have incentives consistent with the JDM (Jones and Davis). Finally, the fundamental attribution error (bias) may occur due to people's use of the availability heuristic (Nisbett and Ross 1980). That is, person-related causes may be more salient to third-party evaluators than other causes or, in the extreme, the only causes about which third parties have information (Heider 1958; Gilbert and Malone 1995).

The attribution theory literature only briefly addresses the extent to which the above processing regularities may lead third parties to have low-quality understanding and, if so, how this understanding can be improved. Clearly, third parties can make many errors and exhibit various biases using any form of attribution-based processing, but there is little information regarding the extent to which these errors and biases ultimately result in low-quality understanding (Funder 1987; Cheng and Novick 1990). For example, there is no empirical evidence on how often a single cause accounts for most of the variance in a person's JDM quality. Further, even if JDM quality cannot be explained by a single cause in most cases, quickly accessing a single-cause structure and evaluating JDM as being caused by this single factor may be "adaptive" (i.e., have more benefits than costs). That is, if a single cause is the largest cause of JDM in a given situation, the third party often will be correct in her evaluation. For example, if investment-banking incentives explain 70% of the variance in stock recommendations, it may not be worthwhile for a third party to search for and retain information about other causes or engage in more complicated processing to learn about other causes of analysts' recommendation quality.

In other words, attribution theory tends to focus on normative prescriptions (e.g., the use of covariation-based analysis) and agreement with others as criteria for determining the quality of third parties' attributions. Although these clearly are important criteria for evaluating quality generally, researchers are not able to compare the findings using these criteria to those using other criteria and, thus, are somewhat limited in the conclusions they can draw. In particular, there is little information about the quality of third parties' attributions using actual-outcome criteria to assess quality. For example, there is little evidence about the extent to which person-related factors versus other factors explain people's behavior (Cheng and Novick 1990; Gilbert and Malone 1995).

Attribution theory also has made little progress in exploring methods for improving third parties' understanding of others' behavior. To date, the literature suggests two ideas. First, if third parties are not cognitively overloaded, that is, engaged in too many effortful activities, they may spontaneously correct for errors such as the fundamental attribution error (Gilbert et al. 1988). Thus, a method for improving understanding would be to remove from the environment factors that might cause cognitive overload (e.g., the requirement to perform other tasks). Second, prompts to consider multiple causes or making multiple causes otherwise salient to third parties may prevent them from focusing on a single cause. Where multiple causes of behavior exist, this technique may improve third-party evaluations (Wegener and Petty 1997).

Finally, the attribution theory literature is the main literature addressing third parties' ex post evaluations of professionals' JDM. Specifically, there is a great deal of work on the attribution of responsibility and blame. Attribution of responsibility is defined as "a judgment made about the moral accountability of a person of normal capacities, which judgment usually but does not always involve a causal connection between the person being judged and some morally disapproved act or event" (Shaver 1985). Evaluations of responsibility differ from evaluations of the causes of effects (events) in that people are trying to infer something about the relationship between the effect and resulting outcome rather than the effect and various person, task, and environmental causes that precede it (Weiner 1986). The assignment of blame and consequent punishment follow attributions of responsibility and occur only under certain circumstances, for example, in the absence of mitigating circumstances.

Several factors that are relevant (from either a legal or philosophical perspective) to third parties' ex post evaluations of responsibility and blame indeed affect these evaluations (Shaver 1985; Weiner 1995). These factors are reflected in the typical processing steps followed by third parties. The first step is an evaluation of the causes of an effect—here, a particular judgment or decision. Ostensibly, this step proceeds as described above for evaluations of factors affecting JDM; thus, it seems reasonable to expect that responsibility and blame attributions are affected by the same relevant person, task, and environmental variables described above (Shaver; Weiner), as well as by the same errors and biases. This processing step results in evaluations that causes of JDM do or do not directly involve a person. For example, a third party might conclude that poor JDM quality resulted from lack of effort. The next step is to determine whether any particular individual is responsible for the effect (or, perhaps in the case of accounting professionals, a particular firm). As part of this step, the third party may consider whether the person causes are controllable; a cause such as lack of effort clearly would be controllable (Shaver and Drown 1986; Weiner 1986; Fiske and Taylor 1991; Schlenker et al. 1994). If the causes are not considered controllable (e.g., the person was coerced), responsibility likely will not be attributed to the identified individual. Third parties also may consider whether the standards governing the situation are clear and whether they are binding on the identified individual (Schlenker et al.).

If the causes are considered controllable and the standards clear and binding, the next step involves determining a level of responsibility for the individual. Levels of responsibility include "causality," "foreseeability," and "intentionality" (Heider 1958; Shaver 1985).[17] Holding someone responsible at the causality level means that she is thought to be causally related to the effect (e.g., an auditor's lack of effort led to a low-quality audit opinion). Holding someone responsible at the foreseeability level means that the third party believes that a person-related cause accounts for the effect, and the person was able to foresee the negative outcome that occurred (e.g., investors losing money).[18] The highest level of responsibility (intentionality) is attributed to a person who is thought to have caused the effect, foreseen the related negative outcome, and desired that the negative outcome occur.

[17]Another level of responsibility is "association," in which someone is attributed responsibility for an effect even when she has no causal relation to the effect.
[18]An alternate definition of foreseeability is that the person was able to foresee the risks involved in the situation, as well as the likelihood and severity of possible negative outcomes (Karlovac and Darley 1988).

These levels of responsibility, then, are positively related to the amount of blame and punishment that are attributed to a person. However, before blame is assigned, the person subject to blame may offer justifications or excuses. Justifications are claims that the effect and related outcome are not negative, in contrast to the views of the third party (Shaver 1985). For example, a person may claim that her behavior served a greater social purpose and, in this way, is positive overall. Excuses are statements that are intended to shift focus from person-related, controllable causes to non-person-related causes or uncontrollable person-related factors (Weiner 1995), or to say that the rules were not clear, were irrelevant to the situation, or were not binding on the person (Schlenker et al. 2001). If justifications or excuses are accepted by third parties, responsibility, blame, and punishment may be decreased either somewhat or entirely (Schlenker et al.). In addition, as the level of care taken to prevent negative outcomes increases, evaluations of responsibility and blame by third parties decrease (Karlovac and Darley 1988).[19]

Unfortunately, third parties' attributions of responsibility and blame also can be affected by irrelevant variables. The most important of these is the outcome itself. For example, juries evaluating auditors know about the auditors' opinion decision and also about negative outcomes such as the existence of material misstatements or bankruptcy. As described in Chapter 3, people have difficulty ignoring knowledge of outcomes even in situations such as legal settings, where standards dictate that legal responsibility is based on the quality of the JDM and, thus, that outcomes are irrelevant (e.g., Causey and Causey 1991). Consistent with this, research indicates that third parties evaluate JDM more negatively when they have knowledge of negative outcomes than when they do not (e.g., Karlovac and Darley 1988; Hawkins and Hastie 1990; Plous 1993). In addition, the severity of the outcome, which typically is considered irrelevant to JDM quality, can affect third parties' evaluations of responsibility and blame. Specifically, results suggest that when third parties are dissimilar to the professionals being evaluated, as would normally be the case with jurors evaluating accountants, they attribute more responsibility to the professionals for more severe outcomes (e.g., Walster 1966; Fincham and Jaspars 1980; Burger 1981; Weiner 1995).[20] Further, excuses are more likely to be accepted if they are accompanied by salient information and the professional is confident when offering the excuse (Schlenker et al. 2001); clearly, these factors may not be related to the "quality" of the excuses. Finally, negative affect in third parties can influence their responsibility attributions; this negative affect can occur simply after learning about negative outcomes (Kadous 2001). Affect in third parties clearly is not relevant to making judgments of responsibility and blame regarding professionals' JDM.

Clearly, if the irrelevant factors described above affect third parties' evaluations of professionals' responsibility and blame, these evaluations can be in error or biased.[21] Additional errors or bias can occur because third parties sometimes make a

---

[19]Level of care is similar to the negligence concept used in litigation against auditors and others.

[20]The opposite maintains when third parties are similar to the persons being evaluated (i.e., as severity increases, attributed responsibility decreases). This phenomenon is known as "defensive attribution" because people apparently are trying to protect themselves from ever being held responsible for a similar event (Shaver 1970). They believe their association to an event to be a possibility because of their similarity to the person involved.

[21]Similar to attributions of causes of others' JDM, however, it is difficult to make statements about the quality of these ex post attributions because the literature focuses on a limited number of criteria when evaluating the quality of these attributions.

responsibility evaluation first then engage in motivated reasoning to support their evaluation (Weiner 1995). This may occur if third parties have some sort of stake in the outcome of the responsibility evaluation or because they need to believe in a "just world" in which someone is held responsible for a negative event (Shaver 1985). In the latter case, third parties tend to be biased upward in their responsibility assessments. For example, they may attribute a "foreseeability" level of responsibility to a professional when a "causality" level is more appropriate. Unfortunately, little systematic evidence exists about how to improve third parties' evaluations of professionals' responsibility. The accounting literature, however, provides a few examples. Lowe and Reckers (1994) show that asking jurors to evaluate the probability of other possible outcomes reduces, but does not eliminate, the effect of outcomes on jurors' evaluations of auditors' JDM. Kadous (2001) shows that telling jurors to attribute their negative affect to a source other than the accounting professionals eliminates the impact of outcomes on jurors' evaluations.

To summarize, attribution theory proposes that third parties explicitly attempt to determine the causes of professionals' JDM quality and think of these causes in terms of person-related causes versus other types of causes. Key person-related causes on which third parties focus are abilities and motivation. In ascertaining causes, third parties may use covariation information and conduct a "mental ANOVA" or, instead, attempt to match effect information to knowledge structures or intuitive theories held in memory. When they are unable to match to information in memory, they may engage in more extensive processing and search for and evaluate additional information. Irrespective of the process used, third parties make a number of errors and exhibit a number of biases when making attributions about causes of JDM. These can occur with covariation-based and memory retrieval–based processes. One bias that is specific to third-party evaluations is the fundamental attribution error, in which third parties tend to attribute JDM more frequently to person-related causes than to other causes. Unfortunately, very little information about the quality of third parties' attributions and methods of improving them exists. It is reasonable to assume, however, that at least some of the errors and biases discussed earlier lower the quality of attributions. Therefore, it also is reasonable to conduct further research using different criteria for attribution "performance."

Similarly, attribution theory speaks to ex post evaluations of professionals' JDM, evaluations that often are done for the purposes of assigning responsibility and blame. These evaluations involve attributions regarding causes, as above, as well as reasoning regarding the appropriate level of responsibility. This reasoning includes consideration of the controllability of causes, the extent to which rules are clear and binding on a professional, and the extent to which the professional may have foreseen and intended a negative outcome related to her JDM. Blame evaluations follow responsibility assessments and also are affected by justifications and excuses. Responsibility and blame evaluations can be in error or biased as well. Some of this occurs because they are affected by irrelevant factors such as outcome severity and the confidence of the professional when communicating excuses. Similar to evaluations of causes, there is little information about the quality of third parties' ex post understanding of professionals' JDM, but again, it is reasonable to assume that the documented errors or biases can decrease this quality and, thus, that investigating methods of improving ex post understanding is important.

Persuasion and Communication Theories

Another set of theories that is relevant to third-party understanding of accounting professionals' JDM relates to how third parties react to persuasive messages (including judgments and decisions) communicated to them from various message producers (e.g., advertisers).[22] These theories do not posit that third parties deliberately search for causes of producers' "message quality." Yet they are pertinent to the discussion in this chapter because they predict that both relevant and irrelevant factors affect third parties' evaluation of producers and their messages. In particular, this literature originated the concept of "source credibility" and informs us about the factors that third parties consider when evaluating the "credibility" of a source, as well as the effects of "source credibility" on third parties' reactions to and use of the messages produced by those sources.[23] Consistent with this, the accounting literature often appeals to the persuasion literature when investigating third-party understanding of professionals' JDM.

A major theory in this literature is the Elaboration Likelihood Model (ELM) (Petty and Cacioppo 1981, 1986; Petty and Wegener 1998, 1999).[24] This descriptive theory proposes that third parties are affected by (relevant) person-related causes, task-related causes, and environmental causes of message (JDM) quality when reacting to messages. However, third parties also are affected by irrelevant factors (i.e., variables that theoretically are not related to message quality). For example, their evaluation of message (JDM) quality may be affected by the physical attractiveness of the person delivering the message (Petty and Wegener 1998). The ELM also posits that third parties exhibit differences as to how they evaluate messages.

Key person-related factors that can affect third parties' reactions to messages produced by professionals include source credibility, attractiveness, and power (Hovland et al. 1953; Birnbaum and Stegner 1979; Petty and Wegener 1998). *Source credibility* encompasses both expertise and trustworthiness, factors that are relevant to message (JDM) quality. Expertise refers to the competence of the message provider to generate a correct message (e.g., an analyst's ability to provide an accurate earnings forecast), whereas trustworthiness refers to the message provider's willingness to provide a high-quality message, specifically the message she considers to be most correct.[25] For example, an analyst may be competent enough to provide an accurate earnings forecast but choose to provide an upwardly biased forecast in order to encourage investors to buy a firm's stock.[26] The analyst may be motivated to do this, for example, because she is compensated partially on the basis of trading volume. *Source attractiveness* typically is considered irrelevant to message (JDM) quality; this person-related factor refers both to physical attractiveness and to how likable the message producer is. *Source power* refers to the extent to which the message producer can sanction the third party if she does not accept the producer's message. This factor likely

---

[22]Note that most of this literature focuses on evaluations done from afar, that is, with no interaction between message producer (e.g., accounting professional) and third party.

[23]A related literature on "cascaded inference" proposes a normative model for considering factors such as source credibility when evaluating information (e.g., Schum and Martin 1982).

[24]The Heuristic-Systematic Model (Chaiken 1980; Chaiken et al. 1996; Chen and Chaiken 1999) is another important theory in this area. Because it has many similarities to the ELM, it is discussed only when there are important differences.

[25]Correctness of messages can be defined similarly to correctness of JDM (see Chapter 2).

[26]This choice may be strategic or due to reasoning motivated to reach this desired conclusion.

is irrelevant to message quality but clearly can affect a third party's reaction to a producer's message. Other person-related factors that typically are considered irrelevant to message quality but that can affect third-party reactions include the message producer's speed of speech and demographic characteristics (Petty and Wegener).

Third parties are affected also by various task-related factors when reacting to messages (Hovland et al. 1953; Petty and Wegener 1998). In this context, "task-related factors" refers to elements of the persuasive message. First, messages can be consistent or inconsistent with a third party's preexisting views. For example, a creditor may expect a qualified opinion, and an auditor can issue either an unqualified opinion or a qualified opinion. Second, messages such as analysts' recommendations can be supported by arguments that vary as to quality, quantity, the manner in which they are framed (positively or negatively), and the order in which they are presented. Argument framing and argument order typically are considered irrelevant to message quality, but it is not clear to what extent other task-related factors are relevant to the reactions of third parties. To determine the relevance of argument quantity, it is necessary to know, for example, what constitutes a "single" argument. Nevertheless, it seems reasonable that at least some of these other task-related factors also are not related to message (JDM) quality and, thus, should not have an impact on third parties' reaction to messages.

Environmental factors affecting reactions to messages include whether there are any sorts of distractions, the mode in which messages are communicated (e.g., in a newspaper article or on television), and the extent to which messages are repeated. Distractions likely are irrelevant to message quality and, thus, should not affect reactions thereto. Mode of communication is irrelevant if mode is chosen randomly by the message producer or is not under her control; however, mode of communication may reflect message quality if the producer chooses the mode. For example, analysts may choose to communicate less accurate forecasts in writing rather than on television in the hope that fewer investors will notice the forecasts. Repetition of messages likewise may or may not be relevant to third-party reactions. If repetition of an analyst's forecast simply reflects, for example, newspapers' need to fill space, it likely is not relevant. However, repetition may reflect something relevant to third-party reactions, for example, the newsworthiness of the story. Other environmental factors include whether third parties receive a warning about the content of an upcoming message. In real-world accounting settings, this factor likely is relevant to third-party reactions in many cases because it reflects some sort of signaling on the part of the message producer. Finally, the ELM proposes that third parties themselves can differ in their reactions to messages because of variation in their knowledge, demographic characteristics, abilities, and personality. The most important of these is knowledge; its effects on third-party reactions will be discussed shortly.

Similar to attribution theory, persuasion theories document regularities in the cognitive processes third parties use when evaluating and reacting to messages. Specifically, these theories posit that people engage in varying amounts of processing of messages, ranging from thorough, effortful processing of the key issues and arguments contained in the message (called "central route" processing by the ELM and "systematic" processing by the HSM) to minimal, low-effort processing (called "peripheral route" processing by the ELM and "heuristic" processing by the HSM). In turn, the extent and depth of processing affect the extent to which messages have effects on third parties' reactions. Most important, third parties' reactions to messages and their providers often affect their decisions (Perloff 1993; Petty and Wegener 1998).

In minimal processing situations, evaluators do not think about message-related arguments; instead, they take shortcuts to determine how to evaluate a message (i.e., whether to accept it or reject it).[27] An example of minimal processing is an investor reacting positively to the stock recommendation of a Goldman Sachs analyst simply because Goldman Sachs is a well-known brokerage firm. As another example, an investor might count the number of supporting arguments for an analyst's recommendation and evaluate the recommendation positively based on the heuristic that "a message that can be supported by a large number of arguments must be correct" (Chen and Chaiken 1999). Thorough, effortful processing means that evaluators "elaborate" each argument related to a message; this includes retrieving argument-relevant information from memory, searching for additional information, and evaluating evidence about each argument.

More specifically, persuasion theories posit that third parties can engage in processing at all points along a continuum (called the "elaboration continuum" in the ELM) between the low-effort and high-effort varieties when evaluating messages and their providers. These theories propose that the probability of processing occurring at some point in this continuum is determined by evaluators' abilities and motivation. When motivation and abilities both are high, evaluators of messages engage in high-effort processing. When motivation and abilities both are low, evaluators engage in low-effort processing. When either motivation or abilities are more moderate, the relative amounts of low-effort and high-effort processing change.

Motivation to process a message is affected primarily by the personal relevance and consequences of the message (Fiske and Taylor 1991; Petty and Wegener 1998). So, for example, a bank loan officer is more likely to exert high effort when evaluating the auditor's report for her personal client as opposed to auditors' reports for other bank clients she might come in contact with, for example, as part of a loan committee. Similarly, motivation is enhanced when the evaluator is accountable for her evaluation and when she acts individually rather than as part of a group. Other factors, including the extent to which a message is inconsistent with an existing knowledge structure and individual differences in the desire to process information, can enhance motivation. Abilities to process the key elements of a message are affected by differences in individual processing abilities and variation in the opportunity to process the message, which varies with message repetition and distraction. Abilities to process may be affected also by time pressure (Chen and Chaiken 1999) and prior knowledge about a topic (Petty and Wegener).

Persuasion theories posit that all person, task, and environmental variables can affect third-party understanding of messages (and their providers) through low-effort or high-effort processing. For example, the perceived competence of the message provider may serve as a simple cue on which a low-effort evaluation is based; here, a third party might simply accept as valid a message from a source perceived to be highly competent with no further processing. On the other hand, the perceived competence of the provider may affect the additional information a third party gathers when assessing

---

[27]The ELM allows for "unconscious" shortcuts (e.g., the effects of *mere exposure*) (Fiske and Taylor 1991; Perloff 1993). This phenomenon means that simply because people are exposed to a message multiple times, they evaluate it more favorably. In other words, there is no explicit use of a heuristic related to exposure and a positive evaluation. The HSM, by contrast, specifies that people explicitly access from memory heuristics such as "experts' statements are valid."

the arguments contained in a message, gathering additional information for a source perceived to be of low competence.

As is the case with attribution-based evaluations, third parties can make errors and exhibit biases when (more passively) reacting to messages produced by individuals such as accounting professionals. First, as mentioned above, research indicates that third parties react to factors that are theoretically unrelated or experimentally manipulated to be unrelated to message (JDM) quality such as the attractiveness and speed of speech of the message provider, the framing and order of arguments supporting the message, and environmental distractions. Third-party evaluations that are conditioned on both irrelevant and relevant factors likely are of lower quality than those conditioned solely on relevant factors. Second, when third parties engage in lower-effort processing, using shortcuts to react to messages, they clearly can make errors and exhibit biases. For example, shortcuts can involve the use of heuristics, and the use of heuristics creates predictable biases (see Chapter 5).

Third, even if third parties engage in higher-effort processing, this processing still can lead to biased evaluations. The most important factor contributing to biased evaluations in third parties is their possession of (organized) knowledge about the topic. When third parties have knowledge about the topic, they may inadvertently interpret message-related arguments as confirming of their own positions and produce counter-arguments against disconfirming evidence (Petty and Wegener 1999). Another form of bias that can occur even with higher-effort processing is that people can confound relevant and irrelevant factors when reacting to messages. For example, people may interpret evidence about a message provider as indicating that she is competent (when she actually is not) simply because she is attractive (Petty and Wegener 1998). Fourth, although the ELM proposes that third parties are motivated to be correct in their evaluations of others' JDM, the HSM allows for third parties to be motivated to reach a desired conclusion (see Chapters 3 and 7). One desired conclusion is a third party's prior belief regarding the causes of someone else's JDM. When third parties are motivated in this fashion, they may, for example, selectively use heuristics to support their position and, as such, have predictable biases. Overall, the persuasion and communication literature tends to rely mostly on normative criteria for evaluating quality of third-party understanding, similar to attribution theory. However, this literature sometimes manipulates factors to be irrelevant to JDM quality, thus establishing an actual-outcome performance criterion for assessing quality. This allows for more broad-based conclusions regarding the quality of third-party reactions to persuasive messages.

Based on these criteria, the persuasion literature strongly suggests that the above-documented errors and biases lower quality of third-party understanding of others' JDM. Consistent with this, the literature recently has documented that third parties sometimes attempt to correct their evaluations of others because they perceive there is bias in those evaluations. For example, if an investor believes that she has accepted an analyst's stock recommendation simply because the analyst is well dressed when she appears on television, the investor may try to undo the influence of the analyst's appearance on her reaction. Specifically, the Flexible Correction Model (FCM) posits that, if people are motivated and able to search for possible biasing factors such as physical attractiveness and indeed believe that their reactions are biased, they then will attempt to undo the biases (Wegener and Petty 1995, 1997). People will be able to undo a bias if they also are motivated and able to make such corrections. Corrections are based on intuitive theories of how biases operate and the magnitude of such biases. Using the investor example, if the investor believes she has been heavily positively influenced by an analyst's stock recommendation because of her appearance (and she is motivated and able to apply this theory to her evaluation), she will try to significantly lessen her positive evaluation of the analyst's recommendation.

To date, the literature on the FCM is relatively silent about the factors that affect motivation and abilities to search for biases, as well as about the factors that affect motivation and abilities to undue biases. One possible motivator to search for biases is the presence of some sort of prompt to do so, such as one provided by the experimenter (Wegener and Petty 1995; Petty et al. 1998). Another is an unexpected reaction by the third party to a particular message (Wilson et al. 2002). Otherwise, little is known about this correction process. What is known is that the process often goes awry; people can correct too much (i.e., in too great a magnitude) for biases, correct for biases that do not exist, or correct in the wrong direction (Wegener and Petty 1995, 1997).

In summary, persuasion and communication theories posit that third parties are affected by various factors when reacting to professionals' JDM. Some of these factors are "true causes" of the professionals' JDM (e.g., competence), whereas some of these factors are theoretically irrelevant to JDM (e.g., physical attractiveness). These theories include a larger number of factors that can affect third parties' evaluations than does attribution theory; further, they do not focus as heavily on person-related causes. Like attribution theory, persuasion theories allow for multiple amounts and types of processing of information about professionals' JDM. The amount and type of processing, ranging from thorough processing of all JDM-related information to minimal, low-effort processing that may rely on a single cue, is determined by the third party's motivation and abilities. A third party's motivation is determined mostly by the consequences she faces based on the professional's judgment or decision. Abilities to process are affected by individual differences in abilities, knowledge, time pressure, and other factors.

Persuasion and communication theories also posit that third parties' reactions to professionals' JDM exhibit errors and biases and, as such, likely are of low quality in many situations. Many of these errors and biases occur because reactions are influenced by factors that are unrelated to JDM (e.g., confidence of the professional). In addition, low-effort processing often involves the use of heuristics, which leads to predictable biases. Further, prior knowledge about the topic of interest can bias reactions because third parties are able to engage in motivated reasoning that supports their existing knowledge. This literature indicates that third parties sometimes spontaneously correct their reactions if they are motivated and able to do so. These corrections are based on intuitive theories about how certain factors affect their understanding (e.g., "physical attractiveness has made my reaction more positive than it ought to be"). Unfortunately, however, the literature offers little information about what creates motivation and abilities to correct for errors and biases in reactions to others' JDM.

Other Theories

There are other theories that can inform our understanding of third-party understanding of accounting professionals' JDM. First is theory on *judge–advisor systems* (JAS); these systems consist of "one or more persons in the role of advisor who formulate judgments or recommended alternatives and communicate these to the person in the role of the judge" (Sniezek and Buckley 1995).[28] For our purposes, the judge is the third party and the advisor is the professional. Definitions of JAS also typically note that there are economic consequences of the judge's decision for both the judge and the advisor. For example, an investor who accepts the advice of a broker clearly has investment returns that are affected by this advice, and the broker's compensation is affected by the investor's trade. Most important, the JAS literature indicates that third parties' evaluations of professionals' JDM affect the third parties' own JDM quality.

Research on JAS indicates that many factors affect third parties' understanding of professionals' JDM. Similar to the findings related to persuasion theories, some factors are related to JDM quality, whereas other factors are not. Person factors that affect third parties' evaluation of professionals' JDM include amount of training and experience, prior accuracy, and confidence (Sniezek and Buckley 1995; Harvey and Fischer 1997; Harvey et al. 2000; Yaniv and Kleinberger 2000; Sniezek and Van Swol 2001). Note that, in the experimental settings used in JAS studies, all these factors may be manipulated to be relevant or irrelevant to JDM quality. In real-world settings, training, experience, and prior accuracy are likely to be related to current JDM quality, whereas confidence is not. Yet professionals' confidence plays a large role in third parties' evaluations of professionals' JDM in this literature (Sniezek and Buckley; Yates et al. 1996; Sniezek and Van Swol; Price and Stone 2004; Van Swol and Sniezek 2005). Finally, the raw number of correct judgments a professional makes positively affects third parties' evaluations of the professional, irrespective of the professional's overall accuracy rate (Yates et al.). Thus, professionals who are prolific at making judgments and decisions may receive more positive overall evaluations of their JDM than do less prolific but overall more correct professionals.

Task-related and environmental factors that affect third parties' evaluations of professionals' JDM include the timing of the provision of advice (before or after the third party has made a preliminary judgment or decision), which is unrelated to the quality of professionals' JDM (at least in experimental settings). Receiving advice before considering the evidence oneself tends to decrease the quality of third parties' understanding of professionals' JDM (Sniezek and Buckley 1995). In addition, the mere presence of advice tends to create social pressure that leads third parties to evaluate the advice and the professionals who provide it somewhat positively even if there is no evidence to support this understanding (Harvey and Fischer 1997). Finally, third parties evaluate sets of professionals and their advice more positively if those professionals are consistent in their advice and if the professionals use redundant information (Sniezek and Buckley; Budescu and Rantilla 2000; Budescu et al. 2003). Again, these factors may not be related to the quality of the professionals' JDM, but a preference for or misunderstanding of the relative value of redundant information is consistent with findings in other contexts (e.g., Schum and Martin 1982; Soll 1999). Unlike other literatures, the JAS literature goes on to document that the effect of these factors on third parties' evaluations of professionals' JDM affect the third parties' own JDM quality.

According to the JAS literature, third parties themselves differ as to how they make evaluations of professionals' JDM. Third parties with less domain experience or

---

[28]The JAS literature sometimes assumes an interpersonal relationship between judge and advisor and sometimes does not.

knowledge tend to evaluate professionals' JDM more positively, irrespective of its quality vis-à-vis an actual outcome (Sniezek and Van Swol 2001). In addition, the difference in level of experience between the third party and professional tends to have a positive effect on the evaluation of professionals' JDM, again irrespective of its quality (Harvey and Fischer 1997). These findings suggest that inexperienced third parties have lower-quality understanding of professionals' JDM. A factor that can improve the quality of third parties' understanding of professionals' JDM is monetary incentives (Sniezek et al. 2004).

Little is known in this literature about cognitive processing regularities that occur during third parties' evaluations of professionals' JDM. A recent model (Jungermann and Fischer 2005) proposes that a key mediator between factors affecting third parties' evaluation of professionals' JDM and those evaluations is trust. Indeed, studies show that factors affecting third parties' understanding, such as confidence of professionals and their own experience, are positively related to trust (Sniezek and Van Swol 2001). More specifically, this model notes that third parties rely primarily on trust in the professional to determine whether or not to accept or reject a particular piece of advice, rather than following more normative JDM principles related to evaluating all possible alternatives based on a complete set of evidence. Another recent idea (Price and Stone 2004) is that third parties use a "confidence heuristic" to evaluate professionals' JDM. In particular, they use a professional's confidence as a proxy for or cue to her knowledge, ability, and other factors that are related to JDM quality.

The JAS literature documents several errors and biases that can occur when third parties evaluate professionals' JDM. First, the above findings suggest that factors that are manipulated to be unrelated to professionals' JDM (and often are normatively unrelated as well) affect third parties' evaluations thereof. This may occur because evaluations are mediated by trust, and factors irrelevant to JDM quality affect trust. Second, there are differences among third parties with regard to the quality of their understanding; these differences are based on a comparison of third parties' evaluations of professionals' JDM to professionals' JDM compared to an actual outcome. Third, use of a confidence heuristic clearly can lead to errors in understanding given that confidence often is unrelated to professionals' JDM quality. Fourth, third parties tend to engage in "egocentric discounting" (Yaniv and Kleinberger 2000; Yaniv 2004), meaning that they weight their own JDM more heavily than that of professionals (if the two conflict), irrespective of the relative quality of their JDM. Further, the more knowledge third parties have about the domain, the more they tend to discount professionals' judgments and decisions. The posited reason for this is that people know the reasons for their own JDM but do not know as much about the professionals' reasons, and having more knowledge means knowing more reasons. In turn, knowing more reasons bolsters the weight placed on their JDM. Clearly, if professionals have higher-quality JDM than do third parties, third parties' understanding of professionals' JDM will be in error. Overall, then, this literature documents that errors and biases do lead to lower-quality third-party understanding, defined as third-party understanding vis-à-vis actual outcomes. Also unlike other literatures, this literature tends to document that problems in third-party understanding lead to lowered-quality individual JDM for the third parties.

Unfortunately, the JAS literature is so young that little information concerning ways of improving third parties' understanding of professionals' JDM exists. Some authors are pragmatic in noting that, even if third parties' evaluations are faulty, their combination of the advice of even a randomly selected professional with their own judgment or decision is likely to lead to improvement of their JDM through the reduction of random error (e.g., Yaniv 2004). In other words, the literature notes that low-quality third-party evaluations may not necessarily lead to low JDM quality on the part of third parties simply because the aggregation of someone else's JDM with their own JDM can lead to higher-quality JDM than might otherwise be the case (see Chapter 7). Nevertheless, it seems likely that third-party understanding of professionals' JDM could be improved, and as a consequence, third parties' own JDM could be improved.

Another body of work that is relevant to third-party understanding of accounting professionals' JDM is that on how people generally make judgments about causes (e.g., Einhorn and Hogarth 1986). These studies present descriptive models and findings that indicate that people focus on certain cues as being indicative of causality; when these cues are present to a large degree, people judge a particular factor to be a cause of a particular effect. These cues include covariation between the proposed cause and the effect. For example, if the presence of qualified audit opinions is highly correlated with companies going bankrupt, people may conclude that impending bankruptcy is a cause of qualified opinions (or vice versa). People also consider temporal order when assessing causality and judge causation to be more likely if the factor in question immediately precedes the effect. Thus, if an All-Star analyst is highly accurate at earnings forecasts in the year after she is named as such, the abilities underlying the All-Star designation may be thought to be the cause of the accuracy. A third cue people consider is contiguity in time between a particular factor and an effect, with high contiguity leading to higher probability judgments that the factor is a cause. If an audit firm issues a qualified opinion on a company that goes bankrupt 10 years later, impending bankruptcy is less likely to be considered a cause of the audit opinion. Finally, some studies indicate that people consider the extent to which causes resemble effects (e.g., they look for "large" causes for "large" effects). For example, investors may have difficulty believing that a computer glitch could cause a multibillion dollar error in a firm's financial statements. Instead, they may believe that management fraud must be the culprit.

In judging whether a particular factor is the cause of a particular effect, then, people retrieve from memory or search for information about these "cues to causality." For example, an investor viewing a strong buy recommendation from an analyst may consider the extent to which this type of recommendation occurs when analysts have investment-banking ties with firms they are covering (part of covariation). After assessing the strength of each cue, models propose that people consider alternative plausible causes of an effect (Einhorn and Hogarth 1986). For example, an investor may consider that the cause of the strong buy recommendation is that the analysts' assessment of the firm truly leads her to believe in strong earnings potential. The final judgment of the probability that a factor has caused a particular effect is the gross strength of the cues to causality for that factor, taken as a set, less the strength of alternative explanations.

Most important, some of these cues to causality likely are relevant to evaluating others' JDM, whereas others are not. Covariation clearly is relevant; factors typically must be strongly related to effects to be true causes of those effects. Temporal order may or may not be relevant to determining causes. Something that immediately precedes an effect may be the result of the expectation of that effect rather than a cause of the effect per se. Similarly, contiguity in time may or may not be relevant to determining causes; in the world of accounting, there may be relationships between causes and effects that are quite long term (for example, consider the relationship between customer satisfaction and financial results). The extent to which causes resemble effects likely is often irrelevant to the evaluations of others' JDM. Given the likely irrelevance of some "cues to causality," at least in some situations, third-party evaluations based on this form of processing often may be in error or biased. Because this literature is meant to be descriptive, however, it normally does not focus on people's "performance" at evaluating causes or on methods of improving these evaluations.[29]

This final set of literatures focuses more specifically on the evaluation of others' JDM as opposed to evaluations of the more general constructs of "behavior" or "messages." Work on both JAS and causal reasoning indicates that both relevant and irrelevant person, task, and environmental factors affect third parties' evaluations of professionals' JDM. Unfortunately, little is known about the processes by which these factors affect evaluations; this is likely due to the relative youth of these literatures. Consistent with other work, third parties are shown to make errors and exhibit biases in JAS settings, and they likely do so in causal reasoning settings as well. Further, these errors and biases probably lead to lower-quality understanding. To date, the largest demonstrated reason for these is the focus on irrelevant factors. In addition, third parties' knowledge of the domain can lead them to excessively discount the advice of professionals. Finally, similar to other fields, little evidence on improving these evaluations exists.

Summary of Theories

Theories related to third-party understanding of accounting professionals' JDM are quite diverse and differ in a number of significant ways. However, they also exhibit some common themes. This section summarizes these differences and commonalities.

First, the theories differ as to whether they posit that people are explicitly attempting to understand JDM and determine its causes or, instead, are simply reacting to professionals' JDM and, in this process, being affected by the causes of JDM. Attribution theory and the literature on JAS and causal reasoning suggest explicit attempts to understand professionals' JDM, whereas persuasion theories indicate more passive reactions to JDM-related causes. It may be the case in accounting that individuals with more passive reactions (e.g., unsophisticated investors), could be trained to be more active in attempting to understand causes of others' JDM. Second, the JAS literature addresses situations where the person whose JDM is being evaluated is a professional whose judgment is being used by a third party and also specifies that there are economic consequences of the JDM to both the third party and the professional. This scenario most closely matches the accounting setting; other literatures

---

[29]A final literature that may be pertinent to third-party evaluations of others' JDM is the literature indicating that people attend to irrelevant cues and fail to attend to relevant cues when making their own technical judgments and decisions (see Chapters 3, 5, and 6). People may make these errors because they lack knowledge regarding the situation, because they have incorrect intuitive theories regarding information that is presented to them, or because they use certain processes such as heuristics that often lead to correct JDM but sometimes do not.

examine the understanding of behavior, communicated messages, and the like, and do not specify particular roles for the third party and the person whose JDM is being understood. Unfortunately, however, unlike most accounting settings, the JAS literature allows for interactions between the third party and the professional. As mentioned earlier, there is an opportunity for accounting researchers to develop a better theory regarding how third parties specifically understand the JDM of others (as opposed to more general constructs such as behavior), where the others are in professional positions and operate from afar. For example, the finding in the JAS literature that third parties evaluate advice and advisors positively simply because they are present (perhaps due to social pressure) does not apply to accounting settings where there is no interaction.

Third, attribution theory suggests that third parties emphasize person-related causes in their understanding of others' JDM, whereas other literatures indicate that third parties focus on or are affected by person, task, and environmental causes. These literatures also list a larger number of possible causes of JDM. As discussed further below, the accounting literature to date focuses mostly on whether third parties understand person-related causes of JDM; however, it is not clear whether this is because researchers believe that third parties in accounting settings focus on these or, instead, because it is simpler to measure and manipulate these factors. It clearly is of interest, for example, to learn whether investors understand that analysts assigned to cover firms with high earnings predictability are likely to have more accurate earnings forecasts.

Fourth, attribution theory suggests that people focus mostly on "true causes" when understanding others' JDM but may make errors when processing this information. Other literatures, however, document a number of irrelevant causes that people focus on or allow to lower the quality of their understanding, for example, professionals' confidence, physical attractiveness, and the framing of arguments in a message.[30] The suggestions for improving third parties' understanding differ depending on the source of difficulties. Given the focus of accounting research on improving JDM, understanding the extent to which third parties in accounting settings are influenced by irrelevant factors clearly is important. Fifth, attribution and persuasion theories suggest that people sometimes spontaneously correct their understanding of others' JDM, whereas other literatures do not. Understanding the extent to which third parties in accounting may engage in these correction attempts and, more important, how successful they are when correcting their understanding also is critical from the perspective of improving JDM. Sixth, attribution theory and the ELM assume that third parties are motivated to be correct in their understanding of others' JDM (Darley and Goethals 1980; Kelley and Michela 1980), whereas the HSM also allows for third parties to be motivated to reach desired conclusions. The types of errors and biases that arise from differentially motivated processing are clearly of interest to accounting researchers examining third parties whose motivations may differ. For example, investors may be motivated to reach the conclusion that a mutual fund manager's JDM is of high quality because they have invested a great deal of money in the fund.

Finally, a very important difference across the literatures is the manner in which they measure the quality of third-party understanding. Although most of the literatures

---

[30]Note that these statements are not related to attribution of responsibility, where the literature shows that irrelevant factors can affect third parties' ex post understanding of others' JDM.

appear to focus on performance rather than process, there are differences in the criteria used to assess performance. Attribution theory tends to rely on normative prescriptions and agreement with others. The persuasion literature uses both normative prescriptions and actual outcomes, whereas the JAS literature focuses mostly on actual outcomes. Furthermore, the JAS literature links the quality of third-party understanding to the quality of third parties' JDM based on their use of professionals' advice. This information ultimately is crucial because the use of third parties' JDM, in many contexts in accounting, is for the purpose of improving one's own JDM. The difficulty created by the use of different performance criteria comes in making predictions about quality in any given accounting setting where both these criteria and others may be relevant.

Commonalities among the literatures include the following. First, to the extent that processing mechanisms are specified, theories allow for multiple amounts and forms of processing to underlie third parties' evaluations of others' JDM. Attribution theory specifies that people may use extensive covariation-based analysis (or extensive processing of other sorts) or instead rely on less effortful matching to information contained in memory. Similarly, persuasion theories specify that people may engage in extensive processing of message-related information or, instead, rely on low-effort processes such as the use of heuristics. In other words, people tend to exert effort to process in a "data driven" manner in some cases, but in other cases process in a less effortful "memory driven" manner (Hewstone 1989). Third parties in accounting likely differ in this manner as well; for example, extent of processing may be affected by the incentives they have to correctly understand professionals' JDM, and these incentives can vary greatly. Consequently, understanding the differences in errors and biases that result from different forms of processing is important in accounting.

Another common theme among the literatures is that people often focus on irrelevant factors when understanding causes of JDM. However, also common to the literatures is that there is little explication of why this is the case. For example, why do people focus on gender? Are people using this as a proxy for something else that they believe to be relevant to JDM quality but, unfortunately, they have chosen the wrong proxy, or do they truly believe gender is relevant to JDM (when, in fact, it may not be)? If the latter is the case, why do people believe this? Is it because of factors such as media coverage? Another possibility is that researchers believe that a factor is irrelevant based on theory but the factor is relevant empirically. For example, gender may be irrelevant to analysts' earnings forecasts from a theoretical perspective because it reflects, for example, personality and ability differences that are not relevant to the earnings forecast task. However, empirically, there may be a relation between gender and JDM quality because, say, men analysts receive more and better resources than women analysts. This could occur for political or sociological reasons (e.g., an "old boys' network"). Without a clear understanding of why third parties use or are affected by these factors in their evaluations of others' JDM (including the possibility that the factors indeed are relevant), it is difficult to suggest methods for improving their JDM.

Finally, common to the literatures is that there generally is little consideration of methods for improving JDM. Perhaps this is because of the relative youth of the literatures or the focus on description; nevertheless, examining methods for improving third parties' understanding of JDM clearly is important for accounting research.

8-3 DIFFERENCES AMONG THIRD PARTIES' UNDERSTANDING OF ACCOUNTING PROFESSIONALS' JDM

This section summarizes the differences among third parties that can affect their understanding of accounting professionals' JDM. Some of these differences are discussed above, whereas some are new to this section.[31] The most interesting of these differences is knowledge about the domain in question; some theories propose that knowledge has a positive effect on the quality of third parties' evaluations, whereas other theories propose the opposite. Specifically, we can interpret attribution theory to imply that the quality of covariation knowledge (or of knowledge structures and intuitive theories) has a positive impact on the quality of attributions about causes of JDM. This is because people often determine causes based on covariation-based analysis or matching to the knowledge they have stored in memory; therefore, the better these types of knowledge, the better the attributions. On the other hand, persuasion and communication theories propose that knowledge can have a negative impact on third parties' evaluations of others' JDM because it allows them to engage in reasoning that is motivated to support their preexisting beliefs about causes of that JDM, and these preexisting beliefs may be incorrect. The literature on JAS also proposes a possible negative effect of domain-related knowledge on third-party evaluations. In particular, increases in the amount of knowledge lead to greater discounting of the JDM provided by professionals, even when the professionals have higher-quality JDM than do the third parties.[32]

Another difference among third parties that can affect their evaluations is the extent to which they are motivated to reach an "accurate" understanding of others' JDM. Here, theories are consistent in suggesting that greater accuracy-related motivation leads to higher-quality understanding. Attribution theory implies that this is the case because greater motivation likely leads to covariation-based processing. Similarly, persuasion theories propose that greater motivation leads to more effortful processing, which typically results in higher-quality reactions to professionals' JDM (e.g., ones that are unaffected by irrelevant factors). Along with this, greater motivation creates a higher chance that a third party will spontaneously correct for any biases she believes exist in her understanding of others' JDM. The JAS literature finds similar results.

In addition to knowledge and motivation, there are other differences among third parties that can affect their understanding of others' JDM. First, people have differences in "attributional styles" (Hewstone 1989). These styles likely reflect personality factors. For example, some people have a pessimistic style, in which they are prone to evaluate negative outcomes (such as low-quality JDM) as being caused by person-related factors (Fiske and Taylor 1991). Second, third parties exhibit differences in their intuitive theories (Dweck et al. 1993; Hong et al. 1997; Levy and Dweck 1998; McConnell 2001). "Entity theorists" assume that personal characteristics are fixed, whereas "incremental theorists" believe that personal characteristics are malleable. As a consequence, entity theorists tend to attribute effects to person-related factors

---

[31]It seems plausible that all the variables affecting individual, technical JDM described in Chapters 3 through 7 can affect third parties' understanding of (social judgments about) others' JDM. However, this section discusses only those person variables specifically considered by the third-party evaluation literature.
[32]On the other hand, this literature also notes that too little knowledge can be problematic for evaluations in that low-knowledge people may be too positive in their evaluations of the quality of JDM of professionals.

because their beliefs cause them to focus on these. Further, they continue to focus on person-related causes even when other causes are made highly salient (Levy and Dweck). Incremental theorists give fewer attributions to person-related causes (Dweck et al.).

Knowledge and accuracy-related motivation are two key differences among third parties that can affect the quality of their understanding of others' JDM. This is not surprising given that knowledge and motivation are two key variables affecting one's own technical JDM. However, of particular interest for accounting is that knowledge is not always thought to have positive effects on third-party understanding. This seems counter-intuitive and deserves further investigation. Motivation to be accurate normally is thought to positively affect the quality of third-party understanding. Yet little is known about the relative roles of motivation and knowledge (that is, if they both have positive effects), and learning about these roles is important for improving third-party understanding. For example, would sophisticated investors have a better understanding of the factors affecting analysts' JDM because they have greater knowledge, greater motivation, or both? Finally, other factors also likely affect the quality of third-party understanding, and little evidence exists on these. This also seems to be an area deserving further attention. For example, are third parties who work in groups better able to understand others' JDM? Given the number of factors that impinge on third parties when evaluating others' JDM, it seems reasonable that there are important factors besides knowledge and motivation that lead to differences in the quality of their evaluations.

8-4 INDIVIDUALS' UNDERSTANDING OF THEIR OWN JDM

This section discusses *self-insight,* or individuals' understanding of the factors that affect their own JDM and its consequent quality. Although self-insight is not a topic that is unique to accounting, it clearly is important in accounting research. Self-insight affects people's learning from experience, willingness to use decision aids, and selection of jobs or tasks to perform (e.g., Nisbett and Ross 1980). For example, if an auditor erroneously believes that her previously poor JDM is due to a lack of effort, she may exert more effort yet continue to have poor JDM. As another example, an auditor who overestimates her knowledge may choose not to use a decision aid and consequently perform poorly. In addition, not using a decision aid may lead to greater attribution of responsibility in litigation against the auditor (e.g., Lowe et al. 2002). In other words, self-insight can affect the extent to which people improve their JDM quality in the long term or exhibit high-quality JDM in the short term, and lowered JDM quality clearly can lead to serious economic consequences. Self-insight's moderating role in the effectiveness of JDM improvement methods is also of research interest, especially if accounting professionals vary in their level of self-insight. This seems likely given that factors such as experience can be related to self-insight (e.g., Anderson 2005).

There are a variety of perspectives on and methods for studying self-insight; this section discusses methods as they relate to each theoretical perspective. One area of research examining self-insight is attribution theory. Attribution theory proposes that people may actively search for the causes of their own behavior, similar to how they search for the causes of others' behavior, and that there is variation in the extent to which people engage in this search. For example, if people do not obtain a goal, they are more likely to attempt to understand the causes of their failure to reach the goal (Weiner 1985; Hewstone 1989; Försterling 2001). Also similar to what occurs with third parties evaluating others, people tend to focus on abilities, motivation, task difficulty, and luck as the key causes of their own JDM (Darley and Goethals 1980).

Attribution theory also proposes that people exhibit the same cognitive processing regularities when analyzing the causes of their own JDM as they do when analyzing the causes of other people's JDM. Thus, they are prone to the same errors and biases discussed earlier (Nisbett and Ross 1980). For example, overall, people attribute more of the variance in their own JDM to person-related causes than to other causes (Watson 1982). Also similar to third parties, people who are attempting to understand their own behavior can miss relevant causes (Nisbett and Ross).

However, people exhibit further errors and biases in self-insight; this is despite the fact that they should have more knowledge about themselves than about others. The main one of these is that people exhibit the *self-serving attribution bias* (Hewstone 1989; Försterling 2001). This means that they tend to attribute good outcomes to person-related causes but bad outcomes to other causes such as task difficulty or bad luck. Possible explanations for this phenomenon include reasoning motivated by preservation of self-esteem, strategic impression management, and memory that tends to store person-related causes with good outcomes but not with bad outcomes. This bias is akin to offering excuses to oneself for one's poor (JDM) outcomes (Schlenker and Weigold 1992). As is the case with third parties, people often will accept their own excuses. Further, the self-insight literature in this area also documents that people will attribute variation in their behavior to irrelevant factors (Nisbett and Ross 1980). Many of these errors and biases may be caused by people relying on intuitive theories about the causes of behavior because they cannot or, for some reason, do not access their memory to obtain information relevant to assessing true causes, for example, covariation information (Nisbett and Ross). Because intuitive theories about the causes of behavior often are incorrect, self-insight can suffer.[33]

Generally, then, the attribution theory literature suggests that people are relatively poor at understanding the causes of their own behavior vis-à-vis normative prescriptions or agreement with others (Nisbett and Ross 1980). In turn, as discussed earlier, this suggests that the quality of JDM can suffer in both the short term and the long term.[34] Studying self-insight from an attribution-theory perspective typically involves examining people's attributed causes for good versus bad outcomes and comparing the relative frequencies of person-related and non-person-related attributions across the types of outcomes. An additional method for examining self-insight in this literature is to compare the relative frequency of person-related versus non-person-related attributions made by individuals for their own behavior to these same frequencies when attributions are made by third parties for the same individuals' behavior. Resulting

---

[33]Consistent with this, in domains where people are explicitly trained in JDM strategies, they have good self-insight because they have access to these strategies (i.e., their intuitive theories are correct) (Nisbett and Ross 1980).

[34]An exception is that some authors argue that the self-serving attribution bias is useful because it leads people to persist in tasks when they otherwise would not (e.g., Weiner 1985). Specifically, if people attribute bad outcomes to non-person-related causes, they may be more motivated in future experiences with a task. This is particularly true if they can avoid attributing bad outcomes to their lack of abilities (Darley and Goethals 1980). In other words, although self-insight may not be good, this actually has positive effects on future JDM.

differences, often termed the *actor-observer bias* (e.g., Jones and Nisbett 1971), may indicate a lack of self-insight for the individuals examining their own behavior. Without knowing the true frequencies of causes, however, both of these methods are subject to the criticism that they are not properly measuring self-insight. More generally, without comparisons of individuals' "performance" at understanding their JDM to multiple criteria, it is difficult to make broad-based conclusions regarding their level of understanding.

Self-insight literature that is related to attribution theory is that on "naive realism" (e.g., Van Boven et al. 1999, 2003; Pronin et al. 2002a, 2002b; Pronin et al. 2004). *Naive realism* means that people believe that their views on matters (including their JDM) are shared fairly universally by others. As a consequence of this belief, when people view others whose beliefs (JDM) differ from their own, they tend to attribute those differences to the operation of biases in others' beliefs and the lack of biases in their own beliefs. This attributional pattern results both from motivation to preserve self-esteem and because people tend to consult intuitive theories when evaluating the causes of others' behavior but use introspection when explaining the causes of their own behavior.[35] People's introspection is error prone, but they do not realize this. These findings suggest poor self-insight. Unfortunately, the method typically used in this literature is to rate oneself relative to one's peers; there normally is no comparison of people's actually exhibited biases (as determined by comparison to an external criterion) to their ratings of themselves. In other words, this literature uses only an agreement with others criterion for evaluating quality. Thus, although people may have poor self-insight using this criterion, it is not clear what findings would appear if other criteria were used to evaluate self-insight quality.

Other literature that examines self-insight is the expertise literature (see Chapter 3). Specifically, this literature suggests that, as people become more practiced with tasks, their cognitive processing becomes more automatic (Anderson 2005). This means that it is less available for conscious description. As a consequence, it may be more difficult for more experienced individuals to understand the factors that affect their JDM than it is for less experienced individuals. In other words, self-insight may be negatively related to experience. Consistent with this, the findings related to the use of verbal protocols as a method for examining people's insight into their cognitive processing (a typical method for examining insight in this literature) indicate that it may be more difficult to obtain from experts protocols that accurately reflect processes, where accuracy means that the protocols produce results similar to other empirical measures of processes or results that are consistent with theory (Ericsson and Simon 1996). This literature typically does not speak to the absolute level of quality of self-insight in novices and experts, but rather the differences based on experience. Furthermore, the literature typically does not focus on ways of improving self-insight.

A final piece of literature on self-insight is the judgment and decision-making literature that examines people's understanding of their use of multiple information cues in experimental settings (Doherty and Reilly 2001). Self-insight here typically is assessed by correlating the actual weights placed on cues (empirically derived from ANOVA or regression analysis) to subjective weights obtained from subjects postexperimentally. In other words, this literature tends to assess the quality of self-insight

---

[35]Note that this part of the theory runs counter to attribution theory.

using an actual outcome criterion that focuses on cue weights. Subjective weights normally are elicited by asking subjects to divide 100 points among cues to reflect their relative importance or usage (Cook and Stewart 1975).[36] Other methods for assessing self-insight include comparing the quality of judgments made on a holdout sample using subjective weights to the quality of those made using actual weights. Similarly, researchers can correlate the predicted judgments obtained from an analysis that uses subjective weights to one that uses actual weights (Reilly and Doherty 1992). This method is particularly useful if information cues are correlated with each other (see Chapter 5). A recently introduced method is to present subjects with a list of cue weight sets used by all the subjects in the study and ask them to recognize their own set of weights (Reilly and Doherty 1989, 1992).

There are varying opinions on the quality of and biases in self-insight in this literature. With regard to quality, much of the early literature indicates relatively low self-insight (e.g., Slovic and Lichtenstein 1971). However, more recent studies indicate that people may have relatively high self-insight under certain circumstances (Doherty and Reilly 2001), specifically in experimental situations where they make repeated judgments and choices using a limited set of information cues.[37] Even under these circumstances, however, people tend to overestimate weights for cues that are relatively unimportant (based on their actual weights) and underestimate weights for cues that are relatively important. This may occur because people believe they consider more cues than they actually do; typically, the variance in people's JDM can mostly be accounted for by a small number of cues (Slovic and Lichtenstein). Nevertheless, the conclusions regarding the quality of self-insight generally are more positive in this literature.

Similar to the situation with the literature on third-party understanding, theories and findings regarding self-insight are quite diverse. One reason for this is that self-insight studies also use very different criteria for assessing the quality of self-insight. The literatures that conclude that people have poor self-insight tend to compare it to normative prescriptions and others' self-insight. On the other hand, literatures that show greater levels of self-insight tend to compare it to actual outcomes (or similar empirical measures). Even in situations where people have relatively high insight, however, they tend to exhibit certain errors and biases such as overestimating (underestimating) the importance of factors that are not of much relevance (of great relevance) to their JDM. Further, there are new errors and biases that appear in the self-insight domain (e.g., the self-serving attribution bias and the tendency to believe that others exhibit more JDM biases than oneself). In addition, it may be the case that more experienced individuals have poorer self-insight than less experienced individuals. Thus, it appears that further work on self-insight is useful and ultimately should lead to researching methods for improvement. For example, one method for improvement may be attempting to infer one's own characteristics by carefully focusing on one's choices (Wilson and Dunn 2004).

---

[36]There are a number of other techniques for eliciting subjective weights, such as asking subjects to allocate 100 points to the most important cue then smaller numbers of points to remaining cues based on how important they are relative to the most important cue. Cook and Stewart (1975) find no differences in self-insight based on these elicitation techniques.
[37]In addition, self-insight appears to be better when subjects are asked to recognize their cue weight set from a list than to generate it themselves (Reilly and Doherty 1992).

FIGURE 8-2   Third Parties who Use Accounting Professionals' JDM

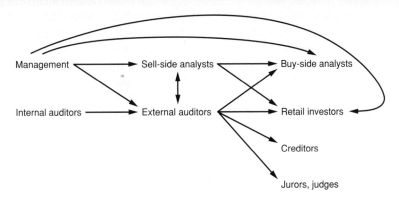

8-5   ACCOUNTING STUDIES ON THIRD PARTIES' UNDERSTANDING OF ACCOUNTING PROFESSIONALS' JDM

This section reviews accounting studies that examine various third parties' understanding of accounting professionals' JDM. In contrast to prior chapters, which focus solely on studies that document individual behavior, this chapter also includes studies that document market-level outcomes. The reason for this is that much of the work in this area is at the market level. That is, studies often examine investors' evaluation of managers' or analysts' JDM by examining market-level outcomes. Thus, omitting this material would provide an incomplete picture of what we know about third parties' evaluation of accounting professionals' JDM quality. Further, studies typically examine third parties' understanding of factors empirically related to JDM quality or whose relevance has been established by professional standards.[38]

The following discussion of studies is organized around the third parties involved in understanding JDM and the particular accounting professionals whose JDM is being evaluated. These third parties and their relationships to accounting professionals are depicted in Figure 8-2. The first part of this section covers studies examining analysts', investors', and auditors' understanding of managers' JDM. This section also includes studies that examine understanding of internal auditors' JDM by external auditors. After this, studies about investors' evaluation of analysts' JDM are discussed. Finally, studies examining investors', jurors', and others' understanding of auditors are discussed.

Third Parties' Understanding of Managers' and Internal Auditors' JDM

One study examines analysts' understanding of managers' JDM. Williams (1996) archivally examines the effects of management's prior forecast accuracy and establishes that prior accuracy is related to current accuracy. She then finds that analysts'

---

[38]Occasionally, studies that examine elements of theories related to third-party understanding of JDM (e.g., attribution theory) also are included even if there is no particular link to JDM quality of the factors examined.

forecast revisions are not differentially affected by management's prior accuracy when current forecasts indicate bad news; however, when management's current forecasts indicate good news, analysts' forecasts are affected by management's prior accuracy. This interaction likely reflects analysts' belief that management has greater incentives to voluntarily issue good news versus bad news forecasts (discussed further below).

Two studies examine investors' reactions to managers' forecasts conditional on managers' accuracy. Hirst et al. (1999) experimentally demonstrate that investors predict higher future earnings when management's prior forecast accuracy is said to be high rather than when it is said to be low. In another experiment, Hirst et al. (2003) examine the effects of reconciliations of prior estimates to actual outcomes on investors' ability to detect opportunistic versus accurate reporting by management in those estimates. Investors are able to detect these differences only when reconciliations describe the effect of errors in estimates on the balance sheet and income statement. When reconciliations simply report actual outcomes, there are no differences in investors' evaluation of management's reporting, even though the accuracy of the reporting is manipulated. Overall, then, findings regarding third parties' understanding of the effect of managers' prior accuracy (its relevance and sign) on their current JDM are somewhat mixed.

Next, several archival studies examine investors' price reactions to voluntary management disclosures to examine if these reactions vary with incentives that can affect managers' JDM. As mentioned earlier, managers may have greater incentives to voluntarily disclose good news than bad news (e.g., McNichols 1989). Consistent with this, price reactions to disclosures that contain bad news are larger than reactions to good-news disclosures (e.g., Skinner 1994; Soffer et al. 2000; Hutton et al. 2003). Hutton et al. also find that investors react to good-news disclosures only when they are accompanied by supplemental statements that are verifiable. Rogers and Stocken (2005) examine investors' reactions to management forecasts and show that the market responds differentially to forecasts with more versus less bias when the forecasts indicate good news but not when they indicate bad news. In addition, the difficulty of forecasting affects investors' ability to detect bias, with greater difficulty lessening their ability; as a consequence, managers strategically bias their forecasts more when forecasting difficulty is high. Frost (1997) studies disclosures made by managers of financially distressed and nondistressed firms and finds that investors react more to positive disclosures from nondistressed firms, consistent with their recognition that distressed firms have greater incentives to issue positive disclosures. Generally, then, it appears that investors understand the relevance and directional relationship of managers' incentives to JDM.

A number of studies examine investors' understanding of or reaction to management's attributed causes for firm performance. Managers' JDM quality is not directly linked to firm performance, but it is reasonable to assume such a link and, therefore, a link between causes of JDM and causes of firm performance. Staw et al. (1983) code attributed causes for performance appearing in letters to shareholders for high-performing and low-performing firms (firms with large increases or decreases in earnings per share, respectively). Subsequent stock price changes are positively associated with the extent to which the attributed causes enhance management's image. However, in this study, it is not clear if these reactions are "incorrect" because high-performing firms are those that tend to list these person-related causes for performance, whereas low-performing firms tend to list task or environmental causes. Baginski et al. (2000) focus on attributions associated with managers' earnings forecasts and find that there is a stronger price reaction to the unexpected earnings component of forecasts accompanied by attributions than to those unaccompanied by attributions. Further, the reaction to forecasts attributing earnings to non-person-related (i.e., non-management-related) causes is stronger than to forecasts attributing earnings to management-related causes. It is important to note that, consistent with Staw et al., attributed causes accompanying bad (good) news forecasts tend to be non person related (person related). Baginski et al. (2004) extend this study to show that the effects of attributions continue to be significant after controlling for various factors that affect attributions such as firm size and industry. Although non-person-related attributions tend to drive these results, it is nevertheless of importance that attributed causes per se may affect investor reactions. In other words, this study separates the effects of the attributed causes from the characteristics of the firms with which they are associated, suggesting that perhaps investor reactions are incorrectly influenced by management's suggested causes of firm performance (and, by implication, of their JDM). Finally, Kaplan et al. (1990) experimentally examine subjects' decisions about buying a stock based on various types of management letters to shareholders. Subjects receiving letters that include excuses for poor performance are no more likely to buy than subjects receiving no letter, whereas subjects receiving letters with justifications for past actions are more likely to buy. Note that Kaplan et al. do not manipulate or suggest any relation of these factors to management's JDM. Overall, however, it appears that investors may not fully understand the relevance (or irrelevance) to managers' JDM of statements they make in shareholder letters and in other situations such as voluntary disclosures.

The next set of studies examines auditors' evaluation of management's JDM. The most likely motivation for these studies is that auditing standards prescribe that auditors consider the reliability of evidence obtained during audits, one form of which is information provided by management. Specifically, many studies examine whether evidence obtained from management is evaluated less positively than is evidence obtained from another party. This is expected to be the case if auditors recognize management's incentives to provide favorable evidence. However, a countervailing force is that management may also be expected to have greater knowledge about a particular financial reporting issue than does another party. At any rate, although studies based on these notions do not necessarily provide evidence that management's JDM quality is higher or lower than that of other parties and, thus, any information about the level of quality of third-party understanding, they are included in this section because of their practical importance and reliance on some of the key theories discussed earlier in the chapter.

Joyce and Biddle (1981b) find that auditors who receive information from the client's credit manager make judgments about the probability of collecting a receivable that are no different from those who receive information from an independent credit agency when this manipulation is done between subjects; when the manipulation is done within subjects, the independent agency's information is considered more reliable. Reimers and Fennema (1999) use a similar task and report similar between-subjects results for auditors assigned to the preparer role, that is, no effect for source of evidence; however, auditors acting in the role of reviewer view client-provided evidence as less reliable. Hirst (1994) reports that auditors make larger revisions to their judgments of the probability of an account misstatement when evidence comes from other auditors than when it comes from management. Peterson and Wong-on-Wing (2000) provide auditor subjects with an explanation for a fluctuation that comes from either the client or an audit supervisor and observe no differences in the extent to which auditors choose tests that exhibit confirmation bias toward the explanation. Finally, Caster and Pincus (1996) report that auditors are more likely to suggest an audit adjustment when evidence comes from a credit agency rather than from the client. All these studies examine whether auditors understand the relevance and directional relationship between the source of evidence (management versus other) and its quality; they find mixed results, consistent with the multiple differences reflected in the JDM of management and other individuals.

Other studies examine auditors' understanding of managers' JDM when managers' competence, integrity (trustworthiness), or incentives are manipulated within the study. Again, these studies rely on intuitive and professional-standards-based notions about the signs of the relations of these factors to management's JDM quality (positive, positive, and negative, respectively). Starting with studies about competence, Danos and Imhoff (1982) show that auditors weight management's past accuracy at making financial forecasts as the most important factor when evaluating the reasonableness of current forecasts (as compared to other competence factors and environmental factors). Rebele et al. (1988) find that auditors place more weight on evidence from management when management is described as having high competence. Knechel and Messier (1990) report that auditors place less weight on management's credibility when they receive evidence indicating an account is collectible than when they receive evidence indicating otherwise; this finding likely reflects third parties' belief that there is an interaction between management competence and incentives. Anderson et al.'s (1994) auditor subjects rate the likelihood of a management explanation for a ratio fluctuation being correct to be higher when management is described as being highly competent. Anderson and Marchant (1989) examine auditors' evaluations of managers' competence and integrity. Auditors rate the diagnosticity of information about positive competence behaviors higher than information about negative competence behaviors, but they rate the diagnosticity of negative integrity behaviors higher than that of positive integrity behaviors. In addition, more extreme behaviors of any type are rated as more diagnostic. Overall, these studies document that auditors understand the relevance and directional relationship of managers' competence to their JDM. Some studies examine differential weighting of competence and other factors related to managers' JDM; there is no way of assessing the correctness of these weightings because there is no criterion for such.

Several studies examine auditors' evaluation of management's JDM conditional on management integrity or incentives. Peecher (1996) examines the extent to which integrity affects auditors' judgments about the likelihood that a client's explanation for a fluctuation is correct under conditions that vary the client's desired conclusion. When integrity is high, it has a larger effect on the judgments of auditors who face conditions that motivate them to accept the client's desired conclusion; when integrity is low, it has no differential effect across conditions. The former result is consistent with motivated reasoning, whereas the latter is consistent with conservatism. Haynes (1999) finds that auditors place more weight on management integrity than on evidence diagnosticity when evaluating the probability of error in an account. Goodwin (1999) finds that auditors suggest more conservative accounting treatments when management integrity is low. Jenkins and Haynes (2003) report that client integrity has no effect on the extent to which auditors' judgments reflect clients' desired conclusions. In other words, auditors do not place differential weight on integrity in order to reach a desired conclusion, inconsistent with the findings of Peecher. Similar to the studies on competence, these studies examine auditors' understanding of the relevance, sign, and weighting of managers' integrity. Findings regarding understanding of relevance and sign are mixed, and there is no criterion for evaluating the findings regarding understanding of weighting.

Studies related to management incentives include Danos and Imhoff (1983), who show that auditors evaluating the reasonableness of management forecasts place the most weight on the extent to which management compensation is tied to forecast accuracy. Anderson et al. (2004) report that auditors judge the likelihood of misstatement to be higher when managers face greater incentives for earnings management; auditors are also less willing to rely on management-provided information in this case. Finally, Wong-on-Wing et al. (1989) manipulate the extent to which management has a choice in a transaction and the extent to which the transaction deviates from what other companies do. Auditors attribute the reason for the transaction mostly to management (rather than to external factors) when managers have a choice and the transaction deviates greatly. However, these attributions do not affect auditors' subsequent judgments about accounting for the transaction. Auditors appear to understand the relevance and directional relation of managers' incentives to managers' JDM but do not always reflect this understanding in their own JDM.

Finally, a number of studies examine external auditors' evaluation of internal auditors. These studies generally examine auditors' understanding of the signs and weightings of the factors suggested by auditing standards as important in this evaluation: competence, objectivity (similar to integrity and/or trustworthiness), and quality of prior work. Little work demonstrates that these factors affect internal auditors' JDM quality, but their having positive relations to quality seem plausible. Abdel-Khalik et al. (1983) report that auditors place the most weight on objectivity when making planning judgments. Brown (1983) reports similar findings and that quality of internal auditors' prior work affects these judgments. Schneider (1984, 1985) finds that auditors view the quality of internal auditors' prior work and competence as most important, followed by objectivity, and that their evaluations affect the extent to which they rely on internal auditors to conduct audit work. Margheim (1986) documents similar findings, except that internal auditor trustworthiness has no impact on external auditors' reliance. Messier and Schneider (1988) find that competence ranks ahead of objectivity and prior work in evaluations of internal auditors. Finally, DeZoort et al. (2001) find that external auditors believe that internal auditors' receiving incentive-based compensation or working in a consulting role reduces their objectivity; however, only the compensation factor affects external auditors' reliance decisions. Here, auditors appear to understand the relevance and signed relations of these internal auditor factors on their JDM. With regard to understanding of weights, there is no criterion for assessing this.

This section reviews studies on analysts', investors', and auditors' understanding of the factors that affect managers' JDM quality, as well as studies on external auditors' understanding of internal auditors' JDM quality. The studies use different methods and draw on different theories but tend to focus on whether third parties understand the relevant factors that affect managers' (or internal auditors') JDM quality. That is, they tend not to examine whether third parties incorrectly focus on irrelevant factors such as confidence when evaluating managers' (or internal auditors') JDM. The only exception to this is the study by Baginski et al. (2004), whose findings suggest that investors may incorrectly be influenced by statements made by management in conjunction with earnings forecasts. This focus makes sense given the relative youth of this literature.

The studies mostly focus on whether third parties use relevant factors and understand their directional relationship to JDM. Relevance of factors sometimes is established empirically (through either measurement or manipulation), whereas in other cases it is established by reference to professional standards. Only one study examines analysts' understanding of managers' JDM; this study documents that analysts appear to understand the effects of prior accuracy and incentives on JDM quality. Several studies examine whether investors understand the factors affecting managers' JDM. Investors often appear to understand the effects of incentives (to reach desired conclusions) and the effects of managers' prior accuracy on current JDM quality. However, investors appear to not understand the effects of factors such as task complexity.

The literature on auditors evaluating managers' JDM shows that auditors sometimes evaluate managers more negatively than others who provide evidence and sometimes do not. This may mean that auditors do not understand the relevance of the source of evidence or, more likely, that they understand that managers may have greater knowledge that helps them provide correct evidence in addition to having greater incentives that would lead them to provide positively biased evidence. When factors related to knowledge or incentives alone are manipulated, auditors appear to understand each factor's relevance and directional relation to managers' JDM quality. However, the findings are more mixed when management integrity alone is manipulated. The literature on external auditors' evaluations of internal auditors indicates that external auditors understand the relevance and directional effect on JDM of the factors prescribed by auditing standards. Finally, many studies in this area examine auditors' cue weightings, but there is no criterion against which to compare these to determine their correctness.

Third Parties' Understanding of Analysts' JDM

As shown in Figure 8-2, several parties, that is, investors (including retail investors and buy-side analysts) and auditors, may use the JDM of sell-side analysts as inputs to their own JDM. There are a number of studies in this area that can be divided into two basic groups: those that examine whether investors understand the effects of incentives on analysts' JDM and those that examine whether investors understand other factors that affect analysts' JDM, including knowledge and various task characteristics.

A number of archival studies examine investors' reactions to forecasts made by analysts with varying incentives. Dugar and Nathan (1995) report that the market reacts more strongly to reports issued by analysts who do not have an investment-banking relationship with a client than to those issued by analysts with such a relationship, consistent with their finding that investment-banking analysts issue more optimistic forecasts and recommendations. Lin and McNichols (1998) find no differences in the market reaction to buy recommendations issued by analysts working at brokerage firms who are serving as lead underwriters at the time of the recommendation versus those from analysts at unaffiliated firms. However, the market does react more negatively to hold recommendations issued by underwriter analysts. These findings are somewhat inconsistent with the study's finding that underwriter analysts' recommendations are significantly more favorable than unaffiliated analysts'. Michaely and Womack (1999) report that the market reacts less strongly to buy recommendations from underwriter analysts than to similar recommendations from nonunderwriter analysts, consistent with the recommendations of underwriter analysts being of lower quality, as measured by stock returns. Francis and Soffer (1997) find a larger market reaction to earnings forecast revisions that accompany buy recommendations than to those that accompany hold or sell recommendations; their reasoning is that investors place more weight on earnings forecasts when recommendations are more likely to be affected by incentives.

Two experimental studies examine investors' evaluations of analysts' JDM under varying incentives.[39] These studies do not demonstrate the relation of the incentives to analysts' JDM quality, but the research discussed above supports this relation. Hirst et al.'s (1995) student subjects believe that incentives play a larger role in analysts' favorable reports when those reports come from investment-banking analysts. However, they do not reflect these beliefs in their judgments about stock performance. When subjects receive unfavorable reports, incentives do affect stock performance judgments; performance is rated lower when an unfavorable report comes from an investment-banking analyst. Cote's (2000) investment club member subjects believe analyst credibility to be lower when they have higher priors regarding analyst optimism in earnings forecasts and also when they receive an optimistic (versus a pessimistic) forecast within the experiment, where optimism versus pessimism is meant to proxy for incentive differences. In turn, their beliefs about credibility influence the extent to which they rely on an analyst's forecast in revising their own earnings forecasts. Studies of understanding of analysts' incentives, then, tend to find that investors understand the relevance and directional effect on JDM of these incentives. Investors also may understand that incentives interact with other factors in affecting analysts' JDM, although such interactions have not been empirically demonstrated.

A number of studies examine investors' reactions to other factors that affect analysts' JDM quality. Two studies investigate the differential market reaction to forecasts made by analysts receiving awards versus those not receiving awards. It is well established in these and other studies that the receipt of awards is positively associated with forecast accuracy. Stickel (1992) documents a larger market reaction to upward forecast revisions made by award winners; however, there is no difference in reaction to downward revisions. Gleason and Lee (2003) show a larger market reaction to both upward and downward forecast revisions made by award-winning analysts. Thus, investors appear to understand the relevance and directional relation of awards to analysts' JDM.

Mikhail et al. (1997) show that the market reaction to forecasts from analysts with five or more years of forecasting experience for a particular firm is greater than that for analysts with less experience, consistent with experience being positively related to forecast accuracy. They also find that the market reaction to recommendation upgrades is stronger when the upgrades come from experienced analysts, but there is no differential reaction based on experience to recommendation downgrades. Again,

---

[39]Ackert et al. (1996, 1997) also examine students' reactions to biased forecast information, but the studies are set in an abstract context.

this finding may reflect investors' understanding of a possible interactional effect of experience and incentives. Based on prior findings that previous forecast accuracy is associated with current forecast accuracy, Park and Stice (2000) investigate whether there is a greater market reaction to revisions issued by analysts with higher prior accuracy and find this result. Maines (1990, 1996) experimentally examines the effect of redundancy among forecasts and individual forecasters' prior accuracy on people's assessments of the accuracy of a consensus forecast. Subjects tend to appropriately consider prior accuracy but frequently have difficulty incorporating redundancy in their assessments of consensus forecast accuracy. The effect of both variables on the quality of the consensus forecast is established in the experimental setting. Overall, investors appear to understand the relevance and directional effect of experience and prior accuracy on individual analysts' JDM quality but do not appear to understand the effect of redundancy on consensus forecasts' quality.

Remaining studies examine the impact of investors' reactions to multiple factors empirically shown to be associated with analysts' forecast accuracy. Wiedman (1996) shows that the market reaction to analysts' forecast is related to firm size and dispersion in forecasts; further, firms' number of lines of business is not associated with investor reactions, consistent with its not being associated with relative forecast accuracy. Clement and Tse (2003) examine investors' reactions to prior forecast accuracy, brokerage firm size, forecast frequency, analyst experience, forecast age, and number of firms and industries followed by analysts. Market reaction results indicate that investors react only to prior accuracy, brokerage firm size, and forecast age. Further, investors react positively to forecast age when it is negatively associated with accuracy, and weights placed on factors by investors do not correspond to weights from the accuracy model. Bonner et al. (2003) investigate sophisticated versus unsophisticated investors' reactions to the following factors: forecast age, analyst experience, analyst turnover, forecast frequency, brokerage firm size, award status, and number of firms and industries followed. Again, these factors are shown to be related to analysts' forecast accuracy. Bonner et al. focus on the extent to which predictions from investors' models match those from the environmental accuracy model and find that sophisticated investors' reactions better match the environmental model. This occurs because sophisticated investors are more correct when determining the signs and weights of the relations of the factors to analysts' accuracy. This is particularly true when focusing on the two variables that provide the greatest explanatory power for current forecast accuracy—prior accuracy and forecast age. This set of studies, then, indicates that investors understand the relevance and directional relation of only some factors related to analysts' forecast accuracy; further, they often misunderstand the relative cue weightings.

Although multiple third parties likely are influenced by the work of analysts, studies to date focus exclusively on investors' understanding of analysts' JDM. Several studies focus on whether investors understand the impact of analysts' incentives to reach desired conclusions (and their resulting motivation) and find that investors mostly appear to understand incentives' directional influence on analysts' JDM. In addition, investors may understand that incentives interact with other factors to affect analysts' JDM.

Additional studies examine whether investors understand the directional effect of other factors that may reflect ability and knowledge, such as experience, receipt of awards, and prior accuracy. Investors mostly appear to understand the relevance and directional effects of these factors as well, consistent with third parties' being focused on person-related causes. Findings on whether investors understand the effects of task-related causes on JDM (e.g., factors that reflect task complexity such as number of firms followed) are less positive; investors appear not to understand the relevance of these factors. Further, unsophisticated investors believe that forecast age has a positive relation to analysts' accuracy when the opposite is the case (sophisticated investors do appear to understand age's directional relation to analysts' JDM). Finally, sophisticated investors appear to have a higher quality of understanding with regard to the relative importance (weightings) of factors that affect analysts' JDM.

Third Parties' Understanding of External Auditors' JDM

A number of parties evaluate the quality of external auditors' JDM. These include analysts, investors, creditors, and jurors and judges. One study examines the effect of independence factors on investors' evaluations of auditors' JDM. Although previous studies do not clearly demonstrate a link between these factors and actual independence, or between actual independence and auditors' JDM quality, regulators and professional standards suggest that there are such relations.[40] Dopuch et al. (2003) experimentally investigate the effects of disclosure of nonaudit fees and feedback about the accuracy of auditors' reports on investors' perceptions of auditors' independence. Dopuch et al. find that the disclosure of nonaudit fees does not increase the accuracy of investors' understanding of auditors' independence except when the disclosures indicate independence and the auditors truly are independent (as shown by feedback about their reports). Further, these disclosures reduce the accuracy of investors' understanding when auditors are truly (not truly) independent and the disclosures indicate that auditors are not (are) independent.

A number of studies examine creditors' evaluations of factors related to auditors' JDM. The relation of these factors to JDM quality is intuitive or professional-standards based. Knapp's (1985) loan officer subjects believe that several variables affect auditors' ability to resist pressure from management regarding financial reporting choices. These variables include the extent to which the reporting issue is dealt with by technical standards, the client's financial condition, the provision of nonaudit services, and the level of competition the audit firm faces. Lowe and Pany (1995) investigate loan officers' perceptions of auditor independence and financial statement reliability, as well as their decisions to grant a loan, in a situation where the audit firm performs nonaudit services for the client under varying conditions. They find that auditor independence is perceived to be higher when an audit firm's nonaudit services are provided by a separate division; however, this factor does not affect the perceived reliability of financial statements or the decision to grant a loan. Further, the length of the relationship between client and auditor does not affect any of these variables. However, the size of the nonaudit services affects all three dependent variables. Because it is not clear to what extent these factors truly are related to auditors' JDM, it is difficult to draw conclusions about the quality of loan officers' understanding of auditors' JDM.

---

[40]Survey studies similarly suggest these relations. For example, Schroeder et al. (1986) and Knapp (1991) find that audit committee members perceive a number of factors to be related to auditor quality, including audit firm size, audit firm tenure, and individual auditors' independence and experience.

Finally, several studies report on judges' and juries' understanding of auditors' JDM quality. A number of these studies document that third parties evaluate the quality of an auditor's JDM to be lower when there is a negative outcome rather than a positive outcome associated with the JDM (Anderson et al. 1993; Lowe and Reckers 1994; Kinney and Nelson 1996; Anderson et al. 1997b; Kadous 2000, 2001). Outcomes are legally and normatively irrelevant to the assessment of others' JDM. In addition, Anderson et al. (1993) show that judges evaluate the relevance of negative (positive) cues to be greater when there is a negative (positive) outcome, meaning that outcomes can affect evaluations through interpretation of information cues. Lowe and Reckers also document that asking jurors to judge the probability of other specified outcomes mitigates the negative effect of outcomes on their understanding. Anderson et al. (1997b), however, find that this technique is not effective with judges; instead, asking judges to consider that auditors face stakeholders other than investors eliminates the negative effect of outcomes. Kadous (2001) instructs jurors to attribute any negative affect they experience to being a juror (rather than to the auditors); this instruction also eliminates the effect of outcomes on their evaluations of auditors' JDM.

Further studies examine issues other than outcome effects. Arrington et al. (1985) show that business owners tend to attribute negative outcomes associated with auditors' JDM to person- (auditor-) related causes, consistent with attribution theory. Rennie (1995) reports that students, proxying for jurors, rate auditors more responsible for failing to detect a financial statement misstatement when the auditors use an unusual audit procedure. Clearly, failing to detect a misstatement is low-quality JDM, but there is no link between the unusualness of the audit procedure to JDM quality other than the perceptual link created by the experiment. Bonner et al. (1998) archivally document that auditors are more likely to be sued when frauds involve fictitious transactions or are of a more frequent variety. Their hypothesis is based on plaintiffs' attorneys anticipating that jurors will attribute greater responsibility to auditors for missing these types of frauds, even if there is no relation between the type of fraud and auditors' JDM quality. (However, this is not shown.) Again, in these studies, it is difficult to draw conclusions about the quality of third parties' evaluation of auditors' JDM because the studies tend not to link the examined factors to auditors' JDM (except perhaps intuitively). In contrast, Kadous (2000) shows that jurors evaluate higher-quality audit work more positively only when the consequences of audit failure are moderate; when consequences are severe, there is no effect of true quality on evaluation of auditors as reflected by guilt ratings and verdicts. Further, these differences appear to occur because jurors create higher standards of due care for auditors associated with failures having severe consequences, contrary to legal prescriptions. In other words, jurors appear to have low-quality understanding here.

Finally, two studies examine the effects of auditors' decision-aid use on evaluations of their JDM. Again, it is not known whether decision-aid use by auditors increases their JDM quality, but such a positive effect is plausible based on previous findings in psychology (see Chapter 9). Anderson et al. (1995) report that judges attribute more responsibility for failure to detect a misstatement to auditors who use but do not follow all the recommendations of a decision aid related to analytical procedures versus those who do not have an aid available. However, auditors who fully use the aid are not attributed lower responsibility. Lowe et al. (2002) manipulate auditors' use of a decision aid and the decision aid's reliability in an investigation of jurors' evaluations of auditors' JDM in a case involving fraud. When the aid is described as reliable, jurors attribute more responsibility for missing the fraud (lower-quality JDM) to auditors who choose to override the aid and less responsibility to auditors who follow the aid when it is incorrect than to those who have no aid. This last set of studies more likely demonstrates that jurors and judges at least somewhat understand the relevance and directional relation of decision-aid use to auditors' JDM.

Several studies examine third parties' understanding of factors affecting auditors' JDM. Only one study examines investors, who appear to not understand fully the effects of independence-related factors. A few studies examine creditors' understanding, but it is difficult to draw conclusions because they do not establish the relation of the examined factors to auditors' JDM. The bulk of the studies examines jurors' and judges' understanding of auditors' JDM, perhaps consistent with the notion that attempts to understand auditors' JDM frequently arise in ex post evaluation contexts. Many of these studies demonstrate that jurors and judges do not understand that outcomes are not relevant to auditors' JDM quality. However, various techniques may mitigate this misunderstanding. Other studies of jurors and judges focus on a variety of other factors. Some of the studies rely on only intuitive notions about the relation of these factors to auditor JDM quality; again, then, it is difficult to conclude about jurors' and judges' understanding of the factors. In studies that examine decision-aid use by auditors, jurors and judges do appear to understand the relevance and directional relation of this factor to auditors' JDM. However, a study that examines outcome severity, a factor that is irrelevant to auditors' JDM quality, finds that jurors do not understand this.

Summary

As is the case in psychology, the accounting literature on the quality of third-party understanding finds mixed results with regard to that quality; some studies document good understanding, whereas other studies do not. Further, within studies, third parties understand the effect of some factors on JDM but do not understand the effects of other factors. More specifically, third parties evaluating managers' JDM seem to understand the relevance and directional effects of managers' knowledge, abilities, and incentives on their JDM but may not understand the effects of various relevant and irrelevant task-related factors. Similar findings appear with third parties' understanding analysts' JDM. Work on third-party understanding of auditors' JDM focuses mostly on the effects of outcomes on jurors and judges' ex post evaluations of auditors and finds that (irrelevant) outcomes influence these evaluations. Overall, then, studies related to managers and analysts focus mostly on whether third parties use relevant factors and understand their directional effects on JDM, whereas studies related to understanding auditors' JDM mostly examine whether third parties are influenced by irrelevant factors (when they should not be). One reason for the mixed findings may be that, similar to psychology, accounting studies on third-party understanding rely on a number of different theoretical backgrounds and methods. Another, more likely, reason is that third parties understanding accounting professionals' JDM are similar to third parties evaluating others' behavior in many domains. For example, they sometimes do not use relevant cues and sometimes use irrelevant cues. In addition, they sometimes understand directional relations between factors and JDM and sometimes do not. Overall, then, third parties evaluating accounting professionals' JDM may be subject to the same errors and biases as are third parties in other situations.

However, the third-party understanding literature in accounting differs from that in psychology in a number of ways. For the most part, the accounting literature has proceeded in a relatively logical fashion. That is, early studies focused principally on documenting whether third parties understand that particular cues are related to JDM and the signs of these cues' relationships. More important, these studies frequently established the relevance and sign of JDM-related factors empirically. In some cases, studies relied on professional standards to establish this information. In either case, there is a strong and justifiable criterion underlying the JDM factors being studied. By contrast, in psychology, studies sometimes use intuitive notions of the relevance of factors to JDM.

More recent studies have proceeded beyond third-party understanding of the relevance and directional effect of relevant cues to examine their understanding of irrelevant cues' irrelevance and the weighting of relevant cues. Again, these studies use either empirical or professional-standards-based criteria for irrelevance and cue weighting and, thus, use an important criterion for measuring third parties' "performance" at understanding. What is needed at this point is more work along these lines. In particular, researchers need to go beyond focusing on person-related factors (both relevant and irrelevant) to examine whether third parties understand the effects of task-related and environmental factors (besides incentives) that affect accounting professionals' JDM. The literature on the effects of these factors on professionals' own JDM establishes that these variables matter, so researchers can proceed to examine whether third parties understand their relevance and directional effects. Further, given the dearth of information available to third parties about some factors affecting professionals' JDM (e.g., ability) it is important to examine whether third parties are using appropriate measures for factors whose relevance and directional relation they appear to understand. A similar statement can be made about studying third parties' cue weights; third parties may be trying to understand the relative importance of JDM factors in a complex environment (e.g., one in which the JDM factors are correlated with each other). Accounting research also needs to examine whether there are differences among third parties as to their understanding of professionals' JDM; a variety of third parties rely on accounting-related JDM, and they likely differ significantly on many characteristics such as knowledge and incentives. Very little work in this regard exists currently. Further, once studies on these issues have reached a critical mass, researchers should move on to examine methods for improving third parties' understanding of accounting-related JDM.

Perhaps the most important avenue for future research in this area is the examination of third party–accounting professional relationships other than those described above and shown in Figure 8-2. For example, regulators recently have focused a great deal of attention on analysts' JDM, yet there is no literature on the quality of their understanding of the factors affecting analysts' earnings forecasts, stock recommendations, and other JDM outputs. Along with this, regulators likely attempt to understand managers' JDM, yet we know little about how well they do so. Perhaps the most important relationships omitted from the literature to date are those that go in the opposite direction, that is, from accounting-related professionals to third parties. These relationships reflect the notion that accounting-related professionals know that third parties may misunderstand the determinants of their JDM and, as a result, behave strategically to capitalize on this misunderstanding. Examples of such behavior have been mentioned throughout this chapter, but virtually no research examines whether accounting-related professionals such as managers, analysts, and auditors strategically exploit others' misunderstanding of their JDM.[41] Given the serious consequences that can result from such behavior, this research is extremely important.

8-6   ACCOUNTING STUDIES ON SELF-INSIGHT

Managers' Understanding of Their JDM

A number of studies examine managers' self-insight regarding company performance. As mentioned earlier, although there is no explicit link of managers' individual JDM quality to company performance in these studies, such a link can be assumed. These studies all rely on attribution theory and examine the self-serving attribution bias. Staw et al. (1983) find that the more negative are shareholder letters, the more likely managers are to attribute causes of firm performance to non-person-related factors rather than person-related (management-related) factors, consistent with the self-serving bias. These differences likely are not true self-insight differences, however. Instead, they appear to reflect strategic attempts at impression management (this is evidenced by differences in managers' sales of stock between the two types of firms). Bettman and Weitz (1983) also examine shareholder letters and find that letters suggest non-management-related, unstable, and uncontrollable causes more frequently for poor financial performance than for good performance. Further, there is evidence that both cognitive processing biases and motivated reasoning underlie these differences.

Salancik and Meindl (1984) similarly find more management-related reasons suggested as causes of good performance and more other reasons suggested as causes of bad performance. In addition, firms with unstable performance are more likely to suggest management-related reasons for good performance than are stable firms and are less likely to suggest other reasons as causes of bad performance. The authors suggest that these differences reflect cognitive processing biases in self-insight for unstable firms and strategic impression management for stable firms. Aerts (1994) documents similar findings for firms with good financial performance but finds no difference in the frequency of management-related causes versus non-management-related causes for firms with bad performance. He also finds that firms with good performance tend to use more accounting than nonaccounting language when describing causes. In addition, stable firms with poor performance tend to use more accounting language than do unstable firms with poor performance. Aerts suggests that this finding reflects stable firms' attempts to appear less defensive by obscuring their attributed causes with technical details. Aerts (2005) finds that listed companies provide more attributions in shareholder letters than do unlisted companies. Further, listed companies use relatively more excuses, denials, and justifications than do unlisted companies. Aerts (2005) interprets these attributional differences as reflecting strategic impression management. Finally, Baginski et al. (2000) examine attributions associated with managers' earnings forecasts and find that attributions are more likely to accompany bad news forecasts than good news forecasts. Further, attributions accompanying bad (good) news forecasts tend to be non-management-related causes (management-related causes).

---

[41]For exceptions, see Bloomfield (1997) and Zimbelman and Waller (1999).

Accounting studies of managers' self-insight all rely on attribution theory and focus on the self-serving attribution bias, and findings are consistent with findings in psychology. That is, there is strong evidence for the self-serving bias in statements by managers that appear in shareholder letters and accompany earnings forecasts. The accounting literature also finds evidence that this bias may reflect strategic impression management, motivated reasoning, or other cognitive factors. In other words, it is not clear that this "bias" always is intentional (strategic). Further, we know little about to what extent managers' self-insight is of high or low quality in these situations because studies typically do not compare the "quality" of the attributions to some criterion. Instead, consistent with psychology, they compare the types of attributions across categories of financial outcomes. Given that there are no other studies of managers' self-insight, it therefore is difficult to draw conclusions about its quality.

Analysts', Investors', and Loan Officers' Understanding of Their JDM

Several studies examine the self-insight of individuals engaged in financial or credit analysis tasks. Mear and Firth (1987a) report that analysts judging risk and return of stocks have relatively poor self-insight into the weights they place on various cues, as evidenced by the correlation between their subjectively reported weights and their actual weights derived from regressions. Wright (1977b, 1979) reports findings similar to Mear and Firth for students predicting stock prices.

Slovic (1969) and Slovic et al. (1972) examine the self-insight of stockbrokers making stock recommendations. The first study employs only two brokers and reports good insight for one and a medium level of insight for the other based on a comparison of subjective weights to actual weights. The second study reports relatively poor self-insight for brokers but relatively good self-insight for students included in the study; in fact, the authors report a negative correlation between experience and insight. Savich (1977) reports that students have good self-insight when making stock purchase decisions based on accounting information. Finally, Zimmer (1980) examines the self-insight of bank loan officers who make judgments about bankruptcy and finds that self-insight, as measured by the correlation between their predicted judgment accuracy and actual judgment accuracy, is very low.

Studies examining analysts', investors', and loan officers' self-insight typically assess self-insight by comparing subjective cue weights to empirically derived cue weights. Findings using this method are mixed; self-insight ranges from quite poor to very good. However, the studies also differ on a number of other criteria, such as the number of information cues presented to subjects and the types of subjects used. Given the small number of studies in the area, it is difficult to draw conclusions about what might account for the varying levels of self-insight detected by these studies.

Auditors' Understanding of Their JDM

A number of experimental studies examine auditors' self-insight; most of them ask auditors to distribute 100 points across information cues to indicate their relative importance. The studies then correlate these ratings to actual cue weights derived from ANOVA or regression models. The first set of studies asks auditors to rate the quality of internal controls for payroll, a task generally considered to be fairly easy. Ashton (1974a) finds that auditors have quite high insight in this task; he also finds no relation of experience to self-insight. Ashton and Brown (1980) find similar results.

Ashton and Kramer (1980) document high insight for both auditors and students in a similar task, with auditors' insight being somewhat higher. Hamilton and Wright (1982) report similar findings, except that the students' insight in their study is as high as that of the auditors. Joyce (1976) extends these studies to examine auditors' judgments about hours to allocate to audit areas based on internal control cues and finds somewhat lower self-insight than do the studies by Ashton (1974a), Ashton and Brown (1980), and Ashton and Kramer (1980). He also finds that experienced and inexperienced auditors have similar levels of insight.

In a study of inherent risk judgments, Colbert (1988) reports that auditors have self-insight that is somewhat lower than that reported in the internal control studies; this study occurred at a time when inherent risk was a relatively new concept for auditors. Danos and Imhoff (1982) ask auditor subjects to rank the importance of cues affecting their judgments of the reasonableness of financial forecasts. They do not report numerical data regarding self-insight, but the auditors appear to have reasonably high insight. Messier (1983) reports high self-insight among audit partners making materiality and disclosure judgments and no relation between experience and insight. Brown (1983) reports somewhat lower insight for auditors making judgments regarding reliance on internal auditors; there also is no effect of experience on insight in this study. Johnson and Kaplan (1991) compare the insight of accountable and nonaccountable auditors making judgments about inventory obsolescence. They find a medium level of insight for accountable subjects and a significantly lower level of insight for nonaccountable subjects. Finally, in the sole auditing study relying on attribution theory to examine self-insight, Arrington et al. (1985) find that auditors are less likely to attribute negative audit-related outcomes to person-related causes than to other types of causes, consistent with the self-serving attribution bias.

With the exception of the Arrington et al. (1985) study, studies of auditors' self-insight rely on a comparison of subjective cue weights to objective cue weights, similar to the literature on analysts, investors, and loan officers. However, studies of auditors tend to find relatively good self-insight using this method. Again, there are several possible explanations for this difference. One is that many of the studies in this area measure self-insight in a payroll internal control evaluation task that gives auditors a small number of information cues. Perhaps, then, auditors appear to have better self-insight than other accounting professionals because of the tasks researchers have used. On the other hand, perhaps auditors differ in some way from other professionals that allows them to have better self-insight (e.g., their training or the extent to which their environment is structured). Without direct comparisons of auditors to other professionals and a consideration of these sorts of factors, however, these comments are speculative.

The self-insight literature in accounting is limited and relatively old. Self-insight does not appear to be a topic of much interest among accounting researchers currently. Although studies of self-insight per se may not be considered to cover enough ground to "make a contribution," continued study of self-insight seems important because of the impact of self-insight on people's willingness to consider and fully engage in methods of improving JDM such as their use of decision aids. Thus, future research should focus on the extent to which accounting professionals' self-insight moderates the effectiveness of various improvement methods.

8-7 SUMMARY

This chapter discusses the literature on third-party and self understanding of the factors that affect JDM quality. Specifically, the chapter reviews evidence on the processes by which third parties evaluate others' JDM and the factors that affect these evaluations (including differences among third parties). Where possible, the chapter also discusses what is known about the quality of third-party evaluations and methods of improving these evaluations, if such methods are needed. The chapter also briefly discusses the various approaches to and findings regarding the study of self-insight.

Findings regarding third-party understanding in accounting are somewhat difficult to compare to findings in psychology because the two literatures use different criteria for ascertaining the "correctness" of third-party understanding. With this caveat in mind, a comparison indicates that these findings are fairly similar. Third parties appear to understand the effects of some factors that are relevant to accounting professionals' JDM, most notably their incentives, knowledge, and abilities. These variables also are those most frequently studied by accounting researchers, consistent with psychology's focus on relevant person-related factors and incentives. Where studies examine other variables (e.g., relevant and irrelevant task-related variables), third parties often appear to not understand their effects on professionals' JDM. Overall, third parties evaluating accountants sometimes do (do not) understand the effects of various factors, both relevant and irrelevant, on accountants' JDM quality. Further, and also similar to psychology, third parties similarly exhibit mixed results with regard to understanding the directional relation and appropriate weightings of factors related to accountants' JDM quality.

More important, these mixed findings suggest several directions for future research. Much of the accounting work on third-party understanding empirically establishes the effects of various factors on professionals' JDM quality, and this trend should continue. In other words, researchers must know how factors are related to JDM before examining whether third parties understand these relations. Assuming that empirical evidence indicates that factors beyond knowledge, abilities, and incentives contribute substantially to accounting professionals' JDM, researchers should examine whether third parties understand the effects of these other factors. For example, one variable that explains a large portion of the variance in analysts' forecast accuracy is the age of the forecast. Fortunately, in this literature, studies have examined whether investors understand the impact of this variable. However, in other literatures, less attention has been paid to task-related and other person and environmental factors. These studies are particularly important because many of these variables can be controlled by accounting professionals (e.g., the difficulty of the tasks they choose to perform). Similar to this, if professionals understand that third parties use inappropriate measures of relevant factors, they may try to increase the level of these measures they possess. For example, if analysts know that investors use media coverage as a proxy for their competence, they may invest in activities to increase their media coverage (activities that have no effect on their JDM). Further, researchers should examine whether third parties understand that certain factors are theoretically irrelevant to professionals' JDM. Given that the psychology literature frequently demonstrates that third parties are affected by these, it would not be surprising to find that third parties evaluating accountants also are affected (and the limited evidence to date supports this). As is the case with many other factors, accountants may be able to strategically manipulate some of these factors in order to influence third-party evaluations. An example mentioned earlier is that professionals may try to increase the confidence they portray to third parties if they know that third parties are inappropriately swayed by confidence. Along with these investigations, of course, researchers should explore the processes that account for third parties' understanding or misunderstanding of factors that relate to accounting professionals' JDM. In this way, accounting research can make a contribution to psychology, given that psychology theories do not always clearly specify process mechanisms. More generally, accounting research can contribute to psychology by learning how third parties specifically evaluate professionals' JDM from "afar."

The accounting and psychology literatures are similar also with regard to areas that need a great deal more research. First, it is unclear to what extent third parties in accounting (or elsewhere) actively attempt to understand causes of JDM rather than passively reacting to causal factors. Whether causal understanding is active or passive is important for suggesting methods of improving this understanding. Second, very little work in both areas addresses methods of improving third-party understanding. Although the "quality" of this understanding often is not known, the presence of persistent errors and biases suggests that this quality could be improved. Once accounting researchers have a better understanding of how third parties understand accounting professionals' JDM, they should proceed to study methods of improvement. Note that regulators may believe that they are far ahead of researchers in this regard. For example, the recent regulated separation of investment banking from other parts of brokerage firms suggests that regulators believe investors are incapable of understanding the effects of incentives on analysts' JDM and, thus, they have to remove the effects of those incentives altogether. Such beliefs clearly are open to empirical investigation, and evidence suggests that regulators' beliefs may be incorrect. Third, relatively little is known in both areas about how differences among third parties, most notably knowledge, may affect the quality of their understanding. Given the diverse groups of third parties who use accounting professionals' JDM, further research in this area clearly is important. Relatedly, research may indicate that different methods of improvement are necessary for different types of third parties.

The self-insight literature in accounting is similar to that in psychology in that it relies on a number of diverse theories and methods and produces mixed results regarding the quality of accounting professionals' self-insight. Because some of the findings indicate relatively poor self-insight among accounting professionals, future research is important. However, it is not clear whether such work can stand on its own. Rather, it seems more reasonable to consider studying the moderating effects self-insight can have on the effectiveness of JDM improvement methods, such as decision aids.

CHAPTER

Methods for Improving JDM

This chapter addresses the remaining questions in the framework, as highlighted in Figure 9-1. Specifically, it addresses JDM improvement methods that cause changes to the person, the task, or the environment, and which attempt to reduce either across-person or within-person variation in JDM quality or to raise a uniformly low level of JDM quality to an "acceptably high" level.[1] While discussing these changes, the chapter also addresses whether they are viable in practice. Because accounting is a highly regulated field, and also a highly competitive field, some changes that are theoretically feasible are not practically feasible. For example, time pressure may have a negative effect on auditors' JDM but a change related to this variable (e.g., reducing time pressure), may not be feasible because auditing firms typically charge clients fixed fees and, thus, must keep time spent on audits at a level that allows for a profit to be made.

This chapter proceeds as follows. The next section introduces a framework for understanding the effects of changes related to person, task, and environmental variables that are meant to improve JDM. The chapter then discusses three classes of JDM improvement methods that are used frequently in accounting settings. These methods are instruction, experience, and feedback; personnel screening practices, including selection, assignment to tasks, and promotion based on performance appraisals; and decision aids such as checklists and statistical models. The chapter uses the framework to describe how these methods can improve JDM and discusses the accounting research related to each method. In addition, the chapter makes note of factors that moderate their effectiveness. Next, the chapter applies the framework to a few examples of the person, task, and environmental causes of variation in or low levels of JDM quality discussed in Chapters 3 through 7. A final section summarizes.

9-1 FRAMEWORK FOR JDM IMPROVEMENT METHODS

Figure 9-1 categorizes methods for improving JDM quality as changes related to the person, task, or environment. This categorization is useful in that it helps readers remember that there are a variety of methods of attempting to improve JDM. These methods, by definition, must make changes related to person variables, task variables, or environmental variables because these categories of variables cover all the factors

---

[1]An "acceptably high" level of JDM quality will be determined by a given firm for a given task or, perhaps, by regulators in some instances. It likely is a level whose benefits exceed its costs.

FIGURE 9-1 Framework for JDM Research in Accounting

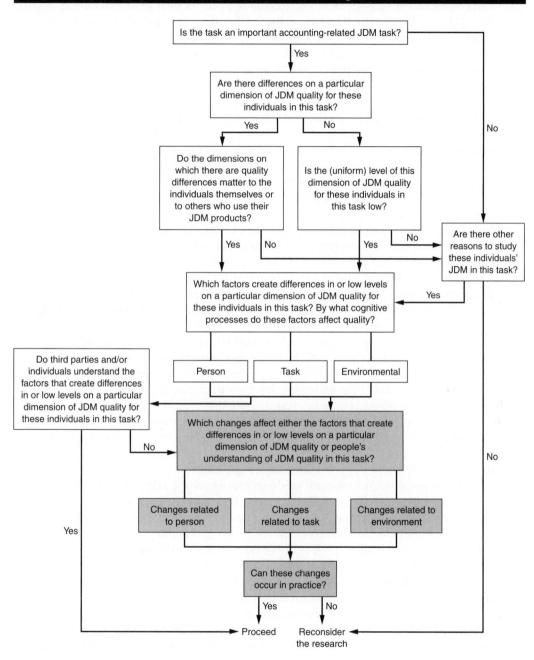

that affect JDM quality. However, this classification of improvement methods is not universally accepted. For example, extrinsic motivators such as accountability may be considered changes related to the person (rather than changes to the environment) in that they are meant to increase the person's level of motivation. A decision aid, instead of being considered a change to the task, may be thought of as a change to the environment in the sense that people are being provided with an additional resource.

Because of this lack of agreement, this section introduces another potentially useful framework for discussing JDM improvement methods. This framework comes from understanding that there are a finite number of general methods that can improve JDM that is of less than "acceptably high" quality. It adopts the simplifying assumptions that only one variable affects JDM quality and that this variable has either a positive or a negative effect, on average, on JDM quality. If the variable in question has a positive effect on JDM quality, there are two general methods for improving JDM that is less than acceptably high. The first general method is to increase the level of the variable. For example, suppose that knowledge content is the only variable affecting JDM. Knowledge content can be increased by a variety of techniques, for example, instruction or assignment of high-knowledge individuals to the task. The second general method for improving JDM when the variable of interest is one that positively affects JDM is to remove or decrease the effects of a moderator that is reducing the variable's positive effect. For example, people may have the appropriate knowledge but not be able to retrieve it from memory because of interference from task-related information. Again, there are multiple specific possibilities for implementing this method as it relates to knowledge content (e.g., changing task-related information or supplementing the task with a decision aid). Whether these two general methods are classified as causing changes related to person, task, or environmental variables in a particular situation clearly is less important than understanding their potential effectiveness. Such an understanding depends on the researcher learning whether there is a low level of the factor in question present in accounting professionals or, instead, whether the factor is present but JDM quality is not being as positively affected by the factor as it could be because of some moderating factor. In other words, researchers must explore fully the JDM framework's (Figure 9-1's) previous research questions.

The remaining three general methods for improving JDM quality relate to situations where variables have a negative effect on JDM quality. The most common situation underlying JDM quality that is reduced by a negative-effect variable likely is that the variable is present in too great a quantity. If this is the case, improving JDM quality involves either decreasing the quantity of the variable or putting in place a moderator that reduces the variable's effect when a high level of that variable exists. Irrelevant information that causes a dilution effect (see Chapter 6) is an example of a negative-effect variable. A specific method for improving JDM quality if there is too much irrelevant information is to reduce the amount of such information available to or used by accounting professionals. However, given that the amount of irrelevant information present in an environment may be difficult to control, a firm instead could use the second general method—put in place or increase the level of some factor that will moderate the negative effect of this variable. For example, the firm could ask its professionals to use a decision aid that requires them to evaluate information's relevance to a hypothesis under consideration. The third general method for a negative-effect variable is appropriate if the variable is present in only a small quantity but its negative effect is being exacerbated by a moderator. For example, the negative effect of irrelevant information can be exacerbated by accountability. In this case, the appropriate method involves reducing the effect of the moderator, most likely by removing it from the environment. If this is not feasible, the situation might require putting in place yet another factor that reduces the exacerbating effect of the moderator. Note that this third general method related to negative-effect variables will not be discussed extensively because the JDM literature, in its focus on improving JDM quality, typically does not focus on moderators that exacerbate negative JDM effects of various factors.

Finally, one caveat that always applies when discussing methods for improving JDM is that a given method may not be effective because of the manner in which it is implemented or the manner in which it is received by the persons for whom it is intended. For example, instruction is one method that theoretically can increase knowledge content. However, if the instructor is unable to properly organize and deliver lectures, this method may not have a positive effect on knowledge content and, therefore, JDM quality. To the extent that research documents that such factors are moderators of the effectiveness of changes designed to improve JDM quality, this chapter (and other chapters that discuss variables that can serve as JDM improvement methods) describes their effects.

9-2   INSTRUCTION, PRACTICE, AND FEEDBACK

Definitions and Background

This section discusses the effects of the JDM improvement methods of instruction, practice, and feedback with the focus being primarily on their effects on JDM through knowledge content and structure.[2] *Instruction* is defined as "events deliberately planned to support learning" (Gredler 2005). The psychology literature defines "learning" in a variety of ways, ranging from acquisition of knowledge to a change in performance (Baddeley 1990). This chapter defines *learning* as acquisition of knowledge because of the chapter's focus on the effects of improvement methods on the determinants of JDM quality. *Practice* is defined as the repetition of a task (Reber 1995), and *feedback* is information about one or more elements of JDM that comes to the decision maker after she makes a judgment or decision. These JDM improvement methods clearly are viable in practice, given the current prevalence of their use.

There are a variety of forms of instruction, practice, and feedback. Instruction includes formal classroom activities and activities students do in preparation for classroom activities.[3] Formal classroom activities can be carried out in a university setting or in training programs provided by firms, professional organizations, and the like (Driscoll 2005). This section focuses on the following instructional activities: reading text, listening to lectures, reading worked-out example problems, answering short objective questions, generating and answering one's own questions, and working problems or

---

[2]Instruction, practice, and feedback can also affect cognitive processes and other variables such as motivation. This section restricts discussion to the effects of these variables on knowledge for parsimony.
[3]Some instruction does not involve formal classroom meetings. For example, universities have begun to offer some courses through distance learning programs, and firms sometimes provide instruction through interactive software that is accessed by each individual in the most convenient setting for her. The discussion that follows regarding the effects of instruction may not generalize to these settings.

solving longer cases.[4] As can be inferred from this list, some instructional activities involve practice (e.g., working problems). Clearly, practice also occurs outside instructional contexts (e.g., on the job). In this chapter, "practice" will also be used to refer to more passive phenomena such as hearing others talk about having performed tasks. In this regard, then, practice is akin to informal instruction. Also, although it is somewhat unconventional, this chapter will use the term practice to refer to what normally is deemed *experience,* that is, being present at an event. Finally, as discussed in Chapter 7, feedback can be *outcome feedback,* in which a person receives the "correct answer" (e.g., to a problem worked as part of instruction or for a JDM task practiced on the job) or *cognitive feedback,* in which a person receives some information about either her cognitive processing or properties of the JDM task or both.

Instruction, practice, and feedback are not unique to accounting environments. However, they are critically important to public accounting firms and other organizations that employ accounting-related professionals. First, these firms look to universities for properly trained entry-level professionals, and in response, universities frequently change their curricula; thus, an understanding of the effects of instruction, practice, and feedback is important to accounting educators. In addition, firms typically provide opportunities for continuing education to their employees. In fact, many accounting professionals are required to have continuing education in order to retain their professional designations (e.g., CPAs and CFAs). Firms' investments in instructional programs can be enormous, and instructional programs are the most often used technique for enhancing worker productivity (Salas and Cannon-Bowers 2001; Arthur et al. 2003; Salas and Kosarzycki 2003). Yet firms (likely including firms that employ accounting professionals) often are reluctant to incorporate research findings into their training programs (Salas and Kosarzycki). Further, in accounting, instruction, practice, and feedback can vary as to amounts and type across tasks, supervisors, and firms (Belkaoui and Picur 1987; Bonner and Pennington 1991). The combination of these factors suggests that firms that employ accounting professionals may have at least some costly instruction, practice, and feedback systems that are ineffective.

Instruction, Practice, and Feedback Effects

Instruction, practice, and feedback have positive effects on knowledge content and knowledge structure on average. In turn, knowledge content and knowledge structure typically have positive effects on JDM quality. Thus, instruction, practice, and feedback are changes that can increase the level of "good" variables, that is, those that positively affect JDM quality.

As a brief review, *knowledge content* refers to the quantity and specific pieces of information stored in long-term memory. There are three types of knowledge of importance in accounting settings: *episodic knowledge* for details of personal experiences, *declarative knowledge* of facts and concepts, and *procedural knowledge* of if-then rules for performing skilled tasks. Declarative and procedural knowledge are referred to collectively as *semantic knowledge,* or knowledge that extracts meaning from the details of items. *Knowledge structure* refers to the extent to which and the ways in which that information is organized. Episodic and declarative knowledge can be organized

---

[4]For a more complete list of classroom activities that can be considered under the auspices of instruction, see Bonner (1999).

into hierarchical networks, schemas, or scripts, whereas procedural knowledge typically is thought to be organized in a simple list format.

JDM quality is affected positively by knowledge content through the speed and probability of retrieving that knowledge from memory. Speed and probability of retrieval are positive functions of the strength of knowledge and task information, whereas strength of knowledge is a positive function of the frequency and recency of encounters with the information. However, strength decreases with lengthy time lags since activation. JDM quality can be affected positively by knowledge structures through the activation and retrieval of multiple, related items of knowledge; these effects are intensified when knowledge structures are activated more frequently. Further, the effects typically are more positive when knowledge structures are organized "correctly" (e.g., are consistent with professional standards).

Before covering how instruction, practice, and feedback specifically affect knowledge content and structure, it is important to provide some general discussion about how people acquire and organize semantic knowledge (both declarative and procedural) and episodic knowledge. Normally, for people to acquire declarative knowledge and episodic knowledge, information must enter memory through the process of encoding. Encoding involves three steps (Klatzky 1980; Baddeley 1990; Anderson 2000, 2005). First, people must sense information either visually or auditorily so the information can enter a sensory store. Second, people must attend to the information in one of the sensory stores for it to enter short-term (or working) memory, which also is a temporary and limited-capacity holding place. Third, people must rehearse (repeat) material in a meaningful way, and do so rapidly, for it to move from short-term memory to long-term memory.[5] One way of rehearsing information meaningfully is to elaborate upon it with additional information; this additional information often comes from preexisting knowledge (Gredler 2005). If such rehearsal occurs, people can remember even the most trivial of details. However, in everyday settings, the information moved from short-term memory to long-term memory more likely includes important details of events and concepts (episodic knowledge), as well as meaningful interpretations of events and concepts (declarative knowledge). One exception to this general encoding scenario occurs for episodic knowledge of the frequency of events. This type of knowledge does not require rehearsal for it to be stored in long-term memory; as such, it is said to be gained relatively "automatically" (Zacks and Hasher 2002).

The organization of declarative knowledge and episodic knowledge into knowledge structures is the subject of much debate (e.g., Conway 1997; Lamberts and Shanks 1997; Markman 1999). People gradually integrate new knowledge with existing knowledge while encoding that new knowledge (Anderson and Schunn 2000), yet the mechanisms by which this occurs are controversial and likely differ depending on the type of structure being created. Consider declarative knowledge structures for categories as an example. Some theories posit that these structures are developed inductively (i.e., by experiencing instances of an object or event and making note of correlations between the object or event and various attributes) as well as by reasoning about the similarity of the object or event to other items (Murphy and Medin 1985; Anderson 2000). For

---

[5]Many factors can disrupt the flow of information into memory during these three steps. In other words, factors can disrupt the sensing of information, the attention paid to information, and the rehearsal of information. Discussion of these factors is beyond the scope of this book. (For more information, see Klatzky [1980]; Eysenck [1982]; Baddeley [1990]; Anderson [2000]; Schacter [2001].)

example, people may learn that cats and dogs are different concepts because of their distinguishing features, but they may learn also that both are part of the category "domestic animals" by noting that they both tend to live indoors and interact with humans. Other authors posit a role for people's existing naive, or intuitive, theories in the formation of knowledge structures (Heit 1997). For example, people may have an intuitive theory that domestic animals have fur; thus, they may not classify a goldfish as a domestic animal.

Finally, procedural knowledge is acquired and organized somewhat differently than are declarative knowledge and episodic knowledge (Anderson and Fincham 1994; Anderson et al. 1997a; Anderson and Schunn 2000). In the early stages of doing JDM tasks, learners use declarative knowledge and various general problem-solving strategies such as working backward from the goal. As they begin to have exposure to examples (as well as information about the examples' solutions) and are able to reference those examples in memory or elsewhere (e.g., in a textbook), they begin to rely on the strategy of reasoning by analogy from the examples. Learners then compile procedural knowledge by accessing declarative knowledge and analogizing from examples; this compilation involves extracting general principles in the form of if-then rules. They then apply these if-then rules to further examples. If the rules are successful for solving problems, they gain strength in memory; if they are unsuccessful, they are discarded. Rules may be unsuccessful if learners extract the wrong principle through their combination of declarative knowledge and analogical reasoning from examples; this may occur if, for example, learners choose examples that are similar to the current situation based on superficial rather than meaningful features (Ross 1989).

With this general backdrop, this section now can focus on the effects of instruction, practice, and feedback on semantic knowledge content and structure.[6] Declarative knowledge content mostly is the product of instruction. In particular, the instructional activities that best facilitate the acquisition of declarative knowledge are those that do not involve practice—reading texts, listening to lectures, answering short questions, and generating and answering questions (Bonner 1999). Texts and lectures aid the first step of encoding declarative knowledge by presenting information to people. To aid in the second encoding step, instruction can draw attention to key pieces of information. For example, texts and lectures can use headings and formatting to draw attention; in addition, asking students to answer short objective questions can draw attention. These types of instruction can aid the third encoding step (meaningful rehearsal) through facilitating elaboration. For instance, texts and lectures can provide links to previously covered material using diagrams and explicit discussion of the links. Students can also be asked to generate and answer questions. These instructional activities also can aid the acquisition of declarative knowledge by directly teaching strategies that aid encoding, such as mnemonics, imagery, and the PQ4R technique, which specifies several steps for studying a textbook (Anderson 2005). Further, they can increase the strength of declarative knowledge in memory through repetition of material, which requires that students activate the material frequently. For example, repetition can be accomplished through summaries in texts and lectures and through asking questions.

---

[6]Episodic knowledge will not be discussed further because, by definition, it is acquired through personal experience, which is considered part of "practice" in this chapter.

Although instruction is the most efficient manner of promoting declarative knowledge acquisition, practice and feedback also can play a role (Anderson and Schunn 2000). Practice and feedback activities that present and focus on key pieces of declarative knowledge can aid in the first and second encoding steps. Further, practice and feedback can activate declarative knowledge and, thus, increase its strength in memory.

The instructional activities that lead to declarative knowledge acquisition (reading texts, listening to lectures, and asking and answering questions) can have positive effects on declarative knowledge structures as well (Anderson 2000). For example, a text or lecture can directly provide a desired knowledge structure through an outline or a drawing of the structure. Texts and lectures also facilitate the organization of knowledge into appropriate structures through section headings and subheadings and through discussion of how various pieces of knowledge relate to each other (Gredler 2005). In addition, instruction can provide lists of relevant attributes of categories, as well as lists of features that distinguish one category from another.

Declarative knowledge structures also may be acquired through practice and feedback. For example, as described above, people may acquire category structures by experiencing instances of those categories and engaging in inductive reasoning. In addition, both outcome and cognitive feedback can assist in the development of categories. For example, a staff auditor could be told that a procedure that recalculates sales invoice totals does not aid with the sales existence objective, but rather the sales valuation objective. In accounting, it seems likely that learners develop declarative knowledge structures in both ways.

To acquire procedural knowledge, learners must interact in some way with JDM problems (Woolfolk 1998; Committee on Developments 2000; Gredler 2005). Interaction with problems is necessary because procedural knowledge is compiled through this interaction. Further, learners need feedback about their understanding of the problems. Although the instructional activities of reading texts and listening to lectures are important for setting the stage for procedural knowledge acquisition (Bonner 1999), the principal issue here is whether interaction with problems should occur through instruction or practice. Specifically, people can interact with problems through reading worked-out example problems or by doing problems themselves. Conventional wisdom indicates that "practice makes perfect," but recent research indicates that there are many situations in which learners acquire more procedural knowledge by reading worked-out examples than by working problems. (See Atkinson et al. [2000] for a review.)[7] Given that many textbooks and lectures include these examples, that students like to rely on worked-out examples, and that learning from worked-out examples can be substantially less time consuming, these findings are practically important (Chi and Bassok 1989). They may be especially important in firms that employ accounting professionals given the voluminous amount of material that typically must be included in training programs.

In order for worked-out examples to create superior learning conditions for procedural knowledge, however, at least three conditions must be met.[8] First, the examples must be structured in a manner that reduces the load on short-term memory and better directs attention than does working problems (Ward and Sweller 1990; Atkinson

---

[7]Chi et al. (1994) also explore whether worked-out examples can aid in the acquisition of declarative knowledge.

[8]Other conditions that may be important are reviewed by Atkinson et al. (2000).

et al. 2000). Working problems can impose a heavy load on short-term memory because people use general strategies such as working backward from a goal; these strategies require that they hold in short-term memory the end goal, multiple subgoals related to the end goal, and so on. Working problems can also direct attention away from acquiring procedural knowledge because people focus intensely on reaching the goal of solving the problem rather than on learning the appropriate procedures.

However, worked-out examples can cause similar problems because they typically are formatted based on visual appeal and other factors not based on learning research (Sweller et al. 1990). Typical worked-out examples include a statement of the problem, step-by-step procedures for solving a problem, and information about how these procedures meet various goals inherent in the solution process (Atkinson et al. 2000). Many worked-out examples include additional information such as diagrams. When examples include additional information that is not integrated with the text, learning may be reduced because people are forced to attempt to hold the two sets of information in short-term memory; many people are unable to do this (Ward and Sweller 1990; Sweller et al.; Sweller and Chandler 1994). Further, attention is directed away from learning and toward integrating the information. In addition, if examples do not integrate goals and the steps that relate to those goals, short-term memory load can be increased because people must store this information separately. Instead, if goals and steps are integrated, people may be able to store the integrated information as a "chunk"; in addition, attention is focused directly on the procedures to be learned (Sweller and Chandler). Finally, if worked-out examples contain redundant information, they may not lead to greater learning because the redundancy taxes short-term memory.

The second condition that is necessary for people to acquire more procedural knowledge from reading worked-out examples than from working problems is that they adequately explain the examples to themselves (Anderson and Schunn 2000; Atkinson et al. 2000).[9] Learners must self-explain because worked-out examples typically do not explain all elements of the solution process; for example, they may not explain why each step occurs. More important, the active engagement of the learner in self-explanation seems to be superior to, for example, hearing lectures on the information omitted by examples (Chi and Bassok 1989). "Adequate" self-explanation means that learners accurately and completely interpret the examples and, thus, successfully complete repairs to the incorrect knowledge and intuitive theories they have brought to the instructional setting (Chi 2000). There appear to be two types of self-explanation strategies that can aid in this endeavor: "anticipative reasoning" and "principle-based explaining" (Renkl 1997; Atkinson et al.). The former strategy involves predicting the next step in a worked-out example and checking one's prediction against the example. The latter strategy involves understanding the underlying conceptual structure of the problem and inferring procedures from this structure. These strategies do not appear to be related to abilities; however, learners who are good principle-based explainers appear also to have some prior knowledge. Fortunately, evidence indicates that these self-explaining strategies can be learned through instruction (Bielaczyc et al. 1995; Chi).

The third condition is that learners do not have a great deal of prior domain knowledge. Several studies have found that people with high domain knowledge gain

---

[9]Note that self-explanation is distinct from elaboration in that learners are attempting to make sense of the text rather than provide links to new material that can help retain or retrieve that material (Chi 2000).

as much or more procedural knowledge from working problems as they do from reading worked-out examples (Renkl et al. 1998; Tuovinen and Sweller 1999; Kalyuga et al. 2001a, 2001b). This occurs because prior knowledge helps direct attention toward learning procedures while working problems; it also allows learners to hold more information in short-term memory than they would otherwise because much of the necessary knowledge already exists in long-term memory.

Depending on the above conditions, then, acquisition of procedural knowledge may or may not require practice. However, most evidence indicates that people cannot acquire procedural knowledge without feedback (Ross 1988). If people read worked-out examples, feedback is part of the examples themselves. That is, the worked-out examples, by definition, include information about individual if-then rules and the final solution. Thus, the issue of whether people can acquire knowledge without feedback pertains to situations in which they work problems. In these situations, feedback can come from an instructor or, if practice is done on the job, feedback can come from a supervisor.

In general, feedback that accompanies practice must be timely, complete, accurate, and credible for people to acquire procedural knowledge. More specifically, this feedback also normally must be cognitive feedback (or cognitive feedback along with outcome feedback). It generally is difficult for people to acquire procedural knowledge from outcome feedback alone because people infer incorrect if-then rules from outcomes affected by noise or because they continuously change their rules in response to varying outcomes (Balzer et al. 1989). Exceptions to this general finding occur when tasks are very simple (Hirst and Luckett 1992) or when people know a causal theory of the task prior to receiving outcome feedback (Camerer 1981b). Simple tasks are those for which there are very few procedural rules and/or there is very little noise. In this case, inferring procedures from outcomes is dramatically easier. When people have prior knowledge, they are better able to infer correct procedures from outcomes because their knowledge directs them toward these procedures.[10]

Unfortunately, although instruction, practice, and feedback can have substantial positive effects on knowledge content and knowledge structure, there are many moderators that can reduce their positive effects. Many of these moderators are person variables pertaining to the learner.[11] Task and environmental factors also can moderate the effectiveness of instruction, practice, and feedback. Finally, elements of instruction, practice, and feedback themselves can create variability in the extent to which they have positive effects on knowledge.

---

[10]For several reasons, the discussion regarding the effects of instruction, practice, and feedback on knowledge content and structure does not include information about "transfer of learning." First, *transfer of learning* is a term with many meanings (Singley and Anderson 1989; Bransford and Schwartz 1999; Committee on Developments 2000; Haskell 2001; Mayer 2002). These range from the application of individual if-then rules learned in the context of one type of problem to a different type of problem to the use of prior knowledge when acquiring new knowledge. Meanings such as the latter clearly overlap with the discussion in this section on initial learning. Second, much of the discussion related to "teaching for transfer" also overlaps with the discussion in this section. That is, many of the principles advocated in the transfer literature (e.g., providing feedback and ensuring sufficient student motivation) also are relevant to the initial learning of material. Third, much of the literature on the "failure to transfer" discusses reasons people do not access or use knowledge stored in memory. These issues are covered in earlier discussions of knowledge content and structure (Chapter 3) and cognitive processing (Chapter 5).

[11]Characteristics of the instructor also can moderate the effectiveness of instruction. To the extent research documents these characteristics, they are discussed under the section on characteristics of instruction.

Person variables that moderate the effects of instruction, practice, and feedback include abilities, intrinsic motivation, and various personality characteristics. A large body of literature indicates that people better acquire knowledge content and knowledge structures from instruction if they are higher in general intelligence and/or verbal abilities (Wexley 1984; Hunter 1986; Tannenbaum and Yukl 1992; Ree et al. 1995; Ackerman 1999; Lohman 1999; Day et al. 2001; Salas and Cannon-Bowers 2001; Salgado et al. 2001). Further, learners who have high intrinsic motivation also better acquire knowledge from instruction (Wexley; Dillon 1986; Resnick 1989; Revelle 1989; Tannenbaum and Yukl; Committee on Developments 2000; Salas and Cannon-Bowers; Driscoll 2005; Salgado and Fruyt 2005).[12] Intrinsic motivation can derive, for example, from need for achievement or self-efficacy. Personality characteristics that can moderate the effects of instruction on knowledge include goal orientation; some people have "learning goals" (goals to master the material), whereas other people have "performance goals" (goals to perform well on instruments that evaluate learning or performance). People with learning goals tend to sustain motivation even when they are attempting to master difficult-to-acquire knowledge, whereas people with performance goals may give up when they face too much difficulty (Committee on Developments; Salas and Cannon-Bowers; Driscoll). As other examples, highly anxious people are less likely to acquire knowledge from instruction (Revelle), as are those who are less open to new experiences (Salgado and Fruyt).

An important person-variable moderator is the prior knowledge of learners. This moderator is discussed above with regard to the effects of practice and outcome feedback on procedural knowledge. To reiterate, people who have higher-quality declarative knowledge are more likely to acquire correct procedural knowledge in these situations and others (Vosniadou 1989). "Higher quality" declarative knowledge includes greater amounts of correct information stored in memory as well as knowledge that is organized around correct domain principles.

In addition, people with higher-quality prior declarative knowledge in a domain are more likely to acquire further high-quality declarative knowledge content and structures from instruction and to do so faster (e.g., Chiesi et al. 1979; Heit 1997). Although encoding of declarative knowledge generally can be described as a three-step process in which information ultimately becomes knowledge in memory, people do not simply "record" the new declarative knowledge. Rather, they "construct" the new declarative knowledge by interpreting the information presented to them in light of their existing knowledge (Resnick 1989; Committee on Developments 2000; Gredler 2005). Clearly, then, the extent to which existing declarative knowledge is correct influences the extent to which new declarative knowledge is correct (Heit). Although this may seem obvious, it often is overlooked by instructors who assume that students bring correct declarative knowledge into an instructional setting (Committee on Developments). In fact, students frequently bring incorrect or incomplete declarative knowledge and incorrect intuitive theories into the instructional setting, and these incorrect ideas cause them to selectively attend to and perhaps misinterpret new information (Heit; Schwartz and Bransford 1998; Committee on Developments). High-quality prior

---

[12]Anderson's (2000) discussion implies that motivation does not moderate the effects of instruction on knowledge based on the finding that people acquire knowledge when they have attended to it, even if they do not intend to acquire it. The discussion here focuses on the effect that motivation has when learners intend to learn the material.

knowledge content also helps people acquire new knowledge (and do so faster) because it allows for better and more elaborations (Bransford et al. 1989; Kyllonen and Woltz 1989; Resnick; Gredler).[13] Finally, high-quality declarative knowledge structures also can facilitate the acquisition of declarative knowledge. They do so by lightening the load on short-term memory (Kyllonen and Woltz; Woolfolk 1998; Gredler); people are able to hold more new information in memory because they can use "chunks."

Characteristics of the task for which knowledge is being acquired and characteristics of the environment also can moderate the effects of instruction, practice, and feedback. The complexity of the task can serve as a motivator for acquiring knowledge (Committee on Developments 2000). Tasks that are sufficiently complex to challenge people, but not overwhelm them, can stimulate motivation to acquire knowledge. A key environmental variable is the extent to which organizations emphasize training programs and frame them positively; higher levels of this factor can enhance people's acquisition of knowledge (Tannenbaum and Yukl 1992; Salas and Cannon-Bowers 2001). Finally, the adequacy of the time given for learning also can moderate the effects of instruction, practice, and feedback (Committee on Developments).

Not surprisingly, various elements of instruction, practice, and feedback themselves can moderate their effects on knowledge content and structure. Starting with instruction, the content of instruction obviously is a key moderator of its effects on knowledge. High-quality instructional content derives from a high-quality cognitive task analysis. This entails creating a detailed inventory of the items of knowledge and cognitive processes needed to complete a task successfully along with sequencing those items so knowledge items that require prerequisite knowledge follow the prerequisites (Tannenbaum and Yukl 1992; Anderson 2000; Anderson and Schunn 2000; Salas and Cannon-Bowers 2001; Mayer 2004). Instructors (and textbook authors) sometimes do not conduct a complete task analysis and, as such, omit important content. Further, for particular types of knowledge, instruction should include certain types of content. For example, to promote knowledge of concepts, instruction needs to include many examples and nonexamples of the concepts, labels and definitions for the concepts, and listings of relevant attributes (Woolfolk 1998; Committee on Developments 2000).

A second element of instruction that can moderate its positive effects is the specific instructional activity employed. As mentioned earlier, acquisition of declarative knowledge is facilitated by reading text, hearing lectures, answering instructor-provided questions, and generating and answering one's own questions. By contrast, acquisition of procedural knowledge is facilitated by reading text, hearing lectures, and reading worked-out example problems or solving problems. Third, the sequencing of instructional activities may affect the acquisition of knowledge. One issue here relates to the acquisition of declarative knowledge about concepts, that is, whether the traditional instructional activities of hearing lectures and reading texts should precede or follow exposure to examples and nonexamples (see earlier discussion). Schwartz and Bransford (1998) argue that students should engage in active comparison of examples and nonexamples of concepts first to learn about distinctive features. This then sets the

---

[13]People also may differ in their knowledge of how to learn (referred to as *metacognitive knowledge*). People who have more metacognitive knowledge learn more (Resnick 1989; Woolfolk 1998). In fact, possession of such knowledge may override the moderating effects of abilities (Woolfolk).

stage for learning principles regarding these distinctive features from text or lecture; otherwise, students may not fully learn these principles.

Fourth, variations within specific instructional activities can moderate the positive effects of instruction on knowledge. For example, studies (e.g., McNamara et al. 1996; McNamara and Kintsch 1996) show that students with low prior knowledge in a domain learn better when reading textbooks that are coherent in their writing, whereas students with high prior knowledge learn better when reading low-coherence texts. Although these findings may seem somewhat odd, the authors argue that high-knowledge students face too simple a task if given a high-coherence text, one so simple it may not promote learning. By contrast, when given a low-coherence text, they are forced to focus and draw inferences while reading.[14] As another example, there is debate about whether making textbooks more interesting can increase learning. Some evidence indicates that more interesting texts decrease knowledge acquisition (e.g., Harp and Mayer 1998), but other evidence indicates that more interesting texts promote learning (e.g., Fernald 1989).[15]

Practice and feedback can vary also as to their positive effects on knowledge. First, the quality of practice can vary. Ericsson and his colleagues (Ericsson et al. 1993; Ericsson 1996) argue that people who engage in "deliberate practice" learn more and perform better than those who do not. *Deliberate practice* is defined as practice by highly motivated individuals that occurs outside a paid work environment and is done alone; it also involves activities that are designed by an instructor to be specific to the individual's particular learning needs and includes high-quality feedback. Even though this type of practice is most applicable to persons in domains such as sports and music, Ericsson et al. argue that these elements of practice can enhance acquisition of all types of procedural knowledge. However, Anderson and Schunn (2000) suggest that deliberate practice simply is a term for describing practice that truly is spent on learning rather than on extraneous activities. A second dimension of practice whose effects are better established is whether practice is "spaced" or "massed" (Baddeley 1990). Practice leads to better learning when learning is spread over a number of days rather than done in one or a few days. Further, within individual days, material is learned better if repeated exposures to the material are spaced over the day rather than shown mostly in sequence.

Feedback can vary on many dimensions. (See Chapter 7 for a lengthier discussion.) As mentioned above, the most effective feedback is timely, complete, accurate, and credible. As the time lag between JDM and the receipt of feedback increases, the learning effects of feedback diminish (Anderson 2005). As the completeness of feedback itself or the completeness with which people process the feedback diminishes, so do its positive effects on knowledge (Hogarth 1987). Further, as the accuracy of feedback or the perceived accuracy of feedback (credibility) decrease, the positive effects on knowledge also decrease. In the former case, the reduced knowledge effects clearly

---

[14]Similar to this, findings indicate that students with high abilities learn better with less structured instructional activities, whereas students with low abilities learn better with more structured activities (Snow 1989). The explanation for this also is similar; people with high abilities need the lack of structure to motivate them to work hard at learning the material.

[15]By contrast, research generally indicates that learners' inherent interest in a topic leads to increased learning from instruction (Tobias 1994) and that interesting instructional environments, for example, those that include humor, tend to promote learning (Committee on Developments 2000; Driscoll 2005).

are due to the poor content of the feedback; in the latter case, they are due to people being less likely to use the feedback.

Studying the effects of instruction, practice, and feedback on knowledge content and structure is best accomplished through manipulation in experiments. There are several reasons for this. First, detailed and separate measurement of instruction, practice, and feedback is inherently difficult. For example, it is difficult for people to recall the amount of time spent during instruction on activities that did not involve practice versus those that did involve practice. Researchers could attempt to measure such items without asking individuals directly; for example, they could examine the contents of a textbook to ascertain how much of the text involves working problems. However, such a measurement technique is fraught with difficulties (e.g., students may not have worked the problems). An extreme alternative to such detailed questions is measuring instruction, practice, and feedback with coarse questions such as those that ask how many years of experience someone has with a particular task. These questions (or archival gathering of similar data, say, from employment records) likely lead to far more accurate responses but suffer from the larger problem of not being able to provide any information about the separate effects of these three variables. In addition, coarse measures of experience confound the effects of instruction, practice, and feedback with those of personnel screening. That is, people with greater experience may have that simply because they have been selected to continue in the organization (Davis et al. 1997); they may have been selected because they had more knowledge to begin with (rather than acquiring it through the additional experience they have been provided) or for some other reason, such as greater abilities.

Some studies have taken an approach between these extremes. For example, Bonner et al. (1992) ask tax practitioners several questions about the amount of coursework, whether coursework was primarily problem based, amount of time spent doing tasks, and the like; then they factor analyze the questions to determine if questions generally related to instruction, practice, and feedback load together. Bonner and Pennington (1991) gather data from an audit firm's training schedule and manuals, performance evaluation forms, and other internal documents, and examine whether instruction, practice, and feedback-related measures are correlated with each other. Despite being less extreme, these intermediate measurement techniques still suffer from problems. In addition to the inherent difficulties related to measuring instruction, practice, and feedback, these factors often are partially or completely confounded with other variables in the environment in which accounting professionals work. For example, if researchers measure the amount of feedback available for a particular task, they might also be measuring the existence and difficulty of firm-imposed goals (e.g., Locke 1967). For these reasons, then, manipulation of instruction, practice, and feedback is preferred.

Accounting Studies on Instruction and Practice

This section reviews accounting studies that examine the effects of instruction and practice on knowledge (studies examining feedback effects were discussed in Chapter 7).[16] Unless otherwise stated, studies do not distinguish between declarative knowledge and procedural knowledge. Beginning with studies on producers of

---

[16]This section includes articles from *Issues in Accounting Education,* given its prominence in publishing studies related to instruction.

accounting information, three studies examine instruction and practice effects in managerial accounting contexts. Stone et al. (2000) measure the knowledge of a large number of management accountants. They measure instruction and practice using years of experience and report that more experienced management accountants have less entry-level (textbook-based) knowledge but greater industry knowledge and tacit managerial knowledge than do less experienced accountants. Dearman and Shields (2001) measure management accountants' amount of coursework and number of years working in cost accounting and cost management, as well as their volume-based and activity-based cost knowledge content and structure. They predict that cost accounting instruction and practice are related to volume-based knowledge content and structure but find that only cost accounting practice is related to knowledge content. Measures of instruction are not related either to content or to structure, and practice is not related to knowledge structure. Similarly, they predict that cost management instruction and practice are related to activity-based knowledge but find that only cost-management practice is related to activity-based knowledge structures. In an interesting study, Luft and Shields (2001) examine the effects of experience with different accounting systems on students' learning of the relation of investments in intangibles to future profits. Students who practice with systems that expense intangibles learn less than those who practice with systems that capitalize intangibles.

A number of studies examine the effects of instruction and practice on users of accounting information, specifically in financial accounting contexts. These studies typically present data from students enrolled in the first financial accounting course or the intermediate accounting course. Several studies examine the effects of moderators such as abilities on the effects of instruction and practice in this course. Eskew and Faley (1988) find that abilities and prior knowledge (as measured by SAT scores, high school and college grades, and previous math and accounting courses) are positively related to knowledge gained in the first course (as measured by exam scores). Ward et al. (1993) find that math ACT scores are positively related to the first course grade, and Gist et al. (1996) find that SAT scores, general college grades, and grades in calculus are positively related to the first course grades (for minority students). Booker (1991) similarly reports that ACT scores are positively related to intermediate accounting grades (for minority students). Tyson (1989) shows that women students, who report higher levels of need for achievement, obtain higher grades in all accounting courses than men students. However, Doran et al. (1991) report that men students earn higher grades in the second accounting course and are no different from women students in the first course; they also show that being an accounting major and having higher ACT scores and GPAs lead to higher grades in these courses.

Remaining studies examine a variety of issues, including questions related to specific forms and sequences of instructional activities. Edmonds and Alford (1989) vary the complexity of the presentation of information in the first accounting course and find that students with the less complex presentation perform better on the first exam that follows this presentation but not on subsequent exams. Kachelmeier et al. (1992) study the effect of a computerized learning aid that includes worked-out examples related to pension accounting. Students receiving the aid score higher on an exam related to this material than do other students.

Gobeil and Phillips (2001) examine the effects of prior accounting knowledge and whether a case is written in a narrative (story based) versus traditional format on students' acquisition and application of knowledge related to a case that requires that they estimate an acceptable range for reported earnings. The story format case is thought to be more interesting. Students with high knowledge acquire more case information, as measured by recall of case facts, but there is no effect of case style. However, low-knowledge students who read a story-based case better apply their knowledge when estimating earnings than do those reading a traditional case; case format has no effect on high-knowledge students' application of knowledge. Phillips and Vaidyanathan (2004) examine whether students learn more when cases precede versus follow lectures, consistent with the suggestions of Schwartz and Bransford (1998). They examine learning by assessing performance in two cases about financial viability (the second case occurs after both groups have received both the first case and lecture). In the first case, students receiving the lecture before the case identify more relevant concepts that are part of the lecture and fewer irrelevant concepts. However, students receiving the case before the lecture identify more relevant concepts that are not part of the lecture. Further, in the second case, the case-before-lecture students identify more relevant instructed and uninstructed concepts, and there are no differences in the identification of irrelevant concepts. Crandall and Phillips (2002) find that students who receive cases that are hypertext linked to conceptual text better apply their knowledge to new cases than students who receive no links. Finally, Halabi et al. (2005) examine the effects of prior accounting knowledge and reading worked-out examples versus working problems on students' learning about adjusting entries. Students with prior knowledge report memory load that is unaffected by form of instruction, whereas students with no prior knowledge report lower load when facing worked-out examples. However, only prior knowledge affects the total amount of knowledge gained about adjusting entries.

Two studies examine more general instruction and practice issues in a financial accounting context. Herz and Schultz (1999) examine students' acquisition of declarative and procedural knowledge related to converting cash-based income to accrual-based income. Students first hear a lecture on the subject then practice a large number of problems and receive feedback. Students gain declarative knowledge from the lecture; further, this knowledge does not improve with practice. They acquire procedural knowledge from the practice and feedback, and their responses to procedural knowledge questions become quicker with practice, consistent with the knowledge becoming more automated. Stone and Shelley (1997) examine the effects of a change in a university's curriculum from a predominantly lecture-based curriculum to one employing a large number of unstructured cases on students' acquisition of declarative and procedural knowledge in financial accounting (as well as in auditing, management accounting, tax, and other areas). The curriculum has virtually no effect on the acquisition of declarative knowledge but does have some effects on procedural knowledge. One complicating factor in this study is that students self-selected into one of the two curricula, and students with higher abilities tended to select the new curriculum.

A final set of studies related to instruction and practice in financial accounting examines the effects of students' beliefs about learning on their acquisition of knowledge. Phillips (1998) finds that the extent to which students believe knowledge is uncertain is positively associated with their performance on an unstructured financial reporting case (perhaps reflecting procedural knowledge acquisition) but not associated with performance on multiple-choice exams (perhaps reflecting declarative knowledge acquisition). Similarly, Phillips (2001) finds that case performance is associated with a belief that knowledge is complex.

The next group of studies examines instruction and practice effects in tax settings. Bonner et al. (1992) measure a number of instruction and practice variables; a factor analysis suggests these variables capture general time in practice, practice in corporate tax planning, current corporate tax client base, amount of general university tax instruction, amount of corporate tax instruction, and amount of case-based instruction. They then relate these factor-based measures to measures of declarative and procedural corporate tax knowledge. Amount of university instruction and amount of case-based instruction are positively related to measures of declarative knowledge. Practice in corporate tax planning and general time in practice are positively related to measures of procedural knowledge. There are some negative relations between instruction or experience and knowledge, consistent with the exploratory nature of the study.

Remaining studies examine more specific instructional issues. Anderson et al. (1989, 1990b) examine the effects of instructing students using conceptual material, worked-out examples, and cases that contain conceptual material, examples, and explanations of the examples on their ability to identify and apply the correct tax rule to a given problem. Anderson et al. (1989) study a situation in which there is no preexisting financial accounting knowledge that can conflict with the tax rule, whereas Anderson et al. (1990b) study a situation in which such a conflict exists. The first study finds that students receiving examples are better able than cases- or concepts-trained students to apply a tax rule but less able to identify the correct rule to apply. The second study finds that students receiving cases are better at both rule identification and application. Schadewald and Limberg (1990) find that students who generate elaborations when reading tax rules recall more rules than do students who read explanations provided by the instructor, reflecting greater knowledge content. Hermanson (1994) finds similar results. Roberts and Ashton (2003) examine the effects of reading text on tax accountants' and students' acquisition of declarative knowledge related to tax research and performance in a tax research task. Subjects who read the text acquire knowledge and perform better than those who do not.

The auditing area contains a number of studies on the effects of instruction and practice. Many of these studies examine differences between experienced and inexperienced auditors' (or students') knowledge content or structure, using length of experience as a measure of instruction and practice. Weber (1980) finds that auditors who read a list of internal controls recall more controls than do students, indicating greater knowledge content. They also cluster their recall more by control category, indicating more structured knowledge. Frederick (1991) similarly finds that auditors recall more internal controls and cluster their recall more than do students. Tubbs (1992) asks students and auditors either to list as many sales cycle errors as they can or to estimate the probability of occurrence of one of eight sales cycle errors. Experienced auditors list more errors than do students, indicating greater knowledge content. Results from the probability estimation task indicate that experienced auditors structure errors more around control objectives than do students. Christ (1993) asks inexperienced and experienced auditors to perform an audit planning task then recall information from the task. Experienced auditors recall more information and, to some extent, show greater structure to their knowledge. Finally, a number of studies indicate that experienced auditors have more accurate knowledge of the frequency of financial statement errors than do inexperienced auditors and students, along with greater general knowledge about errors and more appropriately structured error knowledge (Libby and Frederick 1990; Nelson 1993a; Frederick et al. 1994; Solomon et al. 1999; however, see Ashton [1991] for an exception).

Other studies in auditing examine more specific instruction and practice effects. Libby and Tan (1994), reanalyzing the data of Bonner and Lewis (1990), examine the effects of various practice measures and ability on knowledge related to four different audit tasks. They conjecture that abilities are more important to the acquisition of knowledge in less structured tasks. They find that a general experience measure is related to knowledge in all tasks, whereas an industry experience measure also is related to knowledge in a specialized industry task. Abilities are related to knowledge in two of the three tasks where this relationship is predicted and unrelated to knowledge in the one situation where no relationship is predicted.

Bonner and Pennington (1991) develop archival measures of the amount of overall instruction auditors receive for several audit JDM tasks as well as the amount of instruction they receive before practice and find that both these measures are related to JDM quality in those tasks (and JDM quality is shown to be affected by knowledge). Bonner and Walker (1994) examine the effects of two forms of instruction, practice, and two forms of feedback on the acquisition of procedural knowledge related to ratio analysis. Subjects receiving instruction alone or practice alone generally do not acquire procedural knowledge (feedback results are summarized in Chapter 7). Bonner et al. (1997) demonstrate that declarative knowledge structures can be obtained through instruction; further, the presence of instructed knowledge structures improves the acquisition of error frequency knowledge from practice.

The remaining studies examine the effects of variations in particular instructional activities or practice. Butt (1988) studies the effects of form of exposure to accounting error or generic stimuli frequency data (summarized, individual presentations of stimuli, or a combination of summaries and individual presentations) and general audit experience on the acquisition of frequency knowledge. When frequency knowledge is measured in absolute form, subjects who receive individual presentations of items have greater knowledge than other subjects, but there is no effect for audit experience. When frequency knowledge is measured in relative form, audit experience also has a positive effect on knowledge. When generic stimuli are used, presentation format affects knowledge acquisition no matter how this is measured, but audit experience does not.

Choo and Tan (1995) examine the effects of various forms of elaboration on students' acquisition of knowledge about substantive tests, as measured by their cue weights. They find that the combination of student-generated and instructor-assisted elaboration leads to the greatest knowledge gains, followed by those with instructor-assisted elaboration. Students using either no elaboration techniques or only their own elaborations do not acquire knowledge. Earley (2001) compares the effects of self-explanation to those of cognitive feedback (or combined explanation and feedback) in a real estate valuation task. Both self-explanation and cognitive feedback have positive effects on procedural knowledge acquisition (as measured by performance on the task), and their combination yields the largest effect. In addition, subjects who exhibit the most reasoning in their self-explanations gain the most procedural knowledge. Earley (2003) uses a similar task and documents that subjects who receive information about the correct answer prior to self-explaining exhibit greater reasoning in those explanations than do those who receive outcome feedback (i.e., receive the answer after explaining). In addition, reasoning is positively related to procedural knowledge.

Finally, Pei and Reneau (1990) and Gal and Steinbart (1992) examine various issues related to computer-based instruction. Pei and Reneau train students in two different methods of classifying internal controls to instantiate initial knowledge structures then further train them using an expert system that employs a knowledge structure that is either consistent or inconsistent with the initial knowledge structure. Students who receive an expert system that is consistent with their initial knowledge structure learn more from that system, as indicated by greater quantity of recalled internal controls, greater clustering of recalled internal controls, and greater recognition of internal controls. Gal and Steinbart vary the extent to which computer-based instruction prompts students to think about solutions to control weakness or financial statement error problems and the extent to which the instruction requires students to reason backward (from effect to cause) rather than to reason forward. Neither manipulation affects learning, as measured by students' performance on later tasks.

Similar to the psychology literature, the accounting literature on instruction and experience tends to find that people acquire declarative knowledge through instruction and procedural knowledge through some combination of practice and feedback. However, reading worked-out examples appears to be a promising substitute for practice, and future research should continue to explore boundary conditions for the effectiveness of this technique given that it may speed up procedural knowledge acquisition and lower firms' training costs substantially. Also similar to psychology, abilities and prior knowledge appear to lead to faster and greater knowledge acquisition. Characteristics of instruction such as choice and sequencing of instructional activities also appear to affect knowledge acquisition, but there are not enough studies to draw general conclusions. What might be of interest in this regard is to gain a better understanding of how firms currently conduct their training sessions, as well as the constraints they face. For example, is there adequate time to have participants work cases then hear lectures then work cases again? As another example, to what extent are firms using traditional classroom-based instructional activities such as lecturing to a group of professionals rather than relying on individualized activities such as interactive software? Similarly, to what extent are firms relying on instruction as opposed to day-to-day experience with other possible learning tools such as decision aids? How effective are these other tools for promoting knowledge acquisition? Research in this area could have a greater impact on practice if researchers understand firms' current learning conditions as well as their constraints.

It seems most important, however, to step back and examine the larger picture of the environment in which people gain knowledge about accounting issues. Of particular interest here is how accounting systems themselves affect learning. The study by Luft and Shields (2001) provides a good example of how a system (via its use of capitalization or expensing) may either increase or decrease people's knowledge about important accounting issues. More generally, it seems plausible that the regulatory environment (e.g., the presence of relatively more principles-based versus rules-based standards) can affect how people learn. A second issue of interest is how people's intuitive theories about accounting affect their learning. Given the prevalence of magazine, newspaper, and even television coverage of accounting-related issues today, it seems likely that misinformation about accounting reaches people who use accounting for important judgments and decisions (e.g., investors and marketing managers). It would be interesting to document the prevalence and effects of these theories on learning and JDM.

9-3   PERSONNEL SCREENING

Definitions and Background

This section discusses the effects of various personnel practices, jointly termed *personnel screening,* on various factors that affect JDM quality. Specifically, discussion centers around *selection* of the individuals from an applicant pool to whom job offers are made, *assignment* of existing personnel to various positions and tasks within an organization, and *promotion* of individuals to new positions based on *performance appraisals.*[17] These personnel practices can have an impact on JDM quality by affecting various person variables such as knowledge, abilities, intrinsic motivation, and personality characteristics. In addition, these practices, although not directly affecting task variables, can affect the characteristics of the tasks faced by a particular individual. For example, assignment of personnel to tasks may be based partially on the complexity of those tasks (e.g., Prawitt 1995; Abdolmohammadi 1999). Personnel practices may also contain elements of environmental variables that can affect JDM quality. For instance, performance appraisals may provide feedback to individuals. Thus, personnel screening can affect JDM quality through a variety of factors. However, because the personnel psychology literature tends to focus on the effects of these practices on person variables, this section adopts a similar focus. Clearly, given the current extent of these practices' use, they will continue to be a viable JDM improvement method.

Personnel screening involves a variety of activities. Starting with selection, an organization can employ several techniques to assess person variables of interest; this chapter focuses on tests, interviews, reference letters, and the collection of information via application forms and similar vehicles. Assignment of existing staff consists of specifying the particular tasks individuals will perform within the positions for which they were hired initially. For example, public accounting firms hire many staff auditors each year and assign them to particular client engagements. Such assignment can be more detailed. For instance, within a particular client engagement, some tasks are assigned to audit staff and some tasks are assigned to more experienced personnel. Assignment can also involve the shuffling of existing personnel among tasks. For example, accounting firms often reassign auditors to new clients. Performance appraisals can include face-to-face discussions and written reports. These appraisals are used for many purposes, including identification of training needs, determination of pay, and promotion

---

[17]Discussion of *recruiting* practices (activities meant to identify potential high-quality applicants and to attract them to become part of the applicant pool) is beyond the scope of this section. However, recruiting may be important to individual JDM quality within organizations because of its effects on the characteristics of the applicant pool from which employees ultimately are selected. Research on recruiting is relatively recent, but there are some well-established findings. For example, providing realistic job previews leads to higher-quality applicants (as measured by qualifications and later job performance). Further discussion can be found in Barber (1998), Rynes and Cable (2003), and Saks (2005). This section also does not discuss the relationship of performance appraisals to monetary incentives and to subsequent performance because Chapter 7 discusses the effects of monetary incentives on JDM quality.

to new positions; this chapter focuses on their use for promotion.[18] They also may be used as inputs to selection and assignment processes, as discussed further below.

Personnel screening is not unique to firms that employ accounting professionals. Clearly, however, these methods of affecting determinants of JDM quality are extremely relevant to these firms. First, high-quality personnel practices (those consistent with extant research) may be positively related to firm performance (e.g., Huselid 1995; Huselid et al. 1997; Terpstra and Rozell 1997a; Schmidt and Hunter 1998).[19] Second, as is the case with instructional programs, firms' investments in personnel programs are quite large (Schmitt and Chan 1998). Third and also similar to the situation with instructional programs, firms often do not engage in high-quality personnel practices (Terpstra and Rozell 1997b). For example, many firms do not use tests of abilities as part of the selection process even though these typically are the most predictive of job performance and among the least costly (Schmidt and Hunter; Ones et al. 2005). As another example, firms typically provide little motivation for performance appraisers to make high-quality appraisals, even though lack of motivation leads to many problems in appraisals such as overly lenient ratings (Arvey and Murphy 1998). Reasons for not using high-quality personnel practices include lack of familiarity, incorrect beliefs about usefulness, legal concerns, and lack of resources (Terpstra and Rozell 1997b).

Given how pervasive these findings are, they likely apply to firms that employ accounting-related professionals. More important, there is substantial variation in both the number and types of personnel practices used by firms, including those in the accounting area (Cleveland et al. 1989; Wilk and Cappelli 2003). For example, public accounting firms vary as to the universities they target for hiring. In addition, public accounting firms have different assignment strategies depending on how structured they are (Prawitt 1995). Given the large costs of personnel practices and the existence of variation in these practices across firms that employ accounting-related professionals, it seems likely that at least some of these firms have costly personnel practices that do not lead to higher levels of the person variables of interest (e.g., abilities).

Personnel Selection, Assignment, and Performance Appraisal Effects

Personnel selection, assignment, and promotion based on performance appraisals can have positive effects on knowledge, abilities, and other person variables such as intrinsic motivation that have average positive effects on performance (JDM quality).[20]

---

[18]Promotion is one of the most often cited purposes of performance appraisals (Murphy and Cleveland 1995). However, performance appraisals typically are used simultaneously for multiple purposes (Jiambalvo et al. 1983; Cleveland et al. 1989), and multiple purposes sometimes create conflicts for raters. For example, the promotion use of appraisals may lead raters to focus more on factors that positively affect job performance, whereas the training use of appraisals may lead raters to focus more on factors that negatively affect job performance.

[19]However, recent work questions whether high-quality personnel practices lead to high levels of firm performance or, instead, whether firms that experience high performance then have the resources to engage in high-quality personnel practices (Wright et al. 2005).

[20]The personnel psychology literature focuses on job performance rather than JDM quality per se. For accounting professionals (and others), job performance consists of both "technical performance," which includes the quality of judgments and decisions, and "contextual performance" (Borman and Motowildo 1993). *Contextual performance* refers to behaviors that contribute to a firm but do not relate directly to technical activities. For example, mentoring and encouraging other people can contribute to a firm by increasing the others' technical performance. Both technical performance and contextual performance affect performance ratings and personnel decisions based on those ratings (Landy and Shankster 1994; Borman et al. 1995).

Further, these personnel practices sometimes focus on personality characteristics that are believed to be positively related to performance. Overall, then, these practices are thought to have a positive effect on various person variables by increasing the level of these variables vis-à-vis what the level would be were the practices not used. In other words, personnel selection, assignment, and promotion based on performance appraisals are like instruction, practice, and feedback in that they tend to increase the level of variables that are either known or believed to positively affect JDM quality.[21]

One major personnel practice is selection. Personnel selection involves two major processes that are aimed at choosing individuals from a pool of applicants. The first is creating a selection system for each type of position within an organization (Schmitt and Chan 1998). Theoretically, this phase involves several steps, each of which can contribute to increasing knowledge, abilities, intrinsic motivation, and certain personality characteristics. The first step is job analysis, which entails precisely specifying the behaviors and tasks required by a given job and valued by the organization, as well as the person variables that are likely to have a positive impact on the required behaviors and task performance (Schmitt and Chan; Voskuijl 2005). As part of job analysis, firms must specify what is meant by "performance"; as discussed in Chapter 2, performance (here, JDM quality) often has multiple dimensions. Second, firms should develop and determine that measures for multiple performance dimensions and for the person variables predicted to be important to those performance dimensions are reliable (using standard techniques for determining reliability).[22] Third, firms should collect data using the developed measures and validate their predictions regarding important person variables (i.e., determine if the person variables are related to performance as predicted).[23] The best way of doing this is to use statistical techniques such as regression analysis.

If done properly, each of these steps can contribute to increases in the levels of the specified person variables. For example, job analysis that specifies the key person variables and validation studies that support their effects on job performance lead firms to focus on these variables during the actual selection process. Proper development of measures of person variables has a positive effect on the extent to which hired individuals actually possess these characteristics. Further, all these steps can contribute to the face validity of selection techniques, which positively affects applicants' reactions to these techniques; in turn, applicants' reactions to selection techniques positively affect their interest in an organization (Schmitt and Chan 1998).

The second major phase of the selection process is for the organization to use the developed system to identify applicants who possess the desired characteristics for a position.[24] Similar to the first phase, this phase can lead to higher levels of knowledge,

---

[21]Note that most of the person variables on which personnel practices focus cannot be altered by other mechanisms. Abilities and personality characteristics are relatively fixed characteristics in adults. Although firms can provide extrinsic motivators such as monetary incentives to deal with intrinsic motivation issues, there likely also is a minimum level of intrinsic motivation that is necessary for accounting-related positions. Finally, with regard to knowledge, instructional programs for some types of knowledge may be prohibitively costly or take too long for employees to complete (Jones et al. 2001).

[22]Sometimes, measures for variables such as abilities are commercially available, so firms do not have to develop them.

[23]An additional element of selection system development (and refinement) that firms may want to consider is empirical examination of the sources of applicants that tend to produce the best employees (Schmitt and Chan 1998).

[24]This phase may consist of several sequential subphases, such as initial screening, an on-campus portion, and an office visit. A detailed discussion of each of these subphases is beyond the scope of this section.

abilities, and other person variables by focusing efforts on measuring these variables and through the provision of reliable measures for selectors to use. However, this phase may entail making further choices about how best to measure person variables. That is, firms may not be able to or choose not to use the methods used in the initial development of the system. Inability to use methods used earlier occurs when applicants do not yet possess the characteristics of interest. For example, firms may use knowledge tests to measure current employees' job-related knowledge. Applicants for jobs do not have as extensive job-related knowledge as do current employees, however, so selection systems instead may include measures of factors that predict the acquisition of knowledge (e.g., ability tests) or measures of what job-related knowledge applicants may possess (e.g., grades). The choice to not use methods used in the initial development of the system instead may be based on concerns about applicants' reactions to the methods and, thus, the potential effects on hiring capable employees. For example, some firms are concerned about ability tests because of perceptions that they disadvantage minority applicants (e.g., Guion 1998).[25] Indeed, to have effective selection systems, firms should attempt to increase applicants' positive attitudes toward selection procedures, for example, by explaining the procedures to them (Schmitt et al. 2003).

The specific measures used in the actual selection process discussed by this section include ability tests and other written instruments for gathering specific information (e.g., personality questionnaires and application forms), reference letters, and interviews. Note that these measurement techniques do not match up one-for-one with the underlying person variables of interest. To the extent possible, the ensuing discussion explicates which variables are measured by each technique.

Ability tests have been shown to be the most valid predictor of job performance across many fields for employees hired into positions for which they have no experience; many accounting-related positions are such entry-level positions (e.g., Hunter and Hunter 1984; Hunter 1986; Schmidt and Hunter 1998, 2004). The reason for this finding is that abilities are positively related to the acquisition of technical knowledge, which then has a positive impact on performance. In particular, most of the variation in performance that is accounted for by abilities can be explained by a single "general intelligence" factor; tests of more specific abilities have no incremental predictive validity beyond this measure (Salgado et al. 2001).

Another written vehicle for collecting information is the personality questionnaire.[26] In recent years, these questionnaires have revolved around measuring the "Big Five" personality variables: conscientiousness, emotional stability, extroversion, agreeableness, and openness to new experiences (Digman 1990). Conscientiousness and emotional stability appear to be related to performance in many fields and to have incremental predictive validity beyond ability tests (Salgado et al. 2001; Salgado and Fruyt 2005).[27] Agreeableness and extroversion appear to matter to performance in some jobs, and agreeableness also has incremental predictive validity (beyond ability

---

[25]A recent study (Hunter and Schmidt 2000) suggests that these tests do not create disadvantages for minorities.

[26]Because these questionnaires involve self-reports, there is concern about applicants faking their responses for purposes of impression management or giving incorrect answers due to lack of self-insight. These problems do not seem to substantially affect the link between personality measures and performance, however (Guion 1998).

[27]These conclusions, however, are still being debated (e.g., Hough and Oswald 2000; Hough and Ones 2001; Cook 2004).

tests). Similarly, integrity tests, which produce composite measures of conscientiousness, emotional stability, and agreeableness, are related to performance and have incremental predictive validity beyond both ability tests and measures of conscientiousness (Sackett and Wanek 1996), so the combination of an ability test and an integrity test produces one of the highest predictive validities (Schmidt and Hunter 1998).

The key issue is whether personality questionnaires capture the intended personality characteristics. Evidence supporting this is that, as predicted, personality measures are related more to contextual job performance than to technical job performance (Schmitt et al. 2003). Further, they are related to tacit job knowledge (see Chapter 3), which is proposed to mediate the relation of personality to contextual performance (Landy and Shankster 1994; Borman et al. 1997; Motowildo 2003). In addition, the measures from these questionnaires typically are not correlated with ability test measures (Schmidt and Hunter 1998). However, personality questionnaires may capture person variables beyond personality characteristics. For example, conscientiousness (and integrity) questions likely capture intrinsic motivation (Schmitt et al.); indeed, the effect of conscientiousness on performance is similar to the effect of motivation on performance, that is, it has a positive effect on technical knowledge, which, in turn, positively affects technical performance (Motowildo).

Personnel selection systems collect other information in writing through application forms, résumés, transcripts, and similar vehicles. This information includes individuals' demographic characteristics, work experience, level of education, grades, extracurricular activities and personal interests, and previous test scores. Firms may collect these data to measure a variety of person variables, including knowledge, abilities, intrinsic motivation, and personality characteristics. They may intend to use them as supplements to other measures or as substitutes in cases where other methods cannot be used (e.g., knowledge tests) or where methods may engender negative applicant reactions (e.g., ability tests). With regard to their predictive validity, Schmidt and Hunter (1998) show that education and interests have relatively low validity overall as well as low incremental validity over ability tests, whereas age has no predictive validity for job performance. Hunter and Hunter (1984) show that grades have relatively low validity. Reference letters, although frequently used by organizations, typically have low predictive validity for job performance; this is likely due to their being almost uniformly positive (Schmidt and Hunter; Salgado et al. 2001; Cook 2004). Finally, job experience has low to moderate predictive validity in situations where applicants have relevant job experience (and incremental validity over ability test measures) (McDaniel et al. 1988; Schmidt and Hunter 1998, 2004; Schmidt et al. 1988; Quiñones et al. 1995). Validities for experience measures are greatest when experience is between zero and five years, when it is measured based on amount (e.g., number of times a task is performed) rather than total time spent, when it is measured based on specific tasks rather than at the job level, and for low-complexity jobs.

The most popular selection technique is the interview, which typically is done face-to-face. Some firms rely exclusively on interviews during the selection process (Salgado et al. 2001). Interviews can have high predictive validity for job performance if they are structured (Huffcutt and Arthur 1994; Schmitt and Chan 1998; Cortina et al. 2000; Cook 2004; Born and Scholarios 2005); further, they have substantial incremental validity over ability tests, so the combination of structured interviews and ability tests also produces high validity. Structured interviews are those that include detailed questions developed from job analyses. They require that the same questions be asked in exactly the same format and order for each applicant. In addition, structured interviews include detailed rating scales for each question and require that ratings be given for each answer. For example, they may use "behaviorally anchored rating scales," which list particular behaviors that indicate high, medium, and low levels of each dimension being rated (Schmitt and Chan; Dipboye 2005). Structured interviews also constrain interviewers from asking follow-up questions and elaborating on required questions.[28] These types of interviews may also require that interviewers take notes and participate in training prior to interviewing (Campion et al. 1997).[29] Finally, structured interviews differ from unstructured interviews in that they tend to focus on different issues (Huffcutt et al. 2001). Specifically, structured interviews tend to ask questions related to job knowledge, interpersonal skills, and organizational fit, whereas unstructured interviews tend to focus on education, experience, and interests.

Perhaps the most important issue about interviews is which person variables they actually capture. Ratings from structured interviews have been shown to be somewhat correlated with measures of job knowledge, ability tests, and measures of interpersonal skills, creativity, and leadership (Schmidt and Hunter 1998; Cortina et al. 2000; Huffcutt et al. 2001; Cook 2004). However, there is mixed evidence regarding the extent to which structured interview ratings are correlated with personality questionnaire measures (Barrick et al. 2000; Cortina et al.; Roth et al. 2005).

Another major personnel practice is assignment of existing personnel to tasks and positions; this practice also can have positive effects on knowledge, abilities, intrinsic motivation, and other person variables relevant to JDM quality. Assignment of just-hired personnel to tasks and jobs is based on perceptions of characteristics that are needed for these tasks and jobs; these perceptions likely come from the selection process. Thus, the extent to which initial assignment leads to higher levels of relevant person variables is related to the extent to which the selection process does so (Guion 1998). Assignment of existing (experienced) employees to tasks and jobs likely is based substantially on the extent to which they possess the characteristics perceived to be related to performance in those tasks and jobs. At this point, assessments of employee characteristics likely come from the performance appraisals that are used for promotion and other purposes. Thus, the extent to which this type of assignment has a positive influence on "good" person variables is related to the effectiveness of performance appraisals.

Promotions based on performance appraisal ratings can positively affect knowledge, abilities, and other person variables by choosing for promotion people with higher levels of these variables. Indeed, research indicates that performance ratings are related to such variables (Landy and Farr 1980; Schmidt et al. 1986, 1988; Borman et al. 1991, 1995; Schmidt and Hunter 2004).[30] Specifically, this can occur if appraisals that

---

[28]However, Huffcutt and Arthur (1994) find little decrease in validity when interviewers are allowed to ask follow-up questions.

[29]Research has attempted to examine which elements of structured interviews enhance their predictive validity. These elements are still unclear, but the following may be important: using job analysis as a basis for questions, asking the same questions of each person, having to rate each answer, and training (Conway et al. 1995; Campion et al. 1997).

[30]This section assumes that performance appraisals consist of judgmental ratings made by one person (typically a supervisor) for each employee vis-à-vis specified standards. This is the most commonly used performance appraisal technique (Landy and Farr 1980). Alternatively, firms may appraise performance by comparing employees to one another. For example, they may use forced distributions to provide appraisals.

assess only overall performance correctly reflect the relationship of these variables to performance or if appraisals correctly rate each of the relevant person variables separately then give nonzero weights to these separate ratings in overall assessments.[31] Clearly, the person variables included in performance appraisal processes should be those shown to be related to performance (e.g., through validation studies used to develop personnel selection practices). To be of the highest quality, performance appraisal systems should include several additional elements (Murphy and Cleveland 1995; Guion 1998). For example, items on appraisal forms should be pretested for understanding and face validity and analyzed to establish their construct validity. Along with this, high-quality appraisal systems utilize raters who have knowledge of the jobs for which performance is being rated. They also train raters with regard to the meaning of the rated factors and proper procedures for using the rating forms, including how to use rating scales. Raters who provide appraisals should also have sufficient opportunities to observe and make records of their subordinates' work, and they should be motivated to provide correct appraisals. Finally, appraisal systems should clearly specify performance standards.

Unfortunately, as mentioned earlier, firms often do not use the highest-quality personnel practices (those described above). At the outset, then, the probability that these practices have positive effects on knowledge and other person variables relevant to performance can be decreased substantially. In addition, there are a number of moderators of the positive effects of existing personnel selection, assignment, and performance appraisal/promotion processes. A large number of these moderators pertain to the people involved in personnel practices.

Starting with personnel selection, the quality of system development can be negatively affected by characteristics of the persons participating in development (Morgeson and Campion 1997; Guion 1998). First, firms typically choose several "subject matter experts" to conduct job analyses and to choose and establish the reliability of measures of person variables of interest (Landy and Shankster 1994; Schmitt and Chan 1998). As discussed in Chapter 8, third parties evaluating others' JDM quality often make errors, so these experts may not truly be the most knowledgeable about the jobs and the determinants of performance therein. In addition, even knowledgeable people can make errors in the job analysis process. For example, they may rely on preformed stereotypes about job requirements rather than conducting careful analyses. Second, system development also requires choosing and determining the reliability of measures of performance. For this step, firms often rely on ratings produced by the performance appraisal process. As discussed below, these ratings can be affected by a number of errors and biases. Third, system development requires validation of the measured variables' relation to performance; this process also can be moderated by characteristics of people involved. Individuals involved in validation may not use statistical techniques; instead, they may rely on intuitive analysis. When conducting intuitive analyses, people can make many errors (see Chapter 5). For example, when

---

[31]Establishing the correctness of performance appraisals is quite difficult (Sulsky and Balzer 1988; Balzer and Sulsky 1992; Murphy and Cleveland 1995; Murphy and DeShon 2000). Various methods for doing so include comparing raters' appraisals to those of "expert" raters, comparing one rater's appraisals to those of another rater, and examining ratings for the presence of particular errors. There are problems with each method. For example, expert raters may not be experts. As another example, raters may agree with each other but both be incorrect because they share particular biases.

assessing covariation intuitively, people tend not to use all the information that should be used; specifically, they tend to focus on instances where performance is high and a performance determinant such as ability also is high (e.g., Shaklee and Tucker 1980; Crocker 1981).

Person-variable moderators of the effectiveness of the actual selection process typically relate to the interview process, the combination of various measures to create overall ratings of applicants, and applicants' reactions to selection methods. The interview process can lead to less positive outcomes with regard to the person variables of interest for a variety of reasons. First, interviewers often are influenced by irrelevant factors, both in rating various dimensions of individuals and in their overall ratings. These include gender, ethnicity, age, weight, height, and attractiveness (Schmitt and Chan 1998; Hosoda et al. 2003; Cook 2004; Dipboye 2005). These factors may affect interviewers by invoking knowledge structures related to such factors (i.e., stereotypes); these knowledge structures then guide later parts of the interview. Second, interviewers may implicitly make decisions regarding applicants before the interview begins based on the information they have about grades and other characteristics. In other words, interviewers may seek to confirm these decisions through the questions they ask or the manner in which they ask them or by engaging in motivated reasoning regarding interviewees' answers. Third, interviewers may frame the interview as a vehicle for rejecting applicants; like other types of framing, this framing may influence the manner in which they ask questions and interpret answers.

Persons involved in the actual selection process also may make errors and exhibit certain biases when combining dimension ratings to form overall ratings for applicants. This occurs because such combination is most frequently done subjectively (by the selectors) rather than mechanically (Born and Scholarios 2005). As is true in other situations, persons combining cues to make overall judgments can be inconsistent in applying their own judgment policies, changing the weights given to various factors across applicants (e.g., Dougherty et al. 1986; Ganzach et al. 2000; Dipboye 2005). Further, there can be substantial differences in the judgment policies used by different selectors within a firm (Graves and Karren 1992).

A third person-variable moderator of the effectiveness of the actual selection process is applicant reactions to selection methods; these reactions affect applicants' decisions about whether to accept jobs and, thus, the levels of knowledge, abilities, and other determinants of performance that ultimately exist among employees. In general, applicants have more positive reactions to methods that are perceived to be job related, not personally intrusive, not unfair, and that allow for a personal meeting with the selector(s) (Anderson et al. 2001). These characteristics of methods likely reflect applicants' confidence in selectors' capabilities to do a competent job when evaluating them as well as their beliefs about how well they will fare under each method (Rynes and Connerley 1993; Landy and Shankster 1994). More specifically, interviews and reference letters receive relatively high ratings, whereas integrity tests and personality questionnaires receive moderate ratings; ability tests receive relatively low ratings (Rynes and Connerley). Attitudes toward ability ratings can be made more favorable if applicants are informed about how they are job related; further, applicants prefer contextually specific ability tests over general tests (Ones et al. 2005).

Characteristics of the people participating in the process also can moderate the positive effects of assignment and performance appraisal on knowledge, abilities, and other person variables related to performance. The first characteristic of interest is the knowledge of system participants. Evidence indicates that people form beliefs about others' knowledge by imputing their own knowledge to others then adjusting based on differences between themselves and those others (Nickerson 1999). In other words, people assume that others know what they know as a default then adjust this belief upward or downward depending on differences in characteristics they believe affect knowledge. For example, an antique collector may assume that another collector knows what she knows about antiques and adjust downward based on the fact that the other person has less experience collecting. Clearly, after repeated interaction with another, one's beliefs about the other's knowledge are modified so this default-adjustment process is needed only when one lacks information about a particular piece of knowledge possessed by the other. This process can affect personnel assignment and performance appraisal given the central role of perceptions about employees' knowledge in both processes and given that persons making assignment and performance appraisal judgments and decisions likely have knowledge that differs from that of employees. Thus, they may make errors in their assessment of employees' knowledge, and the extent of these errors can differ across employees assuming that there is variation in the difference between employees' knowledge and that of persons making assignments and appraisals for which these personnel do not properly adjust.

A second knowledge factor that can affect performance appraisal in particular is knowledge of outcomes related to employees' job performance. As discussed in Chapter 3, people should ignore these outcomes when making their appraisals (assuming that outcomes are not used as a measure of job performance), but they typically do not. For example, a senior auditor evaluating a staff auditor's work related to internal control evaluation should do so based on whether the staff auditor followed professional standards and firm policy (along with other applicable criteria) rather than based on whether a serious internal control weakness was discovered later.

A number of other characteristics of raters can moderate the extent to which performance appraisals used for promotions are correct and, thus, reflect person variables relevant to performance (Landy and Farr 1980; Judge and Ferris 1993; Murphy and Cleveland 1995; Wayne and Liden 1995; Guion 1998; Schmitt and Chan 1998; Guion and Highhouse 2006). First, lack of experience with performance appraisals decreases the correctness of ratings. Second, raters who have lower job performance themselves give less correct ratings to their subordinates than do high-performing raters. Third, raters provide higher ratings of individuals who are like themselves in some way, for example, as to race (dubbed the "similar to me" effect). Fourth, raters provide higher ratings to individuals with whom they get along well. Fifth, raters are affected by the extent to which the gender of the one being rated matches their stereotypes of the gender roles implied by a job. Specifically, men receive more favorable ratings than do women in what are considered traditionally male jobs, whereas women receive more favorable ratings than men in what are considered traditionally female jobs (although the latter set of differences is smaller). Sixth, raters may have intuitive (and, thus, incorrect) theories about job performance and the factors related to it and use these theories rather than specified procedures. For example, Schmidt et al. (1986) find that raters rely on experience rather than job knowledge in rating workers with more than five years of experience, despite the fact that experience beyond five years in their setting does not increase performance. Seventh, performance ratings can exhibit "halo effects," in that ratings of multiple separate dimensions of performance (and, thus, overall performance ratings) are inappropriately affected by the rater's beliefs about one salient dimension of performance or the rater's global impression of the person being rated.

The above rater characteristics likely affect their ratings through cognitive processes. For example, less experienced raters likely lack knowledge of the rating process and, consequently, use incorrect cues, weight cues inappropriately, and so on. Raters giving higher ratings to individuals to whom they are similar have greater positive affect for those persons, and affect is used as a cue in performance ratings (Judge and Ferris 1993). Another possible explanation for the similar-to-me effect, as well as for halo effects and for gender-role stereotyping effects, is that raters do not engage in extensive processing of all the information available about those being rated at the appraisal point. Instead, raters may rely on their categorizations of individuals that are derived from some salient feature of the individual, for example, prior performance (Feldman 1981; Guion 1998). These categorizations affect the behaviors that are observed as part of the appraisal process, the behaviors that are recalled at the time of the appraisal, the interpretation of behaviors, and the reconstruction of information that cannot be recalled.[32] In other words, as discussed in Chapter 5, raters seek evidence that confirms their categorizations of subordinates. Thus, for example, halo effects may result from a positive general impression of a subordinate that leads a rater to recall only positive information related to separate performance dimensions or to reconstruct positive information using the prototypical member of the "good performer" category.

It is only when employees' behavior departs from initial categorizations or when they are not easily categorized that raters tend to engage in extensive, time-consuming processing. In general, the greater the time spent on processing, the more likely ratings are to be correct (Ilgen et al. 1993). However, extensive processing of employee information during performance appraisal may be conducted using attribution-theory-like processing (see Chapter 8). This means that raters may seek to determine the extent to which an employee's performance is caused by her characteristics (internal attributions) or by other factors (external attributions). In so doing, they may exhibit errors such as the fundamental attribution error; again, this means that raters consider internal factors to be more important than external factors in causing job performance. Thus, if raters encounter a plausible internal factor early in the appraisal process, they may not consider further information and, therefore, draw the wrong conclusions regarding employees' performance and the factors that affect it (e.g., Wood and Mitchell 1981).

In addition to these cognitive processing errors, raters may exhibit strategic behavior that leads to lower-quality ratings and, thus, lessens the positive effects of performance appraisal on various person variables related to employees' performance (JDM quality). For example, raters intentionally may be lenient in their ratings (i.e., give high ratings to most employees) because they want to avoid conflict, because they want to make the unit they manage look better, or because they want to obtain

---

[32]Recall of information about those being rated frequently may occur because firms do not require detailed recordkeeping as part of the appraisal process or because raters prefer to rely on their memories.

monetary rewards for their subordinates (Murphy and Cleveland 1995; Guion 1998; Fletcher and Perry 2001). In these cases, raters may fill in appraisal forms after having made decisions about ratings so as to make the forms consistent with the ratings.

A final person-variable moderator of the positive effects of the performance appraisal process is supervisor-focused influence tactics used by subordinates. For example, subordinates may try to flatter supervisors by commenting on their appearance, the quality of their work, etc. (e.g., Kipnis and Schmidt 1988). Subordinates who use these tactics are perceived by supervisors as being more similar to them and, thus, rated more highly (e.g., Wayne and Ferris 1990; Wayne and Liden 1995; Wayne et al. 1997).

Task variables also can moderate the positive effects of the selection process on various person-variable determinants of JDM quality (performance). With regard to selection, measures of abilities become more important to predicting performance as job-related tasks become more complex (Ree et al. 1995; Ones et al. 2005). This is consistent with higher-complexity jobs requiring more knowledge and greater abilities leading to greater job-related knowledge (see Chapter 6). Job complexity also may moderate the relations of various personality measures to performance, with these relations being the largest when jobs are of medium complexity (Salgado and Fruyt 2005). Little is known about task variables' moderating effects on assignment and appraisal processes. Recent work suggests that presentation format issues such as those described in Chapter 6 may arise during the appraisal process (e.g., Lipe and Salterio 2002; Banker et al. 2004).

Environmental variables also can reduce the positive effects of the selection, assignment, and performance appraisal/promotion processes. First, at the selection point, societal beliefs and legal pressures can cause firms to not use methods that are highly valid, such as ability tests (Guion 1998; Hunter and Schmidt 2000). Second, if the incentive system linking performance to pay is ineffective, the selection system's attempts to find people who will perform well may be for naught because those people may quickly exit the organization (Schmitt and Chan 1998). Alternatively, a positive link between performance ratings and pay (i.e., an effective incentive system) can lead supervisors to be overly lenient in their performance ratings (see above). Third, accountability during selection processes may improve appraisers' measurement of relevant person variables if focused on processes but worsen measurement if focused on outcomes (Dipboye 2005). However, failing to hold appraisers accountable for their ratings appears to lower the quality of those ratings (Mero and Motowildo 1995). In general, failing to motivate performance appraisers (e.g., by tying their pay to the correctness of their appraisals) lessens the quality of performance ratings (Arvey and Murphy 1998).

Finally, elements of various selection, assignment, and performance appraisal/ promotion methods themselves can moderate their positive effects on person-variable determinants of JDM quality. Starting with selection, despite their inferior reliability and predictive validity, organizations overwhelmingly prefer unstructured interviews to structured interviews during selection (Hough and Oswald 2000) partially because they believe structured interviews are not as useful (Terpstra and Rozell 1997b). Also, as discussed earlier, certain methods of measuring person variables during selection are more effective. For example, interviews produce less reliable measures of abilities and personality characteristics than, respectively, tests and questionnaires.

There are a number of elements of performance appraisals per se that moderate their positive effects. First, if firms use something other than performance ratings in order to avoid the problems discussed above, they may introduce further problems into the process. For example, job-related outcomes such as production or financial results are affected by factors other than individuals' performance, and these factors can vary across individuals and jobs (Schmitt and Chan 1998; Hough and Oswald 2000; Motowildo 2003). Second, training related to performance appraisals varies as to its effectiveness (Woehr and Huffcutt 1994). The least effective type of training, termed "rater error training," explains common errors and biases such as halo effects to raters and admonishes raters to avoid them. "Performance dimension training," in which raters learn about the factors being evaluated during appraisal, is only slightly more effective. The most effective training is "frame of reference training," in which raters learn about performance standards, the factors being evaluated, and examples of behaviors for each of these factors; they also receive practice and feedback related to appraisals. Third, the quality of performance ratings is lowered somewhat if scales use numerical or adjectival anchors (e.g., "very good") rather than behavioral anchors that describe specific behaviors indicating poor, average, and good performance (Landy and Farr 1980). Fourth, the quality of ratings decreases as the time lag between employees' work and the performance appraisal increases (Heneman and Wexley 1983; Ilgen et al. 1993). Fifth, as the amount of information used in appraisal decreases, so does its quality (Heneman and Wexley).

Studies of the effects of personnel selection, assignment, and promotion and performance appraisal processes on person variables that have a positive effect on JDM quality frequently involve archival or survey data. This is not surprising given the large number of moderator variables that can have an effect on these processes, as well as the extent to which high-quality personnel practices are not used in practice. As a result, researchers may be drawn toward examining the effects of these personnel practices as used rather than attempting to experimentally manipulate practices that firms are unlikely to adopt and attempting to control for or manipulate a large number of moderating variables. These are reasonable concerns, but there also are many problems associated with studying the effects of these factors archivally. The first is the presence of correlated variables. For example, there is substantial correlation among the uses of performance appraisal systems (Cleveland et al. 1989). Specifically, firms that tend to use performance appraisals for promotion purposes also tend to use these appraisals for training, employee feedback, and so on. Thus, a researcher who attempts to examine the effects of performance appraisal–based promotions on employee characteristics such as knowledge may also be examining the effects of training, feedback, and other factors on these characteristics. The second problem is that moderators in this area can have multiple effects, some of which can offset each other. For instance, as performance appraisers gain experience, they gain knowledge about the appraisal process; such knowledge typically leads to higher-quality ratings. On the other hand, appraisers also gain more knowledge about their firm, employees' jobs, and their own job as they gain experience. If they impute this knowledge to their employees and do not adjust sufficiently for their employees' lack of experience, the quality of their performance ratings can be decreased. Archival data often do not allow the researcher to disentangle such effects. For these reasons and others such as an interest in having firms raise the quality of their personnel practices, there is a great need for experimental studies in this area.

Accounting Studies on Selection, Assignment, and Performance Appraisal Effects

This section reviews accounting studies that examine the effects of personnel selection, assignment, and performance appraisal/promotion processes on factors that affect JDM quality. Most of these studies relate to public accounting firms and, more specifically, the audit function.

Starting with studies on selection, in one study that focuses on a diverse group of potential employers of accounting students, Pasewark et al. (1988) collect data from students about their grades, work experience, and extracurricular activities, as well as the number of on-campus interviews, office visits, and job offers they receive. Findings relating to what were then the "Big Eight" firms show that grades and activities are important to obtaining on-campus interviews, grades are important to obtaining office visits, and activities are important to job offers. For smaller public accounting firms, grades appear to matter the most, affecting all three outcomes. For private companies, the only factor related to any outcome is grades, which is related to job offers. In another similarly diverse study, Ahadiat and Smith (1994) collect ratings of importance of various applicant characteristics from many different potential employers. They find that employers perceive several factors to be important, with professional conduct, reliability, ethical standards, and communication skills ranking the highest. Work experience, academic achievement, and extracurricular activities rank lower, perhaps explaining the frequent nonsignificance of these variables in the Pasewark et al. study. Also similar to the earlier study, there are differences in rankings of these factors across types of employers. Kirsch et al. (1993) conduct an experiment with students and public accounting recruiters and find that simulated hiring decisions differ between these groups. These differences partially reflect differential weights placed on the factors under examination. For example, students weight communication skills most highly, whereas recruiters rate this cue the lowest among the six provided.

Studies examining personnel assignment include Blocher (1979), who collects archival data on the performance evaluations of audit seniors over the course of several assignments. He finds that the performance ratings of seniors who are assigned to the same client during at least two periods do not change. Further, seniors who are assigned consecutively to multiple clients within the same industry show declining performance ratings over time. However, seniors who are assigned consecutively to clients in different industries show no change in ratings. There are a number of factors that can influence these ratings, such as learning, changes in raters, and so forth, so it is unclear what these differences reflect.

Prawitt (1995) experimentally examines the effects of audit firm structure and environmental complexity (levels of inherent risk and control risk) on staffing assignments made by audit managers. He finds that managers from structured firms tend to assign less experienced staff to tasks and recommend the use of less experienced persons as reviewers. Further analysis suggests that these findings reflect the fact that structured firms' auditors tend to face less complex tasks than do unstructured firms' auditors. In addition, unstructured firm managers tend to increase the experience level of assigned staff and reviewers more than do structured firm managers when faced with high levels of environmental complexity; this appears to be due to structured firm managers' relying on specialists under these circumstances rather than more experienced generalists. Consistent with Prawitt's findings, Abdolmohammadi (1999) provides survey findings that indicate that firms assign less experienced individuals to more structured tasks.

O'Keefe et al. (1994b) use survey and archival data to document that the complexity and risk of audits are positively related to the total number of hours worked by auditors at almost all levels of engagement. In this instance, complexity is measured by the client's overall size, size of foreign operations, and auditor assessments, and risk is measured by leverage, public status, and auditor assessments. Increases in risk typically lead to higher proportions of work being performed by the most experienced auditors, whereas increases in complexity sometimes lead to relatively more work being done by staff auditors. The latter finding simply may reflect the need for more of the work that tends to be done by staff auditors. Stein et al. (1994), using the O'Keefe et al. data, find similar effects for complexity across two industries but also find that increases in risk tend to lead to more work by experienced auditors for financial firms but more work by less experienced auditors for manufacturing firms. Hackenbrack and Knechel (1997) find that increasing risk leads to greater relative use of more experienced auditors, whereas increasing client size leads to greater relative use of less experienced auditors.

Studies related to performance appraisal include several in managerial accounting settings. Stone et al. (2000) obtain archival data on the performance of management accountants of varying ranks and measure with a questionnaire their technical (general entry-level and industry-related) knowledge, tacit job knowledge, and abilities. They find that entry-level technical knowledge decreases with rank and that industry knowledge and tacit job knowledge increase with rank. Abilities do not differ across ranks. Wier et al. (2002) use archival data on performance evaluations and promotions for a large number of management accountants and find that performance appraisals at the staff and senior ranks are positively correlated, possibly reflecting either the effects of prior impressions or abilities. However, there is a negative correlation between time to be promoted from staff to senior and time to be promoted from senior to manager. They also find that promotions to senior are based more on performance vis-à-vis one's peers, whereas promotions to manager are based more on performance vis-à-vis standards.

Xu and Tuttle (2005) manipulate accounting information and hypothetical subordinate work style and ask graduate students to act as supervisors appraising subordinates' performance. They also measure work styles of the students; they are classified as "adaptors" (those who seek to solve problems in a structured, precise fashion) or as "innovators" (those who are more creative in their problem solving). Accounting information indicates that the plant being run by the hypothetical subordinate is performing above the industry average or below the industry average. They find that supervisors like subordinates more when they are described as having work styles similar to those of the supervisors. Further, the extent to which supervisors like subordinates affects the attributions they make for good versus poor accounting information. Specifically, supervisors attribute good performance (as suggested by accounting information) more to internal than to external factors for subordinates they like, and they attribute bad performance more to internal than to external factors for subordinates they dislike. Along with this, performance evaluations are positively related to the attribution of good performance to internal factors. However, attributions do not affect performance evaluations when accounting information indicates poor performance.

Although not directly related to performance appraisal, a study by Rowe (2004) is informative as to its effects. This study finds that student subjects acting as designers of management control systems do not fully understand the extent to which internal factors versus external factors affect the performance of subordinates working under those systems. Specifically, they underestimate the capability of a particular type of control system for reducing free-rider problems among subordinates working in teams. Finally, as discussed in Chapter 3, a number of studies find that knowledge of outcomes affects performance appraisals in management accounting contexts (Lipe 1993; Tan and Lipe 1997; Frederickson et al. 1999; Ghosh and Lusch 2000). In addition, Frederickson et al. find that outcome effects increase as appraisers gain more experience with outcome-based appraisal systems.

Studies of performance appraisal in public accounting contexts include Jiambalvo et al. (1983), who experimentally examine the appraisals of hypothetical staff accountants of partners, managers, and seniors in auditing, tax, and consulting units of public accounting firms. They find substantial disagreement among individuals within each unit as to weights placed on the manipulated factors (e.g., employees' knowledge) and as to overall appraisals. There also is disagreement across units. Appraisers are highly consistent in applying their rating policies, however. Kida (1984c) conducts a similar study with audit seniors and managers and also finds substantial disagreement across individuals as to cue weights and overall evaluations. Wright (1982) finds higher levels of agreement among senior auditors and that high-performing senior auditors make appraisals that are very similar to those of low-performing senior auditors.

Ferris and Larcker (1983) obtain archival and survey data relating to staff auditors to measure their knowledge (as assessed by grades and other educational attainments), organizational commitment, motivation, similarity to supervisors, physical attractiveness, performance ratings, and salaries. Performance ratings are related to only organizational commitment and motivation, whereas salaries are related to knowledge and physical attractiveness. The lack of the relation of knowledge to performance ratings and the fact that different factors affect performance ratings and salaries may reflect the fact that the staff auditors in this study were relatively new and, thus, unlikely to vary much as to knowledge gained on the job. Tan and Libby (1997) obtain archival performance ratings of staff auditors, seniors, and managers and collect from them questionnaire measures of technical knowledge, tacit job knowledge, and abilities. Staff auditors with high performance ratings have significantly higher technical knowledge than staff with low ratings; there are no differences in abilities or tacit job knowledge. Seniors with high performance ratings have significantly higher technical knowledge and abilities, but not tacit job knowledge, than do seniors with low ratings. Finally, managers with high ratings have greater tacit job knowledge than managers with low ratings, but are no different with regard to technical knowledge or abilities.

Remaining studies in the public accounting context examine specific performance appraisal issues as opposed to the more general studies above. Harrell and Wright (1990) develop behaviorally anchored rating scales and ask seniors and managers to use these scales in addition to the performance appraisal scales in place to rate staff auditors as well as answer several survey questions. They find that seniors and managers feel that the behaviorally anchored scales better capture staff's performance than do conventional scales. They also find that the behaviorally anchored scales are valid from the perspectives that ratings on these scales are related to salary increases, promotions, and ratings of retention desirability. Luckett and Hirst (1989) manipulate the type of feedback audit seniors and managers receive regarding their performance appraisals of hypothetical staff auditors. Some receive no feedback, some receive feedback as to the "correct" overall evaluation (as given by three partners in the firm), some receive feedback as to the "correct" cue weights (also as given by the partners), and some receive both outcome feedback and the cue-weight task properties feedback. All the groups receiving feedback have substantially higher agreement among themselves than do the no-feedback subjects, and they also have cue weights that are closer to the "correct" weights.

Kennedy and Peecher (1997) examine the issue of whether auditors impute their technical knowledge to other auditors when evaluating those other auditors. They ask several pairs of managers and seniors (seniors and staff) who have experience working together to answer knowledge questions and rate the probability that their subordinates can answer the questions. They find that supervisors (managers and seniors) rely on their perceived knowledge to assess their subordinates' (seniors' and staff's) knowledge. In addition, the extent to which they overestimate their subordinates' knowledge increases with the actual knowledge gap between themselves and their subordinates. Tan and Jamal (2001) investigate whether audit managers are influenced by their prior impressions of seniors with whom they have worked extensively when appraising the quality of their current work. The seniors being evaluated have previous performance ratings of outstanding or average. Managers who have either outstanding or average performance ratings rate the performance of both types of seniors first based on memos that contain their identities then several weeks later with identities removed. They find that average managers rate the current work of seniors with prior outstanding ratings more favorably than that of seniors with prior average ratings when the seniors' identities are revealed, but they rate the work no differently when the identities are not revealed. Outstanding managers, on the other hand, rate the current work of outstanding and average seniors to be similar in both identity-known and identity-unknown conditions (consistent with the evaluations of this work made by partners in the firm). Thus, they conclude that outstanding managers rate seniors' current work more objectively.

Three studies examine attribution-type behavior related to auditor performance appraisals. Kaplan and Reckers (1985) examine the appraisals of a hypothetical senior auditor whose current work is described as poor. They manipulate the senior's past work as being good or poor and the client history as being stable or unstable. Seniors and managers provide appraisals and give more internal attributions when the senior's prior work is poor and the client history is stable. Kaplan and Reckers (1993), using a similar task, manipulate whether the senior's work has been improving or deteriorating over time and whether the senior provides an explanation that implicates client problems for her current poor performance. Other seniors providing appraisals give fewer internal attributions when the hypothetical senior offers an explanation and when she has an improving work history. Further, performance appraisals are positively affected by the extent of external attribution. Crant and Bateman (1993) ask staff, seniors, and managers to appraise the performance of a hypothetical staff auditor and manipulate whether the staff's performance is poor, whether she attributes her performance to herself or to external factors, and whether she employs a "self-handicapping" strategy by offering descriptions of how difficult the work will be before she performs it. The auditors' appraisals are affected not only by the actual performance, but also by the staff's attribution and self-handicapping. Specifically, appraisals of staff whose performance is poor are more positive when an external attribution is provided (versus an internal attribution), but attributions do not affect appraisals when performance is good. Appraisals of staff whose performance is poor are more positive when the staff uses self-handicapping (versus when she does not); appraisals of those with good performance are less positive when the staff uses self-handicapping.

As is the case in psychology, accounting studies indicate that personnel screening practices can lead to higher amounts of person variables such as knowledge and abilities. However, these practices sometimes are affected by irrelevant factors such as knowledge of outcomes, similarity of the appraiser to the person being evaluated, the appraiser's own knowledge, and impression management tactics. Further, people can vary greatly as to the weights they place on factors that are relevant to personnel screening. Beyond this, accounting studies of personnel screening tend not to focus on many of the issues studied in psychology (e.g., the predictive validity of different selection techniques).

Future research in this area probably should focus on assignment and performance appraisal rather than selection. It seems unlikely that individuals involved in selecting persons for accounting-related positions differ in any substantive way from those studied in the personnel psychology literature. Further, it seems unlikely that firms will change selection procedures based on research because of the apparently entrenched beliefs people have about various techniques such as unstructured interviews. Assignment studies such as that by Prawitt (1995) can increase our understanding not only of the effects of assignment per se, but also of how firms make tradeoffs between personnel-related improvement techniques and other JDM improvement methods such as decision aids. Studies of performance appraisal and related promotions may be difficult to conduct because of the lack of publicly available data or the willingness of firms to provide such private information. Experimental studies may be helpful in this regard, but they should employ professional subjects rather than students. Of particular interest in this area is how accounting information may interact with performance appraisal processes (as in the study by Xu and Tuttle [2005]). More generally, it would be of interest to ascertain how factors that are somewhat unique to the accounting environment, such as the presence of desired conclusions and professional standards, affect this process. Another interesting topic for future research is whether promotion processes that are based on performance appraisal systems that combine both accounting (financial) and nonfinancial measures are better than traditional promotion processes at increasing the levels of desired person variables.

9-4   DECISION AIDS

Definitions and Background

This section covers the effects of a variety of remedies collectively referred to as "decision aids." *Decision aids* are "tools that assist the decision maker in gathering, processing, or analyzing information for a decision" (Brown and Eining 1997). As this definition suggests, decision aids typically are thought to have positive effects on the quality of cognitive processing, specifically memory retrieval, information search, problem representation, hypothesis generation, and hypothesis and evidence evaluation (see Chapter 5).[33] In turn, various aspects of these cognitive processes can have positive effects on JDM quality. Thus, like instruction, practice, feedback, and personnel screening, decision aids can have positive effects on "good" variables (those that positively affect JDM quality). Some decision aids can also reduce the effects of factors that moderate the positive effects of knowledge on JDM. In addition, because decision aids are task-specific, they can change task variables. Many of these changes reduce the level of task variables that typically have negative effects on JDM quality. For example, they can reduce task complexity by reducing the amount of information a person has to process. Similarly, by imposing a standard presentation format and response mode, decision aids can promote higher agreement among individuals and within individuals over time (two dimensions of JDM quality). With a few exceptions, as discussed below, decision aids are feasible for practical implementation and already are being widely used.

Decision aids come in many shapes and sizes. They range from simple instructions such as "consider multiple perspectives" to complex *decision support systems,* which are computer-based interactive systems that include databases and mathematical models for operating on the data (Benbasat and Nault 1990), and *expert systems,* which are computational models of expert JDM that use symbolic reasoning (often in the form of if-then rules) rather than mathematical calculations (Luconi et al. 1986). Even though expert systems are meant to replace people, the literature contains many examples of expert systems being used in more of an advisory role (e.g., Liang 1988; Brown 1991a). Although both decision support systems and expert systems are used in accounting settings (e.g., Abdolmohammadi 1987; Messier and Hansen 1987; Michaelsen and Messier 1987; Brown 1991a), discussion of the theory and empirical evidence regarding their effects on JDM quality is beyond the scope of this section. However, to the extent accounting studies examine the use of these systems as decision aids, they are included in the discussion below.

Decision aids are not at all unique to accounting settings. Nevertheless, decision aids are an extremely relevant JDM improvement method in these settings. First, many accounting professionals and others who use accounting information already employ a number of decision aids in their daily work. For example, auditors use structured audit procedures that include checklists and audit programs. Personal finance magazines provide checklists for investors to use when making investment decisions. Second, similar to the other improvement methods discussed in this chapter, the monetary investment in decision aids by firms that employ accounting professionals can be enormous (e.g., Brown 1991a), and some of these investments may reap no positive returns because of lack of organizational support and similar factors (e.g., Gill 1995). Third, firms sometimes develop decision aids based on intuitive notions about how to improve JDM rather than relying on research and often do not examine their actual effects on JDM (O'Leary 1987; Ashton and Willingham 1989). As a consequence, aids

---

[33]Through repeated use, decision aids may have an effect on the acquisition of knowledge (learning). Discussion of decision aids' learning effects is beyond the scope of this section. For studies in accounting related to this issue, see, for example, Böer and Livnat (1990); Murphy (1990); Pei and Reneau (1990); Eining and Dorr (1991); Gal and Steinbart (1992); Steinbart and Accola (1994); Odom and Dorr (1995); Glover et al. (1997); Rose and Wolfe (2000); and Rose (2005). There are other possible effects of decision aids such as increased motivation and dissemination of expert-level knowledge throughout a firm, that also are beyond the scope of this section (e.g., Ashton and Willingham 1989; Messier 1995).

sometimes may not be effective at improving JDM because they are not directed at the underlying causes of lower-quality JDM. Further, their developers may not be aware of the potential negative effects of decision aids (see below). Along with this, there is variation in the types of decision aids used across firms, tasks, and people. For example, public accounting firms that are considered "semistructured" tend to prefer expert systems and replacement of people with models more than do other types of firms (Abdolmohammadi 1991). As another example, people who are more overconfident are less likely to rely on any type of decision aid (Arkes et al. 1986). Thus, there clearly are possible negative economic consequences of decision aids in some situations given their costs, the manner in which they are developed, and the variation in their use and form across situations.

Studying the effects of most types of decision aids is best done through manipulation in experiments. Archival study of decision aids likely is fraught with a number of difficulties. First, firms are likely to either employ or not employ decision aids for a given task; thus, it may not be possible to compare aided JDM quality to unaided JDM quality within a single task and a single firm. If such comparisons are made across firms, there may be many confounding factors such as the knowledge of the individuals doing the task. For similar reasons, it does not make sense to compare aided JDM in one task to unaided JDM in another task. Experiments can hold such confounding factors constant. Second, aids used in practice may combine various types of JDM improvement techniques. For example, an aid may contain a checklist and mathematical combination of information elicited by the checklist. Even if it were possible to compare aided JDM for a particular task to unaided JDM for that same task within a single firm, it would be unclear whether the checklist or the mathematical combination or both affect aided JDM. An experiment can manipulate specific techniques and hold others constant. Third, people often do not like to rely on decision aids, particularly those that remove them from the JDM process to a large extent (Larrick 2004). An archival study could address this by searching for evidence that people are using aids such as completed checklists. However, such evidence may be unreliable (e.g., people fill out checklists for documentation purposes but do not really use them for JDM) or unavailable because there are no specific records related to the use of aids. An experimental researcher can track the use of aids by, for example, presenting the experiment on a computer. An exception to this discussion occurs for two types of aids: replacing people with a statistical model derived from data on actual outcomes and relevant information cues (an environmental model) and combining people's JDM with that from an environmental model. Here, archival research clearly can make a contribution if people's judgments or decisions, as well as information cues that may be related to the JDM, are publicly available. For example, much of the research on the quality of analysts' earnings forecasts compares the forecasts to those derived from time series models or to a combination of the two.

The next several sections discuss the effects of various types of decision aids. Specifically, these are memory aids, brief instructions, decomposition, and aids that are based on statistical models. Before discussing the specific aids, however, this section covers two issues that are pertinent to all types of aids. The first issue, mentioned earlier, is that of whether people will rely on decision aids. The second issue is that decision aids can be implemented using a variety of formats. The simplest format issue is whether the decision aid is on paper or is computerized. Beyond this, a number of format issues arise. This section focuses on one of the key format issues related to decision aids—the use of graphs versus tables.

Factors Affecting Reliance on Decision Aids

Before discussing specific aids, it is important to understand factors that affect people's reliance on decision aids. Reliance can range from no use of the decision aid whatsoever, that is, completely ignoring it, working around it, or trying to "outsmart it" (Brown and Jones 1998), to full reliance, in which people do all the tasks required by the decision aid. Further, in cases where aids contain recommendations or answers, such as in the case of aids that employ statistical models, full reliance implies use of the aid's answer as one's own judgment or decision. Clearly, reliance can lie between none and full. Partial reliance may mean that an individual does only some of the tasks required by the aid; it also may mean that an individual considers the aid's recommendation as one information cue when making her judgment or decision but also considers other cues (Brown and Jones).

Many factors appear to impinge on people's willingness to rely on decision aids. Starting with factors that negatively affect reliance, people generally do not like aids that are known to be less than 100% correct (and decision aids always are imperfect) because they like the idea of explaining all the variance in JDM-related outcomes (Dawes 1979; Arkes et al. 1986; Einhorn 1986). Further, people tend to be overconfident in their own knowledge and abilities (see Chapter 4), so they feel that they can make better judgments and decisions than the imperfect ones suggested by an aid. For example, people believe that they can incorporate complexities that are not incorporated into aids, such as high-level interactions among cues (Kleinmuntz 1990). The more overconfident people are, the less likely they are to rely on aids (Arkes et al.).[34] In addition, people dislike technological change and do not enjoy the intimation that their JDM has been of less than high quality in the past (Larrick 2004). As a consequence of all these factors, people generally tend not to be fond of decision aids.

Exacerbating people's tendencies not to rely on aids are monetary incentives to produce high-quality JDM (Arkes et al. 1986). As discussed in Chapter 7, the imposition of monetary incentives can lead people to continuously change strategies in an effort to receive the incentive payment; such inconsistency leads to lower-quality JDM. Also, if people receive outcome feedback about their JDM as they proceed through several cases, they are less likely to use an aid because the feedback further points out the imperfections in the aid (Arkes et al.). Another factor that can reduce reliance on aids is the provision of information about tradeoffs that must be made in decision settings. Tradeoffs create conflict (Kottemann and Davis 1991), and as discussed in Chapter 5, people may prefer to avoid conflict during cognitive processing. If aids are computerized and people are reluctant to use computers, this factor also can reduce reliance (Brown and Eining 1997). More generally, people often do not understand the basis for the decision aid and, consequently, are less likely to believe in the decision aid's usefulness (Kleinmuntz 1990; Larrick 2004). Finally, if the decision aid offers the use of multiple cognitive processing strategies that vary as to cognitive effort required,

---

[34] As described in Chapter 4, little is known about what causes differences in overconfidence. For example, levels of knowledge and abilities have relatively low associations with overconfidence (Lichtenstein and Fischhoff 1977; Mabe and West 1982; Oskamp 1982).

people tend to rely on the strategies requiring the least effort (Todd and Benbasat 1991, 1992, 1994, 2000). Unfortunately, these strategies also tend to be the least likely to improve JDM quality. In this case, reliance on the aid per se is not affected; rather, it is reliance on the best strategy one can extract from the aid that is affected. Although this lack of full reliance can increase the efficiency aspect of JDM quality, it clearly can have a negative effect on other JDM quality elements.

Several factors can increase reliance on decision aids. First, given people's ideas about the imperfections in aids, the provision of information that an aid produces or leads to high-quality JDM tends to encourage its use (Fuerst and Cheney 1982; Powell 1991; Davis and Kottemann 1995). Similar to this, providing people with feedback about the quality of their unaided or partially aided JDM versus the quality of their JDM were they to fully rely on an aid can encourage the use of aids (Arkes et al. 1986; Davis and Kottemann). Note that this feedback is different from feedback regarding an individual's aided JDM quality per se; as mentioned above, such feedback tends to discourage use of aids.

Increased reliance on relatively complex decision aids can be facilitated by user involvement in development and user training (Fuerst and Cheney 1982; Guimaraes et al. 1992; Larrick 2004). Further, if decision aids are supported by top management (Guimaraes et al. 1992) and top management is viewed as credible (Larrick 2004), their perceived usefulness and resulting user reliance can be increased. People also rely more on aids that allow their input and interaction (e.g., decision support systems) rather than those that simply "spit out" an answer, perhaps because the former give an "illusion of control" (e.g., Davis and Kottemann 1994). Relatedly, people may prefer to rely on aids that explain why they provide the recommended responses (e.g., Ye and Johnson 1995). Further, the more user friendly the aid, the more likely people are to rely on it (Timmermans and Vlek 1994; Brown and Jones 1998).

A number of studies in accounting examine decision aid reliance issues in tasks related to users and producers of accounting information. Several investigate subjects' willingness to rely on a decision aid consisting of a rule for predicting bond ratings. The rule mechanically combines information from financial ratios and presents both a bond rating "score" and a recommended rating. Ashton (1990) provides this aid to auditors, who are told that use of the aid results in eight correct ratings in a group of sixteen cases. Very few subjects rely exclusively on the aid, although the aid does affect their JDM. Reliance is reduced when they both receive the aid and face monetary incentives, outcome feedback, or the requirement to justify their choices. Whitecotton and Butler (1998) allow some of their student subjects to select the financial ratios to include in the Ashton aid, whereas others receive the best set of ratios. Subjects who are involved in choosing the ratios rely on the aid more frequently. Kaplan et al. (2001) manipulate whether auditor subjects are informed about the Ashton aid's 50% accuracy rate and also measure auditors' locus of control. Auditors who are informed or who have an internal locus of control rely less on the aid. A second study shows that student subjects with an internal locus of control rely less on the aid only when they are not involved in choosing the ratios; when they are, there are no effects due to locus of control. Whitecotton (1996) examines decision aid reliance by financial analysts and students judging whether earnings will be more or less than expected in the following year. The decision aid here also is a rule that utilizes financial ratios to predict the probability of earnings exceeding expectations. It has a 75% accuracy rate, of which

346 CHAPTER 9   Methods for Improving JDM

subjects are made aware. Confidence has a negative effect on decision aid reliance, but experience does not. Finally, Nelson et al. (2003) report that investors' reliance on a decision aid for their investment decisions is negatively related to their confidence.

Remaining studies focus on auditing tasks. Anderson et al. (2003) show that auditors given explanations for a ratio fluctuation from a decision aid consider those explanations more sufficient for explaining the fluctuation than when the same explanations ostensibly are provided by the client. Ye and Johnson (1995) give auditors an aid related to analytical procedures and find that they are more willing to rely on the aid if it provides justifications of the procedures it uses and a list of the data used to make a recommendation. Eining et al. (1997) report that auditors rely more on an expert system related to fraud risk assessment than a statistical model; they argue this is because the expert system they employ is a more interactive decision aid that also explains its recommendations. Boatsman et al. (1997) show that penalties related to incorrect decisions affect reliance on an aid's recommendations. Specifically, these penalties lead to increases in shifting JDM away from the aid's recommendations and decreases in ignoring the aid; however, overall, ignoring the aid is quite prevalent. Finally, several surveys of auditors (Abdolmohammadi 1991, 1999; Abdolmohammadi and Usoff 2001) indicate that auditors believe that the vast majority of audit tasks are best performed by humans with no aids.

Accounting findings to date appear to be consistent with those in psychology in documenting people's general distaste for decision aids. Also consistent with psychology, decreased aid reliance can result from the provision of incentives or outcome feedback, or the requirement to justify one's JDM. Further, overconfidence and knowledge of an aid's accuracy rate (if not very high) can result in decreased reliance. However, if the aid is interactive or people are involved with its development, reliance can increase. Future research in this area should continue to examine the effects on aid reliance of factors that are important in accounting environments (e.g., the presence of a desired conclusion that leads to motivated reasoning and whether there is professional guidance related to the JDM). Of particular interest is the regulatory and legal environment that accounting professionals face given that reliance (or lack of reliance) on decision aids can have both negative and positive economic consequences. For instance, if decision aids are viewed as a type of professional standard (Jennings et al. 1993), relying on the aid's recommendations could be viewed favorably during legal proceedings, whereas not relying on the aid's recommendations could be viewed unfavorably.

Effects of Decision Aid Format

As mentioned earlier, decision aids can vary widely as to type. Along with this, aids' format can vary on many dimensions, and format differences can affect cognitive processing and subsequent JDM quality. For example, aids can be in black and white or color. Information cues can be organized in lists or matrices, individual cues within these organizations can appear in different orders, and the cues can be stated in terms of numbers or words (Kleinmuntz and Schkade 1993). Further, information cues can be presented sequentially or simultaneously. Information can be displayed in the form of graphs or tables (Vessey 1991). Decision aids can elicit JDM using a variety of response modes and can be on paper or computerized. Computerized aids can also vary the presentation of information cues for each decision maker; for example, lists of items can be customized depending on information entered by each individual (Brown and Eining 1997). Clearly, there can be many more format variations.

Discussion of most of these format variations is beyond the scope of this book. For example, the effects of presenting an aid on a computer rather than on paper involve complex issues of human–computer interaction (e.g., Carroll 1997; Olson and Olson 2003). Because decision aids tend to be task specific, other format issues are effectively task characteristics and, as such, the reader is referred to Chapter 6 regarding the effects of order of information, sequential versus simultaneous presentation, and response mode.

This section focuses on the effects of graphical versus tabular presentation because a number of studies in accounting examine these effects, and the use of graphs in accounting-related displays is widespread (e.g., DeSanctis 1984). For example, firms frequently use graphs in annual reports (Jarvenpaa and Dickson 1988). The effects of graphs versus tables can occur through alteration of task complexity and through direct influence on cognitive processing. These effects, however, occur differentially across various types of tasks. Vessey (1991) categorizes tasks as "elementary" or "higher level decision-making" tasks. Elementary tasks require the perception of overall patterns in data. For example, they may require looking for trends, comparing or interpolating values, and discerning relationships between variables. They primarily involve the acquisition of information needed for JDM. Higher level decision-making tasks require that people obtain, evaluate, and combine individual data points (information cues). In other words, they involve both information acquisition and evaluation. Vessey's theory is that graphical presentations facilitate the cognitive processing required by elementary tasks, whereas tabular presentations facilitate the processing required by higher level tasks. To the extent that there is a match between presentation and type of task, then, task complexity is lessened and cognitive processing improved. Her review of a number of studies supports this theory to a large extent. In addition, the time series forecasting literature indicates that graphs may facilitate linear series forecasting (Harvey 2001).

Hwang and Wu (1990) focus on the effects of graphs and tables contingent on task complexity and find an interaction; specifically, graphs lead to higher JDM quality when tasks are of medium complexity. For tasks of low or high complexity, there is no difference in JDM quality due to tables versus graphs. Their findings suggest that there may be effects beyond the match or mismatch of data presentation and required cognitive processing. Overall, then, this literature focuses on the notion of "cognitive fit," or the match between the graphical or tabular presentation and the type of JDM task being completed. It seems possible that there are other factors that impinge on this fit, such as individual differences. Finally, studies indicate that judgments or decisions that are aided with both tables and graphs tend to be of higher quality than those aided with tables alone (Vessey 1991).

A number of studies related to users and producers of accounting information compare the effects of tables to those of a particular kind of graphical presentation called "schematic faces." *Schematic faces* portray information cues by varying the presentation of different parts of the face (e.g., the eyes, nose, ears, etc.). Moriarity (1979) reports that accountants and students make more accurate bankruptcy predictions and take less time when using graphical faces than when using tables. MacKay and Villareal (1987) show that student subjects with faces are no more accurate overall at this task, although they do take less time. However, subjects are better at predictions for non-bankrupt firms with faces and better at predictions for bankrupt firms with tables. In addition, women make more accurate predictions than men when using faces. Umanath and Vessey (1994) find that students receiving traditional graphs make more accurate bankruptcy predictions than students receiving either faces or tables. In addition, subjects receiving faces are as accurate as those receiving tables. Faces subjects also take more time than the other groups. They suggest that these findings reflect bankruptcy prediction's requirements for both information acquisition and information evaluation; the graphs they provide maintain underlying data so subjects are able to engage in both activities better than they are with faces. Further, the graphs promote information acquisition better than do the tables because of their summarizing features. Stock and Watson (1984) report that student and faculty subjects predicting bond rating changes are more accurate and efficient with faces. Amer's (1991) student subjects receive a numerical table, a bar graph, a polygon display, or a schematic face and are asked to either predict bond ratings or determine if a firm has violated its debt covenants (the latter is considered an "elementary" task by Vessey's [1991] definition). There are no effects of presentation format type on JDM quality in the bond-rating task, although subjects are more accurate in the debt-covenant task if they receive a table or bar graph rather than a face or a polygon display.

DeSanctis and Jarvenpaa (1989) ask student subjects to forecast several financial statement amounts using a tabular presentation of data, a graphical presentation (bar charts), or a combined presentation (bar charts with numbers). Subjects with the combined presentation, after sustained practice, make the most accurate forecasts, followed by the subjects with graphs, then those with tables. Frownfelter-Lohrke (1998) manipulates aid format similarly and asks student subjects to predict a firm's financial condition (considered an "elementary task") and estimate earnings per share (considered a "higher level task"). She finds very few differences in accuracy or time taken based on format.

Four studies use inventory production simulation tasks. Benbasat and Schroeder's (1977) subjects receive information in either a table or a graph, but all subjects receive numerical summary data as well. Subjects with graphs have lower overall costs (the objective of the task) and take no more time. However, Lucas (1981) finds the opposite results with regard to cost performance, and Remus (1984) finds no differences. Remus (1987) reports that subjects with tables have lower costs in a low-complexity setting, but subjects with graphs have lower costs in a medium-complexity setting. Finally, Wright (1995) examines graphs versus tables in an auditing setting. He reports that auditors given both tables and graphs (line and bar charts) exhibit higher accuracy overall in loan-related tasks than do those given tables only. However, these effects are driven by differences in the most complex judgment; there are no effects in less complex tasks.

Accounting studies tend to find that graphical decision aid formats lead to either equivalent or greater JDM quality than do tabular formats. These findings are somewhat inconsistent with theory from other fields that suggests tabular formats may be better for "higher level" JDM tasks. It may be the case that experimental studies in accounting have simplified tasks to the extent that any advantages of tables cannot be realized. Similar to psychology, the combination of graphs and tables tends to produce greater JDM quality than tables alone. Although results in accounting are perhaps more internally consistent than those in psychology, this does not mean that further research on graphs versus tables in accounting is unimportant. There are at least two issues that bear further investigation. One is the development of theory; accounting researchers could contribute in this area given that findings here are somewhat different than those in other areas despite the fact that accounting-related tasks vary in the ways discussed by Vessey (1991). The second key issue is the impact of misleading graphs on JDM in accounting. Jarvenpaa and Dickson (1988) note, for example, that many graphs that are included in annual reports are distorted and, therefore, misleading. Experimental studies to date have used appropriate graphs and, therefore, cannot examine the potential harmful impact of graphs on the JDM of users of such information.

Effects of Memory Aids

The first type of decision aid considered in this section is *memory aids,* whose general purpose is to assist individuals in recovering from memory knowledge that is relevant to a given JDM task.[35] For example, auditors sometimes use lists of internal controls as an aid to evaluating a client's control system. Specifically, memory aids affect the cognitive processes of memory retrieval and hypothesis generation; the latter occurs because hypotheses often are taken directly from memory rather than generated on the spot. Because people tend not to retrieve all relevant information or generate all plausible hypotheses, the use of memory aids can lead to an increase in the quantity of relevant items retrieved or hypotheses generated. To the extent that an individual's knowledge for these items is accurate, memory aids can have positive effects on JDM quality (as discussed in Chapter 5, these effects may occur directly or through information search and other cognitive processes). In addition, memory aids can reduce the ill effects of moderators of knowledge content and knowledge structure effects. For example, memory aids can attempt to reduce the effects of task-related information that causes output interference or prompt individuals to retrieve certain types of information that they might not retrieve spontaneously (e.g., base rates). Finally, by focusing attention on relevant items, memory aids can assist in reducing the effects of irrelevant information. Overall, then, memory aids can increase the quality of two cognitive processes—memory retrieval and hypothesis generation—facets of which are positively related to JDM quality, obviate the effects of factors that moderate the positive effects of knowledge content and structure, and reduce the negative effects of irrelevant information.

This section discusses three specific types of memory aids that are used in practice: lists, examples, and "fault trees."[36] *Lists* are sequential records of items that are relevant to a particular JDM task. These lists can be of specific items that are contained in episodic memory but that might not be retrieved otherwise. For example, an auditor may use last year's work papers to find a list of internal controls that were in place for a particular client. More typically, however, lists contain items stored in semantic memory such as general types of controls that a company might employ for a particular

---

[35]Clearly, these aids also may provide knowledge that people currently do not have stored in memory.
[36]The memory aids discussed in this chapter are "external aids" rather than "internal aids" (e.g., Intons-Peterson and Fournier 1986). In addition to using external aids, people can attempt to enhance memory retrieval using internal-to-memory strategies such as rehearsal. These strategies are not particularly relevant in professional settings where large amounts of information must be used.

control objective; an auditor would use such a list to obtain information to evaluate this year's control risk. *Examples* (sometimes called "prompts") are specific instances of an important item, typically an instance from a category of items relevant to JDM. These normally relate to semantic knowledge as well. For example, rather than listing all possible types of controls that might ensure that a particular control objective is achieved, an audit firm might provide its staff with an example. *Fault trees* are hierarchical representations of a particular type of semantic knowledge—the possible causes of particular events. They proceed from the event at the top of the tree down to categories of possible causes then farther down to specific examples of causes within those categories (e.g., Russo and Kolzow 1994). They are used for diagnostic tasks such as determining the cause of an unexpected fluctuation in a financial ratio. For example, an auditor might view a fault tree for a fluctuation in the gross margin ratio that lists "sales errors" and "inventory errors" as categories of causes, as well as specific examples of errors under these categories.

Lists and fault trees can increase the number of items retrieved from memory (and the number of hypotheses that are generated from memory) by activating information that might not be activated otherwise (see Chapter 3). Similarly, by providing inventories of relevant items, lists and fault trees can negate the moderating effects of factors such as output interference that reduce the quality of retrieval. Further, by requiring people to focus on the information provided, lists and fault trees can implicitly steer them away from attending to and being influenced by irrelevant information (Harvey 2001). Examples can assist with retrieval by activating information that is linked to related information in memory; the retrieval of this related information then is facilitated through spreading activation. In addition, the examples themselves may be items that would not otherwise be retrieved because of memory retrieval problems.

Unfortunately, these memory aids do not always achieve the objectives of increasing the quality of memory retrieval (or hypothesis generation) and of obviating the impact of factors that moderate positive effects of knowledge. One reason is that people may not use the provided memory aids; as discussed above, there are a variety of reasons people generally shy away from decision aids. In the area of memory, people prefer to rely on long-term memory in order to circumvent processing constraints (Simon 1990). Along with this, people can be highly overconfident about the accuracy of their memory, meaning that they may not feel the need to refer to a memory aid (e.g., Moeckel and Plumlee 1989). Fortunately, professionals may be more willing to refer to memory aids when information is important to their JDM (Sprinkle and Tubbs 1998).

In addition, elements of the memory aids themselves can reduce their positive effects. Designers of lists and fault trees likely attempt to make these aids as complete and accurate as possible while keeping their size manageable (e.g., small enough to fit on one page or screen) (Russo and Kolzow 1994; Van Schie and Van der Pligt 1994). As a result, rather than containing every possible relevant item, lists may omit a few items and fault trees frequently include a category called "all others." Although the impact of the omission of items from lists has not been studied extensively, the effect likely is that people are less apt to retrieve those items than if they were included on the list. When fault trees include an "all others" category, people tend to overestimate the probability of items explicitly listed and, thus, underestimate the probability of items included in the "all others" group (e.g., Fischhoff et al. 1978; Mehle et al. 1981; Gettys et al. 1986; Dubé-Rioux and Russo 1988; Russo and Kolzow). There are several explanations for this phenomenon. The most prominent of these are the salience of the presented items (versus the lack of salience of the items not presented) (e.g., Russo and Kolzow) and the use of anchoring and adjustment whereby people start by assigning equal probabilities to listed categories then insufficiently anchor and adjust given their beliefs about differences in the likelihoods of causes (e.g., Fox and Clemen 2005). Underestimation of the probability of the "all others" category is reduced somewhat if fault-tree users generate and rate the probabilities of further causes of an event (Mehle et al.; Dubé-Rioux and Russo; Russo and Kolzow) or if they have high levels of domain knowledge (Johnson et al. 1991b; Ofir 2000). A final problem with lists and fault trees may be that they provide the perception that included information cues are of equal importance given that no explicit cue weightings are included.

Examples pose a different sort of problem. As discussed in Chapter 3, task-related information can cause output interference, or the inhibition of retrieval of knowledge from memory, for individuals with well-organized knowledge. An example contained in a memory aid is one type of this task-related information. Specifically, the provision of an example can cause people to retrieve no more, and sometimes less, information from memory than they would without the example (e.g., Rundus 1973; Roediger 1974; Nickerson 1984). Further, as the number of examples increases, these inhibiting effects also increase because each example can create interference (Rundus). The extent to which an example is viewed to be typical of a category may increase the effects of output interference (Mervis and Rosch 1981). More typical members are, by definition, stronger in memory and more likely to be reretrieved, thus causing interference. Finally, examples, lists, and fault trees all may increase the level of task variables (vis-à-vis unaided judgment) that have a negative effect on JDM quality. For example, lists may impose a particular frame on decision makers; a decision aid related to internal control evaluation may list control strengths rather than control weaknesses. As discussed in Chapter 6, framing a judgment in terms of strengths could lead auditors to focus too little on weaknesses and, consequently, make an incorrect evaluation of controls. As another example, memory aids may prescribe a certain order of information processing.

Studies examining memory aid effects in accounting all pertain to auditors. Starting with studies that examine lists and fault trees, Purvis (1989) finds that auditors collect more information about internal controls when given a list than when asked to document their internal control evaluation using a flowchart or a memo. However, subjects given lists are less likely than other subjects to collect certain key pieces of information because of the omission of those items from the list. Pincus (1989) examines the effects of a list on auditors' fraud judgments. Subjects with a list collect far more information than those without a list; further, they collect relatively equal proportions of information indicating fraud, information indicating no fraud, and information that is neutral with respect to fraud, whereas no-list subjects focus heavily on information indicating fraud. Unfortunately, these differences lead list subjects to make less accurate assessments of fraud risk for a case where fraud is involved and to be no better in their assessments in a no-fraud case. Asare and Wright (2004) similarly find that auditors who use a list make lower assessments of fraud than those not using a list. In addition, auditors who use a standard audit program (another form of list) design an audit program that is less effective at detecting fraud. Eining et al. (1997) find that auditors with a list-type aid are no better at differentiating between fraud and no-fraud cases than are unaided subjects.

Bonner et al. (1996) find that auditors given a list of errors contained in various transaction cycle and control objective categories are better able to apply their knowledge to conditional probability judgments that are inconsistent with their knowledge structures than are those without a list. Further, auditors' application of knowledge to judgments consistent with their knowledge structures is not harmed by using the list. Two studies examine the effects of list aids in analytical procedures settings. Blocher et al. (1983) show that auditors given a list of suggested analytical procedures plan more of such procedures. Anderson et al. (1997c) report that auditors given a list that is dominated by error-related hypotheses for a ratio fluctuation give higher probabilities for an error being the cause of the fluctuation than do those given a list dominated by non-error hypotheses.

Remaining studies examine the effect of examples. Note that some of these studies do not intend to use examples as memory aids; nevertheless, their results may be informative as to the effect of these aids. Four studies (Libby 1985; Libby and Frederick 1990; Church and Schneider 1993, 1995) examine the effect of providing an example of an error that could explain a ratio fluctuation. Libby and Frederick's experienced auditors generate more errors from the transaction cycle to which an example belongs (versus no-example subjects) if it is a low-frequency (atypical) example but not if it is a high-frequency (typical) example. However, inexperienced auditors' hypothesis generation is not affected by the example. Libby finds no effect of example on the type of hypotheses generated and attributes this to the example being typical. Church and Schneider find that auditors generate fewer errors from the example's transaction cycle when they view either a typical or an atypical example and argue that this is because they restrict the number of alternative categories of errors from which auditors can generate hypotheses.

Two studies examine the effect of examples using recall of presented materials, rather than retrieval from memory. Pei and Tuttle (1999) ask auditors to rate the probability of hypothesized causes of a ratio fluctuation then recall those causes either with no examples, high-plausibility (typical) examples, or low-plausibility (atypical) examples. Subjects receiving the low-plausibility examples recall fewer causes than do no-example subjects, whereas high-plausibility example subjects' recall is no different from that of no-example subjects. In another experiment, low-plausibility subjects recall fewer causes than no-example subjects when errors are high in severity but recall more causes than no-example subjects when errors are low in severity. Finally, Frederick (1991) reports that both experienced and inexperienced auditors recall fewer internal controls than do subjects with no examples when they study those controls organized by control objective and receive examples; when they study controls organized by sequence, examples mostly do not affect recall.

Results of accounting research on lists and examples parallel those from psychology. First, lists tend to lead to the retrieval of or focus on more information overall, but this does not always lead to greater JDM quality. One reason is that list-aided individuals are less likely to focus on items omitted from lists than are unaided subjects. A second reason may be that people place equal weight on listed items when, instead, they should weight cues unequally based on their diagnosticity for the judgment at hand; this appears to be a particular problem for fraud judgments. In one study where cues were weighted mechanically, list aids did improve JDM quality (Bonner et al. 1996). The provision of examples (versus no examples) appears not to improve accounting

JDM quality and sometimes can decrease it. These effects are partially due to output interference but may reflect many other factors that are as yet unknown. There appear to be many memory aids used in professional practice, and accounting researchers have only scratched the surface with regard to their effects. For instance, it seems important to understand the inferences people may draw from lists (e.g., that cues should be weighted equally or that more important cues are listed first). These inferences likely are unfounded in most cases, yet if developers are unaware of their existence, they can cause aided JDM to be of lower quality than unaided JDM. The negative JDM effects of examples are particularly worrisome given how intuitively appealing they may be to aid developers. Research on factors that can mitigate these negative effects would therefore be useful. Finally, the effects of these types of aids in areas other than auditing would be of interest.

Effects of Brief Instructions

Another type of decision aid is *brief instructions* about how to make judgments and decisions; for example, people may be exhorted to "consider multiple perspectives." This type of decision aid typically aims to increase the quality of cognitive processing. It can also reduce the negative effects of task characteristics, as described further below. Brief instructions can be of a wide variety of types. One type that is not discussed extensively here is *warnings,* which instruct people to avoid certain biases. For example, a warning may state that people judge the ex ante probability of an event higher than they would otherwise once they know the event has occurred and that they should avoid this hindsight bias. Such warnings normally are ineffective at improving JDM quality (Fischhoff 1982; Arkes 1991; Plous 1993), likely because they do not address the cognitive underpinnings of errors and biases in JDM.

Instead, this section focuses on two types of brief instructions that have been the focus of accounting research because they currently are used in practice or could be implemented relatively easily. One type of instruction tells people to provide *explanations,* or reasons that support their JDM. Another type of instruction asks people to provide *counter-explanations;* these can be reasons their judgment or decision is incorrect or reasons another judgment or decision is correct. Similar to counter-explanations are instructions that ask people to *consider alternatives.* Here, people are asked to generate other possible judgments or decisions (in particular, they are sometimes asked to "consider the opposite" judgment or decision), but they do not necessarily elaborate on the additional alternatives with explanations.

Explanation as a decision aid often is incorporated into organizational systems; that is, people are asked to document reasons for their judgments and decisions (Koehler 1991). For example, auditors write memos that explain their judgments regarding whether there are material misstatements present in accounts. Further, people have a natural propensity to explain things (Keil 2006). Requiring explanation ostensibly can encourage people to retrieve, search for, and evaluate more information than they otherwise would, and evaluate the information more carefully because it promotes accountability (and motivation) for higher-quality JDM. In other words, explanation may increase the quality of several cognitive processes and, thus, the quality of resulting JDM. Unfortunately, this motivation occurs in a setting where there is a desired conclusion—one's original judgment or decision. As discussed in Chapters 3 and 7, motivation to reach a desired conclusion often does not result in higher-quality processing because people tend to direct their retrieval and search toward only supporting reasons and evaluate ambiguous evidence as supportive of their desired conclusion.[37] In fact, the requirement to explain can result in reduced-quality processing (and JDM) if it causes people to focus on easily accessible reasons that are of less relevance to the task than are less accessible reasons (Larrick 2004).

In contrast, instructions to counter-explain or consider alternatives typically are effective at improving cognitive processing (e.g., Koriat et al. 1980; Lord et al. 1984; Hoch 1985; Hirt and Markman 1995). They do lead people to retrieve, search for, and evaluate more information than they would in the absence of the instructions; they obviously can lead also to the generation of additional hypotheses and changes to problem representations. All these effects occur because this type of instruction requires that people shift away from their original frame of reference (their judgment or decision) (Koehler 1991). In turn, they activate different parts of their knowledge structures—those associated with alternatives—and this spreads activation to different information. In addition, such instructions can reduce the negative effects of certain task variables.

In general, instructions to counter-explain or consider alternatives can reduce the effects of cognitive processing biases that occur as a result of knowledge being structured in memory and activation spreading only to items associated with the initial judgment or decision (Arkes 1991). First, they can reduce the effects of explanation described above.[38] They can also reduce confirmation bias and other errors in hypothesis evaluation such as focusing only on evidence related to the hypothesis under consideration (Arkes; Larrick 2004). Further, such instructions may be useful in reducing the effects of overconfidence by asking people to consider reasons that do not support their proposed JDM (Koriat et al. 1980). With regard to task variables, instructions to counter-explain or consider alternatives can reduce the effect of outcome information (one type of irrelevant information) and, thus, hindsight bias, by asking people to consider reasons a different outcome might have occurred (Arkes et al. 1988). They can reduce the effects of task framing by forcing people to consider different frames (Plous 1993). Finally, they can reduce the fundamental attribution error by getting people to consider non-person-related causes when evaluating others' JDM (Heath et al. 1998).

However, the effectiveness of counter-explanation and consideration of alternatives at improving cognitive processing can be reduced under some circumstances. First, if people are asked to list too many counter-explanations or additional alternatives, the difficulty of generating these may convince people that their earlier JDM was

---

[37]A phenomenon termed the *explanation effect* (e.g., Hirt and Sherman 1985; Anderson and Sechler 1986) refers to the tendency for experimental subjects asked to explain a given predicted outcome to increase their estimates of the probability that outcome will occur. In professional accounting settings, the prediction to be explained often is the individual's own judgment or decision. In this situation, increased belief in one's JDM typically does not occur through explanation (Koehler 1991), but rather through desired conclusion–motivated cognitive processing. Nevertheless, there are some situations in accounting settings in which a particular event is provided (e.g., when a client provides a hypothesis for an unusual outcome such as a ratio fluctuation). In these situations, the explanation effect may apply.

[38]These instructions may not eliminate the effects of explanation because there is something of a primacy effect that occurs when explanation and counter-explanation are juxtaposed, and explanation typically comes first. There are many possible reasons for this, including output interference from the reasons generated as part of explanation (Hoch 1984).

indeed correct (Sanna et al. 2002). Similarly, if people are asked to explain or consider an implausible alternative, this improvement technique may not be effective (Sherman et al. 1985; Hirt and Markman 1995). More generally, people who are knowledgeable about a task appear to consider the ease of accessing counter-explanations or alternatives and use this subjective experience as a cue to determining whether their original judgment or decision is correct (Schwarz 1998; Sanna et al.). If people can be convinced to attribute this subjective experience to some other factor, the moderating effect of ease of accessibility can be reduced (Sanna and Schwarz 2003). Finally, of course, if people choose not to rely on these types of aids, their effectiveness can be diminished.

Several studies in accounting investigate the effects of instructions to explain, counter-explain, or consider alternatives. Studies related to producers and users of accounting information include Moser (1989), who asks investment club members to generate reasons that support and do not support a specific amount of increase in a company's earnings then to judge the probability of this increase. Subjects who generate relatively more supporting reasons make higher probability judgments. Order of generation affects the relative proportion of supporting reasons provided, with those providing supporting reasons first having a higher proportion. Kadous et al. (2006) report that analysts asked to generate two reasons management's plans to improve profits may fail make lower earnings forecasts (and are, thus, less biased) than analysts who give no counter-explanations. However, the forecasts of analysts asked to generate twelve counter-explanations are no different from those of control subjects. A second experiment replicates these results with students and also shows that having people read either a small or large number of counter-explanations leads to lower earnings forecasts than if they do not read any counter-explanations. The effect of the large number of counter-explanations occurs in this second experiment because reading them does not cause subjects to experience difficulty accessing the explanations, unlike generating them.

In auditing, Anderson and Wright (1988) report that students in an internal control evaluation task exhibit the explanation effect when given events to explain, but experienced auditors do not. Three studies examine the effects of explanation and counter-explanation of a nonerror cause for a ratio fluctuation, information provided by the client. Koonce (1992) reports that auditors asked to explain provide higher probability judgments that the cause is correct than do auditors who do not explain this cause. In addition, auditors who explain and counter-explain judge the probability of the nonerror cause to be lower than do explanation-only subjects. However, those who counter-explain then explain (rather than vice versa), assess higher probabilities for the cause, indicating a recency effect. Anderson and Koonce (1995) investigate whether providing additional information to auditors regarding the nonerror cause will reduce the effects of explanation on their judgments about the probability that the cause is correct. This additional information is helpful in two cases: when the cause indeed is correct and when the cause is incorrect and auditors quantify the effects of the additional information. Koonce and Phillips (1996) study whether the difficulty of comprehending client-provided information about the cause reduces the effects of explanation; auditors with difficult-to-comprehend information judge the probability of the nonerror cause to be lower than do those with easy-to-comprehend information.

Other auditing studies include Kennedy (1995), who asks students to estimate other subjects' sales predictions. Subjects are given either high or low sales outcomes, and half are asked to counter-explain the outcome. The (irrelevant) outcome information affects subjects' estimates when they do not counter-explain, but counter-explanation eliminates this curse of knowledge effect. Cushing and Ahlawat (1996) document that auditors asked to first explain their initial going-concern judgment then view information and revise the judgment are not affected by the order of information, whereas those who do not explain exhibit a recency effect. In other words, explanation improves JDM here.

Studies investigating the effects of consideration of alternatives include Heiman (1990), who shows that auditors provided with alternative hypotheses for a set of ratio fluctuations decrease their probability judgments for the initially presented alternative. In addition, auditors who self-generate two or more alternative hypotheses also reduce their probability estimates. In a second experiment, auditors who view five alternatives reduce their probability judgments more than those who view two alternatives; however, strength of alternatives has no effect on the auditors' judgments. Emby and Finley (1997) ask auditors to evaluate evidence related to internal controls and substantive test planning under one of two frames: control risk or control strength. In addition, some auditors are asked to evaluate the direction and relevance of each piece of evidence, whereas others are not. This manipulation is not exactly like counter-explanation or the consideration of alternatives, but Emby and Finley suggest that it similarly focuses attention away from only one perspective. They find that auditors who do not rate evidence are subject to framing effects, whereas those who rate evidence are not.

Remaining studies examine whether consideration of alternatives can reduce the hindsight bias. Reimers and Butler (1992) give auditors either an internal control evaluation task or an opinion choice task, varying the presence and type of outcome information (consistent or inconsistent with the evidence) as well as the presence of instructions to consider the inconsistent outcome. The effect of the inconsistent outcome on auditors' judgments is reduced in the presence of the decision aid. Lowe and Reckers (2000) examine a situation in which they believe auditors would want to exhibit hindsight bias and whether instructions to consider specific alternatives will engender this behavior. Specifically, they ask auditors whether there should be an adjustment to inventory for obsolescence issues in a case where the firm subsequently experiences obsolete inventory and, as a consequence of violating debt covenant restrictions, goes bankrupt. Auditors with this outcome information make higher judgments about the need for adjustment than do those without the information; in addition, auditors asked to consider the legal exposure of the case give similarly high judgments as do those with outcome information. Auditors given instructions to consider multiple possible outcomes move toward the higher judgments but not as completely as those given the legal-exposure instructions.

Two studies examine the reduction of hindsight bias among evaluators of auditors' JDM. Anderson et al. (1997b) report that judges evaluating the appropriateness of an audit partner's decision to not adjust inventory for obsolescence exhibit hindsight bias when given negative outcome information, but hindsight bias is not reduced when they are instructed to consider specific alternative positive outcomes. However, hindsight bias is reduced when judges are instructed to consider alternative stakeholders for auditors' decisions (e.g., employees of the client firm). Clarkson et al. (2002) ask students to assume they are jurors evaluating auditors' JDM quality in a case where a firm receives an unqualified opinion and subsequently goes bankrupt. Some subjects receive no outcome information, whereas other subjects receive either outcome information with no instructions or with one of three types of instructions: (1) a warning to ignore the outcome information, (2) a warning to ignore the outcome with an explanation as to why, or (3) a warning with instructions to consider the effects of the jurors' evaluation on the auditors. Surprisingly, subjects with even the weakest warning have somewhat reduced hindsight bias, whereas those with the second and third types of instructions show no hindsight bias.

Similar to the findings in psychology, accounting studies document that explanation tends not to improve JDM quality and may decrease it. However, counter-explanation and other factors such as experience and quantification of given information may reduce any negative effects of explanation. Accounting studies show also that counter-explanation and consideration of alternatives improve JDM quality. In particular, in addition to obviating the effects of explanation, counter-explanation and consideration of alternatives can reduce the effects of framing, order of information, and irrelevant information such as actual outcomes. However, these aids' effectiveness can be reduced if people are asked to generate too many counter-explanations or alternatives. It also seems possible that the effects of brief instructions can be reduced by other factors in the accounting environment such as circumstances that lead to motivated reasoning. Such effects could occur in several ways such as reducing the number or quality of counter-explanations or alternatives that people generate, increasing the number or quality of explanations originally generated to offset the counter-explanations or alternatives, or simply ignoring the aid and claiming the inability to generate other items. The effects of such moderators seem particularly important to understand given the apparent ease with which this type of decision aid can be implemented and its consistent positive effects in research to date.

Effects of Decomposition

Another important type of decision aid is *decomposition,* a technique which breaks JDM tasks down into smaller parts then combines the answers from the smaller parts to obtain an overall judgment or decision (Raiffa 1968). Although it is not necessary that the combination of answers be done mathematically, it often is the case that decomposition also involves such *mechanical combination.* A simple example of decomposition is asking loan officers to rate (measure) each information cue related to bankruptcy separately then combine those ratings using predetermined weights to obtain a judgment of the probability of a loan applicant going bankrupt. The decomposed tasks do not always involve measuring individual information cues. Instead, decomposition can require that subjects both select and measure information cues. Decomposition is used widely in some accounting fields, such as auditing (Messier 1995).

Decomposition can increase the quality of several cognitive processes. First, when the decomposed task provides information cues, decomposition clearly can assist people in retrieving and searching for a complete set of relevant information. Relatedly, decomposition can serve to reduce the negative effects of heuristics used during processing. For example, a decomposition aid can require the estimation of base rates, a relevant item that may be ignored otherwise if people use the representativeness heuristic. Clearly, increasing the likelihood that people attend to such relevant information can improve JDM quality. Second, it can assist in the hypothesis and evidence evaluation phase by allowing people to focus on small subsets of information separately rather than focusing on all the required information at once; in the latter case, some relevant information may not be used because of short-term memory limitations. In other words, decomposition can reduce task complexity by reducing the amount of information to be processed at a given time. In so doing, decomposition may allow people to use compensatory processing rather than noncompensatory processing (see Chapter 5), and the use of compensatory processing often is associated with higher-quality JDM. Third, decomposition that uses mechanical combination can assist in the combination of evidence by forcing the use of the appropriate cue signs and weights, combination in an appropriate manner (e.g., multiplicatively or additively), and consistent combination across people and situations. All of these factors can increase the quality of JDM. Indeed, evidence from psychology indicates that decomposition often improves JDM (e.g., Einhorn 1974; Armstrong et al. 1975; Lyness and Cornelius 1982; MacGregor et al. 1988; Ravinder et al. 1988; MacGregor and Lichtenstein 1991; Kleinmuntz et al. 1996).

However, decomposition and mechanical combination are not always effective at decreasing task complexity or at improving cognitive processing (or moderating the negative effects of processing-related factors such as heuristics). With regard to task complexity, decomposition increases the number of steps in a task; this can increase task complexity (Goodwin and Wright 1993). In addition, the component tasks must be familiar to people; if not, their lack of clarity can raise task complexity and reduce JDM quality (MacGregor et al. 1988; Goodwin and Wright). With regard to cognitive processing, if decomposition requires the choice of information cues, it may not improve JDM quality and in fact may decrease it because mechanically selected cues inevitably will be the most relevant; thus, human-selected cues can only equal or fall short of this ideal. Further, if mechanical combination is not employed, decomposition aids can reduce JDM quality vis-à-vis unaided JDM. This can occur because people now make errors on more subparts of the task than they would consider otherwise. Even if mechanical combination is employed, if responses to subparts exhibit systematic bias (positively correlated errors), decomposition-aided JDM can be of lower quality than unaided JDM. As such, it is recommended that the subparts be constructed so as to be independent and also so they produce minimal error, for example, by being familiar to users (Ravinder et al. 1998; MacGregor and Lichtenstein 1991; Kleinmuntz et al. 1996). Decomposition and mechanical combination aids are less effective (vis-à-vis unaided judgment) when uncertainty is low because unaided judgment is relatively good in these situations (MacGregor and Armstrong 1994; MacGregor 2001). Finally, people may choose not to rely on a decomposition aid, in which case there can be no positive impact on processing. One unique reason this may occur is that decomposition aids can give people the opportunity to work backward from a desired judgment and fill in component answers that are consistent with this judgment (e.g., Kachelmeier and Messier 1990).

Accounting studies on decomposition mostly pertain to auditors.[39] Jiambalvo and Waller (1984) and Daniel (1988) examine auditors' assessments of test of details risk

---

[39] A number of studies examine the quality of decomposed judgments requiring cue selection and combination (Abdel-Khalik and El-Sheshai 1980; Lewis et al. 1988; Simnett and Trotman 1989; Simnett 1996) but do not compare decomposed judgments to holistic judgments. As such, they are not included here.

made either globally or through decomposition using the audit risk model. Jiambalvo and Waller find no differences between global and decomposed/intuitively combined judgments; however, judgments constructed through mechanical combination are substantially different from those constructed using intuitive combination. The results of mechanical combination indicate that the auditors are not using the audit risk model properly. Daniel finds similar results. Libby and Libby (1989) report that auditors whose decomposed judgments about internal controls are mechanically combined have higher JDM quality, as measured by agreement with an expert panel's judgments and agreement among themselves, than do auditors making global judgments. Bonner et al. (1996) show that auditors make substantial errors when estimating the probability that an audit objective is violated conditional on a particular transaction cycle; however, when this probability judgment is decomposed into its components and the component estimates are aggregated mechanically, errors are reduced. In addition, when auditors make estimates of the probability that a transaction cycle is violated conditional on a particular audit objective (a judgment consistent with their knowledge structures), decomposition does not reduce JDM quality.

Eining et al. (1997) provide auditors with a decomposition aid and find that these subjects are better at discriminating between fraud and no-fraud cases than are both unaided subjects and subjects with a list-type aid. They also have the highest level of consensus. Zimbelman (1997) asks auditors to do planning work for accounts receivable and varies whether assessment of inherent risk is holistic or decomposed to focus separately on the risks of errors and fraud. Auditors with decomposed risk assessments spend more time reading fraud-related cues but do not appear to be more sensitive to differential fraud risk when planning tests and budgeting hours for test work. Instead, decomposition subjects plan more tests in both low- and high-fraud-risk cases. Wilks and Zimbelman (2004) report that auditors making decomposed assessments of elements of fraud risk (attitudes, incentives, and opportunities) make different fraud risk assessments than auditors making holistic judgments but only in a low-fraud-risk case. This appears to occur because decomposition subjects are more sensitive to cues regarding incentives and opportunities in the low-risk case than are holistic judgment subjects.

Butler (1985) examines decomposition's effects on sampling risk judgments. His decomposition aid requires auditors to explicitly assess factors that are relevant to sampling risk but that often are ignored. Although the aid group's mean sampling risk judgments are no different from those of a control group, their decisions to accept or reject an account balance that can be implied from these judgments are more frequently correct. Kachelmeier and Messier (1990) examine decomposition's effects on sample size decisions. Auditors who receive a decomposition aid that allows them to combine component judgments themselves choose larger sample sizes than do unaided subjects; the authors posit this is because the aid forces auditors to focus on all cues relevant to sample size. However, consistent with auditors' working backward from a desired sample size (and smaller sample sizes being more desirable), sample sizes generated by mechanical combination of assessed components are larger than those of the decomposition-intuitive combination group. Finally, Benbasat and Schroeder (1977) show that student subjects receiving a decomposition aid related to an inventory production task have better JDM quality as measured by costs incurred but take more time to make decisions.

Decomposition aids' effects in accounting studies are similar to those in psychology. Decomposition generally tends to improve JDM quality, particularly when mechanical combination also is used. However, accountants may work around these aids, and decomposition aids also may operate like lists in that they lead to a focus on more information overall, but this focus does not necessarily result in better JDM quality.

Given that decomposition aids are intuitively appealing and, thus, frequently used in auditing practice, future research in accounting could examine factors that might lessen the previously documented negative consequences of these aids in auditing. It also seems possible that decomposition aids could be used to improve the quality of JDM in other areas of accounting, for example, investor and managerial JDM.

Effects of Bootstrapping, Replacement with Model, and Combination of Human and Model JDM

Finally, a number of decision aids involve the use of statistical models.[40] These statistical models typically are developed using techniques such as regression analysis and can pertain to either the environment or the person (see Chapter 5). For example, an environmental model related to bankruptcy prediction can be developed using actual bankruptcy outcomes as the dependent variable. Similarly, a model of a person's bankruptcy predictions can be developed using those predictions as the dependent variable. One specific model-related aid is *bootstrapping,* which refers to the technique of creating a model of an individual's judgments or decisions then replacing the individual with her model for future JDM. *Replacing individuals with a model* entails developing an environmental model then having the model make judgments or decisions rather than the individual. Individuals play no role in this situation once the model is developed. A step back from replacement, in the sense that an individual's JDM has an influence on the final JDM, is to *combine individual JDM with the JDM produced by a statistical (environmental) model.* As described further below, these types of aids can increase the quality of cognitive processing and moderate the negative effects of many task and environmental variables.

The main purpose of bootstrapping is to remove inconsistencies from an individual's cognitive processing. Specifically, an individual's model consistently applies the cue weights derived through statistical analysis and consistently combines the weighted cues, whereas the unaided individual may change cue weights and combination rules across situations or within situations over time for a variety of reasons. These inconsistencies include ignoring relevant cues under some circumstances. Reasons for inconsistencies can be as simple as fatigue. However, they can also be induced by task complexity, framing, order of presentation of cues, presentation format, response mode, and environmental variables that might induce "motivated" cue weighting in some situations but not others (e.g., accountability to a client who has a desired conclusion). Further, because a person's model consistently applies only nonzero cue weights, bootstrapping removes the influence of irrelevant information cues that an individual might consider were she not to use her own model in future judgments.

---

[40]Models normally are linear additive models. See Chapter 5 and Dawes and Corrigan (1974) for discussion of the appropriateness of these types of models.

For all these reasons, bootstrapping normally improves JDM quality (e.g., Goldberg 1970; Dawes 1979; Camerer 1981a; Kleinmuntz 1990).[41]

Replacing people with statistical models of the environment, also called "proper linear models" (Dawes 1979), can improve the quality of cognitive processing first by increasing consistency of application of cue weights and combination rules. As such, replacement can negate the effects of the factors described above that can induce inconsistent cue weighting. Further replacement can completely eliminate the influence of irrelevant information cues and negate the effects of factors that can cause individuals not to use all the cues they normally would focus on (e.g., task complexity or motivated reasoning induced by environmental variables). Further, given that people sometimes ignore relevant cues altogether, replacing people with environmental models may increase the number of relevant cues considered for JDM. If, as Dawes says: "the whole trick [to high-quality JDM] is to decide which variables to look at," this may be the most important effect of replacing people with an environmental model. Finally, people sometimes use incorrect cue weights and combination rules (see Chapter 5), so replacement can improve these elements of processing. This may not be as important as the inclusion of all relevant cues given that equal-weight linear models often can perform as well as those using statistically derived weights (Dawes and Corrigan 1974; Dawes). Nevertheless, all these factors can contribute to higher-quality JDM when individuals are replaced with environmental models (e.g., Sawyer 1966; Dawes and Corrigan; Dawes et al. 1989; Kleinmuntz 1990; Grove et al. 2000).

Combining human JDM with a model's JDM is another way of using statistical models as a decision aid. Combination can occur in one of two ways: the individual can use the output of a model as an input to her JDM or a third party (including a computer) can combine the individual's JDM with the output of the model using a predetermined rule such as averaging. Assuming that combination results in a nonzero weight being placed on the model's output, combined JDM can be of higher quality than unaided human JDM for all the reasons that replacement with a model improves JDM. It seems intuitive that the improvement brought by this aid would not be as substantial as that brought by replacement because the unaided and, thus, possibly inconsistent and otherwise error-prone or biased judgment also receives nonzero weight. However, it is possible for combined JDM to be of higher quality than both unaided JDM and model-replaced JDM because humans have certain advantages over models (Blattberg and Hoch 1990). For example, people may be able to use cues that are not included in the model to make better judgments and decisions in certain situations. These cues are not included in models because they are not diagnostic of JDM-related outcomes over a number of cases (Dawes et al. 1989). However, they can be substantially (or perfectly) diagnostic in limited instances. An example, which had led to these cues' designation as *broken leg cues*, relates to predicting whether someone will go to a movie on a given day (Meehl 1954). If the judge knows that the person in question has a broken leg, she can predict with a high level of certainty that the person will not go to a movie. However, this occurs so rarely that it likely would not be included in a general

---

[41]Bootstrapped models are also called "improper linear models" because they may not be based on a full set of relevant cues or contain the cue weights or combination rules that would be derived from an analysis of environmental outcomes (Dawes 1979; Kleinmuntz 1990). Thus, statements about their effects as "aids" refer to the JDM quality they produce as compared to the unaided judgments of the individuals from whom the models are derived.

model predicting attendance at movies. Humans also may be able to identify new variables that should be considered when the environment changes.

Naturally, JDM that is aided by decision aids involving statistical modeling is not always of higher quality than unaided JDM. Perhaps the main reason this occurs is that people refuse to rely on these types of aids. Consistent with this, they are not widely used in practice (Hastie and Dawes 2001). General reasons related to reliance clearly pertain here (see above), but there also are further reasons. For example, people often believe that models, particularly those that involve only a few cues, must have missed something relevant, for example, a broken leg cue (Peterson and Pitz 1986). Further, people fear losing their jobs if they believe they can be replaced by models. A lack of understanding of statistics also is a prominent factor leading people to not use model-based aids (Grove and Meehl 1996).

Other factors that moderate positive effects of model-based aids include the following. First, it sometimes is the case that JDM-related outcomes do not exist or are hard to measure or track. When this is the case, replacing people with an environmental model obviously is not feasible. The inability to use an environmental model is perhaps the main reason that bootstrapping is considered (Goldberg 1970; Camerer 1981a; Armstrong 2001b) because bootstrapping does not deal with a number of causes of low-quality JDM that environmental models can address, such as failure to use all relevant cues (Kleinmuntz 1990). Second, with regard to combination of model and human JDM, most situations are not affected by broken leg cues. Thus, although combination can improve JDM as compared to unaided judgment (and model-replaced judgment as well) in a few cases, replacement with a model tends to produce greater quality over a series of situations (Dawes et al. 1989). This occurs because people believe that there are far more unusual situations than truly is the case. Finally, if the statistical model is not of high quality, which can occur for many reasons such as lack of knowledge on the part of the model's developer, any of these model-based decision aids may not produce JDM that is of higher quality than unaided JDM.

Studies in accounting examine the impact of all three types of statistical-model-based aids. Starting with bootstrapping, Libby (1976a) finds that loan officers outperform their own models when making bankruptcy predictions. However, other studies of loan officers find the opposite result (Zimmer 1981) or no difference between human judgments and bootstrapped judgments (Abdel-Khalik and El-Sheshai 1980). Lewis et al. (1988) report that municipal analysts' predictions of bond ratings are of equal quality to bootstrapped predictions. Ebert and Kruse (1978) find that bootstrapping leads to more accurate judgments of stock returns than those made by analysts themselves. Mear and Firth (1987b), however, find no difference between analysts and bootstrapped models for this task. Ashton (1982) shows that bootstrapped models are more accurate than managers at predicting number of pages of advertising in a magazine. Kida (1980) and Simnett and Trotman (1989) report that auditors making bankruptcy predictions are as accurate as bootstrapped models.

Studies examining replacement with a model include several related to analysts' and management's earnings forecasts. Archival studies of analysts typically find that buy-side and sell-side analysts make more accurate forecasts than do a wide variety of univariate and multivariate time series models (e.g., Elton and Gruber 1972; Brown and Rozeff 1978; Crichfield et al. 1978; Ruland 1978; Collins and Hopwood 1980; Brown et al. 1987; O'Brien 1988; Hopwood and McKeown 1990; also see Armstrong [1983] for a review). Occasionally, the best model constructed by researchers is as accurate as analysts (e.g., Elton and Gruber; Hopwood and McKeown). Analysts appear to be more accurate than models because they have a timing advantage and because they are better at using information (Brown et al.). Similarly, archival studies find that management forecasts frequently are more accurate than those of time series models (Copeland and Marioni 1972; Ruland; however, see Lorek et al. [1976]).

Other studies of users and producers examine replacement with a model in experimental settings. Ebert and Kruse (1978) report that a regression model is more accurate at stock return predictions than are buy-side analysts. Mear and Firth (1987b) report similar findings. Ashton (1982, 1984) shows that a regression model is more accurate than individual managers' predictions of advertising pages. Walker and McClelland (1991) report that managers' predictions of sales volume are less accurate than those made by a time series model but are not less accurate than those from a regression model. Lewis et al. (1988) report that municipal analysts are less accurate than a regression model of municipal bond ratings because they choose cues with lower diagnosticity than does the model; however, they are equally accurate when the model is applied to a validation sample. Abdel-Khalik and El-Sheshai (1980) show that loan officers' predictions of bankruptcy are less accurate than are those of a discriminant analysis model, again because of failure to choose the best cues. Messier and Hansen (1988), using the data from this study, show that an expert system also outperforms the loan officers. Moriarity (1979) reports that accountants are more accurate at predicting bankruptcy than a particular discriminant analysis model, whereas Stock and Watson (1984) find no difference between accountants and a different model.

Studies of auditors versus models include several related to bankruptcy judgments and related going-concern opinion choices. Kida (1980) reports similar accuracy of auditors and a discriminant model at making bankruptcy predictions in an experimental setting. Simnett and Trotman (1989) and Simnett (1996) report that a discriminant model is more accurate than auditors, primarily because auditors do not choose the best cues. Using archival data, two early studies report that auditors' going-concern opinion choices are not as accurate as those of discriminant models (Altman 1982; Levitan and Knoblett 1985); however, a recent study (Hopwood et al. 1994) indicates no differences. Ponemon and Wendell (1995) report that statistical sampling models produce more theoretically correct sample choices than auditors do. Bell and Carcello (2000) show that a regression model is more accurate at assessing fraud risk for cases where fraud exists and is no different from auditors in cases where there is no fraud. Finally, two studies compare the JDM quality of auditors and expert systems. Boritz and Wensley (1992) show that the judgments of auditors and those produced by an expert system designed to generate audit plans are evaluated by other auditors to be similar as to their compliance with professional standards and also as to efficiency. Johnson et al. (1993) show that an expert system based on a theory of deception tactics can better detect fraud than auditors.

A number of studies examine combination of human JDM and model JDM. One set investigates whether researcher-combined predictions of earnings are of higher quality than analysts' predictions. Using archival data, Newbold et al. (1987), Guerard (1987), Lobo and Nair (1990), and Lobo (1991) report that earnings forecasts produced by a combination of analysts' and time series forecasts are more accurate than unaided analysts. However, Conroy and Harris (1987) report that such a combination is more accurate than unaided analysts only when horizons are long and there are only a few analysts following a company. Finally, Lobo (1992) reports that the gain in accuracy due to combination is largest when horizons are long and when analysts' forecasts vary greatly.

Another set of studies experimentally examines people's use of the output of a statistical model, that is, individuals' own combination of their JDM and the model's JDM. Several examine combination by users and producers of accounting information in the context of earnings or sales forecasts. Whitecotton's (1996) and Ghosh and Whitecotton's (1997) analyst and student subjects are more accurate at predicting whether earnings will exceed expectations with the model's output than without; further, the more they agree with the model's predictions, the more accurate they are. Goodwin and Fildes (1999) find that students' sales forecasts are more accurate when they use a model's output than without the model. Two studies compare combined JDM to that of the model alone rather than the human alone. Wolfe and Flores (1990) and Flores et al. (1992) show that a model's earnings forecasts are more accurate when adjusted by loan officers; however, adjustment-related improvements (over the model alone) occur only when model forecasts are relatively inaccurate.

Ashton (1990, 1992) reports that auditors are more accurate at predicting bond ratings when presented with a statistical model's output than when making unaided judgments. Whitecotton and Butler (1998) find the same results with students. Whitecotton et al. (1998) report that students' model-aided bond rating predictions are more accurate than unaided predictions. However, these combined judgments are not as accurate as those of the model alone. Eining et al. (1997) show that auditors using the output of a logit model are better able to discriminate among varying levels of fraud than are unaided auditors; they also exhibit greater consensus. Kowalczyk and Wolfe (1998) report that the judgments of auditors receiving output from an expert system indicating substantial doubt (no substantial doubt) about a firm's ability to continue as a going concern are different (not different) from those receiving no recommendation. In addition, those receiving the substantial doubt recommendation continue to believe this recommendation in the face of inconsistent evidence; this is a negative JDM effect of a decision aid that is akin to anchoring.

Overall, findings from accounting studies examining model-based aids are somewhat similar to those from psychology. One area of exception occurs for bootstrapping, where findings mostly indicate that humans and models are equivalent. These results may reflect the fact that experimental tasks in accounting have presented subjects with limited numbers of cues, so there is little inconsistency in humans' weighting and combination of cues. Libby (1976b) also suggests that accounting professionals may be using nonlinear models, and bootstrapping does not capture such JDM strategies. With regard to replacement with models, almost all experimental studies find that judgments and decisions made by environmental models are superior to those of humans, consistent with psychological findings. However, archival studies of analysts' and managers' earnings forecasts indicate that humans outperform a variety of time series models. Brown et al. (1987) show this finding is partially due to a timing advantage on the part of humans; however, they also suggest that analysts use information better than do models. Finally, combinations of human and model-based JDM tend to be better than either human or model JDM alone; the advantages of combination appear most when models are not particularly accurate. These findings are also consistent with those in psychology.

Given the low likelihood that humans will allow themselves to be replaced with their own models or environmental models, it seems prudent to focus future research on combined model-based and human JDM. In particular, research could continue to focus on factors that can increase or decrease reliance on model-based aids.

Summary

This section has examined the effects of several types of decision aids, specifically memory aids, brief instructions, decomposition, and statistical model-based aids. In addition, the section discusses issues related to reliance on aids and the use of graphs versus tables in aids. Findings regarding decision aids' effects in accounting mostly are consistent with those from psychology with a couple of key exceptions. First, graphical presentations appear to lead to better or equivalent JDM in accounting, whereas the psychology literature posits that tables are better for "higher level" JDM tasks. Second, accounting studies tend to find that the JDM produced by bootstrapped models is no better than or is worse than human JDM. The first differential finding is worth pursuing because of the widespread use of graphs, whereas the second likely is not, given that bootstrapping does not appear to be an acceptable aid in most people's eyes.

9-5   APPLYING THE FRAMEWORK—CHANGES RELATED TO PERSON VARIABLES, TASK VARIABLES, AND ENVIRONMENTAL VARIABLES

Having discussed in depth the effects of three commonly used improvement methods— instruction (and practice and feedback), personnel screening, and decision aids—this section applies the framework for determining JDM improvement methods described in Section 9-1 to examples of person, task, and environmental variables. Specifically, these variables are knowledge content, task complexity, and accountability. Most of the discussion that follows comes from the preceding sections of this chapter or from earlier chapters.

Knowledge content is a variable that has an average positive effect on JDM quality. As such, if knowledge content is the cause of less than acceptable JDM quality, there are two classes of improvement methods that are relevant. First, if knowledge content is not at a high enough level, improvement methods must focus on raising the level. Several methods can accomplish this (assuming that the conditions under which they are effective apply, for example, people are motivated to learn). Instruction, practice, and feedback can raise the level of relevant knowledge, as can personnel screening practices. For example, selection can focus on hiring people who possess the necessary knowledge. Similarly, assignment and promotion can be used to place people with the requisite knowledge into particular positions. People theoretically can also be replaced with high-quality environmental models, although this often is not practically feasible because of resistance to being replaced. If the knowledge content issue relates to people not having multiple types of relevant knowledge, it may be feasible to replace an individual with a group of people who collectively possess all the necessary types of knowledge.[42] On the other hand, the practical costs of convening a group may preclude

---

[42]If lack of a single type of knowledge is the problem, the use of a group likely is unnecessary.

the use of this method. Also, some types of decision aids provide the requisite knowledge to the decision maker at the time it is needed and also may assist her in acquiring the knowledge over time.

The second class of improvement methods for a positive-effect variable is pertinent when the variable is at a high enough level but there is some factor present that moderates its effects. In this situation, improvement methods must attempt to remove the moderator from the environment or otherwise reduce its effects. With regard to knowledge content, these moderators are factors that inhibit the retrieval of knowledge from memory. One culprit is task-related information that causes output interference. Removing or reducing the effects of task-related information that causes output interference can be accomplished in several possible ways. First, the information can be removed from the task. For example, if it is discovered that a decision aid employing examples is causing interference, the examples can be removed from the aid. Further, the aid could be changed to include all relevant information, for example, in a list format, to ensure that it is retrieved (if the aid is used properly). Second, another factor can be put in place that works against such task-related information. For instance, if a firm believes that the provision of examples in a decision aid has certain benefits, they could alter the aid to provide examples from multiple categories to try to reduce the interference that would be caused by examples from a single category. Alternatively, the firm could maintain the original examples in an aid but couple it with another type of aid such as instructions to consider alternatives. Clearly, these latter two examples could be very costly and, thus, might be less likely to be chosen in practice.

Other causes of the failure to retrieve relevant knowledge reflect various aspects of cognitive processing. One is the use of heuristics during JDM. For example, if people use the representativeness heuristic, they may not retrieve knowledge of base rates. A specific improvement method related to retrieval of base rates is to point out the causal relation of base rates to outcomes. More generally, which improvement methods can reduce the use of heuristics? As discussed in Chapter 5, people use heuristics when they have some knowledge that is relevant for a task but do not possess knowledge of task-specific strategies or solutions. In other words, because people lack knowledge of certain types, they are more likely to use heuristics that can cause them to fail to retrieve some of the knowledge they do possess. Improvement methods, then, would be those that increase the level of the missing knowledge (e.g., practice and feedback or personnel screening). A second cognitive processing feature that can lead to failure to retrieve relevant knowledge is motivated reasoning that is caused by the presence of some desired conclusion (i.e., a judgment or decision that has positive monetary or other consequences associated with it). Here, people may retrieve only knowledge that is consistent with the desired conclusion. Improving this aspect of cognitive processing obviously could imply removing the desired conclusion from the environment. This seems infeasible in most practical situations, so methods likely have to focus on working against biased retrieval. One possibility is to employ a decision aid that requires counter-explanation or consideration of alternatives. However, in practice, it is possible that strong motivation to reach the desired conclusion can affect how this aid is used (e.g., by limiting the number of counter-explanations considered or through biased interpretation of their plausibility). In this case, it may be necessary to put in place factors that provide motivation to reach a correct judgment or decision that is stronger than the motivation to reach the desired conclusion. Such factors include legal penalties, negative consequences during performance appraisal, and the like. Overall, then, there are many ways of reducing the effects of moderators here, so an understanding of the moderators that exist clearly is important when proceeding to consider improvements.

The task-variable example used to apply the improvement-method framework is task complexity. Task complexity, on average, has a negative effect on JDM quality. Consequently, the first class of improvement methods involves reducing the level of task complexity. This can be accomplished by increasing the level of structure or level of information clarity in the task. Sometimes, these goals are accomplished by changing the task. For example, a firm could reduce the amount of information it requires its employees to evaluate in a particular JDM task. Alternatively, the goals can be accomplished through the provision of a decision aid. For example, decomposition aids can increase the level of structure for many tasks. Both these methods seem practically feasible.

The second class of improvement methods pertains to putting in place or increasing the level of moderators that reduce complexity's negative effects.[43] Which specific method makes sense depends on the mechanisms by which complexity negatively affects JDM quality as well as the potential moderators that reduce the negative effects. One mechanism by which complexity negatively affects JDM quality is the taxing of memory and processing limitations, which is reduced by the possession of organized knowledge and/or abilities. In this case, then, methods must relate to increasing the level of knowledge (e.g., practice and feedback) or the level of abilities (e.g., personnel screening). Another mechanism by which complexity negatively affects JDM quality is that people restructure tasks (inappropriately) to match their knowledge; in this case, improvement methods must allow people to better retrieve and apply their knowledge to the existing task. Practically feasible decision aids such as checklists and decomposition address these issues. Finally, task complexity can reduce JDM quality because people choose lower-effort processing strategies to compensate for additional effort required by complex tasks; overall, they wish to keep costs lower than task-related benefits. In this case, improvement methods must focus on increasing task-related benefits (e.g., by tying monetary incentives to JDM quality). Such methods may not always be possible given regulatory and other restrictions in accounting settings.

The final example used to illustrate application of the framework is the environmental variable of accountability. Accountability to a party with an unknown view, on average, increases JDM quality, whereas accountability to a party with a known view increases JDM quality only if that known view is correct. Given that it is difficult to specify ex ante the conditions under which a known view is correct, this section focuses on only the first type of accountability. If this type of accountability is known to be a cause of less than acceptable JDM quality, improving JDM hinges on raising the level of accountability or reducing the effects of moderators. Raising the level of accountability may entail making someone accountable for their JDM; this does not seem to be a practical solution because most people already are accountable.

Therefore, improvement methods likely must focus on reducing moderators' effects. One moderator is lack of knowledge and/or abilities. The levels of these factors can be increased as discussed above. Another moderator is informing people of

---

[43] As mentioned earlier, this chapter does not focus on the third general category of improvement methods for negative-effects variables, that is, removing the effects of moderators that exacerbate their negative effects.

accountability requirements post-JDM; this timing problem is easily changed. A final moderator is the perceived credibility of the party to whom one is held accountable. If credibility is too low, accountability may not have a positive effect on JDM. Thus, improvement requires either changing the party to a more credible one or altering the credibility of the person already in place. Factors that are relevant to credibility, such as knowledge, can be altered practically in many ways. Alternatively, firms may choose to alter factors that affect perceived credibility but that likely are irrelevant thereto, for example, by providing training in communication skills.

The discussion above assumes that JDM is affected by only one variable. This clearly is not the case most of the time. Thus, one difficulty in attempting to determine how to improve JDM quality is understanding the individual and possible interactive effects of multiple variables. Along with this, improvement methods related to one variable may create problems vis-à-vis other variables. For example, using performance appraisal to select high-ability individuals for promotion may decrease the motivation of lower-ability individuals. Even if JDM is affected by only one variable, these examples illustrate the importance of understanding the mechanisms by which the variable is affecting JDM negatively or failing to affect JDM as positively as possible, again emphasizing the importance of placing research questions related to improvement methods at the end of the JDM framework shown in Figure 9-1.

9-6 SUMMARY

This chapter reviews the literature on JDM improvement methods, focusing on the effects of instruction, practice, and feedback; personnel screening practices; and decision aids. Specifically, discussion centers around the person variables, task variables, or environmental variables that are affected by these methods and these variables' consequent effects on JDM. In addition, each section covers the factors that can moderate these methods' effectiveness. Unfortunately, the number of such factors is rather large for each type of improvement technique. Given how costly each of these methods is, further study of how to lessen moderators' impact is important if only from a practical perspective.

Findings regarding the effects of these methods in accounting tend to parallel those in psychology with the exception of the effects of graphs versus tables and bootstrapping. As mentioned earlier, the first differential finding is worth pursuing, whereas the second probably is not. In addition to aiding theory development in the area of decision aid format, accounting researchers have the opportunity to build theory for other improvement methods. For example, understanding the effects of accounting systems per se on knowledge acquisition seems critically important given that standard-setters likely assume that there are no such effects, or at least no negative effects. As shown by Luft and Shields (2001), the choice to require expensing of intangibles can impede system users' learning about how intangibles affect future profits. Along with this, it is important to understand how factors that are somewhat unique to accounting settings interact with various improvement methods. For instance, how do professional standards, regulatory and legal threats, and conclusions desired by clients and other constituents, affect accounting professionals' use of decision aids? If such interactive effects can decrease the quality of JDM, are there factors already in place in the environment that serve to mitigate them (e.g., the review process)? Further, it is important to document and understand the effects of recent innovations in JDM improvement methods, such as Internet-based decision aids (Edwards and Fasolo 2001).

Perhaps most important, JDM improvement methods other than those discussed in this chapter are worthy of further investigation. Chapter 7 discusses research to date for many of these methods (e.g., accountability and monetary incentives) as well as possible future research. However, a number of possible improvement methods have not been the subject of extensive study and clearly deserve further examination. Some of these methods relate to people's self-initiated attempts to correct their JDM processes based on a perception that they are flawed (e.g., Wilson et al. 2002). Others involve organizational changes such as the use of consultation in public accounting firms (e.g., Salterio and Denham 1997). Still others involve changes in larger systems such as the legal system. Unfortunately, like other improvement methods, these methods likely have many moderators that can attenuate their effectiveness. For example, legal outcomes can be influenced by a number of irrelevant factors such as pretrial publicity and realized outcomes (e.g., Kramer et al. 1990; Kadous 2001).

The most important of these in today's environment may be those that have been under scrutiny recently. Specifically, various elements of professional standards (e.g., the choice of rules or principles) and elements of the regulatory and organizational environment (e.g., the separation of research from investment banking in brokerage firms) have been the focus of politicians, standard-setters, and the general public in recent times. They have been under scrutiny both for the negative JDM effects they may have caused and because people appear to believe that changing standards, regulations, and organizational setups can solve many JDM problems that previously existed. This is not at all clear because these types of improvement methods may not address the underlying causes of low-quality JDM. For example, rather than simplifying matters (by making financial reporting treatments clear), relatively more rules-based standards could increase task complexity by increasing the amount of information to be processed (Nelson 2003). Further, people who previously made strategic use of standards, regulations, and particular organizational setups likely can find ways to work around new versions of these factors. Finally, the main method that many people advocate for improving individuals' JDM is having them attempt to function in a market. Although markets can help people improve their JDM (e.g., Waller et al. 1999; Chewning et al. 2004), they do not eliminate all errors and biases (e.g., Tuttle et al. 1997). Thus, further study of how markets do and do not improve JDM clearly is important.

CHAPTER

10

Conclusion

This book concludes by contemplating future research using two approaches. The first approach is to summarize what we have learned vis-à-vis the JDM framework used to organize this book and to suggest future research based on "holes" identified by this discussion. In particular, the summary addresses the extent to which the questions in the JDM framework have been answered, as well as how findings in accounting differ from those in psychology. The summary also speculates as to which issues appear to be the "big potatoes" for future research based on framework-related research to date.[1] The second approach to considering future research involves stepping away from the framework in an attempt to identify issues that might not be recognized if one were to focus intensively and exclusively on the framework. In particular, this approach leads to a call for more descriptive research on the current environment in which accounting-related judgments and decisions are made. Specific elements of this environment that may be important are discussed. Finally, stepping away from the framework leads to a conclusion that we need to put more "accounting" into JDM research in accounting.

10-1 FUTURE RESEARCH BASED ON A SUMMARY OF FRAMEWORK-RELATED JDM RESEARCH TO DATE

This book reviews JDM research related to producers, users, auditors, and regulators of accounting information as well as research related to evaluators' of these individuals' work products. The book is organized around the questions posed by the JDM framework, as shown in Figure 10-1.

Two general types of conclusions can be drawn about the extent to which the questions in the framework have been answered and, thus, about future research that derives from noticing "holes" in the extant literature. First, we know a great deal about the individual JDM of external auditors across a wide variety of tasks. We know somewhat less about analysts' and tax professionals' JDM. And we know fairly little about the individual JDM of managerial accountants, investors, managers, investment advisors, brokers, mutual fund managers, internal auditors, corporate directors, standard-setters, and regulators and other evaluators of accountants' work (e.g., judges and juries).[2] Further, most of what we know about auditors' and tax professionals' JDM comes from experimental studies, and much of what we know about analysts' JDM comes from archival

---

[1] As mentioned in Chapter 1, this is Bill Kinney's terminology.
[2] Note, however, that research on auditor JDM is waning (Kinney 2005), whereas research on investors and analysts appears to be increasing.

FIGURE 10-1 Framework for JDM Research in Accounting

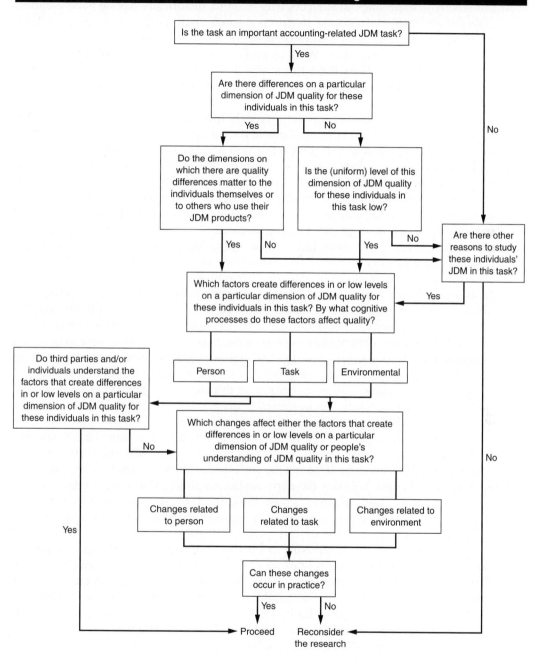

studies. Neither of these conclusions is particularly surprising given the differential availability of experimental subjects, with auditors historically having been the most plentiful and easiest to access in group settings such as firm training programs. Research grants related to studies of auditors' JDM also likely explain the overall prevalence of work on auditors. Work on analysts being somewhat plentiful reflects the availability of data on their JDM; this availability, along with general interest in information intermediaries by archival researchers, also likely explains the prevalence of archival work in this area.

These observations suggest very strongly that there are a number of areas for future research (i.e., answering questions in the framework about the key participants in the accounting arena whose JDM is not well understood). A word of warning with regard to this research direction, however, is that it is crucial to learn about and focus on the defining characteristics of the tasks and environments faced by these individuals, as well as any distinct personal characteristics they may possess, rather than replicating studies related to auditors, tax professionals, or analysts. In other words, the importance of task analysis (see Chapter 1) cannot be overemphasized. For example, managers today face enormous time pressure when making decisions regarding product lines and prices because of global competition that makes speed to market a critical success factor (Gleick 2000). Although time pressure is a salient feature of other areas of accounting, it may create different outcomes in this managerial setting or work through different processes. For example, managers may accept inaccurate cost data to make speedy decisions; in other settings, time pressure often leads to incomplete processing. Finally, these observations suggest that experiments can shed more light on the behavior of analysts, whereas nonexperimental methods could be useful for studying auditors and tax professionals.[3] In general, it would be useful to have more archival work based on psychology theories because of this method's advantages for answering specific JDM questions (e.g., those related to economic consequences) (see Chapter 1 and Koonce and Mercer [2005]).[4]

Second, with regard to the progression of research through the framework, accounting research generally has progressed quite logically, with the earliest studies documenting differences in JDM quality for specific tasks and specific individuals of interest. For example, consider the early studies on auditors' internal control evaluation (e.g., Ashton 1974b). Following these early studies, research proceeded to understanding factors that create differences in auditors' internal control judgments. For example, the literature examined experience-related differences (e.g., Ashton and Kramer 1980), eventually progressing to a better understanding of the specific person variables captured by measures of experience, such as evidence evaluation processes (Bonner 1990). Research then examined other types of variables affecting internal control judgments, such as the task variables of order of information (e.g., Ashton and Ashton 1988) and framing (e.g., Emby 1994) and the environmental variables of feedback (e.g., Waller and Felix 1984) and group processing (e.g., Trotman and Yetton 1985). In addition, studies examining the impact of various person, task, and environmental

---

[3]Clearly, many different methods can be used to study the JDM of individuals about whom we know little to date.
[4]An increase in archival JDM work also might stimulate greater effects of JDM studies in general on archival economics-based work; this impact historically has been rather insignificant (Gibbins and Swieringa 1995).

variables often documented the cognitive processes by which these variables affect JDM. Finally, more recent research has examined the effects of improvement methods on the factors that affect auditors' internal control judgments. For example, studies have examined the effects of decision aids on reducing framing effects (e.g., Emby and Finley 1997) and on increasing cue weighting consistency (e.g., Libby and Libby 1989).

One major exception to the logical progression of research on JDM issues, however, is that researchers have tended to leap over the framework's question about economic consequences of JDM quality. After documenting variation in JDM quality, research generally has investigated JDM determinants assuming that the variation has economic effects on the individuals making the judgments and decisions and/or on others who rely on their work. This assumption likely is warranted in most cases, but it is important now to step back and question the assumption, particularly when considering research on understudied tasks. Clearly, one reason for leaping over this question is the predominant use of experiments in JDM research and the relatively greater difficulty of demonstrating economic consequences with experiments. However, it often is possible to look to the archival economics-based literature to find supporting evidence for this assumption; doing so seems particularly important going forward. If evidence does not exist, documenting economic consequences is an important topic for future research.

Another issue is that research has tended to move from understanding the determinants of JDM quality to examining methods that can improve JDM quality. An alternative direction to follow after learning about determinants is to examine whether third parties who use accountants' JDM understand these determinants. This alternative has been of less interest in the past than the study of improvement methods even though both follow logically from the previous question in the framework. Future research on third-party understanding is particularly important, however, given that one of the core functions of accounting information is its use by third parties to make economically significant decisions.[5]

With regard to specific questions in the framework, the following summary comments and future research suggestions can be offered. Determining whether a task is an accounting-related task likely is a matter of taste, whereas determining whether a task is important can be based on either taste or research. Both bases have been used in previous research, although the basis for this determination sometimes is not specifically stated. Future research should make the basis for determining task importance clear. The second question in the framework is one about which we now know much, at least with regard to specific tasks; what we know is that there frequently is substantial variation in JDM quality. Further, this is similar to what has been found in psychology. As mentioned earlier, however, there are some JDM tasks about which we know very little (including whether there is variation in JDM quality in these tasks), such as most of the tasks performed by internal auditors.

The third question in the framework is one area for which we have less knowledge, as mentioned above. To the extent research has addressed this question, however,

---

[5]There are other more minor exceptions as well. For example, early work on the effects of financial reporting standards (e.g., the use of LIFO versus FIFO) tended to assume that there was variation in financial statement users' JDM without documenting such. Many studies that found no effects of these factors may simply have been documenting that there is little variation in such judgments. Although this seems highly unlikely, it nevertheless highlights the need to consider earlier questions in the framework.

there typically are substantial consequences both for the individuals and for third parties. Note that psychology research tends not to examine this question; as discussed in Chapter 1, it is included in the framework because of its importance in a professional field. Future research should not only examine economic consequences for the accounting professionals involved (e.g., job turnover for analysts), but also focus on economic consequences for third parties. This suggestion reflects the role of accounting in our society and also reflects the fact that economic consequences for third parties are perhaps one of the largest incentives many accounting professionals face. For example, analysts face an incentive related to generating investor trades but may also face a large disincentive caused by the possibility of investor litigation.

The next question in the framework—the factors creating variation in JDM quality—is the subject of most accounting JDM research and, as such, this section returns to it below after briefly discussing the remaining questions in the framework. Remaining questions relate to third parties' and individuals' understanding of the factors that affect their accounting-related JDM and methods of improving JDM quality. Overall, there is less research related to these questions, but findings to date are similar to those in psychology. Going forward, the issues that seem to be of the most importance regarding third parties' understanding include documenting to what extent third parties, in particular unsophisticated third parties such as individual investors, actively attempt to understand the determinants (or even the quality of) accounting professionals' JDM. In addition, to the extent they do attempt to actively understand, how good is their understanding of the myriad factors that can affect JDM quality and their measurement of those factors using incomplete, noisy, and perhaps inaccurate data? For example, do investors use poor proxies such as experience to capture analysts' knowledge, abilities, and other personal characteristics? With regard to JDM improvement methods, the most practically important overall question may be this: Which factors in the environment actually are effective improvement methods? For instance, the effects of the personnel screening and decision aids methods discussed in Chapter 9 are reduced by so many moderators that it is not clear how often these methods actually improve JDM quality. This also is true of the environmental variables discussed in Chapter 7, for example, monetary incentives, accountability, and standards and regulations. Perhaps the most effective improvement methods are instruction (along with practice and feedback), markets, and legal and regulatory penalties for low-quality JDM.

Returning to the question of JDM determinants, a variety of person, task, and environmental variables have been studied and the findings regarding these variables' directional effects on JDM, as well as the moderators of their effects, are remarkably similar to those in psychology. Exceptions include the following. In the area of person variables, findings regarding personal involvement are not as negative as those in psychology, that is, personal involvement does not always lead to lower-quality JDM. Further, auditors appear to be less likely (than psychology studies' subjects and other persons of interest to accounting researchers) to exhibit confirmation bias. They also appear to choose consistent (and conservative) problem representations, which, in turn, lead them to focus more on negative information than do others. This finding is the essence of "professional skepticism" and is of particular importance from the perspective that third parties may try to manipulate accounting professionals through the provision of a particular representation for a task. Similarly, auditors and tax professionals both appear to be less susceptible to the effects of task framing. Auditors' cognitive processing is such that they are less likely to ignore or underweight base rates and are better at considering the effects of sample sizes on outcomes than are other types of individuals.

Overall, it may seem disappointing that most findings regarding JDM determinants are similar to those in psychology, but it has been extremely important to document the extent to which accountants are "normal" for two reasons. First, intuition may have led researchers to believe otherwise. Researchers' intuition may suggest that accounting professionals are more sophisticated than are others and, further, that the forces surrounding them (such as the threat of litigation and monetary penalties) lead to their JDM being of significantly higher quality than that of others. For example, we may believe that sophistication and external forces keep accountants' JDM from being negatively affected by irrelevant task variables such as order of information. However, research often has informed us that such intuition may be incorrect.

Second, firms and regulators often base changes to practice on intuition; sometimes this intuition has led them to assume that accounting professionals are not like other individuals with regard to the determinants of JDM quality, and sometimes it has. Given that accountants sometimes are like "normal" people and sometimes are not, firms and regulators then can make two types of errors. For example, Congress recently changed the regulation of auditors' behavior by instituting an independent board for oversight (rather than relying on peer review). In so doing, Congress mandated that a certain number of members of the new independent regulatory board should not have extensive accounting knowledge (Kinney 2005). Here, the implied intuition is that task-specific knowledge is not important for understanding situations and making high-quality evaluations of others' work, at least for this regulatory body. In other words, intuition assumes that these regulators are not like "normal" people, whereas research evidence most likely would indicate otherwise. As another example, recent audit reforms require mandatory partner rotation, likely based on the intuition that personal involvement has negative effects on JDM quality (e.g., Levitt 2003). Here, the implied intuition is that auditors are "normal"; however, research often indicates that auditors' personal involvement does not lead to lower-quality JDM. In general, then, research that finds results either similar to or dissimilar to those in psychology has the potential to contribute to both theory development among researchers as well as to accounting practice. Further, research that finds dissimilar results can contribute to theory development in psychology.

Given the above findings, which person, task, and environmental variables, or elements thereof, are now the "big potatoes" in the area of JDM determinants? Although each of Chapters 3 through 7 provides a detailed summary of these variables' effects and specific suggestions for important future research, it seems crucial at this point to take the largest view possible. Clearly, the basket of "big potatoes" in the area of JDM determinants will continue to include knowledge and certain environmental factors that affect motivation (i.e., monetary incentives and accountability) along with the cognitive processes through which these factors affect JDM. In the past, JDM researchers in accounting often thought of motivating factors as those related solely to promoting higher JDM quality (e.g., more accurate judgments). What may be of more interest today, however, is how these motivators can be coupled with desired conclusions and lead to motivated reasoning (Kunda 1990). In fact, although previously we may have thought of knowledge and motivation as a combination of variables leading to high-quality professional JDM, we now may see this combination as treacherous; the more knowledgeable professionals are, the better they may be at reasoning that is motivated toward accepting a desired (but incorrect and potentially harmful) conclusion. A third factor that combines with knowledge and motivation that can allow such conclusions to occur in our regulated environment is the nature of accounting and auditing standards per se. That is, if highly knowledgeable and conclusion-motivated professionals can reach these conclusions within such an environment, does some of the blame lie with standards that may allow these conclusions to be considered "correct"? This sort of notion underlies, for example, the debate about rules-based versus principles-based financial reporting standards (e.g., Schipper 2003), even though it appears that this element of the standards simply may alter the manner in which motivated reasoning is carried out (Maines et al. 2003).

Personal involvement is another important and understudied person variable. Most accounting professionals make repeated judgments, unlike students in psychology experiments. Further, regulators' intuition appears to be that this factor may negatively affect JDM (e.g., Levitt 2003), whereas research evidence to date suggests that it may not. Such a disconnect may reflect regulators' focus on the motivation to reach a desired conclusion that might be produced by personal involvement, whereas, in reality, there are other effects of personal involvement (e.g., learning) that offset such negative effects.

Other (static) person variables pertain to individual differences, for example, abilities and personality factors. Research in psychology concludes that these variables have practical importance (e.g., Lubinski 2000), but it is not clear that such a strong statement can be made about all such variables in accounting. For example, as Trotman (2005) notes, if auditing firms discover that persons with varying personalities respond differentially to decision aids, it seems unlikely that the firms will respond by encouraging some people to use the aids while discouraging others. The remaining person variables with the greatest practical importance in accounting seem to be abilities, affect, confidence, and personal motives regarding fairness and other socially desirable outcomes. Starting with abilities, research could have practical implications from the standpoint that abilities cannot be acquired through instruction, but rather must be screened at the points of hiring and promotion; thus, research examining the relative importance of knowledge and abilities to particular tasks continues to be important. Affect and confidence have been the subject of a great deal of work on investor JDM; this work has shown that these factors can negatively affect returns and create market inefficiencies. (See, for example, Hirshleifer [2001] and Barberis and Thaler [2003] for reviews). However, there are many opportunities here to gain further understanding of the processes by which these factors can negatively affect JDM, along with related improvement methods. Study of improvement methods that are particularly germane to accounting situations seems of the most importance (e.g., the evaluation of investments on a portfolio basis rather than a case-by-case basis for reducing the negative effects of confidence) (Nelson et al. 2003). Studies of the effects of social motives are sparse; thus, there are many opportunities in this area (Sprinkle 2003). Examining their effects in conjunction with or as opposed to other motivating factors (e.g., monetary incentives) seems particularly important. For example, do social motives typically carry a desired conclusion? If so, are these desired conclusions similar to those related to other motivators (e.g., monetary incentives)? If not, do such desired conclusions (or the desire to be accurate if no such conclusions are tied to social motives) work against the effects of other motivators' desired conclusions?

Studies of cognitive processing factors clearly continue to be important as part of studying the effects of other key person, task, and environmental variables. However, it also seems critical to learn more about the accounting environment and how elements of this environment affect the processes people exhibit. In particular, it is important to understand to what extent these processes have been adapted to the environment and, thus, might be able to produce high-quality JDM when quality is defined as accuracy vis-à-vis actual outcomes rather than vis-à-vis normative theories (e.g., Asare and Wright 1995).

One important example of a variable whose effects on processes and subsequent JDM deserves further study is task complexity. Psychologists have documented a number of responses to complexity, one of which is simplification of processes (e.g., people switch from compensatory to noncompensatory processing). In accounting settings, it seems that there may be specific responses to complexity that have not yet been documented. Consider the task complexity faced by the individual investor. First she has to decide the type of investment vehicle in which she is interested, for example, mutual funds or individual stocks. Then she has to narrow her choices from a set of thousands of possibilities and acquire and process information about each of the members of the narrowed set. What cognitive processes do investors use to deal with such complexity? For example, do they consider the universe of possibilities at all, say, by examining a listing of mutual funds available? Or, instead, do they simply start with a small set that has garnered their attention (Barber and Odean 2006)? What factors make stocks or mutual funds "attention grabbers"? News coverage of a firm or the stock's price is one such factor (Barber and Odean), but there are others, such as word of mouth among neighbors and friends (Hong et al. 2004). Most important, are there conditions under which such noncompensatory processing responses can lead to high-quality JDM?

Another issue related to task variables that deserves further study is the extent to which they are used strategically by various players in accounting settings and how strategic use affects the JDM of the accounting professionals who interact with these players, as well as that of third parties who rely on the professionals' work. As discussed in Chapter 6, it seems quite plausible that managers can use task variables such as irrelevant information, redundant information, and order of information in an attempt to manipulate auditors' JDM. If managers engage in such behavior, in what situations does it occur (e.g., situations where there is weak or no evidence to support a desired conclusion)? How can auditors and others protect themselves against being influenced by these irrelevant task factors? A final issue that is critically important is to understand how the choices made by standard-setters affect users of accounting information. In other words, we need to better understand how characteristics of accounting systems and tasks affect JDM; this issue is discussed further in the next section.

With regard to environmental variables, as discussed above, the effects of factors that motivate individuals to reach desired conclusions clearly deserve further study. However, the evidence consistently indicates that accounting professionals, including those who should not do so because of standards discouraging such behavior, engage in motivated reasoning. At this point, what would be of more interest is to understand how professionals respond to conflicting motivators. Conflicts in motivators can be created by the combined presence of desired-conclusion motivators and "be correct" kinds of motivators, or by the presence of motivators that suggest different desired conclusions. At this point, we know very little about the JDM effects of conflicting incentives. (For exceptions, see Barrick et al. [2004] and Chen et al. [2006]).[6] Is the response to these incentives dictated solely by the utility provided by various outcomes (e.g., monetary rewards and penalties and socially desirable outcomes such as praise by one's superiors) or, for example, can it be affected also by the types of accounting standards in place (Nelson 2003)? What types of methods can improve JDM if the influence of desired (and incorrect) conclusion motivators is too strong? For example, are changes in organizational setups, restrictions on services, and other regulatory interventions, such as those recently imposed on analysts and auditors, the best ways of potentially constraining such "bad behavior"? As discussed above, are these methods even effective at improving JDM, or instead, should regulators focus solely on increasing penalties? Finally, one environmental variable that is relatively unique to accounting is the review process. Further study of this process, in particular, the strategic interactions between reviewer and the one being reviewed, and theory development such as that provided by Rich et al. (1997a) are critically important.

10-2 FUTURE RESEARCH BASED ON THE CURRENT ACCOUNTING ENVIRONMENT

There are a number of opportunities for interesting and practically important future research based on the analysis of framework-related research to date. Another approach for generating research questions is to step away from the framework and think more broadly. Specifically, researchers first need to consider the current environment in which accounting-related judgments and decisions are made and determine whether there are important variables or issues not captured explicitly by the framework. Second, researchers need to use what has been learned about accountants' JDM to date, along with the current literature in psychology, to develop theories about how accounting per se affects JDM.

The environment in which accounting-related judgments and decisions are made today is extraordinarily complex. It bears little resemblance to the environment many researchers knew when they were employed in practice or began their careers as accounting professors (Kinney 2005). As such, the need for studies that describe characteristics of the environment is enormous. Recent studies describing the valuation models used by analysts (Demirakos et al. 2004), how individual investors use financial statements (Hodge 2003), and the extent to which pro forma earnings are reported (Entwistle et al. 2006) are good examples of the types of information researchers need for finding new (and possibly big) potatoes. Unfortunately, it is difficult to obtain current descriptive evidence on some important accounting environments. For example, as Kinney notes, auditing firms have very few incentives (and many disincentives) regarding disclosure of their current auditing practices and procedures. Perhaps younger members of the academic profession, those who have had recent work experience, can assist in providing this descriptive evidence.

---

[6]Similarly, we know little about how people respond to conflicting motivators that pertain to multiple tasks or multiple dimensions of a single task (Sprinkle 2003).

This chapter can offer only a few examples of changes in the environment that might lead to future research opportunities. One is the proliferation of the financial media. In the past 10 years or so, the size and accessibility of the financial media has increased dramatically. There now are dozens of personal finance publications as well as standard business outlets that cover financial news and thousands of financial Web sites (Bartiromo 2001). Further, television coverage of financial issues now is commonplace. In particular, coverage of some of the key players in the capital market such as analysts has grown substantially. Media coverage is an influential factor for investors and, consequently, for managers and analysts who provide information to investors, as well as for auditors whose reports are relied on by investors. For example, the finance literature indicates that media coverage of firms affects stock prices (Busse and Green 2002; Gadarowski 2004) and that investors who buy highly covered stocks suffer lower returns (Barber and Odean 2006). Although many accounting researchers have commented on the potential effects of the media in the capital market (e.g., how their increased coverage of earnings announcements vis-à-vis analysts' forecasts has created incentives for earnings management), JDM research in accounting typically has not considered media coverage to be an important factor. (For exceptions, see Mutchler et al. [1997]; Joe [2003]; Louis et al. [2005]; and Bonner et al. [2006]). Consistent with this, this book's framework has been applied only to producers, users, auditors, and regulators of accounting information as well as evaluators of their work, and not to members of the media.

There are many roles that the media may play in accounting JDM settings that suggest research opportunities and also suggest that members of the financial media should be added to the list of key players addressed by the framework. First, as implied by the stock price effects described above, the media likely plays an information intermediary role. How does media coverage affect individuals' JDM in this role? For example, as posited by Barber and Odean (2006), does it serve simply as an attention-focusing mechanism? Alternatively, the media may serve as an apparently credible outlet of information for users of accounting information as well. That is, people may look to the media to provide unbiased information about accounting issues, consistent with the media's general role to be accurate reporters of events. However, members of the media face constraints such as severe time deadlines that may cause them not to focus on the credibility that readers and viewers place in their reporting (Bonner et al. 2006). In addition, despite the enormity of media outlets, there are size limits on what can be reported. Thus, the media must selectively attend to accounting issues when deciding what to cover; this means their accounting coverage will be incomplete and likely biased toward "interesting" stories rather than being representative of the population of accounting issues. As a simple example, the media tends to cover audit failures rather than audit successes. If users of accounting information assume that media coverage of accounting events implies credibility and is representative of the population of stories, many elements of cognitive processes and consequent JDM quality can be negatively affected. Perhaps the most serious possible effect of the media as an information intermediary is that users of accounting information allow media coverage to substitute for accounting information in their analysis (i.e., become the sole source of information). For example, an investor may decide to buy a stock because she sees a highly confident analyst giving a buy recommendation on television. She may never look at the financial statements or listen to the analyst's evaluation of the facts leading to earnings and stock price forecasts. Finally, the proliferation of the media means that there may be an increase in the level of certain task variables that have negative effects on JDM. For example, media outlets often report the same stories (e.g., those originated by the Associated Press), leading to repetition of information. A larger number of media outlets can mean enormous repetition. As another example, voluntary disclosures occur through media outlets; thus, the media may unwittingly participate in the strategic framing of information initiated by managers.

A related important factor in today's accounting environment is rapid advances in information technology. Some of these advances have led to the proliferation of media coverage (e.g., the ability to obtain real-time stock quotes means that media coverage of these real-time prices is of interest to many investors). Although accounting researchers have recognized that technology has changed the way practitioners operate, it is not clear that we have a fundamental understanding of how technology affects accounting JDM. For example, is technology (its types, its accessibility, its costs, etc.) simply another environmental variable that should be added to the set of interesting variables to study? If so, what effects does it have on accounting JDM quality and what factors moderate these effects? Alternatively, do we tend to think of certain elements of technology as JDM improvement methods? For example, Hodge et al. (2004) examine whether technology can improve investors' use of accounting information. If technology is considered an improvement method, for example, a type of decision aid, how effective is it at improving JDM, and do general decision aid issues, such as resistance to reliance, pertain to technology? Yet another possibility is that technology has fundamentally altered the world of accounting so the tasks accountants now perform are no longer the tasks traditionally studied by researchers (e.g., Elliott 1992; Hunton 2002). This possibility would suggest that researchers might need to start over in the framework, having analyzed and redefined today's accounting tasks. As Hunton notes, such work likely requires teaming up with information systems researchers. Finally, and perhaps most important, technology already has and may continue to change accounting systems. For example, one of the fundamental principles of accounting today is aggregation of detailed information (discussed further below). Technology allows for real-time and more organized access to disaggregated information (Wallman 1997). Technology also allows users to customize the detailed information they access. In turn, this means that the attestation function must focus on processes businesses use to generate data rather than on a single (standardized and summarized) end product of those processes—the quarterly or annual financial statement. In summary, because of the multiple possible conceptualizations and effects of technology, it is not evident how technology should be incorporated into the JDM framework.

A third factor that may be of import in today's environment is the existence of record numbers of individual investors (Bartiromo 2001) and the intuitive (naive) theories they may have about other people's behavior as well as about accounting and financial issues. For example, when making investments for retirement purposes, people often divide their contributions evenly across the funds offered by retirement plans (Benartzi and Thaler 2001), perhaps because of an intuitive theory that their employer finds all the funds equally desirable. In general, intuitive theories abound and can have significant effects on people's behavior and JDM (e.g., Nisbett and Ross 1980; Soll 1999). Although intuitive theories typically have been of interest to social psychologists who study how people form impressions of others' behavior, they likely play a role in accounting settings given that people have intuitive theories about information more generally (Soll 1999). Perhaps the easiest way of convincing oneself of the validity of this statement is to consider the "wild ideas" that students bring to accounting courses. To date, however, virtually no accounting JDM research has examined the effects of these theories, perhaps because they are not an obvious person variable. (For exceptions, see Koonce et al. [2005a, 2005b].)

An example of an intuitive theory that investors may have about accounting issues is that accounting rules are "cut and dried." As a consequence, in situations where accounting misstatements are discovered in audited financial statements, investors may believe the fault for missing these misstatements lies mostly with the auditors in their (intuitively theorized) role as "rule checkers" and initiate litigation against the auditors. This example shows that the effects of investors' intuitive theories also may negatively affect people who supply them with information, for example, managers, auditors, analysts, and perhaps even the media. In fact, media coverage may have increased the extent of intuitive theories people have about accounting-related issues as well as their confidence therein. Years ago, when financial news coverage was essentially unheard of, people may not have had intuitive theories about accounting issues, or if they did, they likely would have doubted their validity and placed their trust in money managers instead. Today's media coverage (along with the technology to deliver it in a speedy and entertaining fashion) may convince people that they have highly credible theories about accounting. This could occur because people can process media coverage related to their accounting theories in a fashion that supports these theories. For example, if people have a theory that auditors are to blame for accounting failures, they need only selectively attend to media reports that are consistent with this. Overall, then, there are a number of opportunities in this area, including documenting intuitive theories that exist and how they vary across individuals, their effects on JDM (which likely are negative), and methods of improving JDM if negatively affected by these theories.[7]

A final, and perhaps the most important, realization that comes from stepping away from the framework is that JDM research in accounting traditionally has not focused significantly on accounting systems. One likely reason for this is that the state of theory development in psychology was such that accounting researchers were unable to make predictions about the effects of various elements of accounting systems. Thus, although there were several studies in this area in the early days of JDM research, much of the work was atheoretical. By contrast, accounting researchers today can draw on a large body of theory in psychology and combine this with their institutional knowledge of accounting to develop theories that predict the effects of accounting systems on JDM.

How might researchers begin to develop such theories? First, they must delineate the elements of accounting systems that can affect JDM. But, prior to this, researchers must define "accounting" and "accounting research." *Accounting* can be defined as "a system of providing quantitative information, primarily financial in nature, about economic entities that is intended to be useful in making economic decisions" (Accounting

---

[7]More generally, it is important to understand how individual investors process accounting information and how their JDM affects market-level outcomes. In other words, it is of interest to bring behavioral finance findings regarding individual investors' general behavior to bear in specific accounting contexts.

Principles Board 1970). *Accounting research* can be defined as "knowledge of the individual and aggregate effects of alternative standardized business measurement and reporting structures" (Kinney 2001).

Examining these definitions suggests the key facets of accounting systems that deserve empirical study and theory development. First, accounting quantifies, or numerically measures, detailed items—business transactions, events, and states. For standardized quantification to occur, accounting requires principles and rules related to measuring items, as well as principles and rules regarding the types of things that should be measured. Second, accounting classifies and labels things; it places them into groups of items and gives these groups of items names, such as "accounts receivable." Such classification also requires principles and rules as to the types of items that belong in specific groups in order to achieve a standardized structure. Third, accounting uses these classifications to summarize (aggregate) detailed information; for example, it combines all entries to accounts receivable to determine one overall number for this group of items at a particular point in time. Fourth, accounting organizes the summarized information into a format that is meant to be useful for decision making then communicates this organized, summarized information to key decision makers. For example, items considered to be assets are grouped together and shown on the balance sheet in an annual report. Again, this organization requires a set of rules and principles to achieve standardization. Along with standardized presentation of quantitative information, accounting also prescribes standardized presentation (and classification) of information that either cannot be or is not measured (e.g., choices of accounting methods, causes of market risk, etc.).

Fortunately, JDM research in accounting has begun to develop theories for all these elements of accounting systems. Starting with quantification, Kadous et al. (2005) develop theory by recognizing that quantification has effects on JDM via persuasion; they rely on attribution theory and other psychology theories that pertain to persuasion. (Also see Elliott [2006].) Wright (2005), in his commentary on this article, suggests that development of theory regarding quantification effects could be enhanced by considering other theories such as measurement theory, cascaded inference theory, and causal reasoning theory. Theory development on quantification effects could rely also on psychological findings regarding people's numerical interpretations of verbal expressions (see Chapter 6) because verbally expressing information is an obvious alternative to quantified expression.

Theory development for the second element of accounting systems, classification and labeling, also has received some attention. For example, Hopkins (1996) relies on theories of categorization and memory retrieval to predict how particular accounting classifications for hybrid securities affect JDM. In managerial accounting, Lipe and Salterio (2002) focus on the effects categorization has on problem representations and subsequent processing of balanced scorecard information. Koonce and colleagues (Hodder et al. 2001; Koonce et al. 2005a, 2005b) examine the effects of labeling financial instruments and their related risks. They rely on research from marketing and other areas regarding the effects of labels and consider intuitive theories that people might have about various labels as well as about particular concepts such as risk. Further attention to the work on intuitive theories here likely will be fruitful for theory development. For example, terms such as assets and liabilities appear to be value laden (again, think of some of the "wild ideas" students have about what these words mean).

Because classification also dictates placement of items in financial reports, theory development also should consider this issue. Maines and McDaniel (2000) develop a framework for predicting the effects of differential placement of comprehensive income information that relies on psychology theories relating to information encoding and evidence evaluation.

The third element of accounting systems—aggregation—has not received recent attention. Theory development here likely requires considering the multiple differences that can occur when people see and use aggregated versus disaggregated information. For example, when using aggregated information, there can be no order effects because there is one number. With disaggregated information, order effects can occur. Further, when using disaggregated information, people may selectively search for particular pieces of that information, whereas they see or can search for only one piece of aggregated information. In addition, when facing disaggregated information that is customized for specific uses (e.g., performance measures that are customized for varying business units), they may focus on only the information that is common across reports rather than the unique items (Lipe and Salterio 2000). As a result, any benefits of the customization aspect of disaggregation can be lost. However, disaggregated information may facilitate learning because people can see how summarized figures have been calculated. There are a number of other possible effects of aggregation that can lead to various theories in psychology.

The final element of accounting systems—presentation and communication of information—also likely reflects a number of underlying variables for which separate theories may exist in psychology. For example, accounting information can be communicated on paper or electronically. It can be communicated in color or black and white, using tables or graphs, with different font sizes, and so forth. Furthermore, standardized presentation rules may dictate that accounting information appear in either the financial statements or the footnotes, and such placement, as discussed above, can affect JDM through various psychological processes. Finally, of course, the timing of communication can vary. For example, prior to Regulation FD, analysts often received information about companies prior to its being disclosed to the general public.

Surrounding all these elements of systems per se are the principles and rules used to create standardized measurement, classification, aggregation, and presentation. Theory development regarding elements of these principles and rules also is occurring. For example, Nelson (2003) discusses various facets of principles- versus rules-based standards, such as their complexity, the cognitive processes they can or cannot elicit (e.g., analogical reasoning), and the implicit incentives they may create. Rules and principles also sometimes allow for different accounting treatments. To develop theory regarding differential treatment again requires considering, at a very detailed level, the variation created by this choice. This variation sometimes results in differential classification, sometimes results in differential placement, and so forth.

Overall, then, given the state of theory development in psychology, JDM researchers in accounting seem well positioned to use their institutional knowledge to develop theories of how accounting per se affects JDM, and some of this type of work has begun. Although it may not be possible to develop one unified theory of the JDM effects of accounting, it does seem possible ultimately to combine elements of some of the separate theories that are being developed to create a broader framework for predicting the individual JDM effects of a particular accounting issue.

10-3 SUMMARY

This chapter concludes by considering future directions for JDM research in accounting. These suggestions are based on an examination of framework-related research to date as well as broader issues that appear when one steps away from the framework. Although many detailed suggestions for future research are provided in earlier chapters, this chapter also contains a number of interesting possibilities to consider.

JDM research in accounting (and psychology) has come a long way since the publication of Libby's (1981) book. We have matured greatly as a discipline and as individual researchers. The challenge for the future is to focus more on factors that are important, and perhaps unique, to accounting environments and develop our own theories about their effects on individual JDM.

References

Abarbanell, J., and V. Bernard. "Tests of Analysts' Overreaction/Underreaction to Earnings Information as an Explanation for Anomalous Stock Price Behavior." *Journal of Finance* (July 1992): 1181–1207.

Abbott, A. *The System of Professions: An Essay on the Division of Expert Labor.* Chicago: The University of Chicago Press, 1988.

Abdel-Khalik, A. "The Effect of Aggregating Accounting Reports on the Quality of the Lending Decision: An Empirical Investigation." *Journal of Accounting Research* (1973): S104–38.

Abdel-Khalik, A., and K. El-Sheshai. "Information Choice and Utilization in an Experiment on Default Prediction." *Journal of Accounting Research* (Autumn 1980): 325–42.

Abdel-Khalik, A., D. Snowball, and J. Wragge. "The Effects of Certain Internal Audit Variables on the Planning of External Audit Programs." *The Accounting Review* (April 1983): 215–27.

Abdolmohammadi, M. "Bayesian Inference Research in Auditing: Some Methodological Suggestions." *Contemporary Accounting Research* (Fall 1985): 76–94.

Abdolmohammadi, M. "Decision Support and Expert Systems in Auditing: A Review and Research Directions." *Accounting and Business Research* (Spring 1987): 173–85.

Abdolmohammadi, M. "Factors Affecting Auditors' Perceptions of Applicable Decision Aids for Various Audit Tasks." *Contemporary Accounting Research* (Spring 1991): 535–48.

Abdolmohammadi, M. "A Comprehensive Taxonomy of Audit Task Structure, Professional Rank and Decision Aids for Behavioral Research." *Behavioral Research in Accounting* (1999): 51–92.

Abdolmohammadi, M., and P. Berger. "A Test of the Accuracy of Probability Assessment Techniques in Auditing." *Contemporary Accounting Research* (Fall 1986): 149–65.

Abdolmohammadi, M., and C. Usoff. "A Longitudinal Study of Applicable Decision Aids for Detailed Tasks in a Financial Audit." *International Journal of Intelligent Systems in Accounting, Finance & Management* (September 2001): 139–54.

Abdolmohammadi, M., and A. Wright. "An Examination of the Effects of Experience and Task Complexity on Audit Judgments." *The Accounting Review* (January 1987): 1–13.

Abdolmohammadi, M., and A. Wright. "A Multi-Attribute Investigation of Elicitation Techniques in Tests of Account Balances." *Behavioral Research in Accounting* (1992): 63–79.

Accounting Principles Board. Statement No. 4 — "Basic Concepts and Accounting Principles Underlying Financial Statements of Business Enterprises." New York: American Institute of Certified Public Accountants, 1970.

Ackerman, P. "Individual Differences and Skill Acquisition." In *Learning and Individual Differences: Advances in Theory and Research,* edited by P. Ackerman, R. Sternberg, and R. Glaser. New York: W.H. Freeman and Company, 1989.

Ackerman, P. "Traits and Knowledge as Determinants of Learning and Individual Differences: Putting It All Together." In *Learning and Individual Differences: Process, Trait, and Content Determinants,* edited by P. Ackerman, P. Kyllonen, and R. Roberts. Washington, DC: American Psychological Association, 1999.

Ackert, L., and G. Athanassakos. "Prior Uncertainty, Analyst Bias, and Subsequent Abnormal Returns." *Journal of Financial Research* (Summer 1997): 263–73.

Ackert, L., B. Church, and M. Shehata. "What Affects Individuals' Decisions to Acquire Forecasted Information?" *Contemporary Accounting Research* (Fall 1996): 379–99.

Ackert, L., B. Church, and M. Shehata. "An Experimental Examination of the Effects of Forecast Bias on Individuals' Use of Forecasted Information." *Journal of Accounting Research* (Spring 1997): 25–42.

Adams, J. "Toward an Understanding of Inequity." *Journal of Abnormal and Social Psychology* (No. 5 1963): 422–36.

Adams, J. "Inequity in Social Exchange." *Advances in Experimental Social Psychology* (1965): 267–99.

Adamson, R. "Functional Fixedness as Related to Problem Solving: A Repetition of Three Experiments." *Journal of Experimental Psychology* (October 1952): 288–91.

Adelson, B. "When Novices Surpass Experts: The Difficulty of a Task May Increase with Expertise." *Journal of Experimental Psychology: Learning, Memory, and Cognition* (July 1984): 483–95.

Adelson, B., and E. Soloway. "The Role of Domain Experience in Software Design." *IEEE Transactions on Software Engineering* (November 1985): 1351–60.

Aerts, W. "On the Use of Accounting Logic as an Explanatory Category in Narrative Accounting Disclosures." *Accounting, Organizations and Society* (May–July 1994): 337–53.

Aerts, W. "Picking up the Pieces: Impression Management in the Retrospective Attributional Framing of Accounting Outcomes." *Accounting, Organizations and Society* (August 2005): 493–517.

Agnew, N., K. Ford, and P. Hayes. "Expertise in Context: Personally Constructed, Socially Selected, and Reality-Relevant?" In *Expertise in Context,* edited by P. Feltovich, K. Ford, and R. Hoffman. Cambridge, MA: The MIT Press, 1997.

Agoglia, C., T. Kida, and D. Hanno. "The Effects of Alternative Justification Memos on the Judgments of Audit Reviewees and Reviewers." *Journal of Accounting Research* (March 2003): 33–46.

Ahadiat, N., and K. Smith. "A Factor-Analytic Investigation of Employee Selection Factors of Significance to Recruiters of Entry-Level Accountants." *Issues in Accounting Education* (Spring 1994): 59–79.

Ahlawat, S. "Order Effects and Memory for Evidence in Individual versus Group Decision Making in Auditing." *Journal of Behavioral Decision Making* (March 1999): 71–88.

Ajzen, I. "Intuitive Theories of Events and the Effects of Base-Rate Information on Prediction." *Journal of Personality and Social Psychology* (May 1977): 303–14.

Aldag, R., and S. Fuller. "Beyond Fiasco: A Reappraisal of the Groupthink Phenomenon and a New Model of Group Decision Processes." *Psychological Bulletin* (May 1993): 533–52.

Alloy, L., and N. Tabachnik. "Assessment of Covariation by Humans and Animals: The Joint Influence of Prior Expectations and Current Situational Information." *Psychological Review* (January 1984): 112–49.

Alper, T. "Task-Orientation versus Ego-Orientation in Learning and Retention." *American Journal of Psychology* (1946): 224–38.

Altman, E. "Financial Ratios, Discriminant Analysis and the Prediction of Corporate Bankruptcy." *Journal of Finance* (September 1968): 589–609.

Altman, E. "Accounting Implications of Failure Prediction Models." *Journal of Accounting, Auditing and Finance* (Fall 1982): 4–19.

Aly, H., and J. Duboff. "Statistical versus Judgment Sampling: An Empirical Study of Auditing the Accounts Receivable of a Small Retail Store." *The Accounting Review* (January 1971): 119–28.

Amer, T. "An Experimental Investigation of Multi-Cue Financial Information Display and Decision Making." *Journal of Information Systems* (Fall 1991): 18–34.

Amer, T., K. Hackenbrack, and M. Nelson. "Between-Auditor Differences in the Interpretation of Probability Phrases." *Auditing: A Journal of Practice & Theory* (Spring 1994): 126–36.

Amer, T., K. Hackenbrack, and M. Nelson. "Context-Dependence of Auditors' Interpretations of the SFAS No. 5 Probability Expressions." *Contemporary Accounting Research* (Fall 1995): 25–39.

American Institute of Certified Public Accountants. *Report of the Special Committee on Assurance Services.* New York: AICPA, 1996.

American Institute of Certified Public Accountants. *Statements on Auditing Standards.* New York: AICPA, 2004.

Amir, E., and Y. Ganzach. "Overreaction and Underreaction in Analysts' Forecasts." *Journal of Economic Behavior and Organization* (November 1998): 333–47.

Anderson, B., and M. Maletta. "Auditor Attendance to Negative and Positive Information: The Effect of Experience-Related Differences." *Behavioral Research in Accounting* (1994): 1–20.

Anderson, B., and M. Maletta. "Primacy Effects and the Role of Risk in Auditor Belief-Revision Processes." *Auditing: A Journal of Practice & Theory* (Spring 1999): 75–89.

Anderson, C., and E. Sechler. "Effects of Explanation and Counterexplanation on the Development and Use of Social Theories." *Journal of Personality and Social Psychology* (January 1986): 24–34.

Anderson, J. *Learning and Memory: An Integrated Approach,* 2nd ed. New York: John Wiley, 2000.

Anderson, J. *Cognitive Psychology and Its Implications,* 6th ed. New York: Worth Publishers, 2005.

Anderson, J., and J. Fincham. "Acquisition of Procedural Skills From Examples." *Journal of Experimental Psychology: Learning, Memory, and Cognition* (November 1994): 1322–40.

Anderson, J., J. Fincham, and S. Douglass. "The Role of Examples and Rules in the Acquisition of a Cognitive Skill." *Journal of Experimental Psychology: Learning, Memory, and Cognition* (July 1997a): 932–45.

Anderson, J., M. Jennings, S. Kaplan, and P. Reckers. "The Effect of Using Diagnostic Decision Aids for Analytical Procedures on Judges' Liability Judgments." *Journal of Accounting and Public Policy* (Spring 1995): 33–62.

Anderson, J., M. Jennings, D. Lowe, and P. Reckers. "The Mitigation of Hindsight Bias in Judges' Evaluation of Auditor Decisions." *Auditing: A Journal of Practice & Theory* (Fall 1997b): 20–39.

Anderson, J., S. Kaplan, and P. Reckers. "The Effects of Output Interference on Analytical Procedures Judgments." *Auditing: A Journal of Practice and Theory* (Fall 1992): 1–13.

Anderson, J., S. Kaplan, and P. Reckers. "The Effects of Interference and Availability from Hypotheses Generated by a Decision Aid upon Analytical Procedures Judgments." *Behavioral Research in Accounting* (1997c): S1–20.

Anderson, J., D. Lowe, and P. Reckers. "Evaluation of Auditor Decisions: Hindsight Bias Effects and the Expectation Gap." *Journal of Economic Psychology* (December 1993): 711–37.

Anderson, J., K. Moreno, and J. Mueller. "The Effect of Client versus Decision Aid as a Source of Explanations upon Auditors' Sufficiency Judgments: A Research Note." *Behavioral Research in Accounting* (2003): 1–11.

Anderson, J., and C. Schunn. "Implications of the ACT-R Learning Theory: No Magic Bullets." In *Advances in Instructional Psychology: Educational Design and Cognitive Science,* vol. 5, edited by R. Glaser. Mahwah, NJ: Lawrence Erlbaum Associates, 2000.

Anderson, M. "A Comparative Analysis of Information Search and Evaluation Behavior of Professional and Non-Professional Financial Analysts." *Accounting, Organizations and Society* (No. 5 1988): 431–46.

Anderson, M., U. Anderson, R. Helleloid, E. Joyce, and M. Schadewald. "Internal Revenue Service Access to Tax Accrual Workpapers." *The Accounting Review* (October 1990a): 857–74.

Anderson, N., M. Born, and N. Cunningham-Snell. "Recruitment and Selection: Applicant Perspectives and Outcomes." In *Handbook of Industrial, Work & Organizational*

Psychology, vol. 1: *Personnel Psychology,* edited by N. Anderson, D. Ones, H. Sinangil, and C. Viswesevaran. Thousand Oaks, CA: Sage Publications, 2001.

Anderson, U., K. Kadous, and L. Koonce. "The Role of Incentives to Manage Earnings and Quantification in Auditors' Evaluations of Management-Provided Information." *Auditing: A Journal of Practice & Theory* (March 2004): 11–27.

Anderson, U., and L. Koonce. "Explanation as a Method for Evaluating Client-Suggested Causes in Analytical Procedures." *Auditing: A Journal of Practice & Theory* (Fall 1995): 124–32.

Anderson, U., L. Koonce, and G. Marchant. "The Effects of Source-Competence Information and Its Timing on Auditors' Performance of Analytical Procedures." *Auditing: A Journal of Practice & Theory* (Spring 1994): 137–48.

Anderson, U., and G. Marchant. "The Auditor's Assessment of the Competence and Integrity of Auditee Personnel." *Auditing: A Journal of Practice & Theory* (1989): S1–16.

Anderson, U., G. Marchant, and J. Robinson. "Instructional Strategies and the Development of Tax Expertise." *The Journal of the American Taxation Association* (Spring 1989): 7–23.

Anderson, U., G. Marchant, J. Robinson, and M. Schadewald. "Selection of Instructional Strategies in the Presence of Related Prior Knowledge." *Issues in Accounting Education* (Spring 1990b): 41–58.

Anderson, U., and W. Wright. "Expertise and the Explanation Effect." *Organizational Behavior and Human Decision Processes* (October 1988): 250–69.

Andreassen, P. "On the Social Psychology of the Stock Market: Aggregate Attributional Effects and the Regressiveness of Prediction." *Journal of Personality and Social Psychology* (September 1987): 490–96.

Andreassen, P., and S. Kraus. "Judgmental Extrapolation and the Salience of Change." *Journal of Forecasting* (September 1990): 347–72.

Anzai, Y. "Learning and Use of Representations for Physics Expertise." In *Toward a General Theory of Expertise: Prospects and Limits,* edited by K. Ericsson and J. Smith. New York: Cambridge University Press, 1991.

Argote, L., R. Devadas, and N. Malone. "The Base-Rate Fallacy: Contrasting Processes and Outcomes of Group and Individual Judgment." *Organizational Behavior and Human Decision Processes* (August 1990): 296–310.

Argote, L., M. Seabright, and L. Dyer. "Individual versus Group Use of Base-Rate and Individuating Information." *Organizational Behavior and Human Decision Processes* (August 1986): 65–75.

Arkes, H. "Costs and Benefits of Judgment Errors: Implications for Debiasing." *Psychological Bulletin* (November 1991): 486–98.

Arkes, H. "Overconfidence in Judgmental Forecasting." In *Principles of Forecasting: A Handbook for Researchers and Practitioners,* edited by J. Armstrong. Boston: Kluwer, 2001.

Arkes, H., L. Boehm, and G. Xu. "Determinants of Judged Validity." *Journal of Experimental Social Psychology* (November 1991): 576–605.

Arkes, H., R. Dawes, and C. Christensen. "Factors Influencing the Use of a Decision Rule in a Probabilistic Task." *Organizational Behavior and Human Decision Processes* (February 1986): 93–110.

Arkes, H., D. Faust, T. Guilmette, and K. Hart. "Eliminating the Hindsight Bias." *Journal of Applied Psychology* (May 1988): 305–7.

Arkes, H., C. Hackett, and L. Boehm. "The Generality of the Relation between Familiarity and Judged Validity." *Journal of Behavioral Decision Making* (April–June 1989): 81–94.

Armstrong, J. "Relative Accuracy of Judgemental and Extrapolative Methods in Forecasting Annual Earnings." *Journal of Forecasting* (October–December 1983): 437–47.

Armstrong, J. "Combining Forecasts." In *Principles of Forecasting: A Handbook for Researchers and Practitioners,* edited by J. Armstrong. Boston: Kluwer Academic Publishers, 2001a.

Armstrong, J. "Judgmental Bootstrapping: Inferring Experts' Rules for Forecasting." In *Principles of Forecasting: A Handbook for Researchers and Practitioners,* edited by J. Armstrong. Boston: Kluwer Academic Publishers, 2001b.

Armstrong, J., W. Denniston Jr., and M. Gordon. "The Use of the Decomposition Principle in Making Judgments." *Organizational Behavior and Human Performance* (October 1975): 257–63.

Arnold, V., and S. Sutton, ed. *Behavioral Accounting Research: Foundations and Frontiers.* Sarasota, FL: American Accounting Association, 1997.

Arnold, V., S. Sutton, S. Hayne, and C. Smith. "Group Decision Making: The Impact of Opportunity-Cost Time Pressure and Group Support Systems." *Behavioral Research in Accounting* (2000): 69–96.

Arrington, C., C. Bailey, and W. Hopwood. "An Attribution Analysis of Responsibility Assessment for Audit Performance." *Journal of Accounting Research* (Spring 1985): 1–20.

Arrow, J. *Essays in the Theory of Risk-Bearing.* Chicago: Markham, 1971.

Arthur, W., Jr., W. Bennett Jr., P. Edens, and S. Bell. "Effectiveness of Training in Organizations: A Meta-Analysis of Design and Evaluation Features." *Journal of Applied Psychology* (April 2003): 234–45.

Arunachalam, V., and G. Beck. "Functional Fixation Revisited: The Effects of Feedback and a Repeated Measures Design on Information Processing Changes in Response to an Accounting Change." *Accounting, Organizations and Society* (January–March 2002): 1–25.

Arvey, R., and K. Murphy. "Performance Evaluation in Work Settings." *Annual Review of Psychology* (1998): 141–68.

Asare, S. "The Auditor's Going-Concern Decision: Interaction of Task Variables and the Sequential Processing of Evidence." *The Accounting Review* (April 1992): 379–93.

Asare, S., and L. McDaniel. "The Effects of Familiarity with the Preparer and Task Complexity on the Effectiveness of the Audit Review Process." *The Accounting Review* (April 1996): 139–59.

Asare, S., G. Trompeter, and A. Wright. "The Effect of Accountability and Time Budget on Auditors' Testing Strategies." *Contemporary Accounting Research* (Winter 2000): 539–60.

Asare, S., and A. Wright. "Normative and Substantive Expertise in Multiple Hypotheses Evaluation." *Organizational Behavior and Human Decision Processes* (December 1995): 171–84.

Asare, S., and A. Wright. "Evaluation of Competing Hypotheses in Auditing." *Auditing: A Journal of Practice and Theory* (Spring 1997a): 1–13.

Asare, S., and A. Wright. "Hypothesis Revision Strategies in Conducting Analytical Procedures." *Accounting, Organizations and Society* (November 1997b); 737–55.

Asare, S., and A. Wright. "A Note on the Interdependence between Hypothesis Generation and Information Search in Conducting Analytical Procedures." *Contemporary Accounting Research* (Summer 2003): 235–51.

Asare, S., and A. Wright. "The Effectiveness of Alternative Risk Assessment and Program Planning Tools in a Fraud Setting." *Contemporary Accounting Research* (Summer 2004): 325–52.

Asch, S. "Studies on Independence and Conformity: I. A Minority of One against a Unanimous Majority." *Psychological Monographs,* no. 416 (1956).

Ashford, S., and L. Cummings. "Feedback as an Individual Resource: Personal Strategies of Creating Information." *Organizational Behavior and Human Performance* (December 1983): 370–98.

Ashford, S., and L. Cummings. "Proactive Feedback Seeking: The Instrumental Use of the Information Environment." *Journal of Occupational Psychology* (March 1985): 67–79.

Ashton, A. "An Empirical Study of Budget-Related Predictions of Corporate Executives." *Journal of Accounting Research* (Autumn 1982, Part I): 440–49.

Ashton, A. "A Field Test of Implications of Laboratory Studies of Decision Making." *The Accounting Review* (July 1984): 361–75.

Ashton, A. "Experience and Error Frequency Knowledge as Potential Determinants of Audit Expertise." *The Accounting Review* (April 1991): 218–39.

Ashton, A., and R. Ashton. "Aggregating Subjective Forecasts: Some Empirical Results." *Management Science* (December 1985): 1499–1508.

Ashton, A., and R. Ashton. "Sequential Belief Revision in Auditing." *The Accounting Review* (October 1988): 623–41.

Ashton, R. "Cue Utilization and Expert Judgments: A Comparison of Independent Auditors with Other Judges." *Journal of Applied Psychology* (August 1974a): 437–44.

Ashton, R. "An Experimental Study of Internal Control Judgments." *Journal of Accounting Research* (Spring 1974b): 143–57.

Ashton, R. "Cognitive Changes Induced by Accounting Changes: Experimental Evidence on the Functional Fixation Hypothesis." *Journal of Accounting Research* (1976): S1–17.

Ashton, R. "A Descriptive Study of Information Evaluation." *Journal of Accounting Research* (Spring 1981): 42–61.

Ashton, R. *Research in Audit Decision Making: Rationale, Evidence, and Implications.* Vancouver, Canada: The Canadian Certified General Accountants' Research Foundation, 1983.

Ashton, R. "Combining the Judgments of Experts: How Many and Which Ones?" *Organizational Behavior and Human Decision Processes* (December 1986): 405–14.

Ashton, R. "Pressure and Performance in Accounting Decision Settings: Paradoxical Effects of Incentives, Feedback, and Justification." *Journal of Accounting Research* (1990): S148–80.

Ashton, R. "Effects of Justification and a Mechanical Aid on Judgment Performance." *Organizational Behavior and Human Decision Processes* (July 1992): 292–306.

Ashton, R. "A Review and Analysis of Research on the Test-Retest Reliability of Professional Judgment." *Journal of Behavioral Decision Making* (July–September 2000): 277–94.

Ashton, R., and A. Ashton. "Evidence-Responsiveness in Professional Judgment: Effects of Positive versus Negative Evidence and Presentation Mode." *Organizational Behavior and Human Decision Processes* (June 1990): 1–19.

Ashton, R., and A. Ashton, ed. *Judgment and Decision-Making Research in Accounting and Auditing.* Cambridge, MA: Cambridge University Press, 1995.

Ashton, R., and P. Brown. "Descriptive Modeling of Auditors' Internal Control Judgments: Replication and Extension." *Journal of Accounting Research* (Spring 1980): 269–77.

Ashton, R., and S. Kramer. "Students as Surrogates in Behavioral Accounting Research: Some Evidence." *Journal of Accounting Research* (Spring 1980): 1–15.

Ashton, R., and J. Willingham. "Using and Evaluating Audit Decision Aids." In *Auditing Symposium IX: Proceedings of the 1988 Touche Ross/University of Kansas Symposium on Auditing Problems,* edited by R. Srivastava and J. Rebele. Lawrence: University of Kansas, 1989.

Atkinson, A., R. Kaplan, and S. Young. *Management Accounting,* 4th ed. Upper Saddle River, NJ: Prentice-Hall, 2003.

Atkinson, J., and W. Reitman. "Performance as a Function of Motive Strength and Expectancy of Goal-Attainment." *Journal of Abnormal and Social Psychology* (1956): 361–66.

Atkinson, R., S. Derry, A. Renkl, and D. Wortham. "Learning from Examples: Instructional Principles from the Worked Examples Research." *Review of Educational Research* (Summer 2000): 181–214.

Austin, J., and J. Vancouver. "Goal Constructs in Psychology: Structure, Process, and Content." *Psychological Bulletin* (November 1996): 338–75.

Awasthi, V., and J. Pratt. "The Effects of Monetary Incentives on Effort and Decision Performance: The Role of Cognitive Characteristics." *The Accounting Review* (October 1990): 797–811.

Babad, E. "Can Accurate Knowledge Reduce Wishful Thinking in Voters' Predictions of Election Outcomes?" *The Journal of Psychology* (May 1995): 285–300.

Babad, E. "Wishful Thinking among Voters: Motivational and Cognitive Influences." *International Journal of Public Opinion Research* (Summer 1997): 105–25.

Babad, E., M. Hills, and M. O'Driscoll. "Factors Influencing Wishful Thinking and Predictions of Election Outcomes." *Basic and Applied Social Psychology* (December 1992): 461–76.

Babad, E., and Y. Katz. "Wishful Thinking— Against All Odds." *Journal of Applied Social Psychology* (December 1991): 1921–38.

Babad, E., and E. Yacobos. "Wish and Reality in Voters' Predictions of Election Outcomes." *Political Psychology* (March 1993): 37–54.

Bacon, F. "Credibility of Repeated Statements: Memory for Trivia." *Journal of Experimental Psychology: Human Learning and Memory* (May 1979): 241–52.

Baddeley, A. *Human Memory: Theory and Practice.* Boston: Allyn and Bacon, 1990.

Baginski, S., J. Hassell, and W. Hillison. "Voluntary Causal Disclosures: Tendencies and Capital Market Reaction." *Review of Quantitative Finance and Accounting* (December 2000): 371–89.

Baginski S., J. Hassell, and M. Kimbrough. "Why Do Managers Explain Their Earnings Forecasts?" *Journal of Accounting Research* (March 2004): 1–29.

Ball, R., and E. Bartov. "How Naive Is the Stock Market's Use of Earnings Information?" *Journal of Accounting and Economics* (June 1996): 319–37.

Ballou, B. "The Relationship between Auditor Characteristics and the Nature of Review Notes for Analytical Procedure Working Papers." *Behavioral Research in Accounting* (2001): 25–48.

Balzer, W., M. Doherty, and R. O'Connor. "Effects of Cognitive Feedback on Performance." *Psychological Bulletin* (November 1989): 410–33.

Balzer, W., and L. Sulsky. "Halo and Performance Appraisal Research: A Critical Examination." *Journal of Applied Psychology* (November 1992): 975–85.

Balzer, W., L. Sulsky, L. Hammer, and K. Sumner. "Task Information, Cognitive Information, or Functional Validity Information: Which Components of Cognitive Feedback Affect Performance?" *Organizational Behavior and Human Decision Processes* (October 1992): 35–54.

Bamber, E. "Expert Judgment in the Audit Team: A Source Reliability Approach." *Journal of Accounting Research* (Autumn 1983): 396–412.

Bamber, E. "Opportunities in Behavioral Accounting Research." *Behavioral Research in Accounting* (1993): 1–29.

Bamber, E., and J. Bylinski. "The Effects of the Planning Memorandum, Time Pressure and Individual Auditor Characteristics on Audit Managers' Review Time Judgments." *Contemporary Accounting Research* (Fall 1987): 127–43.

Bamber, E., and R. Ramsay. "An Investigation of the Effects of Specialization in Audit Workpaper Review." *Contemporary Accounting Research* (Fall 1997): 501–13.

Bamber, E., and R. Ramsay. "The Effects of Specialization in Audit Workpaper Review on Review Efficiency and Reviewers' Confidence." *Auditing: A Journal of Practice and Theory* (Fall 2000): 147–57.

Bamber, E., R. Ramsay, and R. Tubbs. "An Examination of the Descriptive Validity of the Belief-Adjustment Model and Alternative Attitudes to Evidence in Auditing." *Accounting, Organizations and Society* (April–May 1997): 249–68.

Bamber, E., R. Watson, and M. Hill. "The Effects of Group Support System Technology on Audit Group Decision Making." *Auditing: A Journal of Practice and Theory* (Spring 1996): 122–33.

Bandura, A. *Self-Efficacy: The Exercise of Control.* New York: W. H. Freeman and Company, 1997.

Banker, R., H. Chang, and M. Pizzini. "The Balanced Scorecard: Judgmental Effects of Performance Measures Linked to Strategy." *The Accounting Review* (January 2004): 1–23.

Barber, A. *Recruiting Employees: Individual and Organizational Perspectives.* Thousand Oaks, CA: Sage Publications, 1998.

Barber, B., R. Lehavy, M. McNichols, and B. Trueman. "Can Investors Profit from the Prophets? Security Analyst Recommendations and Stock Returns." *Journal of Finance* (April 2001): 531–63.

Barber, B., and T. Odean. "Boys Will Be Boys: Gender, Overconfidence, and Common Stock Investment." *The Quarterly Journal of Economics* (February 2001): 261–92.

Barber, B., and T. Odean. "All that Glitters: The Effect of Attention and News on the Buying Behavior of Individual and Institutional Investors." Working paper, 2006.

Barberis, N., and R. Thaler. "A Survey of Behavioral Finance." In *Handbook of the Economics of Finance,* edited by G. Constantinides, M. Harris, and R. Stulz. Amsterdam: North-Holland, 2003.

Barefield, R. "The Effects of Aggregation on Decision Making Success: A Laboratory Study." *Journal of Accounting Research* (Autumn 1972): 229–42.

Bar-Hillel, M. "The Base-Rate Fallacy in Probability Judgments." *Acta Psychologica* (May 1980): 211–33.

Barnes, P., and J. Webb. "Management Information Changes and Functional Fixation: Some Experimental Evidence from the Public Sector." *Accounting, Organizations and Society* (No. 1 1986): 1–18.

Baron, J. *Thinking and Deciding,* 3rd ed. New York: Cambridge University Press, 2000.

Barrett, M. "Accounting for Intercorporate Investments: A Behavior Field Experiment." *Journal of Accounting Research* (1971): S50–65.

Barrick, J., C. Cloyd, and B. Spilker. "The Influence of Biased Tax Research Memoranda on Supervisors' Initial Judgments in the Review Process." *Journal of the American Taxation Association* (Spring 2004): 1–19.

Barrick, M., G. Patton, and S. Haugland. "Accuracy of Interviewer Judgments of Job Applicant Personality Traits." *Personnel Psychology* (Winter 2000): 925–51.

Bartiromo, M. *Use the News: How to Separate the Noise from the Investment Nuggets and Make Money in Any Economy.* New York: Harper Collins Publishers, 2001.

Bartov, E., D. Givoly, and C. Hayn. "The Rewards to Meeting or Beating Earnings Expectations." *Journal of Accounting and Economics* (June 2002): 173–204.

Baskerville, R. "Hofstede Never Studied Culture." *Accounting, Organizations and Society* (January 2003): 1–14.

Baumeister, R., and M. Leary. "The Need to Belong: Desire for Interpersonal Attachments as a Fundamental Human Motive." *Psychological Bulletin* (May 1995): 497–529.

Baumeister, R., and L. Newman. "How Stories Make Sense of Personal Experiences: Motives that Shape Autobiographical Narratives." *Personality and Social Psychology Bulletin* (December 1994): 676–90.

Bazerman, M., J. Curhan, and D. Moore. "Negotiation." *Annual Review of Psychology* (2000): 279–314.

Beach, L., and T. Mitchell. "A Contingency Model for the Selection of Decision Strategies." *Academy of Management Review* (July 1978): 439–49.

Beaver, W. *Financial Reporting: An Accounting Revolution,* 3rd ed. Upper Saddle River, NJ: Prentice Hall, 1998.

Beck, R. *Motivation: Theories and Principles,* 4th ed. Upper Saddle River, NJ: Prentice Hall, 2000.

Becker, D. "The Effects of Choice on Auditors' Intrinsic Motivation and Performance." *Behavioral Research in Accounting* (1997): 1–19.

Bedard, J., and S. Biggs, "The Effect of Domain-Specific Experience on Evaluation of Management Representations in Analytical Procedures." *Auditing: A Journal of Practice and Theory* (1991a): S77–90.

Bedard, J., and S. Biggs. "Pattern Recognition, Hypotheses Generation, and Auditor Performance in Analytical Task." *The Accounting Review* (July 1991b): 622–42.

Bedard, J., S. Biggs, and J. Maroney. "Sources of Process Gain and Loss from Group Interaction in Performance of Analytical Procedures." *Behavioral Research in Accounting* (1998): S207–33.

Bedard, J., and K. Johnstone. "Earnings Manipulation Risk, Corporate Governance Risk, and Auditors' Pricing and Planning Decisions." *The Accounting Review* (April 2004): 277–304.

Bédard, J. "Expertise and Its Relation to Audit Decision Quality." *Contemporary Accounting Research* (Fall 1991): 198–222.

Bédard, J., and M. Chi. "Expertise in Auditing." *Auditing: A Journal of Practice and Theory* (1993): S21–45.

Bédard, J., and T. Mock. "Expert and Novice Problem-Solving Behavior in Audit Planning." *Auditing: A Journal of Practice and Theory* (1992): S1–20.

Begg, I., A. Anas, and S. Farinacci. "Dissociation of Processes in Belief: Source Recollection, Statement Familiarity, and the Illusion of Truth." *Journal of Experimental Psychology: General* (December 1992): 446–58.

Begg, I., and V. Armour. "Repetition and the Ring of Truth: Biasing Comments." *Canadian Journal of Behavioural Science* (April 1991): 195–213.

Begg, I., V. Armour, and T. Kerr. "On Believing What We Remember." *Canadian Journal of Behavioural Science* (July 1985): 199–214.

Belkaoui, A. "The Impact of Socio-Economic Accounting Statements on the Investment Decision: An Empirical Study." *Accounting, Organizations and Society* (No. 3 1980): 263–83.

Belkaoui, A., and R. Picur. "Sources of Feedback in a CPA Firm." *Journal of Business Finance & Accounting* (Summer 1987): 175–86.

Bell, D. "Regret in Decision Making under Uncertainty." *Operations Research* (September–October 1982): 961–81.

Bell, D. "Risk Premiums for Decision Regret." *Management Science* (October 1983): 1156–66.

Bell, J. "The Effect of Presentation Form on the Use of Information in Annual Reports." *Management Science* (February 1984): 169–85.

Bell, T., and J. Carcello. "A Decision Aid for Assessing the Likelihood of Fraudulent Financial Reporting." *Auditing: A Journal of Practice & Theory* (Spring 2000): 169–84.

Belsky, G. "Why Smart People Make Major Money Mistakes." *Money* (July 1995): 76–85.

Ben Zur, H., and S. Breznitz. "The Effect of Time Pressure on Risky Choice Behavior." *Acta Psychologica* (February 1981): 89–104.

Benartzi, S., and R. Thaler. "Naive Diversification Strategies in Defined Contributions Saving Plans." *The American Economic Review* (March 2001): 79–98.

Benbasat, I., and A. Dexter. "Value and Events Approaches to Accounting: An Experimental Evaluation." *The Accounting Review* (October 1979): 735–49.

Benbasat, I., and A. Dexter. "Individual Differences in the Use of Decision Support Aids." *Journal of Accounting Research* (Spring 1982): 1–11.

Benbasat, I., and B. Nault. "An Evaluation of Empirical Research in Managerial Support Systems." *Decision Support Systems* (May 1990): 203–26.

Benbasat, I., and R. Schroeder. "An Experimental Investigation of Some MIS Design Variables." *MIS Quarterly* (March 1977): 37–49.

Benson, E. "Intelligent Intelligence Testing." *Monitor on Psychology* (February 2003): 48–51.

Berg, J., L. Daley, J. Dickhaut, and J. O'Brien. "Controlling Preferences for Lotteries on Units of Experimental Exchange." *Quarterly Journal of Economics* (May 1986): 281–306.

Berg, J., J. Dickhaut, and K. McCabe. "The Individual versus the Aggregate." In *Judgment and Decision-Making Research in Accounting and Auditing,* edited by R. Ashton and A. Ashton. Cambridge, MA: Cambridge University Press, 1995.

Bernard, V., and J. Thomas. "Evidence that Stock Prices Do Not Fully Reflect the Implications of Current Earnings for Future Earnings." *Journal of Accounting and Economics* (December 1990): 305–40.

Bernardi, R. "Fraud Detection: The Effect of Client Integrity and Competence and Auditor Cognitive Style." *Auditing: A Journal of Practice & Theory* (1994): S68–84.

Berton, L., and S. Adler. "CPA's Nightmare: How Audit of a Bank Cost Price Waterhouse $338 Million Judgment." *Wall Street Journal* (August 14, 1992): A1, A7.

Bettman, J., and B. Weitz. "Attributions in the Board Room: Causal Reasoning in Corporate Annual Reports." *Administrative Science Quarterly* (July 1983): 165–83.

Beyer, S., and E. Bowden. "Gender Differences in Self-Perceptions: Convergent Evidence from Three Measures of Accuracy and Bias." *Personality and Social Psychology Bulletin* (February 1997): 157–72.

Beyth-Marom, R. "How Probable Is Probable? A Numerical Translation of Verbal Probability Expressions." *Journal of Forecasting* (July–September 1982): 257–69.

Beyth-Marom, R., and B. Fischhoff. "Diagnosticity and Pseudodiagnosticity." *Journal of Personality and Social Psychology* (December 1983): 1185–95.

Bhattacharjee, S., T. Kida, and D. Hanno. "The Impact of Hypothesis Set Size on the Time Efficiency and Accuracy of Analytical Review Judgments." *Journal of Accounting Research* (Spring 1999): 83–100.

Bielaczyc, K., P. Pirolli, and A. Brown. "Training in Self-Explanation and Self-Regulation Strategies: Investigating the Effects of Knowledge Acquisition Activities on Problem Solving." *Cognition and Instruction* (April 1995): 221–52.

Bierstaker, J., J. Bedard, and S. Biggs. "The Role of Problem Representation Shifts in Auditor Decision Processes in Analytical Procedures." *Auditing: A Journal of Practice and Theory* (Spring 1999): 18–36.

Bierstaker, J., and S. Wright. "A Research Note Concerning Practical Problem-Solving Ability as a Predictor of Performance in Auditing Tasks." *Behavioral Research in Accounting* (2001): 49–62.

Biggs, S. "Financial Analysts' Information Search in the Assessment of Corporate Earning Power." *Accounting, Organizations and Society* (No. 3/4 1984): 313–23.

Biggs, S., J. Bedard, B. Gaber, and T. Linsmeier. "The Effects of Task Size and Similarity on the Decision Behavior of Bank Loan Officers." *Management Science* (August 1985): 970–87.

Biggs, S., W. Messier Jr., and J. Hansen. "A Descriptive Analysis of Computer Audit Specialists' Decision-Making Behavior in Advanced Computer Environments." *Auditing: A Journal of Practice and Theory* (Spring 1987): 1–21.

Biggs, S., and T. Mock. "An Investigation of Auditor Decision Processes in the Evaluation of Internal Controls and Audit Scope Decisions." *Journal of Accounting Research* (Spring 1983): 234–54.

Biggs, S., T. Mock, and P. Watkins. "Auditor's Use of Analytical Review in Audit Program Design." *The Accounting Review* (January 1988): 148–61.

Biggs, S., M. Selfridge, and G. Krupka. "A Computational Model of Auditor Knowledge and Reasoning Processes in the Going-Concern Judgment." *Auditing: A Journal of Practice and Theory* (1993): S82–99.

Biggs, S., and J. Wild. "An Investigation of Auditor Judgment in Analytical Review." *The Accounting Review* (October 1985): 607–33.

Birnbaum, M., and B. Mellers. "Bayesian Inference: Combining Base Rates with Opinions of Sources Who Vary in Credibility." *Journal of Personality and Social Psychology* (October 1983): 792–804.

Birnbaum, M., and S. Stegner. "Source Credibility in Social Judgment: Bias, Expertise, and the Judge's Point of View." *Journal of Personality and Social Psychology* (January 1979): 48–74.

Birnberg, J., and M. Shields. "The Role of Attention and Memory in Accounting Decisions." *Accounting, Organizations and Society* (No. 3/4 1984): 365–82.

Birnberg, J., and J. Shields. "Three Decades of Behavioral Accounting Research: A Search for Order." *Behavioral Research in Accounting* (1989): 23–74.

Blattberg, R., and S. Hoch. "Database Models and Managerial Intuition: 50% Model + 50% Manager." *Management Science* (August 1990): 887–99.

Blocher, E. "Performance Effects of Different Audit Staff Assignment Strategies." *The Accounting Review* (July 1979): 563–73.

Blocher, E., R. Esposito, and J. Willingham. "Auditors' Analytical Review Judgments for Payroll Expense." *Auditing: A Journal of Practice & Theory* (Fall 1983): 75–91.

Blocher, E., R. Moffie, and R. Zmud. "Report Format and Task Complexity: Interaction in Risk Judgments." *Accounting, Organizations and Society* (No. 6 1986): 457–70.

Bloom, R., P. Elgers, and D. Murray. "Functional Fixation in Product Pricing: A Comparison of Individuals and Groups." *Accounting, Organizations and Society* (No. 1 1984): 1–11.

Bloomfield, R. "Strategic Dependence and the Assessment of Fraud Risk: A Laboratory Study." *The Accounting Review* (October 1997): 517–38.

Bloomfield, R., R. Libby, and M. Nelson. "Communication of Confidence as a Determinant of Group Judgment Accuracy." *Organizational Behavior and Human Decision Processes* (December 1996): 287–300.

Bloomfield, R., R. Libby, and M. Nelson. "Confidence and the Welfare of Less-Informed Investors." *Accounting, Organizations and Society* (November 1999): 623–47.

Bloomfield, R., R. Libby, and M. Nelson. "Underreactions, Overreactions, and Moderated Confidence." *Journal of Financial Markets* (May 2000): 113–37.

Bloomfield, R., R. Libby, and M. Nelson "Do Investors Overrely on Old Elements of the Earnings Time Series?" *Contemporary Accounting Research* (Spring 2003): 1–31.

Boatsman, J., C. Moeckel, and B. Pei. "The Effects of Decision Consequences on Auditors' Reliance on Decision Aids in Audit Planning." *Organizational Behavior and Human Decision Processes* (August 1997): 211–47.

Boehm, L. "The Validity Effect: A Search for Mediating Variables." *Personality and Social Psychology Bulletin* (June 1994): 285–93.

Böer, G., and J. Livnat. "Using Expert Systems to Teach Complex Accounting Issues." *Issues in Accounting Education* (Spring 1990): 108–19.

Bond, M., and P. Smith. "Cross-Cultural Social and Organizational Psychology." *Annual Review of Psychology* (1996): 205–35.

Bonner, S. "Experience Effects in Auditing: The Role of Task-Specific Knowledge." *The Accounting Review* (January 1990): 72–92.

Bonner, S. "Is Experience Necessary in Cue Measurement? The Case of Auditing Tasks." *Contemporary Accounting Research* (Fall 1991): 253–69.

Bonner, S. "A Model of the Effects of Audit Task Complexity." *Accounting, Organizations and Society* (April 1994): 213–34.

Bonner, S. "Choosing Teaching Methods Based on Learning Objectives: An Integrative Framework." *Issues in Accounting Education* (February 1999): 11–39.

Bonner, S., J. Davis, and B. Jackson. "Frontiers in Experimental Tax Research: Experimental Economics and Tax Professional Judgment." In *A Guide to Tax Research Methodologies*, edited by C. Enis. Sarasota, FL: American Accounting Association, 1991.

Bonner, S., J. Davis, and B. Jackson. "Expertise in Corporate Tax Planning: The Issue Identification Stage." *Journal of Accounting Research* (1992): S1–28.

Bonner, S., R. Hastie, G. Sprinkle, and S. Young. "A Review of the Effects of Financial Incentives on Performance in Laboratory Tasks: Implications for Management Accounting." *Journal of Management Accounting Research* (2000): 19–64.

Bonner, S., J. Hugon, and B. Walther. "Investor Reaction to Celebrity Analysts: The Case of Earnings Forecast Revisions." Working paper, 2006.

Bonner, S., and B. Lewis. "Determinants of Auditor Expertise." *Journal of Accounting Research* (1990): S1–20.

Bonner, S., R. Libby, and M. Nelson. "Using Decision Aids to Improve Auditors' Conditional Probability Judgments." *The Accounting Review* (April 1996): 221–40.

Bonner, S., R. Libby, and M. Nelson. "Audit Category Knowledge as a Precondition to Learning from Experience." *Accounting, Organizations and Society* (July 1997): 387–410.

Bonner, S., Z. Palmrose, and S. Young. "Fraud Type and Auditor Litigation: An Analysis of SEC Accounting and Auditing Enforcement Releases." *The Accounting Review* (October 1998): 503–32.

Bonner, S., and N. Pennington. "Cognitive Processes and Knowledge as Determinants of Auditor Expertise." *Journal of Accounting Literature* (1991): 1–50.

Bonner, S., and G. Sprinkle. "The Effects of Monetary Incentives on Effort and Task Performance: Theories, Evidence, and a Framework for Research." *Accounting, Organizations and Society* (May 2002): 303–45.

Bonner, S., and P. Walker. "The Effects of Instruction and Experience on the Acquisition of Auditing Knowledge." *The Accounting Review* (January 1994): 157–78.

Bonner, S., B. Walther, and S. Young, "Sophistication-Related Differences in Investors' Models of the Relative Accuracy of Analysts' Forecast Revisions." *The Accounting Review* (July 2003): 679–706.

Boockholdt, J. "Comptronix, Inc.: An Audit Case Involving Fraud." *Issues in Accounting Education* (February 2000): 105–28.

Booker, Q. "A Case Study of the Relationship between Undergraduate Black Accounting Majors' ACT Scores and Their Intermediate Accounting Performance." *Issues in Accounting Education* (Spring 1991): 66–73.

Boritz, J. "The Effect of Information Presentation Structures on Audit Planning and Review Judgments." *Contemporary Accounting Research* (Spring 1985): 193–218.

Boritz, J., and A. Wensley. "Evaluating Expert Systems with Complex Outputs: The Case of Audit Planning." *Auditing: A Journal of Practice & Theory* (Fall 1992): 14–29.

Borman, W., M. Hanson, and J. Hedge. "Personnel Selection." *Annual Review of Psychology* (1997): 299–337.

Borman, W., and S. Motowildo. "Expanding the Criterion Domain to Include Elements of Contextual Performance." In *Personnel Selection in Organizations,* edited by N. Schmitt and W. Borman. San Francisco: Jossey-Bass, 1993.

Borman, W., L. White, and D. Dorsey. "Effects of Ratee Task Performance and Interpersonal Factors on Supervisor and Peer Performance Ratings." *Journal of Applied Psychology* (January 1995): 168–77.

Borman, W., L. White, E. Pulakos, and S. Oppler. "Models of Supervisory Job Performance Ratings." *Journal of Applied Psychology* (November 1991): 863–72.

Born, M., and D. Scholarios. "Decision Making in Selection." In *The Blackwell Handbook of Personnel Selection,* edited by A. Evers, N. Anderson, and O. Voskuijl. Malden, MA: Blackwell Publishing, 2005.

Bouwman, M. "Expert versus Novice Decision Making in Accounting: A Summary." *Accounting, Organizations and Society* (No. 3/4 1984): 325–27.

Bouwman, M., and W. Bradley. "Judgment and Decision Making, Part II: Expertise, Consensus and Accuracy." In *Behavioral Accounting Research: Foundations and Frontiers,* edited by V. Arnold and S. Sutton. Sarasota, FL: American Accounting Association, 1997.

Bouwman, M., P. Frishkoff, and P. Frishkoff. "How Do Financial Analysts Make Decisions? A Process Model of the Investment Screening Decision." *Accounting, Organizations and Society* (No. 1 1987): 1–29.

Bower, G. "Mood and Memory." *American Psychologist* (February 1981): 129–48.

Bower, G., and J. Forgas. "Mood and Social Memory." In *Handbook of Affect and Social Cognition,* edited by J. Forgas. Mahwah, NJ: Lawrence Erlbaum Associates, 2001.

Bransford, J., and D. Schwartz. "Rethinking Transfer: A Simple Proposal with Multiple Implications." *Review of Research in Education* (1999): 61–100.

Bransford, J., N. Vye, L. Adams, and G. Perfetto. "Learning Skills and the Acquisition of Knowledge." In *Foundations for a Psychology of Education,* edited by A. Lesgold and R. Glaser. Hillsdale, NJ: Lawrence Erlbaum Associates, 1989.

Braun, K. "The Disposition of Audit-Detected Misstatements: An Examination of Risk and Reward Factors and Aggregation Effects." *Contemporary Accounting Research* (Spring 2001): 71–99.

Braun, R. "The Effect of Time Pressure on Auditor Attention to Qualitative Aspects of Misstatements Indicative of Potential Fraudulent Financial Reporting." *Accounting, Organizations and Society* (April 2000): 243–59.

Brazel, J., C. Agoglia, and R. Hatfield. "Electronic versus Face-to-Face Review: The Effects of Alternative Forms of Review on Auditors' Performance." *The Accounting Review* (October 2004): 949–66.

Brehmer, A., and B. Brehmer. "What Have We Learned about Human Judgment from Thirty Years of Policy Capturing?" In *Human Judgment: The SJT View,* edited by B. Brehmer and C. Joyce. New York: North-Holland, 1988.

Brehmer, B. "Cue Utilization and Cue Consistency in Multiple-Cue Probability Learning." *Organizational Behavior and Human Performance* (October 1972): 286–96.

Brehmer, B. "Single-cue Probability Learning as a Function of the Sign and Magnitude of the Correlation between Cue and Criterion." *Organizational Behavior and Human Performance* (June 1973): 377–95.

Brehmer, B. "In One Word: Not from Experience." *Acta Psychologica* (August 1980): 223–41.

Brehmer, B., J. Kuylenstierna, and J. Liljergen. "Effects of Function Form and Cue Validity on the Subjects' Hypotheses in Probabilistic Inference Tasks." *Organizational Behavior and Human Performance* (June 1974): 338–54.

Brenner, L., D. Koehler, V. Liberman, and A. Tversky. "Overconfidence in Probability and Frequency Judgments." *Organizational Behavior and Human Decision Processes* (March 1996): 212–19.

Bricker, R., and M. DeBruine. "The Effects of Information Availability and Cost on Investment Strategy Selection: An Experiment." *Behavioral Research in Accounting* (1993): 30–57.

Briers, M., C. Chow, N. Hwang, and P. Luckett. "The Effects of Alternative Types of Feedback on Product-Related Decision Performance: A Research Note." *Journal of Management Accounting Research* (1999): 75–92.

Broadbent, D. *Decision and Stress.* London: Academic Press, 1971.

Brockner, J. "The Escalation of Commitment to a Failing Course of Action: Toward

Theoretical Progress." *Academy of Management Review* (January 1992): 39–61.

Brody, R., and S. Kaplan. "Escalation of Commitment among Internal Auditors." *Auditing: A Journal of Practice and Theory* (Spring 1996): 1–15.

Bromiley, P., and S. Curley. "Individual Differences in Risk Taking." In *Risk-Taking Behavior,* edited by J. Yates. New York: John Wiley, 1992.

Brown, C. "Human Information Processing for Decisions to Investigate Cost Variances." *Journal of Accounting Research* (Spring 1981): 62–85.

Brown, C. "Causal Reasoning in Performance Assessment: Effects of Cause and Effect Temporal Order and Covariation." *Accounting, Organizations and Society* (No. 3 1985): 255–66.

Brown, C. "Diagnostic Inference in Performance Evaluation: Effects of Cause and Event Covariation and Similarity." *Contemporary Accounting Research* (Fall 1987): 111–26.

Brown, C. "Expert Systems in Public Accounting: Current Practice and Future Directions." *Expert Systems with Applications* (January 1991a): 3–18.

Brown, C., M. Peecher, and I. Solomon. "Auditors' Hypothesis Testing in Diagnostic Inference Tasks." *Journal of Accounting Research* (Spring 1999): 1–26.

Brown, C., and I. Solomon. "Effects of Outcome Information on Evaluations of Managerial Decisions." *The Accounting Review* (July 1987): 564–77.

Brown, C., and I. Solomon. "Auditor Configural Information Processing in Control Risk Assessment." *Auditing: A Journal of Practice and Theory* (Fall 1990): 17–38.

Brown, C., and I. Solomon. "Configural Information Processing in Auditing: The Role of Domain-Specific Knowledge." *The Accounting Review* (January 1991): 100–119.

Brown, C., and I. Solomon. "An Experimental Investigation of Explanations for Outcome Effects on Appraisals of Capital-Budgeting Decisions." *Contemporary Accounting Research* (Fall 1993): 83–111.

Brown, D., and M. Eining. "Judgment and Decision Making, Part IV: Information Technology and Decision Aids." In *Behavioral Accounting Research: Foundations and Frontiers,* edited by V. Arnold and S. Sutton. Sarasota, FL: American Accounting Association, 1997.

Brown, D., and D. Jones. "Factors that Influence Reliance on Decision Aids: A Model and an Experiment." *Journal of Information Systems* (Fall 1998): 75–94.

Brown, L. "Forecast Selection When All Forecasts Are Not Equally Recent." *International Journal of Forecasting* (November 1991b): 349–56.

Brown, L. "A Temporal Analysis of Earnings Surprises: Profits versus Losses." *Journal of Accounting Research* (September 2001): 221–41.

Brown, L., R. Hagerman, P. Griffin, and M. Zmijewski. "Security Analyst Superiority Relative to Univariate Time-Series Models in Forecasting Quarterly Earnings." *Journal of Accounting and Economics* (April 1987): 61–87.

Brown, L., and J. Han. "Do Stock Prices Fully Reflect the Implications of Current Earnings for Future Earnings for AR1 Firms?" *Journal of Accounting Research* (Spring 2000): 149–64.

Brown, L., and E. Mohammad. "Profiting from Predicting Individual Analyst Earnings Forecast Accuracy." Working paper, Georgia State University, 2001.

Brown, L., and M. Rozeff. "The Superiority of Analyst Forecasts as Measures of Expectations: Evidence from Earnings." *The Journal of Finance* (March 1978): 1–16.

Brown, P. "Independent Auditor Judgment in the Evaluation of Internal Audit Functions." *Journal of Accounting Research* (Autumn 1983): 444–55.

Brown, P., G. Foster, and E. Noreen. *Security Analyst Multi-Year Earnings Forecasts and the Capital Markets.* Sarasota, FL: American Accounting Association, 1985.

Brownell, P. "Participation in Budgeting, Locus of Control, and Organizational Effectiveness." *The Accounting Review* (October 1981): 844–60.

Brownell, P. "A Field Study Examination of Budgetary Participation and Locus of Control." *The Accounting Review* (October 1982): 766–77.

Brownell, P. "The Motivational Impact of Management-by-Exception in a Budgetary Context." *Journal of Accounting Research* (Autumn 1983): 456–72.

Brownell, P., and A. Dunk. "Task Uncertainty and Its Interaction with Budgetary Participation and Budget Emphasis: Some Methodological Issues and Empirical Investigation." *Accounting, Organizations and Society* (No. 8 1991): 693–703.

Brownell, P., and M. Hirst. "Reliance on Accounting Information, Budgetary Participation, and Task Uncertainty: Tests of a Three-Way Interaction." *Journal of Accounting Research* (Autumn 1986): 241–49.

Brownell, P., and M. McInnes. "Budgetary Participation, Motivation, and Managerial Performance." *The Accounting Review* (October 1986): 587–600.

Bruine de Bruin, W., and G. Keren. "Order Effects in Sequentially Judged Options Due to the Direction of Comparison." *Organizational Behavior and Human Decision Processes* (September–November 2003): 91–101.

Bruner, J., and H. Tajfel. "Cognitive Risk and Environmental Change." *Journal of Abnormal and Social Psychology* (1961): 231–41.

Bruns, W., Jr. "Inventory Valuation and Management Decisions." *The Accounting Review* (April 1965): 345–57.

Brunswik, E. *The Conceptual Framework of Psychology.* Chicago: University of Chicago Press, 1952.

Buchheit, S. "Fixed Cost Magnitude, Fixed Cost Reporting Format, and Competitive Pricing Decisions: Some Experimental Evidence." *Contemporary Accounting Research* (Spring 2004): 1–24.

Buchman, T. "An Effect of Hindsight Bias on Predicting Bankruptcy with Accounting Information." *Accounting, Organizations and Society* (No. 3 1985): 267–86.

Budescu, D., and A. Rantilla. "Confidence in Aggregation of Expert Opinions." *Acta Psychologica* (June 2000): 371–98.

Budescu, D., A. Rantilla, H. Yu, and T. Karelitz. "The Effects of Asymmetry among Advisors on the Aggregation of Their Opinions." *Organizational Behavior and Human Decision Processes* (January 2003): 178–94.

Budescu, D., S. Weinberg, and T. Wallsten. "Decisions Based on Numerically and Verbally Expressed Uncertainties." *Journal of Experimental Psychology: Human Perception and Performance* (May 1988): 281–94.

Budner, S. "Intolerance for Ambiguity as a Personality Variable." *Journal of Personality* (1962): 29–50.

Bull, C., A. Schotter, and K. Weigelt. "Tournaments and Piece Rates: An Experimental Study." *Journal of Political Economy* (February 1987): 1–33.

Burger, J. "Motivational Biases in the Attribution of Responsibility for an Accident: A Meta-Analysis of the Defensive-Attribution Hypothesis." *Psychological Bulletin* (November 1981): 496–512.

Burgstahler, D., and I. Dichev. "Earnings Management to Avoid Earnings Decreases and Losses." *Journal of Accounting and Economics* (December 1997): 99–126.

Busse, J., and T. Green. "Market Efficiency in Real Time." *Journal of Financial Economics* (September 2002): 415–37.

Butler, S. "Application of a Decision Aid in the Judgmental Evaluation of Substantive Test of Details Samples." *Journal of Accounting Research* (Autumn 1985): 513–26.

Butler, S. "Anchoring in the Judgmental Evaluation of Audit Samples." *The Accounting Review* (January 1986): 101–11.

Butt, J. "Frequency Judgments in an Auditing-Related Task." *Journal of Accounting Research* (Autumn 1988): 315–30.

Butt, J., and T. Campbell. "The Effects of Information Order and Hypothesis Testing Strategies on Auditors' Judgments." *Accounting, Organizations and Society* (No. 5/6 1989): 471–79.

Byrnes, J., D. Miller, and W. Schafer. "Gender Differences in Risk Taking: A Meta-Analysis." *Psychological Bulletin* (May 1999): 367–83.

Calegari, M., and N. Fargher. "Evidence that Prices Do Not Fully Reflect the Implication of Current Earnings for Future Earnings: An Experimental Markets Approach." *Contemporary Accounting Research* (Fall 1997): 397–433.

Camerer, C. "General Conditions for the Success of Bootstrapping Models." *Organizational Behavior and Human Performance* (June 1981a): 411–22.

Camerer, C. "The Validity and Utility of Expert Judgment." Ph.D. dissertation, University of Chicago, 1981b.

Camerer, C. "The Rationality of Prices and Volumes in Experimental Markets." *Organizational Behavior and Human Decision Processes* (May 1992): 237–72.

Camerer, C. "Individual Decision Making." In *The Handbook of Experimental Economics,* edited by J. Kagel and A. Roth. Princeton, NJ: Princeton University Press, 1995.

Camerer, C., and E. Johnson. "The Process-Performance Paradox in Expert Judgment: How Can Experts Know So Much and Predict So Badly?" In *Toward a General Theory of Expertise: Prospects and Limits,* edited by K. Ericsson and J. Smith. New York: Cambridge University Press, 1991.

Camerer, C., G. Loewenstein, and M. Weber. "The Curse of Knowledge in Economic Settings: An Experimental Analysis." *Journal of Political Economy* (October 1989): 1232–54.

Campbell, D. "Task Complexity: A Review and Analysis." *Academy of Management Review* (January 1988): 40–52.

Campbell, D., and K. Gingrich. "The Interactive Effects of Task Complexity and Participation on Task Performance: A Field Experiment." *Organizational Behavior and Human Decision Processes* (October 1986): 62–80.

Campbell, D., and D. Ilgen. "Additive Effects of Task Difficulty and Goal Setting on Subsequent Task Performance." *Journal of Applied Psychology* (June 1976): 319–24.

Campbell, D., and J. Stanley. *Experimental and Quasi-Experimental Designs for Research.* Boston: Houghton Mifflin, 1963.

Campion, M., D. Palmer, and J. Campion. "A Review of Structure in the Selection Interview." *Personnel Psychology* (Autumn 1997): 655–702.

Cannon-Bowers, J., E. Salas, and S. Converse. "Shared Mental Models in Expert Team Decision Making." In *Individual and Group Decision Making,* edited by N. Castellan Jr. Hillsdale, NJ: Lawrence Erlbaum Associates, 1993.

Carhart, M. "On Persistence in Mutual Fund Performance." *Journal of Finance* (March 1997): 57–82.

Carnes, G., G. Harwood, and R. Sawyers. "A Comparison of Tax Professionals' Individual and Group Decisions When Resolving Ambiguous Tax Questions." *Journal of the American Taxation Association* (Fall 1996): 1–18.

Carroll, J. *Human Cognitive Abilities: A Survey of Factor-Analytic Studies.* New York: Cambridge University Press, 1993.

Carroll, J. "Human-Computer Interaction: Psychology as a Science of Design." *Annual Review of Psychology* (1997): 61–83.

Carroll, J., and E. Johnson. *Decision Research: A Field Guide.* Newbury Park, CA: Sage Publications, 1990.

Casey, C., Jr. "The Usefulness of Accounting Ratios for Subjects' Predictions of Corporate Failure: Replication and Extensions." *Journal of Accounting Research* (Autumn 1980a): 603–13.

Casey, C., Jr. "Variation in Accounting Information Load: The Effect on Loan Officers' Predictions of Bankruptcy." *The Accounting Review* (January 1980b): 36–49.

Casey, C. "Prior Probability Disclosure and Loan Officers' Judgments: Some Evidence of the Impact." *Journal of Accounting Research* (Spring 1983): 300–307.

Casey, C., and T. Selling. "The Effect of Task Predictability and Prior Probability Disclosure on Judgment Quality and Confidence." *The Accounting Review* (April 1986): 302–17.

Castellan, N., Jr. "Paradoxes in Individual and Group Decision Making: A Plea for Models." In *Individual and Group Decision Making,* edited by N. Castellan Jr. Hillsdale, NJ: Lawrence Erlbaum Associates, 1993.

Caster, P., and K. Pincus. "An Empirical Test of Bentham's Theory of the Persuasiveness of Evidence." *Auditing: A Journal of Practice & Theory* (1996): S1–22.

Causey, D., and S. Causey. *Duties and Liabilities of Public Accountants,* 4th ed. Starkville, MO: Accountant's Press, 1991.

Chaiken, S. "Heuristic versus Systematic Information Processing and the Use of Source versus Message Cues in Persuasion." *Journal of Personality and Social Psychology* (November 1980): 752–66.

Chaiken, S., W. Wood, and A. Eagly. "Principles of Persuasion." In *Social Psychology: Handbook of Basic Principles,* edited by E. Higgins and A. Kruglanski. New York: The Guilford Press, 1996.

Chalos, P. "Financial Distress: A Comparative Study of Individual, Model, and Committee

Asessments." *Journal of Accounting Research* (Autumn 1985): 527–43.

Chalos, P., and S. Pickard. "Information Choice and Cue Use: An Experiment in Group Information Processing." *Journal of Applied Psychology* (November 1985): 634–41.

Chalos, P., and M. Poon. "Participation and Performance in Capital Budgeting Teams." *Behavioral Research in Accounting* (2000): 199–229.

Chang, C., J. Ho, and W. Liao. "The Effects of Justification, Task Complexity and Experience/Training on Problem-Solving Performance." *Behavioral Research in Accounting* (1997): S98–116.

Chang, C., S. Yen, and R. Duh. "An Empirical Examination of Competing Theories to Explain the Framing Effect in Accounting-Related Decisions." *Behavioral Research in Accounting* (2002): 35–64.

Chang, D., and J. Birnberg. "Functional Fixity in Accounting Research: Perspective and New Data." *Journal of Accounting Research* (Autumn 1977): 300–312.

Chang, J., and G. Monroe. "A Research Note on the Effects of Gender and Task Complexity on an Audit Judgment." *Behavioral Research in Accounting* (2001): 111–25.

Chang, O., D. Nichols, and J. Schultz. "Taxpayer Attitudes toward Tax Audit Risk." *Journal of Economic Psychology* (September 1987): 299–309.

Chapman, G., and E. Johnson. "The Limits of Anchoring." *Journal of Behavioral Decision Making* (December 1994): 223–42.

Chapman, G., and E. Johnson. "Anchoring, Activation, and the Construction of Values." *Organizational Behavior and Human Decisions Processes* (August 1999): 115–53.

Chapman, G., and E. Johnson. "Incorporating the Irrelevant: Anchors in Judgments of Belief and Value." In *Heuristics and Biases: The Psychology of Intuitive Judgment,* edited by T. Gilovich, D. Griffin, and D. Kahneman. New York: Cambridge University Press, 2002.

Chase, W., and H. Simon. "Perception in Chess." *Cognitive Psychology* (January 1973): 55–81.

Chatman, J., D. Caldwell, and C. O'Reilly. "Managerial Personality and Performance: A Semi-Idiographic Approach." *Journal of*

Research in Personality* (December 1999): 514–45.

Chen, Q., J. Francis, and W. Jiang. "The Role of Forecast Patterns in Conveying Analysts' Predictive Ability." Working paper, 2006.

Chen, S., and S. Chaiken. "The Heuristic-Systematic Model in Its Broader Context." In *Dual-Process Theories in Social Psychology,* edited by S. Chaiken and Y. Trope. New York: The Guilford Press, 1999.

Cheng, M., P. Luckett, and A. Schulz. "The Effects of Cognitive Style Diversity on Decision-Making Dyads: An Empirical Analysis in the Context of a Complex Task." *Behavioral Research in Accounting* (2003a): 39–62.

Cheng, M., A. Schulz, P. Luckett, and P. Booth. "The Effects of Hurdle Rates on the Level of Escalation of Commitment in Capital Budgeting." *Behavioral Research in Accounting* (2003b): 63–85.

Cheng, P., and L. Novick. "A Probabilistic Contrast Model of Causal Induction." *Journal of Personality and Social Psychology* (April 1990): 545–67.

Chenhall, R., and D. Morris. "The Effect of Cognitive Style and Sponsorship Bias on the Treatment of Opportunity Costs in Resource Allocation Decisions." *Accounting, Organizations and Society* (No. 1 1991): 27–46.

Chenhall, R., and D. Morris. "The Role of Post Completion Audits, Managerial Learning, Environmental Uncertainty and Performance." *Behavioral Research in Accounting* (1993): 170–86.

Chesley, G. "Elicitation of Subjective Probabilities: A Review." *The Accounting Review* (April 1975): 325–37.

Chesley, G. "The Elicitation of Subjective Probabilities: A Laboratory Study in an Accounting Context." *Journal of Accounting Research* (Spring 1976): 27–48.

Chesley, G. "Subjective Probability Elicitation: The Effect of Congruity of Datum and Response Mode on Performance." *Journal of Accounting Research* (Spring 1977): 1–11.

Chesley, G. "Subjective Probability Elicitation Techniques: A Performance Comparison." *Journal of Accounting Research* (Autumn 1978): 225–41.

Chesley, G. "Interpretation of Uncertainty Expressions." *Contemporary Accounting Research* (Spring 1986): 179–199.

Chevalier, J., and G. Ellison. "Are Some Mutual Fund Managers Better than Others? Cross-Sectional Patterns in Behavior and Performance." *Journal of Finance* (June 1999a): 875–99.

Chevalier, J., and G. Ellison. "Career Concerns of Mutual Fund Managers." *The Quarterly Journal of Economics* (May 1999b): 389–432.

Chewning, E., Jr., M. Coller, and B. Tuttle. "Do Market Prices Reveal the Decision Models of Sophisticated Investors? Evidence from the Laboratory." *Accounting, Organizations and Society* (November 2004): 739–58.

Chewning, E., Jr., and A. Harrell. "The Effect of Information Load on Decision Makers' Cue Utilization Levels and Decision Quality in a Financial Distress Decision Task." *Accounting, Organizations and Society* (No. 6 1990): 527–42.

Chi, M. "Self-Explaining: The Dual Processes of Generating Inference and Repairing Mental Models." In *Advances in Instructional Psychology: Educational Design and Cognitive Science,* vol. 5, edited by R. Glaser. Mahwah, NJ: Lawrence Erlbaum Associates, 2000.

Chi, M., and M. Bassok. "Learning from Examples via Self-Explanations." In *Knowing, Learning, and Instruction: Essays in Honor of Robert Glaser,* edited by L. Resnick. Hillsdale, NJ: Lawrence Erlbaum Associates, 1989.

Chi, M., N. de Leeuw, M. Chiu, and C. LaVancher. "Eliciting Self-Explanations Improves Understanding." *Cognitive Science* (July 1994): 439–77.

Chi, M., P. Feltovich, and R. Glaser. "Categorization and Representation of Physics Problems by Experts and Novices." *Cognitive Science* (April–June 1981): 121–25.

Chi, M., R. Glaser, and M. Farr, ed. *The Nature of Expertise.* Hillsdale, NJ: Lawrence Erlbaum Associates, 1988.

Chiesi, H., G. Spilich, and J. Voss. "Acquisition of Domain-Related Information in Relation to High and Low Domain Knowledge." *Journal of Verbal Learning and Verbal Behavior* (June 1979): 257–73.

Chong, V., and K. Chong. "Budget Goal Commitment and Informational Effects of Budget Participation on Performance: A Structural Equation Modeling Approach." *Behavioral Research in Accounting* (2002): 65–86.

Choo, F. "Cognitive Scripts in Auditing and Accounting Behavior." *Accounting, Organizations and Society* (No. 5/6 1989): 481–93.

Choo, F. "Auditors' Judgment Performance Under Stress: A Test of the Predicted Relationship by Three Theoretical Models." *Journal of Accounting, Auditing and Finance* (Summer 1995): 611–41.

Choo, F. "Auditors' Knowledge Content and Judgment Performance: A Cognitive Script Approach." *Accounting, Organizations and Society* (May 1996): 339–59.

Choo, F., and K. Tan. "Effect of Cognitive Elaboration on Accounting Students' Acquisition of Auditing Expertise." *Issues in Accounting Education* (Spring 1995): 27–45.

Choo, F., and K. Trotman. "The Relationship between Knowledge Structure and Judgments for Experienced and Inexperienced Auditors." *The Accounting Review* (July 1991): 464–85.

Chow, C. "The Effects of Job Standard Tightness and Compensation Scheme on Performance: An Exploration of Linkages." *The Accounting Review* (October 1983): 667–85.

Chow, C., T. Lindquist, and A. Wu. "National Culture and the Implementation of High-Stretch Performance Standards: An Exploratory Study." *Behavioral Research in Accounting* (2001): 85–109.

Christ, M. "Evidence on the Nature of Audit Planning Problem Representations: An Examination of Auditor Free Recalls." *The Accounting Review* (April 1993): 304–22.

Christensen, A., and P. Hite. "A Study of the Effect of Taxpayer Risk Perceptions on Ambiguous Compliance Decisions." *Journal of the American Taxation Association* (Spring 1997): 1–18.

Chung, J., and G. Monroe. "A Research Note on the Effects of Gender and Task Complexity on an Audit Judgment." *Behavioral Research in Accounting* (2001): 111–25.

Church, B. "An Examination of the Effect that Commitment to a Hypothesis Has on Auditors' Evaluations of Confirming and Disconfirming Evidence." *Contemporary Accounting Research* (Spring 1991): 513–34.

Church, B., and A. Schneider. "Auditors' Generation of Diagnostic Hypotheses in Response to a Superior's Suggestion:

Interference Effects." *Contemporary Accounting Research* (Fall 1993): 333–50.

Church, B., and A. Schneider. "Internal Auditors' Memory for Financial-Statement Errors." *Behavioral Research in Accounting* (1995): 17–36.

Cialdini, R., and M. Trost. "Social Influence, Social Norms, Conformity, and Compliance." In *The Handbook of Social Psychology,* 4th ed., edited by D. Gilbert, S. Fiske, and G. Lindzey. Boston: McGraw-Hill, 1998.

Clancey, W. "Acquiring, Representing, and Evaluating a Competence Model of Diagnostic Strategy." In *The Nature of Expertise,* edited by M. Chi, R. Glaser, and M. Farr. Hillsdale, NJ: Lawrence Erlbaum, 1988.

Clarkson, P., C. Emby, and V. Watt. "Debiasing the Outcome Effect: The Role of Instructions in an Audit Litigation Setting." *Auditing: A Journal of Practice & Theory* (September 2002): 7–20.

Clemen, R. "Combining Forecasts: A Review and Annotated Bibliography." *International Journal of Forecasting* (No. 4 1989): 559–83.

Clement, M. "Analyst Forecast Accuracy: Do Ability, Resources, and Portfolio Complexity Matter?" *Journal of Accounting and Economics* (July 1999): 285–303.

Clement, M., and S. Tse. "Do Investors Respond to Analysts' Forecast Revisions as if Forecast Accuracy Is All That Matters?" *The Accounting Review* (January 2003): 227–49.

Clement, M., and S. Tse. "Financial Analyst Characteristics and Herding Behavior in Forecasting." *The Journal of Finance* (February 2005): 307–41.

Clements, J. "Are You Irrational or Thrill-Seeking When It Comes to Risky Investments?" *The Wall Street Journal* (June 4, 1996): C1.

Cleveland, J., K. Murphy, and R. Williams. "Multiple Uses of Performance Appraisal: Prevalence and Correlates." *Journal of Applied Psychology* (January 1989): 130–35.

Cloyd, C. "Prior Knowledge, Information Search Behaviors, and Performance in Tax Research Tasks." *Journal of the American Taxation Association* (1995): S82–107.

Cloyd, C. "Performance in Tax Research Tasks: The Joint Effects of Knowledge and Accountability." *The Accounting Review* (January 1997): 111–31.

Cloyd, C., and B. Spilker. "The Influence of Client Preferences on Tax Professionals' Search for Judicial Precedents, Subsequent Judgments and Recommendations." *The Accounting Review* (July 1999): 299–322.

Cloyd, C., and B. Spilker. "Confirmation Bias in Tax Information Search: A Comparison of Law Students and Accounting Students." *Journal of the American Taxation Association* (Fall 2000): 60–71.

Cloyd, C., J. Pratt, and T. Stock. "The Use of Financial Accounting Choice to Support Aggressive Tax Positions: Public and Private Firms." *Journal of Accounting Research* (Spring 1996): 23–43.

Cohen, J., and T. Kida. "The Impact of Analytical Review Results, Internal Control Reliability, and Experience on Auditors' Use of Analytical Review." *Journal of Accounting Research* (Autumn 1989): 263–76.

Cohen, J., and G. Trompeter. "An Examination of Factors Affecting Audit Practice Development." *Contemporary Accounting Research* (Winter 1998): 481–504.

Cohen, L., and K. Kelly. "Loose Leash—NYSE Turmoil Poses Question: Can Wall Street Regulate Itself?" *Wall Street Journal* (December 31, 2003): A1.

Colbert, J. "Inherent Risk: An Investigation of Auditors' Judgments." *Accounting, Organizations and Society* (No. 2 1988): 111–21.

Collins, A., and E. Loftus. "A Spreading-Activation Theory of Semantic Processing." *Psychological Review* (November 1975): 407–28.

Collins, W., and W. Hopwood. "A Multivariate Analysis of Annual Earnings Forecasts Generated from Quarterly Forecasts of Financial Analysts and Univariate Time-Series Models." *Journal of Accounting Research* (Autumn 1980): 390–406.

Committee on Developments in the Science of Learning and Committee on Learning Research and Educational Practice, Commission on Behavioral and Social Sciences and Education, National Research Council. *How People Learn: Brain, Mind, Experience, and School.* Washington, DC: National Academy Press, 2000.

Conroy, R., and R. Harris. "Consensus Forecasts of Corporate Earnings: Analysts' Forecasts and Time Series Methods." *Management Science* (June 1987): 725–38.

Conway, J., R. Jako, and D. Goodman. "A Meta-Analysis of Interrater and Internal Consistency Reliability of Selection Interviews." *Journal of Applied Psychology* (September 1995): 565–79.

Conway, M., ed. *Cognitive Models of Memory.* Cambridge, MA: MIT Press, 1997.

Cook, D. "The Effect of Frequency of Feedback on Attitudes and Performance." *Journal of Accounting Research* (1967): S213–24.

Cook, D. "The Impact on Managers of Frequency of Feedback." *Academy of Management Review* (September 1968): 263–77.

Cook, E., and T. Kelley. "Auditor Stress and Time-Budgets." *The CPA Journal* (July 1988): 83–86.

Cook, M. *Personnel Selection: Adding Value through People,* 4th ed. West Sussex, England: John Wiley & Sons, 2004.

Cook, R., and T. Stewart. "A Comparison of Seven Methods for Obtaining Subjective Descriptions of Judgmental Policy." *Organizational Behavior and Human Performance* (February 1975): 31–45.

Cook, T., and D. Campbell. *Quasi-Experimentation: Design & Analysis Issues for Field Settings.* Boston: Houghton Mifflin, 1979.

Cooksey, R. *Judgment Analysis: Theory, Methods, and Applications.* San Diego, CA: Academic Press, 1996.

Copeland, R., and R. Marioni. "Executives' Forecasts of Earnings per Share versus Forecasts of Naive Models." *The Journal of Business* (October 1972): 497–512.

Corless, J. "Assessing Prior Distributions for Applying Bayesian Statistics in Auditing." *The Accounting Review* (July 1972): 556–66.

Cortina, J., N. Goldstein, S. Payne, H. Davison, and S. Gilliland. "The Incremental Validity of Interview Scores Over and Above Cognitive Ability and Conscientiousness Scores." *Personnel Psychology* (Summer 2000): 325–51.

Cote, J. "Analyst Credibility: The Investor's Perspective." *Journal of Managerial Issues* (Fall 2000): 352–62.

Cote, J., and D. Sanders. "Herding Behavior: Explanations and Implications." *Behavioral Research in Accounting* (1997): 20–45.

Covaleski, M., J. Evans III, J. Luft, and M. Shields. "Budgeting Research: Three Theoretical Perspectives and Criteria for Selective Integration." *Journal of Management Accounting Research* (2003): 3–49.

Crandall, D., and F. Phillips. "Using Hypertext in Instructional Material: Helping Students Link Accounting Concept Knowledge to Case Applications." *Issues in Accounting Education* (May 2002): 163–83.

Crant, J., and T. Bateman. "Assignment of Credit and Blame for Performance Outcomes." *Academy of Management Journal* (February 1993): 7–27.

Craswell, A., J. Francis, and S. Taylor. "Auditor Brand Name Reputations and Industry Specialization." *Journal of Accounting & Economics* (December 1995): 297–322.

Creyer, E., J. Bettman, and J. Payne. "The Impact of Accuracy and Effort Feedback and Goals on Adaptive Decision Behavior." *Journal of Behavioral Decision Making* (January–March 1990): 1–16.

Crichfield, T., T. Dyckman, and J. Lakonishok. "An Evaluation of Security Analysts' Forecasts." *The Accounting Review* (July 1978): 651–68.

Crocker, J. "Judgment of Covariation by Social Perceivers." *Psychological Bulletin* (September 1981): 272–92.

Crosby, M. "Implications of Prior Probability Elicitation on Auditor Sample Size Decisions." *Journal of Accounting Research* (Autumn 1980): 585–93.

Crosby, M. "Bayesian Statistics in Auditing: A Comparison of Probability Elicitation Techniques." *The Accounting Review* (April 1981): 355–65.

Crowne, D., and D. Marlowe. "A New Scale of Social Desirability Independent of Psychopathology." *Journal of Consulting Psychology* (1960): 349–54.

Crystal, G. *In Search of Excess: The Overcompensation of American Executives.* New York: W.W. Norton & Company, 1991.

Cuccia, A. "The Effects of Increased Sanctions on Paid Tax Preparers: Integrating Economic and Psychological Factors." *Journal of the American Taxation Association* (Spring 1994): 41–66.

Cuccia, A., K. Hackenbrack, and M. Nelson. "The Ability of Professional Standards to

Mitigate Aggressive Reporting." *The Accounting Review* (April 1995): 227–48.

Cuccia, A., and G. McGill. "The Role of Decision Strategies in Understanding Professionals' Susceptibility to Judgment Biases." *Journal of Accounting Research* (Autumn 2000): 419–35.

Curley, S., J. Yates, and R. Abrams. "Psychological Sources of Ambiguity Avoidance." *Organizational Behavior and Human Decision Processes* (October 1986): 230–56.

Cushing, B., and S. Ahlawat. "Mitigation of Recency Bias in Audit Judgment: The Effect of Documentation." *Auditing: A Journal of Practice & Theory* (Fall 1996): 110–22.

Damasio, A. *Descartes' Error: Emotion, Reason, and the Human Brain.* New York: HarperCollins, 1994.

Daniel, K., D. Hirshleifer, and A. Subrahmanyam. "Investor Psychology and Security Market Under- and Overreactions." *The Journal of Finance* (December 1998): 1839–85.

Daniel, K., D. Hirshleifer, and S. Teoh. "Investor Psychology in Capital Markets: Evidence and Policy Implications." *Journal of Monetary Economics* (January 2002): 139–209.

Daniel, S. "Some Empirical Evidence about the Assessment of Audit Risk in Practice." *Auditing: A Journal of Practice & Theory* (Spring 1988): 174–81.

Danos, P., and E. Imhoff. "Auditor Review of Financial Forecasts: An Analysis of Factors Affecting Reasonableness Judgments." *The Accounting Review* (January 1982): 39–54.

Danos, P., and E. Imhoff Jr. "Factors Affecting Auditors' Evaluations of Forecasts." *Journal of Accounting Research* (Autumn 1983): 473–94.

Darley, J., and G. Goethals. "People's Analyses of the Causes of Ability-Linked Performances." In *Advances in Experimental Social Psychology,* vol. 13, edited by L. Berkowicz. New York: Academic Press, 1980.

Daroca, F. "Informational Influences on Group Decision Making in a Participative Budgeting Context." *Accounting, Organizations and Society* (No. 1 1984): 13–32.

Das, S., C. Levine, and K. Sivaramakrishnan. "Earnings Predictability and Bias in Analysts'

Earnings Forecasts." *The Accounting Review* (April 1998): 277–94.

Das, S., and H. Zhang. "Rounding-up in Reported EPS, Behavioral Thresholds, and Earnings Management." *Journal of Accounting and Economics* (April 2003): 31–50.

Davis, F., and J. Kottemann. "User Perceptions of Decision Support Effectiveness: Two Production Planning Experiments." *Decision Sciences* (January–February 1994): 57–78.

Davis, F., and J. Kottemann. "Determinants of Decision Rule Use in a Production Planning Task." *Organizational Behavior and Human Decision Processes* (August 1995): 145–57.

Davis, F., G. Lohse, and J. Kottemann. "Harmful Effects of Seemingly Helpful Information on Forecasts of Stock Earnings." *Journal of Economic Psychology* (June 1994): 253–67.

Davis, J. *Group Performance.* Reading, MA: Addison-Wesley, 1969.

Davis, J. "Experience and Auditors' Selection of Relevant Information for Preliminary Control Risk Assessments." *Auditing: A Journal of Practice and Theory* (Spring 1996): 16–37.

Davis, J., and J. Mason. "Similarity and Precedent in Tax Authority Judgment." *Journal of the American Taxation Association* (Spring 2003): 53–71.

Davis, J., and I. Solomon. "Experience, Expertise, and Expert-Performance Research in Public Accounting." *Journal of Accounting Literature* (1989): 150–64.

Davis, L., M. Dwyer, and G. Trompeter. "A Note on Cross-Sectional Tests for Knowledge Differences." *Behavioral Research in Accounting* (1997): 46–59.

Dawes, R. "The Robust Beauty of Improper Linear Models in Decision Making." *American Psychologist* (July 1979): 571–82.

Dawes, R., and B. Corrigan. "Linear Models in Decision Making." *Psychological Bulletin* (February 1974): 95–106.

Dawes, R., D. Faust, and P. Meehl. "Clinical versus Actuarial Judgment." *Science* (March 31, 1989): 1668–74.

Day, E., W. Arthur Jr., and D. Gettman. "Knowledge Structures and the Acquisition of a Complex Skill." *Journal of Applied Psychology* (October 2001): 1022–33.

Dearman, D., and M. Shields. "Cost Knowledge and Cost-Based Judgment Performance."

Journal of Management Accounting Research (2001): 1–18.

Deaux, K., and T. Emswiller. "Explanations of Successful Performance on Sex-Linked Tasks: What Is Skill for the Male Is Luck for the Female." *Journal of Personality and Social Psychology* (January 1974): 80–85.

Deaux, K., and E. Farris. "Attributing Causes for One's Own Performance: The Effects of Sex, Norms, and Outcomes." *Journal of Research in Personality* (March 1977): 59–72.

Dechow, P., A. Hutton, and R. Sloan. "The Relation between Analysts' Forecasts of Long-Term Earnings Growth and Stock Price Performance Following Equity Offerings." *Contemporary Accounting Research* (Spring 2000): 1–32.

Deci, E., G. Betley, J. Kahle, L. Abrams, and J. Porac. "When Trying to Win: Competition and Intrinsic Motivation." *Personality and Social Psychology Bulletin* (March 1981): 79–83.

Degeorge, F., J. Patel, and R. Zeckhauser. "Earnings Management to Exceed Thresholds." *Journal of Business* (January 1999): 1–33.

DeGroot, A. "Perception and Memory versus Thought: Some Old Ideas and Recent Findings." In *Problem Solving,* edited by B. Kleinmuntz. New York: Wiley, 1966.

Demirakos, E., N. Strong, and M. Walker. "What Valuation Models Do Analysts Use?" *Accounting Horizons* (December 2004): 221–40.

Demski, J., and G. Feltham. "Economic Incentives in Budgetary Control Systems." *The Accounting Review* (April 1978): 336–59.

DeSanctis, G. "Computer Graphics as Decision Aids: Directions for Research." *Decision Sciences* (Fall 1984): 463–87.

DeSanctis, G., and S. Jarvenpaa. "Graphical Presentation of Accounting Data for Financial Forecasting: An Experimental Investigation." *Accounting, Organizations & Society* (No. 5/6 1989): 509–25.

Desberg, P., and J. Taylor. *Essentials of Task Analysis.* Lanham, MD: University Press of America, 1986.

DeZoort, F., R. Houston, and M. Peters. "The Impact of Internal Auditor Compensation and Role on External Auditors' Planning Judgments and Decisions." *Contemporary Accounting Research* (Summer 2001): 257–81.

DeZoort, F., and A. Lord. "An Investigation of Obedience Pressure Effects on Auditors' Judgments." *Behavioral Research in Accounting* (1994): S1–30.

DeZoort, F., and A. Lord. "A Review and Synthesis of Pressure Effects Research in Accounting." *Journal of Accounting Literature* (1997): 28–85.

DeZoort, F., and S. Salterio. "The Effects of Corporate Governance Experience and Financial-Reporting and Audit Knowledge on Audit Committee Members' Judgments." *Auditing: A Journal of Practice and Theory* (September 2001): 31–47.

Dichev, I., and T. Janes. "Lunar Cycle Effects in Stock Returns." *The Journal of Private Equity* (No. 4 2003): 8–29.

Dickhaut, J. "Alternative Information Structures and Probability Revisions." *The Accounting Review* (January 1973): 61–79.

Diener, E., and E. Suh. "National Differences in Subjective Well-Being." In *Well-Being: The Foundations of Hedonic Psychology,* edited by D. Kahneman, E. Diener, and N. Schwarz. New York: Russell Sage Foundation, 1999.

Dietrich, J., S. Kachelmeier, D. Kleinmuntz, and T. Linsmeier. "Market Efficiency, Bounded Rationality, and Supplemental Business Reporting Disclosures." *Journal of Accounting Research* (September 2001): 93–117.

Digman, J. "Personality Structure: Emergence of the Five-Factor Model." *Annual Review of Psychology* (1990): 417–40.

Dilla, W., and D. Stone. "Representations as Decision Aids: The Asymmetric Effects of Words and Numbers on Auditors' Inherent Risk Judgments." *Decision Sciences* (Summer 1997): 709–43.

Dillard, J., N. Kauffman, and E. Spires. "Evidence Order and Belief Revision in Management Accounting Decisions." *Accounting, Organizations and Society* (No. 7 1991): 619–33.

Dillon, R. "Issues in Cognitive Psychology and Instruction." In *Cognition and Instruction,* edited by R. Dillon and R. Sternberg. San Diego, CA: Academic Press, 1986.

Dipboye, R. "The Selection/Recruitment Interview: Core Processes and Contexts." In *The Blackwell Handbook of Personnel Selection,* edited by A. Evers, N. Anderson, and O. Voskuijl. Malden, MA: Blackwell Publishing, 2005.

Ditto, P. and D. Lopez. "Motivated Skepticism: Use of Differential Decision Criteria for Preferred and Nonpreferred Conclusions." *Journal of Personality and Social Psychology* (October 1992): 568–84.

Ditto, P., J. Scepansky, G. Munro, A. Apanovitch, and L. Lockhart. "Motivated Sensitivity to Preference-Inconsistent Information." *Journal of Personality and Social Psychology* (July 1998): 53–69.

Doherty, M., C. Mynatt, R. Tweney, and M. Schiavo. "Pseudodiagnosticity." *Acta Psychologica* (March 1979): 111–21.

Doherty, M., and B. Reilly. "Assessing Self-Insight via Policy Capturing and Cognitive Feedback." In *The Essential Brunswik: Beginnings, Extensions, Applications,* edited by K. Hammond and T. Stewart. New York: Oxford University Press, 2001.

Dopuch, N. "Another Perspective on the Use of Deception in Auditing Experiments." *Auditing: A Journal of Practice and Theory* (Fall 1992): 109–12.

Dopuch, N., R. King, and R. Schwartz. "An Experimental Investigation of Retention and Rotation Requirements." *Journal of Accounting Research* (June 2001): 93–117.

Dopuch, N., R. King, and R. Schwartz. "Independence in Appearance and in Fact: An Experimental Investigation." *Contemporary Accounting Research* (Spring 2003): 79–114.

Dopuch, N., and J. Ronen. "The Effects of Alternative Inventory Valuation Methods—An Experimental Study." *Journal of Accounting Research* (Autumn 1973): 191–211.

Doran, B., M. Bouillon, and C. Smith. "Determinants of Student Performance in Accounting Principles I and II." *Issues in Accounting Education* (Spring 1991): 74–84.

Dougherty, T., R. Ebert, and J. Callender. "Policy Capturing in the Employment Interview." *Journal of Applied Psychology* (January 1986): 9–15.

Dowen, R. "Analyst Reaction to Negative Earnings for Large Well-Known Firms." *Journal of Portfolio Management* (Fall 1996): 49–55.

Driscoll, M. *Psychology of Learning for Instruction,* 3rd ed. Upper Saddle River, NJ: Pearson Education, 2005.

Driver, M. "Integrative Style Test." Working paper, University of Southern California, 1971.

Driver, M., and T. Mock. "Human Information Processing, Decision Style Theory, and Accounting Information Systems." *The Accounting Review* (July 1975): 490–508.

Dubé-Rioux, L., and J. Russo. "An Availability Bias in Professional Judgment." *Journal of Behavioral Decision Making* (March 1988): 223–37.

DuCette, J., and S. Wolk. "Cognitive and Motivational Correlates of Generalized Expectancies for Control." *Journal of Personality and Social Psychology* (June 1973): 420–26.

Dudycha, L., and J. Naylor. "Characteristics of the Human Inference Process in Complex Choice Behavior Situations." *Organizational Behavior and Human Performance* (September 1966): 110–28.

Dugar, A., and S. Nathan. "The Effect of Investment Banking Relationships on Financial Analysts' Earnings Forecasts and Investment Recommendations." *Contemporary Accounting Research* (Fall 1995): 131–60.

Duncker, K. "On Problem-Solving." *Psychological Monographs,* no. 270 (1945).

Dunk, A. "Budget Emphasis, Budgetary Participation and Managerial Performance: A Note." *Accounting, Organizations and Society* (No. 4 1989): 321–24.

Dusenbury, R. "The Effect of Prepayment Position on Individual Taxpayers' Preferences for Risky Tax-Filing Options." *Journal of the American Taxation Association* (Spring 1994): 1–16.

Dweck, C., Y. Hong, and C. Chiu. "Implicit Theories: Individual Differences in the Likelihood and Meaning of Dispositional Inference." *Personality and Social Psychology Bulletin* (October 1993): 644–56.

Dyckman, T. "The Effects of Alternative Accounting Techniques on Certain Management Decisions." *Journal of Accounting Research* (Spring 1964a): 91–107.

Dyckman, T. "On the Investment Decision." *The Accounting Review* (April 1964b): 285–95.

Dyckman, T., R. Hoskin, and R. Swieringa. "An Accounting Change and Information

Processing Changes." *Accounting, Organizations and Society* (No. 1 1982): 1–11.

Dye, R. "The Trouble with Tournaments." *Economic Inquiry* (January 1984): 147–49.

Eames, J., and S. Glover. "Earnings Predictability and the Direction of Analysts' Earnings Forecast Errors." *The Accounting Review* (July 2003): 707–24.

Eames, M., S. Glover, and J. Kennedy. "The Association between Trading Recommendations and Broker-Analysts' Earnings Forecasts." *Journal of Accounting Research* (March 2002): 85–104.

Earley, C. "Knowledge Acquisition in Auditing: Training Novice Auditors to Recognize Cue Relationships in Real Estate Valuation." *The Accounting Review* (January 2001): 81–97.

Earley, C. "A Note on Self-Explanation as a Training Tool for Novice Auditors: The Effects of Outcome Feedback Timing and Level of Reasoning on Performance." *Behavioral Research in Accounting* (2003): 111–24.

Earley, P., and T. Lituchy. "Delineating Goal and Efficacy Effects: A Test of Three Models." *Journal of Applied Psychology* (February 1991): 81–98.

Easterbrook, J. "The Effect of Emotion on Cue Utilization and the Organization of Behavior." *Psychological Review* (1959): 183–201.

Ebert, R., and T. Kruse. "Bootstrapping the Security Analyst." *Journal of Applied Psychology* (January 1978): 110–19.

Eccles, J., and A. Wigfield. "Motivational Beliefs, Values, and Goals." *Annual Review of Psychology* (2002): 109–32.

Eddy, D. "Probabilistic Reasoning in Clinical Medicine: Problems and Opportunities." In *Judgment under Uncertainty: Heuristics and Biases,* edited by D. Kahneman, P. Slovic, and A. Tversky. New York: Cambridge University Press, 1982.

Edland, A., and O. Svenson. "Judgment and Decision Making under Time Pressure: Studies and Findings." In *Time Pressure and Stress in Human Judgment and Decision Making,* edited by O. Svenson and A. Maule. New York: Plenum Press, 1993.

Edmonds, T., and R. Alford. "Environmental Complexity and the Level of Information Processing by Introductory Accounting Students." *Issues in Accounting Education* (Fall 1989): 345–58.

Edwards, W., and B. Fasolo. "Decision Technology." *Annual Review of Psychology* (2001): 581–606.

Eger, C., and J. Dickhaut. "An Examination of the Conservative Information Processing Bias in an Accounting Framework." *Journal of Accounting Research* (Autumn 1982, Part II): 711–23.

Eggleton, I. "Patterns, Prototypes, and Predictions: An Exploratory Study." *Journal of Accounting Research* (1976): S68–131.

Eggleton, I. "Intuitive Time-Series Extrapolation." *Journal of Accounting Research* (Spring 1982): 68–102.

Eilifsen, A., W. Knechel, and P. Wallage. "Application of the Business Risk Audit Model: A Field Study." *Accounting Horizons* (September 2001): 193–208.

Einhorn, H. "The Use of Nonlinear, Noncompensatory Models in Decision Making." *Psychological Bulletin* (March 1970): 221–30.

Einhorn, H. "Expert Measurement and Mechanical Combination." *Organizational Behavior and Human Performance* (February 1972): 86–106.

Einhorn, H. "Expert Judgment: Some Necessary Conditions and an Example." *Journal of Applied Psychology* (October 1974): 562–71.

Einhorn, H. "Overconfidence in Judgment." In *New Directions for Methodology of Social and Behavioral Science: Fallible Judgment in Behavioral Research,* edited by R. Shweder and D. Fiske. San Francisco: Jossey-Bass, 1980.

Einhorn, H. "Accepting Error to Make Less Error." *Journal of Personality Assessment* (Fall 1986): 387–95.

Einhorn, H., and R. Hogarth. "Unit Weighting Schemes for Decision Making." *Organizational Behavior and Human Performance* (April 1975): 171–92.

Einhorn, H., and R. Hogarth. "Confidence in Judgment: Persistence of the Illusion of Validity." *Psychological Review* (September 1978): 395–416.

Einhorn, H., and R. Hogarth. "Behavioral Decision Theory: Processes of Judgment and Choice." *Annual Review of Psychology* (1981): 53–88.

Einhorn, H., and R. Hogarth. "Judging Probable Cause." *Psychological Bulletin* (January 1986): 3–19.

Einhorn, H., R. Hogarth, and E. Klempner. "Quality of Group Judgment." *Psychological Bulletin* (January 1977): 158–72.

Eining, M., and P. Dorr. "The Impact of Expert System Usage on Experiential Learning in an Auditing Setting." *Journal of Information Systems* (Spring 1991): 1–16.

Eining, M., D. Jones, and J. Loebbecke. "Reliance on Decision Aids: An Examination of Auditors' Assessment of Management Fraud." *Auditing: A Journal of Practice & Theory* (Fall 1997): 1–19.

Elliott, B. "Are Investors Influenced by Pro Forma Emphasis and Reconciliations in Earnings Announcements?" *The Accounting Review* (January 2006): 113–33.

Elliott, R. "The Third Wave Breaks on the Shores of Accounting." *Accounting Horizons* (June 1992): 61–85.

Elstein, A., L. Shulman, and S. Sprafka. *Medical Problem Solving: An Analysis of Clinical Reasoning.* Cambridge, MA: Harvard University Press, 1978.

Elton, E., and M. Gruber. "Earnings Estimates and the Accuracy of Expectational Data." *Management Science* (April 1972): B-409–24.

Emby, C. "Framing and Presentation Mode Effects in Professional Judgment: Auditors' Internal Control Judgments and Substantive Testing Decisions." *Auditing: A Journal of Practice and Theory* (1994): S102–27.

Emby, C., and D. Finley. "Debiasing Framing Effects in Auditors' Internal Control Judgments and Testing Decisions." *Contemporary Accounting Research* (Summer 1997): 55–77.

Emby, C., and M. Gibbins. "Good Judgment in Public Accounting: Quality and Justification." *Contemporary Accounting Research* (Spring 1988): 287–313.

Entwistle, G., G. Feltham, and C. Mbagwu. "Financial Reporting Regulation and the Reporting of Pro Forma Earnings." *Accounting Horizons* (March 2006): 39–55.

Epley, N., and T. Gilovich. "Putting Adjustment Back in the Anchoring and Adjustment Heuristic." In *Heuristics and Biases: The Psychology of Intuitive Judgment,* edited by T. Gilovich, D. Griffin, and D. Kahneman. New York: Cambridge University Press, 2002.

Ericsson, K., ed. *The Road to Excellence: The Acquisition of Expert Performance in the Arts and Sciences, Sports and Games.* Mahwah, NJ: Lawrence Erlbaum, 1996.

Ericsson, K., R. Krampe, and C. Tesch-Römer. "The Role of Deliberate Practice in the Acquisition of Expert Performance." *Psychological Bulletin* (November 1993): 363–406.

Ericsson, K., and A. Lehman. "Expert and Exceptional Performance: Evidence on Maximal Adaptations to Task Constraints." *Annual Review of Psychology* (1996): 273–305.

Ericsson, K., and W. Oliver. "Methodology for Laboratory Research on Thinking: Task Selection, Collection of Observations, and Data Analysis." In *The Psychology of Human Thought,* edited by R. Sternberg and E. Smith. New York: Cambridge University Press, 1988.

Ericsson, K., and H. Simon. *Protocol Analysis: Verbal Reports as Data.* Cambridge, MA: MIT Press, 1996.

Ericsson, K., and J. Smith, ed. *Toward a General Theory of Expertise: Prospects and Limits.* New York: Cambridge University Press, 1991.

Erickson, M., B. Mayhew, and W. Felix Jr. "Why Do Audits Fail? Evidence from Lincoln Savings and Loan." *Journal of Accounting Research* (Spring 2000): 165–94.

Eskew, R., and R. Faley. "Some Determinants of Student Performance in the First College-Level Financial Accounting Course." *The Accounting Review* (January 1988): 137–47.

Estes, R., and J. Hosseini. "The Gender Gap on Wall Street: An Empirical Analysis of Confidence in Investment Decision Making." *The Journal of Psychology* (November 1988): 577–90.

Evans, C., and K. Dion. "Group Cohesion and Performance: A Meta-Analysis." *Small Group Research* (May 1991): 175–86.

Evans, J., V. Heiman-Hoffman, and S. Rau. "The Accountability Demand for Information." *Journal of Management Accounting Research* (Fall 1994): 24–42.

Eysenck, M. *Attention and Arousal: Cognition and Performance.* Berlin: Springer, 1982.

Eysenck, M. *A Handbook of Cognitive Psychology.* London: Erlbaum, 1986.

Fagley, N., and P. Miller. "The Effect of Framing on Choice: Interactions with Risk-Taking Propensity, Cognitive Style, and Sex." *Personality and Social Psychology Bulletin* (September 1990): 496–510.

Fama, E. "Agency Problems and the Theory of the Firm." *Journal of Political Economy* (April 1980): 288–307.

Farmer, T., L. Rittenberg, and G. Trompeter. "An Investigation of the Impact of Economic and Organizational Factors on Auditor Independence." *Auditing: A Journal of Practice and Theory* (Fall 1987): 1–14.

Feingold, A. "Gender Differences in Personality: A Meta-Analysis." *Psychological Bulletin* (November 1994): 429–56.

Feldman, J. "Beyond Attribution Theory: Cognitive Processes in Performance Appraisal." *Journal of Applied Psychology* (April 1981): 127–48.

Felix, W. "Evidence on Alternative Means of Assessing Prior Probability Distributions for Audit Decision Making." *The Accounting Review* (October 1976): 800–807.

Fernald, L. "Tales in a Textbook: Learning in the Traditional and Narrative Modes." *Teaching of Psychology* (October 1989): 121–24.

Ferris, K., and D. Larcker. "Explanatory Variables of Auditor Performance in a Large Public Accounting Firm." *Accounting, Organizations and Society* (No. 1 1983): 1–11.

Fields, T., T. Lys, and L. Vincent. "Empirical Research on Accounting Choice." *Journal of Accounting and Economics* (September 2001): 255–307.

Financial Analysts Federation and Institute of Chartered Financial Analysts. *Standards of Practice Handbook: The Code of Ethics and The Standards of Professional Conduct,* 4th ed. New York: Financial Analysts Federation, 1988.

Fincham, F., and J. Jaspars. "Attribution of Responsibility: From Man the Scientist to Man as Lawyer." *Advances in Experimental Social Psychology* (1980): 81–138.

Finucane, M., A. Alhakami, P. Slovic, and S. Johnson. "The Affect Heuristic in Judgments of Risks and Benefits." *Journal of Behavioral Decision Making* (January–March 2000): 1–17.

Fischer, C., M. Wartick, and M. Mark. "Detection Probability and Taxpayer Compliance: A Review of the Literature." *Journal of Accounting Literature* (1992): 1–46.

Fischhoff, B. "Perceived Informativeness of Facts." *Journal of Experimental Psychology: Human Perception and Performance* (May 1977): 349–58.

Fischhoff, B. "Debiasing." In *Judgment under Uncertainty: Heuristics and Biases,* edited by D. Kahneman, P. Slovic, and A. Tversky. New York: Cambridge University Press, 1982.

Fischhoff, B., and R. Beyth-Marom. "Hypothesis Evaluation from a Bayesian Perspective." *Psychological Review* (July 1983): 239–60.

Fischhoff, B., P. Slovic, and S. Lichtenstein. "Fault Trees: Sensitivity of Estimated Failure Probabilities to Problem Representations." *Journal of Experimental Psychology: Human Perception and Performance* (May 1978): 330–44.

Fisher, J., and T. Selling. "The Outcome Effect in Performance Evaluation: Decision Process Observability and Consensus." *Behavioral Research in Accounting* (1993): 58–77.

Fiske, S., D. Kinder, and W. Larter. "The Novice and the Expert: Knowledge-Based Strategies in Political Cognition." *Journal of Experimental Social Psychology* (July 1983): 381–400.

Fiske, S., and S. Taylor. *Social Cognition,* 2nd ed. New York: McGraw-Hill, 1991.

Fleishman, E. "Toward a Taxonomy of Human Performance." *American Psychologist* (December 1975): 1127–49.

Fletcher, C., and E. Perry. "Performance Appraisal and Feedback: A Consideration of National Culture and a Review of Contemporary Research and Future Trends." In *Handbook of Industrial, Work, & Organizational Psychology,* vol. 1: *Personnel Psychology,* edited by N. Anderson, D. Ones, H. Sinangil, and C. Viswesvaran. Thousand Oaks, CA: Sage Publications, 2001.

Flores, B., D. Olson, and C. Wolfe. "Judgmental Adjustment of Forecasts: A Comparison of Methods." *International Journal of Forecasting* (March 1992): 421–33.

Fong, G., D. Krantz, and R. Nisbett. "The Effects of Statistical Training on Thinking about Everyday Problems." *Cognitive Psychology* (July 1986): 253–92.

Ford, J., N. Schmitt, S. Schechtman, B. Hults, and M. Doherty. "Process Tracing Methods:

Contributions, Problems, and Neglected Research Questions." *Organizational Behavior and Human Decision Processes* (February 1989): 75–117.

Forgas, J. "Mood and Judgment: The Affect Infusion Model (AIM)." *Psychological Bulletin* (January 1995): 39–66.

Försterling, F. *Attribution: An Introduction to Theories, Research and Applications.* Philadelphia, PA: Taylor & Francis Group, 2001.

Fox, C., and R. Clemen. "Subjective Probability Assessment in Decision Analysis: Partition Dependence and Bias Toward the Ignorance Prior." *Management Science* (September 2005): 1417–32.

France, M. "The New Accountability." *Business Week* (July 26, 2004): 30–34.

Francis, J., and D. Philbrick. "Analysts' Decisions as Products of a Multi-Task Environment." *Journal of Accounting Research* (Autumn 1993): 216–30.

Francis, J., and L. Soffer. "The Relative Informativeness of Analysts' Stock Recommendations and Earnings Forecast Revisions." *Journal of Accounting Research* (Autumn 1997): 193–211.

Frank, R. *Choosing the Right Pond.* New York: Oxford University Press, 1985.

Frederick, D. "Auditors' Representation and Retrieval of Internal Control Knowledge." *The Accounting Review* (April 1991): 240–58.

Frederick, D., V. Heiman-Hoffman, and R. Libby. "The Structure of Auditors' Knowledge of Financial Statement Errors." *Auditing: A Journal of Practice & Theory* (Spring 1994): 1–21.

Frederick, D., and R. Libby. "Expertise and Auditors' Judgments of Conjunctive Events." *Journal of Accounting Research* (Autumn 1986): 270–90.

Frederickson, J., S. Peffer, and J. Pratt. "Performance Evaluation Judgments: Effects of Prior Experience under Different Performance Evaluation Schemes and Feedback Frequencies." *Journal of Accounting Research* (Spring 1999): 151–65.

Freeman, M., and D. Miller. "Effects of Locus of Control and Pacing on Performance of and Satisfaction with a Simulated Inspection Task." *Perceptual and Motor Skills* (December 1989): 779–85.

Friedman, J. "Aiming to Elevate the Conduct of Analysts." *Los Angeles Times* (August 19, 2002): C1.

Frisch, D., and R. Clemen. "Beyond Expected Utility: Rethinking Behavioral Decision Research." *Psychological Bulletin* (July 1994): 46–54.

Frisch, D., and S. Jones. "Assessing the Accuracy of Decisions." *Theory & Psychology* (February 1993): 115–35.

Froot, K., D. Scharfstein, and J. Stein. "Herd on the Street: Informational Inefficiencies in a Market with Short-Term Speculation." *Journal of Finance* (September 1992): 1461–84.

Frost, C. "Disclosure Policy Choices of UK Firms Receiving Modified Audit Reports." *Journal of Accounting and Economics* (July 1997): 163–87.

Frownfelter-Lohrke, C. "The Effects of Differing Information Presentations of General Purpose Financial Statements on Users' Decisions." *Journal of Information Systems* (Fall 1998): 99–107.

Fuerst, W., and P. Cheney. "Factors Affecting the Perceived Utilization of Computer-Based Decision Support Systems in the Oil Industry." *Decision Sciences* (October 1982): 554–69.

Funder, D. "Errors and Mistakes: Evaluating the Accuracy of Social Judgment." *Psychological Bulletin* (January 1987): 75–90.

Funder, D. "Personality." *Annual Review of Psychology* (2001): 197–221.

Gadarowski, C. "Financial Press Coverage and Expected Stock Returns." Working paper, Cornell University, 2004.

Gal, G., and P. Steinbart. "Interface Style and Training Task Difficulty as Determinants of Effective Computer-Assisted Knowledge Transfer." *Decision Sciences* (January–February 1992): 128–43.

Gallagher, K. "An Analyst Can be Key to Big Deals: Expertise Lends Credibility to Manager of Stock Offering." *The Milwaukee Journal Sentinel* (April 20, 1996): B1.

Ganguly, A., J. Kagel, and D. Moser. "The Effects of Biases in Probability Judgments on Market Prices." *Accounting, Organizations and Society* (No. 8 1994): 675–700.

Ganzach, Y., A. Kluger, and N. Klayman. "Making Decisions from an Interview: Expert

Measurement and Mechanical Combination." *Personnel Psychology* (Spring 2000): 1–20.

Gardner, H. *Intelligence Reframed: Multiple Intelligences for the 21st Century.* New York: Basic Books, 1999.

Gasparino, C. "Analysts' Contracts Link Pay to Deal Work." *Wall Street Journal* (May 6, 2002): C1.

Geis, F. "Self-Fulfilling Prophecies: A Social Psychological View of Gender." In *The Psychology of Gender,* edited by A. Beall and R. Sternberg. New York: Guilford Press, 1993.

Gentner, D., and A. Stevens. *Mental Models.* Hillsdale, NJ: Lawrence Erlbaum Associates, 1983.

Gervais, S., and T. Odean. "Learning to Be Overconfident." *Review of Financial Studies* (Spring 2001): 1–27.

Gettys, C., and S. Fisher. "Hypothesis Plausibility and Hypothesis Generation." *Organizational Behavior and Human Performance* (August 1979): 93–110.

Gettys, C., T. Mehle, and S. Fisher. "Plausibility Assessments in Hypothesis Generation." *Organizational Behavior and Human Decision Processes* (February 1986): 14–33.

Ghosh, D. "De-escalation Strategies: Some Experimental Evidence." *Behavioral Research in Accounting* (1997): 88–112.

Ghosh, D., and R. Lusch. "Outcome Effect, Controllability and Performance Evaluation of Managers: Some Field Evidence from Multi-Outlet Businesses." *Accounting, Organizations and Society* (May 2000): 411–25.

Ghosh, D., and S. Whitecotton. "Some Determinants of Analysts' Forecast Accuracy." *Behavioral Research in Accounting* (1997): S50–68.

Gibbins, M. "Deception: A Tricky Issue for Behavioral Research in Accounting and Auditing." *Auditing: A Journal of Practice and Theory* (Fall 1992): 113–26.

Gibbins, M., and J. Newton. "An Empirical Exploration of Complex Accountability in Public Accounting." *Journal of Accounting Research* (Autumn 1994): 165–86.

Gibbins, M., S. Salterio, and A. Webb. "Evidence about Auditor–Client Management Negotiation Concerning Client's Financial Reporting." *Journal of Accounting Research* (December 2001): 535–63.

Gibbins, M., and R. Swieringa. "Twenty Years of Judgment Research in Accounting and Auditing." In *Judgment and Decision-Making Research in Accounting and Auditing,* edited by R. Ashton and A. Ashton. Cambridge, MA: Cambridge University Press, 1995.

Gibbins, M., and K. Trotman. "Audit Review: Managers' Interpersonal Expectation and Conduct of the Review." *Contemporary Accounting Research* (Fall 2002): 411–44.

Gigerenzer, G., U. Hoffrage, and H. Kleinbolting. "Probabilistic Mental Models: A Brunswikian Theory of Confidence." *Psychological Review* (October 1991): 506–28.

Gigerenzer, G., P. Todd, and the ABC Research Group. *Simple Heuristics that Make Us Smart.* New York: Oxford University Press, 1999.

Gigone, D., and R. Hastie. "The Common Knowledge Effect: Information Sharing and Group Judgment." *Journal of Personality and Social Psychology* (No. 5 1993): 959–74.

Gigone, D., and R. Hastie. "Proper Analysis of the Accuracy of Group Judgments." *Psychological Bulletin* (January 1997): 149–67.

Gilbert, D., and P. Malone. "The Correspondence Bias." *Psychological Bulletin* (January 1995): 21–38.

Gilbert, D., B. Pelham, and D. Krull. "On Cognitive Busyness: When Person Perceivers Meet Persons Perceived." *Journal of Personality and Social Psychology* (May 1988): 733–40.

Gill, T. "Early Expert Systems: Where Are They Now?" *MIS Quarterly* (March 1995): 51–81.

Gilovich, T., and D. Griffin. "Introduction—Heuristics and Biases: Then and Now." In *Heuristics and Biases: The Psychology of Intuitive Judgment,* edited by T. Gilovich, D. Griffin, and D. Kahneman. New York: Cambridge University Press, 2002.

Gist, W., H. Goedde, and B. Ward. "The Influence of Mathematical Skills and Other Factors on Minority Student Performance in Principles of Accounting." *Issues in Accounting Education* (Spring 1996): 49–60.

Givoly, D., and J. Lakonishok. "The Information Content of Financial Analysts' Earnings Forecasts." *Journal of Accounting and Economics* (March 1979): 165–85.

Glaser, R., and M. Chi. Overview to *The Nature of Expertise,* edited by M. Chi, R. Glaser, and

M. Farr. Hillsdale, NJ: Lawrence Erlbaum, 1988.

Gleason, C., and C. Lee. "Analyst Forecast Revisions and Market Price Discovery." *The Accounting Review* (January 2003): 193–225.

Gleick, J. *Faster: The Acceleration of Just about Everything.* New York: Vintage, 2000.

Glover, S. "The Influence of Time Pressure and Accountability on Auditors' Processing of Nondiagnostic Information." *Journal of Accounting Research* (Autumn 1997): 213–26.

Glover, S., D. Prawitt, and B. Spilker. "The Influence of Decision Aids on User Behavior: Implications for Knowledge Acquisition and Inappropriate Reliance." *Organizational Behavior and Human Decision Processes* (November 1997): 232–55.

Gobeil, J., and F. Phillips. "Relating Case Presentation Style and Level of Student Knowledge to Fact Acquisition and Application in Accounting Case Analyses." *Issues in Accounting Education* (May 2001): 205–22.

Goldberg, L. "Man versus Model of Man: A Rationale, Plus Some Evidence, for a Method of Improving on Clinical Inferences." *Psychological Bulletin* (July 1970): 422–32.

Gonedes, N., N. Dopuch, and S. Penman. "Disclosure Rules, Information Production, and Capital Market Equilibrium: The Case of Forecast Disclosure Rules." *Journal of Accounting Research* (Spring 1976): 89–137.

Goodwin, J. "The Effects of Source Integrity and Consistency of Evidence on Auditors' Judgments." *Auditing: A Journal of Practice & Theory* (Fall 1999): 1–16.

Goodwin, P., and R. Fildes. "Judgmental Forecasts of Time Series Affected by Special Events: Does Providing a Statistical Forecast Improve Accuracy?" *Journal of Behavioral Decision Making* (February 1999): 37–53.

Goodwin, P., and G. Wright. "Improving Judgmental Time Series Forecasting: A Review of the Guidance Provided by Research." *International Journal of Forecasting* (August 1993): 147–61.

Graham, J. "Herding among Investment Newsletters: Theory and Evidence." *Journal of Finance* (February 1999): 237–68.

Graham, J., and C. Harvey. "Market Timing Ability and Volatility Implied in Investment Newsletters' Asset Allocation Recommendations." *Journal of Financial Economics* (November 1996): 397–421.

Gramling, A. "External Auditors' Reliance on Work Performed by Internal Auditors: The Influence of Fee Pressure on this Reliance Decision." *Auditing: A Journal of Practice and Theory* (1999): S117–35.

Graves, L., and R. Karren. "Interviewer Decision Processes and Effectiveness: An Experimental Policy-Capturing Investigation." *Personnel Psychology* (Summer 1992): 313–40.

Gredler, M. *Learning and Instruction: Theory into Practice,* 5th ed. Upper Saddle River, NJ: Pearson Education, 2005.

Green, D., and J. Swets. *Signal Detection Theory and Psychophysics.* Oxford: John Wiley, 1966.

Greenberg, J., and R. Folger. "Procedural Justice, Participation, and the Fair Process Effect in Groups and Organizations." In *Basic Group Process,* edited by P. Paulus. New York: Springer-Verlag, 1983.

Greenberg, P., and R. Greenberg. "Social Utility in a Transfer Pricing Situation: The Impact of Contextual Factors." *Behavioral Research in Accounting* (1997): 113–53.

Greeno, J. "Indefinite Goals in Well-structured Problems." *Psychological Review* (November 1976): 479–91.

Greer, W., Jr. "Theory versus Practice in Risk Analysis: An Empirical Study." *The Accounting Review* (July 1974): 496–505.

Griffin, D., and A. Tversky. "The Weighing of Evidence and the Determinants of Confidence." *Cognitive Psychology* (July 1992): 411–35.

Grinblatt, M., S. Titman, and R. Wermers. "Momentum Investment Strategies, Portfolio Performance, and Herding: A Study of Mutual Fund Behavior." *American Economic Review* (December 1995): 1088–1105.

Grove, W., and P. Meehl. "Comparative Efficiency of Information (Subjective, Impressionistic) and Formal (Mechanical, Algorithmic) Prediction Procedures: The Clinical-Statistical Controversy." *Psychology, Public Policy, and Law* (May 1996): 293–323.

Grove, W., D. Zald, B. Lebow, B. Snitz, and C. Nelson. "Clinical versus Mechanical Prediction: A Meta-Analysis." *Psychological Assessment* (March 2000): 19–30.

Gruber, M. "Another Puzzle: The Growth in Actively Managed Mutual Funds." *Journal of Finance* (July 1996): 783–810.

Guerard, J., Jr. "Linear Constraints, Robust-Weighting and Efficient Composite Modeling." *Journal of Forecasting* (July–September 1987): 193–99.

Guilford, J. *Personality.* New York: McGraw-Hill, 1959.

Guimaraes, T., M. Igbaria, and M. Lu. "The Determinants of DSS Success: An Integrated Model." *Decision Sciences* (March–April 1992): 409–30.

Guion, R. *Assessment, Measurement, and Prediction for Personnel Decisions.* Mahwah, NJ: Lawrence Erlbaum, 1998.

Guion, R., and S. Highhouse. *Essentials of Personnel Assessment and Selection.* Mahwah, NJ: Lawrence Erlbaum, 2006.

Gully, S., D. Devine, and D. Whitney. "A Meta-Analysis of Cohesion and Performance: Effects of Level of Analysis and Task Interdependence." *Small Group Research* (November 1995): 497–520.

Gupta, M., and R. King. "An Experimental Investigation of the Effect of Cost Information and Feedback on Product Cost Decisions." *Contemporary Accounting Research* (Spring 1997): 99–127.

Gupta, P., N. Umanath, and M. Dirsmith. "Supervision Practices and Audit Effectiveness: An Empirical Analysis of GAO Audits." *Behavioral Research in Accounting* (1999): 27–49.

Gutner, T. "Women & Co.: Will Citi Get it Right?" *Business Week* (October 29, 2001): 96.

Guzzo, R., and M. Dickson. "Teams in Organizations: Recent Research on Performance and Effectiveness." *Annual Review of Psychology* (1997): 307–38.

Guzzo, R., R. Jette, and R. Katzell. "The Effects of Psychologically Based Intervention Programs on Worker Productivity: A Meta-Analysis." *Personnel Psychology* (Summer 1985): 275–91.

Guzzo, R., E. Salas, and Associates. *Team Effectiveness and Decision Making in Organizations.* San Francisco: Jossey-Bass, 1995.

Hackenbrack, K. "Implications of Seemingly Irrelevant Evidence in Audit Judgment." *Journal of Accounting Research* (Spring 1992): 126–36.

Hackenbrack, K., and W. Knechel. "Resource Allocation Decisions in Audit Engagements." *Contemporary Accounting Research* (Fall 1997): 481–99.

Hackenbrack, K., and M. Nelson. "Auditors' Incentives and Their Application of Financial Accounting Standards." *The Accounting Review* (January 1996): 43–59.

Hackman, R. "Toward Understanding the Role of Tasks in Behavioral Research." *Acta Psychologica* (August 1969): 97–128.

Halabi, A., J. Tuovinen, and A. Farley. "Empirical Evidence on the Relative Efficiency of Worked Examples versus Problem-Solving Exercises in Accounting Principles Instruction." *Issues in Accounting Education* (February 2005): 21–32.

Halpern, D. *Sex Differences in Cognitive Abilities,* 3rd ed. Mahwah, NJ: Lawrence Erlbaum, 2000.

Hamilton, R., and W. Wright. "Internal Control Judgments and Effects of Experience: Replications and Extensions." *Journal of Accounting Research* (Autumn 1982, Part II): 756–65.

Hammersley, J., K. Kadous, and A. Magro. "Cognitive and Strategic Components of the Explanation Effect." *Organizational Behavior and Human Decision Processes* (May 1997): 149–58.

Hammond, K. *Human Judgment and Social Policy: Irreducible Uncertainty, Inevitable Error, Unavoidable Injustice.* New York: Oxford University Press, 1996.

Hammond, K., and T. Stewart. *The Essential Brunswik: Beginnings, Explications, Applications.* New York: Oxford University Press, 2001.

Hammond, K., T. Stewart, B. Brehmer, and D. Steinmann. "Social Judgment Theory." In *Human Judgment and Decision Processes,* edited by M. Kaplan and S. Schwartz. New York: Academic Press, 1975.

Hand, J. "A Test of the Extended Functional Fixation Hypothesis." *The Accounting Review* (October 1990): 740–63.

Hansen, R. "Commonsense Attribution." *Journal of Personality and Social Psychology* (December 1980): 996–1009.

Harding, N., and K. Trotman. "Hierarchical Differences in Audit Workpaper Review Performance." *Contemporary Accounting Research* (Winter 1999): 671–84.

Harp, S., and R. Mayer. "How Seductive Details Do Their Damage: A Theory of Cognitive Interest in Science Learning." *Journal of Educational Psychology* (August 1998): 414–34.

Harper, R., Jr., W. Mister, and J. Strawser. "The Impact of New Pension Disclosure Rules on Perceptions of Debt." *Journal of Accounting Research* (Autumn 1987): 327–30.

Harrell, A. "The Decision-Making Behavior of Air Force Officers and the Management Control Process." *The Accounting Review* (October 1977): 833–41.

Harrell, A., and P. Harrison. "An Incentive to Shirk, Privately Held Information, and Managers' Project Evaluation Decisions." *Accounting, Organizations and Society* (October 1994): 569–77.

Harrell, A., and A. Wright. "Empirical Evidence on the Validity and Reliability of Behaviorally Anchored Rating Scales for Auditors." *Auditing: A Journal of Practice & Theory* (Fall 1990): 134–49.

Harrison, G., and J. McKinnon. "Cross-Cultural Research in Management Control Systems Design: A Review of the Current State." *Accounting, Organizations and Society* (July–August 1999): 483–506.

Harrison, K., and L. Tomassini. "Judging the Probability of a Contingent Loss: An Empirical Study." *Contemporary Accounting Research* (Spring 1989): 642–48.

Harrison, P., and A. Harrell. "Impact of 'Adverse Selection' on Managers' Project Evaluations." *Academy of Management Journal* (June 1993): 635–43.

Harrison, P., S. West, and J. Reneau. "Initial Attributions and Information-Seeking by Superiors and Subordinates in Production Variance Investigations." *The Accounting Review* (April 1988): 307–20.

Harvey, D., J. Rhode, and K. Merchant. "Accounting Aggregation: User Preferences and Decision Making." *Accounting, Organizations and Society* (No. 3 1979): 187–210.

Harvey, N. "Improving Judgment in Forecasting." In *Principles of Forecasting: A Handbook for Researchers and Practitioners,* edited by J. Armstrong. Boston: Kluwer Academic Publishers, 2001.

Harvey, N., and I. Fischer. "Taking Advice: Accepting Help, Improving Judgment, and Sharing Responsibility." *Organizational Behavior and Human Decision Processes* (May 1997): 117–33.

Harvey, N., C. Harries, and I. Fischer. "Using Advice and Assessing Its Quality." *Organizational Behavior and Human Decision Processes* (March 2000): 252–73.

Hasher, L., D. Goldstein, and T. Topping. "Frequency and the Conference of Referential Validity." *Journal of Verbal Learning and Verbal Behavior* (February 1977): 107–12.

Haskell, R. *Transfer of Learning: Cognition, Instruction, and Reasoning.* San Diego, CA: Academic Press, 2001.

Hastie, R., and R. Dawes. *Rational Choice in an Uncertain World: The Psychology of Judgment and Decision Making.* Thousand Oaks, CA: Sage Publications, 2001.

Hastie, R., and B. Park. "The Relationship between Memory and Judgment Depends on Whether the Judgment Task Is Memory-Based or On-Line." *Psychological Review* (July 1986): 258–68.

Hastie, R., and K. Rasinski. "The Concept of Accuracy in Social Judgment." In *The Social Psychology of Knowledge,* edited by D. Bar-Tal and A. Kruglanski. New York: Cambridge University Press, 1988.

Hausman, T. "Executive Pay (A Special Report)." *Wall Street Journal* (April 8, 1999): R9.

Hawkins, S., and R. Hastie. "Hindsight: Biased Judgments of Past Events after the Outcomes Are Known." *Psychological Bulletin* (May 1990): 311–27.

Hawkins, S., and S. Hoch. "Low-Involvement Learning: Memory without Evaluation." *Journal of Consumer Research* (September 1992): 212–25.

Hawkins, S., S. Hoch, and J. Meyers-Levy. "Low-Involvement Learning: Repetition and Coherence in Familiarity and Belief." *Journal of Consumer Psychology* (July 2001): 1–11.

Hayes, R. "The Impact of Trading Commission Incentives on Analysts' Stock Coverage Decisions and Earnings Forecasts." *Journal of*

Accounting Research (Autumn 1998): 299–320.

Haynes, C. "Auditors' Evaluation of Evidence Obtained through Management Inquiry: A Cascaded-Inference Approach." *Auditing: A Journal of Practice & Theory* (Fall 1999): 87–104.

Hayward, M., and W. Boeker. "Power and Conflicts of Interest in Professional Firms: Evidence from Investment Banking." *Administrative Science Quarterly* (March 1998): 1–22.

Healy, P., and J. Wahlen. "A Review of the Earnings Management Literature and Its Implications for Standard Setting." *Accounting Horizons* (December 1999): 365–83.

Heath, C., and R. Gonzalez. "Interaction with Others Increases Decision Confidence but Not Decision Quality: Evidence against Information Collection Views of Interactive Decision Making." *Organizational Behavior and Human Decision Processes* (March 1995): 305–26.

Heath, C., R. Larrick, and J. Klayman. "Cognitive Repairs: How Organizational Practices Can Compensate for Individual Shortcomings." *Research in Organizational Behavior* (1998): 1–37.

Heider, F. *The Psychology of Interpersonal Relations.* Hillsdale, NJ: Lawrence Erlbaum Associates, 1958.

Heiman, V. "Auditors' Assessments of the Likelihood of Error Explanations in Analytical Review." *The Accounting Review* (October 1990): 875–90.

Heiman-Hoffman, V., D. Moser, and J. Joseph. "The Impact of an Auditor's Initial Hypothesis on Subsequent Performance at Identifying Actual Errors." *Contemporary Accounting Research* (Spring 1995): 763–79.

Heintz, J., and G. White. "Auditor Judgment in Analytical Review—Some Further Evidence." *Auditing: A Journal of Practice and Theory* (Spring 1989): 22–39.

Heit, E. "Knowledge and Concept Learning." In *Knowledge, Concepts, and Categories,* edited by K. Lamberts and D. Shanks. Cambridge, MA: MIT Press, 1997.

Helleloid, R. "Hindsight Judgments about Taxpayers' Expectations." *Journal of the American Taxation Association* (Spring 1988): 31–46.

Hendrickxx, L., C. Vlek, and H. Oppewal. "Relative Importance of Scenario Information and Frequency Information in the Judgment of Risk." *Acta Psychologica* (September 1989): 41–63.

Heneman, R., and K. Wexley. "The Effects of Time Delay in Rating and Amount of Information Observed on Performance Rating Accuracy." *Academy of Management Journal* (December 1983): 677–86.

Henry, R. "Improving Group Judgment Accuracy: Information Sharing and Determining the Best Member." *Organizational Behavior and Human Decision Processes* (May 1995): 190–97.

Henry, R., J. Kmet, E. Desrosiers, and A. Landa. "Examining the Impact of Interpersonal Cohesiveness on Group Accuracy Interventions: The Importance of Matching versus Buffering." *Organizational Behavior and Human Decision Processes* (January 2002): 25–43.

Henry, R., O. Strickland, S. Yorges, and D. Ladd. "Helping Groups Determine Their Most Accurate Member." *Journal of Applied Social Psychology* (July 1996): 1153–70.

Hermanson, D. "The Effect of Self-Generated Elaboration on Students' Recall of Tax and Accounting Material: Further Evidence." *Issues in Accounting Education* (Fall 1994): 301–18.

Herz, P., and J. Schultz Jr. "The Role of Procedural and Declarative Knowledge in Performing Accounting Tasks." *Behavioral Research in Accounting* (1999): 1–26.

Hewstone, M. *Causal Attribution: From Cognitive Processes to Collective Beliefs.* Cambridge, MA: Blackwell Publishers, 1989.

Hill, G. "Group versus Individual Performance: Are N + 1 Heads Better Than One?" *Psychological Bulletin* (May 1982): 517–38.

Hilton, R., R. Swieringa, and M. Turner. "Product Pricing, Accounting Costs and Use of Product-Costing Systems." *The Accounting Review* (April 1988): 195–218.

Hinsz, V., R. Tindale, and D. Vollrath. "The Emerging Conceptualization of Groups as Information Processors." *Psychological Bulletin* (January 1997): 43–64.

Hirsch, M., Jr. "Disaggregated Probabilistic Accounting Information: The Effect of Sequential Events on Expected Value Maximization Decisions." *Journal of Accounting Research* (Autumn 1978): 254–69.

Hirshleifer, D. "Investor Psychology and Asset Prices." *The Journal of Finance* (August 2001): 1533–97.

Hirshleifer, D., and T. Shumway. "Good Day Sunshine: Stock Returns and the Weather." *Journal of Finance* (June 2003): 1009–32.

Hirst, D. "Auditors' Sensitivity to Source Reliability." *Journal of Accounting Research* (Spring 1994): 113–26.

Hirst, D., and P. Hopkins. "Comprehensive Income Reporting and Analysts' Valuation Judgments." *Journal of Accounting Research* (1998): S47–75.

Hirst, D., P. Hopkins, and J. Wahlen. "Fair Values, Income Measurement, and Bank Analysts' Risk and Valuation Judgments." *The Accounting Review* (April 2004): 453–72.

Hirst, D., K. Jackson, and L. Koonce. "Improving Financial Reports by Revealing the Accuracy of Prior Estimates." *Contemporary Accounting Research* (Spring 2003): 165–93.

Hirst, D., and L. Koonce. "Audit Analytical Procedures: A Field Investigation." *Contemporary Accounting Research* (Fall 1996): 457–86.

Hirst, D., L. Koonce, and J. Miller. "The Joint Effect of Management's Prior Forecast Accuracy and the Form of Its Financial Forecasts on Investor Judgment." *Journal of Accounting Research* (1999): S101–24.

Hirst, D., L. Koonce, and P. Simko. "Investor Reactions to Financial Analysts' Research Reports." *Journal of Accounting Research* (Autumn 1995): 335–51.

Hirst, M., and S. Lowy. "The Linear Additive and Interactive Effects of Budgetary Goal Difficulty and Feedback on Performance." *Accounting, Organizations and Society* (No. 5 1990): 425–36.

Hirst, M., and P. Luckett. "The Relative Effectiveness of Different Types of Feedback in Performance Evaluation." *Behavioral Research in Accounting* (1992): 1–22.

Hirst, M., and P. Yetton. "The Effects of Budget Goals and Task Interdependence on the Level of and Variance in Performance: A Research Note." *Accounting, Organizations and Society* (April 1999): 205–16.

Hirt, E., and K. Markman. "Multiple Explanation: A Consider-an-Alternative Strategy for Debiasing Judgments." *Journal of Personality and Social Psychology* (December 1995): 1069–86.

Hirt, E., and S. Sherman. "The Role of Prior Knowledge in Explaining Hypothetical Events." *Journal of Experimental Social Psychology* (November 1985): 519–43.

Ho, J., and R. May. "Auditors' Causal Probability Judgments in Analytical Procedures for Audit Planning." *Behavioral Research in Accounting* (1993): 78–101.

Ho, J., and W. Rodgers. "A Review of Accounting Research on Cognitive Characteristics." *Journal of Accounting Literature* (1993): 101–130.

Ho, T., and R. Michaely. "Information Quality and Market Efficiency." *Journal of Financial and Quantitative Analysis* (March 1988): 53–70.

Hoch, S. "Availability and Interference in Predictive Judgments." *Journal of Experimental Psychology: Learning, Memory and Cognition* (October 1984): 649–62.

Hoch, S. "Counterfactual Reasoning and Accuracy in Predicting Personal Events." *Journal of Experimental Psychology: Learning, Memory, and Cognition* (October 1985): 719–31.

Hodder, L., L. Koonce, and M. McAnally. "SEC Market Risk Disclosures: Implications for Judgment and Decision Making." *Accounting Horizons* (March 2001): 49–70

Hodge, F. "Hyperlinking Unaudited Information to Audited Financial Statements: Effects on Investor Judgments." *The Accounting Review* (October 2001): 675–91.

Hodge, F. "Investors' Perceptions of Earnings Quality, Auditor Independence, and the Usefulness of Audited Financial Information." *Accounting Horizons* (2003): S37–48.

Hodge, F., J. Kennedy, and L. Maines. "Does Search-Facilitating Technology Improve the Transparency of Financial Reporting?" *The Accounting Review* (July 2004): 687–703.

Hoffman, P. "The Paramorphic Representation of Clinical Judgment." *Psychological Bulletin* (March 1960): 116–31.

Hoffman, R., ed. *The Psychology of Expertise: Cognitive Research and Empirical AI.* New York: Springer-Verlag, 1992.

Hoffman, V., and J. Patton. "Accountability, the Dilution Effect, and Conservatism in Auditors' Fraud Judgments." *Journal of Accounting Research* (Autumn 1997): 227–37.

Hofstede, G. *Culture's Consequences: International Differences in Work-Related Values.* Beverly Hills, CA: Sage Publications, 1980.

Hofstedt, T., and J. Kinard. "A Strategy for Behavioral Accounting Research." *The Accounting Review* (January 1970): 38–54.

Hogarth, R. "Beyond Discrete Biases: Functional and Dysfunctional Aspects of Judgmental Heuristics." *Psychological Bulletin* (September 1981): 197–217.

Hogarth, R. *Judgement and Choice,* 2nd ed. New York: John Wiley, 1987.

Hogarth, R. "Accounting for Decisions and Decisions for Accounting." *Accounting, Organizations and Society* (July 1993): 407–24.

Hogarth, R., and H. Einhorn. "Order Effects in Belief Updating: The Belief-Adjustment Model." *Cognitive Psychology* (January 1992): 1–55.

Hollingshead, A., J. McGrath, and K. O'Connor. "Group Task Performance and Communication Technology: A Longitudinal Study of Computer-Mediated versus Face-to-Face Work Groups." *Small Group Research* (August 1993): 307–33.

Holt, D. "Auditors and Base Rates Revisited." *Accounting, Organizations and Society* (No. 6 1987): 571–78.

Holt, D., and P. Morrow. "Risk Assessment Judgments of Auditors and Bank Lenders: A Comparative Analysis of Conformance to Bayes' Theorem." *Accounting, Organizations and Society* (August 1992): 549–59.

Hong, H., and J. Kubik. "Analyzing the Analysts: Career Concerns and Biased Earnings Forecasts." *Journal of Finance* (February 2003): 313–51.

Hong, H., J. Kubik, and A. Solomon. "Security Analysts' Career Concerns and Herding of Earnings Forecasts." *RAND Journal of Economics* (Spring 2000): 121–44.

Hong, H., J. Kubik, and J. Stein. "Social Interaction and Stock-Market Participation." *The Journal of Finance* (February 2004): 137–63.

Hong, Y., C. Chiu, C. Dweck, and R. Sacks. "Implicit Theories and Evaluative Processes in Person Cognition." *Journal of Experimental Social Psychology* (May 1997): 296–323.

Hopkins, P. "The Effect of Financial Statement Classification of Hybrid Financial Instruments on Financial Analysts' Stock Price Judgments." *Journal of Accounting Research* (1996): S33–50.

Hopkins, P., R. Houston, and M. Peters. "Purchase, Pooling, and Equity Analysts' Valuation Judgments." *The Accounting Review* (July 2000): 257–81.

Hopwood, W., and J. McKeown. "Evidence on Surrogates for Earnings Expectations within a Capital Market Context." *Journal of Accounting, Auditing & Finance* (Summer 1990): 339–63.

Hopwood, W., J. McKeown, and J. Mutchler. "A Reexamination of Auditor versus Model Accuracy within the Context of the Going-Concern Opinion Decision." *Contemporary Accounting Research* (Spring 1994): 409–31.

Hoskin, R. "Opportunity Cost and Behavior." *Journal of Accounting Research* (Spring 1983): 78–95.

Hosoda, M., E. Stone-Romero, and O. Coats. "The Effects of Physical Attractiveness on Job-Related Outcomes: A Meta-Analysis of Experimental Studies." *Personnel Psychology* (Summer 2003): 431–62.

Hough, L., and D. Ones. "The Structure, Measurement, Validity, and Use of Personality Variables in Industrial Work, and Organizational Psychology." In *Handbook of Industrial, Work & Organizational Psychology,* vol. 1: *Personnel Psychology,* edited by N. Anderson, D. Ones, H. Sinangil, and C. Viswesvaran. Thousand Oaks, CA: Sage Publications, 2001.

Hough, L., and F. Oswald. "Personnel Selection: Looking Toward the Future—Remembering the Past." *Annual Review of Psychology* (2000): 631–64.

Houghton, K. "Accounting Data and the Prediction of Business Failure: The Setting of Priors and the Age of Data." *Journal of Accounting Research* (Spring 1984): 361–68.

Houston, R. "The Effects of Fee Pressure and Client Risk on Audit Seniors' Time Budget Decisions." *Auditing: A Journal of Practice and Theory* (Fall 1999): 70–86.

Houston, R., M. Peters, and J. Pratt. "The Audit Risk Model, Business Risk and Audit-Planning Decisions." *The Accounting Review* (July 1999): 281–98.

Hovland, C., I. Janis, and H. Kelley. *Communication and Persuasion: Psychological Studies of Opinion Change.* New Haven, Connecticut: Yale University Press, 1953.

Hronsky, J., and K. Houghton. "The Meaning of a Defined Accounting Concept: Regulatory Changes and the Effect on Auditor Decision Making." *Accounting, Organizations and Society* (March 2001): 123–39.

Huber, G. "Cognitive Style as a Basis for MIS and DSS Design: Much Ado about Nothing?" *Management Science* (May 1983): 567–79.

Huffcutt, A., and W. Arthur Jr. "Hunter and Hunter (1984) Revisited: Interview Validity for Entry-Level Jobs." *Journal of Applied Psychology* (March 1994): 184–90.

Huffcut, A., J. Conway, P. Roth, and N. Stone. "Identification and Meta-Analytic Assessment of Psychological Constructs Measured in Employment Interviews." *Journal of Applied Psychology* (September 2001): 897–913.

Hugon, J. "Effects of Redundancy in Media Coverage on Nonprofessional Investors' Earnings Forecasts." Working paper, Georgia State University, 2006.

Humphreys, M., and W. Revelle. "Personality, Motivation, and Performance: A Theory of the Relationship between Individual Differences and Information Processing." *Psychological Review* (April 1984): 153–84.

Hunter, J. "Cognitive Ability, Cognitive Aptitudes, Job Knowledge, and Job Performance." *Journal of Vocational Psychology* (December 1986): 340–62.

Hunter, J., and R. Hunter. "Validity and Utility of Alternative Predictors of Job Performance." *Psychological Bulletin* (July 1984): 72–98.

Hunter, J., and F. Schmidt. "Racial and Gender Bias in Ability and Achievement Tests: Resolving the Apparent Paradox." *Psychology, Public Policy, and Law* (February 2000): 151–58.

Hunton, J. "Mitigating the Common Information Sampling Bias Inherent in Small-Group Discussion." *Behavioral Research in Accounting* (2001): 171–94.

Hunton, J. "Blending Information and Communication Technology with Accounting Research." *Accounting Horizons* (March 2002): 55–67.

Hunton, J., and R. McEwen. "An Assessment of the Relation between Analysts' Earnings Forecast Accuracy, Motivational Incentives and Cognitive Information Search Strategy." *The Accounting Review* (October 1997): 497–515.

Hunton, J., R. McEwen, and S. Bhattacharjee. "Toward an Understanding of the Risky Choice Behavior of Professional Financial Analysts." *Journal of Psychology and Financial Markets* (December 2001): 182–89.

Hunton, J., B. Wier, and D. Stone. "Succeeding in Managerial Accounting, Part 2: A Structural Equations Analysis." *Accounting, Organizations and Society* (November 2000): 751–62.

Hursch, C., K. Hammond, and J. Hursch. "Some Methodological Considerations in Multiple Cue Probability Studies." *Psychological Review* (January 1964): 42–60.

Huselid, M. "The Impact of Human Resource Management Practices on Turnover, Productivity, and Corporate Financial Performance." *Academy of Management Journal* (June 1995): 635–72.

Huselid, M., S. Jackson, and R. Schuler. "Technical and Strategic Human Resource Judgement Effectiveness as Determinants of Firm Performance." *Academy of Management Journal* (February 1997): 171–88.

Hussein, M., and A. Rosman. "The Ex Ante Role of Behavioral Research in Setting Financial Accounting Policy." In *Behavioral Accounting Research: Foundations and Frontiers,* edited by V. Arnold and S. Sutton. Sarasota, FL: American Accounting Association, 1997.

Hutton, A., G. Miller, and D. Skinner. "The Role of Supplementary Statements with Management Earnings Forecasts." *Journal of Accounting Research* (December 2003): 867–90.

Hwang, M., and B. Wu. "The Effectiveness of Computer Graphics for Decision Support: A Meta-Analytical Integration of Research Findings." *Database* (Fall 1990): 11–20.

Hyatt, T., and D. Prawitt. "Does Congruence between Audit Structure and Auditors' Locus of Control Affect Job Performance?" *The Accounting Review* (April 2001): 263–74.

Ilgen, D., J. Barnes-Farrell, and D. McKellin. "Performance Appraisal Process Research in the 1980s: What Has It Contributed to Appraisals in Use?" *Organizational Behavior and Human Decision Processes* (April 1993): 321–68.

Institutional Investor Web site. "Research and Rankings: The 2002 All-America Research Team." (February 23, 2003), http://www.institutionalinvestor.com.

Intons-Peterson, M., and J. Fournier. "External and Internal Memory Aids: When and How Often Do We Use Them?" *Journal of Experimental Psychology: General* (August 1986): 267–80.

Iselin, E. "The Effects of Information Load and Information Diversity on Decision Quality in a Structured Decision Task." *Accounting, Organizations and Society* (No. 2 1988): 147–64.

Iselin, E. "The Impact of Information Diversity on Information Overload Effects in Unstructured Managerial Decision Making." *Journal of Information Science* (August 1989): 163–73.

Isen, A., and N. Geva. "The Influence of Positive Affect on Acceptable Level of Risk: The Person with a Large Canoe Has a Large Worry." *Organizational Behavior and Human Decision Processes* (April 1987): 145–54.

Isen, A., and R. Patrick. "The Effects of Positive Feelings on Risk Taking: When the Chips Are Down." *Organizational Behavior and Human Performance* (April 1983): 194–202.

Ismail, Z., and K. Trotman. "The Impact of the Review Process in Hypothesis Generation Tasks." *Accounting, Organizations and Society* (July 1995): 345–57.

Jackson, B., and V. Milliron. "Tax Compliance Research: Findings, Problems, and Prospects." *Journal of Accounting Literature* (No. 5 1986): 125–65.

Jacob, J., T. Lys, and M. Neale. "Expertise in Forecasting Performance of Security Analysts." *Journal of Accounting and Economics* (November 1999): 51–82.

Jacoby, J., A. Kuss, D. Mazursky, and T. Troutman. "Effectiveness of Security Analyst Information Accessing Strategies: A Computer Interactive Assessment." *Computers in Human Behavior* (No. 1 1985): 95–113.

Jacoby, J., D. Mazursky, T. Troutman, and A. Kuss. "When Feedback Is Ignored: Disutility of Outcome Feedback." *Journal of Applied Psychology* (August 1984): 531–45.

Jacoby, J., T. Troutman, A. Kuss, and D. Mazursky. "Experience and Expertise in Complex Decision Making." In *Advances in Consumer Research,* vol. 13, edited by R. Lutz. Provo, UT: Association for Consumer Research, 1986.

Jaffe, J., and J. Mahoney. "The Performance of Investment Newsletters." *Journal of Financial Economics* (August 1999): 289–307.

Jamal, K., P. Johnson, and R. Berryman. "Detecting Framing Effects in Financial Statements." *Contemporary Accounting Research* (Fall 1995): 85–105.

Jamal, K., and H. Tan. "Can Auditors Predict the Choices Made by Other Auditors?" *Journal of Accounting Research* (December 2001): 583–97.

Janis, I. *Groupthink,* 2nd ed. Boston: Houghton Mifflin, 1982.

Jarvenpaa, S., and G. Dickson. "Graphics and Managerial Decision Making: Research Based Guidelines." *Communications of the ACM* (June 1988): 764–74.

Jeffrey, C. "The Relation of Judgment, Personal Involvement, and Experience in the Audit of Bank Loans." *The Accounting Review* (October 1992): 802–20.

Jenkins, G., Jr., A. Mitra, N. Gupta, and J. Shaw. "Are Financial Incentives Related to Performance? A Meta-Analytic Review of Empirical Research." *Journal of Applied Psychology* (October 1998): 777–87.

Jenkins, J., and C. Haynes. "The Persuasiveness of Client Preferences: An Investigation of the Impact of Preference Timing and Client Credibility." *Auditing: A Journal of Practice & Theory* (March 2003): 143–54.

Jennings, D., T. Amabile, and L. Ross. "Informal Covariation Assessment: Data-Based versus Theory-Based Judgments." In *Judgment under Uncertainty: Heuristics and Biases,* edited by D. Kahneman, P. Slovic, and A. Tversky. New York: Cambridge University Press, 1982.

Jennings, M., D. Kneer, and P. Reckers. "The Significance of Audit Decision Aids and Precase Jurists' Attitudes on Perceptions of Audit Firm Culpability and Liability." *Contemporary Accounting Research* (Spring 1993): 489–507.

Jensen, M. "Corporate Budgeting Is Broken— Let's Fix It." *Harvard Business Review* (November 2001): 94–101.

Jensen, R. "An Experimental Design for Study of Effects of Accounting Variations in Decision Making." *Journal of Accounting Research* (Autumn 1966): 224–38.

Jiambalvo, J. "Performance Evaluation and Directed Job Effort: Model Development and Analysis in a CPA Firm Setting." *Journal of Accounting Research* (Autumn 1979): 436–55.

Jiambalvo, J., and W. Waller. "Decomposition and Assessments of Audit Risk." *Auditing: A Journal of Practice & Theory* (Spring 1984): 80–88.

Jiambalvo, J., D. Watson, and J. Baumler. "An Examination of Performance Evaluation Decisions in CPA Firm Subunits." *Accounting, Organizations and Society* (No. 1 1983): 13–29.

Jiambalvo, J., and N. Wilner. "Auditor Evaluation of Contingent Claims." *Auditing: A Journal of Practice & Theory* (Fall 1985): 1–11.

Joe, J. "Why Press Coverage of a Client Influences the Audit Opinion." *Journal of Accounting Research* 41 (March 2003): 109–34.

Johnson, E. "Expertise and Decision under Uncertainty: Performance and Process." In *The Nature of Expertise,* edited by M. Chi, R. Glaser, and M. Farr. Hillsdale, NJ: Lawrence Erlbaum, 1988.

Johnson, E. "Auditor Memory for Audit Evidence: Effects of Group Assistance, Time Delay, and Memory Task." *Auditing: A Journal of Practice and Theory* (Spring 1994): 36–56.

Johnson, E., and A. Tversky. "Affect, Generalization, and the Perception of Risk." *Journal of Personality and Social Psychology* (July 1983): 20–31.

Johnson, L. "An Empirical Investigation of the Effects of Advocacy on Preparers' Evaluations of Judicial Evidence." *Journal of the American Taxation Association* (Spring 1993): 1–22.

Johnson, P., A. Durán, F. Hassebrock, J. Moller, M. Prietula, P. Feltovich, and D. Swanson. "Expertise and Error in Diagnostic Reasoning." *Cognitive Science* (September 1981): 235–83.

Johnson, P., S. Grazioli, and K. Jamal. "Fraud Detection: Intentionality and Deception in Cognition." *Accounting, Organizations and Society* (July 1993): 467–88.

Johnson, P., K. Jamal, and R. Berryman. "Effects of Framing on Auditor Decisions." *Organizational Behavior and Human Decision Processes* (October 1991a): 75–105.

Johnson, R., R. Rennie, and G. Wells. "Outcome Trees and Baseball: A Study of Expertise and List-Length Effects." *Organizational Behavior and Human Decision Processes* (December 1991b): 324–40.

Johnson, V., and S. Kaplan. "Experimental Evidence on the Effects of Accountability on Auditor Judgments." *Auditing: A Journal of Practice & Theory* (1991): S96–107.

Johnson, W. "'Representativeness' in Judgmental Predictions of Corporate Bankruptcy." *The Accounting Review* (January 1983): 78–97.

Johnstone, K., J. Bedard, and S. Biggs. "Aggressive Client Reporting: Factors Affecting Auditors' Generation of Financial Reporting Alternatives." *Auditing: A Journal of Practice and Theory* (March 2002): 47–65.

Jones, E., and K. Davis. "From Acts to Dispositions: The Attribution Process in Person Perception." In *Advances in Experimental Social Psychology,* vol. 2, edited by L. Berkowitz. New York: Academic Press, 1965.

Jones, E., and R. Nisbett. "The Actor and the Observer: Divergent Perceptions of the Causes of Behavior." In *Attribution: Perceiving the Causes of Behavior,* edited by E. Jones, D. Kanouse, H. Kelley, R. Nisbett, S. Valins, and B. Weiner. Morristown, NJ: General Learning Press, 1971.

Jones, R., J. Sanchez, G. Parameswaran, J. Phelps, C. Shoptaugh, M. Williams, and S. White. "Selection or Training? A Two-Fold Test of the Validity of Job-Analytic Ratings of Trainability." *Journal of Business and Psychology* (Spring 2001): 363–89.

Jonsson, A., and C. Allwood. "Stability and Variability in the Realism of Confidence Judgments over Time, Content Domain, and Gender." *Personality and Individual Differences* (March 2003): 559–74.

Josephs, R., R. Larrick, C. Steele, and R. Nisbett. "Protecting the Self from Negative

Consequences of Risky Decisions." *Journal of Personality and Social Psychology* (January 1992): 26–37.

Joyce, E. "Expert Judgment in Audit Program Planning." *Journal of Accounting Research* (1976): S29–60.

Joyce, E., and G. Biddle. "Anchoring and Adjustment in Probabilistic Inference in Auditing." *Journal of Accounting Research* (Spring 1981a): 120–45.

Joyce, E., and G. Biddle. "Are Auditors' Judgments Sufficiently Regressive?" *Journal of Accounting Research* (Autumn 1981b): 323–49.

Joyce, E., R. Libby, and S. Sunder. "Using the FASB's Qualitative Characteristics in Accounting Policy Choices." *Journal of Accounting Research* (Autumn 1982, Part II): 654–75.

Judge, T., and G. Ferris. "Social Context of Performance Evaluation Decisions." *Academy of Management Journal* (February 1993): 80–105.

Jung, C. *Psychological Types.* New York: Harcourt Brace, 1923.

Jungermann, H. "Inferential Processes in the Construction of Scenarios." *Journal of Forecasting* (October–December 1985): 321–27.

Jungermann, H., and K. Fischer. "Using Expertise and Experience for Giving and Taking Advice." In *The Routines of Decision Making,* edited by T. Betsch and S. Haberstroh. Mahwah, NJ: Lawrence Erlbaum Associates, 2005.

Kachelmeier, S. "Do Cosmetic Reporting Variations Affect Market Behavior? A Laboratory Study of the Accounting Emphasis on Unavoidable Costs." *Review of Accounting Studies* (No. 2 1996): 115–40.

Kachelmeier, S., J. Jones, and J. Keller. "Evaluating the Effectiveness of a Computer-Intensive Learning Aid for Teaching Pension Accounting." *Issues in Accounting Education* (Fall 1992): 164–78.

Kachelmeier, S., S. Limberg, and M. Schadewald. "A Laboratory Market Examination of the Consumer Price Response to Information about Producers' Costs and Profits." *The Accounting Review* (October 1991): 694–717.

Kachelmeier, S., and W. Messier Jr. "An Investigation of the Influence of a Nonstatistical Decision Aid on Auditor Sample Size Decisions." *The Accounting Review* (January 1990): 209–26.

Kadous, K. "The Effects of Audit Quality and Consequence Severity on Juror Evaluations of Auditor Responsibility for Plaintiff Losses." *The Accounting Review* (July 2000): 327–41.

Kadous, K. "Improving Jurors' Evaluations of Auditors in Negligence Cases." *Contemporary Accounting Research* (Fall 2001): 425–44.

Kadous, K., S. Kennedy, and M. Peecher. "The Effect of Quality Assessment and Directional Goal Commitment on Auditors' Acceptance of Client-Preferred Accounting Methods." *The Accounting Review* (July 2003): 759–78.

Kadous, K., L. Koonce, and K. Towry. "Quantification and Persuasion in Managerial Judgment." *Contemporary Accounting Research* (Fall 2005): 643–86.

Kadous, K., S. Krische, and L. Sedor. "Using Counter-Explanation to Limit Analysts' Forecast Optimism." *The Accounting Review* (March 2006): 377–98.

Kadous, K., and A. Magro. "The Effects of Exposure to Practice Risk on Tax Professionals' Judgements and Recommendations." *Contemporary Accounting Research* (Fall 2001): 451–75.

Kadous, K., and L. Sedor. "The Efficacy of Third-Party Consultation in Preventing Managerial Escalation of Commitment: The Role of Mental Representations." *Contemporary Accounting Research* (Spring 2004): 55–82.

Kahle, J., and R. White. "Tax Professional Decision Biases: The Effects of Initial Beliefs and Client Preferences." *Journal of the American Taxation Association* (2004): S1–29.

Kahneman, D. *Attention and Effort.* Englewood Cliffs, NJ: Prentice-Hall, 1973.

Kahneman, D. "New Challenges to the Rationality Assumption." *Journal of Institutional and Theoretical Economics* (March 1994): 18–36.

Kahneman, D., and S. Frederick. "Representativeness Revisited: Attribute Substitution in Intuitive Judgment." In *Heuristics and Biases: The Psychology of Intuitive Judgment,* edited by T. Gilovich, D. Griffin, and D. Kahneman. New York: Cambridge University Press, 2002.

Kahneman, D., P. Slovic, and A. Tversky. *Judgment under Uncertainty: Heuristics and Biases.* Cambridge, England: Cambridge University Press, 1982.

Kahneman, D., and A. Tversky. "Subjective Probability: A Judgment of Representativeness." *Cognitive Psychology* (July 1972): 430–54.

Kahneman, D., and A. Tversky. "On the Psychology of Prediction." *Psychological Review* (July 1973): 237–51.

Kahneman, D., and A. Tversky. "Prospect Theory: An Analysis of Decision under Risk." *Econometrica* (March 1979): 263–91.

Kahneman, D., and A. Tversky. "The Simulation Heuristic." In *Judgment under Uncertainty: Heuristics and Biases,* edited by D. Kahneman, P. Slovic, and A. Tversky. New York: Cambridge University Press, 1982.

Kahneman, D., and A. Tversky. "Choices, Values, and Frames." *American Psychologist* (April 1984): 341–50.

Kahneman, D., and A. Tversky, ed. *Choices, Values, and Frames.* New York: Russell Sage Foundation and Cambridge University Press, 2000.

Kalyuga, S., P. Chandler, and J. Sweller. "Learning Experience and Efficiency of Instructional Guidance." *Educational Psychology* (March 2001a): 5–23.

Kalyuga, S., P. Chandler, J. Tuovinen, and J. Sweller. "When Problem Solving Is Superior to Studying Worked Examples." *Journal of Educational Psychology* (September 2001b): 579–88.

Kamstra, M., L. Kramer, and M. Levi. "Losing Sleep at the Market: The Daylight Saving Anomaly." *The American Economic Review* (September 2000): 1005–11.

Kamstra, M., L. Kramer, and M. Levi. "Winter Blues: A SAD Stock Market Cycle." *The American Economic Review* (March 2003): 324–43.

Kanfer, R. "Task-Specific Motivation: An Integrative Approach to Issues of Measurement, Mechanisms, Processes, and Determinants." *Journal of Social and Clinical Psychology* (No. 2 1987): 237–64.

Kanfer, R. "Motivation Theory and Industrial and Organizational Psychology." In *Handbook of Industrial and Organizational Psychology,* edited by M. Dunnette and L. Hough.

Palo Alto, CA: Consulting Psychologists Press, 1990.

Kaplan, S., C. Moeckel, and J. Williams. "Auditors' Hypothesis Plausibility Assessments in an Analytical Review Setting." *Auditing: A Journal of Practice and Theory* (Fall 1992): 50–65.

Kaplan, S., S. Pourciau, and P. Reckers. "An Examination of the Effect of the President's Letter and Stock Advisory Service Information on Financial Decisions." *Behavioral Research in Accounting* (1990): 63–92.

Kaplan, S., and P. Reckers. "An Examination of Auditor Performance Evaluation." *The Accounting Review* (July 1985): 477–87.

Kaplan, S., and P. Reckers. "An Examination of Information Search during Initial Audit Planning." *Accounting, Organizations and Society* (No. 5/6 1989): 539–50.

Kaplan, S., and P. Reckers. "An Examination of the Effects of Accountability Tactics on Performance Evaluation Judgments in Public Accounting." *Behavioral Research in Accounting* (1993): 101–23.

Kaplan, S., P. Reckers, S. West, and J. Boyd. "An Examination of Tax Reporting Recommendations of Professional Tax Preparers." *Journal of Economic Psychology* (December 1988): 427–43.

Kaplan, S., J. Reneau, and S. Whitecotton. "The Effects of Predictive Ability Information, Locus of Control, and Decision Maker Involvement on Decision Aid Reliance." *Journal of Behavioral Decision Making* (January 2001): 35–50.

Karau, S., and K. Williams. "Social Loafing: A Meta-Analytic Review and Theoretical Integration." *Journal of Personality and Social Psychology* (October 1993): 681–706.

Karlovac, M., and J. Darley. "Attribution of Responsibility for Accidents: A Negligence Law Analogy." *Social Cognition* (No. 6 1988): 287–318.

Karpoff, J., and J. Lott. "The Reputational Penalty Firms Bear from Committing Criminal Fraud." *Journal of Law and Economics* (October 1993): 757–802.

Kassirer, J. "Diagnostic Reasoning." *Annals of Internal Medicine* (June 1989): 893–900.

Kassirer, J., and R. Kopelman. "Cognitive Errors in Diagnosis: Instatiation, Classification, and

Consequences." *American Journal of Medicine* (April 1989): 433–41.

Keil, F. "Explanation and Understanding." *Annual Review of Psychology* (2006): 227–54.

Kelley, H. "Attribution Theory in Social Psychology." In *Symposium on Motivation,* edited by D. Levine. Lincoln: University of Nebraska Press, 1967.

Kelley, H. "Attribution in Social Interaction." In *Attribution: Perceiving the Causes of Behavior,* edited by E. Jones, D. Kanouse, H. Kelley, R. Nisbett, S. Valins, and B. Weiner. Morristown, NJ: General Learning Press, 1971a.

Kelley, H. "Causal Schemata and the Attribution Process." In *Attribution: Perceiving the Causes of Behavior,* edited by E. Jones, D. Kanouse, H. Kelley, R. Nisbett, S. Valins, and B. Weiner. Morristown, NJ: General Learning Press, 1971b.

Kelley, H. "The Processes of Causal Attribution." *American Psychologist* (February 1973): 107–28.

Kelley, H., and J. Michela. "Attribution Theory and Research." *Annual Review of Psychology* (1980): 457–501.

Kelley, T., and L. Margheim. "The Impact of Time Budget Pressure, Personality, and Leadership Variables on Dysfunctional Auditor Behavior." *Auditing: A Journal of Practice and Theory* (Spring 1990): 21–42.

Kenis, I. "Effects of Budgetary Goal Characteristics on Managerial Attitudes and Performance." *The Accounting Review* (January 1979): 707–21.

Kennedy, J. "Debiasing Audit Judgment with Accountability: A Framework and Experimental Results." *Journal of Accounting Research* (Autumn 1993): 231–45.

Kennedy, J. "Debiasing the Curse of Knowledge in Audit Judgment." *The Accounting Review* (April 1995): 249–73.

Kennedy, J., and M. Peecher. "Judging Auditors' Technical Knowledge." *Journal of Accounting Research* (Autumn 1997): 279–93.

Kennedy, J., D. Kleinmuntz, and M. Peecher. "Determinants of the Justifiability of Performance in Ill-Structured Audit Tasks." *Journal of Accounting Research* (1997): S105–23.

Kerr, D., and D. Ward. "The Effects of Audit Task on Evidence Integration and Belief Revision." *Behavioral Research in Accounting* (1994): 21–43.

Kerr, N., and R. Tindale. "Group Performance and Decision Making." *Annual Review of Psychology* (2004): 623–55.

Kerr, N., R. MacCoun, and G. Kramer. "Bias in Judgment: Comparing Individuals and Groups." *Psychological Review* (October 1996): 687–719.

Kessler, L., and R. Ashton. "Feedback and Prediction Achievement in Financial Analysis." *Journal of Accounting Research* (Spring 1981): 146–62.

Keys, D. "Confidence Interval Financial Statements: An Empirical Investigation." *Journal of Accounting Research* (Autumn 1978): 389–99.

Khorana, A. "Top Management Turnover: An Empirical Investigation of Mutual Fund Managers." *Journal of Financial Economics* (March 1996): 403–27.

Kida, T. "An Investigation into Auditors' Continuity and Related Qualification Judgments." *Journal of Accounting Research* (Autumn 1980): 506–23.

Kida, T. "The Effect of Causality and Specificity on Data Use." *Journal of Accounting Research* (Spring 1984a): 145–52.

Kida, T. "The Impact of Hypothesis-Testing Strategies on Auditors' Use of Judgment Data." *Journal of Accounting Research* (Spring 1984b): 332–40.

Kida, T. "Performance Evaluation and Review Meeting Characteristics in Public Accounting Firms." *Accounting, Organizations and Society* (No. 2 1984c): 137–47.

Kida, T., K. Moreno, and J. Smith. "The Influence of Affect on Managers' Capital Budgeting Decisions." *Contemporary Accounting Research* (Fall 2001): 477–94.

Kida, T., and J. Smith. "The Encoding and Retrieval of Numerical Data for Decision Making in Accounting Contexts: Model Development." *Accounting, Organizations and Society* (October–November 1995): 585–610.

Kida, T., J. Smith, and M. Maletta. "The Effects of Encoded Memory Traces for Numerical Data on Accounting Decision Making." *Accounting, Organizations and Society* (July–August 1998): 451–66.

King, R. "An Experimental Investigation of Self-Serving Biases in an Auditing Trust Game:

The Effect of Group Affiliation." *The Accounting Review* (April 2002): 265–84.

Kinney, W., Jr. "Empirical Accounting Research Design for Ph.D. Students." *The Accounting Review* (April 1986): 338–50.

Kinney, W., Jr. "Accounting Scholarship: What Is Uniquely Ours?" *The Accounting Review* (April 2001): 275–84.

Kinney, W., Jr. "Twenty-Five Years of Audit Deregulation and Re-Regulation: What Does It Mean for 2005 and Beyond?" *Auditing: A Journal of Practice & Theory* (2005): S89–109.

Kinney, W., Jr., and M. Nelson. "Outcome Information and the 'Expectation Gap': The Case of Loss Contingencies." *Journal of Accounting Research* (Autumn 1996): 281–99.

Kinney, W., Jr., and W. Uecker. "Mitigating the Consequences of Anchoring in Auditor Judgments." *The Accounting Review* (January 1982): 55–69.

Kipnis, D., and S. Schmidt. "Upward-Influence Styles: Relationship with Performance Evaluations, Salary, and Stress." *Administrative Science Quarterly* (December 1988): 528–42.

Kirsch, R., P. Leathers, and K. Snead. "Student versus Recruiter Perceptions of the Importance of Staff Auditor Performance Variables." *Accounting Horizons* (December 1993): 58–69.

Klammer, T., and S. Reed. "Operating Cash Flow Formats: Does Format Influence Decisions?" *Journal of Accounting and Public Policy* (Autumn 1990): 217–35.

Klatzky, R. *Human Memory,* 2nd ed. New York: W.H. Freeman and Company, 1980.

Klayman, J. "Varieties of Confirmation Bias." In *The Psychology of Learning and Motivation,* vol. 32: *Decision Making from a Cognitive Perspective,* edited by J. Busemeyer, D. Medin, and R. Hastie. San Diego, CA: Academic Press, 1995.

Klayman, J., J. Soll, C. González-Vallejo, and S. Barlas. "Overconfidence: It Depends on How, What, and Whom You Ask." *Organizational Behavior and Human Decision Processes* (September 1999): 216–47.

Kleinmuntz, B. "Why We Still Use Our Heads Instead of Formulas: Toward an Integrative Approach." *Psychological Bulletin* (May 1990): 296–310.

Kleinmuntz, D., M. Fennema, and M. Peecher. "Conditioned Assessment of Subjective Probabilities: Identifying the Benefits of Decomposition." *Organizational Behavior and Human Decision Processes* (April 1996): 1–15.

Kleinmuntz, D., and D. Schkade. "Information Displays and Decision Processes." *Psychological Science* (July 1993): 221–27.

Kluger, A., and A. DeNisi. "The Effects of Feedback Interventions on Performance: A Historical Review, a Meta-Analysis, and a Preliminary Feedback Intervention Theory." *Psychological Bulletin* (March 1996): 254–84.

Knapp, M. "Audit Conflict: An Empirical Study of the Perceived Ability of Auditors to Resist Management Pressure." *The Accounting Review* (April 1985): 202–11.

Knapp, M. "Factors that Audit Committee Members Use as Surrogates for Audit Quality." *Auditing: A Journal of Practice & Theory* (Spring 1991): 35–52.

Knechel, W., and W. Messier Jr. "Sequential Auditor Decision Making: Information Search and Evidence Evaluation." *Contemporary Accounting Research* (Spring 1990): 386–406.

Koehler, D. "Explanation, Imagination, and Confidence in Judgment." *Psychological Bulletin* (November 1991): 499–519.

Koonce, L. "Explanation and Counterexplanation During Audit Analytical Review." *The Accounting Review* (January 1992): 59–76.

Koonce, L., U. Anderson, and G. Marchant. "Justification of Decisions in Auditing." *Journal of Accounting Research* (Autumn 1995): 369–84.

Koonce, L., M. Lipe, and M. McAnally. "Judging the Risk of Financial Instruments: Problems and Potential Remedies." *The Accounting Review* (July 2005a): 871–95.

Koonce, L., M. McAnally, and M. Mercer. "How Do Investors Judge the Risk of Financial Items?" *The Accounting Review* (January 2005b): 221–41.

Koonce, L., and M. Mercer. "Using Psychology Theories in Archival Financial Accounting Research." *Journal of Accounting Literature* (2005): 175–214.

Koonce, L., and F. Phillips. "Auditors' Comprehension and Evaluation of Client-Suggested Causes in Analytical Procedures."

Behavioral Research in Accounting (1996): 32–48.

Koriat, A. "How Do We Know that We Know? The Accessibility Model of the Feeling of Knowing." *Psychological Review* (October 1993): 609–39.

Koriat, A., M. Goldsmith, and A. Pansky. "Toward a Psychology of Memory Accuracy." *Annual Review of Psychology* (2000): 481–537.

Koriat, A., S. Lichtenstein, and B. Fischhoff. "Reasons for Confidence." *Journal of Experimental Psychology: Human Learning & Memory* (March 1980): 107–18.

Kottemann, J., and F. Davis. "Decisional Conflict and User Acceptance of Multicriteria Decision-Making Aids." *Decision Sciences* (September–October 1991): 918–26.

Kowalczyk, T., and C. Wolfe. "Anchoring Effects Associated with Recommendations from Expert Decision Aids: An Experimental Analysis." *Behavioral Research in Accounting* (1998): S147–69.

Kramer, G., N. Kerr, and J. Carroll. "Pretrial Publicity, Judicial Remedies, and Jury Bias." *Law and Human Behavior* (October 1990): 409–38.

Kramer, L. "Intraday Stock Returns, Time-Varying Risk Premia, and Diurnal Mood Variation." Working paper, University of Toronto, 2000.

Kramer, W., and R. Runde. "Stocks and the Weather: An Exercise in Data Mining or yet Another Capital Market Anomaly?" *Empirical Economics* (1997): 637–41.

Krawczyk, K. "The Influence of Tax Law Requirements and Organization of Client Facts on Professional Judgment." *Behavioral Research in Accounting* (1994): S97–120.

Kren, L. "Budgetary Participation and Managerial Performance: The Impact of Information and Environmental Volatility." *The Accounting Review* (July 1992): 511–26.

Kruglanski, A. "The Psychology of Being 'Right': The Problem of Accuracy in Social Perception and Cognition." *Psychological Bulletin* (November 1989): 395–409.

Krull, G., Jr., P. Reckers, and B. Wong-on-Wing. "The Effect of Experience, Fraudulent Signals and Information Presentation Order on Auditors' Beliefs." *Auditing: A Journal of Practice & Theory* (Fall 1993): 143–53.

Kühberger, A. "The Framing of Decisions: A New Look at Old Problems." *Organizational Behavior and Human Decision Processes* (May 1995): 230–40.

Kühberger, A. "The Influence of Framing on Risk Decisions: A Meta-Analysis." *Organizational Behavior and Human Decision Processes* (July 1998): 23–55.

Kühberger, A., M. Schulte-Mecklenbeck, and J. Perner. "The Effects of Framing, Reflection, Probability, and Payoff on Risk Preference in Choice Tasks." *Organizational Behavior and Human Decision Processes* (June 1999): 204–31.

Kuhn, K., and J. Sniezek. "Confidence and Uncertainty in Judgmental Forecasting: Differential Effects of Scenario Presentation." *Journal of Behavioral Decision Making* (December 1996): 231–47.

Kunda, Z. "The Case for Motivated Reasoning." *Psychological Bulletin* (November 1990): 480–98.

Kunda, Z. *Social Cognition: Making Sense of People.* Cambridge, MA: The MIT Press, 1999.

Kyle, A., and F. Wang. "Speculation Duopoly with Agreement to Disagree: Can Overconfidence Survive the Market Test?" *The Journal of Finance* (December 1997): 2073–90.

Kyllonen, P., and D. Woltz. "Role of Cognitive Factors in the Acquisition of Cognitive Skill." In *Abilities, Motivation, & Methodology: The Minnesota Symposium on Learning and Individual Differences,* edited by R. Kanfer, P. Ackerman, and R. Cudeck. Hillsdale, NJ: Lawrence Erlbaum Associates, 1989.

Lakonishok, J., A. Shleifer, and R. Vishny. "The Impact of Institutional Trading on Stock Prices." *Journal of Financial Economics* (August 1992): 23–44.

Lamberts, K., and D. Shanks, ed. *Knowledge, Concepts, and Categories.* Cambridge, MA: MIT Press, 1997.

Landy, F., and J. Farr. "Performance Rating." *Psychological Bulletin* (January 1980): 72–107.

Landy, F., and L. Shankster. "Personnel Selection and Placement." *Annual Review of Psychology* (1994): 261–96.

Langer, E., and J. Roth. "Heads I Win, Tails It's Chance: The Illusion of Control as a Function of the Sequence of Outcomes in a Purely

Chance Task." *Journal of Personality and Social Psychology* (December 1975): 951–55.

Langley, M. "Big Companies Get Low Marks for Lavish Executive Pay." *Wall Street Journal* (June 9, 2003): C1.

Larrick, R. "Motivational Factors in Decision Theories: The Role of Self-Protection." *Psychological Bulletin* (May 1993): 440–50.

Larrick. R. "Debiasing." In *Blackwell Handbook of Judgment & Decision Making,* edited by D. Koehler and N. Harvey. Malden, MA: Blackwell Publishing, 2004.

Larson, J., P. Foster-Fishman, and C. Keys. "Discussion of Shared and Unshared Information in Decision-Making Groups." *Journal of Personality and Social Psychology* (September 1994): 446–61.

Latané, B., K. Williams, and S. Harkins. "Many Hands Make Light the Work: The Causes and Consequences of Social Loafing." *Journal of Personality and Social Psychology* (June 1979): 822–32.

Lau, C., L. Low, and I. Eggleton. "The Impact of Reliance on Accounting Performance Measures on Job-Related Tension and Managerial Performance: Additional Evidence." *Accounting, Organizations and Society* (July 1995): 359–81.

Laughlin, P., and A. Ellis. "Demonstrability and Social Combination Processes on Mathematical Intellective Tasks." *Journal of Experimental Social Psychology* (May 1986): 177–89.

Lawler, E., III. *Motivation in Work Organizations.* San Francisco: Jossey-Bass, 1994.

Lawrence, M., R. Edmundson, and M. O'Connor. "The Accuracy of Combining Judgemental and Statistical Forecasts." *Management Science* (December 1986): 1521–32.

Lazear, E., and S. Rosen. "Rank-Order Tournaments as Optimum Labor Contracts." *Journal of Political Economy* (October 1981): 841–64.

Lenney, E. "Women's Self-Confidence in Achievement Settings." *Psychological Bulletin* (January 1977): 1–13.

Lerner, J., and P. Tetlock. "Accounting for the Effects of Accountability." *Psychological Bulletin* (March 1999): 255–75.

Lesgold, A., H. Rubinson, P. Feltovich, R. Glaser, D. Klopfer, and Y. Wang. "Expertise in a Complex Skill: Diagnosing X?Ray Pictures." In *The Nature of Expertise,* edited by M. Chi, R. Glaser, and M. Farr. Hillsdale, NJ: Lawrence Erlbaum, 1988.

Levin, I., and G. Gaeth. "How Consumers Are Affected by the Framing of Attribute Information." *Journal of Consumer Research* (December 1988): 374–78.

Levin, I., S. Schneider, and G. Gaeth. "All Frames Are Not Created Equal: A Typology and Critical Analysis of Framing Effects." *Organizational Behavior and Human Decision Processes* (November 1998): 149–88.

Levine, J., and R. Moreland. "Progress in Small Group Research." *Annual Review of Psychology* (1990): 585–634.

Levine, J., L. Resnick, and E. Higgins. "Social Foundations of Cognition." *Annual Review of Psychology* (1993): 585–612.

Levitan, A., and J. Knoblett. "Indicators of Exceptions to the Going Concern Assumption." *Auditing: A Journal of Practice and Theory* (Fall 1985): 26–39.

Levitt, A. "The SEC's Repair Job." *Wall Street Journal* (February 10, 2003): A14.

Levy, S., and C. Dweck. "Trait- versus Process-Focused Social Judgment." *Social Cognition* (Spring 1998): 151–72.

Lewis, B. "Expert Judgment in Auditing: An Expected Utility Approach." *Journal of Accounting Research* (Autumn 1980): 594–602.

Lewis, B., and J. Bell. "Decisions Involving Sequential Events: Replications and Extensions." *Journal of Accounting Research* (Spring 1985): 228–39.

Lewis, B., J. Patton, and S. Green. "The Effects of Information Choice and Information Use on Analysts' Predictions of Municipal Bond Rating Changes." *The Accounting Review* (April 1988): 270–82.

Lewis, B., M. Shields, and S. Young. "Evaluating Human Judgments and Decision Aids." *Journal of Accounting Research* (Spring 1983): 271–85.

Liang, T. "Expert Systems as Decision Aids: Issues and Strategies." *Journal of Information Systems* (Spring 1988): 41–50.

Libby, R. "Accounting Ratios and the Prediction of Failure: Some Behavioral Evidence." *Journal of Accounting Research* (Spring 1975): 150–61.

Libby, R. "Man versus Model of Man: Some Conflicting Evidence." *Organizational Behavior and Human Performance* (June 1976a): 1–12.

Libby, R. "Man versus Model of Man: The Need for a Nonlinear Model." *Organizational Behavior and Human Performance* (June 1976b): 23–26.

Libby, R. *Accounting and Human Information Processing: Theory and Applications.* Englewood Cliffs, NJ: Prentice-Hall, 1981.

Libby, R. "Availability and the Generation of Hypotheses in Analytical Review." *Journal of Accounting Research* (Autumn 1985): 648–67.

Libby, R. "Experimental Research and the Distinctive Features of Accounting Settings." In *The State of Accounting Research as We Enter the 1990s,* edited by T. Frecka. Champaign: University of Illinois, 1989.

Libby, R. "The Role of Knowledge and Memory in Audit Judgment." In *Judgment and Decision-Making Research in Accounting,* edited by R. Ashton and A. Ashton. Cambridge, England: Cambridge University Press, 1995.

Libby, R., and R. Blashfield. "Performance of a Composite as a Function of the Number of Judges." *Organizational Behavior and Human Performance* (April 1978): 121–29.

Libby, R., and D. Frederick. "Experience and the Ability to Explain Audit Findings." *Journal of Accounting Research* (Autumn 1990): 348–67.

Libby, R., and W. Kinney Jr. "Does Mandated Audit Communication Reduce Opportunistic Corrections to Manage Earnings Forecasts?" *The Accounting Review* (October 2000): 383–404.

Libby, R., and P. Libby. "Expert Measurement and Mechanical Combination in Control Reliance Decisions." *The Accounting Review* (October 1989): 729–47.

Libby, R., and M. Lipe. "Incentives, Effort, and the Cognitive Processes Involved in Accounting-Related Judgments." *Journal of Accounting Research* (Autumn 1992): 249–73.

Libby, R., and H. Tan. "Modeling the Determinants of Audit Expertise." *Accounting, Organizations and Society* (November 1994): 701–16.

Libby, R., and H. Tan. "Analysts' Reactions to Warnings of Negative Earnings Surprises." *Journal of Accounting Research* (Autumn 1999): 415–35.

Libby, R., and K. Trotman. "The Review Process as a Control for Differential Recall of Evidence in Auditor Judgments." *Accounting, Organizations and Society* (August 1993): 559–74.

Libby, R., K. Trotman, and I. Zimmer. "Member Variation, Recognition of Expertise, and Group Performance." *Journal of Applied Psychology* (February 1987): 81–87.

Lichtenstein, S., and B. Fischhoff. "Do Those Who Know More Also Know More about How Much They Know?" *Organizational Behavior and Human Performance* (December 1977): 159–83.

Lichtenstein, S., B. Fischhoff, and L. Phillips. "Calibration of Probabilities: The State of the Art to 1980." In *Judgment under Uncertainty: Heuristics and Biases,* edited by D. Kahneman, P. Slovic, and A. Tversky. New York: Cambridge University Press, 1982.

Lichtenstein, S., and J. Newman. "Empirical Scaling of Common Verbal Phrases Associated with Numerical Probabilities." *Psychonomic Science* (No. 10 1967): 563–64.

Lin, H., and M. McNichols. "Underwriting Relationships, Analysts' Earnings Forecasts and Investment Recommendations." *Journal of Accounting and Economics* (February 1998): 101–27.

Lindberg, D., and M. Maletta. "An Examination of Memory Conjunction Errors in Multiple Client Audit Environments." *Auditing: A Journal of Practice and Theory* (March 2003): 127–41.

Lindquist, T. "Fairness as an Antecedent to Participative Budgeting: Examining the Effects of Distributive Justice, Procedural Justice and Referent Cognitions on Satisfaction and Performance." *Journal of Management Accounting Research* (Fall 1995): 122–47.

Lipe, M. "Analyzing the Variance Investigation Decision: The Effects of Outcomes, Mental Accounting, and Framing." *The Accounting Review* (October 1993): 748–64.

Lipe, M. "Individual Investors' Risk Judgments and Investment Decisions: The Impact of Accounting and Market Data." *Accounting, Organizations and Society* (October 1998): 625–40.

Lipe, M., and S. Salterio. "The Balanced Scorecard: Judgmental Effects of Common and Unique Performance Measures." *The Accounting Review* (July 2000): 283–98.

Lipe, M., and S. Salterio. "A Note on the Judgmental Effects of the Balanced Scorecard's Information Organization." *Accounting, Organizations and Society* (August 2002): 531–40.

Littlepage, G., and A. Mueller. "Recognition and Utilization of Expertise in Problem-Solving Groups: Expert Characteristics and Behavior." *Group Dynamics: Theory, Research, and Practice* (December 1997): 324–28.

Littlepage, G., G. Schmidt, E. Whisler, and A. Frost. "An Input-Process-Output Analysis of Influence and Performance in Problem-Solving Groups." *Journal of Personality and Social Psychology* (November 1995): 877–89.

Littlepage, G., and H. Silbiger. "Recognition of Expertise in Decision-Making Groups: Effects of Group Size and Participation Patterns." *Small Group Research* (August 1992): 344–55.

Livingston, J. "Management-Borne Costs of Fraudulent and Misleading Financial Reports." Ph.D. dissertation, University of Rochester, 1997.

Lo, A., and D. Repin. "The Psychophysiology of Real-Time Financial Risk Processing." *Journal of Cognitive Neuroscience* (No. 3 2002): 323–39.

Lobo, G. "Alternative Methods of Combining Security Analysts' and Statistical Forecasts of Annual Corporate Earnings." *International Journal of Forecasting* (May 1991): 57–63.

Lobo, G. "Analysis and Comparison of Financial Analysts', Time Series, and Combined Forecasts of Annual Earnings." *Journal of Business Research* (May 1992): 269–80.

Lobo, G., and R. Nair. "Combining Judgmental and Statistical Forecasts: An Application to Earnings Forecasts." *Decision Sciences* (Spring 1990): 446–60.

Locke, E. "Motivational Effects of Knowledge of Results: Knowledge or Goal Setting?" *Journal of Applied Psychology* (No. 4 1967): 324–29.

Locke, E. "The Motivation Sequence, the Motivation Hub, and the Motivation Core." *Organizational Behavior and Human Decision Processes* (December 1991): 288–99.

Locke, E., and G. Latham. *A Theory of Goal Setting and Task Performance.* Englewood Cliffs, NJ: Prentice-Hall, 1990.

Locke, E., K. Shaw, L. Saari, and G. Latham. "Goal-Setting and Task Performance: 1969–1980." *Psychological Bulletin* (July 1981): 125–52.

Loewenstein, G., and D. Schkade. "Wouldn't It Be Nice? Predicting Future Feelings." In *Well-Being: The Foundations of Hedonic Psychology,* edited by D. Kahneman, E. Diener, and N. Schwarz. New York: Russell Sage Foundation, 1999.

Loewenstein, G., E. Weber, C. Hsee, and N. Welch. "Risk as Feelings." *Psychological Bulletin* (March 2001): 267–86.

Lohman, D. "Minding Our P's and Q's: On Finding Relationships between Learning and Intelligence." In *Learning and Individual Differences: Process, Trait, and Content Determinants,* edited by P. Ackerman, P. Kyllonen, and R. Roberts. Washington, DC: American Psychological Association, 1999.

Lohse, G., and E. Johnson. "A Comparison of Two Process Tracing Methods for Choice Tasks." *Organizational Behavior and Human Decision Processes* (October 1996): 28–43.

Loomes, G., and R. Sugden. "Regret Theory: An Alternative Theory of Rational Choice under Uncertainty." *Economic Journal* (December 1982): 805–24.

Lopes, L. "Decision Making in the Short Run." *Journal of Experimental Psychology: Human Learning and Memory* (September 1981): 377–85.

Lopes, L. "Between Hope and Fear: The Psychology of Risk." *Advances in Experimental Social Psychology* (1987): 255–95.

Lord, A. "Pressure: A Methodological Consideration for Behavioral Research in Auditing." *Auditing: A Journal of Practice and Theory* (Fall 1992): 89–108.

Lord, C., M. Lepper, and E. Preston. "Considering the Opposite: A Corrective Strategy for Social Judgment." *Journal of Personality and Social Psychology* (December 1984): 1231–43.

Lorek, K., C. McDonald, and D. Patz. "A Comparative Examination of Management Forecasts and Box-Jenkins Forecasts of Earnings." *The Accounting Review* (April 1976): 321–30.

Louis, H., J. Joe, and D. Robinson. "Managers' and Investors' Responses to Media Exposure of Board Ineffectiveness." Working paper, Pennsylvania State University, University Park, 2005.

Low, K-Y. "The Effects of Industry Specialization on Audit Risk Assessment and Audit-Planning Decisions." *The Accounting Review* (January 2004): 201–19.

Lowe, D., and K. Pany. "CPA Performance of Consulting Engagements with Audit Clients: Effects on Financial Statement Users' Perceptions and Decisions." *Auditing: A Journal of Practice & Theory* (Fall 1995): 35–53.

Lowe, D., and P. Reckers. "The Effects of Hindsight Bias on Jurors' Evaluations." *Decision Sciences* (May–June 1994): 401–26.

Lowe, D., and P. Reckers. "The Use of Foresight Decision Aids in Auditors' Judgments." *Behavioral Research in Accounting* (2000): 97–118.

Lowe, D., P. Reckers, and S. Whitecotton. "The Effects of Decision-Aid Use and Reliability on Jurors' Evaluations of Auditor Liability." *The Accounting Review* (January 2002): 185–202.

Lubinski, D. "Scientific and Social Significance of Assessing Individual Differences: 'Sinking Shafts at a Few Critical Points.'" *Annual Review of Psychology* (2000): 405–44.

Lucas, H., Jr. "An Experimental Investigation of the Use of Computer-Based Graphics in Decision Making." *Management Science* (July 1981): 757–68.

Luckett, P., and I. Eggleton. "Feedback and Management Accounting: A Review of Research into Behavioural Consequences." *Accounting, Organizations and Society* (No. 4 1991): 371–94.

Luckett, P., and M. Hirst. "The Impact of Feedback on Inter-Rater Agreement and Self Insight in Performance Evaluation Decisions." *Accounting, Organizations and Society* (No. 5/6 1989): 379–87.

Luconi, F., T. Malone, and M. Scott Morton. "Expert Systems: The Next Challenge for Managers." *Sloan Management Review* (Summer 1986): 3–14.

Luft, J. "Bonus and Penalty Incentives: Contract Choice by Employees." *Journal of Accounting and Economics* (September 1994): 181–206.

Luft, J. "Fairness, Ethics and the Effect of Management Accounting on Transactions Costs." *Journal of Management Accounting Research* (1997): 199–216.

Luft, J., and R. Libby. "Profit Comparisons, Market Prices and Managers' Judgments about Negotiated Transfer Prices." *The Accounting Review* (April 1997): 217–29.

Luft, J., and M. Shields. "Why Does Fixation Persist? Experimental Evidence on the Judgment Performance Effects of Expensing Intangibles." *The Accounting Review* (October 2001): 561–87.

Luft, J., and M. Shields. "Mapping Management Accounting: Graphics and Guidelines for Theory-Consistent Empirical Research." *Accounting, Organizations and Society* (February–April 2003): 169–249.

Lundeberg, M., P. Fox, and J. Punccohar. "Highly Confident but Wrong: Gender Differences and Similarities in Confidence Judgments." *Journal of Educational Psychology* (March 1994): 114–21.

Lusk, E. "Cognitive Aspects of Annual Reports: Field Independence/Dependence." *Journal of Accounting Research* (Autumn 1973): 191–202.

Lyness, K., and E. Cornelius III. "A Comparison of Holistic and Decomposed Judgment Strategies in a Performance Rating Simulation." *Organizational Behavior and Human Performance* (February 1982): 21–38.

Lys, T., and L. Soo. "Analysts' Forecast Precision as a Response to Competition." *Journal of Accounting, Auditing and Finance* (Fall 1995): 751–65.

Mabe, P., and S. West. "Validity of Self-Evaluation of Ability: A Review and Meta-Analysis." *Journal of Applied Psychology* (June 1982): 280–96.

MacDonald, A., Jr. "Revised Scale for Ambiguity Tolerance: Reliability and Validity." *Psychological Reports* (June 1970): 791–98.

MacDonald, E. "The Making of an Expert Witness: It's in the Credentials." *Wall Street Journal* (February 8, 1999): B1, B4.

MacGregor, D. "Time Pressure and Task Adaptation: Alternative Perspectives on Laboratory Studies." In *Time Pressure and Stress in Human Judgment and Decision Making,* edited by O. Svenson and A. Maule. New York: Plenum Press, 1993.

MacGregor, D. "Decomposition for Judgmental Forecasting and Estimation." In *Principles of Forecasting: A Handbook for Researchers and Practitioners,* edited by J. Armstrong. Boston: Kluwer Academic Publishers, 2001.

MacGregor, D., and J. Armstrong. "Judgemental Decomposition: When Does It Work?" *International Journal of Forecasting* (December 1994): 495–506.

MacGregor, D., and S. Lichtenstein. "Problem Structuring Aids for Quantitative Estimation." *Journal of Behavioral Decision Making* (June 1991): 101–16.

MacGregor, D., S. Lichtenstein, and P. Slovic. "Structuring Knowledge Retrieval: An Analysis of Decomposed Quantitative Judgments." *Organizational Behavior and Human Decision Processes* (December 1988): 303–23.

MacKay, D., and A. Villarreal. "Performance Differences in the Use of Graphics and Tabular Displays of Multivariate Data." *Decision Sciences* (Fall 1987): 535–46.

Magee, R., and J. Dickhaut. "Effects of Compensation Plans on Heuristics in Cost Variance Investigations." *Journal of Accounting Research* (Autumn 1978): 294–314.

Maines, L. "The Effect of Forecast Redundancy on Judgments of a Consensus Forecast's Expected Accuracy." *Journal of Accounting Research* (1990): S29–47.

Maines, L. "The Role of Behavioral Accounting Research in Financial Accounting Standard Setting." *Behavioral Research in Accounting* (1994): 204–12.

Maines, L. "An Experimental Examination of Subjective Forecast Combination." *International Journal of Forecasting* (June 1996): 223–33.

Maines, L., E. Bartov, P. Fairfield, D. Hirst, T. Iannaconi, R. Mallett, C. Schrand, D. Skinner, and L. Vincent. "Evaluating Concepts-Based versus Rules-Based Approaches to Standard Setting." *Accounting Horizons* (March 2003): 73–89.

Maines, L., and J. Hand. "Individuals' Perceptions and Misperceptions of Time Series Properties of Quarterly Earnings." *The Accounting Review* (July 1996): 317–36.

Maines, L., and L. McDaniel. "Effects of Comprehensive-Income Characteristics on Nonprofessional Investors' Judgments: The Role of Financial-Statement Presentation Format." *The Accounting Review* (April 2000): 179–207.

Maines, L., L. McDaniel, and M. Harris. "Implications of Proposed Segment Reporting Standards for Financial Analysts' Investment Judgments." *Journal of Accounting Research* (1997): S1–33.

Maital, S., R. Filer, and J. Simon. "What Do People Bring to the Stock Market (Besides Money)? The Economic Psychology of Stock Market Behavior." In *Handbook of Behavioral Economics,* edited by B. Gilad and S. Kaish. Greenwich, CT: JAI Press, 1986.

Maletta, M. "An Examination of Auditors' Decisions to Use Internal Auditors as Assistants: The Effect of Inherent Risk." *Contemporary Accounting Research* (Spring 1993): 508–25.

Maletta, M., and T. Kida. "The Effect of Risk Factors on Auditors' Configural Information Processing." *The Accounting Review* (July 1993): 681–91.

Malkiel, B. *A Random Walk Down Wall Street.* New York: W.W. Norton & Co., 1999.

Marchant, G. "Analogical Reasoning and Hypothesis Generation in Auditing." *The Accounting Review* (July 1989): 500–513.

Marchant, G. "Accounting Changes and Information Processing: Some Further Empirical Evidence." *Behavioral Research in Accounting* (1990a): 93–103.

Marchant, G. "Discussion of the Determinants of Auditor Expertise." *Journal of Accounting Research* (1990b): S21–28.

Marchant, G., J. Robinson, U. Anderson, and M. Schadewald. "Analogical Transfer and Expertise in Legal Reasoning." *Organizational Behavior and Human Decision Processes* (April 1991): 272–90.

Marchant, G., J. Robinson, U. Anderson, and M. Schadewald. "The Use of Analogy in Legal Argument: Problem Similarity, Precedent, and Expertise." *Organizational Behavior and Human Decision Processes* (June 1993): 95–119.

Margheim, L. "Further Evidence on External Auditors' Reliance on Internal Auditors." *Journal of Accounting Research* (Spring 1986): 194–205.

Markman, A. *Knowledge Representation.* Mahwah, NJ: Lawrence Erlbaum Associates, 1999.

Matsui, T., A. Okada, and R. Mizuguchi. "Expectancy Theory Prediction of the Goal Theory Postulate 'The Harder the Goals, the Higher the Performance.'" *Journal of Applied Psychology* (February 1981): 54–58.

Matsumoto, D. "Management's Incentives to Avoid Negative Earnings Surprises." *The Accounting Review* (July 2002): 483–514.

Maule, A., and G. Hockey. "State, Stress, and Time Pressure." In *Time Pressure and Stress in Human Judgment and Decision Making,* edited by O. Svenson and A. Maule. New York: Plenum Press, 1993.

Mawhinney, T. "Intrinsic x Extrinsic Motivation: Perspectives from Behaviorism." *Organizational Behavior and Human Performance* (December 1979): 411–40.

Mayer, R. *The Promise of Educational Psychology,* vol. II: *Teaching for Meaningful Learning.* Upper Saddle River, NJ: Pearson Education, 2002.

Mayer, R. "Teaching of Subject Matter." *Annual Review of Psychology* (2004): 715–44.

McCartney, S., and H. Evans. "After the Bomb, Expert Opinions Flood the Media." *Wall Street Journal* (April 21, 1995): B1.

McClelland, D. *The Achieving Society.* Princeton, NJ: Van Nostrand Reinhold, 1961.

McClelland, D., J. Atkinson, R. Clark, and E. Lowell. *The Achievement Motive.* New York: Appleton-Century-Crofts, 1953.

McClure, J. "Discounting Causes of Behavior: Are Two Reasons Better than One?" *Journal of Personality and Social Psychology* (January 1998): 7–20.

McConnell, A. "Implicit Theories: Consequences for Social Judgments of Individuals." *Journal of Experimental Social Psychology* (May 2001): 215–27.

McDaniel, L. "The Effects of Time Pressure and Audit Program Structure on Audit Performance." *Journal of Accounting Research* (Autumn 1990): 267–85.

McDaniel, L., L. Maines, and R. Martin. "Evaluating Financial Reporting Quality: The Effects of Financial Expertise versus Financial Literacy." *The Accounting Review* (2002): S139–67.

McDaniel, M., F. Schmidt, and J. Hunter. "Job Experience Correlates of Job Performance." *Journal of Applied Psychology* (No. 2 1988): 327–30.

McEwen, R., and J. Hunton. "Is Analyst Forecast Accuracy Associated with Accounting Information Use?" *Accounting Horizons* (March 1999): 1–16.

McGhee, W., M. Shields, and J. Birnberg. "The Effects of Personality on a Subject's Information Processing." *The Accounting Review* (July 1978): 681–97.

McIntyre, E. "Current-Cost Financial Statements and Common-Stock Investments Decisions." *The Accounting Review* (July 1973): 575–85.

McKeown, J., J. Mutchler, and W. Hopwood. "Towards an Explanation of Auditor Failure to Modify the Audit Opinions of Bankrupt Companies." *Auditing: A Journal of Practice and Theory* (1991): S1–13.

McLeod, P. "An Assessment of the Experimental Literature on Electronic Support of Group Work: Results of a Meta-Analysis." *Human-Computer Interaction* (No. 3 1992): 257–80.

McMillan, J., and R. White. "Auditors' Belief Revisions and Evidence Search: The Effect of Hypothesis Frame, Confirmation Bias, and Professional Skepticism." *The Accounting Review* (July 1993): 443–65.

McNamara, D., and W. Kintsch. "Learning from Texts: Effects of Prior Knowledge and Text Coherence." *Discourse Processes* (October 1996): 247–88.

McNamara, D., E. Kintsch, N. Songer, and W. Kintsch. "Are Good Texts Always Better? Interactions of Text Coherence, Background Knowledge, and Levels of Understanding in Learning from Text." *Cognition and Instruction* (No. 1 1996): 1–43.

McNees, S. "The Uses and Abuses of 'Consensus' Forecasts." *Journal of Forecasting* (December 1992): 703–10.

McNichols, M. "Evidence of Informational Asymmetries from Management Earnings Forecasts and Stock Returns." *The Accounting Review* (January 1989): 1–27.

Mear, R., and M. Firth. "Cue Usage and Self-Insight of Financial Analysts." *The Accounting Review* (January 1987a): 176–82.

Mear, R., and M. Firth. "Assessing the Accuracy of Financial Analyst Security Return

Predictions." *Accounting, Organizations and Society* (No. 4 1987b): 331–40.

Meehl, P. *Clinical versus Statistical Prediction.* Minneapolis, MN: University of Minnesota Press, 1954.

Meehl, P., and A. Rosen. "Antecedent Probability and the Efficiency of Psychometric Signs, Patterns, or Cutting Scores." *Psychological Bulletin* (May 1955): 194–216.

Mehle, T., C. Gettys, C. Manning, S. Baca, and S. Fisher. "The Availability Explanation of Excessive Plausibility Assessments." *Acta Psychologica* (November 1981): 127–40.

Mellers, B., and A. McGraw. "Anticipated Emotions as Guides to Choice." *Current Directions in Psychological Science* (December 2001): 210–14.

Mendenhall, R. "Evidence of Possible Underweighting of Earnings-Related Information." *Journal of Accounting Research* (Spring 1991): 170–80.

Merchant, K. "The Design of the Corporate Budgeting System: Influences on Managerial Behavior and Performance." *The Accounting Review* (October 1981): 813–29.

Mero, N., and S. Motowildo. "Effects of Rater Accountability on the Accuracy and Favorability of Performance Ratings." *Journal of Applied Psychology* (May 1995): 517–24.

Mervis, C., and E. Rosch. "Categorization of Natural Objects." *Annual Review of Psychology* (1981): 89–115.

Messier, W., Jr. "The Effect of Experience and Firm Type on Materiality/Disclosure Judgments." *Journal of Accounting Research* (Autumn 1983): 611–18.

Messier, W., Jr. "Research in and Development of Audit Decision Aids." In *Judgment and Decision-Making Research in Accounting and Auditing,* edited by R. Ashton and A. Ashton. Cambridge, MA: Cambridge University Press, 1995.

Messier, W., Jr., and J. Hansen. "Expert Systems in Auditing: The State of the Art." *Auditing: A Journal of Practice & Theory* (Fall 1987): 94–105.

Messier, W., Jr., and J. Hansen. "Inducing Rules for Expert System Development: An Example Using Default and Bankruptcy Data." *Management Science* (December 1988): 1403–15.

Messier, W., Jr., and A. Schneider. "A Hierarchical Approach to the External Auditor's Evaluation of the Internal Auditing Function." *Contemporary Accounting Research* (Spring 1988): 337–53.

Messier, W. F., Jr., and R. Tubbs. "Recency Effects in Belief Revision: The Impact of Audit Experience and the Review Process." *Auditing: A Journal of Practice & Theory* (Spring 1994): 57–72.

Meyer, D., and R. Schvaneveldt. "Meaning, Memory Structure and Mental Processes." In *The Structure of Human Memory,* edited by C. Cofer. San Francisco: W.H. Freeman and Co., 1976.

Meyer, J., and I. Gellatly. "Perceived Performance Norm as a Mediator in the Effect of Assigned Goal on Personal Goal and Task Performance." *Journal of Applied Psychology* (August 1988): 410–20.

Meyers-Levy, J. "Gender Differences in Information Processing: A Selectivity Interpretation." In *Cognitive and Affective Responses to Advertising,* edited by P. Cafferata and A. Tybout. Lexington, MA: Lexington Books, 1986.

Meyvis, T., and C. Janiszewski. "Consumers' Beliefs about Product Benefits: The Effect of Obviously Irrelevant Product Information." *Journal of Consumer Research* (March 2002): 618–35.

Mia, L. "Managerial Attitude, Motivation and the Effectiveness of Budget Participation." *Accounting, Organizations and Society* (No. 5 1988): 465–75.

Mia, L. "The Impact of Participation in Budgeting and Job Difficulty on Managerial Performance and Work Motivation: A Research Note." *Accounting, Organizations and Society* (No. 4 1989): 347–57.

Michaelson, R., and W. Messier Jr. "Expert Systems in Taxation." *The Journal of the American Taxation Association* (Spring 1987): 7–21.

Michaely, R., and K. Womack. "Conflict of Interest and the Credibility of Underwriter Analyst Recommendations." *Review of Financial Studies,* special (1999): 653–86.

Mieg, H. *The Social Psychology of Expertise: Case Studies in Research, Professional Domains, and Expert Roles.* Mahwah, NJ: Lawrence Erlbaum, 2001.

Mikhail, M., B. Walther, and R. Willis. "Do Security Analysts Improve Their Performance with Experience?" *Journal of Accounting Research* (1997): S131–57.

Mikhail, M., B. Walther, and R. Willis. "Does Forecast Accuracy Matter to Security Analysts?" *The Accounting Review* (April 1999): 185–200.

Mikhail, M., B. Walther, and R. Willis. "Do Security Analysts Exhibit Persistent Differences in Stock Picking Ability?" *Journal of Financial Economics* (October 2004): 67–91.

Miller, G. "The Magical Number Seven, Plus or Minus Two: Some Limits on Our Capacity for Processing Information." *Psychological Review* (March 1956): 81–97.

Miller, J. "Information Input Overload and Psychopathology." *American Journal of Psychiatry* (February 1960): 695–704.

Miller, P., and N. Fagley. "The Effects of Framing, Problem Variations, and Providing Rationale on Choice." *Personality and Social Psychology Bulletin* (October 1991): 517–22.

Milliron, V. "A Behavioral Study of the Meaning and Influence of Tax Complexity." *Journal of Accounting Research* (Autumn 1985): 794–816.

Mills, T. "The Effect of Cognitive Style on External Auditors' Reliance Decisions on Internal Audit Functions." *Behavioral Research in Accounting* (1996): 49–73.

Miner, J. *Theories of Organizational Behavior.* Hinsdale, IL: The Dryden Press, 1980.

Mladenovic, R., and R. Simnett. "Examination of Contextual Effects and Changes in Task Predictability on Auditor Calibration." *Behavioral Research in Accounting* (1994): 178–203.

Mock, T. "The Value of Budget Information." *The Accounting Review* (July 1973): 520–34.

Mock, T., T. Estrin, and M. Vasarhelyi. "Learning Patterns, Decision Approach, and Value of Information." *Journal of Accounting Research* (Spring 1972): 129–53.

Mock, T., A. Wright, M. Washington, and G. Krishnamoorthy. "Auditors' Uncertainty Representation and Evidence Aggregation." *Behavioral Research in Accounting* (1997): S123–47.

Moeckel, C. "The Effect of Experiences on Auditors' Memory Errors." *Journal of Accounting Research* (Autumn 1990): 368–87.

Moeckel, C. "Two Factors Affecting an Auditor's Ability to Integrate Audit Evidence." *Contemporary Accounting Research* (Fall 1991): 270–92.

Moeckel, C., and R. Plumlee. "Auditors' Confidence in Recognition of Audit Evidence." *The Accounting Review* (October 1989): 653–66.

Moeckel, C., and J. Williams. "The Role of Source Availability in Inference Verification." *Contemporary Accounting Research* (Spring 1990): 850–58.

Moore, D., T. Kurtzberg, C. Fox, and M. Bazerman. "Positive Illusions and Forecasting Errors in Mutual Fund Investment Decisions." *Organizational Behavior and Human Decision Processes* (August 1999): 95–114.

Moreno, K., and S. Bhattacharjee. "The Impact of Pressure from Potential Client Business Opportunities on the Judgments of Auditors across Professional Ranks." *Auditing: A Journal of Practice and Theory* (March 2003): 13–28.

Moreno, K., T. Kida, and J. Smith. "The Impact of Affective Reactions on Risky Decision Making in Accounting Contexts." *Journal of Accounting Research* (December 2002): 1331–49.

Morgeson, F., and M. Campion. "Social and Cognitive Sources of Potential Inaccuracy in Job Analysis." *Journal of Applied Psychology* (September 1997): 627–55.

Moriarity, S. "Communicating Financial Information through Multidimensional Graphics." *Journal of Accounting Research* (Spring 1979): 205–24.

Moriarity, S., and F. Barron. "Modeling the Materiality Judgments of Audit Partners." *Journal of Accounting Research* (Autumn 1976): 320–41.

Morris, N., and W. Rouse. "Review and Evaluation of Empirical Research in Troubleshooting." *Human Factors* (October 1985): 503–30.

Moscovici, S. "Social Influence and Conformity." In *The Handbook of Social Psychology,* 3rd ed., edited by G. Lindzey and E. Aronson. New York: Random House, 1985.

Moser, D. "The Effects of Output Interference, Availability, and Accounting Information on Investors' Predictive Judgments." *The Accounting Review* (July 1989): 433–48.

Moser, D. "Does Memory Affect Judgment? Self-Generated versus Recall Memory Measures." *Journal of Personality and Social Psychology* (April 1992): 555–63.

Moser, D., J. Birnberg, and S. Do. "A Similarity Strategy for Decisions Involving Sequential Events." *Accounting, Organizations and Society* (May–July 1994): 439–58.

Moser, D., J. Evans, and C. Kim. "The Effects of Horizontal and Exchange Inequity on Tax Reporting Decisions." *The Accounting Review* (October 1995): 619–34.

Motowildo, S. "Job Performance." In *Handbook of Psychology,* vol. 12: *Industrial and Organizational Psychology,* edited by W. Borman, D. Ilgen, and R. Klimoski. Hoboken, NJ: John Wiley & Sons, 2003.

Mueller, J., and J. Anderson. "Decision Aids for Generating Analytical Review Alternatives: The Impact of Goal Framing and Audit-Risk Level." *Behavioral Research in Accounting* (2002): 157–77.

Mullen, B., and C. Copper. "The Relation between Group Cohesiveness and Performance: An Integration." *Psychological Bulletin* (March 1994): 210–27.

Munk, C. "Analysts' Roles Evolve with Incentives." *Wall Street Journal* (May 21, 2003): A1.

Murphy, D. "Expert System Use and the Development of Expertise in Auditing: A Preliminary Investigation." *Journal of Information Systems* (Fall 1990): 18–35.

Murphy, G., and D. Medin. "The Role of Theories in Conceptual Coherence." *Psychological Review* (July 1985): 289–316.

Murphy, K., and J. Cleveland. *Understanding Performance Appraisal: Social, Organizational, and Goal-Based Perspectives.* Thousand Oaks, CA: Sage Publications, 1995.

Murphy, K., and R. DeShon. "Interrater Correlations Do Not Estimate the Reliability of Job Performance Ratings." *Personnel Psychology* (Winter 2000): 873–900.

Murthy, U., and D. Kerr. "Comparing Audit Team Effectiveness via Alternative Modes of Computer-Mediated Communication." *Auditing: A Journal of Practice and Theory* (March 2004): 141–52.

Mussweiler, T., and F. Strack. "Hypothesis-Consistent Testing and Semantic Priming in the Anchoring Paradigm: A Selective Accessibility Model." *Journal of Experimental Social Psychology* (March 1999): 136–64.

Mussweiler, T., and F. Strack. "Numeric Judgments under Uncertainty: The Role of Knowledge in Anchoring." *Journal of Experimental Social Psychology* (September 2000a): 495–518.

Mussweiler, T., and F. Strack. "The Use of Category and Exemplar Knowledge in the Solution of Anchoring Tasks." *Journal of Personality and Social Psychology* (June 2000b): 1038–52.

Mussweiler, T., and F. Strack. "The Semantics of Anchoring." *Organizational Behavior and Human Decision Processes* (November 2001): 234–55.

Mussweiler, T., F. Strack, and T. Pfeiffer. "Overcoming the Inevitable Anchoring Effect: Considering the Opposite Compensates for Selective Accessibility." *Personality and Social Psychology Bulletin* (September 2000): 1142–50.

Mutchler, J., W. Hopwood, and J. McKeown. "The Influence of Contrary Information and Mitigating Factors on Audit Opinion Decisions on Bankrupt Companies." *Journal of Accounting Research* (Autumn 1997): 295–310.

Myers, I., and M. McCaulley. *Manual: A Guide to the Development and Use of the Myers-Briggs Type Indicator.* Palo Alto, CA: Consulting Psychologists Press, 1985.

Naylor, J., and R. Clark. "Intuitive Inference Strategies in Interval Learning Tasks as a Function of Validity Magnitude and Sign." *Organizational Behavior and Human Performance* (No. 4 1968): 378–99.

Naylor, J., and T. Dickinson. "Task Structure, Work Structure, and Team Performance." *Journal of Applied Psychology* (June 1969): 167–77.

Naylor, J., and E. Schenck. "The Influence of Cue Redundancy upon the Human Inference Process for Tasks of Varying Degrees of Predictability." *Organizational Behavior and Human Performance* (No. 1 1968): 47–61.

Nelson, M. "The Effects of Error Frequency Knowledge and Accounting Knowledge on Error Diagnosis in Analytical Review." *The Accounting Review* (October 1993a): 804–24.

Nelson, M. "The Learning and Application of Frequency Knowledge in Audit Judgment." *Journal of Accounting Literature* (1993b): 185–211.

Nelson, M. "Strategies of Auditors: Evaluation of Sample Results." *Auditing: A Journal of Practice and Theory* (Spring 1995): 34–49.

Nelson, M. "Behavioral Evidence on the Effects of Principles- and Rules-Based Standards." *Accounting Horizons* (March 2003): 91–104.

Nelson, M. "A Review of Experimental and Archival Conflicts-of-Interest Research in Auditing." In *Conflicts of Interest: Challenges and Solutions in Business, Law, Medicine, and Public Policy,* edited by D. Moore, D. Cain, G. Loewenstein, and M. Bazerman. Cambridge, MA: Cambridge University Press, 2005.

Nelson, M., R. Bloomfield, J. Hales, and R. Libby. "The Effect of Information Strength and Weight on Behavior in Financial Markets." *Organizational Behavior and Human Decision Processes* (November 2001): 168–96.

Nelson, M., J. Elliott, and R. Tarpley. "Evidence from Auditors about Managers' and Auditors' Earnings Management Decisions." *The Accounting Review* (2002): S175–202.

Nelson, M., and W. Kinney Jr. "The Effect of Ambiguity on Loss Contingency Reporting Judgments." *The Accounting Review* (April 1997): 257–74.

Nelson, M., S. Krische, and R. Bloomfield. "Confidence and Investors' Reliance on Disciplined Trading Strategies." *Journal of Accounting Research* (2003): 503–23.

Nelson, M., R. Libby, and S. Bonner. "Knowledge Structure and the Estimation of Conditional Probabilities in Audit Planning." *The Accounting Review* (January 1995): 27–47.

Newberry, K., P. Reckers, and R. Wyndelts. "An Examination of Tax Practitioner Decisions: The Role of Preparer Sanctions and Framing Effects Associated with Client Condition." *Journal of Economic Psychology* (June 1993): 439–52.

Newbold, P., J. Zumwalt, and S. Kannan. "Combining Forecasts to Improve Earnings per Share Prediction: An Examination of Electric Utilities." *International Journal of Forecasting* (No. 3 1987): 229–38.

Newell, A., and H. Simon. *Human Problem Solving.* Englewood Cliffs, NJ: Prentice-Hall, 1972.

Newton, L. "The Risk Factor in Materiality Decisions." *The Accounting Review* (January 1977): 97–108.

Ng, T., and H. Tan. "Effects of Authoritative Guidance Availability and Audit Committee Effectiveness on Auditors' Judgments in an Auditor-Client Negotiations Context." *The Accounting Review* (July 2003): 801–18.

Nicholson, N. "How Hardwired Is Human Behavior?" *Harvard Business Review* (July–August 1998): 135–47.

Nickerson, R. "Retrieval Inhibition from Part-Set Cuing: A Persistent Enigma in Memory Research." *Memory & Cognition* (November 1984): 531–52.

Nickerson, R. "Confirmation Bias: A Ubiquitous Phenomenon in Many Guises." *Review of General Psychology* (June 1998): 175–220.

Nickerson, R. "How We Know—and Sometimes Misjudge—What Others Know: Imputing One's Own Knowledge to Others." *Psychological Bulletin* (November 1999): 737–59.

Nisbett, R. *The Geography of Thought: How Asians and Westerners Think Differently . . . and Why.* New York: Free Press, 2003.

Nisbett, R., D. Krantz, C. Jepson, and Z. Kunda. "The Use of Statistical Heuristics in Everyday Inductive Reasoning." *Psychological Review* (October 1983): 339–63.

Nisbett, R., and L. Ross. *Human Inference: Strategies and Shortcomings of Social Judgment.* Englewood Cliffs, NJ: Prentice-Hall, 1980.

Nisbett, R., H. Zukier, and R. Lemley. "The Dilution Effect: Nondiagnostic Information Weakens the Implications of Diagnostic Information." *Cognitive Psychology* (April 1981): 248–77.

Nofsinger, J., and R. Sias. "Herding and Feedback Trading by Institutional and Individual Investors." *Journal of Finance* (December 1999): 2263–95.

Nolen-Hoeksema, S., and C. Rusting. "Gender Differences in Well-Being." In *Well-Being: The Foundations of Hedonic Psychology,* edited by D. Kahneman, E. Diener, and N. Schwarz. New York: Russell Sage Foundation, 1999.

Nouri, H., and R. Parker. "The Relationship between Budget Participation and Job Performance: The Roles of Budget Adequacy and Organizational Commitment." *Accounting, Organizations and Society* (July–August 1998): 467–83.

O'Brien, P. "Analysts' Forecasts as Earnings Expectations." *Journal of Accounting and Economics* (January 1988): 53–83.

O'Donnell, E. "Measuring Cognitive Effort During Analytical Review: A Process-Tracing Framework with Experimental Results." *Auditing: A Journal of Practice & Theory* (1996): S100–110.

O'Keefe, T., R. King, and K. Gaver. "Audit Fees, Industry Specialization, and Compliance with GAAS Reporting Standards." *Auditing: A Journal of Practice and Theory* (Fall 1994a): 41–55.

O'Keefe, T., D. Simunic, and M. Stein. "The Production of Audit Services: Evidence from a Major Public Accounting Firm." *Journal of Accounting Research* (Autumn 1994b): 241–61.

O'Leary, D. "Validation of Expert Systems—With Applications to Auditing and Accounting Expert Systems." *Decision Sciences* (Summer 1987): 468–85.

O'Reilly, B. "Why Johnny Can't Invest." *Fortune* (November 9, 1998): 173–78.

Odean, T. "Volume, Volatility, Price, and Profit When All Traders Are Above Average." *The Journal of Finance* (December 1998): 1887–1934.

Odean, T. "Do Investors Trade Too Much?" *The American Economic Review* (December 1999): 1279–98.

Odom, M., and P. Dorr. "The Impact of Elaboration-Based Expert System Interfaces on De-Skilling: An Epistemological Issue." *Journal of Information Systems* (Spring 1995): 1–17.

Ofir, C. "Ease of Recall versus Recalled Evidence in Judgment: Experts versus Laymen." *Organizational Behavior and Human Decision Processes* (January 2000): 28–42.

Ohanian, R. "Construction and Validation of a Scale to Measure Celebrity Endorsers' Perceived Expertise, Trustworthiness, and Attractiveness." *Journal of Advertising* (No. 19 1990): 39–52.

Oliver, B. "A Study of Confidence Interval Financial Statements." *Journal of Accounting Research* (Spring 1972): 154–66.

Olsen, R. "Desirability Bias among Professional Investment Managers: Some Evidence from Experts." *Journal of Behavioral Decision Making* (March 1997): 65–72.

Olsen, R. "Behavioral Finance and Its Implications for Stock-Price Volatility." *Financial Analysts Journal* (March–April 1998): 10–18.

Olsen, R., and C. Cox. "The Influence of Gender on the Perception and Response to Investment Risk: The Case of Professional Investors." *Journal of Psychology and Financial Markets* (No. 1 2001): 29–36.

Olson, G., and J. Olson. "Human–Computer Interaction: Psychological Aspects of the Human Use of Computing." *Annual Review of Psychology* (2003): 491–516.

Ones, D., C. Viswesvaran, and S. Dilchert. "Cognitive Ability in Personnel Selection Decisions." In *The Blackwell Handbook of Personnel Selection,* edited by A. Evers, N. Anderson, and O. Voskuijl. Malden, MA: Blackwell Publishing, 2005.

Opdyke, J., A. Lucchetti, and C. Oster. "Mum's the Word in Wake of Disclosure Rule." *Wall Street Journal* (August 16, 2000): C1.

Ortman, R. "The Effects on Investment Analysis of Alternative Reporting Procedure for Diversified Firms." *The Accounting Review* (April 1975): 298–304.

Oskamp, S. "Overconfidence in Case-Study Judgments." In *Judgment under Uncertainty: Heuristics and Biases,* edited by D. Kahneman, P. Slovic, and A. Tversky. New York: Cambridge University Press, 1982.

Otley, D., and F. Dias. "Accounting Aggregation and Decision-Making Performance: An Experimental Investigation." *Journal of Accounting Research* (Spring 1982): 171–88.

Owhoso, V., W. Messier Jr., and J. Lynch Jr. "Error Detection by Industry-Specialized Teams during Sequential Audit Review." *Journal of Accounting Research* (June 2002): 883–900.

Paese, P., and J. Sniezek. "Influences on the Appropriateness of Confidence in Judgment: Practice, Effort, Information, and Decision-Making." *Organizational Behavior and*

Human Decision Processes (February 1991): 100–130.

Palmrose, Z. "Trials of Legal Disputes Involving Independent Auditors: Some Empirical Evidence." *Journal of Accounting Research* (1991): S149–85.

Paquette, L., and T. Kida. "The Effect of Decision Strategy and Task Complexity on Decision Performance." *Organizational Behavior and Human Decision Processes* (February 1988): 128–42.

Park, C., and E. Stice. "Analyst Forecasting Ability and the Stock Price Reaction to Forecast Revisions." *Review of Accounting Studies* (September 2000): 259–72.

Pasewark, W., J. Strawser, and J. Wilkerson Jr. "Empirical Evidence on the Association between Characteristics of Graduating Accounting Students and Recruiting Decisions of Accounting Employers." *Issues in Accounting Education* (Fall 1988): 388–401.

Patton, J. "An Experimental Investigation of Some Effects of Consolidating Municipal Financial Reports." *The Accounting Review* (April 1978): 402–14.

Payne, J. "Task Complexity and Contingent Processing in Decision Making: An Information Search and Protocol Analysis." *Organizational Behavior and Human Performance* (August 1976): 366–87.

Payne, J. "Contingent Decision Behavior." *Psychological Bulletin* (September 1982): 382–402.

Payne, J., J. Bettman, and E. Johnson. *The Adaptive Decision Maker.* New York: Cambridge University Press, 1993.

Payne, J., M. Braunstein, and J. Carroll. "Exploring Predecisional Behavior: An Alternative Approach to Decision Research." *Organizational Behavior and Human Performance* (August 1978): 366–87.

Peecher, M. "The Influence of Auditors' Justification Processes on Their Decisions: A Cognitive Model and Experimental Evidence." *Journal of Accounting Research* (Spring 1996): 125–40.

Pei, B., and J. Reneau. "The Effects of Memory Structure on Using Rule-Based Expert Systems for Training: A Framework and an Empirical Test." *Decision Sciences* (Spring 1990): 263–86.

Pei, B., P. Reckers, and R. Wyndelts. "The Influence of Information Presentation Order on Professional Tax Judgment." *Journal of Economic Psychology* (March 1990): 119–46.

Pei, B., P. Reckers, and R. Wyndelts. "Tax Professionals' Belief Revision: The Effects of Information Sequence, Client Preference, and Domain Experience." *Decision Sciences* (January–February 1992a): 175–99.

Pei, B., S. Reed, and B. Koch. "Auditor Belief Revisions in a Performance Auditing Setting: An Application of the Belief-Adjustment Model." *Accounting, Organizations and Society* (February 1992b): 169–83.

Pei, B., and B. Tuttle. "Part-Set Cueing Effects in a Diagnostic Setting with Professional Auditors." *Journal of Behavioral Decision Making* (July 1999): 233–56.

Pennington, N. "Comprehension Strategies in Programming." In *Empirical Studies of Programmers: Second Workshop,* edited by G. Olson, S. Sheppard, and E. Soloway. Norwood, NJ: Ablex Publishing Co., 1987a.

Pennington, N. "Stimulus Structures and Mental Representations in Expert Comprehension of Computer Programs." *Cognitive Psychology* (July 1987b): 295–341.

Pennington, N., and R. Hastie. "Evidence Evaluation in Complex Decision Making." *Journal of Personality and Social Psychology* (August 1986): 242–58.

Pennington, N., and R. Hastie. "Explanation-Based Decision Making: Effects of Memory Structure on Judgment." *Journal of Experimental Psychology: Learning, Memory, and Cognition* (July 1988): 521–33.

Pennington, N., and R. Hastie. "Explaining the Evidence: Tests of the Story Model for Juror Decision Making." *Journal of Personality and Social Psychology* (February 1992): 189–206.

Pennington, N., and R. Hastie. "Reasoning in Explanation-Based Decision Making." *Cognition* (October–November 1993): 123–63.

Perloff, R. *The Dynamics of Persuasion.* Hillsdale, NJ: Lawrence Erlbaum, 1993.

Peterson, B., and B. Wong-on-Wing. "An Examination of the Positive Test Strategy in Auditors' Hypothesis Testing." *Behavioral Research in Accounting* (2000): 257–77.

Peterson, C., and L. Beach. "Man as an Intuitive Statistician." *Psychological Bulletin* (July 1967): 29–46.

Peterson, D., and G. Pitz. "Effect of Input from a Mechanical Model on Clinical Judgment." *Journal of Applied Psychology* (January 1986): 163–67.

Pettigrew, T. "The Measurement and Correlates of Category Width as a Cognitive Variable." *Journal of Personality* (December 1958): 532–44.

Petty, R., and J. Cacioppo. "Attitude and Attitude Change." *Annual Review of Psychology* (1981): 357–404.

Petty, R., and J. Cacioppo. *Communication and Persuasion: Central and Peripheral Routesto Attitude Change.* New York: Springer-Verlag, 1986.

Petty, R., and D. Wegener. "Attitude Change: Multiple Roles for Persuasion Variables." In *The Handbook of Social Psychology,* 4th ed., edited by D. Gilbert, S. Fiske, and G. Lindzey. Boston: McGraw-Hill, 1998.

Petty, R., and D. Wegener. "The Elaboration Likelihood Model: Current Status and Controversies." In *Dual-Process Theories in Social Psychology,* edited by S. Chaiken and Y. Trope. New York: The Guilford Press, 1999.

Petty, R., D. Wegener, and P. White. "Flexible Correction Processes in Social Judgment: Implications for Persuasion." *Social Cognition* (Spring 1998): 93–113.

Phelps, R., and J. Shanteau. "Livestock Judges: How Much Information Can an Expert Use?" *Organizational Behavior and Human Performance* (April 1978): 209–19.

Phillips, F. "Accounting Students' Beliefs about Knowledge: Associating Performance with Underlying Belief Dimensions." *Issues in Accounting Education* (February 1998): 113–26.

Phillips, F. "A Research Note on Accounting Students' Epistemological Beliefs, Study Strategies, and Unstructured Problem-Solving Performance." *Issues in Accounting Education* (February 2001): 21–39.

Phillips, F., and G. Vaidyanathan. "Should Case Materials Precede or Follow Lectures?" *Issues in Accounting Education* (August 2004): 305–19.

Pincus, K. "The Efficacy of a Red Flags Questionnaire for Assessing the Possibility of Fraud." *Accounting, Organizations and Society* (No. 1/2 1989): 153–63.

Pincus, K. "Auditor Individual Differences and Fairness of Presentation Judgments." *Auditing: A Journal of Practice and Theory* (Fall 1990): 150–66.

Pincus, K. "Audit Judgment Confidence." *Behavioral Research in Accounting* (1991): 39–65.

Pitz, G., and N. Sachs. "Judgment and Decision: Theory and Application." *Annual Review of Psychology* (1984): 139–63.

Plous, S. *The Psychology of Judgment and Decision Making.* New York: McGraw-Hill, 1993.

Plumlee, M. "The Effect of Information Complexity on Analysts' Use of That Information." *The Accounting Review* (January 2003): 275–96.

Plumlee, R. "The Standard of Objectivity for Internal Auditors: Memory and Bias Effects." *Journal of Accounting Research* (Autumn 1985): 683–99.

Ponemon, L., and D. Gabhart. "Auditor Independence Judgments: A Cognitive-Developmental Model and Experimental Evidence." *Contemporary Accounting Research* (Fall 1990): 227–51.

Ponemon, L., and J. Wendell. "Judgmental versus Random Sampling in Auditing: An Experimental Investigation." *Auditing: A Journal of Practice & Theory* (Fall 1995): 17–34.

Posner, M. "Introduction: What Is It to Be an Expert?" In *The Nature of Expertise,* edited by M. Chi, R. Glaser, and M. Farr. Hillsdale, NJ: Lawrence Erlbaum, 1988.

Powell, J. "An Attempt at Increasing Decision Rule Use in a Judgment Task." *Organizational Behavior and Human Decision Processes* (February 1991): 89–99.

Pratt, J. "Post-Cognitive Structure: Its Determinants and Relationship to Perceived Information Use and Predictive Accuracy." *Journal of Accounting Research* (Spring 1982): 189–209.

Pratt, J., and J. Stice. "The Effects of Client Characteristics on Auditor Litigation Risk Judgments, Required Audit Evidence, and Recommended Audit Fees." *The Accounting Review* (October 1994): 639–56.

Prawitt, D. "Staffing Assignments for Judgment-Oriented Audit Tasks: The Effects of Structured Audit Technology and

Environment." *The Accounting Review* (July 1995): 443–65.

Prechter, R., Jr. "Unconscious Herding Behavior as the Psychological Basis of Financial Market Trends and Patterns." *Journal of Psychology and Financial Markets* (No. 3 2001): 120–25.

Price, P., and E. Stone. "Intuitive Evaluation of Likelihood Judgment Producers: Evidence for a Confidence Heuristic." *Journal of Behavioral Decision Making* (January 2004): 39–57.

Pritchard, R., S. Jones, P. Roth, K. Stuebing, and S. Ekeberg. "Effects of Group Feedback, Goal Setting, and Incentives on Organizational Productivity." *Journal of Applied Psychology* (May 1988): 337–58.

Pronin, E., T. Gilovich, and L. Ross. "Objectivity in the Eye of the Beholder: Divergent Perceptions of Bias in Self versus Others." *Psychological Review* (July 2004): 781–99.

Pronin, E., D. Lin, and L. Ross. "The Bias Blind Spot: Perceptions of Bias in Self versus Others." *Personality and Social Psychology Bulletin* (March 2002a): 369–81.

Pronin, E., C. Puccio, and L. Ross. "Understanding Misunderstanding: Social Psychological Perspectives." In *Heuristics and Biases: The Psychology of Intuitive Judgment,* edited by T. Gilovich, D. Griffin, and D. Kahneman. New York: Cambridge University Press, 2002b.

Purvis, S. "The Effect of Audit Documentation Format on Data Collection." *Accounting, Organizations and Society* (No. 5/6 1989): 551–63.

Quattrone, G. "Overattribution and Unit Formation: When Behavior Engulfs the Person." *Journal of Personality and Social Psychology* (April 1982): 593–607.

Quiñones, M., J. Ford, and M. Teachout. "The Relationship between Work Experience and Job Performance: A Conceptual and Meta-Analytic Review." *Personnel Psychology* (Winter 1995): 887–910.

Raghunandan, K., R. Grimlund, and A. Schepanski. "Auditor Evaluation of Loss Contingencies." *Contemporary Accounting Research* (Spring 1991): 549–69.

Raiffa, H. *Decision Analysis.* Reading, MA: Addison Wesley, 1968.

Raiijmakers, J., and R. Shiffrin. "Search of Associative Memory." *Psychological Review* (March 1981): 93–134.

Ramanathan, K., and W. Weis. "Supplementing Collegiate Financial Statements with Across-Fund Aggregation: An Experimental Inquiry." *Accounting, Organizations and Society* (No. 2 1981): 143–51.

Ramsay, R. "Senior/Manager Differences in Audit Workpaper Review." *Journal of Accounting Research* (Spring 1994): 127–35.

Rau, S., and D. Moser. "Does Performing Other Audit Tasks Affect Going-Concern Judgments?" *The Accounting Review* (October 1999): 493–508.

Ravinder, H., D. Kleinmuntz, and J. Dyer. "The Reliability of Subjective Probabilities Obtained through Decomposition." *Management Science* (February 1988): 186–99.

Rebele, J., J. Heinz, and G. Briden. "Independent Auditor Sensitivity to Evidence Reliability." *Auditing: A Journal of Practice & Theory* (Fall 1988): 43–52.

Reber, A. *The Penguin Dictionary of Psychology,* 2nd ed. New York: Penguin Books, 1995.

Reckers, P., D. Sanders, and R. Wyndelts. "An Empirical Investigation of Factors Influencing Tax Practitioner Compliance." *Journal of the American Taxation Association* (Fall 1991): 30–46.

Reckers, P., and J. Schultz Jr. "Individual versus Group Assisted Audit Evaluations." *Auditing: A Journal of Practice and Theory* (Fall 1982): 64–74.

Reckers, P., and J. Schultz Jr. "The Effects of Fraud Signals, Evidence Order, and Group-Assisted Counsel on Independent Auditor Judgment." *Behavioral Research in Accounting* (1993): 124–44.

Ree, M., T. Carretta, and M. Teachout. "Role of Ability and Prior Job Knowledge in Complex Training Performance." *Journal of Applied Psychology* (November 1995): 721–30.

Reilly, B., and M. Doherty. "A Note on the Assessment of Self-Insight in Judgment Research." *Organizational Behavior and Human Decision Processes* (August 1989): 123–31.

Reilly, B., and M. Doherty. "The Assessment of Self-Insight in Judgment Policies."

Organizational Behavior and Human Decision Processes (December 1992): 285–309.

Reimers, J., and S. Butler. "The Effect of Outcome Knowledge on Auditors' Judgmental Evaluations." *Accounting, Organizations and Society* (February 1992): 185–94.

Reimers, J., and M. Fennema. "The Audit Review Process and Sensitivity to Information Source Objectivity." *Auditing: A Journal of Practice & Theory* (Spring 1999): 117–23.

Reimers, J., S. Wheeler, and R. Dusenbury. "The Effect of Response Mode on Auditors' Control Risk Assessments." *Auditing: A Journal of Practice & Theory* (Fall 1993): 62–78.

Remus, W. "An Empirical Investigation of the Impact of Graphical and Tabular Data Presentations on Decision Making." *Management Science* (May 1984): 533–42.

Remus, W. "A Study of Graphical and Tabular Displays and Their Interaction with Environmental Complexity." *Management Science* (September 1987): 1200–1204.

Renkl, A. "Learning from Worked-Out Examples: A Study on Individual Differences." *Cognitive Science* (January–March 1997): 1–29.

Renkl, A., R. Stark, H. Gruber, and H. Mandl. "Learning from Worked-Out Examples: The Effects of Example Variability and Elicited Self-Explanations." *Contemporary Educational Psychology* (January 1998): 90–108.

Rennie, M. "Factors Affecting Responsibility Assessments after an Audit Failure." *Behavioral Research in Accounting* (1995): 104–21.

Resnick, L. Introduction to *Knowing, Learning, and Instruction: Essays in Honor of Robert Glaser,* edited by L. Resnick. Hillsdale, NJ: Lawrence Erlbaum Associates, 1989.

Revelle, W. "Personality, Motivation, and Cognitive Performance." In *Abilities, Motivation, & Methodology: The Minnesota Symposium on Learning and Individual Differences,* edited by R. Kanfer, P. Ackerman, and R. Cudeck. Hillsdale, NJ: Lawrence Erlbaum Associates, 1989.

Reyna, V., and C. Brainerd. "Fuzzy-Trace Theory and Framing Effects in Choice: Gist Extraction, Truncation, and Conversion.

Journal of Behavioral Decision Making (October–December 1991): 249–62.

Ricchiute, D. "An Empirical Assessment of the Impact of Alternative Task Presentation Modes on Decision-Making Research in Auditing." *Journal of Accounting Research* (Spring 1984): 341–50.

Ricchiute, D. "Presentation Mode, Task Importance, and Cue Order in Experimental Research on Expert Judges." *Journal of Applied Psychology* (May 1985): 367–73.

Ricchiute, D. "Effects of Judgment on Memory: Experiments in Recognition Bias and Process Dissociation in a Professional Judgment Task." *Organizational Behavior and Human Decision Processes* (April 1997): 27–39.

Ricchiute, D. "The Effect of Audit Seniors' Decisions on Working Paper Documentation and on Partners' Decisions." *Accounting, Organizations and Society* (April 1999): 155–71.

Rich, J. "Reviewers' Responses to Expectations about the Client and the Preparer." *The Accounting Review* (April 2004): 497–517.

Rich, J., I. Solomon, and K. Trotman. "The Audit Review Process: A Characterization from the Persuasion Perspective." *Accounting, Organizations and Society* (July 1997a): 481–505.

Rich, J., I. Solomon, and K. Trotman. "Multi-Auditor Judgment/Decision Making Research: A Decade Later." *Journal of Accounting Literature* (1997b): 86–126.

Richardson, S., S. Teoh, and P. Wysocki. "The Walkdown to Beatable Analyst Forecasts: The Role of Equity Issuance and Insider Trading Incentives." *Contemporary Accounting Research* (Winter 2004): 885–24.

Robben, H., P. Webley, R. Weigel, K. Wärneryd, K. Kinsey, D. Hessing, F. Alvira Martin, H. Elffers, R. Wahlund, L. van Langenhove, S. Long, and J. Scholz. "Decision Frame and Opportunity as Determinants of Tax Cheating: An International Experimental Study." *Journal of Economic Psychology* (September 1990): 341–64.

Roberts, M., and R. Ashton. "Using Declarative Knowledge to Improve Information Search Performance." *Journal of the American Taxation Association* (Spring 2003): 21–38.

Robinson, L., and R. Hastie. "Revision of Beliefs When a Hypothesis Is Eliminated from

Consideration." *Journal of Experimental Psychology: Human Perception and Performance* (August 1985): 443–56.

Roediger, H. "Inhibiting Effects of Recall." *Memory & Cognition* (No. 2 1974): 261–69.

Rogers, J., and P. Stocken. "Credibility of Management Forecasts." *The Accounting Review* (October 2005): 1233–60.

Roggeveen, A., and G. Johar. "Perceived Source Variability versus Familiarity: Testing Competing Explanations for the Truth Effect." *Journal of Consumer Psychology* (No. 2 2002): 81–91.

Rohrbaugh, J. "Improving the Quality of Group Judgment: Social Judgment Analysis and the Delphi Technique." *Organizational Behavior and Human Performance* (August 1979): 73–92.

Ronen, J. "Some Effects of Sequential Aggregation in Accounting on Decision-Making." *Journal of Accounting Research* (Autumn 1971): 307–32.

Ronen, J. "Effects of Some Probability Displays on Choices." *Organizational Behavior and Human Performance* (February 1973): 1–15.

Rose, J. "Decision Aids and Experiential Learning." *Behavioral Research in Accounting* (2005): 175–89.

Rose, J., and C. Wolfe. "The Effects of System Design Alternatives on the Acquisition of Tax Knowledge from a Computerized Tax Decision Aid." *Accounting, Organizations and Society* (April 2000): 285–306.

Rosman, A., I. Seol, and S. Biggs. "The Effect of Stage of Development and Financial Health on Auditor Decision Behavior in the Going-Concern Task." *Auditing: A Journal of Practice and Theory* (Spring 1999): 37–54.

Ross, B. "Remindings in Learning and Instruction." In *Similarity and Analogical Reasoning,* edited by S. Vosniadou and A. Ortony. New York: Cambridge University Press, 1989.

Ross, J. "Controlling Variables: A Meta-Analysis of Training Studies." *Review of Educational Research* (Winter 1988): 405–37.

Ross, L. "The Intuitive Psychologist and His Shortcomings: Distortions in the Attribution Process." In *Advances in Experimental Social Psychology,* vol. 10, edited by L. Berkowitz. New York: Academic Press, 1977.

Roth, P., C. Van Iddekinge, A. Huffcutt, C. Eidson Jr., and M. Schmit. "Personality Saturation in Structured Interviews." *International Journal of Selection and Assessment* (December 2005): 261–73.

Rothstein, H. "The Effects of Time Pressure on Judgment in Multiple Cue Probability Learning." *Organizational Behavior and Human Decision Processes* (February 1986): 83–92.

Rotter, J. "Generalized Expectancies for Internal versus External Control of Reinforcement." *Psychological Monographs* (1966): 1–28.

Rouse, W., and N. Morris. "On Looking into the Black Box: Prospects and Limits in the Search for Mental Models." *Psychological Bulletin* (November 1986): 349–63.

Rowe, C. "The Effect of Accounting Report Structure and Team Structure on Performance in Cross-Functional Teams." *The Accounting Review* (October 2004): 1153–80.

Rubinstein, M. "Rational Markets: Yes or No? The Affirmative Case." *Financial Analysts Journal* (May–June 2001): 15–29.

Ruble, T., and R. Cosier. "Effects of Cognitive Styles and Decision Setting on Performance." *Organizational Behavior and Human Decision Processes* (August 1990): 283–95.

Ruland, W. "The Accuracy of Forecasts by Management and by Financial Analysts." *The Accounting Review* (April 1978): 439–47.

Rundus, D. "Negative Effects of Using List Items as Recall Cues." *Journal of Verbal Learning and Verbal Behavior* (February 1973): 43–50.

Russo, R., and K. Kolzow. "Where Is the Fault in Fault Trees?" *Journal of Experimental Psychology: Human Perception and Performance* (February 1994): 17–32.

Rutledge, R. "The Ability to Moderate Recency Effects through Framing of Management Accounting Information." *Journal of Managerial Issues* (Spring 1995): 27–40.

Rutledge, R., and A. Harrell. "The Impact of Responsibility and Framing of Budgetary Information on Group-Shifts." *Behavioral Research in Accounting* (1994): 92–109.

Rynes, S., and D. Cable. "Recruitment Research in the Twenty-First Century." In *Handbook of Psychology,* vol. 12: *Industrial and Organizational Psychology,* edited by W. Borman, D. Ilgen, and R. Klimoski. Hoboken, NJ: John Wiley & Sons, 2003.

Rynes, S., and M. Connerley. "Applicant Reactions to Alternative Selection Procedures." *Journal of Business and Psychology* (Spring 1993): 261–77.

Sackett, P., and J. Wanek. "New Developments in the Use of Measures of Honesty, Integrity, Conscientiousness, Dependability, Trustworthiness, and Reliability for Personnel Selection." *Personnel Psychology* (Winter 1996): 787–829.

Saks, A. "The Impracticality of Recruitment Research." In *The Blackwell Handbook of Personnel Selection,* edited by A. Evers, N. Anderson, and O. Voskuijl. Malden, MA: Blackwell Publishing, 2005.

Salancik, G. "Commitment and Control of Organizational Behavior and Belief." In *New Directions in Organizational Behavior,* edited by B. Staw and G. Salancik. Chicago: St. Clair, 1977.

Salancik, G., and J. Meindl. "Corporate Attributions as Strategic Illusions of Corporate Control." *Administrative Science Quarterly* (June 1984): 238–54.

Salas, E., and J. Cannon-Bowers. "The Science of Training: A Decade of Progress." *Annual Review of Psychology* (2001): 471–99.

Salas, E., and M. Kosarzycki. "Why Don't Organizations Pay Attention to (and Use) Findings from the Science of Training?" *Human Resource Development Quarterly* (Winter 2003): 487–91.

Salgado, J., and F. Fruyt. "Personality in Personnel Selection." In *The Blackwell Handbook of Personnel Selection,* edited by A. Evers, N. Anderson, and O. Voskuijl. Malden, MA: Blackwell Publishing, 2005.

Salgado, J., C. Viswesvaran, and D. Ones. "Predictors Used for Personnel Selection: An Overview of Constructs, Methods and Techniques." In *Handbook of Industrial, Work, & Organizational Psychology,* vol. 1: *Personnel Psychology,* edited by N. Anderson, D. Ones, H. Sinangil, and C. Viswesvaran. Thousand Oaks,CA: Sage Publications, 2001.

Salterio, S. "The Effects of Precedents and Client Position on Auditors' Financial Accounting Policy Judgment." *Accounting, Organizations and Society* (July 1996): 467–86.

Salterio, S., and R. Denham. "Accounting Consultation Units: An Organizational Memory Analysis." *Contemporary Accounting Research* (Winter 1997): 669–91.

Salterio, S., and L. Koonce. "The Persuasiveness of Audit Evidence: The Case of Accounting Policy Decisions." *Accounting, Organizations and Society* (August 1997): 573–87.

Sami, H., and B. Schwartz. "Alternative Pension Liability Disclosure and the Effect on Credit Evaluation: An Experiment." *Behavioral Research in Accounting* (1992): 49–62.

San Miguel, J. "Human Information Processing and Its Relevance to Accounting: A Laboratory Study." *Accounting, Organizations and Society* (No. 4 1976): 357–73.

Sandberg, J. "Some Ideas Are So Bad That Only Team Efforts Can Account for Them." *Wall Street Journal* (September 29, 2004): B1.

Sandler, I., F. Reese, L. Spencer, and P. Harpin. "Person x Environment Interaction and Locus of Control: Laboratory, Therapy, and Classroom Studies." In *Research with the Locus of Control Construct,* vol. 2, edited by H. Lefcourt. New York: Academic Press, 1983.

Sanna, L., and N. Schwarz. "Debiasing the Hindsight Bias: The Role of Accessibility Experiences and (Mis)attributions." *Journal of Experimental Social Psychology* (May 2003): 287–95.

Sanna, L., N. Schwarz, and S. Stocker. "When Debiasing Backfires: Accessible Content and Accessibility Experiences in Debiasing Hindsight." *Journal of Experimental Psychology: Learning, Memory, and Cognition* (May 2002): 497–502.

Saunders, E. "Stock Prices and Wall Street Weather." *The American Economic Review* (December 1993): 1337–45.

Savage, L. *The Foundations of Statistics.* New York: Wiley, 1954.

Savich, R. "The Use of Accounting Information in Decision Making." *The Accounting Review* (July 1977): 642–52.

Sawyer, J. "Measurement and Prediction, Clinical and Statistical." *Psychological Bulletin* (September 1966): 178–200.

Sayre, T., F. Rankin, and N. Fargher. "The Effects of Promotion Incentives on Delegated Investment Decisions: A Note." *Journal of Management Accounting Research* (1998): 313–24.

Schacter, D. *The Seven Sins of Memory.* Boston: Houghton Mifflin, 2001.

Schadewald, M. "Reference Point Effects in Taxpayer Decision Making." *Journal of the American Taxation Association* (Spring 1989): 68–84.

Schadewald, M., and S. Limberg. "Instructor-Provided versus Student-Generated Explanations of Tax Rules: Effect on Recall." *Issues in Accounting Education* (Spring 1990): 30–40.

Schadewald, M., and S. Limberg. "Effect of Information Order and Accountability on Causal Judgments in a Legal Context." *Psychological Reports* (October 1992): 619–25.

Scharfstein, D., and J. Stein. "Herd Behavior and Investment." *American Economic Review* (June 1990): 465–79.

Schepanski, A. "Tests of Theories of Information Processing Behavior in Credit Judgment." *The Accounting Review* (July 1983): 581–99.

Schepanski, A., and D. Kelsey. "Testing for Framing Effects in Taxpayer Compliance Decisions." *Journal of the American Taxation Association* (Fall 1990): 60–77.

Schepanski, A., and T. Shearer. "A Prospect Theory Account of the Income Tax Withholding Phenomenon." *Organizational Behavior and Human Decision Processes* (August 1995): 174–86.

Schipper, K. "Analysts' Forecasts." *Accounting Horizons* (December 1991): 105–21.

Schipper, K. "Academic Accounting Research and the Standard Setting Process." *Accounting Horizons* (December 1994): 61–73.

Schipper, K. "Principles-Based Accounting Standards." *Accounting Horizons* (March 2003): 61–72.

Schisler, D. "An Experimental Examination of Factors Affecting Tax Preparers' Aggressiveness—A Prospect Theory Approach." *Journal of the American Taxation Association* (Fall 1994): 124–42.

Schlenker, B., T. Britt, J. Pennington, R. Murphy, and K. Doherty. "The Triangle Model of Responsibility." *Psychological Review* (October 1994): 632–52.

Schlenker, B., B. Pontari, and A. Christopher. "Excuses and Character: Personal and Social Implications of Excuses." *Personality and Social Psychology Review* (No. 5 2001): 15–32.

Schlenker, B., and M. Weigold. "Interpersonal Processes Involving Impression Regulation and Management." *Annual Review of Psychology* (1992): 133–68.

Schloemer, P., and M. Schloemer. "The Personality Types and Preferences of CPA Firm Professionals: An Analysis of Changes in the Profession." *Accounting Horizons* (December 1997): 24–39.

Schmidt, F., and J. Hunter. "The Validity and Utility of Selection Methods in Personnel Psychology: Practical and Theoretical Implications of 85 Years of Research Findings." *Psychological Bulletin* (September 1998): 262–74.

Schmidt, F., and J. Hunter. "General Mental Ability in the World of Work: Occupational Attainment and Job Performance." *Journal of Personality and Social Psychology* (January 2004): 162–73.

Schmidt, F., J. Hunter, and A. Outerbridge. "Impact of Job Experience and Ability on Job Knowledge, Work Sample Performance, and Supervisory Ratings of Job Performance." *Journal of Applied Psychology* (May 1986): 432–39.

Schmidt, F., J. Hunter, A. Outerbridge, and S. Goff. "Joint Relation of Experience and Ability with Job Performance: Test of Three Hypotheses." *Journal of Applied Psychology* (January 1988): 46–57.

Schmitt, N., and D. Chan. *Personnel Selection: A Theoretical Approach.* Thousand Oaks, CA: Sage Publications, 1998.

Schmitt, N., J. Cortina, M. Ingerick, and D. Wiechmann. "Personnel Selection and Employee Performance." In *Handbook of Psychology,* vol. 12: *Industrial and Organizational Psychology,* edited by W. Borman, D. Ilgen, and R. Klimoski. Hoboken, NJ: John Wiley & Sons, 2003.

Schmitt, N., and A. Dudycha. "Positive and Negative Cue Redundancy in Multiple Cue Probability Learning." *Memory & Cognition* (January 1975): 78–84.

Schmitt, R. "Who Is an Expert? In Some Courtrooms, The Answer Is 'Nobody.'" *Wall Street Journal* (June 17, 1997): A1, A8.

Schneider, A. "Modeling External Auditors' Evaluations of Internal Auditing." *Journal of Accounting Research* (Autumn 1984): 657–78.

Schneider, A. "The Reliance of External Auditors on the Internal Audit Function."

Journal of Accounting Research (Autumn 1985): 911–19.

Schneider, L., and T. Selling. "A Comparison of Compensatory and Noncompensatory Models of Judgment: Effects of Task Predictability and Degrees of Freedom." *Accounting, Organizations and Society* (January 1996): 3–22.

Schneider, S. "Framing and Conflict: Aspiration Level Contingency, the Status Quo, and Current Theories of Risky Choice." *Journal of Experimental Psychology: Learning, Memory, and Cognition* (September 1992): 1040–57.

Schneider, S., and L. Lopes. "Reflection in Preferences under Risk: Who and When May Suggest Why." *Journal of Experimental Psychology: Human Perception and Performance* (November 1986): 535–48.

Schoemaker, P. "When and How to Use Scenario Planning: A Heuristic Approach with Illustration." *Journal of Forecasting* (November 1991): 549–64.

Schoemaker, P. "Multiple Scenario Development: Its Conceptual and Behavioral Foundation." *Strategic Management Journal* (March 1993): 193–213.

Schraagen, J., S. Chipman, and V. Shalin. *Cognitive Task Analysis.* Mahwah, NJ: Lawrence Erlbaum Associates, 2000.

Schroder, H., M. Driver, and S. Streufert. *Human Information Processing.* New York: Holt, Rinehart & Winston, 1967.

Schroeder, M., I. Solomon, and D. Vickrey. "Audit Quality: The Perceptions of Audit-Committee Chairpersons and Audit Partners." *Auditing: A Journal of Practice & Theory* (Spring 1986): 86–94.

Schultz, J., Jr., and P. Reckers. "The Impact of Group Processing on Selected Audit Disclosure Decisions." *Journal of Accounting Research* (Autumn 1981): 482–501.

Schulz, A., and M. Cheng. "Persistence in Capital Budgeting Reinvestment Decisions — Personal Responsibility Antecedent and Information Asymmetry Moderator: A Note." *Accounting and Finance* (March 2002): 73–86.

Schum, D., and A. Martin. "Formal and Empirical Research on Cascaded Inference in Jurisprudence." *Law & Society Review* (No. 17 1982): 105–51.

Schwartz, D., and J. Bransford. "A Time for Telling." *Cognition and Instruction* (No. 4 1998): 475–522.

Schwarz, N. "Accessible Content and Accessibility Experiences: The Interplay of Declarative and Experiential Information in Judgment." *Personality and Social Psychology Review* (No. 2 1998): 87–99.

Schwarz, N. "Feelings as Information: Moods Influence Judgments and Processing Strategies." In *Heuristics and Biases: The Psychology of Intuitive Judgment,* edited by T. Gilovich, D. Griffin, and D. Kahneman. New York: Cambridge University Press, 2002.

Schwarz, N., and G. Clore. "Mood, Misattribution, and Judgments of Well-Being: Informative and Directive Functions of Affective States." *Journal of Personality and Social Psychology* (September 1983): 513–23.

Schwarz, N., F. Strack, D. Hilton, and G. Naderer. "Base Rates, Representativeness, and the Logic of Conversation: The Contextual Relevance of 'Irrelevant' Information." *Social Cognition* (Spring 1991): 67–84.

Scott, T., and P. Tiessen. "Performance Measurement and Managerial Teams." *Accounting, Organizations and Society* (April 1999): 263–85.

Sedor, L. "An Explanation for Unintentional Optimism in Analysts' Earnings Forecasts." *The Accounting Review* (October 2002): 731–53.

Selling, T. "Confidence and Information Usage: Evidence from a Bankruptcy Prediction Task." *Behavioral Research in Accounting* (1993): 237–64.

Selto, F., and J. Cooper. "Control of Risk Attitude in Experimental Accounting Research." *Journal of Accounting Literature* (1990): 229–64.

Shafir, E., and R. LeBoeuf. "Rationality." *Annual Review of Psychology* (2002): 491–517.

Shafir, E., I. Simonson, and A. Tversky. "Reason-Based Choice." *Cognition* (October–November 1993): 11–36.

Shaklee, H., and D. Tucker. "A Rule Analysis of Judgments of Covariation between Events." *Memory & Cognition* (September 1980): 459–67.

Shanteau, J. "Some Unasked Questions about the Psychology of Expert Decision Makers." In *Proceedings of the 1984 IEEE Conference on Systems, Man, and Cybernetics,* edited by M. Elhaway. New York: IEEE, 1984.

Shanteau, J. "Psychological Characteristics of Expert Decision Makers." In *Expert Judgment and Expert Systems,* edited by J. Mumpower, O. Renn, D. Phillips, and V. Uppuluri. Berlin: Springer-Verlag, 1987.

Shanteau, J. "Competence in Experts: The Role of Task Characteristics." *Organizational Behavior and Human Decision Processes* (November 1992a): 252–66.

Shanteau, J. "The Psychology of Experts: An Alternative View." In *Expertise and Decision Support,* edited by G. Wright and F. Bolger. New York: Plenum Press, 1992b.

Shanteau. J., D. Weiss, R. Thomas, and J. Pounds. "Performance-Based Assessment of Expertise: How to Decide if Someone Is an Expert or Not." *European Journal of Operational Research* (January 2002): 253–63.

Shapira, Z. *Risk Taking: A Managerial Perspective.* New York: Russell Sage Foundation, 1995.

Shaver, K. "Attribution: Effects of Severity and Relevance on the Responsibility Assigned for an Accident." *Journal of Personality and Social Psychology* (No. 14 1970): 101–13.

Shaver, K. *The Attribution of Blame: Causality, Responsibility, and Blameworthiness.* New York: Springer-Verlag, 1985.

Shaver, K., and D. Drown. "On Causality, Responsibility, and Self-Blame: A Theoretical Note." *Journal of Personality and Social Psychology* (April 1986): 697–702.

Shelley, M. "Gain/Loss Asymmetry in Risky Intertemporal Choice." *Organizational Behavior and Human Decision Processes* (July 1994): 124–59.

Shelley, M., and T. Omer. "Intertemporal Framing Issues in Management Compensation." *Organizational Behavior and Human Decision Processes* (April 1996): 42–58.

Shelton, S. "The Effect of Experience on the Use of Irrelevant Evidence in Auditor Judgment." *The Accounting Review* (April 1999): 217–24.

Shepperd, J. "Productivity Loss in Performance Groups: A Motivation Analysis." *Psychological Bulletin* (January 1993): 67–81.

Sherden, W. *The Fortune Sellers: The Big Business of Buying and Selling Predictions.* New York: John Wiley & Sons, 1998.

Sherman, S., R. Cialdini, D. Schwartman, and K. Reynolds. "Imagining Can Heighten or Lower the Perceived Likelihood of Contracting a Disease: The Mediating Effect of Ease of Imagery." *Personality and Social Psychology Bulletin* (No. 1 1985): 118–27.

Shields, M. "Some Effects of Information Load on Search Patterns Used to Analyze Performance Reports." *Accounting, Organizations and Society* (No. 4 1980): 429–42.

Shields, M. "Effects of Information Supply and Demand on Judgment Accuracy: Evidence from Corporate Managers." *The Accounting Review* (April 1983): 284–303.

Shields, M. "A Predecisional Approach to the Measurement of the Demand for Information in a Performance Report." *Accounting, Organizations and Society* (No. 3/4 1984): 355–63.

Shields, M., I. Solomon, and W. Waller. "Effects of Alternative Sample Space Representations on the Accuracy of Auditors' Uncertainty Judgments." *Accounting, Organizations and Society* (No. 4 1987): 375–88.

Shields, M., I. Solomon, and W. Waller. "Auditors' Usage of Unaudited Book Values when Making Presampling Audit Value Estimates." *Contemporary Accounting Research* (Fall 1988): 1–18.

Shiller, R. "Outlaw Selective Disclosure? — Yes, Markets Must Be Fair." *Wall Street Journal* (August 10, 2000): A18.

Shiller, R. "Bubbles, Human Judgment, and Expert Opinion." Cowles Foundation Discussion Paper no. 1303, 2001.

Shiller, R., and J. Pound. "Survey Evidence of Diffusing of Interest among Institutional Investors." *Journal of Economic Behavior and Organization* (August 1989): 47–66.

Shiraev, E., and D. Levy. *Introduction to Cross-Cultural Psychology: Critical Thinking and Contemporary Applications.* Boston: Allyn and Bacon, 2001.

Siegel-Jacobs, K., and J. Yates. "Effects of Procedural and Outcome Accountability on Judgment Quality." *Organizational Behavior and Human Decision Processes* (January 1996): 1–17.

Simnett, R. "The Effect of Information Selection, Information Processing and Task Complexity on the Predictive Accuracy of Auditors." *Accounting, Organizations and Society* (October–November 1996): 699–719.

Simnett, R., and K. Trotman. "Auditor versus Model: Information Choice and Information Processing." *The Accounting Review* (July 1989): 514–28.

Simon, H. "A Behavioral Model of Rational Choice." *Quarterly Journal of Economics* (February 1955): 99–118.

Simon, H. "The Structure of Ill Structured Problems." *Artificial Intelligence* (Winter 1973): 181–201.

Simon, H. "Invariants of Human Behavior." *Annual Review of Psychology* (1990): 1–19.

Simon, S. "Boom in Expert Witness Field Unfazed by Cynicism." *Los Angeles Times* (April 15, 1996): A1, A16–A17.

Simonson, I., and B. Staw. "Deescalation Strategies: A Comparison of Techniques for Reducing Commitment to Losing Courses of Action." *Journal of Applied Psychology* (August 1992): 419–26.

Singley, M., and J. Anderson. *The Transfer of Cognitive Skill.* Cambridge, MA: Harvard University Press, 1989.

Sinha, P., L. Brown, and S. Das. "A Re-Examination of Financial Analysts' Differential Earnings Forecast Accuracy." *Contemporary Accounting Research* (Spring 1997): 1–42.

Skinner, D. "Why Firms Voluntarily Disclose Bad News." *Journal of Accounting Research* (Spring 1994): 38–60.

Skov, R., and S. Sherman. "Information-Gathering Processes: Diagnosticity, Hypothesis-Confirmatory Strategies, and Perceived Hypothesis Confirmation." *Journal of Experimental Social Psychology* (March 1986): 93–121.

Slovic, P. "Analyzing the Expert Judge: A Descriptive Study of a Stockbroker's Decision Processes." *Journal of Applied Psychology* (August 1969): 255–63.

Slovic, P. *The Perception of Risk.* Sterling, VA: Earthscan Publishers, 2000.

Slovic, P., M. Finucane, E. Peters, and D. MacGregor. "The Affect Heuristic." In *Heuristics and Biases: The Psychology of Intuitive Judgment,* edited by T. Gilovich, D. Griffin, and D. Kahneman. New York: Cambridge University Press, 2002.

Slovic, P., D. Fleissner, and W. Bauman. "Analyzing the Use of Information in Investment Decision Making: A Methodological Proposal." *Journal of Business* (April 1972): 283–301.

Slovic, P., and S. Lichtenstein. "Comparison of Bayesian and Regression Approaches to the Study of Information Processing in Judgment." *Organizational Behavior and Human Performance* (November 1971): 649–744.

Smith, G. "Toward a Heuristic Theory of Problem Structuring." *Management Science* (December 1988): 1489–1506.

Smith, G. "Inside Fidelity: How the Fund Giant's Stock-Picking Machine Works." *Business Week* (October 10, 1994): 88–96.

Smith, J., and T. Kida. "Heuristics and Biases: Expertise and Task Realism in Auditing." *Psychological Bulletin* (May 1991): 472–89.

Smith, K., J. Dickhaut, K. McCabe, and J. Pardo. "Neuronal Substrates for Choice under Ambiguity, Risk, Gains, and Losses." *Management Science* (June 2002): 711–18.

Smith, V., and M. Walker. "Monetary Rewards and Decision Cost in Experimental Economics." *Economic Inquiry* (April 1993): 245–61.

Sniezek, J. "An Examination of Group Process in Judgmental Forecasting." *International Journal of Forecasting* (No. 2 1989): 171–78.

Sniezek, J., and T. Buckley. "Cueing and Cognitive Conflict in Judge-Advisor Decision Making." *Organizational Behavior and Human Decision Processes* (May 1995): 159–74.

Sniezek, J., and R. Henry. "Accuracy and Confidence in Group Judgment." *Organizational Behavior and Human Decision Processes* (February 1989): 1–28.

Sniezek, J., G. Schrah, and R. Dalal. "Improving Judgement with Prepaid Expert Advice." *Journal of Behavioral Decision Making* (July 2004): 173–90.

Sniezek, J., and L. Van Swol. "Trust, Confidence, and Expertise in a Judge-Advisor System." *Organizational Behavior and Human Decision Processes* (March 2001): 288–307.

Snow, R. "Aptitude-Treatment Interaction as a Framework for Research on Individual Differences in Learning." In *Learning and Individual Differences: Advances in Theory and Research,* edited by P. Ackerman, R. Sternberg, and R. Glaser. New York: W.H. Freeman and Company, 1989.

Snowball, D. "Some Effects of Accounting Expertise and Information Load: An Empirical Study." *Accounting, Organizations and Society* (No. 3 1980): 323–38.

Snyder, M., and N. Cantor. "Testing Hypotheses about Other People: The Use of Historical Knowledge." *Journal of Experimental Social Psychology* (July 1979): 330–42.

Snyder, M., and W. Swann Jr. "Hypothesis-Testing Processes in Social Interaction." *Journal of Personality and Social Psychology* (November 1978): 1202–12.

Soffer, L., S. Thiagarajan, and B. Walther. "Earnings Preannouncement Strategies." *Review of Accounting Studies* (March 2000): 5–26.

Soll, J. "Intuitive Theories of Information: Beliefs about the Value of Redundancy." *Cognitive Psychology* (March 1999): 317–46.

Solomon, I. "Probability Assessment by Individual Auditors and Audit Teams: An Empirical Investigation." *Journal of Accounting Research* (Autumn 1982, Part II): 689–710.

Solomon, I. "Multi-Auditor Judgment/Decision Making Research." *Journal of Accounting Literature* (1987): 1–25.

Solomon, I., A. Ariyo, and L. Tomassini. "Contextual Effects on the Calibration of Probabilistic Judgments." *Journal of Applied Psychology* (August 1985): 528–32.

Solomon, I., and C. Brown. "Auditors' Judgments and Decisions under Time Pressure: An Illustration and Agenda for Research." In *Auditing Symposium XI: Proceedings of the 1992 Deloitte and Touche/University of Kansas Symposium on Audit Problems,* edited by R. Srivastava. Lawrence: University of Kansas. 1992.

Solomon, I., J. Krogstad, M. Romney, and L. Tomassini. "Auditors' Prior Probability Distributions for Account Balances." *Accounting, Organizations and Society* (No. 1 1982): 27–42.

Solomon, I., M. Shields, and O. Whittington. "What Do Industry-Specialist Auditors Know?" *Journal of Accounting Research* (Spring 1999): 191–208.

Sorenson, L. "Outpsyching the Market." *Forbes* (July 11, 1988): 56–57.

Spilker, B. "The Effects of Time Pressure and Knowledge on Key Word Selection Behavior in Tax Research." *The Accounting Review* (January 1995): 49–70.

Spilker, B., and D. Prawitt. "Adaptive Responses to Time Pressure: The Effects of Experience on Tax Information Search Behavior." *Behavioral Research in Accounting* (1997): 172–98.

Spilker, B., R. Worsham Jr., and D. Prawitt. "Tax Professionals' Interpretation of Ambiguity in Tax Compliance and Planning Decision Contexts." *Journal of the American Taxation Association* (Fall 1999): 75–89.

Sporer, S., S. Penrod, D. Read, and B. Cutler. "Choosing, Confidence, and Accuracy: A Meta-Analysis of the Confidence-Accuracy Relation in Eyewitness Identification Studies." *Psychological Bulletin* (November 1995): 313–27.

Spors, K. "Corporate Governance (A Special Report)." *Wall Street Journal* (June 21, 2004): R7.

Sprinkle, G. "The Effect of Incentive Contracts on Learning and Performance." *The Accounting Review* (July 2000): 299–326.

Sprinkle, G. "Perspectives on Experimental Research in Managerial Accounting." *Accounting, Organizations and Society* (February–April 2003): 287–318.

Sprinkle, G., and R. Tubbs. "The Effects of Audit Risk and Information Importance on Auditor Memory During Working Paper Review." *The Accounting Review* (October 1998): 475–502.

Srull, T. "The Role of Prior Knowledge in the Acquisition, Retention, and Use of New Information" *Advances in Consumer Research* (1983): 572–76.

Staël von Holstein, C. "Probabilistic Forecasting: An Experiment Related to the Stock Market." *Organizational Behavior and Human Performance* (August 1972): 130–58.

Stallman, J. "Toward Experimental Criteria for Judging Disclosure Improvement." *Journal of Accounting Research* (1969): S29–43.

Stasser, G., L. Taylor, and C. Hanna. "Information Sampling in Structured and Unstructured Discussions of Three- and Six-Person Groups." *Journal of Personality and Social Psychology* (July 1989): 67–78.

Stasser, G., and W. Titus. "Pooling of Unshared Information in Group Decision Making: Biased Information Sampling During

Discussion." *Journal of Personality and Social Psychology* (June 1985): 1467–78.

Staw, B. "Knee-Deep in the Big Muddy: A Study of Escalating Commitment to a Chosen Course of Action." *Organizational Behavior and Human Performance* (June 1976): 27–44.

Staw, B., P. McKechnie, and S. Puffer. "The Justification of Organizational Performance." *Administrative Science Quarterly* (December 1983): 582–600.

Staw, B., and J. Ross. "Understanding Behavior in Escalation Situations." *Science* (October 1986): 216–20.

Stein, E. "A Look at Expertise from a Social Perspective." In *Expertise in Context: Human and Machine,* edited by P. Feltovich, K. Ford, and R. Hoffman. Menlo Park, CA: AAII Press/MIT Press, 1997.

Stein, M., D. Simunic, and T. O'Keefe. "Industry Differences in the Production of Audit Services." *Auditing: A Journal of Practice & Theory* (1994): S128–42.

Steinbart, P., and W. Accola. "The Effects of Explanation Type and User Involvement on Learning from and Satisfaction with Expert Systems." *Journal of Information Systems* (Spring 1994): 1–17.

Steiner, I. *Group Process and Productivity.* New York: Academic Press, 1972.

Steinmann, D. "The Effects of Cognitive Feedback and Task Complexity in Multiple-Cue Probability Learning." *Organizational Behavior and Human Performance* (April 1976): 168–79.

Sternberg, R. *Practical Intelligence: How Practical and Creative Intelligence Determine Success in Life.* New York: Simon & Schuster, 1996.

Sternberg, R., and J. Horvath. *Tacit Knowledge in Professional Practice: Researcher and Practitioner Perspectives.* Mahwah, NJ: Lawrence Erlbaum Associates, 1999.

Sternberg, R., and J. Kaufman. "Human Abilities." *Annual Review of Psychology* (1998): 479–502.

Stewart, D., and G. Stasser. "Expert Role Assignment and Information Sampling during Collective Recall and Decision Making." *Journal of Personality and Social Psychology* (October 1995): 619–28.

Stewart, T. "Your Company's Most Valuable Asset: Intellectual Capital." *Fortune* (October 3, 1994): 68–74.

Stewart, T., P. Roebber, and L. Bosart. "The Importance of the Task in Analyzing Expert Judgment." *Organizational Behavior and Human Decision Processes* (March 1997): 205–19.

Stickel, S. "Reputation and Performance among Security Analysts." *Journal of Finance* (December 1992): 1811–36.

Stock, D., and C. Watson. "Human Judgment Accuracy, Multidimensional Graphics, and Humans versus Models." *Journal of Accounting Research* (Spring 1984): 192–206.

Stocks, M., and A. Harrell. "The Impact of an Increase in Accounting Information Level on the Judgment Quality of Individuals and Groups." *Accounting, Organizations and Society* (October–November 1995): 685–700.

Stone, D., and W. Dilla. "When Numbers Are Better Than Words: The Joint Effects of Response Representation and Experience on Inherent Risk Judgments." *Auditing: A Journal of Practice & Theory* (1994): S1–19.

Stone, D., J. Hunton, and B. Wier. "Succeeding in Managerial Accounting. Part 1: Knowledge, Ability, and Rank." *Accounting, Organizations and Society* (October 2000): 697–715.

Stone, D., and M. Shelley. "Educating for Accounting Expertise: A Field Study." *Journal of Accounting Research* (1997): S35–61.

Strack, F., and T. Mussweiler. "Explaining the Enigmatic Anchoring Effect: Mechanisms of Selective Accessibility." *Journal of Personality and Social Psychology* (September 1997): 437–66.

Strauss, S., and J. McGrath. "Does the Medium Matter? The Interaction of Task Type and Technology on Group Performance and Member Reactions." *Journal of Applied Psychology* (No. 1 1994): 87–97.

Sulsky, L., and W. Balzer. "Meaning and Measurement of Performance Rating Accuracy: Some Methodological and Theoretical Concerns." *Journal of Applied Psychology* (August 1988): 497–506.

Summers, D., and K. Hammond. "Inference Behavior in Multiple-cue Tasks Involving Both Linear and Nonlinear Relations." *Journal of Experimental Psychology* (No. 5 1966): 751–57.

Sutton, S., and S. Hayne. "Judgment and Decision Making, Part III: Group Processes." In *Behavioral Accounting Research:*

Foundations and Frontiers, edited by V. Arnold and S. Sutton. Sarasota, FL: American Accounting Association, 1997.

Swain, M., and S. Haka. "Effects of Information Load on Capital Budgeting Decisions." *Behavioral Research in Accounting* (2000): 171–98.

Sweller, J., and P. Chandler. "Why Some Material Is Difficult to Learn." *Cognition and Instruction* (No. 3 1994): 185–233.

Sweller, J., P. Chandler, P. Tierney, and M. Cooper. "Cognitive Load as a Factor in the Structuring of Technical Material." *Journal of Experimental Psychology: General* (June 1990): 176–92.

Swieringa, R., M. Gibbins, L. Larsson, and J. Sweeney. "Experiments in the Heuristics of Human Information Processing." *Journal of Accounting Research* (1976): S159–87.

Tan, C., C. Jubb, and K. Houghton. "Auditor Judgments: The Effects of the Partner's Views on Decision Outcomes and Cognitive Effort." *Behavioral Research in Accounting* (1997): S157–75.

Tan, H. "Effects of Expectations, Prior Involvement, and Review Awareness on Memory for Audit Evidence and Judgment." *Journal of Accounting Research* (Spring 1995): 113–35.

Tan, H., and K. Jamal. "Do Auditors Objectively Evaluate Their Subordinates' Work?" *The Accounting Review* (January 2001): 99–110.

Tan, H., and A. Kao. "Accountability Effects on Auditors' Performance: The Influence of Knowledge, Problem-Solving Ability, and Task Complexity." *Journal of Accounting Research* (Spring 1999): 209–23.

Tan, H., and R. Libby. "Tacit Managerial versus Technical Knowledge as Determinants of Audit Expertise in the Field." *Journal of Accounting Research* (Spring 1997): 97–113.

Tan, H., R. Libby, and J. Hunton. "Analysts' Reactions to Earnings Preannouncement Strategies." *Journal of Accounting Research* (March 2002a): 223–46.

Tan, H., and M. Lipe. "Outcome Effects: The Impact of Decision Process and Outcome Controllability." *Journal of Behavioral Decision Making* (December 1997): 315–25.

Tan, H., T. Ng, and B. Mak. "The Effects of Task Complexity on Auditors' Performance: The Impact of Accountability and Knowledge." *Auditing: A Journal of Practice and Theory* (September 2002b): 81–95.

Tan, H., and K. Trotman. "Reviewers' Responses to Anticipated Stylization Attempts by Preparers of Audit Workpapers." *The Accounting Review* (April 2003): 581–604.

Tan, H., and J. Yates. "Financial Budgets and Escalation Effects." *Organizational Behavior and Human Decision Processes* (March 2002): 300–322.

Tan, H., and Yip-Ow, J. "Are Reviewers' Judgements Influenced by Memo Structure and Conclusions Documented in Audit Workpapers?" *Contemporary Accounting Research* (Winter 2001): 663–78.

Tannenbaum, S., and G. Yukl. "Training and Development in Work Organizations." *Annual Review of Psychology* (1992): 399–441.

Terpstra, D., and E. Rozell. "Sources of Human Resource Information and the Link to Organizational Profitability." *The Journal of Applied Behavioral Science* (March 1997a): 66–83.

Terpstra, D., and E. Rozell. "Why Some Potentially Effective Staffing Practices Are Seldom Used." *Public Personnel Management* (Winter 1997b): 483–95.

Tetlock. P. "Accountability and Complexity of Thought." *Journal of Personality and Social Psychology* (July 1983): 74–83.

Tetlock, P. "Accountability: A Social Check on the Fundamental Attribution Error." *Social Psychology Quarterly* (September 1985): 227–36.

Tetlock, P., J. Lerner, and R. Boettger. "The Dilution Effect: Judgmental Bias, Conversational Convention, or a Bit of Both?" *European Journal of Social Psychology* (November–December 1996): 915–34.

Tetlock, P., L. Skitka, and R. Boettger. "Social and Cognitive Strategies for Coping with Accountability: Conformity, Complexity, and Bolstering." *Journal of Personality and Social Psychology* (October 1989): 632–40.

Thaler, R., ed. *Advances in Behavioral Finance.* New York: Russell Sage Foundation, 1993.

Thaler, R. "Mental Accounting Matters." *Journal of Behavioral Decision Making* (September 1999): 183–206.

Thibaut, J., and H. Kelley. *The Social Psychology of Groups.* New Brunswick, NJ: Transaction Publishers, 1991.

Thibaut, J., and L. Walker. *Procedural Justice: A Psychological Analysis.* Hillsdale, NJ: Lawrence Erlbaum, 1975.

Thibodeau, J. "The Development and Transferability of Task Knowledge." *Auditing: A Journal of Practice and Theory* (2003): 47–67.

Thomas, P. "Investing Survey Shows Race Plays a Part." *Wall Street Journal* (June 6, 2001): C 21.

Timmermans, D., and C. Vlek. "An Evaluation Study of the Effectiveness of Multi-Attribute Decision Support as a Function of Problem Complexity." *Organizational Behavior and Human Decision Processes* (July 1994): 75–92.

Tindale, R. "Decision Errors Made by Individuals and Groups." In *Individual and Group Decision Making,* edited by N. Castellan Jr. Hillsdale, NJ: Lawrence Erlbaum Associates, 1993.

Tobias, S. "Interest, Prior Knowledge, and Learning." *Review of Educational Research* (Spring 1994): 37–54.

Todd, P., and I. Benbasat. "An Experimental Investigation of the Impact of Computer Based Decision Aids on Decision Making Strategies." *Information Systems Research* (June 1991): 87–115.

Todd, P., and I. Benbasat. "The Use of Information in Decision Making: An Experimental Investigation of the Impact of Computer-Based Decision Aids." *MIS Quarterly* (September 1992): 373–93.

Todd, P., and I. Benbasat. "The Influence of Decision Aids on Choice Strategies: An Experimental Analysis of the Role of Cognitive Effort." *Organizational Behavior and Human Decision Processes* (October 1994): 36–74.

Todd, P., and I. Benbasat. "Inducing Compensatory Information Processing through Decision Aids that Facilitate Effort Reduction: An Experimental Assessment." *Journal of Behavioral Decision Making* (January–March 2000): 91–106.

Tomassini, L., I. Solomon, M. Romney, and J. Krogstad. "Calibration of Auditors' Probabilistic Judgments: Some Empirical Evidence." *Organizational Behavior and Human Performance* (December 1982): 391–406.

Tramifow, D., and J. Sniezek. "Perceived Expertise and Its Effect on Confidence." *Organizational Behavior and Human Decision Processes* (February 1994): 290–302.

Trombley, M. "Stock Prices and Wall Street Weather: Additional Evidence." *Quarterly Journal of Business and Economics* (Summer 1997): 11–21.

Trompeter, G. "The Effect of Partner Compensation Schemes and Generally Accepted Accounting Principles on Audit Partner Judgment." *Auditing: A Journal of Practice and Theory* (Fall 1994): 56–68.

Trotman, K. "The Review Process and the Accuracy of Auditor Judgments." *Journal of Accounting Research* (Autumn 1985): 740–52.

Trotman, K. "Discussion of 'Judgment and Decision Making Research in Auditing: A Task, Person, and Interpersonal Interaction Perspective." *Auditing: A Journal of Practice & Theory* (2005): S73–87.

Trotman, K., and J. Sng. "The Effect of Hypothesis Framing, Prior Expectations and Cue Diagnosticity on Auditors' Information Choice." *Accounting, Organizations and Society* (No. 5/6 1989): 565–76.

Trotman, K., and Wood, R. "A Meta-Analysis of Studies on Internal Control Judgments." *Journal of Accounting Research* (Spring 1991): 180–92.

Trotman, K., and A. Wright. "Recency Effects: Task Complexity, Decision Mode, and Task-Specific Experience." *Behavioral Research in Accounting* (1996): 175–93.

Trotman, K., and P. Yetton. "The Effect of the Review Process on Auditor Judgments." *Journal of Accounting Research* (Spring 1985): 256–67.

Trotman, K., P. Yetton, and I. Zimmer. "Individual and Group Judgments of Internal Control Systems." *Journal of Accounting Research* (Spring 1983): 286–92.

Troutman, C., and J. Shanteau. "Inferences Based on Nondiagnostic Information." *Organizational Behavior and Human Performance* (June 1977): 43–55.

Trueman, B. "On the Incentives for Security Analysts to Revise Their Earnings Forecasts." *Contemporary Accounting Research* (Fall 1990): 203–22.

Trueman, B. "Analyst Forecasts and Herding Behavior." *The Review of Financial Studies* (Spring 1994): 97–124.

Tubbs, M. "Goal Setting: A Meta-Analytic Examination of the Empirical Evidence." *Journal of Applied Psychology* (August 1986): 474–83.

Tubbs, R. "The Effect of Experience on the Auditor's Organization and Amount of Knowledge." *The Accounting Review* (October 1992): 783–801.

Tubbs, R., W. Messier Jr., and W. Knechel. "Recency Effects in the Auditor's Belief-Revision Process." *The Accounting Review* (April 1990): 452–60.

Tucker, L. "A Suggested Alternative Formulation in the Developments by Hursch, Hammond, and Hursch and by Hammond, Hursch and Todd." *Psychological Review* (November 1964): 528–32.

Tulving, E. "How Many Memory Systems Are There?" *American Psychologist* (April 1985): 385–98.

Tuovinen, J., and J. Sweller. "A Comparison of Cognitive Load Associated with Discovery Learning and Worked Examples." *Journal of Educational Psychology* (June 1999): 334–41.

Turk, R. "Going Shopping with a 'Perfect Size 8' Shows Why There's No Such Thing." *Los Angeles Times* (January 19, 1995): E1.

Turner, C. "Accountability Demands and the Auditor's Evidence Search Strategy: The Influence of Reviewer Preferences and the Nature of the Response (Belief versus Action)." *Journal of Accounting Research* (December 2001): 683–706.

Tuttle, B. "Using Base Rate Frequency Perceptions to Diagnose Financial Statement Error Causes." *Auditing: A Journal of Practice & Theory* (Spring 1996): 104–21.

Tuttle, B., and F. Burton. "The Effects of a Modest Incentive on Information Overload in an Investment Analysis Task." *Accounting, Organizations and Society* (November 1999): 673–87.

Tuttle, B., M. Coller, and F. Burton. "An Examination of Market Efficiency: Information Order Effects in a Laboratory Market." *Accounting, Organizations and Society* (January 1997): 89–103.

Tuttle, B., and M. Stocks. "The Use of Outcome Feedback and Task Property Information by Subjects with Accounting-Domain Knowledge to Predict Financial Distress." *Behavioral Research in Accounting* (1998): 76–107.

Tversky, A. "Elimination by Aspects: A Theory of Choice." *Psychological Review* (July 1972): 281–99.

Tversky, A. "Features of Similarity." *Psychological Review* (July 1977): 327–52.

Tversky, A., and I. Gati. "Studies of Similarity." In *Cognition and Categorization,* edited by E. Rosch and B. Lloyds. Hillsdale, NJ: Lawrence Erlbaum, 1978.

Tversky, A., and D. Kahneman. "Availability: A Heuristic for Judging Frequency and Probability." *Cognitive Psychology* (September 1973): 77–110.

Tversky, A., and D. Kahneman. "Judgment under Uncertainty: Heuristics and Biases." *Science* (September 1974): 1124–31.

Tversky, A., and D. Kahneman. "The Framing of Decisions and the Psychology of Choice." *Science* (January 30, 1981): 453–58.

Tyler, T. "The Psychology of Legitimacy: A Relational Perspective on Voluntary Deference to Authorities." *Personality and Social Psychology Review* (No. 4 1997): 323–45.

Tyson, T. "Grade Performance in Introductory Accounting Courses: Why Female Students Outperform Males." *Issues in Accounting Education* (Spring 1989): 153–60.

Tyszka, T., and P. Zielonka. "Expert Judgments: Financial Analysts versus Weather Forecasters." *Journal of Psychology and Financial Markets* (No. 3 2002): 152–60.

Uecker, W. "The Quality of Group Performance in Simplified Information Evaluation." *Journal of Accounting Research* (Autumn 1982, Part I): 388–402.

Uecker, W., and W. Kinney Jr. "Judgmental Evaluation of Sample Results: A Study of the Type and Severity of Errors Made by Practicing CPAs." *Accounting, Organizations and Society* (No. 3 1977): 269–75.

Umanath, N., and I. Vessey. "Multiattribute Data Presentation and Human Judgment: A Cognitive Fit Perspective." *Decision Sciences* (September–December 1994): 795–824.

Vallone, R., D. Griffin, S. Lin, and L. Ross. "Overconfident Prediction of Future Actions and Outcomes by Self and Others." *Journal of*

Personality and Social Psychology (April 1990): 582–92.

Van Boven, L., A. Kamada, and T. Gilovich. "The Perceiver as Perceived: Everyday Intuitions about the Correspondence Bias." *Journal of Personality and Social Psychology* (December 1999): 1188–99.

Van Boven, L., K. White, A. Kamada, and T. Gilovich. "Intuitions about Situational Correction in Self and Others." *Journal of Personality and Social Psychology* (August 2003): 249–58.

van Breda, M., and K. Ferris. "A Note on the Effect of Prior Probability Disclosure and Information Representativeness on Subject Predictive Accuracy." *Behavioral Research in Accounting* (1992): 140–51.

Van Schie, E., and J. Van der Pligt. "Getting an Anchor on Availability in Causal Judgment." *Organizational Behavior and Human Decision Processes* (January 1994): 140–54.

Van Swol, L., and J. Sniezek. "Factors Affecting the Acceptance of Expert Advice." *British Journal of Social Psychology* (September 2005): 443–61.

Vasarhelyi, M. "Man–Machine Planning Systems: A Cognitive Style Examination of Interactive Decision Making." *Journal of Accounting Research* (Spring 1977): 138–53.

Venuti, E., M. Holtzman, and A. Basile. "Due Professional Care in Cases of High Engagement Risk." *The CPA Journal* (December 2002): 26–33.

Vera-Muñoz, S. "The Effects of Accounting Knowledge and Context on the Omission of Opportunity Costs in Resource Allocation Decisions." *The Accounting Review* (January 1998): 47–72.

Vera-Muñoz, S., W. Kinney Jr., and S. Bonner. "The Effects of Domain Experience and Task Presentation Format on Accountants' Information Relevance Assurance." *The Accounting Review* (July 2001): 405–30.

Vergoossen, R. "Changes in Accounting Policies and Investment Analysts' Fixation on Accounting Figures." *Accounting, Organizations and Society* (August 1997): 589–607.

Vessey, I. "Cognitive Fit: A Theory-Based Analysis of the Graphs versus Tables Literature." *Decision Sciences* (Spring 1991): 219–40.

von Neumann, J., and O. Morgenstern. *Theory of Games and Economic Behavior,* 2nd ed. Princeton, NJ: Princeton University Press, 1947.

Voskuijl, O. "Job Analysis: Current and Future Perspectives." In *The Blackwell Handbook of Personnel Selection,* edited by A. Evers, N. Anderson, and O. Voskuijl. Malden, MA: Blackwell Publishing, 2005.

Vosniadou, S. "Analogical Reasoning as a Mechanism in Knowledge Acquisition: A Developmental Perspective." In *Similarity and Analogical Reasoning,* edited by S. Vosniadou and A. Ortony. New York: Cambridge University Press, 1989.

Voss, J., and T. Post. "On the Solving of Ill-Structured Problems." In *The Nature of Expertise,* edited by M. Chi, R. Glaser, and M. Farr. Hillsdale, NJ: Lawrence Erlbaum Associates, 1988.

Vroom, V. *Work and Motivation.* New York: John Wiley, 1964.

Wagenaar, W. "Generation of Random Sequences by Human Subjects: A Critical Survey of Literature." *Psychological Bulletin* (January 1972): 65–72.

Waggoner, J., and J. Cashell. "The Impact of Time Pressure on Auditors' Performance." *Ohio CPA Journal* (January–April 1991): 27–32.

Walker, K., and L. McClelland. "Management Forecasts and Statistical Prediction Model Forecasts in Corporate Budgeting." *Journal of Accounting Research* (Autumn 1991): 371–81.

Wall Street Journal. "Investors Grapple with Second Year of Losses—Many Owning Stocks and Funds See More Risks in the Market; Painful Lessons Are Learned." (January 7, 2002): R1.

Wall Street Journal. "Linking Pay to Performance Is Becoming a Norm in the Workplace." (April 6, 1999): A1.

Waller, W. "Decision-Making Research in Managerial Accounting: Return to Behavioral-Economics Foundations." In *Judgment and Decision-Making Research in Accounting,* edited by R. Ashton and A. Ashton. Cambridge, England: Cambridge University Press, 1995.

Waller, W., and W. Felix Jr. "The Auditor and Learning from Experience: Some

Conjectures." *Accounting, Organizations and Society* (No. 3/4 1984): 383–406.

Waller, W., and W. Felix Jr. "Auditors' Covariation Judgments." *The Accounting Review* (April 1987): 275–92.

Waller, W., and J. Jiambalvo. "The Use of Normative Models in Human Information Processing Research in Accounting." *Journal of Accounting Literature* (1984): 201–23.

Waller, W., and T. Mitchell. "The Effects of Context on the Selection of Decision Strategies for the Cost Variance Investigation Problem." *Organizational Behavior and Human Performance* (June 1984): 397–413.

Waller, W., and M. Zimbelman. "A Cognitive Footprint in Archival Data: Generalizing the Dilution Effect from Laboratory to Field Settings." *Organizational Behavior and Human Decision Processes* (July 2003): 254–68.

Waller, W., B. Shapiro, and G. Sevcik. "Do Cost-Based Pricing Biases Persist in Laboratory Markets?" *Accounting, Organizations and Society* (November 1999): 717–39.

Wallman, S. "The Future of Accounting and Financial Reporting, Part IV: 'Access' Accounting." *Accounting Horizons* (June 1997): 103–16.

Wallsten, T., and C. Barton. "Processing Probabilistic Multidimensional Information for Decisions." *Journal of Experimental Psychology: Learning, Memory, and Cognition* (September 1982): 361–84.

Wallsten, T., D. Budescu, and R. Zwick. "Comparing the Calibration and Coherence of Numerical and Verbal Probability Judgments." *Management Science* (February 1993): 176–90.

Walo, J. "The Effects of Client Characteristics on Audit Scope." *Auditing: A Journal of Practice and Theory* (Spring 1995): 115–24.

Walster, E. "Assignment of Responsibility for an Accident." *Journal of Personality and Social Psychology* (No. 3 1966): 73–79.

Wang, X. "Framing Effects: Dynamics and Task Domains." *Organizational Behavior and Human Decision Processes* (November 1996): 145–57.

Ward, M., and J. Sweller. "Structuring Effective Worked Examples." *Cognition and Instruction* (No. 1 1990): 1–39.

Ward, S., D. Ward, T. Wilson Jr., and A. Deck. "Further Evidence on the Relationship between ACT Scores and Accounting Performance of Black Students." *Issues in Accounting Education* (Fall 1993): 128–36.

Watson, D. "The Structure of Project Teams Facing Differentiated Environments—An Exploratory Study in Public Accounting Firms." *The Accounting Review* (April 1975): 259–73.

Watson, D. "The Actor and the Observer: How Are Their Perceptions of Causality Divergent?" *Psychological Bulletin* (November 1982): 682–700.

Wayne, S., and G. Ferris. "Influence Tactics, Affect, and Exchange Quality in Supervisor-Subordinate Interactions: A Laboratory Experiment and Field Study." *Journal of Applied Psychology* (October 1990): 487–99.

Wayne, S., and R. Liden. "Effects of Impression Management on Performance Ratings: A Longitudinal Study." *Academy of Management Journal* (February 1995): 232–60.

Wayne, S., R. Liden, I. Graf, and G. Ferris. "The Role of Upward Influence Tactics in Human Resource Decisions." *Personnel Psychology* (Winter 1997): 979–1006.

Webby, R., and M. O'Connor. "Judgemental and Statistical Time Series Forecasting: A Review of the Literature." *International Journal of Forecasting* (March 1996): 91–118.

Weber, R. "Some Characteristics of the Free Recall of Computer Controls by EDP Auditors." *Journal of Accounting Research* (Spring 1980): 214–41.

Wegener, D., and R. Petty. "Flexible Correction Processes in Social Judgment: The Role of Naive Theories in Corrections for Perceived Bias." *Journal of Personality and Social Psychology* (January 1995): 36–51.

Wegener, D., and R. Petty. "The Flexible Correction Model: The Role of Naive Theories of Bias in Bias Correction." In *Advances in Experimental Social Psychology,* vol. 29, edited by M. Zanna. New York: Academic Press, 1997.

Wegener, D., R. Petty, B. Detweiler-Bedell, and W. Jarvis. "Implications of Attitude Change Theories for Numerical Anchoring: Anchor Plausibility and the Limits of Anchor Effectiveness." *Journal of Experimental Social Psychology* (January 2001): 62–69.

Weick, K. "Stress in Accounting Systems." *The Accounting Review* (April 1983): 350–69.

Weiner, B. "'Spontaneous' Causal Thinking." *Psychological Bulletin* (January 1985): 74–84.

Weiner, B. *An Attributional Theory of Motivation and Emotion.* New York: Springer-Verlag, 1986.

Weiner, B. *Judgments of Responsibility: A Foundation for a Theory of Social Conduct.* New York: The Guilford Press, 1995.

Wermers, R. "Mutual Fund Herding and the Impact on Stock Prices." *Journal of Finance* (April 1999): 581–622.

Wexley, K. "Personnel Training." *Annual Review of Psychology* (1984): 519–51.

White, R. "Motivation Reconsidered: The Concept of Competence." *Psychological Review* (1959): 297–333.

White, R., P. Harrison, and A. Harrell. "The Impact of Income Tax Withholding on Taxpayer Compliance: Further Empirical Evidence." *Journal of the American Taxation Association* (Fall 1993): 63–78.

Whitecotton, S. "The Effects of Experience and Confidence on Decision Aid Reliance: A Causal Model." *Behavioral Research in Accounting* (1996): 194–216.

Whitecotton, S., and S. Butler. "Influencing Decision Aid Reliance through Involvement in Information Choice." *Behavioral Research in Accounting* (1998): S182–200.

Whitecotton, S., D. Sanders, and K. Norris. "Improving Predictive Accuracy with a Combination of Human Intuition and Mechanical Decision Aids." *Organizational Behavior and Human Decision Processes* (December 1998): 325–48.

Wiedman, C. "The Relevance of Characteristics of the Information Environment in the Selection of a Proxy for the Market's Expectations for Earnings: An Extension of Brown, Richardson, & Schwager (1987)." *Journal of Accounting Research* (Autumn 1996): 313–24.

Wier, B., D. Stone, and J. Hunton. "Promotion and Performance Evaluation of Managerial Accountants." *Journal of Management Accounting Research* (2002): 189–208.

Wilk, S., and P. Cappelli. "Understanding the Determinants of Employer Use of Selection Methods." *Personnel Psychology* (Spring 2003): 103–24.

Wilkins, T., and I. Zimmer. "The Effect of Leasing and Different Methods of Accounting for Leases on Credit Evaluations." *The Accounting Review* (October 1983): 749–64.

Wilks, J. "Predecisional Distortion of Evidence as a Consequence of Real-Time Audit Review." *The Accounting Review* (January 2002): 51–71.

Wilks, T., and M. Zimbelman. "Decomposition of Fraud-Risk Assessments and Auditors' Sensitivity to Fraud Cues." *Contemporary Accounting Research* (Fall 2004): 719–45.

Williams, P. "The Relation between a Prior Earnings Forecast by Management and Analyst Response to a Current Management Forecast." *The Accounting Review* (January 1996): 103–13.

Willis, R. "Mutual Fund Manager Forecasting Behavior." *Journal of Accounting Research* (December 2001): 707–25.

Wilner, N., and J. Birnberg. "Methodological Problems in Functional Fixation Research: Criticism and Suggestions." *Accounting, Organizations and Society* (No. 1 1986): 71–80.

Wilson, T., D. Centerbar, and N. Brekke. "Mental Contamination and the Debiasing Problem." In *Heuristics and Biases: The Psychology of Intuitive Judgment,* edited by T. Gilovich, D. Griffin, and D. Kahneman. New York: Cambridge University Press, 2002.

Wilson, T., and E. Dunn. "Self-Knowledge: Its Limits, Value, and Potential for Improvement." *Annual Review of Psychology* (2004): 493–518.

Windsor, C., and N. Ashkanasy. "The Effect of Client Management Bargaining Power, Moral Reasoning Development, and Belief in a Just World on Auditor Independence." *Accounting, Organizations and Society* (October–November 1995): 701–20.

Winkler, R. "The Assessment of Prior Distributions in Bayesian Analysis." *Journal of the American Statistical Association* (September 1967): 776–800.

Witkin, H., P. Oltman, E. Raskin, and S. Karp. *A Manual for the Embedded Figures Test.* Palo Alto, CA: Consulting Psychologists Press, 1971.

Wittenbaum, G., A. Hubbell, and C. Zuckerman. "Mutual Enhancement: Toward an Understanding of the Collective Preference for Shared Information." *Journal of Personality and Social Psychology* (November 1999): 967–78.

Woehr, D., and A. Huffcutt. "Rater Training for Performance Appraisal: A Quantitative Review." *Journal of Occupational and Organizational Psychology* (September 1994): 189–205.

Wolfe, C., and B. Flores. "Judgmental Adjustment of Earnings Forecasts." *Journal of Forecasting* (No. 4 1990): 389–405.

Wolfe, M., and N. Pennington. "Memory and Judgment: Availability versus Explanation-Based Accounts." *Memory and Cognition* (June 2000): 624–34.

Wong-on-Wing, B., J. Reneau, and S. West. "Auditors' Perception of Management: Determinants and Consequences." *Accounting, Organizations and Society* (No. 5/6 1989): 577–87.

Wood, R. "Task Complexity: Definition of the Construct." *Organizational Behavior and Human Decision Processes* (February 1986): 60–82.

Wood, R., A. Mento, and E. Locke. "Task Complexity as a Moderator of Goal Effects: A Meta-Analysis." *Journal of Applied Psychology* (August 1987): 416–25.

Wood, R., and T. Mitchell. "Manager Behavior in a Social Context: The Impact of Impression Management on Attributions and Disciplinary Actions." *Organizational Behavior and Human Performance* (December 1981): 356–78.

Woolfolk, A. *Educational Psychology,* 9th ed. Upper Saddle River, NJ: Pearson Education, 1998.

Wright, A. "An Investigation of the Engagement Evaluation Process for Staff Auditors." *Journal of Accounting Research* (Spring 1982): 227–39.

Wright, A. "The Impact of Prior Working Papers on Auditor Evidential Planning Judgments." *Accounting, Organizations and Society* (No. 6 1988a): 595–606.

Wright, A. "Discussion of 'Quantification and Persuasion in Managerial Judgment.'" *Contemporary Accounting Research* (Fall 2005): 687–91.

Wright, A., and J. Bedard. "Decision Processes in Audit Evidential Planning: A Multistage Investigation." *Auditing: A Journal of Practice and Theory* (Spring 2000): 123–43.

Wright, P. "The Harassed Decision Maker: Time Pressures, Distractions, and the Use of

Evidence." *Journal of Applied Psychology* (October 1974): 555–61.

Wright, P., T. Gardner, L. Moynihan, and M. Allen. "The Relationship between HR Practices and Firm Performance: Examining Causal Order." *Personnel Psychology* (June 2005): 409–46.

Wright, S., and A. Wright. "The Effect of Industry Experience on Hypothesis Generation and Audit Planning Decisions." *Behavioral Research in Accounting* (1997): 273–94.

Wright, W. "Financial Information Processing Models: An Empirical Study." *The Accounting Review* (July 1977a): 676–89.

Wright, W. "Self-Insight into the Cognitive Processing of Financial Information." *Accounting, Organizations and Society* (No. 4 1977b): 323–31.

Wright, W. "Properties of Judgment Models in a Financial Setting." *Organizational Behavior and Human Performance* (February 1979): 73–85.

Wright, W. "Empirical Comparison of Subjective Probability Elicitation Methods." *Contemporary Accounting Research* (Fall 1988b): 45–57.

Wright, W. "Superior Loan Collectibility Judgments Given Graphical Displays." *Auditing: A Journal of Practice & Theory* (Fall 1995): 144–53.

Wright, W., Jr., and U. Anderson. "Effects of Situation Familiarity and Financial Incentives on Use of the Anchoring and Adjustment Heuristic for Probability Assessment." *Organizational Behavior and Human Decision Processes* (August 1989): 68–82.

Wright, W., and G. Bower. "Mood Effects on Subjective Probability Assessment." *Organizational Behavior and Human Decision Processes* (July 1992): 276–91.

Wysocki, B., Jr. "Do Investors Confuse Price with Quality? Panagora Bets against Human Foibles." *Wall Street Journal* (December 4, 1996): A2.

Xu, Y., and B. Tuttle. "The Role of Social Influences in Using Accounting Performance Information to Evaluate Subordinates: A Causal Attribution Approach." *Behavioral Research in Accounting* (2005): 191–210.

Yaniv, I. "Receiving Other People's Advice: Influence and Benefit." *Organizational Behavior and Human Decision Processes* (January 2004): 1–13.

Yaniv, I., and E. Kleinberger. "Advice Taking in Decision Making: Egocentric Discounting and Reputation Formation." *Organizational Behavior and Human Decision Processes* (November 2000): 260–81.

Yaniv, I., and Y. Schul. " Elimination and Inclusion Procedures in Judgment." *Journal of Behavioral Decision Making* (September 1997): 211–20.

Yaniv, I., and Y. Schul. "Acceptance and Elimination Procedures in Choice: Noncomplementarity and the Role of Implied Status Quo." *Organizational Behavior and Human Decision Processes* (July 2000): 293–313.

Yates, J. *Judgment and Decision Making.* Englewood Cliffs, NJ: Prentice Hall, 1990.

Yates, J., J. Lee, W. Sieck, I. Choi, and P. Price. "Probability Judgments across Cultures." In *Heuristics and Biases: The Psychology of Intuitive Judgment,* edited by T. Gilovich, D. Griffin, and D. Kahneman. New York: Cambridge University Press, 2002.

Yates, J., L. McDaniel, and E. Brown. "Probabilistic Forecasts of Stock Prices and Earnings: The Hazards of Nascent Expertise." *Organizational Behavior and Human Decision Processes* (June 1991): 60–79.

Yates, J., P. Price, J. Lee, and J. Ramirez. "Good Probabilistic Forecasters: The 'Consumer's' Perspective." *International Journal of Forecasting* (March 1996): 41–56.

Ye, L., and P. Johnson. "The Impact of Explanation Facilities on User Acceptance of Expert Systems Advice." *MIS Quarterly* (June 1995): 157–72.

Yerkes, R., and J. Dodson. "The Relation of Strength of Stimulus to Rapidity of Habit Formation." *Journal of Comparative Neurology and Psychology* (1908): 459–82.

Yetton, P., and P. Bottger. "Individual versus Group Problem Solving: An Empirical Test of a Best-Member Strategy." *Organizational Behavior and Human Performance* (June 1982): 307–21.

Yip-Ow, J., and H. Tan. "Effects of the Preparer's Justification on the Reviewer's Hypothesis Generation and Judgment in Analytical Procedures." *Accounting, Organizations and Society* (February 2000): 203–15.

Young, S. "Participative Budgeting: The Effects of Risk Aversion and Asymmetric Information on Budgetary Slack." *Journal of Accounting Research* (Autumn 1985): 829–42.

Young, S., J. Fisher, and T. Lindquist. "The Effects of Intergroup Competition and Intragroup Cooperation on Slack and Output in a Manufacturing Setting." *The Accounting Review* (July 1993): 466–81.

Yuan, K., L. Zheng, and Q. Zhu. "Are Investors Moonstruck? Lunar Phases and Stock Returns." *The Journal of Empirical Finance* (January 2006): 1–23.

Zacks, R., and L. Hasher. "Frequency Processing: A Twenty-Five Year Perspective." In *Frequency Processing and Cognition,* edited by P. Sedlmeier and T. Betsch. New York, NY: Oxford University Press, 2002.

Zajonc, R. "Emotions." In *The Handbook of Social Psychology,* 4th ed., edited by D. Gilbert, S. Fiske, and G. Lindzey. Boston: McGraw-Hill, 1998.

Zakay, D. "The Impact of Time Perception Processes on Decision Making under Time Stress." In *Time Pressure and Stress in Human Judgment and Decision Making,* edited by O. Svenson and A. Maule. New York: Plenum Press, 1993.

Zemke, R., and T. Kramlinger. *Figuring Things Out: A Trainer's Guide to Needs and Task Analysis.* Reading, MA: Addison-Wesley, 1982.

Zimbelman, M. "The Effects of SAS No. 82 on Auditors' Attention to Fraud Risk Factors and Audit Planning Decisions." *Journal of Accounting Research* (1997): S75–97.

Zimbelman, M., and W. Waller. "An Experimental Investigation of Auditor-Auditee Interaction under Ambiguity." *Journal of Accounting Research* (1999): S135–65.

Zimmer, I. "A Lens Study of the Prediction of Corporate Failure by Bank Loan Officers." *Journal of Accounting Research* (Autumn 1980): 629–36.

Zimmer, I. "A Comparison of the Prediction Accuracy of Loan Officers and Their

Linear-Additive Models." *Organizational Behavior and Human Performance* (February 1981): 69–74.

Zuckerman, M. *Behavioral Expressions and Biosocial Bases of Sensation Seeking.* New York: Cambridge University Press, 1994.

Zukier, H. "The Dilution Effect: The Role of the Correlation and the Dispersion of Predictor Variables in the Use of Nondiagnostic Information." *Journal of Personality and Social Psychology* (December 1982): 1163–74.

Zukier, H., and D. Jennings. "Nondiagnosticity and Typicality Effects in Prediction." *Social Cognition* (No. 2 1983–1984): 187–98.

Index